THE ECONOMICS OF
MONEY AND BANKING

STEPHEN M. GOLDFELD
Princeton University

LESTER V. CHANDLER
Emeritus, Princeton University

THE ECONOMICS OF MONEY AND BANKING

NINTH EDITION

1817

HARPER & ROW, PUBLISHERS, New York

Cambridge, Philadelphia, San Francisco, London,
Mexico City, São Paulo, Singapore, Sydney

Sponsoring Editor: John Greenman
Project Editor: Steven Pisano
Text and Cover Design: Barbara Bert/North 7 Atelier Ltd.
Text Art: Fineline Illustrations, Inc.
Production: Debra Forrest
Compositor: Waldman Graphics, Inc.
Printer and Binder: R. R. Donnelley & Sons Company

THE ECONOMICS OF MONEY AND BANKING Ninth Edition

Library of Congress Cataloging-in-Publication Data

Chandler, Lester Vernon, 1905–
  The economics of money and banking.

  Includes bibliographies and index.
  1. Money. 2. Banks and banking. I. Goldfeld,
Stephen M. II. Title.
HG221.C448 1986   332.4   85-22034
ISBN 0-06-042406-0
International ISBN 0-06-35-0317-4

86 87 88 89 9 8 7 6 5 4 3 2 1

CONTENTS

PREFACE

The field of money and banking has undergone rapid changes in the last few years. Major new legislation, financial innovation, and regulatory actions have combined to alter dramatically the way banks and related financial institutions go about their business. These same developments, coupled with some extraordinary economic circumstances—record-high interest rates, double-digit inflation, deep recessions, and foreign debt crises—have necessitated substantial changes in the conduct of monetary policy. Moreover, the real world of money and banking remains in a state of flux. While this presents a challenge to textbook writers, one we hope we have met, it also means that it is a most exciting time to begin formal study of money and banking.

This edition has been extensively revised and rewritten to reflect the latest developments. Nevertheless, it is quite similar in purpose and approach to the eight editions that have preceded it. It is addressed primarily to undergraduates taking a first course in money and banking. In the selection and presentation of materials we have kept the needs of the students in mind constantly and have not tried to write to our professional colleagues.

This is not an exhaustive treatment of money and banking. It would take a book many times the size of this to deal with the vast amounts of theoretical, legal, institutional, empirical, and historical materials that have been accumulated in the field of money and banking. Since such an encyclopedic treatment is inappropriate for a first course, we have therefore selected what we believe to be the most important principles, processes, and problems and have attempted to deal with them fully enough to clarify their significance and interrelationships.

The ultimate interest of this book is in policy. However, policy cannot be understood without a theory of the interrelationships of money and banking and the functioning of the economy as a whole, a clear understanding of the institutions and processes involved, and an appreciation of the social and historical context within which policy makers operate and by which their policies are shaped. This book, therefore, employs theoretical, institutional, and historical approaches. It emphasizes an evolutionary view, attempting not only to explain how present-day structures, attitudes, and policies evolved, but also to suggest some possible directions of future changes. This view seems particularly appropriate in the light of recent developments.

Major Changes in the Ninth Edition

While this edition retains in its title the seemingly old-fashioned phrase "money and banking," it is thoroughly modern in scope. To be sure, notions of what constitutes both "money" and a "bank" have altered perceptibly in recent years and these changes are examined fully in what follows. Moreover, since the forces that brought about these changes will inevitably provide further stimulus for change, a major goal is to provide the reader with a firm understanding of the dynamic nature of financial institutions and markets.

To accomplish this, the present edition introduces a number of major changes in both the exposition and coverage. The most extensive revisions appear in the new Part II devoted to depository institutions. This includes a new chapter on thrift institutions, documenting the evolution and problems of these institutions and spelling out the nature of financial innovation and legislation affecting the thrifts. More generally, Part II provides an expanded discussion of financial deregulation and innovation, documents the growing similarities among commercial banks and other financial institutions, and analyzes such contemporary issues as interstate banking and nonbank banks. This part also contains a substantially rewritten chapter on depository institutions and the money supply, and a revised and updated discussion of the assets and liabilities held by financial institutions.

The treatment of monetary policy has been extensively revised with particular emphasis on the problems faced by the Federal Reserve in a changing financial environment. A number of other issues related to the Federal Reserve receive new or substantially revised treatment. These include a discussion of the structure and independence of the Federal Reserve, the pricing of Federal Reserve services, and the structure of reserve requirements. Elsewhere in the book, some of the more important changes include the following: a simplification of the treatment of aggregate demand and supply and an expanded analysis of inflation; an expanded and simplified discussion of interest rates and bond prices; and a new discussion of real versus nominal interest rates and the role of inflationary expectations.

A reviewer of a previous edition of this book noted that the book is "easy to respect and hard to love." While the present edition remains a serious book, designed not to insult the reader, we have tried to make it more user-friendly. Concise chapter summaries are now systematically provided, and we have made greater use of demonstration boxes to illustrate principles. We welcome suggestions from readers for other such modifications.

Many individuals have made helpful contributions in the preparation of this edition. For their helpful comments, we would particularly like to thank Richard Edwards of St. Bonaventure University, Walter Rice of California Polytechnic State University, M. Richard Roseman of California State University, and Elinor Solomon of George Washington University. For preparing the *Instructor's Manual* that accompanies the text, Professor Rice is owed a double dose of thanks. Finally, we would like to thank our Princeton friends, Dan Sichel for his valuable assistance, and Barbara Grindle Hickey and Phyllis Durepos for their splendid secretarial help.

Stephen M. Goldfeld
Lester V. Chandler

PART 1

THE NATURE AND FUNCTIONS OF MONEY AND FINANCE

1

MONEY AND THE ECONOMY

One need not be an economist to be acutely aware that money plays an important role in modern life. It is evident, even to the most casual observer, that the behavior of money is vitally important to the operation of the national and international economies. When we recall the events of history, we are reminded that the periods of major economic contraction in the United States were frequently characterized by banking or monetary crises and invariably accompanied by substantial reductions in the stock of money. In particular, significant reductions of the money supply accompanied the major economic contractions of 1873–1879, 1893–1894, 1907–1908, 1920–1921, 1929–1933, and 1937–1938. Banking crises occurred in 1873 and again in 1907.

During our most severe economic contraction, the Great Depression of 1929–1933, we witnessed a collapse of the banking system, with the consequent disappearance via failure or merger of nearly 40 percent of the nation's banks. Newspapers of the 1930s headlined stories of "deflation and depression"; of the drastic decline of output, job opportunities, and prices accompanying the shrinkage of effective demand; of widespread want and suffering while millions of unemployed workers and other productive facilities that were both willing and able to work were standing idle because of insufficient "demand"; and of wholesale failures of debtors to meet their obligations because of the decline of their incomes and of the prices of their assets.

3

These episodes seem to confirm George Bernard Shaw's view that the "lack of money is the root of all evil." Yet at other times, too much money seems to be the problem. Headlines in other periods told different stories—of "inflation," of rising living costs, and of discontent and distress among those whose income and wealth were relatively fixed in terms of money. For example, in the periods surrounding the two world wars—1914–1920 and 1939–1948—prices more than doubled. During each period, the stock of money outstanding likewise more than doubled.

History also provides ample evidence that the movement of money between nations can have an important influence on economic developments throughout the world. In the United States, for instance, we have had to worry about the international position of the dollar, about the continuing deficit in our balance of international payments, the deterioration of our net international reserve position and speculation against the dollar. Difficulties on both the domestic and international fronts are of more than historical interest. Indeed, in the last decade or so, the United States has been struggling to cope with both severe inflation and excessive unemployment. In the mid-1970s, we experienced double-digit inflation for the first time in nearly 30 years, and this was followed rapidly by a severe recession. The same pattern was repeated in the 1980–1982 period as the economy first experienced another bout of higher inflation and then suffered the worst recession of the post-World War II era, with the unemployment rate rising to nearly 11 percent in 1982. To be sure, in the face of this unemployment the rate of inflation fell dramatically from 1981 to 1985. After 1982, as the economy picked up steam, the unemployment rate declined as well. However, as of early 1985 the unemployment rate seemed stuck at over 7 percent, a level that disturbed many policy makers.

On the international front, the early 1980s were marked by the dollar's steady appreciation relative to other currencies and a rising chorus of complaints from foreign countries for the United States to get its financial house in order. Throughout these developments, it was acknowledged that money was playing a critical, if incompletely understood, role. The halls of Congress and the nation's newspapers were filled with a wide range of views as to the proper course for monetary policy.

In short, personal experience as well as some knowledge of history and economics makes it clear to everyone that money plays an important role in the economic system and that the behavior of money is somehow causally related to the behavior of employment, the level of output, the distribution of wealth and income, and so forth. Furthermore, our past experience suggests that it is important for our national well-being that we somehow achieve the "right" amount of money. In a growing economy, the "right" amount of money is usually thought of in terms of the appropriate percentage change of the money supply. In various countries around the world, the task of getting the "right" amount of money falls to the central bank. In the United States, this function is carried out by the Federal Reserve

System, which uses monetary policy to regulate both the supply of money and conditions in financial markets to achieve the officially stated goals of national economic policy—high employment, price stability, and economic growth. But although this may be easy to say, it is distinctly less easy to do.

Indeed, the design of a sound monetary policy requires answers to such thorny questions as these: Just what is money? What are its functions in the economy? And how does money perform these functions? To what extent has money and monetary policy contributed to economic disturbances, and how can monetary policy be used to promote economic objectives generally considered desirable? How does rapid evolutionary change in the nature of the financial system, such as we are currently experiencing, complicate the role of monetary policy? With how much success can we use monetary policy to prevent unemployment, promote a steadily advancing level of output, and maintain a stable purchasing power of the dollar while preserving a basically free enterprise economy?

Such questions are the central concern of this book. Our primary interest throughout is in the functioning of the monetary, credit, and banking systems, and in their relationships to the functioning of the economy as a whole. Though much space will be devoted to historical, structural, and legal aspects of the various institutions that create, transfer, and destroy money, these aspects will not be studied primarily for their own sakes, but rather for their contribution to our understanding of the functioning of the economic system.

THE BASIC FUNCTION OF MONEY

Money has one fundamental purpose in an economic system: to facilitate the exchange of goods and services—to lessen the time and effort required to carry on trade. A person living and working in isolation from others has no use for money. It cannot be eaten or worn or used to promote productive processes; having no occasion to exchange either goods or services with others, such a person has no need for money. Even if a dozen persons lived together in isolation from all others, the use of money would be of only limited benefit to them; they could barter their goods and services among themselves with little loss of time and effort. As groups become larger, however, and wish to increase their degree of specialization and the size of their trade area, they find the direct barter of goods and services increasingly inconvenient and wasteful of time and effort. They therefore search for something that will enable them to escape the inefficient and time-consuming process of barter: they invent money.

We may say, then, that the sole purpose of money in the economic system is to enable trade to be carried on as cheaply as possible in order to make feasible the optimal degree of specialization, with its attendant increase of productivity. We are all familiar with the high degree of specialization that characterizes modern economies—specialization of persons, of business firms, of regions, and of types of capital. We know that without this high degree of specialization, which enables us to utilize the various regions to maximum advantage, to make the most advantageous use of native abilities, to develop skills, to amass huge amounts of specialized and useful knowledge, to employ large aggregations of specialized capital, and to achieve economies of scale, our productive powers and living standards would be far below their present levels. But this specialization would be impossible without an equally highly developed system of exchange or trade. Money is productive, therefore, in the sense that it is an essential part of the modern exchange mechanism and facilitates specialization and production.

BARTER EXCHANGE

We have carefully avoided saying that exchange is impossible without money. People can, of course, carry on trade by a direct bartering of goods and services. Primitive trade was often carried on in this way, and bartering is not unknown even now. Yet pure barter is so wasteful of time and effort that little trade would be feasible if this were the only available method of exchange.

The first serious shortcoming of pure barter is the lack of any common unit in terms of which to measure and state the values of goods and services. (By the *value* of a good or service is meant its *worth*, the quantity of other goods and services that it can command in the market.) In this situation, the value of each article in the market could not be stated simply as one quantity, but would have to be stated in as many quantities as there were kinds and qualities of other goods and services in the market. For example, if there were 500,000 kinds and qualities of goods and services in the market, the value of each would have to be stated in terms of 499,999 others. Moreover, no meaningful accounting system would be possible. A balance sheet would consist of a long physical inventory of the kinds and qualities of the various goods owned and another inventory of those owed. Consequently, the net worth of the person or firm could be ascertained, if at all, only by a prolonged and tedious study of the numerous barter rates of exchange prevailing in the market. Profit and loss statements would be equally difficult to draw up and interpret. A firm could list only the various kinds and qualities of goods and services acquired during the period as income and those paid out as expenses. Again, the net results could be discovered, if at all, only by a laborious study of barter rates of exchange. It is almost inconceivable that even a small department store, not to mention General Motors, could keep meaningful accounts in the absence of a monetary unit.

The second serious disadvantage of barter is often described as "the lack of a double coincidence of wants." Stated more simply, it would happen only rarely that the owner of a good or service could easily find someone who both wanted that commodity more than anything else and possessed the commodity that our trader wanted more than anything else. For example, suppose that a farmer owned a three-year-old draft horse and wished to trade it for a certain kind of two-wheeled cart. To find someone who already owned or could build with maximum economy exactly the kind of cart the farmer wanted and who would be willing to trade it, and who also wanted more than anything else the kind of horse that was being offered, would be a laborious and time-consuming process, if such a person existed at all. The farmer would probably have to accept something less desirable than the cart, or else carry through a number of intermediate barter transactions—for example, trading the horse for a cow, the cow for a boat, the boat for some sheep, and the sheep for the desired cart. Barter presents even more serious difficulties when the articles to be exchanged are not of the same value and cannot be divided without loss of value. Imagine, for example, the plight of the farmer who wanted to trade the horse for a pair of overalls, a hat, three dishes, an aluminum skillet, 50 cartridges, some schoolbooks, and numerous other inexpensive articles.

A third disadvantage of pure barter is the lack of any satisfactory unit in terms of which to write contracts requiring future payments. Contracts involving future payments are an essential part of an exchange economy; individuals must enter into agreements as to wages, salaries, interests, rents, and other prices extending over a period of time. But in a pure barter economy these future payments would have to be stated in terms of specific goods or services. Though this would be possible, it would lead to three grave difficulties: (1) It would often invite controversy as to the quality of the goods or services to be repaid; (2) the parties would often be unable to agree on the specific commodity to be used for repayment; (3) both parties would run the risk that the commodity to be repaid would increase or decrease seriously in value over the duration of the contract (e.g., wheat might rise markedly in value in terms of other commodities, to the debtor's regret, or decrease markedly in value, to the creditor's regret).

A fourth disadvantage of pure barter, which results from its first two shortcomings, is the lack of any method of storing generalized purchasing power. People could store purchasing power for future use only by holding specific commodities or claims against specific commodities. This method of storing purchasing power has often been used, and as we shall see later, is used extensively even today. Yet it has serious disadvantages when it is the only method available. The stored commodity may deteriorate (or appreciate) in value; its storage may be costly; and it may be difficult to dispose of quickly without loss if its holder wishes to buy something else.

Because of the four disadvantages outlined above, pure barter is a highly inefficient means of trade. It was to overcome these difficulties that virtually every society invented some kind of money early in its development.

THE SPECIFIC FUNCTIONS OF MONEY

Money serves its basic purpose as "the great wheel of circulation, the great instrument of commerce" by performing four specific functions, each of which obviates one of the difficulties of pure barter described above. These functions are to serve as: (1) a unit of value, (2) a medium of exchange, (3) a standard of deferred payments, and (4) a store of value. The first two are usually called the *primary* functions of money. The last two are called *derivative* functions because they are derived from the primary functions.

MONEY AS A UNIT OF VALUE

The first function of money has been given many names, of which the most common are *unit of value, standard of value, unit of account, common measure of value,* and *common denominator of value.* Through all these names runs one common idea: The monetary unit serves as the unit in terms of which the value of all goods and services is measured and expressed. As soon as a group develops a monetary unit such as a dollar, a peso, a franc, a pound sterling, or a pengo, the value of each good or service can be expressed as a *price,* by which we mean the number of monetary units for which it will exchange. For example, we say that the value of a certain hat is $10, that beef of a certain grade has a value of $2 a pound, and so on. Ours is certainly a pecuniary society in the sense that values typically are measured and expressed in monetary units.

The practice of measuring the values of goods and services in monetary units greatly simplifies the problem of measuring the exchange values of commodities in the market. One has merely to compare their relative prices in terms of monetary units. For example, if pig iron is $10 per hundredweight and corn is $2.50 per bushel, a hundredweight of pig iron is worth 4 bushels of corn. This practice also simplifies accounting. Assets, liabilities, income, and expenses of all kinds can be stated in terms of common monetary units to be added or subtracted.

Money is not the only common unit of measurement employed in the economic system. Units such as feet, inches, and meters are used to measure linear distance; ounces, grams, pounds, and short tons, to measure weight; gallons, liters, and barrels, to measure liquid volume; and so on. These units of physical measurement are themselves constant quantities. Confusion would surely result if units of physical measurement were to shrink 25 percent one year and expand 10 percent the next. Yet the unit of value (money), perhaps the most important unit of measurement in the economic system, has too often undergone wide fluctuations in its value or *purchasing power.* The latter is the inverse of the average or general level of prices of a large number of goods and services, as measured by the consumer price index, the wholesale price index, or by an index of the prices of all goods and services included in the gross national product.

For example, if the general or average level of prices doubles—i.e., if twice as many dollars are required to buy a given assortment of goods and services— the value or purchasing power of a dollar decreases by 50 percent. But if the general or average level of prices falls by 50 percent—i.e., if only half as many dollars are required to purchase a given assortment of goods and services—then the value or purchasing power of a dollar is doubled. These variations in purchasing power are typically referred to as inflation or de- flation. More specifically, the rate of *inflation* measures the speed with which the purchasing power of money is declining (e.g., 6 percent per year). The corresponding measure when the purchasing power of money is rising is the rate of *deflation*. The consequences of inflation and deflation will be discussed as we proceed.

MONEY AS A MEDIUM OF EXCHANGE

Various names have been given to the second function of money: *medium of exchange, medium of payments, circulating medium,* and *means of pay- ment.* This function of money is served by anything that is generally (not necessarily universally, but very commonly) accepted by people in ex- change for goods and services. The "thing" may be porpoise teeth, bits of gold, copper coins, pieces of paper, or credits on the books of a bank; the only essential requirement of an object to be used as money is that people be willing to accept it in exchange for goods and services. When a group has developed such a mechanism, its members need no longer waste their time and energy in barter. Our farmer can simply sell the horse to the person who offers the most money for it and then buy the supplies from those who offer the best bargain. The Ford worker need not barter his bolt- tightening services directly for the various things that he needs; he can sell his services for money in the most favorable market and spend the money as he sees fit. In the final analysis, all trade is barter; one good or service is traded indirectly for others, with money acting as the intermediary. But by serving this purpose, money greatly increases the ease of trade.

The fact that money is often referred to as *generalized purchasing power* or as *a bearer of options* emphasizes the freedom of choice that the use of money affords. The owners of goods or services need not secure their sup- plies from the people to whom they trade those goods or services; they can use their money to buy the things they want most, from the people who offer the best bargain, and at the time they consider most advantageous.

Here, again, money can function properly only if it maintains a relatively stable purchasing power. If a dollar is a bearer of fluctuating amounts of generalized purchasing power, it is likely to cause confusion and injustice in trade.

MONEY AS A STANDARD OF DEFERRED PAYMENTS

As soon as money comes into general use as a unit of value and a medium of payments, it almost inevitably becomes the unit in terms of which deferred or future payments are stated. Modern economic systems require the existence of a large volume of contracts of this type. Most of these are contracts for the payment of principal and interest on debts in which future payments are stated in monetary units. Some of these contracts run for only a few days or a few months, many run for more than 10 years, and some run for 100 years or more. At the end of 1984, the volume of outstanding debts of American governmental units, nonfinancial business firms, and households was $6.0 trillion. There are also many contracts other than debts that are fixed or semifixed in terms of monetary units; among these are dividends on preferred stock, long-term leases on real estate and other property, and pensions.

The disadvantages of writing contracts for future payments in terms of specific commodities have already been noted. But money is a satisfactory standard of deferred payments only to the extent that it maintains a constant purchasing power through time, or if it changes in value, does so in a predictable way. If there is substantial deflation, especially of an unpredictable sort, it injures the groups that have promised to pay fixed amounts of money and gives windfall gains to those who receive these fixed amounts. If, on the other hand, money loses value through time as a result of inflation, it tends to injure those who have agreed to receive the fixed amounts and lightens the burden of payers.

MONEY AS A STORE OF VALUE

We have already noted the disadvantages of holding specific commodities as a store of value. As soon as money comes to be used as a unit of value and as a generally acceptable means of payment, it is almost certain to be widely used as a store of value. The holders of money are, in effect, holders of generalized purchasing power that can be spent through time as they see fit for the things they want most to buy. They know that it will be accepted at any time for any good or service and that it will remain constant in terms of itself. Money is thus a good store of value with which to meet unpredictable emergencies and especially to pay debts that are fixed in terms of money. This does not mean that money has been a stable and wholly satisfactory store of value; it can meet this test only if its purchasing power does not decline. In actual practice, it has performed this function most capriciously.

Money is not, of course, the only store of value. This function can be served by any valuable asset. One can store value for the future by holding short-term promissory notes, bonds, mortgages, preferred stocks, household furniture, houses, land, or any other kind of valuable goods. The principal advantages of these other assets as a store of value are that they, unlike most forms of money, ordinarily yield an income in the form of interest, profits, rent, or usefulness (as in the case of an auto or a suit of clothes); and they sometimes rise in value in terms of money. On the other hand, these assets have certain disadvantages as a store of value, among which are the following: (1) They sometimes involve storage costs; (2) they may depreciate in terms of money; and (3) they are "illiquid" in varying degrees, because they are not generally acceptable as money and because sometimes the only way to convert them into money quickly is to exchange them at a loss of value.

All persons and business firms are free to choose for themselves the form in which they will store their value, to determine the proportions they will hold in the form of money and in various nonmonetary forms, and to alter these from time to time to achieve what seem to them the most advantageous proportions on the basis of income, safety, and liquidity. The decisions are much influenced by people's expectations as to the future behavior of prices. Other things being equal, if they expect that prices are more likely to rise (i.e., they anticipate inflation), they will be inclined to hold less of their wealth in the form of money and more in other forms. But if they come to believe that prices of other things are less likely to rise and more likely to fall, they will be inclined to hold an increased part of their wealth in the form of money and a smaller part in other forms.

DEFINITION OF MONEY

Having considered the various functions performed by money, we must now ask: What "things" are included in money and what "things" are excluded? Money should be defined precisely, for we shall deal at length with the supply (stock) of money and its behavior. Unfortunately, it is impossible to find a clear-cut answer to this basic question. As one economist has written:

> It is a singular and, indeed, a significant fact that, although money was the first economic subject to attract men's thoughtful attention, and has been the focal centre of economic investigation ever since, there is at present day not even an approximate agreement as to what ought to be designated by the word. The business world makes use of the term in several senses, while among economists there are almost as many different conceptions as there are writers upon money.[1]

This statement was written in 1899 but, as we shall see, it is just as relevant today.

---

[1]A. P. Andrew, "What Ought to Be Called Money," *Quarterly Journal of Economics*, January 1899, p. 219.

TABLE 1–1 Some Things That Have Served as Money

clay	pigs	wool	porcelain	iron
cowry shells	horses	salt	stone	bronze
wampum	sheep	corn	iron	nickel
tortoise shells	goats	wine	copper	paper
porpoise teeth	slaves	beer	brass	leather
whale teeth	rice	knives	silver	playing cards
boar tusks	tea	hoes	gold	debts of individuals
woodpecker scalps	tobacco	pots	electrum	debts of banks
cattle	pitch	boats	lead	debts of governments

EXAMPLES OF MONEY

Anyone who begins the study of money with a belief that there is some one thing that is "by nature" money and has been used as money at all times and in all places will find monetary history very disconcerting, for a most heterogeneous array of things have served as circulating media. An incomplete list is given in Table 1–1.

Some of these things are animal, some vegetable, some mineral; some, such as debts, defy classification. Some are as valuable for nonmonetary purposes as they are in their use as money; some at the other extreme have almost no value in nonmonetary uses. Some are quite durable; other could be classified as perishable. About the only characteristic that all these things had in common was their ability, at some time and place, to achieve general acceptability in payment. And the reasons for their general acceptability certainly varied from place to place and from time to time.[2]

LEGAL DEFINITIONS OF MONEY

Some people have tried to define money in purely legal terms, contending that "money is what the law says it is." Legal provisions are certainly relevant. A "thing" is likely to have difficulty in achieving general acceptability in payments if the law prohibits its use for this purpose, although violations of such laws are far from unknown. Laws can also help a thing to achieve general acceptability by proclaiming it to be money. They may go further and endow it with *legal tender* powers, decreeing that it has the legal power to discharge debts and that a creditor who refuses it may not demand anything else in payment of an existing debt.

[2]The variety of things that have served as money is reflected in our language. For example, the word *pecuniary*, meaning "monetary," comes from the Latin word *pecus*, which means "cattle," while *salary* derives from the Latin word for salt, *salarium*. Similarly, the expression "to shell out," meaning "to pay," reflects the early use of shells as money.

However, legal definitions of money are not satisfactory for purposes of economic analysis. For one thing, people may refuse to accept things that are legally defined as money and may even refuse to sell goods and services to those who offer legal tender in payment. Moreover, things that are not legally defined as money may come to be generally acceptable in payment and even to become a major part of the circulating medium. Checking accounts are an outstanding example, since these have no legal status as money. So legal provisions are an important, but certainly not the only, determinant of the things that do and do not serve as money.

FUNCTIONAL DEFINITIONS OF MONEY

To be useful for economic analysis, the definition of money must be in functional terms. Money includes all those things that perform the functions of money and excludes all others. But this definition raises still other questions, notably, "performs *what* functions?" Two of the functions—those of serving as a unit of value and as a standard of deferred payment—do not help determine which "things" to include in the money supply and which to exclude, for they are abstractions that can relate to many different things. For example, we could measure values in dollars whether or not our money, denominated in dollars, was composed of gold, paper money, or porpoise teeth. And we could state contracts extending over time in dollars without reference to the nature of the things to be used in payment.

Virtually all economists agree that the money supply should include all those things that are in fact generally acceptable in payment of debt and as payment for goods and services. If a thing is in fact generally acceptable in payment and generally used as a medium of payments, it is money, whatever its legal status may be.

In the United States our money supply certainly includes coins and paper money. These items, collectively known as *currency*, are not only generally acceptable, but also are endowed with full legal tender powers. Yet although it is extensively used, currency is not the primary medium of exchange. Most of what is conventionally called money consists of deposits or account balances at commercial banks and other depository institutions such as savings and loan associations or credit unions. Even though such accounts are not considered legal tender, they are generally acceptable as payment. Payments from these accounts are typically made by a *check*, which instructs a commercial bank or a savings and loan association to reduce the payer's account by the amount of the check and to transfer the funds to the recipient of the check.

Accounts from which such transactions are possible are typically called *checkable deposits* or, alternatively, simply *transactions accounts*. The latter, more general term is somewhat more accurate, since payment from such accounts can sometimes be made by direct electronic means, either by telephone or by use of an electronically encoded card. Whatever one chooses to call them, checkable deposits or transactions accounts, along with currency, comprise the most conventional definition of money, denoted by the symbol M-1.

As Table 1–2 indicates, at the end of 1984 the U.S. money supply as measured by M-1 totaled $558.7 billion, with 28 percent in the form of currency and the remaining 72 percent in the form of checkable deposits. Table 1–2 also demonstrates the rather general finding that a growing economy will typically be accompanied by an increasing money supply. For example, from 1964 to 1974 the annual growth of M-1 was 5.5 percent while the corresponding growth rate for the period 1974–1984 was 7.2 percent. Subsequent chapters elaborate on both the sources of this monetary growth and its economic consequences.

MONEY: PAST, PRESENT, AND FUTURE

As should be clear from the previous discussion, the definition of money has long been a controversial matter. Moreover, as one might suspect in such circumstances, the most commonly accepted definition of money has varied from time to time. Through the mid-1970s, the conventional definition of money was taken to be currency plus demand deposits at commercial banks.[3] This was so because demand deposits at commercial banks constituted the *only* form of checkable deposits. Beginning in the 1970s a number of financial instruments emerged that were capable of serving as substitutes for demand deposits in making transactions. A prominent example is the NOW account, an interest-bearing account that permits the holder to withdraw funds by writing what look, smell, and feel like a check, even though it is called a negotiated order of withdrawal (hence the acronym NOW).

Although they were not considered money when they first appeared, NOW accounts obviously serve as a transactions medium and therefore belong in principle in any transactions-based definition of money. Moreover, since NOW accounts are available at savings and loan associations and mutual savings banks—they were originated by a Massachusetts mutual savings bank—any definition of money that focuses exclusively on commercial banks is clearly too restrictive.

As a result of the evolution of the financial systems typified by the NOW account, the definition of M-1 has been expanded in scope several times in the past few years. The consequence of these redefinitions can be seen in Table 1–2, where the item "other checkable deposits" reports the volume of transactions accounts other than demand deposits at commercial banks. As can be seen, by 1984 these accounts amounted to $146 billion, or to 37

[3]In an earlier day, even demand deposits were regarded as a controversial component of money. For example, as late as 1931, H. Parker Willis, a prominent monetary economist of his time, held that checking accounts should be excluded from a definition of money.

TABLE 1–2 The Public's Money Supply on Selected Dates

Type of money	AMOUNT OUTSTANDING (IN BILLIONS OF DOLLARS)		
	December 1964	December 1974	December 1984
Currency	34.3	67.8	158.7
Demand deposits	127.0	207.5	248.6
Traveler's checks	0.5	1.8	5.2
Other checkable deposits	0.1	0.4	146.2
Total (= M-1)	161.9	277.6	558.7

NOTE: The data shown are monthly averages of daily figures and are adjusted for seasonal variation. The latest data appear in the monthly *Federal Reserve Bulletin.*
SOURCE: Board of Governors of the Federal Reserve System.

percent of all checkable deposits. This percentage would be even higher if we included all possible "checkable" accounts in our definition of money.[4]

If anything, our recent experience shows that what constitutes a medium of payment cannot be settled once and for all. Rather, those assets that function as media of payments may well change with advances in technology and with the evolution of institutional practices. The ability to transfer funds by electronic means rather than by shuffling pieces of paper has a dramatic potential for further altering the definition of money. The continued deregulation of financial systems may also require further refinements in defining money. Both electronic funds and deregulation will be considered in more detail below.

NARROW VS. BROAD DEFINITIONS OF MONEY

While the narrow definition of money based on its function as a medium of payment is the most widely accepted money supply concept, a number of economists consider this definition, even as revised, too restrictive. They admit that only currency and checkable deposits are generally accepted in payments, but they prefer to expand the money category to include some other things that have a high degree of "moneyness" and are widely used as a store of value. None would include everything used as a store of value; the concept of money would become meaningless if expanded to include land, structures, livestock, business inventories, and other such risky and illiquid assets. But some economists would include time and savings deposits at all depository institutions and shares of money market mutual

[4]For a detailed treatment of the various financial instruments which are included in M-1, see Chapter 18. One primary omission from the category of checkable accounts is the transaction account held with so-called money market mutual funds. Such accounts are discussed in Chapter 7.

funds. Some would go further and include U.S. Treasury bills and other short-term debts of the federal government and even short-term debts of safe private debtors.

While many of these financial assets have a high degree of moneyness, or *liquidity*, they are not generally accepted in payment. Moreover, in most cases there is at least a short delay or other cost in exchanging them for money in the sense we have defined it. At a practical level, the main problem is knowing where to draw the line. Since all assets possess the quality of moneyness to some degree, any broad definition is likely to have troublesome borderline cases. Consequently, for the most part we shall stick to the relatively narrow definition of money—currency plus checkable deposits.[5]

MONEY AND THE ECONOMY

The study of money and banking is a means for understanding the influence of money and monetary policy on the functioning of our economic system. Indeed, our concern with the definition of money is motivated by the fact that some measure of the money supply is generally used as a guide or tool of monetary policy. If, for example, monetary policy operates by influencing the stock of money, then it is of obvious importance to define money so that it is meaningfully related to the ultimate economic objectives of policymakers.

This book takes as its premise the view that the behavior of money is an important element in explaining observed economic outcomes and that intelligent monetary policies can contribute to the attainment of socially desirable economic goals. While this upbeat view of money and monetary policy is shared by many economists today, this was not always the case. Indeed, many of the writings of the so-called classical economists, who dominated British and American economic thinking in the nineteenth and early twentieth centuries, tended to accord money only an unimportant role. Such a view of the significance, or rather the insignificance, of money was clearly stated by John Stuart Mill:

> It must be evident, however, that the mere introduction of a particular mode of exchanging things for one another by first exchanging a thing for money, and then exchanging the money for something else, makes no difference in the essential character of transactions. . . .
>
> There cannot, in short, be intrinsically a more significant thing, in the economy of society, than money; except in the character of a contrivance of sparing time and labor. It is a machine for doing quickly and commodiously, what would be done, though less quickly and commodiously, without it; and like many other types of machinery, it only exerts a distinct and independent influence of its own when it gets out of order.

[5]We do, however, explicitly consider some broader definitions in Chapter 18.

> The introduction of money does not interfere with the operation of any of the Laws of Value ... The reasons which make the temporary or market value of things depend on the demand and supply, and their average and permanent values upon their cost of production, are as applicable to a money system as to a system of barter. Things which by barter would exchange for one another, will, if sold for money, sell for an equal amount of it, and so will exchange for one another still, though the process of exchanging them will consist of two operations instead of only one. The relations of commodities to one another remain unaltered by money; the only new relation introduced is their relation to money itself; how much or how little money they will exchange for; in other words how the Exchange Value of money itself is determined.[6]

Two aspects of Mill's statement should be noted before jumping to the conclusion that money deserves no more attention than each of the other labor-saving devices in the economy. First, Mill conceded that money "exerts a distinct and independent influence of its own when it gets out of order." This suggests the importance of keeping money "in order" to avoid disturbances. Second, he was speaking primarily of *equilibrium conditions*—those conditions that would rule after sufficient time had elapsed for all factors of production, output, costs, and prices to become so adjusted that there would be no incentive for further changes. Associated with this long-run equilibrium was a presumption that there would be full employment of both labor and capital.

Modern economists tend to give money and monetary policy a more prominent role in their analysis for several reasons. In the first place, they believe money is frequently "out of order" in the sense in which Mill used the term. The coincidence of severe economic contractions and the disruptive behavior of money cited earlier is one reason for this belief. In the second place, economists now devote much more attention to conditions and periods of disequilibrium: to business cycles, periods of unemployment or inflation, and periods of transition from one equilibrium position to another. The late Lord Keynes once quipped, "In the long-run we are all dead." This does not suggest that long-run consequences are unimportant, but it does emphasize that we cannot afford to neglect short runs or disequilibrium conditions which may persist for long periods and have serious social consequences. Indeed, as we shall see later, once economists focused on conditions of less than full employment, it became apparent that expansionary monetary policy was an effective tool for producing increases in both output and employment. It thus became clear that proper monetary management had an important role to play in achieving national economic objectives.

While we believe this view is the correct one, one should be wary of overemphasizing the influence of money. Some reformers, noting that the ability of individuals to obtain goods and services depends on the amount

---

[6]John Stuart Mill, *Principles of Political Economy*, Book III, chap. 7, p. 3.

of money they can command, have erroneously assumed that the same must always hold true for an entire nation. They would therefore abolish poverty and usher in the economic millennium by greatly expanding the money supply. How wonderful it would be if we could all become rich in any real sense simply by creating great batches of money! Unfortunately, it is not that easy. We have already noted that an expansion of money spending may serve to expand real production if it occurs in a period of unemployment, when the labor force and other productive factors are not working at full capacity. Economic policy must not ignore this fact. But neither can it safely ignore the fact that the most monetary policy can do to promote production—and it may not accomplish this without the aid of other economic policies—is to achieve and maintain full employment. It cannot compensate for a lack of natural resources or backward technology or unimaginative and unenterprising economic management or inefficiency in government economic activities.

In other words, a wise monetary policy may help to raise and maintain the actually realized rate of production closer to potential productive capacity (although we should not assume that it can always achieve even this objective). However, monetary policy usually is not one of the major determinants of this potential capacity. Nor is a wise monetary policy by any means the only factor determining the distribution of income and wealth. We shall have wiser monetary policy, and certainly wiser economic policies as a whole, if we recognize the limitations of monetary policy as well as its power.

SUMMARY

1 The direct barter of goods and services is wasteful of time and effort in carrying out trade. The primary inefficiencies of barter stem from the need for a "double coincidence of wants" and the lack of any common unit in which to measure and state the value of goods and services.

2 Money serves the critical function of a medium of exchange, thereby facilitating trade in goods and services. Money enables society to overcome the inefficiencies of barter, permits more trade to take place, and hence enhances our standard of living. Money also functions as a unit of value, a standard of deferred payment, and a store of value.

3 Throughout history, many things have served as money. At the present time, in the United States, the conventional definition of money, denoted by the symbol M-1, consists of currency and checkable deposits. Currency is comprised of coin and paper money. Checkable deposits, also known as transactions accounts, are primarily in the form of checking or demand deposit accounts and, increasingly, NOW accounts.

4 What constitutes an acceptable means of payment, and therefore how one should best define money, has varied considerably in the recent past and can be expected to undergo further changes in the future. Advances in technology, changes in regulations, and financial innovations will contribute to an evolution of the payments mechanism.

5 Money and monetary policy can have a profound impact on the state of the economy. The remaining chapters of this book will explore the connection between money and the economy in substantial detail.

SELECTED READINGS

Board of Governors of the Federal Reserve System, "A Proposal for Redefining the Monetary Aggregates." *Federal Reserve Bulletin*, January 1979, p. 13–42.

———, "The Redefined Monetary Aggregates," *Federal Reserve Bulletin*, February 1980, pp. 97–114.

Galbraith, J. K., *Money, Whence It Came, Where It Went*, Boston, Houghton Mifflin, 1975.

2

KINDS OF MONEY

In the previous chapter we surveyed the various roles played by money in the economy and discussed some modern definitions of money. We also suggested that a rather diverse set of things have formerly functioned as money. In this chapter we examine this evolution and describe the changes that have taken place in the payments media and the monetary system.

The main development is the movement from commodity money, such as gold coins, to credit money, such as checking deposits. After examining the various types of money, we consider the forces that led to the demise of the so-called gold standard and the rise of the modern banking system. This will have two side benefits. First, it will provide a glimpse at the workings of money in an international setting, a topic we return to in later chapters. Second, it will illustrate that, from the first, national economic policy often faced conflicting and potentially irreconcilable objectives—a frustration that policymakers live with to this day.

CLASSIFICATIONS OF MONEY

Money can be classified on several different bases, such as the following: (1) the physical characteristics of the materials of which money is made; (2) the nature of the issuer, such as a government, central bank, or commercial bank; and (3) the relationship between the value of money as money and the value of money as a commodity. We shall use all these classifications, but it will be convenient to start with the third. Table 2–1 shows the various types of money on this basis.

Since 1933, the United States has had only credit or debt money; both full-bodied and representative full-bodied money were discontinued and withdrawn at that time. The latter two should be analyzed, however, for they have played important roles in monetary history and are still remembered nostalgically by many people.

FULL-BODIED MONEY

Full-bodied money is money whose value as a commodity for nonmonetary purposes is as great as its value as money. Most of the early commodity moneys, such as cattle, rice, wool, and boats, were as valuable for non-monetary purposes as they were in their monetary uses. The principal full-bodied moneys in modern monetary systems have been coins of the standard metal when a country is on a metallic standard: a gold standard, a silver standard, or a bimetallic standard using gold and silver. We shall use gold in our examples, but the same principles apply to full-bodied money made of any other commodity.

Full-bodied coins were typically issued by governments. Three steps were involved:

1 Define the gold value of the monetary unit. This may be done in either of two ways, but both amount to the same thing: Stipulate the gold content of the monetary unit or stipulate the money price of each unit of gold.
2 At the stipulated price, purchase all the metal that is offered and coin it without limit and virtually without charge. This prevents the market price of gold from falling below the mint buying price.
3 Permit the melting of coins to get gold for nonmonetary uses and/or stand ready to sell, at the fixed price, all of the commodity that is

TABLE 2–1 Classifications of Money

  I. Full-bodied money
 II. Representative full-bodied money
III. Credit money
    A. Issued by the government
      1. Token coins
      2. Representative token money
      3. Circulating promissory notes
    B. Issued by banks
      1. Circulating promissory notes issued by central banks
      2. Circulating promissory notes issued by other banks
      3. Deposits subject to check

demanded. It is usually unnecessary to give permission to melt coins; people do it anyway if they find that it is the cheapest way to get gold. The effect of this is to prevent the market price of gold from rising above the mint price as long as gold can be acquired for nonmonetary uses.

These three steps yield an arrangement where the price of gold is stabilized in terms of money and assure that full-bodied coins have the same value as money as they have in nonmonetary uses of the metal. However, and this is most important, this does not mean that full-bodied gold coins would have a constant value or purchasing power in terms of other commodities. If the price of a unit of gold is fixed in terms of money, its purchasing power varies reciprocally with the prices of other things. Thus, the purchasing power of gold will fall by half if the price level of other things doubles, and the purchasing power of gold will double if the price level falls by half. There is no reason to expect that the price level of other things will remain constant simply because the price of gold has been stabilized.

This lack of correspondence between the monetary price and the purchasing power of gold stems from a general deficiency of commodity money: There is no necessary relationship between the productive capacity of the economy and the supply of the commodity. There may, for example, be huge new discoveries of gold deposits that produce an increase in the gold supply which exceeds the growth of the ability of the economy to produce goods and services. In such instances inflation results, and the purchasing power of gold in terms of other goods will decline. Alternatively, the productive capacity of the economy may be expanding rapidly relative to the production of gold, and deflation will result. Evidence of both sorts of episodes throughout history leads to the conclusion that there is little merit to leaving the quantity of money to be determined by the vagaries of gold mining and of competing nonmonetary demands for the use of gold.

REPRESENTATIVE FULL-BODIED MONEY

Representative full-bodied money, which is usually made of paper, is in effect a circulating warehouse receipt for full-bodied coins or their equivalent in bullion. The representative full-bodied money itself has no significant value as a commodity, but it "represents" in circulation an amount of metal with a commodity value equal to the value of the money. The gold certificates that circulated in the United States before their recall in 1933 represented fully equivalent amounts of gold coin or gold bullion held by the Treasury as backing for them. The main advantage of representative over full-bodied money is that the latter, involving as it did a physical commodity, typically became quite inconvenient when large sums were transacted. In all other important respects, the two types of full-bodied money are equivalent.

CREDIT MONEY

By credit money, or debt money, we mean any money, except representative full-bodied money, that circulates at a value greater than the commodity value of the material from which it is made. In some cases, the market value of the money material is insignificant, as in the case of most paper money. In other cases, such as copper coins, the market value of the material may be substantial, but still be below the value of the money.

How can a money achieve and maintain a value or purchasing power as money greater than the value of the commodity of which it is made? The usual method is to limit the quantity of the money by preventing the free and unlimited transformation of the commodity into money. The most common way is for the issuing authority to fix the quantity of the particular type of money to be issued and to buy only as much of the money material as is needed for the purpose. The remainder of the supply of that commodity is left for nonmonetary uses. This residual supply may be so large relative to demands for nonmonetary uses that the market value of the commodity will fall far below the value of the money. Note that in this case the issuing authority itself determines the quantity of debt or credit money to be issued and the amount of the money material to be purchased for the purpose.

Credit or debt money can also result as the issuing authority buys all the money material offered to it, but at a price significantly below the monetary or face value of the money into which it is transformed. Suppose, for example, that the monetary authority issues pesos, each containing a half ounce of silver, but stands ready to buy all silver offered to it at a price of only 1 peso an ounce. The issuing authority is clearly in a position to make large gross profits by purchasing silver at 1 peso an ounce and converting each ounce into 2 pesos of money. This gross profit to the issuer is called *seigniorage*. But the main point here is that this is a way of maintaining the value of credit money above the market value of the commodity of which it is made. Each ounce of silver in the form of money is obviously 2 pesos, but the price of silver in the market could fall as low as 1 peso an ounce, the price at which the monetary authority will buy it.

Credit money can take various forms:

1   **TOKEN COINS.** Our coins (half-dollars, quarters, dimes, nickels, and pennies) are indeed the "small change" of our monetary system; they make up only a very small fraction, about 3 percent, of our total money supply. These coins are all token money, with a value as money considerably above the market values of the metals contained in them. In general, the government creates and issues those amounts of the various denominations of coins that the public demands as "small change."

   The history of silver coins provides a vivid example of one potential problem with token money. Until the mid-1960s dollars, half-dollars, and dimes were 90 percent silver and 10 percent alloy. During this period the price of silver remained low enough to keep the market values of the silver in these coins significantly below their face values. The situation changed in the 1960s as nonmonetary demands for silver—demands for silver to be used in silverware, electronics, and photographic film—rose sharply. The market price reached $1.293 an ounce, at which price it became profitable to melt down silver dollars and to exchange silver certificates for the silver bullion backing them. Silver dollars disappeared from circulation; some were converted to bullion for nonmonetary uses, and some were added to rare coin collections. As the market price of silver continued to rise, it became profitable to melt down half-dollars, quarters, and dimes. Congress modified this situation by changing the commodity content of these coins from silver to copper and nickel. Once again, the money value of small change is far above its market value as a commodity. This episode is a good illustration of Gresham's law, which, simply put, states that "bad money drives good money out of circulation." This happens because "bad" money (with less valuable metallic content) is passed on in transactions while individuals try to hold onto or employ in other uses "good" money (with more intrinsic value). In the extreme, if a coin is worth more as a commodity than as money, it will cease to circulate as money.[1]

2   **REPRESENTATIVE TOKEN MONEY.** This is usually paper which is, in effect, a circulating warehouse receipt for token coins or for an equal weight of bullion that has been deposited with the government. This type of money is like representative full-bodied money, except that the coin or bullion held as "backing" is worth less as a commodity than it is as money. Silver certificates, which circulated in varying amounts from 1878 to 1967, are the only example of this type of money in the United States.

3   **CIRCULATING PROMISSORY NOTES ISSUED BY GOVERNMENTS.** Governments also issue credit money in a form that is usually, but sometimes inaccurately, called *circulating promissory notes*. These are usually made of paper and are sometimes called *fiat* money. The only circulating promissory notes issued by the U.S. government and still in circulation are the U.S. notes, or greenbacks, which were issued to assist in financing the Civil War. Over $400 million of them were originally issued, but they were reduced to $347 million by 1878 and have since remained at approximately that level.

Many people oppose the use of government paper money, fearing that it will be issued in excessive amounts. Monetary history provides

---

[1]Another example of Gresham's law is provided by the use of tobacco as commodity money. Tobacco was made legal tender in Virginia in 1642 and was widely used as commodity money for almost 200 years. Debts payable in tobacco leaves were generally discharged with the foulest and lowest-quality tobacco. The good stuff, as Mr. Gresham would predict, was smoked.

a real basis for this fear, since these issues provide an attractive source of revenue to governments. By spending a small amount for paper, engraving, and printing, a government can pay its debts or cover its expenses by producing millions of dollars' worth of paper money. The temptation to sacrifice proper monetary management to budgetary needs is often strong. It should be pointed out, however, that most of the excessive issues of paper money have occurred during war periods when nations felt that their very existence was at stake and when they were in dire need of money to meet military requirements. There is no reason why a properly managed government paper money should not function well.

4 **CIRCULATING PROMISSORY NOTES ISSUED BY PRIVATE BANKS.** Circulating promissory notes issued by privately owned banks have played an important role in monetary systems. Promissory notes issued by state-chartered banks and by the First and Second Banks of the United States provided a large part of the circulating medium in this country before the Civil War, and the national banks chartered by the federal government issued such notes from the time of the Civil War until 1935.

5 **CIRCULATING PROMISSORY NOTES ISSUED BY CENTRAL BANKS.** The largest part of the currency that is used in most advanced countries is in the form of circulating promissory notes issued by central banks, such as our Federal Reserve banks, the Bank of England, and the Bank of France.

6 **CHECKING DEPOSITS AT BANKS.** The major part of the money supply in this country, as well as in most other advanced countries, is in the form of checkable deposits at banks.[2] These so-called deposits are claims of creditors against a bank which can be transferred from one person or firm to another by means of checks or other orders to pay. These claims against banks are generally acceptable in payment of debts and for goods and services. The popularity of checking deposits can be traced to their advantages: (a) They are not so liable to loss or theft as other types of money. (b) They can be transported very cheaply, regardless of the amount of the payment or the distance between payer and payee. (c) Because checks can be written for the exact amount of the payment, there is no need to make change and count bills and coins. (d) When endorsed by the payee, checks serve as a convenient receipt for payment. The principal disadvantage of checking deposits is that checks drawn on them may not be accepted

---

[2]Throughout this chapter, the term *bank* is shorthand for any depository institution supplying checkable deposits. It thus encompasses commercial banks as well as savings and loan associations, mutual savings banks, and credit unions. This is because of recent deregulation under which the functions of these financial institutions are becoming increasingly similar. For a discussion of these growing similarities and of the semantics of banks, see Chapters 5 and 7.

from an unknown person, but this is largely remedied by such devices as certified checks, cashier's checks, and traveler's checks, which in effect guarantee payment to the payee or to anyone to whom he or she transfers the claim.

OVERVIEW

Full-bodied money, representative full-bodied money, and the various types of credit money have all played a role in monetary systems. Modern economies rely almost exclusively on credit money and, in particular, on currency and checkable bank deposits. Despite these developments, through the years the feeling has persisted, at least in some quarters, that money cannot be "good" unless it is based on some commodity—preferably gold.[3] At the risk of repetition, we must reiterate that this is not so. That credit money can be overissued, and on too many occasions has been, is undeniable. But if it is properly limited, credit money can be given a scarcity value and can circulate at least as satisfacorily as any full-bodied money. In fact, with proper management the quantity of credit money can be adjusted to the needs of the economy better than the quantities of a gold or silver full-bodied money. As we shall now see, it was precisely this lack of flexibility that led to the disappearance of commodity money and commodity standards.

MONETARY STANDARDS

It has been common for a country to try to maintain its monetary unit and its various types of money in that unit at a constant value in terms of some commodity. Any commodity could be chosen, but *gold standards* and *silver standards* have been the most used. The first full-bodied money in the United States was, in fact, on a joint gold–silver standard, the most common type of *bimetallic* standard.

BIMETALLISM

In its first major monetary legislation, the Coinage Act of 1791, the United States established a bimetallic standard. It adopted the dollar as its monetary unit and gave it a fixed value in terms of silver and also in terms of gold. The mint price of silver was fixed at $1.293 an ounce and that of gold at $19.395 an ounce. Thus, the "mint ratio" was 15 to 1. In other words, the

---

[3]That the supposed critical role of gold has been stressed by writers of a "conservative" persuasion is well known. Perhaps less well known is Karl Marx's comment that "only in so far as paper money represents gold . . . is it a symbol of value." This may simply serve to show that Freud was on to something when he observed that the human attachment to gold was deep in the subconscious.

mint price of gold was 15 times that of silver. The government stood ready to mint, at these values, all the gold and silver offered to it. And people were free to melt down or export coins. The clear intent of the legislation was to provide the new nation with full-bodied gold and silver coins, gold coins for the larger denominations and silver for the smaller ones.

However, the scheme failed; silver "drove gold out of circulation" because the mint ratio in the United States valued silver more highly relative to gold than did the mint ratios of several other important countries that were also on bimetallic standards. In those countries the mint ratio was $15\frac{1}{2}$ to 1. This discrepancy created an opportunity for a profitable chain of exchanges of gold and silver. For example, a person could get an ounce of gold in the United States, export it to another country in exchange for $15\frac{1}{2}$ ounces of silver, use 15 ounces of the silver to buy an ounce of gold here, and have $\frac{1}{2}$ ounce of silver left to cover expenses and yield a profit. However, gold would have disappeared from circulation in the United States even without such round-robin exchanges. Americans making payments abroad found it cheaper to pay in gold, while foreigners making payments to Americans found it cheaper to pay in silver.

Responding to complaints against the de facto silver standard, Congress attempted to reestablish a bimetallic standard by altering the mint ratio in 1834. Leaving the silver content of the dollar and the mint price of silver unchanged, it lowered the gold content of the dollar so as to raise the mint price of gold from $19.395 to $20.67 an ounce. The new mint ratio was 16 to 1, while that abroad remained at $15\frac{1}{2}$ to 1. The situation was now reversed; the United States' mint parity valued gold more highly relative to silver than did other countries. The results, although apparently unintended, should have been predictable. Gold now drove silver out of circulation. Not only silver dollars but also half-dollars, quarters, and dimes disappeared, creating inconvenience in trade. The nation came to be on a de facto gold standard.

This experience provides another example of the workings of Gresham's law and also suggests the desirability of having a prerequisite in arithmetic for membership in Congress. We turn now to the more basic issue, the operation of a pure gold standard.

THE GOLD STANDARD

While a precise description of the gold standard would vary from place to place and time to time, in its pure form the *gold standard* simply involved the steps already described—namely, the definition of the monetary unit in terms of gold (e.g., by valuing gold at $20.67 an ounce) and the permission of full convertibility between gold and money and between money and gold. This mechanical connection between gold and the monetary unit undoubtedly encouraged confidence in the value of the monetary unit, but it was not without its problems. The most serious of these was that changes in the stock of monetary gold would tend to produce corresponding changes in the stock of money. For example, in the United States, which operated on a relatively pure gold standard from 1879 to 1933, the stock of dollars would increase as new dollars were issued to acquire new gold. This, in turn, would exert an expansionary and potentially inflationary influence on the economy. Alternatively, the stock of money would decrease whenever someone returned dollars to the government in exchange for gold (or melted down gold coins), and this would produce contractionary and deflationary forces. These inflationary and deflationary results often occurred whether they were wanted or not.

How would such changes in the stock of gold occur? One way was via an increase in the domestic production of gold. Indeed, on a number of occasions in U.S. history, new gold discoveries led to substantial increases in the stock of money and were ultimately translated into significant increases in the price level. But this was neither the only nor the most important source of variation in our gold stock. Rather, as in the case of the demise of bimetallism, international factors proved to be of major significance.

Specifically, if a country had an adverse balace of payments—if it was importing more goods and services from other countries than it was exporting to them—this trade deficit had to be covered by shipping gold abroad. While countries kept *gold reserves* to accommodate temporary outflows, a persistently adverse balance of payments would eventually wipe out any stock of reserves. Under such conditions the international "rules of the game" called for the deficit country to deflate its domestic economy and lower its prices. This would tend to make its own products relatively more attractive to foreigners, since they were now cheaper and would make foreign goods relatively less attractive to its own citizens. Thus, exports would be promoted and imports inhibited. With the appropriate degree of deflation, the balance of payments would again "balance" and the gold outflow would cease.[4]

The difficulty with this scenario was that the cure was often more painful than the disease. Deflation of the domestic economy did more than reduce prices; it also tended to reduce output and employment and produce business failures. Increasingly, the social costs associated with such things as higher unemployment, labor unrest, and falling stock prices came to be regarded as too high a price to pay for maintenance of the gold standard. Countries wanted more freedom to issue money to promote output and employment, finance government deficits, or use for other purposes. The final straw in the United States was the Great Depression; in 1933, after several years of deflation and widespread unemployment, we abandoned

[4]For a more complete description of this process, including the role of foreign exchange rates, see Part 6.

the pure gold standard. While a limited gold standard lingered on until 1971, the age of pure gold standards ended in the mid-1930s.[5]

Such marked changes in the monetary role of gold remind us that monetary systems, far from remaining static, are subject to continuous, and sometimes abrupt, changes in both form and function.

THE EVOLUTION OF THE MODERN PAYMENTS MECHANISM

Modern payment systems now rely on credit money in the form of checkable bank deposits as the major component of the money supply. Understanding some of the critical forces that have brought about this development will provide insight into the nature of banks and a basis for forecasting the nature of future developments in the payment mechanism.

COINAGE

Primitive economies overcame the inconvenience of barter by the use of uncoined metals, such as copper, gold, and silver, as circulating media. These metals probably came to be generally acceptable in payment because they were widely desired for religious and ornamental purposes, they did not deteriorate, their large value relative to their weight and bulk make them relatively easy to transport, and so on. At this stage money was not differentiated from the material of which it was made; the metals flowed freely into and out of monetary uses. The use of bullion as money had serious disadvantages, however, especially if payers were not averse to short-weighing and adulteration. Precision weighing apparatuses were not widely available, and assaying was both laborious and inaccurate. Coinage solved both problems. At first coinage amounted merely to an official certification as to the weight and purity of a lump of metal. The imprint of a king's stamp meant in effect, "I hereby certify that this contains a certain weight of metal of a certain purity." The names of many monetary units (such as pounds, lire, livres, and shekels) that were originally units of weight attest to this fact.

THE EVOLUTION OF BANKING

While coinage was an important monetary innovation, both coins and uncoined metal shared some disadvantages for those who held them or used

[5]Not surprisingly, gold makes periodic attempted combacks. As one economist has observed: "Gold is a hardy perennial. It provides a psychological and material safe haven for people all around the world, and its invocation still produces deep-seated visceral reactions in many. It is not surprising, then, that when economic conditions are unfavorable, proposals to strengthen the role of gold in the monetary system find an audience much wider than the 'gold bugs' who have always seen the demise of the gold standard as the negative turning point in Western civilization." R. N. Cooper, "The Gold Standard: Historical Facts and Future Prospects," *Brookings Papers on Economic Activity*, 1982, No. 1, p. 1.

them to make payments. These included (1) the danger of theft or robbery, either in storage or in transporting the commodity or coin; (2) the costs of transporting to make payments over distances; and (3) the absence of interest or any other return on the money.

Largely because of the danger of theft and robbery, the practice arose of leaving gold and silver in the custody of some reputable person (a wealthy merchant, a money changer, or a goldsmith) who owned a strong box or other means of safekeeping. At this stage the "depositor" undoubtedly expected that the custodian would indeed hold all the specie intact. The custodian performed this service as a favor for friends or charged for it. It is also probable that at this initial stage a depositor who wished to make payments would go to the goldsmith or other custodian, get the required amount of coins, and use the coins themselves to make payment. But this was inconvenient; how much easier it would be to transfer claims against the metal. And such claims were at hand, for the goldsmith or other custodian usually gave some sort of evidence to the depositor. One type was a receipt which said in effect, "IOU so many florins." The next step was for payers to make payment by giving these IOUs to a payee. The latter could then claim the specie from the goldsmith, or use the IOU to make payments to others.

As these IOUs came to be used in payments, the bank note was born. A *bank note* is simply a bank debt or promise to pay, evidenced by a piece of paper. The earliest bank notes may have been acceptable only because they were believed to be fully backed by specie. Nevertheless, this was an important step in the evolution of money, since the community was becoming accustomed to using in payment not the precious metals themselves, but paper claims against those metals.

Another method of payment soon developed. The person leaving gold or silver with the "banker" would not receive a piece of paper representing the debt of the banker, but simply a "deposit credit" evidenced by an entry on the bank's books. The practice soon arose of making payments by writing an order on the banker to pay someone else. For example, Jones would write an order on the bank saying, "Pay Smith X florins and charge to my account." Smith might then claim the gold or silver. But as such orders became more widely acceptable in payment, it became increasingly common for payees to leave the specie with the goldsmith or other banker and to pay others by transferring claims to deposits. Thus, deposit claims, not specie itself, came to be used as a means of payment.

The high cost and risk of transporting precious metals over distances created an opportunity for profit that did not go unnoticed by shrewd goldsmiths and merchants. One can imagine a canny goldsmith-banker in Lübeck writing to a counterpart in Genoa[6]

---

[6]The illustrative use of Genoa and florins (a gold coin first issued in thirteenth-century Florence) is meant to convey the important role of the Italians in the development of commercial banking. Indeed, the word *bank* itself derives from the Italian word *banco*, meaning "bench,"

As we both know, trade between our areas has grown rapidly in recent years. Large amounts of specie flow every month from my area to yours, at great cost to the merchants and great risk to property and life. At the same time, almost equally large amounts of specie flow from the Genoa area to the Lübeck area, at comparable cost and risk. We can easily abolish these unnecessary costs, spur the development of trade, and add to our own pitifully low incomes by cooperating with each other. When someone in your area wishes to make a payment in the Lübeck region, you get from him the required amount of specie and give him an order on me to give specie to the payee, and I will do so. Then, when someone in my area wishes to make payments in the Genoa region, I will collect from her the required amount of specie and give her an order on you, which I hope you will honor. We will have to ship specie between Lübeck and Genoa only to the extent that the payments I make for your account and the payments you make for my account do not balance out, and I forecast that the net shipments required will be very small indeed relative to the total payments effected by us. In fairness to our customers and in the interest of promoting our business we should not charge for these services as much as it would cost our customers to ship specie equal to the total value of all payments, but in fairness to ourselves and our families our charges should exceed our actual costs.

Such were the motivations that led to the establishment of business relationships among emerging bankers in the leading commercial centers. Bills of exchange or orders to pay became an increasingly popular way of effecting payments, and the things transferred were claims against goldsmith-bankers or merchant-bankers.

Up to this point we have dealt with only two forces that contributed to the evolution of banking: the disadvantages of full-bodied coins because of their liability to theft and robbery, and the high cost and risk of transporting them. But these two forces alone were sufficient to concentrate large amounts of the precious metals in the hands of an emerging class of bankers. At first these were primarily goldsmiths, money changers, or merchants who took on safekeeping of specie and related functions as a sideline. Gradually, however, these functions increased in relative importance and profitability, and specialized bankers began to emerge. Note that in this earliest stage all deposits and bank notes were fully backed by specie, and the income of the emerging bankers came from charges for safekeeping and for transmitting payments.

Then came a discovery that was to be momentous for the evolution of banking. The emerging bankers discovered that, to meet their promises to pay in specie on demand, they did not need to hold gold and silver equal to 100 percent of their outstanding debts in the form of deposits and bank notes. A banker who was in fact holding specie fully equal to the value of his deposit and bank note liabilities might have put it this way:

---

reflecting the fact that early Italian bankers conducted their business from a bench in the street. Similarly, the term bankruptcy comes from the Italian custom of breaking the bench of a banker who could not pay off his creditors.

> I do not need to hold all that specie because those people are not all going to demand payment at any one time or even over a short period. Of course, there will be withdrawals. Some will want gold or silver for circulation. Also, I must be prepared to pay gold or silver to other banks who acquire claims against me in the form of deposit and bank note claims that I have issued. But such out-payments will be largely balanced by new inflows of gold and silver. I could meet any net drain that is likely to occur if I held gold and silver equal to only a small fraction—perhaps only a tenth—of my outstanding note and deposit liabilities. To hold more is terribly wasteful. Look at all the gold and silver lying there, idle and earning nothing! I think I'll lend out some of it and earn some interest.

And if his conscience was troubled by his contemplated breach of trust, he may have soothed it by replying, "I didn't promise my customers in so many words that I would hold all the gold and silver; I merely promised that I would pay them gold and silver when they asked for it. If I keep the promise why should it be any concern of theirs if I increase my income a little?"

So were banks transformed from mere custodians holding specie reserves equal to 100 percent of the deposit and bank note liabilities into lenders who held specie equal to only a fraction of their liabilities. *Fractional reserve banking* was born. Such banking may indeed have originated as a surreptitious breach of trust. But the secret was soon out, and fractional reserve banking gained widespread support. A banker could now say to the public, in effect:

> It will be our mutual advantage if you leave most of your gold and silver with me and hold and use as money the bank notes and deposits. The advantage to me as a banker is obvious; I can make loans and earn an income. But I will share this with you by providing valuable services at little or no cost to you. If you want currency that is convenient to hold or transport, I will provide you with bank notes. If you want the convenience of checking facilities I will provide those too. I will hold your funds in safekeeping, provide you with checkbooks, make payments for you over long distances, and do much of your bookkeeping for you.

Many banks also paid interest on deposit balances, an advantage not offered by coins. Moreover, those who were depositors often received preferred treatment when they applied for loans.

In these various ways the public was persuaded to hold more and more of its money in the form of bank notes and deposit claims against banks. Increasing proportions of the gold and silver money came to lodge in the banks, there to serve as fractional reserve against the banks' note and deposit liabilities.

The fractional reserve principle gave banks a great power that will be emphasized in later chapters—the power to increase and decrease the total money supply. Banks did not have this power when they issued bank notes and deposits only in exchange for an equal value of gold and silver; they merely substituted in the hands of the public one type of money for another. Suppose, for example, that the public has entrusted $100 of gold and silver to the banks in exchange for bank notes and deposits. This will appear as follows on the balance sheets of the public and the banks:

BALANCE SHEET OF THE PUBLIC		
ASSETS		**LIABILITIES**
Gold and silver	− $100	
Bank notes and deposits	+ $100	

BALANCE SHEET OF THE BANKS		
ASSETS		**LIABILITIES**
Gold and silver	+ $100	Note and deposit liabilities + $100

The public's total holdings of money remain unchanged, its larger holdings of bank notes and deposits being offset by its smaller holdings of gold and silver. And the banks have issued note and deposit liabilities equal to only the $100 of gold and silver surrendered by the public.

Suppose now that, starting from this situation in which both their gold and silver holdings and their note and deposit liabilities are $100, the banks decide they can meet any likely demands for payments if they hold gold and silver reserves equal to only 10 percent of their liabilities. They come to believe that any gold and silver holdings in excess of 10 percent of their liabilities can be used as a basis for lending. Consider two extreme cases:

1. As the banks lend, the borrowers withdraw from the banks gold and silver equal to the full amount of the loans. If the banks lend $90, their holdings of gold and silver will fall by that amount, and they will increase their assets in the form of outstanding loans (debt claims against borrowers) by the same amount. The banks' balance sheets will now appear as follows:

ASSETS		**LIABILITIES**	
Gold and silver	$10	Note and deposit liabilities	$100
Loans	90		

The effect of this transaction is to increase the public's money supply by $90, the amount of the increase in loans. Thus, in addition to the $100 of notes and deposits still held by the public, the borrowers now have the $90 of gold and silver paid out by the banks. So we find that by making loans or buying other assets, the banks can increase the public's money supply even if borrowers take all their loan proceeds in gold and silver.

However, once the public has become accustomed to using bank notes and deposits as money, borrowers are unlikely to withdraw gold and silver equal to the full amount of their borrowings. They are likely to accept bank notes or deposits instead. Let us therefore consider the other extreme case.

2. As the banks lend, the borrowers take all the loan proceeds in the form of bank notes and deposits, and there is no net drain of gold and silver from the banks. Suppose the banks lend $900, giving note or deposit

claims to the borrowers. The balance sheet of the banks will appear as follows:

ASSETS		LIABILITIES	
Gold and silver	$100	Note and deposit liabilities	$1,000
Loans	900		

In this process the banks have increased the public's money supply by $900, and have done so by issuing new note and deposit liabilities in exchange for debt claims against borrowers. The banks feel secure because their gold and silver reserves are still equal to 10 percent of their liabilities. In a sense, each $1 of gold and silver is supporting, or serving as a basis for, $10 of note and deposit liabilities. But most of these notes and deposits were created as banks purchased assets other than money itself. We will analyze these processes in more detail later and also review the process through which banks decrease the total money supply by decreasing their holdings of loans and other debt claims. But have a try at explaining this yourself. What would happen to the money supply if, starting from the last situation described, the banks decreased by $500 their outstanding loans?

In broad outline, these are the processes through which the public came to hold much of its money in the form of claims against banks. Even when full-bodied gold and silver coins were available and the public could have refused to accept or hold anything else, it chose to hold much of its money in the form of bank notes and deposits, and the banks found it profitable to manufacture these claims. Thus, in large part, the development of credit or debt moneys reflected private choices—the public's choices among the various types of money and the choices of bankers as lenders and creators of money.

GOVERNMENT AND CREDIT MONEY

Although the composition of the money supply and the trend toward greater use of credit moneys have been greatly influenced by the choices of the public and the bankers, governments have exerted important influences in many ways. We shall mention here only a few of the most important:

1 Governments themselves have been issuers of credit money. In some cases, the purpose has been to provide more convenient types of money, such as token coins or paper money; in others, it has been to remedy an alleged shortage of money; and in still others, it has been to finance government expenditures. In the United States, government credit money is now issued by the Treasury (coin) and the Federal Reserve (paper money).

2 Governments regulate the availability of full-bodied and representative full-bodied moneys and the redeemability of moneys in precious met-

als. As noted earlier, the trend has been toward more and more restricted redeemability in gold, thus encouraging the expansion and use of credit moneys.

3 Governments influence the establishment and operation of banks in various ways. For example, they have both encouraged the establishment of banks and regulated their operations. At an early stage, they encouraged the issue of bank notes; later they moved toward the abolition of bank notes. And in various ways they regulate the volume of bank deposits. Indeed, one of the major functions of the Federal Reserve is to regulate money creation and money destruction by the banks.

Most of these points will be developed further in later chapters.

RECENT AND PROSPECTIVE DEVELOPMENTS IN THE PAYMENTS MECHANISM

Our discussion of the evolution of banking has traced the emergence of bank deposits as the primary medium of payments. However, recent advances in computer technology and the rapid growth in credit card usage have suggested to some that, just as coin and currency gradually gave way to the convenience and efficiency of checking deposits, such deposits may give way to yet another type of payments mechanism. Indeed, these days we often her the phrases "checkless society," cashless society," and "electronic money." Furthermore, there is ample evidence that neither the banks nor the Federal Reserve is fully content with the payments mechanism as it now stands. A brief review of the reasons for this discontent will provide further insights as to the nature of money and allow us to indulge in a bit of speculation as to the form of future payments media.

COSTS OF THE PAYMENTS SYSTEM

A payments mechanism is merely a set of institutional arrangements by which exchanges of resources are accomplished. Barter, the use of coin or paper currency, and the use of checking deposits are all forms of payment mechanisms. As with any economic institution, the question naturally arises as to whether the existing mechanism is accomplishing its function as cheaply and as efficiently as possible. This is an important issue, since resources devoted to making payments tend to reduce the output of other goods and services that increase economic welfare.

The most obvious costs of the payments mechanism in the United States are the following: the costs of producing the supply of coin and paper currency, the costs of distributing and storing currency, and the costs of clearing checks. The first two categories include the expenses of operating the U.S. mint and the need for such items as cash registers and safes to guard the stock of currency. Although these costs are hardly inconsequential, by far the most important costs are those involved in clearing checks. In 1982 some 35 billion checks were written in the United States. It has been estimated that each check is handled an average of 10 times and passes between $2\frac{1}{3}$ banks before being returned to its source. The cost of this in recent years has been variously estimated to be 40 to 50 cents per check, implying an overall associated clearing cost of at least $14 billion. Projections for future years call for a steady rise in the number of checks processed.

Faced with the prospect for continued growth in the volume of checks, both the banks and the Federal Reserve have become increasingly concerned about the substantial resources devoted to shuffling pieces of paper among various parts of the country. To stem this tide the Federal Reserve has urged the use of wire transfers to replace processing of vast quantities of paper and has issued a set of guidelines for the implementation of "regional (check) clearing centers ... provided with automated clearing and telecommunications capabilities to serve as a basis for transition to widespread checkless—electronic—fund transfers."

Many economists see the natural evolution of these developments as leading to the ultimate emergence of an *electronic funds transfer system (EFTS)*. Some of the ingredients of such a system are already in place. For example, financial institutions and large corporations already transfer funds through electronic wire systems. Another rapidly growing component of our system for transferring funds is the so-called *automatic clearinghouse* (ACH). These are mainly used by business or the government to transfer funds simultaneously to a large number of individuals. For example, a large corporation might use an ACH to pay its employees. It would first prepare a magnetic tape giving, for each employee, the amount to be paid, the numbers of the bank account from which the transfer is to be made and to which it is to be paid, and the date of the transfer. The corporation then transmits the tape to the ACH, either directly or through its own bank, and the ACH then sees to it that the funds are automatically transferred to the bank account of each worker and debited from the accounts of the corporation. A conventional check is not used anywhere in the process.

As far as the individual consumer is concerned, the new wrinkles for transferring funds without checks stem from automatic teller machines and point-of-sale systems. An *automatic teller machine (ATM)* carries out many of the routine tasks for which human bank tellers are responsible. (However, see box.) Via an ATM one can make a deposit, withdraw funds, and transfer funds between savings and checking accounts. ATMs also offer a number of obvious advantages. First and foremost is convenience, since ATMs provide service 24 hours a day, seven days a week. Furthermore, ATMs can be located in a wide variety of settings, such as airports and shopping centers, at substantially lower cost than building a conventional bank branch office.

THE HUMAN SIDE OF BANKING

While ATMs have spread rapidly, as Citibank has discovered there can be some customer resistance to dealing with machines. Citibank, in an economy move, began a program in 1981 of substituting bank machines for human tellers. Depositors with more than $5,000 in any combination of accounts received a sticker to place on their money machine card, and this sticker entitled the customer to wait in line to see a human teller. All other customers were required to deal with an electronic bank machine for routine bank transactions.

The program apparently did not generate much opposition until March 1983 when Citibank extended it to two of its branches in Manhattan. At this point, protest erupted. In reference to the bank's then-prevailing advertising slogan "the Citi Never Sleeps," one outraged customer noted "The Citi may never sleep, but it yawns a lot because it's bored with us poor people. It's a completely elitist policy. What the bank is saying is that if you don't have money, you're going to get rotten service." As the public outcry spread, a bill was introduced in the New York Legislature requiring teller services for all bank customers.

By May 1983, Citibank had had enough, announcing immediate abandonment of the program at its Manhattan branches and signaling its intention to cancel the program at its other branches. A Citibank official, candidly assessing the move, noted, "The policy did smack a little of class distinction, which is not consistent with our interest in serving customers. There was some bad publicity, and publicity can crystallize public opinion."

The number of ATMs had reached 36,000 as of mid-1983. Moreover, individual banks have started linking their ATMs with those of other institutions to create local, regional, and even national networks through which customers of any of the participating institutions may have access to their accounts. It becomes perfectly plausible to imagine a Massachusetts resident vacationing in Aspen, Colorado, who goes to the local shopping center and withdraws cash directly from her own account. Again, in this whole process, the conventional check is nowhere in evidence.

In the long run, however, it may well be the *point-of-sale (POS) terminal* that has the greatest impact on reducing the flow of checks. A POS terminal at the checkout counter of a retail store would enable a customer with appropriate plastic identification to pay for a purchase by instantly transferring funds from his or her bank account to the store's bank account. The customer might have an overdraft privilege at the bank so that purchases could also be made on credit. Alternatively, the POS terminal might be used as a substitute for an ATM, with the clerk at the checkout counter providing the customer with cash.

BARRIERS TO AN EFTS

The technical basis for an EFTS exists at the present time; moreover, as the rapid growth of ATMs illustrates, the components of an EFTS are also now cost effective. Nevertheless, there are substantial economic and legal barriers to a full-fledged EFTS. The economic barriers stem from the relatively high fixed costs associated with the necessary computer hardware and software and the communications links. These costs make an EFTS system attractive only if there are a substantial number of users. This requires that banks overcome the fact that—astonishing as it may seem to computer experts—people like and trust checks.[7] Getting around this requires that bank service charges begin to reflect the true cost of processing a check, something which is only beginning to happen. The legal barriers to an EFTS stem from the view that ATMs and POS terminals are branch banks in disguise and therefore ought to be governed by the laws that apply to branch banking. Similarly, a nationwide EFTS might well run afoul of prohibitions on interstate banking. Both of these important issues will be considered in subsequent chapters.

IMPLICATIONS OF AN EFTS

While the implementation of an EFTS clearly requires that economic and legal problems be surmounted, for purposes of discussion let us assume that at some point in the future we have made the transition. What differences are we likely to observe in the operation of the system as compared with our preset structure? At the most mundane level we would, of course, see a marked reduction in the use of the conventional checking instrument. But what of the volume of deposits and the appropriate definition of the supply of money? Clearly, in such a world, a broader definition of the money supply would be needed, and such a definition would have to include any depository account accessible by electronic means. Equally evident, however, is the fact that the most appropriate definition of money will depend on the precise details of the payments mechanism.

An electronic payments mechanism would undoubtedly have other implications for the operation of the financial system as well. Most important, an EFTS would provide a new element in the ongoing changes in the nature of competition among the various types of financial institutions. Put simply,

[7]Some people have even been known to spend a rainy afternoon going through old checks as a remembrance of things past.

One rather lighthearted summary of the problem of defining money with some observations about an EFTS is contained in the following contribution by Kenneth Boulding:

> We must have a good definition of Money,
> For if we do not, then what have we got,
> But a Quantity Theory of no-one-knows-what,
> And this would be almost too true to be funny.
> Now, Banks secrete something, as bees secrete honey;
> (It sticks to their fingers some, even when hot!)
> But what things are liquid and what things are not,
> Rests on whether the climate of business is sunny.
> For both Stores of Value and Means of Exchange
> Include, among Assets, a very wide range,
> So your definition's no better than mine.
> Still, with credit-card-clever computers, it's clear
> That money as such will one day disappear;
> Then, what isn't there we won't have to define.

*Kenneth Boulding, "A Shakespearean Sonnet, as written by Swinburne and W. S. Gilbert," *Journal of Money, Credit and Banking*, August 1969, p. 555.

just as an EFTS may make obsolete what we think of as "money," it may also play havoc with our thinking about what a "bank" really is. Such changes will probably also mean a further restructuring of government regulation of financial institutions and a rethinking of monetary policy.

We shall return to these issues in a later chapter. For the present, the mere possibility of an electronic transfer system should serve to reemphasize that appropriate definitions, such as that for money, are continually evolving and require constant review in the light of institutional changes in our economy.

SUMMARY

1 Money can be usefully classified into three categories: full-bodied money; representative full-bodied money; and credit money. Full-bodied money or commodity money is money whose value as a commodity is as great as its value as money. A wide variety of commodities have served as money, including cattle, wool, and tobacco, but the principal monetary commodities have been metals such as gold or silver. In some instances, rather than have the metallic commodity circulate directly,

societies have used representative full-bodied money, typically made of paper, but backed by an equivalent value of the metallic commodity.

2 Under a metallic standard such as a gold standard, a country would try to maintain its monetary unit at a constant value in terms of some commodity (e.g., $35 for one ounce of gold). In its pure form, the gold standard permits full convertibility between gold and money. As a result, variations in the stock of money are tied to gold discoveries and not necessarily related to the needs of the economy. The United States abandoned the pure gold standard in 1933; a limited standard prevailed until 1971.

3 Modern economies tend to rely on credit or debt money, which is neither backed by nor made of a commodity whose value is as great as the value of the money. Credit money can be issued by governments or financial institutions. Examples of credit money include token coins, currency issued by the Federal Reserve, and checkable deposits at banks.

4 Through the years, the payments mechanism has undergone many changes. In early times, payments were typically made in commodity money. As banking developed, the transfer of paper claims became more prevalent. This evolved into the widespread use of checks as a means of payment. In the future, payments may be made by electronic transfer systems via automatic teller machines and point-of-sale terminals. Such a development would have dramatic implications for how we should define money and far-reaching consequences for bank regulation and the conduct of monetary policy.

SELECTED READINGS

Angell, N., *The Story of Money*. New York, Harper & Bros., 1929.

Einzig, P., *Primitive Money*, New York, Oxford University Press, 1966.

Flannery, M. J., and D. M. Jaffee, *The Economic Implications of an Electronic Monetary Transfer System*. Lexington, MA, Heath, 1973.

Galbraith, J. K., *Money: Whence It Came, Where It Went*. Boston, Houghton Mifflin, 1975.

Mitchell, G. W. and R. Hodgon, "Federal Reserve and the Payments System," *Federal Reserve Bulletin*, February 1981, pp. 109–116.

3

DEBT, CREDIT, AND FINANCIAL MARKETS AND INSTITUTIONS

Although in some quarters the notion of being in debt has an evil ring, we shall see in this chapter that debt performs a vital role in channeling savings into productive investment. Put another way, just as money (which is in fact a form of debt) enables an economy to overcome the inefficiencies of barter, the existence of a broad range of debt instruments can help in achieving an efficient allocation of resources and a higher rate of economic growth.

After analyzing the economic functions of debt, we turn to the second objective of this chapter: the actual process of debt creation. We examine the vital role of financial markets and financial institutions in transmitting funds from lenders to borrowers or from savers to investors. A firm understanding of the general principles involved will prove critical in later chapters, where we examine the role of money and monetary policy in more detail.

THE NATURE OF CREDIT OR DEBT

Debt and credit are merely the same thing looked at from two different points of view. They are an obligation to pay in the future; and since money is so widely used as a standard of deferred payments, they are usually

41

obligations to pay fixed sums of money. From the point of view of the person to whom the future payment is to be made, the obligation is a *credit;* it is a claim against another person for payment. But from the point of view of the one who is obliged to pay in the future, the obligation is a *debt.* It should be obvious that the amount of debt outstanding at any given time must be equal to the amount of credit outstanding at that time.

Credit or debt usually originates in economic and financial transactions in which creditors surrender something of value at one point in time in exchange for debtors' promises to pay in the future. The "something of value" surrendered may be money, services, goods, or some financial claim such as stocks or bonds. However, the resulting debt is usually payable in money. We are all familiar with the creation of debt by the sale of goods or services "on credit." For example, Ms. Jones buys groceries, promising to pay at the end of the month. A corporation gets raw materials from its suppliers with the understanding that it will pay at the end of the quarter. Much of the outstanding debt at any time has arisen from such extensions of credit by sellers of goods and services. Most of the remainder has arisen out of money-lending transactions in which creditors surrendered money at one point of time in exchange for promises of debtors to pay later, usually with interest.

ECONOMIC FUNCTIONS OF DEBT

The basic economic functions of debt and financial instruments can be understood most easily and clearly by considering a relatively simple society made up of spending units or households. Each household or unit receives during any period, such as a month, some flow of income resulting from the household's or unit's contribution to the value of current output of goods and services. During each income period each unit also spends some amount for the current output of goods and services to be used for consumption purposes. A unit's income and consumption need not be exactly equal during any period. The difference between them will be called *saving.* During any period, therefore, households can be separated into three categories based on their pattern of saving. (1) *Zero savers* are those whose current consumption is exactly equal to their current income. (2) *Positive savers*, or simply *savers*, are those who consume less than their current income. Their saving represents the amount of their current income that they do not use to demand goods and services for their own current consumption. (3) *Negative savers* or *dissavers* are people whose current consumption exceeds their current income. Their consumption demands for output exceed their current incomes.

Let us now explore why a household may elect to be a saver or dissaver during a period, and why it may be a saver in some periods and a dissaver in others.

DEBT AND CONSUMPTION

One problem faced by each household or unit is allocating its consumption through time—i.e., recognizing that with given current and expected future incomes, "the more we consume in one period the less can we consume in others." To achieve maximum total utility or satisfaction through time, each unit would have to take into consideration its current income, expected future income streams, present needs, and expected future needs. At any given time, different units are likely to attach differing relative values to consumption in the present as against consumption in the future. One unit may value present consumption very highly and be willing to sacrifice large amounts of future consumption in order to consume now in excess of its current income. Another may place a much lower premium on present consumption and demand little reward for consuming less than its current income.

Differing time patterns of income and needs contribute strongly to differences in valuations of present versus future consumption. For example, some units may have large needs in the present—such as expensive medical care or educational services for their children—but expect their future needs to be lower. And their current income may be well below that expected in the future. Such units are likely to place a high premium on present consumption and to want to consume in excess of current incomes. Other units may be in the reverse position. Their present needs may be small relative to those expected in the future, when children reach college age or parents face retirement. And their present incomes may be high relative to those expected in the future. Such units are likely to place a low premium on present consumption and to want to consume less than their current incomes.

When households place different relative valuations on present and future consumption, all can be made to feel better off—to increase their total utility—through exchange or trade of present consumption against future consumption. Those units that place lower premiums on present consumption can transfer their current saving, representing claims on current output, to those units that place a higher premium on present consumption. Later, the borrowing units will return consuming power to the lenders, who can then decide whether to use it immediately for consumption or to save it for later. Thus, all units may be enabled to increase their total utilities through an optimal spreading or allocation of their consumption through time.

In the absence of debt or credit, exchanges of present consumption against future consumption are likely to be inefficient and so limited in extent that large potential increases in utility will fail to be realized. Suppose, for example, that a community has not yet invented consumer credit and has available only two types of assets—physical assets and some form of money, such as coins or paper money, which yields no interest. Households that wished to consume in excess of current incomes could do so only by drawing down their money balances or selling their physical assets. They may not have any excess money balances or physical assets that they could sell without serious deprivation or loss.

Those who wish to save are faced with only very limited alternative uses of their saving; they can increase their money balances or buy physical assets. Increased money balances would provide additional liquidity and safety for the saver, but yield no income. Physical assets might yield an income, but be unattractive because of the transactions costs, illiquidity, and risk involved. As a consequence, savers might save less, and in any case, transfers of their money saving to dissavers would be limited.

The situation can be improved by the invention and use of consumer debt or credit. This enables savers to transfer their money saving, representing claims against current output, to dissavers in exchange for their promises to repay in the future.

So consumer credit (or debt) enables households to better space their consumption through time. It also involves the creation of financial instruments that enrich the menu of assets available to savers.

DEBT AND INVESTMENT

Although consumer credit is widely used and the outstanding stock of consumer debt is very large, a much larger part of the total debt outstanding was created in the process of investment or capital formation—the process of adding to the nation's stock of capital goods. The *stock of capital goods* at any point of time is the accumulated stock of goods produced in the past and not yet consumed. An outstanding characteristic of modern industrial societies is the huge stock of capital. Some types of capital render services directly to consumers, such as houses and apartments, which provide shelter and comfort. However, a larger part of the capital stock renders services as instruments in processes of production. Examples are structures and many types of durable equipment used in manufacturing, transportation, communications, and wholesale and retail trade; office buildings; farm machinery and other equipment; business inventories; and so on. In an industrial economy this huge stock of capital is a major reason for the high output per capita. Technological advances and increases in the stock of capital relative to labor are the two principal sources of growth of output per capita and of output per unit of labor. It is partly because of this that we are so interested in processes of capital formation or investment.

Saving is a necessary condition for capital formation. A society could not add to its stock of capital goods if its members insisted on using for current consumption all the income or output that its labor and other productive resources could produce. *Saving*, or abstinence from current consumption, frees some part of available productive resources to produce output to be used to increase the stock of capital. However, although the ability and willingness to save is a necessary condition for capital formation, it is not by itself sufficient to assure that capital formation will occur. The resources that are not used to produce output for current consumption may remain unemployed or go to waste if no one employs them to produce goods to be added to the stock of capital. Thus, investment is another necessary condition for capital formation. *Investment* means the amount spent during a stated period for current output to be used to increase the stock of capital goods. It is through investment that the amounts of income or output, and more basically the productive resources that are saved, are translated into capital accumulation.

One can imagine an economic system in which each household spent for investment in each period an amount exactly equal to its own saving, no more and no less. Such a system would be highly inefficient, for at least two reasons:

1 **DIFFERENCES IN THE MARGINAL PRODUCTIVITY OF CAPITAL.** For some units, including some with high rates of saving, the *marginal productivity of capital*—the addition to output resulting from additions to capital stock—may be very low. There may be many reasons for this—lack of interest or ability in entrepreneurship and management, inadequate education or experience, possession of an already large stock of capital assets, and so on. For other units, including some with low rates of saving, the marginal productivity of capital may be much higher.

2 **DISECONOMIES OF SMALL SCALE.** If each household or unit could command only an amount of capital equal to its own accumulated savings, many enterprises would be too small to achieve the greater output made possible by the economies of scale. They would not be able to amass enough capital of specialized types, to command the necessary array of special talents, or to reap the other economies of large-scale production.

It is therefore clear that if capital is to make its maximum contribution to productivity, ways must be found to transfer savings, and thus the power of investment, to those who can achieve the highest marginal productivity of capital, and that savings must be pooled and used for investment in entities large enough to achieve economies of scale. In some industries the latter requires the pooling of hundreds of millions or even billions of dollars' worth of assets. In this process, a new type of institution differentiated from households—the specialized business firm—appears.

These business firms in turn create financial instruments or claims against themselves. In effect, savers surrender funds to those who wish to invest, receiving in return newly created financial instruments that represent claims against both the income of firms and their assets. Thus, the process of creating real capital usually has its counterpart in the creation of financial claims that are issued to raise the funds used to buy the capital.

Actual financial claims are of two broad types: equity claims and debt claims. *Equity claims*, such as common stock, are shares of ownership in the firm, necessarily involving both the possibilities of profits and the risk of loss. Alternatively, the saver may prefer to hold a *debt claim*, such as a corporate bond. In this case the firm promises to pay a stated amount of interest and to repay a stated amount of principal at a later date. While the factors that influence a saver's choice between equity and debt claims will be touched upon later, here we simply wish to emphasize that large amounts of business investment are financed through the issue of debt and equity claims.[1]

DEBT AND OTHER INSTITUTIONS

For almost all other types of institutions in our society, debt and credit serve functions quite comparable to those served for households and business firms. Other such institutions include federal, state, and municipal governments; educational institutions; churches; charitable institutions; country clubs; fraternities; and many others. In any stated period these institutions receive flows of income and spend for current output. However, many do not wish to spend for output in a period an amount exactly equal to their current income. Some wish to spend for consumption and investment in capital formation an amount less than their current income. They are in a position to extend credit—to transfer to others claims against current output, receiving in return debt or equity claims. Others wish to be deficit units, to buy output to be used for consumption and investment in amounts exceeding their current incomes. Creation of debt claims against themselves enables them to command more output now in exchange for the obligation to repay later.

OVERVIEW

As should be clear by now, in any given year some units—such as households, business firms, or governmental units—spend more for consumption and investment than they receive in current income. These are called *deficit units.* Other units spend less than their current income for consumption

---

[1]In common parlance, those who put their assets in equity or debt claims are said to "make an investment." We will follow the more narrowly defined usage of the term in economics, in which the term *investment* is reserved for additions to the stock of capital used in production. Of course, the two uses may be related—as, for example, when a company issues debt to finance building a factory. But not all purchases of financial claims are associated with investment in the narrower sense. For example, the purchase of financial claims whose proceeds are used for the purchase of an existing factory results in nothing new being created but merely represents a transfer of ownership. Indeed, in recent years there has been some controversy over the role of banks in financing corporate mergers or takeovers.

and investment purposes, and thus are called *surplus units*. By permitting a transfer of resources from surplus to deficit units, debt plays a critical role in achieving an efficient allocation of resources in the economy. As we shall see, this transfer takes place via a set of financial institutions that collectively constitute a *financial system*. As the late Arthur Okun has expressed it, "the key function of a financial system is to offer people the opportunities to invest without saving and to save without investing."

THE STOCK OF OUTSTANDING DEBT

As a result of the transfer of funds from surplus to deficit units, at any point in time there is a stock of debt or credit outstanding. This stock is equal to the total of all debt issues in preceding periods minus amounts retired through repayment or default.

There are a variety of ways to summarize the stock of outstanding debt. One perspective is provided in Table 3–1, which contains data for the stock of credit market instruments on selected dates. A number of features of this table deserve emphasis. One is the huge volume of outstanding credit market debt—approximately $7,100 billion at the end of 1984. Another is the rate of growth of outstanding debt. For the last 20 years the annual growth of outstanding debt has averaged $305 billion, and its annual average growth in the past decade was $471 billion.

To some pessimists, both the size of outstanding debt and its rate of growth are frightening. They lament that we shall never be able to pay off the debt and that as a nation we are borrowing ourselves into bankruptcy. To refute such primitive theses, we do not have to argue that the growth rate of debt has been "just right" or that all debt has been wisely incurred. Several facts are relevant:

TABLE 3-1 Outstanding Credit Market Debt in the United States (end-of-year figures, in billions of dollars)

Type of debt	1964	1974	1984
U.S. government securities	271.4	457.6	1,902.1
State and local obligations	92.9	207.7	539.2
Corporate and foreign bonds	113.9	286.7	639.5
Mortgages	305.7	741.1	2,024.1
Consumer credit	92.6	213.6	638.1
Bank loans	81.2	278.4	593.6
Other debt	68.2	221.5	1,005.8
Total	$1,026.0	$2,406.7	$7,121.0

SOURCE: Board of Governors of the Federal Reserve System, *Flow of Funds Accounts*, various issues.

1 "We owe it to ourselves." Although many consider debt the antithesis of thrift, savers need debt in order to find an outlet for savings. Thus, the debts of some American units are the assets of others.[2]

2 There is no reason why the outstanding debt should be retired or even reduced in total volume. Some debts will be repaid or reduced, and new debt will be created. Much of the debt, especially that incurred by governments or large businesses, will simply be "rolled over"—that is, replaced by new debt when the old debt matures.

3 The increase of total debt and of service charges on that debt has been accompanied by increases in ability to pay, whether this is measured in terms of income or in terms of the value of national assets. For example, between 1946 and 1984 the gross national product at annual rates and at current prices rose from $210 billion to $3,663 billion. The rise in corporate debt has been a financial counterpart of a high rate of investment in plant, equipment, and inventories. State and local government debt has been incurred mainly to finance public investment in new schools, streets, sanitation systems, and so on.

Some additional perspective on the role of debt in the economy can be gleaned from Table 3–2, which gives a more comprehensive snapshot of the stock of outstanding financial instruments for the year 1984. The data, which are taken from the extremely useful *Flow of Funds Accounts* compiled and published by the Federal Reserve System, illustrate the importance of debt for all the major sectors of the economy. Several facts stand out:

1 *Households* are the economy's largest lender group, with total financial assets of $6,609 billion and total liabilities of $2,224 billion. Much of the household-owned debt is highly liquid, being in the form of money or near-money. The major household liabilities are residential mortgages and consumer credit. The excess of financial assets over financial liabilities of $4,385 billion, which might be termed *financial net worth*, is only part of the overall net worth of the household sector. To arrive at total *net worth* one must include net nonfinancial assets, including real estate and other tangible property such as consumer durables. For 1984, total household net worth amounted to a hefty $11,500 billion.

2 *Businesses* as a group are net financial debtors. Most business debts are owed to financial institutions, with the household sector holding the bulk of the equity shares outstanding. Missing from Table 3–2 are the important nonfinancial assets held by businesses in the form of plant, equipment, and inventory.

3 *Governments*, like businesses, have liabilities that exceed their debt claims on other sectors. Federal debt vastly exceeds state and local

[2]This statement, which is specifically illustrated in Table 3–2, needs to be qualified in that a small but growing part of this debt is owed to foreigners.

TABLE 3-2 Financial Assets and Liabilities (year-end 1984, in billions of dollars)

Type of instrument	HOUSEHOLDS		BUSINESS		GOVERNMENT		FINANCIAL	
	Assets	Liabilities	Assets	Liabilities	Assets	Liabilities	Assets	Liabilities
Demand deposits and currency	386.5		87.7		22.3		63.5	623.1
Time and savings accounts	1,868.2		81.4		73.1		77.0	2,139.1
Money market fund shares	209.7							209.7
Life insurance and pension reserves	1,681.8					139.9		1,542.0
Corporate stock	1,492.5						596.9	161.9
Government securities	611.8		34.1	102.4	174.4	1,762.1	1,428.1	525.5
Corporate and foreign bonds	40.2			453.5			535.9	119.6
Mortgages	184.9	1,373.6		648.3	108.8		1,730.4	2.1
Consumer credit		593.6	76.1				517.5	
Bank loans		36.0		543.6			638.1	30.4
Miscellaneous	132.9	220.6	1,121.0	950.5	269.3	81.4	1,188.5	1,116.9
Total	$6,608.5	$2,223.8	$1,400.3	$2,698.3	$647.9	$1,983.4	$6,775.9	$6,470.3

NOTE: Blanks indicate zero or insignificant entries. For a given row in the table, assets and liabilities do not necessarily balance because we have omitted the "Rest of the World" category and because of minor discrepancies in the data.

SOURCE: Board of Governors of the Federal Reserve System, *Flow of Funds Accounts*, various issues.

debt, but includes large amounts of federal obligations held by federal agencies and trust funds (e.g., Social Security) and by the Federal Reserve.

4 *Financial institutions* such as commercial banks, savings and loan associations, and insurance companies have amassed huge amounts of funds. The bulk of their liabilities are owed to the household sector. Their assets are widely distributed in claims against the household, business, and government sectors. They clearly serve as an important middleman between surplus and deficit units, a role we examine in more detail shortly.

As should be evident from this brief survey of the stock of outstanding financial assets and liabilities, debt instruments are a permanent and important feature of any modern economy. We turn now from the critical role served by debt instruments in channeling funds from surplus to deficit units to the actual *process* of channeling funds from lenders to borrowers.

Figure 3–1 schematically illustrates the twin nature of this process. The first way in which funds are transmitted is *direct* finance, in which ultimate borrowers and lenders are directly matched. Typically, such transactions are arranged by brokers or dealers serving as middlemen who maintain markets for trading both new and outstanding issues of debt instruments. The columns in Table 3–2 for households, business, and government give some indication of the extent of direct finance.

The second method of channeling funds from surplus to deficit units is *indirect*, through financial intermediaries. The importance of this channel is indicated by the vast sums in the "financial" column of Table 3–2. A *financial intermediary* is simply a financial institution—such as a commercial bank, a savings bank, a pension fund, or an insurance company—that issues claims against itself (acquired by ultimate lenders) and uses the proceeds to acquire financial claims against others (the ultimate borrowers). The claims issued by financial intermediaries are called *indirect securities*. Since both brokers and financial intermediaries are serving as middlemen, it is not the absence of a middleman that distinguishes direct and indirect finance. Rather, it is the issuance of indirect securities such as savings deposits. The importance of this distinction will become clearer as we proceed.

FIGURE 3–1
Flows of funds via direct and indirect finance

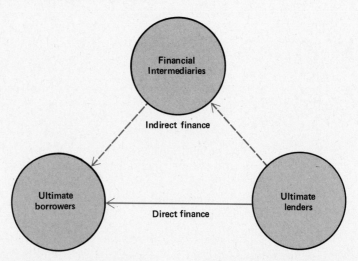

Economic units that raise funds by selling their liabilities to ultimate lenders (direct finance) or to financial intermediaries (indirect finance)

Economic units that acquire financial assets from ultimate borrowers (direct finance) or from financial intermediaries (indirect finance)

FINANCIAL MARKETS AND DIRECT FINANCE

Specialized financial institutions perform services such as gathering and disseminating information about the sources and uses of funds and the creditworthiness of potential borrowers, serving as middlemen between issuers and ultimate buyers of debt and equity claims, and acting as brokers and dealers to facilitate trading in outstanding claims. However, debt, credit, and instruments representing debt and ownership claims could be used even in the absence of these specialized institutions. Deficit units could sell newly created debt or equity claims directly to surplus units. The buyer might then hold the claim until it was redeemed by the issuer. If the buyer wished to sell it, he or she could then search for someone willing to buy it.

Such a simple set of arrangements could function, but only so inefficiently as to increase the cost and inhibit the development of financial processes. For one thing, it could not produce and disseminate the information and analysis required for rational and efficient valuation of claims. Such instruments are only claims against future asset values and future flows of income, and they can be valued rationally only to the extent that buyers and sellers can forecast what these future values are likely to be and the probabilities that they will be realized. This requires information and analysis concerning the past performance of the issuer in meeting its obligations; forecasts of the future performance of the issuer; comparison with other available claims; and so on. If buyers and sellers had to gather and analyze information for themselves, the cost would be so high that only very limited amounts of information would be gathered and analyzed. Ignorance would limit the scope of markets, inhibit regional mobility of funds, and increase risk. Inefficiency in the allocation of funds and of capital investment would be inevitable.

In such a system the creation and sale of new claims would be inefficient and expensive. The issuer would have to seek out buyers, perhaps by ringing doorbells. Markets would be localized, and it would be difficult to move funds from areas of credit plenty to areas of credit scarcity. In the absence of facilities for trading in the stock of outstanding claims, each buyer might hold a security until it matured. If this were necessary, many buyers would be unwilling to acquire claims with longer maturities, or would buy them only at very high yields, because buyers might not want to have these funds unavailable for long periods of time. As an alternative to holding long-term credits, a buyer might seek out other buyers, but this would be time-consuming, and the scarcity of prospective buyers might cause the claim to be sold at low prices. The claims would be illiquid, and the risk of loss of capital value would be high.

To remedy such shortcomings, many types of financial institutions have been developed. We shall now examine two of their other functions: primary distribution of securities and the provision of secondary markets for securities.

PRIMARY DISTRIBUTION OF SECURITIES

Primary distribution of securities means the initial sale of newly created debt or equity claims. This function is best illustrated by *investment banks*, which do not buy securities with the intention of holding them but, like any other merchant, buy for the purpose of resale. Suppose some entity— a corporation or a governmental unit—decides to issue new securities and to sell them through an investment bank or group of investment banks. It may select the investment bank by competitive bidding or through nego- tiation. The investment bank performs four functions:

1 **INVESTIGATION.** This involves analysis of the present status and prob- able future performance of the issuer, the quality of the proposed issue, prices of comparable securities, and prospective market con- ditions. It culminates in the determination of a price for the new issue.

2 **UNDERWRITING.** The investment bank guarantees the issuer a fixed price and assumes the risk of resale. If the issue is small, a single investment bank may underwrite it. If it is larger, two or more in- vestment banks may form an *underwriting syndicate*, each assuming a share of the risk. Some underwriting syndicates include 50 or more investment banks.

3 **WHOLESALE DISTRIBUTION.** In some cases, the underwriters sell at least a part of the issue to other dealers.

4 **RETAIL DISTRIBUTION.** This is the function of selling the new secu- rities to their ultimate buyers. In some cases, the underwriters do this themselves. In others, they sell part of the issue to hundreds of dealers located throughout the nation and even in foreign countries. Their contribution to the regional mobility of funds is evident.

Investment banks are commonly used to distribute issues by corpora- tions, foreign governments, state governments, municipalities and many types of local authorities, and some agencies of the federal government. In a few cases the federal government has distributed its own direct issues through investment banking syndicates. Usually, however, this function is performed for federal securities by the Federal Reserve and commercial banks.

Commercial paper houses are another example of an institution that assists in primary distribution of newly issued short-term claims. *Com- mercial paper*, in this technical sense, refers to short-term promissory notes issued by finance companies and other corporations of high standing. Much of this is sold by the issuer directly to the ultimate buyer, the latter being primarily financial institutions and nonfinancial corporations with funds to invest for short periods. Some commercial paper is issued to dealers, who pay the issuer and distribute the paper to buyers all over the country. Only well-known firms find it feasible to sell their paper in this market.

Institutions engaged in primary distribution of new debt and equity instruments serve to reduce the cost of new issues, to increase the mobility of funds over wide areas, and to improve both the allocation of investible funds and of investment in real capital.

SECONDARY MARKETS FOR SECURITIES

By *secondary markets* we do not mean facilities for the initial sale of new issues, but facilities for trading in outstanding debt and equity claims. If the term were not derogatory, we would call it "the market for secondhand securities." The term *securities* is used here in its broadest sense to include ownership shares and debt obligations of all maturities. Sometimes a distinction is made between *securities markets* or *capital markets*, in which ownership shares and long-term debt obligations are bought and sold, and *money markets*, in which short-term debt obligations are traded.

The secondary securities market in the United States is highly complex, including central securities exchanges and thousands of persons and firms serving as brokers and dealers. Securities dealers buy and sell for their own accounts; they are like any secondhand merchant whose income is derived from the difference between buying price and selling price. However, in serving the brokerage function, brokers do not buy or sell for their own accounts; they act as go-betweens for buyers and sellers. In some cases, they learn who wants to sell and who wants to buy, and then put the prospective buyer and seller in contact with each other so they can enter into a transaction. In others, they act as agent for a buyer or seller.

Some securities command more efficient secondary markets than others. The *marketability* of a security, its ability to be sold quickly without a large decrease in price, depends heavily on at least two factors:

1 **HOW WIDELY ITS ISSUER AND ITS QUALITIES ARE KNOWN.** If both are widely known, there are likely to be many actual and potential buyers who will bid for the security. If only a few know about the security, it may be salable only after a considerable delay or decline of price.
2 **THE AMOUNT OF THE SECURITY OUTSTANDING AND THE NUMBER OF ITS HOLDERS.** If a large amount of it is outstanding and it is widely held, transactions are likely to be frequent and buyers easy to find. But if the amount outstanding is small or most of it is held by only a few, the market for it is likely to be erratic.

Many securities meet both tests and enjoy a continuous market in which individual sellers or buyers can sell or buy considerable amounts quickly with little effect on price. Other securities lack marketability and can be sold only after a delay or a significant decline in price.

The existence of a highly efficient secondary market for a security markedly increases its liquidity and safety of principal value. Its marketability serves one of the requirements of liquidity—the ability to be converted to money quickly. Of course, the other requirement—stability of value—is not assured by the existence of an efficient market. The value of a security may indeed fall because of less optimistic assessments of its issuer, the appearance of more attractive securities, or general changes in financial markets. But the holder is at least assured that there are many potential buyers who will compete for the security at a price commensurate with the prices of comparable issues.

To the extent that secondary markets enhance the expected liquidity and safety of value of securities, issuers of securities can acquire funds at lower costs, which promotes capital formation. Enhanced marketability also makes it less advantageous for buyers to purchase only those securities that mature at or before the time when they will want to use the funds for some other purpose. They can buy issues with longer maturities and recover the money at any time by selling in the secondary market—but only by assuming some risk of loss of value, which may or may not be offset by possibilities of capital gains.

Liquidity through marketability thus helps solve a problem that would exist in a system in which buyers of claims would have to hold them to maturity or could sell them only with difficulty. Deficit units would want to issue large amounts of long-term claims, considering heavy reliance on short-term financing too risky, while buyers would demand short-term claims because they thought they soon would, or might, want to use their money for other purposes.

Let us now survey briefly a few branches of the secondary market for securities, emphasizing functions rather than institutional detail. We start with the national securities exchanges, which include the New York Stock Exchange and the American Stock Exchange in New York City and lesser exchanges in several other cities. The exchanges themselves do not engage in trading. Their functions are to provide physical facilities, including the trading floor; to provide reporting and communications facilities; to determine what issues will be admitted to trading on the exchange; to regulate the conduct of their members; and so on. Actual trading is done by brokers and dealers who are members of the exchanges. These brokers and dealers are interlinked with all parts of the nation and with other countries in various ways. Offers to buy and sell flow through this network to the floor of the exchange from all parts of the country and from other countries. These offers meet on the floor of the exchange, where brokers and dealers conduct what is in effect an auction market, with the securities being sold to those who offer the highest prices. Both equities and bonds of major corporations are traded on these exchanges.

Another type of secondary market for securities is popularly called the *over-the-counter* market. This is not a market in the sense of some central place at which supply and demand meet and at which purchases and sales are consummated. Rather, it is a set of arrangements involving brokers and dealers who are located all over the country and who are linked to one another and to buyers and sellers by telephone, teletype, computers, and written communications (including lists of offers to buy or sell). When an offer to buy or sell is received by a dealer or broker, the broker may sell or buy for his or her own account or for a customer, or communicate the offer to other brokers and dealers in the network. Many types of securities are traded in the over-the-counter market: shares of corporations, corporate bonds and some types of shorter-term corporate debt, debts of foreign governments, debts of the federal government, and debts of states and municipalities.

We deal later with some branches of the over-the-counter market that play important roles in the functioning of the banking and financial system. Among these are the following:

1 The market for U.S. government securities, including dealers who maintain continuous markets for marketable issues of the federal government.
2 The market for negotiable certificates of deposit (CDs), which are transferable instruments representing time-deposit claims against banks.
3 The federal funds market, in which claims against deposits at the Federal Reserve banks are bought and sold.

Such markets play important roles in enhancing the liquidity of some of these assets, in providing liquidity for various financial institutions and others, and in increasing the mobility of funds.

DEVELOPMENT OF FINANCIAL INTERMEDIARIES

The second major channel for transmitting funds from lenders to borrowers is via institutions known as *financial intermediaries.* There are many types of financial intermediaries, such as savings banks, commercial banks, credit unions, and insurance companies, and the details of their operations vary considerably. What they share in common, however, is that they all issue liabilities to the public (e.g., savings deposits and savings and loan shares) and then turn around and use these funds to buy direct securities (e.g., stocks and bonds). To contrast them with the direct securities traded in financial markets, the liabilities of financial intermediaries are termed *indirect securities.*

We have already seen that households and other ultimate owners of savings can and do acquire and hold very large amounts of direct securities. The fact that ultimate owners of savings have the alternative of making up their own portfolios of money and many varieties of direct securities raises key questions: How can a financial intermediary make a living? What can it do for ultimate owners of savings that will induce them to pay an amount large enough for its services to cover its operating costs and leave a profit? In general terms, the answer is that, for at least some savers, a financial intermediary can do what the savers cannot do for themselves, or can do only at higher cost.

Especially for those individuals whose total accumulated savings are not large and for those whose current flow of saving is small, the acquisition and holding of direct securities involves high costs and other disadvantages:

1 **COST OF INFORMATION AND ANALYSIS OF DIRECT SECURITIES.** Many of those who do not acquire expert knowledge about securities in their regular course of business find it costly in terms of time, money, or both to gather and analyze information about any large number of direct securities. This is especially true when people have only small sums to invest.

2 **COST OF BUYING, HOLDING, AND SELLING DIRECT SECURITIES.** Most brokerage fees and other charges for buying and selling vary inversely in percentage terms with the sums involved. Brokers and dealers commonly impose a minimum flat charge in dollars, plus a diminishing percentage charge on sums in excess of that covered by the flat charge. Thus, transactions costs, in percentage terms, are often prohibitive when the sums involved are small or when the securities are to be held only a short time.

3 **COST OF DIVERSIFICATION.** The safety of principal value can be enhanced by holding a variety of direct securities whose prices do not move in a parallel way. Thus, total default risk can be reduced by holding debt claims against a variety of debtors, and greater stability of value may be achieved by holding a wide variety of ownership shares, rather than concentrating on one or a few issues. Wealthy holders, with millions at their disposal, may achieve a high degree of diversification at relatively low cost, but this is not true of those with a smaller volume of assets. These holders must be content with a few issues or incur the high transactions costs involved in buying small amounts of large numbers of issues.

4 **COSTS OF LIQUIDITY.** Most units wish to hold some liquid assets with which to meet foreseen or unforeseen excesses of expenditures over receipts. This can be expensive in terms of foregone income or explicit costs if the only assets available for this purpose are money and direct securities.

These disadvantages and diseconomies of a financial system containing only money itself and direct securities account for the establishment and growth of financial intermediaries. Enterprisers have found a source of profit: Members of the community were willing to accept, on the indirect securities issued by financial intermediaries, a rate of return sufficiently below the rates earned on the direct securities acquired by the intermediaries to cover operating costs and yield a net return. Individual financial intermediaries have succeeded in drawing funds from thousands and even hundreds of thousands of ultimate owners of savings, and many have amassed great pools of assets. Intermediaries with total assets in the hundreds of millions are commonplace, those with assets in the billions are numerous, and there are even some intermediaries with assets over $100 billion.

ECONOMIES OFFERED BY INTERMEDIARIES

The ability of financial intermediaries to survive and prosper is derived from several types of economies of specialization and scale. An intermediary operating with a large pool of funds can command experts in its various functions; reap the increased productivity and lower costs resulting from a high degree of specialization; employ efficient machinery and equipment, such as computers; and often succeed in purchasing services at prices lower than those charged to individual investors. For example, it can gather and analyze information at low cost per unit by spreading the total cost over a large volume of assets. Also, intermediaries can achieve lower transactions costs in buying, holding, and selling direct securities. The preceding sources of economies are highly relevant, but we shall stress the importance of "the law of large numbers." This law is basic to both diversification of assets and the principle of offsetting receipts and withdrawal of funds.

DIVERSIFICATION OF ASSETS

If relevant future events were always predictable, there would be little or no reason for diversifying security holdings. If investors knew in advance what future returns on all securities would be, they would simply put all their funds into the security yielding the highest return. However, perfect certainty is not a characteristic of security markets. No matter how much time one may spend in gathering information, analyzing it, and making forecasts, the best that one can do is identify possible outcomes and estimate a subjective probability distribution for the various possible outcomes. For example, one may estimate the average expected return on a security to be 6 percent, but recognize that there is some probability that the return will be higher and some probability that it will be lower or even negative. Even if one feels confident about the probability distribution, one cannot know which outcome will be realized. Even the improbable can happen. One will, of course, be happy if the actual reutrn is higher than expected. However, one will hardly welcome the risk that the actual outcome will be lower or even negative. If one holds only a single security, one faces a risk that a lower return or even a negative return will depress by a large percentage one's asset value or current income, or both.

Diversification—the holding of more than one security—can decrease the total risk of a portfolio, because lower-than-expected returns on some issues can be offset by higher-than-expected returns on others. However, the extent to which diversification can lower total risk does not depend only on the number of issues held; it depends also on the diversity of behavior of returns on the various securities. Diversification could eliminate risk entirely if returns on different securities were perfectly negatively correlated—if, for example, a fall in the price of one security was always offset exactly by a rise in the price of another. Combining the two risks would eliminate the overall risk. Unfortunately, because all securities are subject to some common forces, it is rarely possible to find securities whose returns are perfectly negatively correlated.

At the other extreme, diversification could not reduce total risk at all if returns on all securities were perfectly positively correlated—if, for example, the prices of all securities always rose or fell simultaneously and in the same proportions. Fortunately, returns on all securities are not perfectly correlated; there is some degree of independence and diverse behavior. This is partly because some issues are subject to forces that do not affect others and partly because forces impinging on all issuers affect them in different ways and degrees. For example, managements of some companies improve while others deteriorate; demands for products of some companies rise while demands for the products of others remain static or decline; companies in different industries are not affected in the same way and degree by such external events as cyclical fluctuations of business, inflation, and deflation; and so on. It is because of some degree of diversity of behavior of different securities that diversification can reduce total risk.

Financial intermediaries are thus reducers of risk and manufacturers of safety. Through diversification of assets, they reduce risk to a degree that could not be achieved, or could be achieved only at higher cost, by the ultimate owners of savings. Operating with a large pool of funds, an intermediary can acquire and hold a large number of different securities; it can buy each in lots large enough to achieve low transaction costs; and through expert management, it may select a combination or portfolio of securities in which the risks best offset one another.

OFFSETTING RECEIPTS AND WITHDRAWALS OF FUNDS

Another fundamental basis for the origin and success of financial intermediaries is the phenomenon of offsetting receipts and withdrawals, which is also related to the law of large numbers. This principle was mentioned briefly in connection with our earlier discussion of commercial banking, but it is also broadly applicable to other types of financial intermediaries. To illustrate the principle, let us assume that some financial intermediary has received funds from a thousand households and has issued to them financial claims against itself, that it stands ready to accept new funds, and that it allows claimants to withdraw funds on demand or after only short notice. The management of the intermediary will expect that during any period some claimants will withdraw funds and others will bring in additional funds. That all claimants will withdraw funds at the same time is highly improbable. On the basis of its own experience and the experience of other intermediaries and based on its knowledge of the income and expenditure flow of its customers, the management will expect that withdrawals will be at least partially, and perhaps fully or more than fully, offset by inflows of funds. It may even estimate a subjective probability distribution of the possible outcomes. For example, it may estimate that during some stated future period there is an 80 percent probability that net inflows will increase its net assets by at least 5 percent, a 95 percent probability that inflows will be at least equal to withdrawals, only a 5 percent probability that net withdrawals will amount to as much as 5 percent of its assets, and only a 1 percent probability that net withdrawals will amount to as much as 10 percent of its assets.

Operating on the basis of such expectations, an intermediary can create and issue to ultimate owners of savings financial claims against itself that are more liquid than the assets that it acquires and holds. For example, the claims that it issues may be fixed in terms of dollars, payable on demand or on short notice, and thus be almost as liquid as money itself. Yet the great bulk of its assets can be in the form of longer-term illiquid securities, such as mortgages or bonds. Expecting that there is only 1 chance in 20 that net withdrawals will amount to as much as 5 percent of its assets and only 1 chance in 100 that such net withdrawals will be as high as 10 percent, it will feel secure in holding no more than 10 percent of its assets in liquid form. Even this small fraction need not all be in the form of money; most of it may be in the form of liquid short-term earning assets, such as obligations of the U.S. Treasury. Its holdings of liquid assets can be even smaller to the extent that it can rely on borrowing to meet net withdrawals.

The transactions costs incurred by an intermediary can be far below those that would be necessary if ultimate owners of savings managed their liquidity individually. To only a minor extent is this due to the fact that an intermediary, buying and selling in large lots, can buy transactions services at lower prices. It is largely the result of the fact that an intermediary need not engage in as many transactions as the individual owner. If the ultimate owners of savings provided their own liquidity, they would have to hold money, which yields no income, or pay transactions costs every time they bought a security and every time they sold a security to get money. However, because of the principle of offsetting receipts and withdrawals, an intermediary needs to sell securities only to the extent of net withdrawals. For example, if its receipts are exactly equal to withdrawals, thus leaving total assets unchanged, the intermediary need not sell any securities regardless of how large gross withdrawals may be.

OVERVIEW

Financial intermediaries are manufacturers of liquidity and safety. The intermediary can create financial claims against itself that have characteristics which differ markedly from those of the assets it acquires and holds. In these ways, intermediaries create financial claims with combinations of safety, liquidity, and yield that conform more closely to the tastes and preferences of many ultimate owners of savings. For these reasons, intermediaries have been able to attract huge amounts of funds. However, intermediaries also provide important benefits to issuers of direct securities, enabling them to issue at lower costs types of securities conforming more closely to the issuers' needs and preferences. For example, a business firm may wish to issue a long-term security that is itself relatively risky and illiquid, while individual investors place a high premium on safety and liquidity and would purchase and hold the security only if rewarded by a very high yield. An intermediary can help to solve such a problem by purchasing the risky and illiquid security conforming to the issuer's preferences and, on the basis of this security, pooled with others, create financial claims conforming to the preferences of investors. It is for this reason that intermediaries are said to intermediate between the preferences of issuers of direct securities and the preferences of asset holders.

It should be quite evident by now that the existence of financial intermediaries leads to a more efficient flow of funds from lenders to borrowers. As a consequence, financial intermediaries, along with financial markets, play an important role in fostering productive investment and economic growth. We look now at some of the principal types of financial intermediaries.

FINANCIAL INTERMEDIARIES: SOME FACTS

Table 3–3 presents a list of the major financial intermediaries, ranked by asset size. A quick run down the list suggests that financial intermediaries display considerable diversity in purpose and in the way in which they channel funds from surplus to deficit units. One of the key distinctions in this regard is whether or not a financial intermediary accepts deposits.

NONDEPOSITORY INSTITUTIONS

Among the major *nondepository* institutions are insurance companies, pension funds, and investment companies. While none of these issue deposit-type claims, they do issue indirect securities with characteristics that differ significantly from those of the direct securities they hold. By far the most important intermediary of this type in terms of total assets are *life insurance companies.* They gather funds by issuing claims against themselves in the

TABLE 3–3 Financial Intermediaries Ranked by Asset Size (year-end 1984, in billions of dollars)

Type of Institution	Asset Size
Commercial banks	$2,013
Savings and loan associations	990
Life insurance companies	692
Private pension funds	623
State and local government retirement funds	355
Sales and consumer finance companies	294
Property and casualty insurance companies	240
Money market funds	210
Mutual savings banks	206
Open-end investment companies	162
Credit unions	116

SOURCE: Board of Governors of the Federal Reserve System, *Flow of Funds Accounts: Assets and Liabilities Outstanding*, Washington, D.C., Various issues.

form of life insurance and annuity policies, which typically combine insurance and savings features. Most of these funds are used to acquire long-term direct securities in such forms as real estate mortgages, corporate bonds and stocks, and government obligations.

Another important nondepository intermediary, *pension funds*, is a key institution in enabling individuals to save for retirement. Funds are acquired through contributions by employers, employees, or both, and claims for retirement pensions are issued to employees. As is the case with insurance companies, pension funds invest in a wide range of marketable securities.

A third nondepository intermediary of note are the *investment companies* that issue ownership claims against themselves and use most of the proceeds to buy a diversified list of corporate stocks or bonds. The holder of investment company shares, therefore, has an equity claim against a diversified portfolio, redeemable directly from the investment company or salable on a stock exchange.

In addition to the private nondepository intermediaries, there are also government-sponsored financial intermediaries such as the Federal National Mortgage Association, commonly dubbed Fanny Mae, which issues its own debt and purchases mortgages on residential real estate.[2] While collectively these nondepository institutions are of considerable economic significance, our main attention in subsequent chapters will be devoted to depository institutions.

[2]Fanny Mae has a number of "friends" with similar functions—namely, Ginny Mae (the Government National Mortgage Association) and Freddie Mac (the Federal Home Loan Mortgage Corporation).

DEPOSITORY INSTITUTIONS

As Table 3–3 reveals, the two largest financial intermediaries are of the depository type. The largest, *commercial banks,* offers a variety of deposit instruments including demand deposits, savings deposits, NOW accounts, and certificates of deposit. As the adjective "commercial" suggests, businesses are important customers of commercial banks, both as depositors and as borrowers. In addition to lending to businesses, commercial banks also purchase government securities and lend to individuals to finance real estate and other consumer purchases. Commercial banks like to portray themselves as "department stores of finance," and it is true that among depository institutions they have the broadest range of deposit-taking and lending powers.

Savings and loan associations (S&Ls) constitute the second largest financial intermediary. They have experienced particularly rapid growth in the postwar period, from less than $10 billion in assets in 1945 to $990 billion in 1984. S&Ls offer a variety of deposit accounts, both savings and transactions, to consumers, and extend a limited amount of credit to businesses and to consumers for purchases other than housing. By far, however, the major use of funds by S&Ls is to issue mortgages on residential real estate. In contrast to the relative short-term maturity of their deposits, many of these mortgages are of very long maturity. The relatively specialized nature of S&Ls, at least as compared to commercial banks, is a matter of both custom and law. This relative specialization is also evident in varying degrees in other depository institutions.

In many respects, *mutual savings banks (MSBs)* are similar to S&Ls. They obtain funds from the same types of sources and they invest primarily in mortgages. However, the lending powers of MSBs are somewhat broader than those of S&Ls, and as a consequence they hold significant quantities of corporate bonds. *Credit unions* also offer savings and transactions accounts to consumers who share some common affiliation, such as place of employment. The primary use of funds by credit unions is for relatively short-term consumer loans for their members.

The final depository institution of note, the *money market mutual fund,* came into existence in the 1970s, but grew dramatically from 1978 to 1984 when total assets expanded from $4 billion to $210 billion. Money market funds issue shares to the public which are easily redeemable. From their inception, these shares combined aspects of both savings and transactions accounts, and over time they have become easier to use for making transactions. Money market funds generally invest in safe short-term financial instruments such as Treasury bills, bank certificates of deposits, and commercial paper issued by well-established corporations. Furthermore, money market funds provide a rate of return to shareholders quite close to the prevailing rate of interest the funds itself earns. As a consequence, as we shall see below, in the late 1970s and the early 1980s money market funds played a critical role in the transformation of the financial system to one unencumbered by ceilings on interest rates payable to depositors.

GOVERNMENT REGULATION OF DEPOSITORY INTERMEDIARIES

Depository financial intermediaries generally issue claims against themselves that are fixed in terms of dollars and have maturities shorter than those of the direct securities they hold. They "borrow short and lend long." This inevitably creates problems of maintaining solvency and liquidity without undue sacrifice of net income. There is risk that the intermediary will become insolvent—that the value of its assets will fall below the value of its liabilities. And there is risk of illiquidity, or inability to pay promptly and in full, even though the intermediary may be solvent if given a longer period in which to sell its assets.

Because of problems such as these, the government has intervened in many ways to regulate and otherwise influence the creation and functioning of financial intermediaries. We will discuss these regulatory issues extensively below; here it will be sufficient to list briefly the major types of regulation.

ASSET REGULATION

In their choice of assets, financial intermediaries are limited in various ways. For one, they may be prohibited from holding certain assets such as common stock. At the other extreme, they may be required to hold other types of assets. Such requirements are often aimed at improving the liquidity of the intermediary.

LIABILITY REGULATION

There are two kinds of regulations affecting liabilities issued by financial intermediaries. One type prohibits the issuance of certain forms of claims. For example, banks are not permitted to offer NOW accounts to business customers. The second type controls the maximum amount of interest that can be paid on various forms of deposits. The prohibition of interest payments on demand deposits is an example of this.

REGULATION OF SERVICE AND STRUCTURE

There is a wide range of potential customer services that are explicitly prohibited to certain financial intermediaries and/or specifically allowed to others. In addition, there exists a set of complex regulations that control, among other things, chartering, branching, and audit and supervision of each type of intermediary.

INSURANCE OF CLAIMS AGAINST FINANCIAL INTERMEDIARIES

Individual accounts are insured up to $100,000 at most commercial banks, mutual savings banks, credit unions, and savings and loan associations.

This has increased the safety and liquidity of these claims, made them more attractive to holders, and enhanced the ability of these institutions to compete for funds. It has also enhanced the geographic mobility of funds.

PROVISION OF LENDING FACILITIES
Because of the very nature of their operations, involving the issue of claims more liquid than most of their assets, it is almost inevitable that financial intermediaries will, at least occasionally, encounter liquidity difficulties. It is because of such experiences that we now have federally sponsored institutions to provide liquidity to financial intermediaries by lending to them or purchasing assets from them.

Regulation has a pervasive influence on the structure of financial intermediaries. Via regulation, the government has tried to produce a safe financial system—one that would be immune from the financial panics so prevalent in our early history. However, financial regulation must also promote an efficient financial system—one that channels funds from lenders to borrowers at the least cost possible. As we shall see below, it has not always been easy for government regulators to achieve a balance between these objectives.

AN OVERVIEW OF THE FINANCIAL SYSTEM

Having looked at its various parts, we are now in a position to survey the American financial system as a whole. It includes three broad sets of elements:

1 Huge amounts of direct securities of widely varying characteristics issued not only by households, business firms, and governmental units, but also by almost every other type of nonfinancial entity. Great stocks of these are outstanding at any point of time and large new issues are typically generated each year.
2 Market facilities for trading in securities—facilities for primary distribution of newly issued securities and secondary market facilities for trading in securities issued earlier. Many securities, whose issuers are well and favorably known, enjoy national and international markets in which they can be bought or sold quickly at competitive prices. When they function efficiently, securities markets add significantly to the liquidity and safety of direct securities.
3 A wide variety of financial intermediaries, which hold huge amounts of direct securities and issue huge amounts of indirect securities with characteristics differing significantly from those of direct securities held. Depository types of intermediaries are outstandingly manufacturers of liquidity.

Understanding this complex financial system will facilitate better understanding of the vital processes of saving, capital accumulation, and determination of the behavior of national income. To be sure, considerable amounts of investment are undertaken by ultimate savers, who finance their investment out of their own current flows of saving without recourse to any branch of the financial markets. However, much investment requires the creation of new securities or trading of old ones. Thus, the saving-investment process involves transactions in financial markets and via financial intermediaries.

A pictorial overview of the entire process is provided in Figure 3–2. The flow of funds from nonfinancial lenders to borrowers is channeled directly through capital markets or indirectly through commercial banks and other nonbank financial intermediaries. As the figure illustrates, the major lender groups are identical to the major borrowing groups. This reflects the fact that financial markets and intermediaries are simply serving as the "middlemen" between lenders and borrowers.

DIRECT VS. INDIRECT FINANCE: SOME DATA

Figure 3–3 documents the actual flow of funds from nonfinancial lenders to nonfinancial borrowers for 1984. It should be emphasized that these data are different in kind from those given in Tables 3–1, 3–2, and 3–3. The earlier

FIGURE 3–2
Direct and indirect flows of funds. SOURCE:
Adapted from William N. Cox, III, "Impairment in
Credit Flow: Fact or Fiction?" *Monthly Review*,
Federal Reserve Bank of Atlanta, February 1970, p. 25.

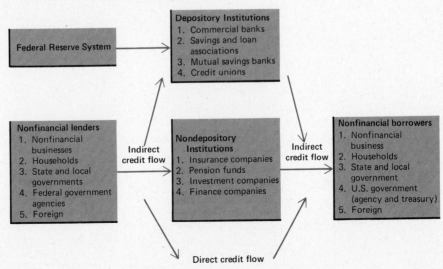

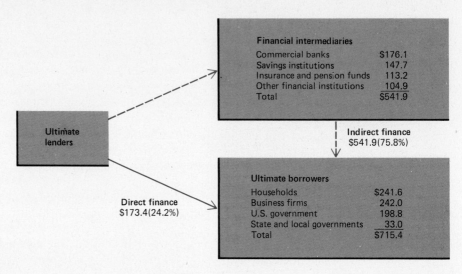

FIGURE 3–3
Total funds raised by domestic nonfinancial sectors in 1984 by direct and indirect finance (in billions of dollars).

data are *financial stocks;* that is, they are dollar amounts outstanding *at a point of time.* The data in Figure 3–3 are *financial flows,* which measure the volume of funds borrowed or lent *during some time period*—in this case, the year 1984. Stocks and flows are related by the fact that a stock of some asset is simply the sum of all previous flows of that asset.[3] Despite this close relationship, it is often useful to look at financial data from both perspectives. This is commonly done when analyzing a business firm. The balance sheet of all the firm's assets and liabilities is a stock concept, while the income (or profit and loss) statement measures financial flows. This distinction between stocks and flows will also play an important role in later chapters, where we consider the relationship between the stock of money outstanding and the flow of national income.

Returning to Figure 3–3, we see that several facts stand out. For one, in 1984 over $700 billion was raised in credit markets by the nonfinancial sector. Households and businesses were the major borrowers, but governments at various levels and foreigners also borrowed sizable sums. A second noteworthy fact is that $542 billion, or approximately three-quarters of the total funds raised, were channeled indirectly through financial intermediaries. Not surprisingly, commercial banks were quantitatively most significant in this regard.

[3]The distinction between stocks and flows applies to real (i.e., physical) as well as financial assets. Thus, for example, the stock of all automobiles outstanding is the cumulated flow of all past net flows of purchases. In this context *net* flow refers to total purchases less depreciation of the existing stock.

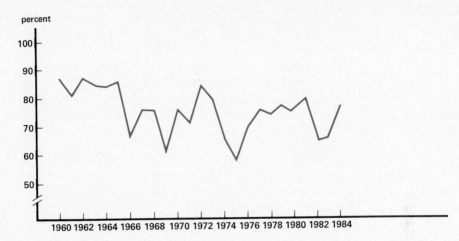

FIGURE 3–4
Percentage of total funds raised by nonfinancial sectors accounted for by indirect finance

While Figure 3–3 provides evidence that indirect finance through financial intermediaries accounted for the bulk of funds channeled through the financial system in 1984, the data in Figure 3–4 indicate that there was nothing special about this particular year. Indeed, from 1960 to 1984, indirect finance accounted on average for 75 percent of all funds—the same fraction as in 1984. There were, of course, years in which financial intermediaries played a somewhat lesser role, such as 1966, 1969, and 1974–1975 and 1982. These years correspond to "credit crunches" or periods of "disintermediation," when financial intermediaries came under severe pressure. But even in these years indirect finance remained the dominant pattern.

SUMMARY

1 By permitting a transfer of resources from surplus to deficit units, *debt* plays a critical role in achieving an efficient allocation of resources in the economy. Financial markets provide the mechanism whereby funds are transferred from surplus to deficit units.

2 Two ways in which funds are transferred from surplus deficit units are known as direct and indirect finance. *Direct* finance takes place when ultimate borrowers and lenders are directly matched, with brokers or dealers serving as middlemen. *Indirect* finance involves the role of a *financial intermediary* that issues indirect securities. Ultimate lenders place their funds with an intermediary, which in turn purchases the primary securities issued by ultimate borrowers.

3 For a number of reasons, financial intermediaries improve the allocation of resources. As compared with individuals, intermediaries are better able to diversify their assets and thus reduce portfolio risk. In addition to manufacturing safety, financial intermediaries also enhance liquidity by creating financial claims that are more liquid than those assets they acquire and hold.

4 As a consequence of the economics of intermediation, financial intermediaries have attracted vast quantities of funds. The major financial intermediaries include depository institutions such as commercial banks, savings and loan associations, mutual savings banks, and money market mutual funds, as well as nondepository institutions such as life insurance companies, pension funds, and investment companies.

5 Government regulation of financial intermediaries takes many forms, including limitations on assets intermediaries may hold and on liabilities they may issue. Government regulation also affects chartering and branching of financial intermediaries and places limits on potential customer services. The government provides insurance of claims against financial intermediaries commonly known as deposit insurance and also stands ready to lend funds to intermediaries should they encounter liquidity difficulties. We will have considerably more to say about the pervasive impact of government on financial intermediaries in subsequent chapters.

SELECTED READINGS

Board of Governors of the Federal Reserve System, *Introduction to Flow of Funds.* Washington, D.C., 1975.

Chandler, L. V., *The Monetary–Financial System.* New York, Harper & Row, 1979.

Goldsmith, R., *Financial Intermediaries in the American Economy since 1900.* Princeton, NJ, Princeton University Press, 1958.

Report of the President's Commission on Financial Structure and Regulation. Washington, D.C., U.S. Government Printing Office, 1971.

Rose, P. S., and D. R. Frazer, *Financial Institutions*, Dallas, Business Publications, Inc., 1980.

Smith, P. F., *Economics of Financial Institutions and Markets.* Homewood, IL, Irwin, 1971.

4

FINANCIAL INSTRUMENTS
AND INTEREST RATES

In Chapter 3 we considered the operation of financial markets in which supplies and demands for funds are brought into balance. These magic words—*market, supply,* and *demand*—should immediately bring to mind another key concept—namely, that of a *market-clearing price.* While the notion of a price that equilibrates supply and demand is simple enough in principle, the details of price setting in financial markets can sometimes be confusing. Part of the reason for this is terminology, since people often refer to both the *price of a financial instrument* and the *price of borrowing money.* These two concepts of price are closely related, but they are not the same. Indeed, this should be apparent from the more common name of the price of borrowed money—the *interest rate.*

The primary purpose of this chapter is to explore the nature of interest rates. Since the borrowing and lending of funds can take place via many different types of financial instruments, we begin by examining the important characteristics of debt instruments. We then introduce the notion of the rate of return yielded by a financial instrument and explain the relationship of this yield to the price of the financial instrument. Next we discuss the various types of interest rates in the marketplace and consider their interconnection. It is perhaps worth emphasizing that this chapter will not provide a complete explanation of how the level of interest rates is set in an economy; that topic will be taken up in Chapter 15. Nevertheless, a firm grasp of the mechanics of interest rates is important if we are to understand the portfolio choices of various groups in the economy and the workings of monetary policy.

ATTRIBUTES OF DEBT INSTRUMENTS

Financial instruments are the evidence of debt that originates in borrowing and lending—that is, in financial transactions in which purchasing power is transferred from surplus spending units to deficit spending units. Examples of financial instruments include Treasury bills issued by the federal government; municipal bonds, which are obligations of state and local governments; bank certificates of deposit; and corporate bonds and commercial paper, which are debts of the business sector. With each of these financial instruments, the holder has a financial claim on the issuer.

In valuing any financial claim and in choosing among alternative financial claims, actual and potential buyers and holders consider the full range of rights and obligations carried by each claim. This suggests that, prior to discussing the interest rate or yield on a financial instrument, it will be helpful to explore some of the important characteristics of financial instruments that can influence the interest rate. We shall concentrate on three attributes: maturity, liquidity, and safety of principal value.[1]

MATURITY

By *maturity* we mean the time that must elapse before the borrower must repay the debt in full. Maturity is most meaningfully measured relative to the current point in time. For example, a bond issued in 1970 and due to be repaid in the year 2000 would have a 30-year maturity at issue but a 15-year maturity in 1985. When issued, most debts have a well-defined maturity that may range from a single day to many years. Two exceptions occur at either end of the maturity spectrum. At one extreme are bonds, called *consols* or *perpetuities*, under which the borrower agrees to make interest payments indefinitely into the future without ever repaying the principal. At one time, consols were in common use in England. At the other end of the spectrum are debts, such as demand deposits in a bank (which are liabilities or debts of the bank to the depositor), which are due on demand. Such debts are due whenever the holder wishes to cash them in, and consequently have no specific maturity.

LIQUIDITY

By the *liquidity* of an asset we mean its capability of being converted into money quickly and without loss of value in terms of money. Money is

[1]Some aspects of these attributes were touched on in Chapter 3.

perfectly liquid; it can be used immediately to pay debts or to spend, and it always remains at a constant value in terms of money. An asset is illiquid to the extent that its conversion into money requires time or entails loss of value either through a decline in its market value or through conversion costs in terms of inconvenience, brokers' fees, dealers' margins, and so on. As we have seen, the actual liquidity of an asset depends in part on the market facilities for it. However, certain assets, even though they are not marketable, can still be quite liquid. For example, the ownership of U.S. savings bonds cannot be transferred, but such bonds can be redeemed with relatively minor inconvenience. In general, a debt instrument is more likely to achieve a high degree of liquidity to the extent that it possesses two characteristics. First, it is a claim on an issuer with an excellent reputation for meeting its obligations promptly and in full. Second, it is of short maturity—payable on demand or within a few months.

Most holders consider liquidity to be a desirable characteristic in an asset and are willing to forgo some income to buy some liquidity. However, holders differ widely in the amounts of liquidity demanded in the form of earning assets and in the amounts of yield they are willing to sacrifice in order to obtain liquidity. Some, expecting or fearing large excesses of spending over receipts in the near future, may be willing to forgo considerable amounts of yield in order to demand large amounts of liquidity in this form. Others, expecting excesses of receipts over payments in the near future, may be willing to sacrifice very little yield to buy liquidity.

To the extent that liquidity requires short maturities, desires of holders may conflict with those of issuers. To the issuer, the short maturity can be a source of illiquidity; it subjects him or her to the possibility of having to repay inconveniently soon or to refinance in an unfavorable market at higher rates of interest.

SAFETY OF PRINCIPAL

By *safety of principal* we mean freedom from risk that the market value of the debt instrument will decline. "Safety" is used here in its relative sense. Instruments that are highly liquid are also highly safe; they are convertible into money not only quickly, but also at a stable price. But some instruments that lack liquidity may be relatively safe; they can be collected or sold without loss over a longer period of time.

Risks of loss of principal value are of two types:

1 **RISK OF DEFAULT.** This is the risk that promised payments of interest and repayment of principal will not be met fully and on schedule. Default risks on debt instruments obviously differ from one issuer to another; the risk of default on debt instruments of the federal government is far below the risk of default on issues of a business concern whose future is doubtful. However, different issues of any given debtor may carry quite different risks of default because of differences

in priority of claim against assets or income, or both. Some classes of debt are given prior claim to a debtor's income or assets, while other classes claim only such income and assets as may remain after satisfaction of all other debts. Other things being equal, holders prefer instruments with lower default risk, but at least some can be induced to hold those with higher default risk if the promised income is higher.

2   **MARKET RISK.** This is the risk that the market price of a debt instrument will decline even if there is no risk of default. As we shall see shortly, this tends to come about when interest rates rise. We return to the issue of market risk after we examine the source of the inverse relationship between interest rates and prices of debt instruments.

YIELD ON DEBT INSTRUMENTS

One of the basic clichés of life is "time is money." Like all clichés, it captures an essential element of truth—namely, that time is valuable. What this means is, faced with a choice of receiving some valuable item today or at some time in the future, a rational individual will prefer to receive it now. This principle applies to such diverse items as houses, land, jewelry, paintings, and money. In the case of a house, for example, receiving it today, as opposed to next year, permits the recipient to earn income by renting it out.

The same principle applies to money. The sum of $100 delivered today, for instance, is clearly worth more than the sum of $100 paid one year from now. The reason is that, as in the case of the house, today's recipient of $100 can earn a return on the funds by "renting" out the money. This is precisely what happens when you take the $100 and deposit it in an interest-bearing bank account or when you purchase a government security. In either instance, it is the prevailing rate of interest that determines the amount of "rent" received. Or as the distinguished economist John Maynard Keynes put it, "The rate of interest is the reward for parting with liquidity for a specified period." That reward, when the cost is deducted becomes the yield.

Generally speaking, by the *yield* of a debt instrument we mean its annual rate of return over cost, taking into consideration not only annual interest payments, but also any difference there may be between cost and sale value. Since it reflects both interest payments and possible capital appreciation or depreciation, such a yield is sometimes called the *effective interest rate*.

To see how we might go about calculating the effective rate of interest for a debt instrument, we shall assume we are dealing with a conventional *bond*, which is an obligation by the seller (or, looked at another way, the borrower of the money) to pay the buyer a fixed sum of dollars per year over the life or maturity of the bond. This fixed sum is called the *coupon*.[2] In addition, when the bond matures, the borrower is obligated to pay the lender the *par value* or *principal* of the bond.

Consider, for example, a bond promising to pay a par value of $1,000 at the end of ten years and $60 (the coupon) at the end of each year. Let us further assume that you are contemplating purchasing this bond at a price P (some numbers are given below) and you want to know what the effective interest rate will be. There are three possible concepts we can apply to this problem—the coupon yield, the current yield, and the yield to maturity. While the yield to maturity will prove to be the best approach, we will better understand this if we consider each of the possible approaches.

THE COUPON YIELD

The *coupon yield* of a bond is simply the coupon expressed as a percentage of the par value of the bond. In the example we are considering, since $60/$1,000 = .06, or 6 percent, the coupon yield of the bond is 6 percent. Since the par value and the coupon remain constant throughout the life of the bond, the coupon yield is likewise constant. The primary defect of the coupon yield as a measure of the effective interest rate is that it ignores the market value or price, P, one pays for the bond. If, for example, the bond is selling for $900, your effective interest rate would be higher than the coupon yield of 6 percent, because when the bond matures in 10 years, you will have a $100 capital gain. (When the bond matures, it is redeemed at its par value of $1,000.) Only if you purchase the bond at par value will the coupon yield properly measure the effective rate of interest.

THE CURRENT YIELD

The *current yield* brings us one step closer to a proper measure by considering both the coupon and the price you pay for the bond. More specifically, the current yield is calculated as the coupon payment (the dollar amount of interest per year) divided by the market price of the bond. In our previous illustration with P = $900, the current yield is $60/$900, or 6.67 percent. If the market price of the bond were $1,100, the current yield would be $60/$1,100, or 5.45 percent. These numbers are qualitatively sensible in that when there is a capital gain to be made, the current yield is higher than the coupon yield. And when a capital loss is involved (e.g., when P = $1,100 and the bond can be redeemed for only $1,000), the current yield is lower than the coupon yield.

---

[2]The reader may be fortunate enough to be related to one of those happy souls whose primary form of work and/or exercise is "clipping" coupons. This phrase stems from the fact that on many bonds the coupon is removed by clipping with scissors (or, perhaps, a gold-plated coupon clipper) and sent to an agent for collection.

Despite this reasonableness, the current yield is also inadequate as a measure of the effective rate of interest since it does not properly treat the potential capital gain or loss. In effect, it fails to take account of the receipts accruing beyond a one-year horizon. As a consequence, it does not distinguish between a 10-year bond with a $60 coupon and selling for $900 and a 1-year bond with the same coupon and price; the current yield on both bonds is 6.67 percent. Yet for the 1-year bond the capital gain of $100 will be realized after one year, whereas in the case of the 10-year bond the person has to wait 10 years. Since "time is money," this aspect of the current yield is clearly undesirable.

THE YIELD TO MATURITY

The *yield to maturity* takes into consideration the current market value, annual interest receipts (the coupon), and the relationship between the current market value and the value at which the debt will be paid off at maturity (the par value). As the name implies, the yield to maturity is calculated under the assumption that the debt instrument is held to maturity. That is, it is sold or redeemed at maturity for its par value.

Precisely how the various elements (coupon, market price, par value) are combined in the yield to maturity is easiest to illustrate if we start with a 1-year bond. More specifically, let us consider a 1-year bond with a coupon of $60 and a market price of $965. An individual who buys this bond for $965 now will receive a coupon payment of $60 one year from now. However, since the bond will mature in one year at the par value of $1,000, the purchaser will also receive a capital gain or capital appreciation of $35 ($1,000 − $965). Thus, the total return for the year will be the sum of the coupon and the capital gain, or $95. Since the initial investment was $965, the yield to maturity will be $95/$965, or 9.84 percent.

As a second example, consider the same 1-year bond which is selling for $1,020. The total return for the year will be $40, consisting of $60 in interest payments *minus* the $20 capital loss. In this instance, the yield to maturity is $40/$1,020, or 3.92 percent.

Taken together, these two examples suggest the intuitively appealing proposition that, given the coupon, the higher the market price of a bond, the lower the yield to maturity or effective interest rate on the bond. This result is really a quite general one, not specific to our examples. To see this more formally, let us turn the problem around and ask what someone would be willing to pay for a bond with a given effective rate of interest.

To make things concrete, let us consider an individual who plans to invest in a 1-year bond at a time when the currently prevailing market yield or effective rate of interest on all such bonds in the marketplace is *i* percent per year. Suppose our potential investor is now offered a debt instrument that carries a promise to pay $1,060 one year later. What will he be willing to pay for this instrument? Our potential buyer will reason as follows: "This piece of paper is of value today only because it represents a claim against money receivable in the future. I will buy it only at such a price that I will receive the going rate of return on my money, and this 'price' is that amount which, if 'rented' at the prevailing yield, would be worth $1,060 a year hence." In other words, the individual wants to determine the amount of money (P) that, if put out at the current yield (i) on this type of obligation, will be worth $1,060 a year from now. That is, we must have

$$P(1 + i) = \$1,060$$

or

$$P = \frac{\$1,060}{1 + i} \tag{1}$$

If the prevailing interest rate is 6 percent, that is, $i = 0.06$, we then have

$$P = \frac{\$1,060}{1.06} = \$1,000$$

Thus, when the market yield is 6 percent, the individual would be willing to pay $1,000 for the asset under consideration. What this means is that when the market effective rate of interest is 6 percent, the future sum of $1,060 is worth $1,000 today. Put another way, we would say that the *present value* of the future sum is $1,000. The process of reducing the future sum to its present value, captured in equation (1), is known as *discounting*. In such cases i is sometimes called the *rate of discount*.

What happens if the interest rate differs from 6 percent? It is evident from our formula that the present value of $1,060 receivable one year hence will be lower if interest rates are higher, and higher if interest rates are lower. For example, if the market yield is 8 percent, the formula becomes

$$P = \frac{\$1,060}{1.08} = \$981.48$$

If, however, the market yield is 4 percent,

$$P = \frac{\$1,060}{1.04} = \$1,019.23$$

The general formula for simple discount is

$$P = \frac{A}{1 + i} \tag{2}$$

where P is the present value, A is the dollar amount receivable at the end of the interest period, and i is the rate of interest for that period stated in hundredths such as 0.08 or 0.04.[3]

[3]Here and later we assume that the interest period is one year and that the interest rate is the rate per year. We also assume that interest is compounded annually. In some cases the interest period is less than a year. For example, it may be six months. In such cases the i in our formula will be the interest rate for half a year and the number of interest periods will be twice as large as it would be if the interest period were one year.

Quite evidently then, as equation (1) or (2) reveals, there is a general inverse relationship between the price of a bond (P) and its yield (i). Moreover, while we have used equation (1) to calculate P for a given value of i, this equation can be turned on its head to solve for i, with a given value for P. In a previous example we saw that a 1-year bond with a $60 coupon and selling for $965 would have a yield to maturity of 9.84 percent. One could get this same result by substituting $P = \$965$ in equation (1) and solving for i, as in

$$\$965 = \frac{\$1,000}{1 + i}$$

so that $i = .0984$. In other words, equation (2) completely characterizes the relationship between the market price of a 1-year bond and its yield and given the appropriate information, can be used to solve for one or the other.

Thus far we have focused on the example of a 1-year bond. The same general ideas carry over to longer-term bonds, but to illustrate this we need to invoke one of the great wonders of the world—compound interest.

YIELDS AND MARKET VALUES WITH COMPOUNDING

We approach the issue by asking what an individual would pay, given an effective rate of interest, for a long-term bond such as the 10-year bond described previously. As before, the answer will be that the individual is willing to pay the present value of the stream of all future payments promised by the bond. While identical in principle, the process of calculating the present value of a long-term bond is a bit more complicated, for two reasons.

First, the obligation is to make a number of payments through time rather than a single payment; second, it involves compound interest or discount. Each prospective buyer will reason as follows: "This obligation is of value only because it represents a claim against $60 at the end of each of the next 10 years and $1,000 at the end of the 10-year period. I will buy it only at such a price that I will receive the going rate of return on my money." The price (P) is the sum of the discounted values of all the individual payments expected in the future. For example, there is some amount of money (P_1) that, if put out at the prevailing yield rate, would be worth $60 a year hence. That is,

$$P_1(1 + i) = \$60$$

or

$$P_1 = \frac{\$60}{1 + i}$$

There is another smaller amount of money (P_2) which, if put out at compound interest at the prevailing rate, would be worth $60 at the end of two years. Compound interest is used because during the second year, interest would be received on the first year's interest. That is,

$$P_2(1 + i)^2 = \$60$$

or

$$P_2 = \frac{\$60}{(1 + i)^2}$$

Similarly, there is a yet smaller amount of money (P_3) that, if put out at compound interest, would be worth \$60 at the end of three years.

$$P_3(1 + i)^3 = \$60$$

or

$$P_3 = \frac{\$60}{(1 + i)^3}$$

The present values of the other interest payments can be arrived at in the same way. There remains the \$1,000 of principal payable at the end of ten years. Its present value is $\$1,000/[(1 + i)^{10}]$. The present value of the bond is the sum of the present values of the various payments to be received on it. That is to say, we have

$$P = \frac{60}{1 + i} + \frac{60}{(1 + i)^2} + \frac{60}{(1 + i)^3} + \cdots + \frac{60}{(1 + i)^{10}} + \frac{1,000}{(1 + i)^{10}} \qquad (3)$$

The general formula for arriving at present value by discounting is

$$P = \frac{A_1}{1 + i} + \frac{A_2}{(1 + i)^2} + \frac{A_3}{(1 + i)^3} + \cdots + \frac{A_n}{(1 + i)^n} + \frac{F}{(1 + i)^n} \qquad (4)$$

where P is the present value, the As are the dollar amounts receivable at the ends of the various interest periods, F is the amount of the principal repayment, i is the rate of discount, and n is the number of interest periods.

By using equation (3), we can now answer the question of what the present value of our 10-year bond will be under alternative interest or discount rates. To do this, we simply plug a value for i into equation (3). The details of this calculation for interest rates of 4, 6, and 8 percent are shown in columns 5, 6, and 7 of Table 4–1. As this table reveals, the present market value of the bond will be \$1,000 if the interest rate is 6 percent, only \$865.80 if the rate is 8 percent, and \$1,162.22 if the rate is 4 percent.

One special case is worth noting because of its simplicity: the case of an obligation to pay fixed annual amounts in perpetuity. In this case, the preceding formula becomes simply

$$P = \frac{A}{i}$$

TABLE 4-1 Discounting and Present Values

		(1)		(2)		(3)		(4)		(5)		(6)		(7)
				VALUES OF COL. (1) AT INTEREST RATES OF						PRESENT VALUES* OF $60 AT END OF INDICATED YEARS AT DISCOUNT RATE OF				
End of year	Formula			4%		6%		8%		4%		6%		8%
1	$(1 + i)$			1.0400		1.0600		1.0800		$57.692		$56.604		$55.556
2	$(1 + i)^2$			1.0816		1.1236		1.1664		55.473		53.400		51.440
3	$(1 + i)^3$			1.1249		1.1910		1.2597		53.340		50.377		47.630
4	$(1 + i)^4$			1.1699		1.2625		1.3605		51.288		47.526		44.102
5	$(1 + i)^5$			1.2167		1.3382		1.4693		49.316		44.836		40.835
6	$(1 + i)^6$			1.2653		1.4185		1.5869		47.419		42.298		37.810
7	$(1 + i)^7$			1.3159		1.5036		1.7138		45.595		39.903		35.009
8	$(1 + i)^8$			1.3686		1.5938		1.8509		43.841		37.645		32.416
9	$(1 + i)^9$			1.4233		1.6895		1.9990		42.155		35.139		30.015
10	$(1 + i)^{10}$			1.4802		1.7908		2.1589		40.534		33.504		27.792
Subtotal										$486.65		$441.61		$402.61
Present value of $1,000 receivable at the end of 10 years										675.57		558.39		463.19
Total										$1,162.22		$1,000.000		$865.80

*The values in columns 5, 6, and 7 are arrived at by dividing $60 by the numbers shown in columns 2, 3, and 4, respectively.

Thus, the present value of the right to receive $60 a year in perpetuity becomes

$$P = \frac{\$60}{0.06} = \$1,000 \quad \text{if the discount rate is 6 percent}$$

$$P = \frac{\$60}{0.04} = \$1,500 \quad \text{if the discount rate is 4 percent}$$

$$P = \frac{\$60}{0.08} = \$750 \quad \text{if the discount rate is 8 percent}$$

As we did with equation (1), we can also use equation (3) to solve for the yield to maturity given the price or market value of the bond. Suppose, for example, that the price is $900. We then have to solve for i in the following equation:

$$900 = \frac{60}{1 + i} + \frac{60}{(1 + i)^2} + \cdots + \frac{60}{(1 + i)^{10}} + \frac{1,000}{(1 + i)^{10}} \tag{5}$$

While the solution is simple to obtain in principle, unlike the case of equation (1), it is not so obvious how you get the answer in practice. Fortunately for investors, there are bond tables which are prepared for precisely this purpose. Figure 4-1 shows a typical page from such a book of tables.

FIGURE 4–1
A standard bond table: 6% coupon

				YEARS AND MONTHS				
Yield	8–3	8–6	8–9	9–0	9–3	9–6	9–9	10–0
4.00	113.93	114.29	114.64	114.99	115.33	115.68	116.01	116.35
4.20	112.43	112.76	113.06	113.37	113.67	113.98	114.27	114.58
4.40	110.96	111.24	111.51	111.79	112.04	112.31	112.57	112.83
4.60	109.51	109.76	109.98	110.22	110.44	110.68	110.89	111.12
4.80	108.09	108.30	108.48	108.69	108.87	109.07	109.25	109.44
5.00	106.68	106.86	107.01	107.18	107.32	107.49	107.63	107.79
5.20	105.30	105.44	105.56	105.69	105.81	105.94	106.05	106.18
5.40	103.94	104.05	104.13	104.23	104.31	104.41	104.49	104.59
5.60	102.60	102.68	102.73	102.80	102.85	102.92	102.96	103.03
5.80	101.29	101.33	101.35	101.39	101.41	101.45	101.46	101.50
6.00	99.99	100.00	99.99	100.00	99.99	100.00	99.99	100.00
6.10	99.35	99.34	99.32	99.32	99.29	99.29	99.26	99.26
6.20	98.71	98.69	98.65	98.64	98.60	98.58	98.54	98.53
6.30	98.08	98.05	97.99	97.96	97.91	97.88	97.83	97.80
6.40	97.45	97.41	97.34	97.30	97.23	97.19	97.12	97.08
6.50	96.83	96.77	96.69	96.63	96.55	96.50	96.42	96.37
6.60	96.22	96.14	96.05	95.98	95.88	95.81	95.72	95.66
6.70	95.61	95.52	95.41	95.33	95.22	95.14	95.03	94.96
6.80	95.00	94.90	94.78	94.68	94.56	94.47	94.35	94.26
6.90	94.40	94.28	94.15	94.04	93.91	93.80	93.68	93.58
7.00	93.80	93.67	93.53	93.41	93.26	93.15	93.01	92.89
7.10	93.21	93.07	92.91	92.76	92.62	92.49	92.34	92.22
7.20	92.62	92.47	92.30	92.15	91.98	91.84	91.68	91.55
7.30	92.03	91.87	91.69	91.53	91.35	91.20	91.03	90.89
7.40	91.46	91.28	91.09	90.92	90.73	90.57	90.38	90.23
7.50	90.88	90.70	90.49	90.31	90.11	89.94	89.74	89.58
7.60	90.31	90.11	89.89	89.71	89.49	89.31	89.11	88.93
7.70	89.75	89.54	89.31	89.11	88.88	88.69	88.48	88.29
7.80	89.18	88.97	88.72	88.51	88.28	88.08	87.85	87.66
7.90	88.63	88.40	88.14	87.92	87.68	87.47	87.23	87.03
8.00	88.07	87.83	87.57	87.34	87.09	86.87	86.62	86.41
8.10	87.53	87.28	87.00	86.76	86.50	86.27	86.01	85.79
8.20	86.98	86.72	86.44	86.19	85.91	85.67	85.41	85.18
8.30	86.44	86.17	85.88	85.62	85.33	85.09	84.81	84.58
8.40	85.90	85.63	85.32	85.05	84.76	84.50	84.22	83.98
8.50	85.37	85.08	84.77	84.49	84.19	83.93	83.64	83.38
8.60	84.84	84.55	84.22	83.94	83.63	83.35	83.05	82.79
8.70	84.32	84.01	83.68	83.39	83.07	82.78	82.48	82.21
8.80	83.80	83.48	83.14	82.84	82.51	82.22	81.91	81.63
8.90	83.29	82.96	82.61	82.30	81.96	81.66	81.34	81.06
9.00	82.77	82.44	82.08	81.76	81.41	81.11	80.78	80.49
9.10	82.27	81.92	81.55	81.23	80.87	80.56	80.22	79.92
9.20	81.76	81.41	81.03	80.70	80.34	80.02	79.67	79.37
9.30	81.26	80.90	80.52	80.17	79.80	79.48	79.12	78.81
9.40	80.76	80.40	80.00	79.65	79.28	78.94	78.58	78.26
9.50	80.27	79.90	79.50	79.14	78.75	78.41	78.05	77.72
9.60	79.78	79.40	78.99	78.63	78.23	77.89	77.51	77.18
9.70	79.30	78.91	78.49	78.12	77.72	77.37	76.99	76.65
9.80	78.82	78.42	77.99	77.62	77.21	76.85	76.46	76.12
9.90	78.34	77.93	77.50	77.12	76.70	76.34	75.94	75.60
10.00	77.86	77.45	77.01	76.62	76.20	75.83	75.43	75.08
10.20	76.93	76.50	76.05	75.64	75.21	74.83	74.41	74.05
10.40	76.00	75.56	75.10	74.68	74.24	73.84	73.42	73.04
10.60	75.09	74.64	74.16	73.73	73.28	72.87	72.44	72.05
10.80	74.20	73.73	73.24	72.80	72.33	71.92	71.47	71.08
11.00	73.31	72.84	72.34	71.88	71.41	70.98	70.53	70.12
11.20	72.45	71.96	71.44	70.98	70.49	70.06	69.90	69.19
11.40	71.59	71.09	70.57	70.10	69.60	69.15	68.68	68.26
11.60	70.75	70.24	69.70	69.22	68.71	68.26	67.78	67.36
11.80	69.91	69.40	68.85	68.36	67.85	67.39	66.90	66.47
12.00	69.10	68.57	68.01	67.52	66.99	66.53	66.03	65.59

SOURCE: *Expanded Bond Values Tables*, Boston, MA, Financial Publishing Co., 1970, p. 589.

To use Figure 4–1 to solve equation (5), we first look down the column headed by 10 years (the maturity of the bond) until we find the number closest to the price 90. (This bond table is calculated on the assumption that the par value of the bond is 100, not 1,000, so the price of 900 in equation (5) translates to 90 in Figure 4–1.) As Figure 4–1 reveals, this occurs at a price of 90.23 which, looking at the left-most column, corresponds to a yield of 7.40 percent.[4] Clearly then, the sample table shown in Figure 4–1, or ones like it, allows us to compute the yield on a bond, given its price, or vice versa.

YIELDS AND MARKET VALUES

We are now in a position to draw together several observations on the relationship between yields and the market values of bonds. From the various formulas presented and the illustrative examples, we clearly see the negative or inverse relationship between the level of market rates and the market value of a debt obligation. Perhaps the easiest way to see this is just to run down a column of Figure 4–1, which shows that a decline in market price is associated (in the first column of Figure 4–1) with a rise in yield.

The numbers presented previously can also be arranged in a slightly different way to bring out another important point—namely, that the longer the maturity of an obligation, the greater is the effect of any given change of market rates of interest on its present value. From our previous examples we can construct Table 4–2. At a market rate of 6 percent, each of three assets is valued at $1,000. If the market rate were 8 percent, while all the bonds have a lower value (the inverse relationship just noted), the decline in value is least for the 1-year bond and greatest for the perpetuity.

MARKET RISK

We can also use these results to reconsider the notion of market risk mentioned earlier. From Table 4–2 it might be inferred that, other things being equal, holders will prefer short maturities over long ones because of their lower market risk, and that they will purchase and hold longer maturities only if rewarded by a higher interest yield. This is sometimes true, but not always. For one thing, longer maturities carry the possibility not only of a larger loss of value if interest rates rise, but also the possibility of a larger capital gain if interest rates fall. When interest rates are expected to fall in the future, the interest yield on longer maturities may be below that on shorter maturities, and holders will expect to make up the difference, or more than the difference, in capital gains.

---

[4]To get a better approximation one would interpolate between the prices 90.23 and 89.58, corresponding to yields of 7.4 and 7.5, respectively. The interpolated yield is 7.44 percent.

TABLE 4–2 Effects of Maturity

Description of debt	PRESENT VALUE IF DISCOUNTED AT		
	6%	4%	8%
An obligation to pay $1,060 at the end of the year	$1,000.00	$1,019.23	$941.48
An obligation to pay $60 annually for ten years and $1,000 at the end of ten years	1,000.00	1,162.22	865.80
An obligation to pay $60 a year in perpetuity	1,000.00	1,500.00	750.00

Moreover, even with given expectations as to the future course of interest rates, different holders are likely to have differing preferences for shorter and longer maturities. Some, expecting to need their funds soon, will prefer short maturities in order to lessen their market risk. Others, looking forward to a very long holding period and wanting an assured rate of return, prefer longer maturities. This also enables them to avoid the expense of buying a succession of shorter maturities. Here again we encounter the important fact of differences among buyers' tastes and preference functions.

OUTSTANDING BONDS

The discussion to this point has been couched in terms of how a potential buyer would value bonds with different payment streams at alternative discount rates or market rates of interest. It is important to emphasize that the relationships we have developed are also relevant for the holder of an *outstanding* debt obligation. Consider, for example, an investor who purchased a perpetuity paying $60 a year when the market interest rate was 6 percent. The purchase price of such a bond clearly must have been $1,000. Now assume that after one year the market rate on *new* perpetuities rises to 8 percent and that our bondholder needs to cash in her existing bond. Since potential purchasers can earn 8 percent by buying new perpetuities, they will be unwilling to settle for a lower rate of return. As the outstanding perpetuity promises to pay only $60 per year, as we have seen it must be priced at $750 to yield 8 percent to the holder. Thus, sale of the perpetuity will produce a capital loss of $250 for the bond owner. While she has earned $60 in interest payments, she will suffer a net loss of $190 on the purchase and subsequent sale of the bond. Given her need for funds and the change in interest rates, our investor obviously would have been better off had she kept the funds in a demand-deposit account paying no interest, although this is not to suggest that this would have been the best option. Purchase of a 1-year bond would have earned the investor some interest and returned her capital intact at the end of the year.

Such is the arithmetic of the negative relationship between the level of market rates of interest and the market values of *outstanding* debt obligations that have maturity values and interest returns which are contractually fixed in terms of dollars. The economic reason for this relationship is that in competitive markets, average yields to maturity on issues already outstanding must be in line with yields on new issues. When yields on new issues are rising, the prices on old issues must fall enough to make their yields equally attractive to investors. And when yields on new issues are falling, investors will bid up the prices of outstanding issues until their yields are no longer higher than those on new issues.

A REALISTIC EXAMPLE

We have explored the relationship between market yields and bond values with artificially chosen bonds, but the same points can be illustrated with reference to some realistic debt instruments. In Table 4–3 we have listed actual historical data on market price and the yield to maturity for two different U.S. government bonds. Both bonds were issued with coupon interest rates of 4 percent but with different terms to maturity. One bond, issued in 1959, had an initial maturity of 21 years, whereas the second, issued a few years later in 1962, was for a 10-year maturity.

As is evident from the table, prices and yields of the outstanding bonds fluctuated substantially and in the expected inverse fashion. In addition, as expected, during the period in which both bonds coexisted, the bond with the longer maturity fluctuated in price over a much wider range (72.44 to 102.50) than the shorter-maturity bond (91.50 to 101.03). This indicates that shorter-maturity bonds, by virtue of being more stable in price, possess greater liquidity.

We noted earlier that many investors consider liquidity to be a desirable characteristic for which they would be willing to sacrifice interest income. To the extent that this is an important consideration, market yields on short-term bonds should be less than those on long-term bonds. However, the data in Table 4–3 indicate that the reverse was true for six of the year-end dates presented.[5] Obviously, liquidity considerations do not fully explain the relationship between these two interest rates. This clearly needs further examination.

VARIETIES OF INTEREST RATES

At various times we shall refer to "the" interest rate, which suggests that there is but one interest rate in a given market at a given time. This is a useful device in making the exposition both simple and brief, but we have

---

[5] These differences need to be interpreted cautiously, since a significant part of the return from the longer-maturity bond is in the form of capital gains, which are taxed at a lower rate.

TABLE 4–3 Year-End Price and Yield for Two 4 Percent United States Government Bonds

| Date | BOND ISSUED 1/23/59 BOND MATURED 2/15/80 | | BOND ISSUED 11/15/62 BOND MATURED 2/15/72 | |
	Market price (in dollars)	Yield to maturity (in percent)	Market price (in dollars)	Yield to maturity (in percent)
1979	98.75	14.42	*	*
1978	93.84	9.93	*	*
1977	93.88	7.17	*	*
1976	95.06	5.75	*	*
1975	88.38	7.32	*	*
1974	86.13	7.30	*	*
1973	85.63	6.92	*	*
1972	87.25	6.25	*	*
1971	87.44	5.98	100.13	2.86
1970	83.25	6.46	97.78	5.46
1969	72.44	8.03	91.50	8.48
1968	83.25	6.01	94.19	6.07
1967	85.06	5.67	93.50	5.80
1966	94.00	4.61	96.50	4.78
1965	94.25	4.56	95.94	4.77
1964	97.88	4.19	98.75	4.21
1963	98.25	4.15	99.19	4.12
1962	101.00	3.92	101.03	3.86
1961	99.56	4.03	*	*
1960	102.50	3.81	*	*
1959	93.69	4.48	*	*

*Prior to issue of bond or subsequent to maturity.

just seen that it is an oversimplification. At any point in time, there is a complex of rates in the market, and these can differ widely and steadily. How can differences in rates persist? Why do lenders not shift their funds from debts with low yields to those with higher yields until all yield differentials have been wiped out?

THE TERM STRUCTURE OF INTEREST RATES

In attempting to answer these questions, it is helpful to begin our analysis with a relatively homogeneous group of financial instruments, the bonds issued by the U.S. government. Since they call for payment in legal tender, such bonds are free of the risk of default, since the government can always print money to meet its obligations. Consequently, the only major differences between various government bonds are with respect to coupon rate and maturity. A group of bonds with a particular combination of coupon rate and maturity is termed an *issue*. We saw two examples of such issues in Table 4–3, but there are, in fact, numerous government issues. For example, on December 31, 1984, there were 219 different issues outstanding. Of these, 72 were short-term, due to mature in one year or less. The bulk of the short-term issues were *Treasury bills*, which are typically issued with maturities of three or six months. However, 28 of the short-term issues had an original maturity exceeding one year. The remaining 147 had maturities running from 1 year to 30 years.

As one might suspect from Table 4–3, the various issues exhibited substantial differences in yields to maturity, with actual yields ranging from about 8 to $11\frac{1}{2}$ percent. These yields are plotted in Figure 4–2, with yields on the vertical axes and the date of maturity (or, equivalently, the number of years to maturity) on the horizontal axes. Clearly, the yields plotted in Figure 4–2 do form a regular pattern, and this has been emphasized by drawing a smooth curve through the data.[6] This curve is known as the *yield curve*, and it portrays the *term structure of interest rates* at a point in time. That is, it shows how the yields to maturity vary with the maturity of the debt instrument on a given date.

As Table 4–3 hinted, the yield curve can take a variety of shapes. The four most common shapes are portrayed in Figure 4–3 and are known as the flat yield curve, the ascending yield curve, the descending yield curve, and the humped yield curve. The ascending yield curve is the "normal" one we had in mind when we suggested that liquidity considerations would tend to make yields on short-term securities less than those on long-term securities. Clearly, however, other shapes are quite common as well. What explains these patterns?

The most commonly given explanation is termed the *expectations theory*, under which the shape of the yield curve is based on investors' expectations of *future* interest rates—in particular, future short-term rates. The nature of this theory can be seen most easily with the aid of an example.

Suppose an individual wishes to invest funds for two years, and for simplicity assume that she considers the following two alternatives: She may purchase a 1-year Treasury security and, when it matures, acquire another 1-year bond; or she may purchase a 2-year bond and hold it until maturity. If our investor is a profit maximizer, she will choose that security (or combination of securities) which gives her the greatest return over the two-year period. For concreteness, suppose that 1-year bonds are currently yielding 7 percent and that our investor expects that 1-year bonds *issued a year from now* will yield 9 percent (this is the expected short-term rate). From one of her options she thus anticipates an average return over the two-year period of roughly 8 percent. Given these expectations, she would buy a 2-year bond only if it yielded more than 8 percent per year, but would

---

[6]The pattern of yields in Figure 4–2 is regular but not precisely so, since there appear to be some outliers off the curve. For the most part these outliers reflect some special features (such as taxes), and these issues are customarily ignored in drawing a yield curve.

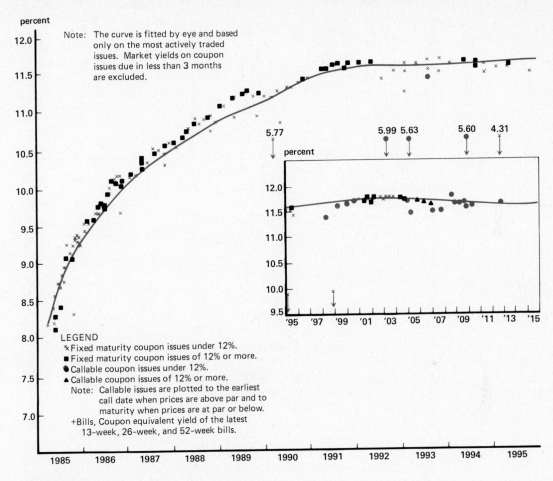

FIGURE 4–2
SOURCE: *Treasury Bulletin*, Winter Issue, Fiscal
1985, p. 33.

purchase a sequence of two 1-year bonds if the two-year rate was less than 8 percent.

If all investors expected a future short-term rate of 9 percent, this line of reasoning would imply that the yield on 2-year bonds would have to be approximately 8 percent for the bond market to be in equilibrium. If it were higher, investors would regard 2-year bonds as a good thing and bid *up* their price (driving *down* their yield) until an 8 percent rate was established and investors were indifferent between the various options. Conversely, if the 2-year bond yield were lower than 8 percent, holders of 2-year bonds would attempt to sell such bonds and buy 1-year bonds (driving bond prices down and bond yields up) until 8 percent rate was established. Thus, *arbitrage* would establish equilibrium in the bond market.

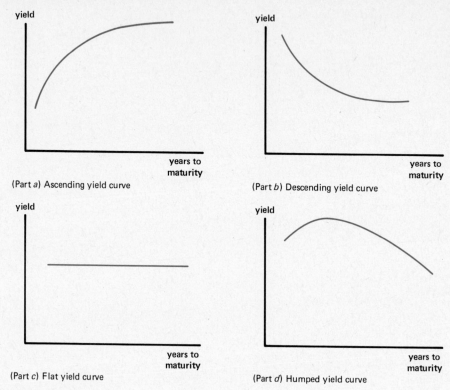

FIGURE 4–3
Common shapes of yield curves

What this example suggests is that, in general, we should find that yields on long-term bonds will be averages of current and expected future short yields. This simple observation is, in fact, sufficient to account for all the possible yield curve patterns portrayed in Figure 4–3. For example, if short-term rates are expected to rise, long-term rates, being an average of current and future short rates, would be above current short rates, producing an ascending yield curve. If lower short-term rates are expected in the future, long-term rates will lie below current short-term rates, giving us a descending yield curve. Finally, if investors expect short-term rates first to rise and then to fall to much lower levels, a humped yield curve will result.

In many respects the expectations theory is a natural extension of the principles on market yields and bond prices. We saw earlier that the actual return from a bond sold before maturity could differ substantially from the yield to maturity that prevailed when the bond was purchased. The expectations theory explicitly recognizes the possibility that individuals may need funds after two, three, or ten years, whatever the maturity of the security they happen to own. What the individual investor is assumed to maximize is the return over some particular *horizon* or *holding period*.

Since different investors will have different holding periods, this serves to bring long-term rates into line to equalize *expected holding period yields* for different horizons.

This is the essence of the expectations theory of the term structure of interest rates. While it provides a reasonably satisfactory explanation of observed yield curves, there are several reasons why it may not hold exactly.

1   **DIVERSE EXPECTATIONS.** Not all investors have the same expectations, so that the arbitrage among various maturities, in some loose sense, responds only to "average" expectations.

2   **TRANSACTIONS COSTS.** Because there are costs, such as brokers' fees, for shifting funds among maturities, complete arbitrage may not take place.

3   **LIQUIDITY CONSIDERATIONS AND UNCERTAINTY.** Investors may not hold expectations with complete confidence and consequently may still prefer short-term maturities because of their liquidity. This would suggest that, for example, if current and all future short-term rates are 6 percent, even though the expectations theory predicts a long rate of 6 percent (a flat yield curve), the actual long-term rate may have to exceed 6 percent to compensate investors for the greater price volatility of long-term bonds.

4   **LONG MATURITY PREFERENCES.** In contrast to those investors who are willing to pay a premium for liquidity, certain groups of investors may prefer longer maturities to better balance the maturity structure of their assets and liabilities. For example, life insurance companies that issue long-term liabilities typically invest in long-term bonds to be assured of a profit regardless of the course of interest rates over the life of the insurance contract. As with the case of liquidity needs, this could lead to a certain amount of bond market *segmentation*, which interferes with the arbitrage process.

THE GENERAL STRUCTURE OF INTEREST RATES

Our discussion of the market for U.S. government securities has documented the existence of numerous interest rates for such bonds. If interest differentials exist within this class of relatively homogeneous securities, it is hardly surprising that an even greater range of possible interest rates emerges once we look at other market instruments. In Figure 4–4 we have plotted a sample of such interest rates for several different types of market instruments. Even this figure conceals many additional interest rate differentials. For example, the single long-term corporate bond rate we have plotted is necessarily an average of many different rates that are paid by corporations with widely different borrowing capabilities. The diversity underlying an average rate is relevant for the other series plotted in the figure as well. This complication aside, what accounts for the general structure of rates portrayed in Figure 4–4?

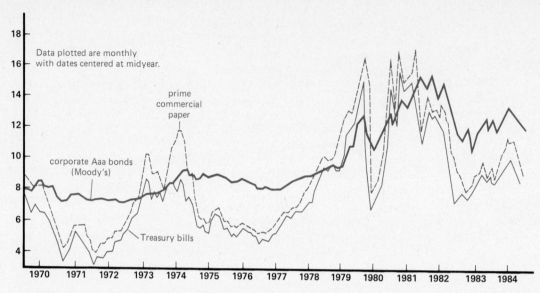

FIGURE 4–4
Selected interest rates, 1970–1984.

Our previous discussion of the term structure has noted some of the possible factors, such as liquidity and market risk. Here we consider a number of additional ones. A factor of primary importance, once we move away from U.S. government securities, is the risk of default. For example, there is a relatively constant differential between the rate on high-grade corporate bonds and the rate on long-term U.S. government securities, and this reflects such a *risk premium*. Perhaps an even more vivid illustration of the risk element is the enormous 4 percentage points difference between interest rates on prime commercial paper and U.S. Treasury bills that prevailed in mid-1974. Like Treasury bills, commercial paper is a short-term instrument. As it is only issued by large and well-known corporations (e.g., General Motors), the historical differential has been a percentage point or less. This might be taken as a measure of the normal risk premium. In mid-1974, however, we were in the midst of the oil crisis, when, at least according to the popular press, safety became of prime concern (especially with Arab oil sheiks). Consequently, the risk premium rose to unprecedented levels. Not coincidentally, mid-1974 was also a period in which short-term rates exceeded long-term ones.

The other noteworthy feature of Figure 4–4 is the record-breaking level of interest rates that prevailed after 1979. Also evident in the figure is a marked increase in interest rate variability during the same period. In March 1980, for example, the Treasury bill rate averaged a whopping $15\frac{1}{2}$ percent. By June 1980, a mere three months later, the Treasury bill rate had plunged to 7 percent; but by December 1980 it was back up close to 16 percent. By historical standards, high and variable interest rates prevailed through the end of the period portrayed in Figure 4–4.[7] We shall have more to say on the causes and consequences of these developments in a later chapter.

In addition to default risk, a number of other explanations of interest rate differentials can be listed more briefly. Among these we have the following:

1 **DIFFERENCES IN COST OF ADMINISTRATION PER DOLLAR OF LOAN PER YEAR.** Interest charges usually include an amount to cover costs of investigating the creditworthiness of the borrower, of holding the loan, and of collecting principal and interest. On some loans, these costs are very low per dollar per year. For example, the annual adminstrative cost per dollar on a very large loan to a corporation whose credit standing need not be investigated may be almost negligible. On the other hand, such costs per dollar of loan per year may be very high on a small installment loan to a consumer when his or her credit standing must be investigated and interest and principal collected in weekly or monthly installments.

2 **DIFFERENCES IN TAXABILITY.** An example of such differences is the fact that income on securities issued by states and municipalities is exempt from federal income taxes, which enables these securities to be sold at lower yield rates. During the two decades ending in 1983 interest rates on municipal securities averaged $1\frac{1}{2}$ percentage points less than the rates on 10-year Treasury bonds.

3 **MARKET IMPERFECTIONS.** Another part of the explanation of interest rate differentials is to be found in imperfections in the credit market, which inhibit the mobility of loan funds from one branch of the market to another. Some of the most important of these are lack of knowledge by lenders or borrowers, legal limitations on the types of loans that can be made by some financial institutions, and differing degrees of monopoly power in the various branches of the market. A variety of restrictions also directly limit the rate of interest on certain types of debt obligations. Here we include state usury laws and legal restrictions that have limited the interest rate the federal government can pay on new long-term issues.

4 **TECHNICAL FEATURES.** A number of technical features of market instruments can also affect their yield. For example, bonds may be *callable* in that the borrower may have the right (usually after a certain date) to prepay the debt. Since borrowers are likely to do this only if interest rates have fallen, investors will generally require some

---

[7]Given the inverse relationships described earlier, the variability in interest rates had its counterpart in the variability in bond prices, with bond prices plummeting while interest rates soared. Declining bond prices naturally meant capital losses for those holding bonds. In early 1982 this prompted the following quip in financial circles. *Question:* How do you become a millionaire in the bond market? *Answer:* Start with two million!

compensation for accepting this feature. On the other hand, certain types of bonds may be *convertible* (e.g., into equities), and some investors may find this a desirable feature.

INFLATION AND THE LEVEL OF INTEREST RATES

As Figure 4–4 suggests, interest rates reached historically high levels in the 1970s and 1980s. As we noted in Chapter 1, these recent periods were also marked by high rates of inflation. These two facts are not a coincidence; rather, they reflect the interplay between the level of inflation and the level of interest rates. To understand this connection, we need to distinguish between what are called nominal and real interest rates.

Nominal interest rates are what we have been talking about all along, namely the rates of interest prevailing in the marketplace for financial instruments. The *real rate of interest*, on the other hand, can be thought of as an inflation-adjusted nominal rate designed to capture the change in purchasing power that results from buying a bond. To clarify this distinction, let us consider an example. Suppose that last year you invested in a 1-year bond with a market yield of 8 percent. Assuming your initial investment was $1,000, this year when the bond matures you will receive a payment of $1,080, reflecting both principal and interest. In this example, your nominal rate of return is 8 percent. Your real rate of return, however, depends on what has happened to the price level over the year that you held the bond. Let us consider two possibilities.

The simplest case is when the price level is unchanged over the period, corresponding to an inflation rate of zero percent. In such a case your $1,080 will enable you to buy 8 percent ($1,080/$1,000) more goods than your initial investment. You have achieved a real rate of return of 8 percent. In other words, when there is no inflation, the nominal rate and the real rate are equal.

Now assume that over the course of the year you have held your bond, the general price level has risen by 5 percent. That is, there has been a 5 percent rate of inflation. As a consequence, your $1,080 will buy less than it would have bought last year. How much less? Well, in terms of last year's purchasing power, exactly 5 percent less. That is, in real purchasing power terms your $1,080 is worth only $1,080/1.05, or $1,028.57. Your real purchasing power has increased only 2.857 percent. We would thus say that the real rate of interest is 2.857 percent.

Two things should be apparent from this example. First, it is approximately true that the real rate of interest is equal to the nominal rate less the rate of inflation. We saw this is exactly true when the inflation rate is zero; when the inflation rate is 5 percent, the real rate is approximately 3 percent (= 8 − 5). Second, as we have illustrated it, it would appear that the real rate of interest can be calculated only *after* we have observed the rate of inflation. But the real rate of interest also has significance in a *forward-looking*, or what economists typically call an *ex ante*, sense.

The easiest way to see this is to consider your decision before you plunk down $1,000 to buy a bond with a nominal rate of interest of 8 percent. You are likely to think to yourself that whether this is a sensible asset to buy depends on what the rate of inflation turns out to be over the life of the bond. If there is a zero rate of inflation, the real rate will be 8 percent; if the inflation rate is 5 percent, the real rate will be roughly 3 percent; if the inflation rate is 8 percent, the real rate would be zero; and for inflation rates above 8 percent, the real rate would be *negative*. Quite obviously then, what rate of inflation you expect or anticipate for the next year is likely to influence your decision to buy the bond. The lower your *inflationary expectations*, the higher the real rate of interest you expect to realize from the bond and the more likely you are to buy it.

Having come this far, we are now in a position to turn this around and deduce that a rise in inflationary expectations is likely to drive up nominal interest rates. The reason is simple. Suppose investors are generally willing to purchase a bond with a nominal yield of 8 percent when they expect an inflation rate of 5 percent. Now suppose that expected inflation rises to 8 percent. Since, as we have seen, this translates into an expected real rate of zero, lenders will no longer be willing to purchase the same 8 percent bond. Only if the nominal interest rate rises above 8 percent so that the anticipated real interest also rises will lenders again be induced to purchase bonds. Indeed, according to one simple theory, the rise in the nominal interest rate would exactly match the increase in the expected rate of inflation. In our example, this would mean that the nominal rate would rise from 8 to 11 percent when the expected inflation rate rose from 5 to 8 percent.

While it need not be the case that there is a simple one-to-one relationship between the nominal rate of interest and the expected rate of inflation, the overall message should be clear: The expected rate of inflation is one general factor that has a direct and positive effect on the level of nominal interest rates.[8]

SUMMARY

1 The *yield to maturity* of a security is the rate of discount that makes the sum of the present values of all future payments equal to its price. Conversely, the *price* or *market value* of a security is equal to the sum of the present values of all future payments accruing to the bondholder.

2 The price, or market value, of a financial instrument results from equi-

---

[8]A one-to-one relationship between nominal interest rates and expected inflation would mean that the real rate of interest is a constant. It is easy to verify that this is not true after the fact, but since inflationary expectations are not directly observable, it is trickier to refute the hypothesis that the expected real rate of interest is constant. Nevertheless, a number of researchers claim to have done so.

librating the forces of supply and demand. The *interest rate* or *yield* on a financial instrument is inversely related to its price. Thus, for example, an increase in the supply of a bond (say, by new issuers who wish to raise additional funds) will tend to reduce the price of the bond and raise the interest rate on the bond. In subsequent chapters we shall discuss how underlying economic developments shift the balance between supply and demand and thus change interest rates. Not surprisingly, the Federal Reserve, through its conduct of monetary policy, is of particular importance in this regard.

3 While the exposition of certain economic principles is often facilitated by the use of a single interest rate, this is a rather marked simplification. As we have seen, there are numerous market rates of interest, and these can differ widely. Moreover, these various rates may not move in a parallel manner through time, although they usually move in the same direction.

4 It is possible to elaborate a substantial number of characteristics of market instruments that explain differences in market yields. As investors differ with respect to preferences, expectations, and opportunities, it would be surprising if they chose to hold their assets in exactly the same form. In fact, there is substantial diversity of asset portfolios across different groups of investors. Or, put another way, because of differences in preferences among buyers and among issuers, securities come to be highly differentiated, with differing claims on assets and income. These come to be reflected in differences in liquidity, safety of principal value, and yield. Holders are presented with a varied menu from which to choose.

SELECTED READINGS

First Boston Corporation, *Handbook of the United States Government and Federal Agencies and Related Money Market Instruments.* Boston, 1970.

Malkiel, B. G., *The Term Structure of Interest Rates: Theory, Empirical Evidence, and Applications.* Morristown, NJ, General Learning Press, 1970.

Stigum, M., *The Money Market: Myth, Reality, and Practice.* Homewood, IL, Dow Jones–Irwin, 1978.

PART 2

COMMERCIAL BANKS
AND OTHER
DEPOSITORY INSTITUTIONS

5

THE STRUCTURE AND REGULATION OF COMMERCIAL BANKING

As we have seen, financial intermediaries play a critical role in channeling funds from lenders to borrowers. Financial intermediaries also offer liabilities that make up the lion's share of the U.S. money supply. Since our ultimate goal is to explore the role of the financial system in the operation of the economy and to understand the workings of monetary policy, we clearly need to investigate the nature and scope of financial intermediaries. A few short years ago, such a discussion would have focused almost exclusively on one type of financial intermediary—the commercial bank. There were many reasons for this.

First, aside from currency, until relatively recently demand deposits were the only assets that counted as "money," and these deposits were the exclusive province of commercial banks. Second, commercial banks were the only financial intermediaries to be affected directly by the Federal Reserve, and thus they served as a fulcrum for monetary policy. Third, commercial banks were by far the most important financial intermediary in terms of sheer size and also in terms of scope of activities. To be sure, even in the old days a text such as this would have pointed out the similarities between bank and nonbank intermediaries. The role of nonbank intermediaries in the workings of monetary policy would also typically be noted. But on the whole such earlier discussions often tended to treat nonbank intermediaries as a pesky pedagogic nuisance. These days, such as approach simply will not work.

What has happened is that institutional, technological, and legal changes have blurred the distinctions between the various types of financial intermediaries. As one illustration, commercial banks have lost their uniqueness in the provision of transactions accounts. Moreover, the rapid changes currently taking place in the financial sector of the economy promise to erode further the distinctiveness of commercial banks. The net result of all this is that nonbank intermediaries can no longer be regarded as appendages to the system.

Nevertheless, commercial banks still deserve to be singled out. Despite recent changes, commercial banks remain the largest and most important of our financial intermediaries, both nationally and internationally. Indeed, as of early 1985 about 90 percent of transactions balances were held at commercial banks. A second reason for singling out commercial banks is that, for largely historical reasons, the vast majority of the laws and regulations governing banking are relatively specific to commercial banking. If only under the law, commercial banks retain a certain uniqueness, and this uniqueness pervades even contemporary discussions of the structure and regulation of financial institutions. For these reasons, we begin our extended discussion of financial intermediaries with an analysis of the structure and regulation of the commercial banking industry.[1]

More specifically, we examine issues such as the following: How are banks born, and how do they die? How did we get so many banks, and is this a good thing? What legal forms can banks take, and does this matter? Is the banking system safe, efficient, and competitive? Who regulates banks, how are they regulated, and why are they regulated? As we attempt to answer these questions, you should gain an appreciation of the complexities of the commercial banking industry and the problems faced by policymakers who are charged with ensuring that the banking system functions smoothly.

DUAL BANKING AND BANK SUPERVISION

If we are to examine commercial banking, we will ultimately need a notion of what constitutes a commercial bank. As we discuss later in this chapter, this is far from being a straightforward matter. For the moment, however, it will suffice to resort to a bit of legal sophistry and define a *commercial bank* as any institution that is chartered to be a commercial bank. As this is meant to suggest, one needs permission to start a bank, and this takes the form of securing a charter to engage in the business of commercial

---

[1]Even in this chapter, which focuses on commercial banks, the role of other financial intermediaries will play an important part, especially when we consider the newest developments.

banking. If one makes a convincing case on grounds of worthiness and need, a commercial bank charter may be obtained from the federal government (through the Comptroller of the Currency) or from the various state banking authorities.

Banks that have been granted charters by the federal government are known as *national banks;* the remainder are called *state banks.* National and state banks exist side by side in every state; hence the characterization of the United States as having a *dual banking system.*[2] As of 1982, roughly two-thirds of the banks had state charters, but they accounted for only 43 percent of total assets (Table 5–1). National banks are evidently less numerous but larger than state banks.

As Table 5–1 indicates, two additional supervisory layers serve to distinguish among banks. The first of these is Federal Reserve membership. All national banks are required to be members of the Federal Reserve System, but membership is optional for state banks. As of 1982, only 10 percent of state banks were members. Overall, therefore, 38 percent of all banks were members, although they had 75 percent of all bank assets.

Another way in which banks can be distinguished from one another is with respect to insurance status. All Federal Reserve member banks are required to have their deposits insured by the Federal Deposit Insurance Corporation (FDIC). While this is optional for state nonmember banks, as shown in Table 5–1 virtually all of these have elected to be insured. (We shall have more to say about the FDIC shortly.)

THE CHOICE OF A CHARTER

Why do banks choose a national or a state charter? As already noted, national banks must join the Federal Reserve, so the choice of a charter is intertwined with the desirability of membership in the Federal Reserve. At least historically, a key element is the nature of reserve requirements im-

[2]The historical reasons for the evolution of a dual banking system are traced in Chapter 9.

TABLE 5–1 Three Ways of Classifying Commercial Banks (as of 1982, year-end)

	Number of banks	Percent of total number	Assets (in billions of dollars)	Percent of total assets
National banks	4,579	31%	$1,070	57%
State banks	10,384	69	801	43
Federal Reserve member banks	5,619	38	1,399	75
Nonmember banks	9,344	62	472	25
FDIC-insured banks	14,437	96	1,861	99
Uninsured banks	526	4	10	1
All commercial banks	14,963	100	1,871	100

posed on members of the Federal Reserve System. While all commercial banks are required to hold some part of their assets in the form of reserves, these requirements are much stiffer for member banks, in terms of both percentage requirements and the form in which reserves must be held. State-chartered banks, aside from having lower percentage requirements, are often permitted to hold earning assets to satisfy reserve requirements. For member banks, reserves pay no interest. The high level of interest rates that has prevailed in recent years has meant that non-interest-bearing reserves carry a substantial opportunity cost. Consequently, banks seeking more advantageous reserve requirements often elect or convert to a state charter.

The differential treatment of reserve requirements for member and non-member banks was substantially changed by legislation passed in 1980. It provides for the imposition of a common set of reserve requirements on all commercial banks.[3] These requirements are being phased in gradually and will be fully in place by 1988. Will this law induce substantial numbers of state banks to switch to national charters or to become members of the Federal Reserve? It seems quite unlikely. One reason is that the 1980 law also reduced some of the advantages of Federal Reserve membership. Formerly, member banks received certain free services from the Federal Reserve. The 1980 law requires the Federal Reserve to charge for these services and make them available to all banks.[4] It seems likely, therefore, that most state banks will find it simpler to stay as they are and deal with a familiar set of laws and regulatory agencies.[5]

REGULATORY PROBLEMS

As expected, the existence of dual banking and the multiplicity of regulatory authorities is a source of complexity (and confusion) in the U.S. banking industry. Even within the federal bureaucracy, harmony does not always reign supreme. At various times considerable controversy has erupted among the Comptroller of the Currency, the FDIC, and the Federal Reserve. Proposals to consolidate these three groups have been advanced on a number of occasions, although with differing visions of which agency would survive the consolidation. We shall consider some of the more recent proposals for the reorganization of the federal regulatory structure in Chapter 10.

Once one introduces both federal and state jurisdictions, even more complexity results. National and state banks are governed by different laws

---

[3]It also imposes reserve requirements on the transactions accounts of other depository intermediaries. The new structure of reserve requirements is discussed in Chapter 12.

[4]For a discussion of the pricing of Federal Reserve services, see Chapter 10.

[5]Capital requirements also tend to be lower for state-chartered banks than for national banks. On the other side, national banks have generally enjoyed more flexibility in the nature of the activities they are permitted to engage in, but even this advantage seems to be eroding with time.

(even in the same state), and banking practices that are prohibited in one state may be permitted in another. Some writers have expressed concern over the fact that individual banks get to choose either a national or a state regulator. The fear, perhaps, is that competition among regulators would lead to banking abuses. Or, put another way, a variation of Gresham's law might apply to bank regulation, with bad regulators driving out good ones. Despite these quirks, dual banking has many staunch defenders, who argue that it stimulates innovation by letting each state function as an experimental laboratory. Others see the same events as threatening to undermine the federal government's oversight of the banking industry. Questions of interpretation aside, later in this chapter we shall see examples of how changes in the nature of banking can be brought about by state actions. The role of state-originated innovations will also figure prominently in Chapter 7 where we will document the changing character of the so-called thrift institutions.

THE NUMBER OF COMMERCIAL BANKS

As noted in Table 5–1, as of the end of 1982, there were 14,963 commercial banks in the United States. This number, however, has fluctuated considerably over time. In 1840 the country had roughly 900 banks. By 1900 the number of banks had expanded to nearly 9,000. This remarkable growth continued up to 1920, at which time there were nearly 30,000 banks in the United States. However, between 1920 and 1940 the trend reversed. The number of banks declined by about 50 percent, falling to roughly 14,000. Since that time it has fluctuated more narrowly, declining a little during the earlier part of the period and showing an increase more recently. This marked variation in the number of banks and the composition of alternative bank types are illustrated in Figure 5–1.

In order to explain changes in the number of commercial banks, it is necessary to examine new bank chartering, bank failures, and bank mergers. The net change in the number of banks during any period is equal to the number of new banks created in the period minus the number that disappear through suspension or voluntary liquidation and also those that disappear by being consolidated or merged into other banks. For convenience we shall refer to these, respectively, as new banks, bank failures, and bank absorptions.

Table 5–2 shows that between the end of 1920 and year-end 1982, the number of banks declined by over 14,000. More than 14,200 new banks were chartered in this period, but these additions were more than offset by over 13,500 failures and nearly 16,000 absorptions of banks through mergers.[6]

---

[6]The careful reader will note some statistical inconsistencies in Table 5–2. These arise partly from discrepancies in the original data and partly from shifts of institutions between the categories of commercial and noncommercial banks.

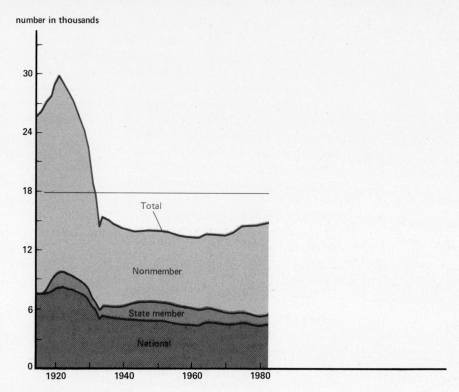

FIGURE 5–1
Commercial banks in the United States. (SOURCE:
Board of Governors of the Federal Reserve
System, *1983 Historical Chart Book,* **Washington,**
D.C., p. 82.)

NEW BANKS

Table 5–2 indicates that more than 14,200 new banks were chartered between 1921 and 1982. The rate of creation of new banks was high in the 1920s, much lower from 1929 through World War II, and higher again in the postwar period, although still considerably below the rates of the 1920s. The rate of creation of new banks depends directly on the supply and willingness of private investors to establish and finance new banks, which presumably is based on prospective profitability, and on the availability of charters from the banking authorities. Both have undergone wide changes since World War I.

Free banking prevailed in the United States during the latter half of the nineteenth century and through World War I; the Comptroller of the Currency and most state banking authorities were empowered to grant charters

TABLE 5–2 Changes in the Number of United States Commercial Banks During Selected Periods, 1920–1982

Period	Number at end of period	New banks	Bank failures	Bank absorptions	Net change during period
1920	29,206				
1921–1929 (inclusive)	23,695	3,253	5,067	3,963	− 5,511
1930–1933 (inclusive)	14,352	674	7,763	2,322	− 9,343
1934–1941 (inclusive)	14,225	890	*	1,127	− 127
1942–1945 (inclusive)	14,011	258	201	327	− 214
1946–1970 (inclusive)	13,688	3,277	252	3,399	− 323
1971–1982 (inclusive)	14,963	3,208	65	1,868	+ 1,275
Total, 1921–1982		14,229	13,572	15,846	− 14,243

*Data not reliable because of some reopenings of banks suspended earlier.
SOURCE: Board of Governors of the Federal Reserve System, *Banking and Monetary Statistics*, Washington, D.C., 1943; Federal Reserve Board, various annual reports, and *Federal Reserve Bulletin*, various issues.

to all who met the requirements of the general banking laws. It was under this policy of free banking that the number of banks grew to more than 29,000 in 1920. Following the banking debacle of the early 1930s, important modifications of the free banking principle resulted from the Banking Act of 1935. Under this law a new bank still must meet the requirements of the relevant general banking laws, but the Comptroller of the Currency may issue a charter for a new national bank and the FDIC may insure the deposits of a new state-chartered bank only if they find it in the public interest to do so after investigating such things as the qualifications and experience of the proposed bank directors and officers, the prospects of success of the new bank, and the need of the community for additional facilities. Most state banking authorities have adopted somewhat similar policies, if only because a new state bank would have but limited chances of success if it were denied deposit insurance.

The prospective profitability of establishing new banks has also fluctuated widely. It is easy to understand why so few new banks were created during the Great Depression and also during and immediately following World War II, when interest rates were abnormally low. However, one might have expected that the rate of new bank creation would have increased even more than it has since about 1950 in view of the generally higher level of interest rates, high and rising levels of economic activity, growth of population, and spread of metropolitan areas. A major part of the explanation is to be found in the growth of branch banking; branch offices have been established in areas that would otherwise have attracted new banks.

BANK ABSORPTIONS

As shown in Table 5–2, between 1920 and 1982, nearly 16,000 banks disappeared through absorption in mergers. The absorption rate was high during the 1920s and somewhat lower from 1930 to 1933. After falling sharply from the end of 1933 to the end of World War II, the absorption rate again rose to high levels in the postwar period. It would be even higher if it were not restricted by the banking authorities and the Department of Justice.

What are the reasons for this high rate of mergers and for pressures toward even higher rates? Mergers can occur only if owners of the bank to be absorbed are willing to sell at a price attractive to the owners and management of the acquiring bank. There are many reasons why the owners of an absorbed bank may be willing to do this. One is the imminence of failure. An unknown number of the absorbed banks would have suspended operations if they had not been bought. Banking authorities have often assisted such mergers. Other reasons for merging include various diseconomies of small scale that come to be reflected in low net earnings, difficulties in providing for management succession at salaries the bank can afford to pay, and the low liquidity and marketability of shares in a small bank.

There are also many reasons why an acquiring bank is willing to pay an attractive price. Since a merger produces a larger bank, the acquiring bank may be able to reap cost savings due to economies of scale. A merger may also offer the possibility of obtaining new lines of business, new customers, or geographic diversification.

BANK FAILURES

Even in the nineteenth and early twentieth centuries, the United States had the dubious distinction of possessing one of the highest, if not the highest, bank failure rates of any important nation with a commercial banking system. Nearly 3,000 banks failed between 1864 and 1920. But the worst was yet to come. Another 5,067 had suspended operations by the end of 1929, and still another 7,763 were defunct by the end of 1933. The mortality rate was especially high among smaller banks, but many large ones also failed.

To generalize about the reasons for failure of any type of business enterprise is difficult, for the reasons vary from case to case. Even in a particular case failure usually results not from a single cause, but from a combination of conditions. Nevertheless, it is possible to isolate some of the most important factors responsible for high failure rates prior to 1934.

As just noted, the era of free banking, which prevailed until the mid-1930s, meant that it was relatively easy—some would say too easy—to start a bank. The net result was "overbanking." For example, it was not unusual for a village with 2,000 inhabitants to have three or more banks. These banks were inevitably small and therefore unable to capitalize on economies of

HOW TO AVOID A BANK FAILURE

A firsthand account of a run on a bank in 1931 brought on by the closing of a neighboring bank.

I told . . . [the staff] what they would have to face in a few hours. "If you want to keep this bank open," I said, "you must do your part. Go about your business as though nothing unusual was happening. . . . We can't break this run today. The best we can do is slow it down. People are going to come here to close out their savings accounts. You are going to pay them. But you are going to pay them very slowly. . . . You know a lot of depositors by sight, and in the past you did not have to look up their signatures, but today when they come here with their deposit books to close out their accounts, you are going to look up every signature card. And take your time about it. And one other thing: When you pay out, don't use any big bills. Pay out in fives and tens, and count slowly." . . .

In the meantime a call had been put through to the Federal Reserve Bank in Salt Lake City to send currency to our [bank]. . . . The armored car that brought funds to us in Ogden arrived on the scene as in the movies when the Union cavalry charged in to save all from the Indians. . . .

Mounting the counter, I raised my hand and called for attention: . . .

"I want to make an announcement. It appears that we are having some difficulty handling our depositors with the speed to which you are accustomed. Many of you have been in line for a considerable time. I just wanted to tell you that instead of closing at the usual hour of three o'clock, we have decided to stay open just as long as there is anyone who desires to withdraw his deposit or make one. Therefore, you people who have just come in can return later this afternoon or evening if you wish. There is no justification for the excitement or the apparent panicky attitude on the part of some depositors. As all of you have seen, we have just had brought up from Salt Lake City, a large amount of currency that will take care of all your requirements. There is plenty more where that came from." (This was true enough—but I didn't say we could get it.)[*]

*Mariner S. Eccles, *Beckoning Frontiers*, New York, Knopf, 1951, pp. 58–60. The bank and Eccles both survived, with Eccles going on to become chairman of the Board of Governors of the Federal Reserve System.

scale. Furthermore, a large percentage of the assets of these small banks were typically in the form of loans to local borrowers. Thus, the banks were likely to be weak in the face of unfavorable economic developments not only in the economy at large, but also in their own localities. And some banks in overbanked areas would have failed even under favorable economic conditions; the adverse economic developments that materialized ensured disaster.

Adverse economic conditions for many banks began in the 1920s with gradual shifts in the location of business brought about in part by the revolution in highway transportation. Prior to the days of hard-surfaced roads, automobiles, and farm trucks, farmers took much of their business to nearby agricultural villages or small towns. Here they sold many of their products, bought supplies, and did their banking. But as new roads and motor vehicles increased the speed and reduced the cost of transportation, farmers took their business (including deposits and borrowing) to the county seat or some other larger city. The smaller village or town was left to wither on the vine; its banks were fortunate if they escaped a less lingering death. Other shifts also contributed to the failures of individual banks: shifts of plants from one area to another, the replacement of small firms by larger ones that did their banking business elsewhere, and so on.

While shifts in the location of business contributed to a substantial number of bank failures, a more important factor was the periods of deflation and depression the economy endured. Bank failures and business depressions are mutually aggravating; a depression tends to break banks, and bank failures deepen a depression. Falling prices, incomes, sales, and employment lessen the abilities of debtors to meet their obligations and thereby threaten both the solvency and the liquidity of banks. Many banks were destroyed or seriously weakened during the sharp deflation starting in May 1920. The failure of agriculture to recover fully during the 1920s injured banks that were dependent on farming. Then came the Great Depression. Thousands of banks failed to survive under its strains, and bank failures and threats of failure played an important role in deepening and prolonging the Depression.

Since 1934 bank failure rates have been much lower than in preceding years. There appear to be many reasons for this, including the protection afforded by better supervision of banks, improved bank management, and more frequent absorptions of weak banks in mergers. However, a basic factor has been the maintenance of high and generally rising levels of income and economic activity. The FDIC, through its role in insuring deposits, merits particular attention in this regard.

THE FEDERAL DEPOSIT INSURANCE CORPORATION (FDIC)

The FDIC was established in direct response to the dramatic number of bank failures experienced in the early 1930s. It began operation in 1934, the year following the worst debacle in banking history, when some 4,000 commercial banks suspended operations. Despite the evident need for deposit insurance, it had many opponents when it was proposed. Indeed, the prestigious American Bankers Association, fighting the idea to the bitter end, declared that "the plan is inherently fallacious ... one of those plausible, but deceptive, human plans that in actual application only serve to render worse the very evils they seek to cure," and further characterized the plan as "unsound, unscientific, unjust, and dangerous."[7] Fortunately for the country, this rhetoric did not prevail. Hindsight has given quite high marks to the FDIC as an effective means of achieving banking stability.

Initially the FDIC insured the first $2,500 of the accounts held by each depositor at each insured bank. This limit has been raised a number of times, most recently in 1980, and now stands at $100,000. The FDIC is financed by annual insurance premiums of 1/12 of 1 percent of total deposits of its member banks. Out of this premium the FDIC pays its operating expenses and adds to insurance reserves, which amounted to some $14 billion at the end of 1982. To make sure that it is unlikely to need these reserves, the FDIC engages in an extensive program of bank examination and supervision that fosters sound management in the banking system. It also helps identify potentially troubled banks to permit corrective action to be taken.

Even under the current system, there remains a sizable volume of uninsured deposits. A very small part of this comes from the roughly 500 state banks that have elected to remain uninsured. The bulk of the uninsured deposits stems from the $100,000 insurance limit, which leaves a surprisingly large volume of deposits uncovered. Indeed, at the end of 1982 more than 25 percent of deposits were uninsured. While some readers may be disturbed by this fact, the practical operating procedures of the FDIC substantially reduce its significance and assure that virtually all depositors will receive full coverage. The primary reason is that the usual method for dealing with bank failure involves the FDIC arranging a merger of the distressed bank with a healthy insured bank. To facilitate a merger, it can purchase assets of the distressed bank or lend funds to it. When a successful merger results depositors suffer no losses, so that the system functions as if full insurance were in effect.

The widespread use of the merger approach, also sometimes called the *deposit assumption method*, has meant that 95 percent of the deposits in banks that failed from 1934 to 1982 were assumed by a healthy bank and therefore, de facto, fully insured. Moreover, even where a merger was not arranged, depositors typically have recovered the vast majority of their uninsured deposits, although a wait of several years is often involved. The funds for paying off the uninsured part of the deposits come from the sale of the failed bank's assets. But despite the historical fact that most unin-

---

[7]Economic Policy Commission, American Bankers Association, *The Guaranty of Bank Deposits*, New York, ABA, 1933, p. 43. The second quote is cited in J. K. Galbraith, *Money*, Boston, Houghton Mifflin, 1975, p. 197.

sured deposits at failed banks end up being covered, there is a loose end in all this. In particular, if a bank appears to be in some difficulty, the big depositors with large sums at risk understandably get nervous. From their point of view, the prudent action would be to withdraw their funds. This, of course, would only add to the bank's difficulties. To head off these withdrawals, the FDIC sometimes finds it necessary to make an announcement explicitly promising to cover all deposits, both insured and uninsured. In 1984 such an action proved necessary when the Continental Illinois Bank of Chicago, then the nation's eighth largest bank, experienced financial difficulties. The guarantee was successful in stablizing the situation in the bank.

By any reasonable standard, the operation of the FDIC has been a significant success. Since its inception in 1934 bank failures have been relatively few in number. Furthermore, those that have occurred have not spread in an infectious way through the banking system. Despite this success, several aspects of the FDIC have come in for questioning. One concerns the issue just discussed—the insurance limit. Some writers have advocated removal of the limit and the provision of 100 percent deposit insurance. The FDIC has taken the position that this erodes "marketplace discipline" and that "discipline can be restored by exposing the largest creditors to some risk of loss."[8] What they have in mind is that the risk of some loss encourages the largest depositors to monitor the condition of the bank and presumably press for more careful bank management. However, as their actions in the case of Continental Illinois suggest, when the chips are down even the FDIC finds this hardnosed attitude to be somewhat unworkable.

A second controversial issue concerns the method of setting the insurance premium paid to the FDIC. As noted before, the premium is 1/12 of 1 percent of total—not just insured—deposits. Many large banks regard the setting of insurance premiums in relation to total deposits as unfair, arguing that this forces them to provide a subsidy to small banks. One reason for this is that small banks have historically had a higher failure rate than large banks, although this has not been true in recent years. From this perspective, they argue that the premium should be higher for small banks. A second reason stems from the fact that large banks have a disproportionately high share of uninsured deposits—that is, a disproportionately large fraction of accounts that exceed the insurance limit. Since premiums are based on total deposits, large banks argue that they are paying for insurance they are not getting.

There are merits in both arguments, and indeed some economists have called for a restructuring of insurance premiums to address these problems, perhaps by relating the insurance premium to the riskiness of a bank's assets. In partial defense of the current system, it should be noted that many of the activities of the FDIC tend to protect (if not insure) all deposits

[8]Federal Deposit Insurance Corporation, *1982 Annual Report*, Washington, D.C., 1983, p. ix.

of its member banks. Consequently, the arguments of the larger banks probably overstate the inequities in the present setup.

ORGANIZATIONAL FORMS IN BANKING

While we have touched on several aspects of the structure of the banking system, our treatment would not be complete without an examination of the various organizational forms found in the United States. By the formidable-sounding phrase "organizational form" we simply mean whether a bank is set up as an independent bank with one office, has branch offices, or is grouped with other banks (or even nonbanks) in some legal or informal way. As we shall see, there is a considerable diversity of organizational forms—a diversity that reflects the legal hodgepodge stemming from our dual banking system.

UNIT BANKS

The most common form of banking in the United States is what is termed *unit banking*. A unit bank is a corporation that operates a single office. Largely as a result of state laws that limited or prohibited branching, unit banks have always dominated American banking. In 1900, for example, 99 percent of the roughly 8,700 banks were unit banks. Today, unit banks account for slightly over one half of all banks. Most unit banks are independent in that they are not controlled by a corporation that controls other banks. Furthermore, the average independent unit bank tends to be relatively small.

BRANCH BANKING

A *branch bank*, as the name suggests, is a banking corporation that directly owns and operates two or more banking offices. Branching can occur through the creation of a new office from scratch, called *de novo branching*, or through the absorption of a bank through merger and the conversion of its facilities into branch offices. Banks often find it more feasible and economical to branch through absorption. For one thing, they may establish branches only with the permission of the banking authorities, and the latter often permit branching by absorption where they would deny *de novo* branches. Also, branching by absorption often gives access to a desirable banking site, brings with it bank assets and an established business, and eliminates one competitor from the local banking market.

Over time there has been a strong trend toward branch banking, with a marked increase in both the number of banks operating branches and the total number of branches. As the data in Table 5–3 show, in 1900 the U.S. banking system was overwhelmingly a unit banking system; of the 8,738

TABLE 5–3 Number of United States Commercial Banks and Branch Offices on Selected Dates (End-of-year figures)

Year	Total number of banks	Number of banks with branches	Total number of branches
1900	8,738	87	119
1920	29,087	530	1,281
1930	22,172	751	3,522
1940	14,344	954	3,525
1950	14,121	1,291	4,721
1960	13,472	2,329	10,216
1970	13,688	3,994	21,424
1982	14,963	7,173	39,479

SOURCE: Board of Governors of the Federal Reserve System, *Banking and Monetary Statistics,* 1940–1970, Washington, D.C., 1976; *Annual Statistical Digest,* various issues.

banks existing at that time, only 87 had even one branch office, and the total number of branches was only 119. In 1920, only 530 of the 29,087 banks operated one or more branches, and the total number of branches was 1,281. Since then, branch banking has continued to grow, interrupted only during the Great Depression. Its growth has been especially rapid since World War II. For example, between 1950 and 1982, the number of banks operating branches increased from 1,291 to 7,173 and the number of branch offices climbed from 4,721 to 39,479. Despite this increase, unit banks still predominate in numbers, although not in total assets.

As a consequence of the expansion of branch banking, the total number of bank facilities has increased markedly since 1950. The expansion of bank facilities via branching is common in other countries as well. For example, both Canada and Great Britain have on the order of only 10 banks; each, however, has many branches. In fact, despite the small number of commercial banks, both countries have more banking facilities per capita than the United States. Branch banking in the United States would expand even faster in the absence of official restrictions. These restrictions stem from the various state laws that govern branch banking—laws that cover a complete spectrum of possibilities.

As of 1951, some 17 states allowed statewide branching, 14 permitted limited branching, and the remaining 17 could be characterized as unit banking states. Over the years the branching laws were liberalized somewhat, and by 1983, 24 states permitted statewide branching, 18 allowed limited branching, and only 8 states prohibited branching. Nevertheless, as of 1983 more than half the states still had restrictions on branching.

A vivid illustration of the differences among states can be seen by comparing California, which has statewide branching, with Texas, a unit banking state. At the beginning of 1983 California had 387 banks, of which 231 maintained 4,493 branching or additional offices. Texas, by contrast, had 1,604 banks, of which 277 maintained 287 additional offices. California had about 12 branches per bank, while Texas had $\frac{1}{6}$ of a branch per bank.

Another point that deserves emphasis is that state branching laws also apply to banks with federal charters. That is, national banks must obey the branching laws of the state in which they are located. This practice, which helps preserve dual banking, stems from congressional acquiescence rather than any constitutional principle. Congressional action is also responsible for the restriction on interstate banking, which was initially prohibited by the 1927 McFadden Act. As noted below, despite this nominal prohibition, numerous forms of interstate banking currently exist. Moreover, substantial forces are working to erode further the restrictions on interstate banking. One of these is the emerging electronic technology that fostered the growth of automatic teller machines (ATMs). In fact, since branching laws were originally designed to deal with brick-and-mortar offices, ATMs and the like are producing considerable strains in interpreting the branching laws as they pertain to both intrastate and interstate branching. We shall examine the branching issue in more detail, but we first need to consider two additional organizational forms.

GROUP BANKING

Aside from branching, the other principal mechanism for establishing multiple-office banking is group or holding company banking. This refers to arrangements under which a corporation has ownership control of two or more separately incorporated banks, which are called is subsidiaries. The latter may be unit banks or branch banks. Also important is the fact that group banks may cross state lines. That is, a holding company may control banks situated in several states.

As in all matters pertaining to bank regulation, state control of group banking is quite varied. About a dozen states prohibit group banking, while more than two dozen have no specific legislation in this area. At the federal level, as a result of the Bank Holding Company Act, there is considerable regulation of bank holding companies. Among the act's most important provisions is that it requires holding companies to register with the Federal Reserve and gives the Federal Reserve power to prescribe the kinds of business activities that are open to bank holding companies.

Like branch banking, group banking has expanded greatly since World War II. By the end of 1982, there were 487 group systems that controlled some 2,900 banks which operated a total of nearly 16,000 branches. These banks held $639 billion of deposits, or about 46 percent of total commercial bank deposits (see Table 5–4). In contrast, in 1965 group banks held only 8 percent of total deposits.

The rapid growth of group banking is attributable to the forces that have stimulated the growth of branch banking and to legal limitations on branch-

TABLE 5–4 Selected Data for One-Bank and Multibank Holding Company Groups (Year-end 1982, dollar amounts in billions)

	Number of groups	Number of banks controlled	Number of branches controlled	Assets	Deposits
One-bank holding companies	3,802	3,777	14,353	$ 602	$ 469
Multibank holding companies	487	2,917	15,586	929	639
Total	4,289	6,694	30,209	$1,531	$1,108

SOURCE: Board of Governors of the Federal Reserve System, *Annual Statistical Digest*, 1982, Washington, D.C., p. 210.

ing. Thus, to a substantial degree group banking has served as a way of getting around intrastate branching laws. This is evidenced by the fact that the vast majority of bank groups are located in states with predominantly unit banking or limited branching. Furthermore, given that group banks may cross state lines, group banking has been a popular device for circumventing prohibitions on interstate branch banking as well.

As we have seen, group banking involves the creation of a holding company that controls two or more banks. Such *multibank* holding companies need to be distinguished from what are known as *one-bank* holding companies. The purpose of a one-bank holding company is not to bring two or more banks under common control; instead, it is to enable a bank to engage in nonbank types of business. The number of one-bank holding companies has expanded rapidly since the mid-1960s. Currently, about one-quarter of the banks are one-bank holding companies, and these banks hold about one-third of total deposits (Table 5–4). Many of the larger banks have reorganized as one-bank holding companies.

CORRESPONDENT RELATIONSHIPS

Despite the growing importance of branch and group banking, unit banks still predominate in the United States. Nevertheless, while most unit banks are independent in a legal sense, they are much less so in a practical one. For most banks this dependence takes the form of *correspondent banking*, an arrangement under which some banks hold deposits with other banks and use these banks as agents in various types of transactions, such as check clearing and collection, purchases and sales of securities, purchases and sales of foreign exchange, and participations in large loans.[9] Nations

---

[9]A loan participation typically occurs when a small bank is unable (for financial or legal reasons) to satisfy a loan request by a big customer. Through its correspondent relationship, the small bank may be able to pass on part of the loan and thus satisfy the customer.

with only a small number of banks, each operating a nationwide system of branches, have no need for such a highly developed domestic correspondent system. In such cases, each bank has an office in the country's major financial center and can reach all parts of the country through its own branches. The importance of correspondent relationships in the United States derives from the structure of our banking system: the facts that most of our thousands of banks operate only one office, that no branch bank is permitted to have branches outside its home state, and that many of our banks are relatively small.

The center of American correspondent banking is New York City, the nation's great financial center. Almost every important bank in the country maintains correspondent relations with at least one large bank in that city. Chicago is the next most important center. In addition, there are many regional centers. The network of correspondent relations is complex, for many banks hold deposits in more than one center, and correspondent banks in one center often have correspondent relations with banks in other centers.

These interbank relations and deposits serve several functions. Among them are the following:

1 **TO OBTAIN CURRENCY AND COIN.** While large banks typically get currency and coin from the Federal Reserve, smaller banks use their correspondents to provide them with vault cash.
2 **TO FACILITATE CHECK CLEARING AND COLLECTION.** Many banks have correspondent banks pay at least some of the checks drawn on them and collect checks on other banks that are deposited with them.
3 **TO FACILITATE DOMESTIC AND FOREIGN PAYMENTS.** A customer of a New Jersey bank may want to make payments with a draft drawn on a New York bank or on some foreign bank. Holding deposits at Chase Manhattan, the New Jersey bank can draw drafts on that bank or on a foreign correspondent of that bank.
4 **TO FACILITATE AGENCY OPERATIONS.** The New Jersey bank may use Chase Manhattan as an agent to buy or sell securities, or to accept or draw drafts. Interbank deposits that can be credited or debited to finance these transactions are helpful.

THE RATIONALE AND ECONOMIC CONSEQUENCES OF BANK REGULATION

Although we have not yet focused specifically on the subject, we have already encountered many of the vast number of ways in which commercial banks are regulated and supervised. Indeed, the health of the banking industry has long been a matter of public interest, and this has fostered laws and regulations governing who can open a bank, what products a bank can offer, what prices a bank can charge, how banks can expand, and what they can do with their funds. Given the pervasive nature of bank regulation, it is important to understand both its rationale, its economic consequences, and its likely future direction. While we have previously noted many forms of bank regulation, it will help to focus the discussion if we have a more complete list before us. Any such list would undoubtedly include the following items:

1 Regulation of entry into banking. A related requirement is that banks have an adequate degree of capitalization before a charter is issued.
2 Regulation of bank branching, through a criterion of community need or through outright legal prohibition of all or particular types of branching.
3 Regulation of bank mergers, by administrative ruling or via the use of antitrust laws.
4 Regulation and supervision of bank assets. For example, banks are prohibited from directly holding certain types of assets, such as common stock or real estate. Bank portfolios are also examined periodically to ensure that they possess an adequate degree of liquidity.
5 Regulation of the allowable set of bank-related activities bank holding companies may engage in.
6 Requirements for, and federal provision and regulation of, deposit insurance.
7 Prohibition of interest payments on demand deposits and restrictions on permissible rates of interest payable on time and saving deposits.

As evidenced by this list, regulation covers almost every aspect of commercial banking. Faced with this welter of regulations, we must naturally ask why it is so extensive, and more specifically why it has taken the form it has.

BASIC GOALS OF REGULATION

An underlying premise of regulation is that commercial banks are of vital importance in the operation of the economy. If banks are to carry out their role successfully, there must be public confidence in the solvency and liquidity of both individual banks and the banking system. As already documented, prior to 1934 public confidence was often severely tried by the instability of the banking system. It is because of this dismal bit of financial history that we find our first theme of modern bank regulation: ensuring the *safety* of banks and the banking system.

Safety, however, is not the only desirable feature of the banking system. It is also of considerable importance that the banking system operate as efficiently as possible. Loosely speaking, in this context efficiency means that banks provide services at as low a cost as possible and that funds are appropriately channeled through banks into their most productive uses.

For this to come about, bank regulations must provide an environment in which banks may exercise individual initiative and respond promptly and flexibly to changing circumstances. Unfortunately, as we shall see, the goal of fostering efficiency in banking often conflicts with the goal of safety.

A related theme in bank regulation concerns competition. Economists have long emphasized the beneficial role of competitive forces in fostering efficiency. In contrast, they have also stressed that monopoly elements and monopolistic practices can hinder efficiency. As we shall see, bank regulation has been rather schizophrenic as regards competition. In one sense bank regulation does seem to have absorbed the lessons of economics, in that it is concerned with monopoly elements. In principle, at least, it is this concern that motivates merger policy. More often than not, however, bank regulation has served to stifle competition. Restrictions on chartering and branching and interest rate ceilings are all examples of limits to competition. These limitations permit banks to charge higher interest rates on loans and permit them to pay lower interest rates on deposits. To be sure, these outcomes were not the goals of public policy. Rather, limits on competition were introduced as a way of assuring a safe and viable banking system.

We now turn to a more detailed consideration of the issues of safety, efficiency, and competition.

SAFETY VS. EFFICIENCY

In the context of banking, safety has various shades of meaning and consequently can be brought about in a variety of ways. One obvious source of safety is provided by the FDIC, which has made deposits safe and promoted the integrity of the payments mechanism. A host of other regulations also contribute to safety, but in a somewhat different manner. Among these are restrictions on entry, assets, liabilities, and bank activities; ceilings on interest rates; and bank examinations. The philosophy behind most of these regulations is that they promote safety by protecting bankers from themselves. That is, they prevent what some see as the danger of banks' pursuing "excessively" risky strategies in the quest for profits. Put another way, these regulations are designed to forestall the possibility of "too much" competition among banks.

Economists who emphasize the importance of efficiency in banking see many of these regulations as misguided. They argue that the main impact of these restrictions is to stifle competition, innovation, and prudent risk taking, and generally to reduce the efficiency of banking. This conflict between safety and efficiency presents a true dilemma in the design of regulation policies. The issues involved can be illustrated by the regulation that prohibits interest payments on demand deposits, or by the interest rate ceilings (Regulation Q) that limit the payment of interest on time and savings deposits.

Control over interest rates payable to depositors dates from 1933. The prevailing view at that time was that "excessive" interest rate competition for deposits had undermined the soundness of the system. As the story goes, this excessive competition drove deposit rates "too high" and then forced banks to seek out risky, high-yielding assets so they could earn enough to pay depositors. The punch line of this story is that the deterioration in the quality of bank portfolios contributed in an important way to the collapse of the banking system in the 1930s.

The validity of this argument is extremely doubtful. For one, subsequent analysis has not revealed any marked deterioration in the quality of bank assets in the 1920s, when excessive competition was alleged to have occurred. Furthermore, whatever the merits of ceilings might have been in the 1930s, the logic of continuing them today is quite minimal. Given the existence of the FDIC and the expanded role of the Federal Reserve after 1933, it strains reason to credit the post-1934 reduction on bank failures to Regulation Q or to the prohibition of interest on demand deposits.

On the other hand, the undesirable effects of these regulations are all too evident. They constrain efficient, well-managed banks from competing effectively for funds and deprive depositors from reaping the benefits of this competition. Furthermore, since competitive forces cannot be squelched by wishful regulations, these regulations tend to force competition into other, often less efficient, channels. One form this may take is the use of gifts or "free" services to attract deposit customers. Alternatively, banks may develop new liabilities to circumvent interest rate ceilings. Finally, other types of financial institutions may step in to take advantage of the restrictions imposed on commercial banks. The rapid emergence of the money market mutual funds, as a way of circumventing Regulation Q ceilings, is a case in point. Given all these developments, it is hardly surprising that interest rate ceilings are largely on their way out. These further developments aside, interest rate ceilings provide a clear example of a restriction designed to promote safety that proved to be a source of inefficiency.

From this and similar episodes many economists have drawn the conclusion that overemphasis is on safety can be detrimental to the health and vitality of the banking system. These economists argue that there is an important distinction between protecting a bank's depositors and protecting the bank itself. The former is clearly a necessary prerequisite for securing public confidence. Protecting the bank—that is, protecting its managers and stockholders—is a different matter. Some economists, while admitting that safety is of prime concern, have even argued that we may have too *few* bank failures. The logic for this position runs roughly as follows.

While failure of any business is not desirable for its own sake, it can perform a useful role in an economy. Specifically, insofar as business failures are brought about by incompetent management, failures serve the socially useful function of sifting out inefficient managers and businesses. To the extent that we artificially short-circuit this mechanism, we guarantee the continued existence of inefficient enterprises.

Those who argue from this perspective would favor eliminating much of the regulation impinging on commercial banks. Banks would then be freer to innovate and to take prudent risks in search of higher profits. At the same time, these economists argue, it would be possible to improve safety by strengthening the deposit insurance system. For one thing, as noted before, we could expand coverage so that all deposits are fully insured. For another, the insurance premium paid to the FDIC could be made to depend on the nature of the risks assumed by the bank. Those banks that were more venturesome in assuming risk would pay a higher premium.

While there is considerable food for thought in this general view, bank regulators have been understandably slow in pursuing policies that might be perceived as reducing bank safety. Nevertheless, there is a clear tendency for competitive pressures, often provided by technological developments, to break down existing regulations or, at the very least, to require a restructuring of existing regulations. Interest rate ceilings are but one example of this; we shall encounter others as we proceed.

COMPETITION IN BANKING

Taking American banking history as a whole, policymakers have shown a distinctly schizophrenic attitude toward competition. Some regulations designed to promote safety have been specifically aimed at curbing "unhealthy" competition. In other respects, public policy has clearly intended to promote competition, at least insofar as it assured the existence of a large number of competing banks. In particular, there has been a longstanding public concern with the dangers of excessive concentration or monopoly power in banking. And the fear that undue concentration would leave resource allocation in the hands of a relatively small number of large banks undoubtedly accounts for the predominance of unit banking in this country.

At first blush, with nearly 15,000 commercial banks, the United States would appear to have a rather high degree of competition. Numbers alone, however, do not ensure competition. Even with a large number of banks in the nation as a whole, there can be many communities served by relatively few banks. In such cases, local borrowers and/or depositors may have few options for obtaining banking services. Banks in such communities may therefore well possess some degree of local monopoly power. That is, they may be shielded from competition with other banks.

How can banks secure and maintain local monopoly power? The answer in part lies in the nature of bank regulatory policy. For example, limits on bank entry and ceiling interest rates on deposits—policies promulgated to promote safety in banking—have undoubtedly contributed to limiting competition in local markets. Somewhat ironically, even those policies aimed at promoting competition may have had anticompetitive effects. In particular, limitations on branching, which were designed to prevent excessive concentration of resources, serve to restrict competition in local markets.

Consequently, policies for avoiding the type of monopoly power traditionally associated with large banks may create opportunities for local monopoly power. While the precise extent of this local power is debatable, it should be clear that promoting competition is more complicated than it might seem at first.

There is also another dimension to this issue. As stressed above, limitations on branch banking have fostered the spread of independent unit banks in the United States. As a consequence, there are many relatively small banks in this country. Indeed, as Table 5–5 indicates, the vast majority of banks—some 10,287 banks, or 70 percent of all banks—each have fewer than $50 million in deposits. These banks hold less than 12 percent of the total deposits in the banking system. Not surprisingly, most of these small banks are located in unit-banking states.

Many economists see the predominance of small banks as an undesirable consequence of branching laws. Their concern is that such banks are likely to be too small to be efficient. That is, they are unable to capitalize on economies of scale that would permit larger banks to provide banking services at lower average cost. The empirical evidence on this score, although open to interpretation, does seem to suggest that there are substantial economies of scale for banks up to some minimum size, which has been variously estimated as anywhere from 10 to 50 million in deposits. Despite this quite large range, the existing evidence does provide support for the position that we have many banks that are too small to be efficient. Furthermore, according to this view, these banks continue because they are somewhat sheltered from the competition of larger banks.

While there is much merit in this line of reasoning, the evidence is not unambiguous, since empirical studies of economies of scale in banking

TABLE 5–5 Size Distribution of All Commercial Banks in the United States, December 31, 1982

Size of banks (In millions of dollars of total deposits)	Number of banks	Percent of number of banks	Total assets (In billions of dollars)	Percent of total assets of all banks
Less than $5	706	4.8	$ 1.7	0.1
$5–10	1,513	10.3	11.6	0.6
$10–25	4,327	29.3	73.2	3.9
$25–50	3,741	25.4	134.0	7.2
$50–100	2,404	16.3	165.2	8.9
$100–500	1,648	11.2	310.6	16.7
$500–1,000	176	1.2	122.3	6.6
$1,000–5,000	184	1.2	372.3	20.0
More than $5,000	45	0.3	672.4	36.1
Total—all banks	14,744	100.0	$1,863.2	100.0

need to be interpreted with care. The main reason is the difficulty in defining precisely what one means by the *output* or *product* of a bank. As department stores of finance, banks produce a variety of outputs, and it is difficult to summarize this variety in a single measure. But this is precisely what those who produce estimates of scale economies have done. Because it is somewhat difficult to pin this issue down quantitatively, opponents of branch banking have understandably been slow in modifying their position. Nevertheless, as documented earlier, branch banking has expanded markedly and should continue to do so in the forseeable future.

Another way of looking at Table 5–5 suggests that restrictions on chartering, mergers, and branching have not been that successful in limiting banking *concentration*. At the other extreme from the small unit banks, we find 229 very large banks, each with assets of over $1 billion. In the aggregate these banks, which amount to only $1\frac{1}{2}$ percent of the number of banks, account for 56 percent of total assets. The sense of largeness is perhaps even more vividly portrayed by Table 5–6, which reports the sizes of the 10 largest commercial banks. Comparing Tables 5–5 and 5–6, we see that the two largest banks have total assets that exceed the assets of the 10,000 smallest banks. These numbers would appear to raise the specter of the more traditional sort of monopoly power.

At the current stage of development most observers of the banking scene tend to regard fears of big-bank monopoly as unfounded. The main reason for this is that there appears to be sufficient competition to keep the big banks "honest." For a particular big bank, this competition stems from other big banks and from the larger number of slightly smaller banks. In addition, large, internationally known corporations have the option of doing business with large foreign banks or of borrowing funds directly from the capital market. Both options provide additional competition.

TABLE 5–6 The 10 Largest Commercial Banks, December 31, 1983

Rank	Name	Assets (In billions of dollars)
1	Citicorp (New York)	$134.7
2	BankAmerica (San Francisco)	121.1
3	Chase Manhattan (New York)	81.9
4	Manufacturers Hanover (New York)	64.3
5	Morgan (J. P.) (New York)	58.0
6	Chemical (New York)	51.1
7	First Interstate Bancorp (Los Angeles)	44.4
8	Continental Illinois (Chicago)	42.1
9	Security Pacific (Los Angeles)	40.4
10	Bankers Trust (New York)	40.0

SOURCE: *Business Week*, April 9, 1984, p. 85.

All of this is not to say that big banks may never present a problem. Technological advances like those that could bring about an electronic funds transfer system could increase the optimum size of banks in the future. But this result is not a foregone conclusion. Indeed, some have argued that computer technology will enhance the ability of smaller institutions to compete. While this remains an open question, other recent developments suggest that the future may provide additional competition for large banks. In particular, a number of large nonbanking firms are expanding their activities into what has been dubbed the "financial services" industry. These developments, which clearly promise increased competition for banks, are part of a larger transformation of the nature of the banking business which is currently underway. Prior to considering these contemporary developments, since it figures prominently in these developments, we need to say a bit more about an organizational form of banking mentioned earlier—the bank holding company.

BANK HOLDING COMPANIES

As our earlier discussion of group banking made clear, bank holding companies are a major component of the American banking environment (see Table 5–4). Moreover, the growth of holding companies provided banks with a way to circumvent a variety of regulations. At first, most of this regulatory sidestepping involved the actions of multibank holding companies—a group arrangement involving two or more separately incorporated banks.

MULTIBANK HOLDING COMPANIES

One reason for the early growth of multibank holding companies is that in many states these organizations were able to get around branching restrictions which often did not apply to groups of banks. This factor remains an important reason for the continued growth of multibank holding companies. Prior to 1956, multibank holding companies were also permitted to own banks in more than one state, thus circumventing prohibitions on interstate branching as well. Furthermore, through their nonbank subsidiaries, multibank holding companies were able to engage in nonbanking activities, including manufacturing and retail selling.

As the scope and size of multibank holding companies increased, concern was expressed over their growing power and the appropriateness of their nonbanking activities. The Bank Holding Company Act of 1956 was a direct response to these concerns. The act prohibited multibank holding companies from engaging in nonbanking activities and restricted their interstate banking activities. While it "grandfathered" existing interstate banking activities, it prohibited any further acquisition of banks across state lines. It did provide that states could enact legislation to permit entry by out-of-state holding companies. Over the next 20 years, however, no states chose to issue such invitations.

ONE-BANK HOLDING COMPANIES

The next round of developments involved the so-called *one-bank holding company*, a corporation that may control a number of subsidiaries, but only one bank. Such institutions were explicitly exempted from the 1956 act. The thinking at the time was that this exemption would enhance the profitability of small banks, which could continue to combine banking and nonbanking activities. To be sure, nothing guaranteed that large banks would not form one-bank holding companies and thus be free to engage in activities that were prohibited both to banks per se and to multibank holding companies. Critics of the situation pointed to the potential for adverse effects on the soundness of banks, conflicts of interest, unfair competition, and undue concentration of financial power—precisely what the 1956 act sought to eliminate.

Nevertheless, over the ensuing decade these fears proved to be rather exaggerated. Large banks did not rush to convert to a one-bank holding company form. Then, in 1966, the floodgates opened. In a relatively short period of time, nearly every large bank in the United States formed a one-bank holding company. Curiously enough, however, the incentive for these conversions was not a sudden urge to engage in nonbanking operations. Rather, this is a theme that will recur again and again, the conversions were motivated by a desire to circumvent interest rate ceilings, which in 1966 were limiting rates payable on all commercial bank liabilities.

The use of the one-banking holding company to get around these ceilings was as simple as it was ingenious. The basic loophole was provided by the fact that bank holding companies were not legally banks and therefore were exempt from interest rate ceilings. What this meant was that bank holding companies could issue their own liabilities at prevailing market rates of interest. The holding company could then turn around and lend the funds to the bank, effectively evading the ceiling.

These developments accomplished two things. By undermining the enforceability of interest rate ceilings, they contributed to the gradual demise of these ceilings. More important for our present purposes, the legacy of this episode was that nearly every large bank in the United States was now part of a one-bank holding company. Since they were exempt from the Bank Holding Company Act, large banks were now poised to take advantage of this loophole and to expand their activities into any nonbanking area of their choosing. The concern expressed a decade earlier resurfaced, and critics called for a change in the law.

In 1970 Congress complied by amending the 1956 Bank Holding Company Act. For all practical purposes, the 1970 amendment restricted one-bank and multibank holding companies to the same range of activities. Thus, the possibility of a one-bank holding company owning a manufacturing firm no longer existed, all bank holding companies were now restricted to *bank-related activities*. While Congress sought to spell out the criteria to be used in defining allowable bank-related activities, the task of actually deciding what was allowable was put in the hands of the Federal Reserve. Table 5–7 contains a recent list of approved and denied activities. Most of the activities that are permitted to holding companies can also be engaged in directly by banks themselves. In recent years, as we shall see shortly, bank holding companies have challenged what they perceive to be the overly narrow interpretation of permissible bank-related activities.

While the general intent of the 1970 amendment was to limit the scope of one-bank holding companies, in at least one important respect the amendment amounted to a substantial liberalization of holding-company operations. In particular, the amendment placed no geographical limits on the operations of nonbanking subsidiaries of bank holding companies. This paved the way for an expansion in interstate banking operations, a development which, along with the evolving scope of bank-related activities, is currently one of the "hot" topics in bank structure and regulation. We conclude this chapter with a brief examination of the relevant issues in these two important and controversial areas.

CURRENT TOPICS IN BANK STRUCTURE AND REGULATION

The banking industry is currently experiencing substantial pressures for change. To a significant extent, these pressures have arisen as altered economic conditions have come into conflict with existing restrictions or regulations conceived in an earlier era. As noted previously, this has been a constant theme in the evolution of banking in the United States. For example, throughout the 1970s steadily rising levels of interest rates made ceilings on rates payable to depositors increasingly a problem for the banks and other depository institutions. Only when it became apparent that these ceilings were being circumvented by financial innovations did lawmakers relent and pass legislation gradually abolishing them.

At the present time, the laws and/or regulations providing the most pressure are those limiting (1) the geographic markets in which banks may participate and (2) the nature of the products banks may offer their customers. More specifically, the controversies concern the extent to which banks can or should be able to operate across state lines and the degree to which banks will be able to expand the range of services they provide. Several developments have served to bring these issues to the forefront. New communications and data processing technology have led to computerization of many financial services. This in turn has blurred both geographic lines and the distinctions between banks and other suppliers of

TABLE 5–7 Permissible and Impermissible Activities for Commercial-Bank Holding Companies

Activities permitted

1. Mortgage banking
2. Finance company
3. Credit card issuance
4. Factoring company
5. Industrial banking
6. Servicing loans
7. Trust company
8. Investment advising
9. General economic information
10. Full-payout leasing
11. Community welfare investments
12. Bookkeeping and data processing services
13. Insurance agent or broker—related to credit extensions in small communities
14. Underwriting credit life and credit accident and health insurance
15. Courier services
16. Management consulting to nonaffiliated banks
17. Issuance and sale of traveler's checks and money orders
18. Performing real estate appraisals
19. Conducting securities brokerage and margin lending
20. Providing advice concerning foreign exchange
21. Acting as a futures commission merchant
22. Buying and selling gold and silver
23. Providing check authorization
24. Performing commercial bank functions at offshore locations
25. Operating a savings and loan if SLA is threatened with harm
26. Brokering options on securities issued or guaranteed by the U.S. government.
27. Executing unsolicited purchases and sales of securities

Activities prohibited

1. Combined sale of mutual funds and insurance
2. General life insurance underwriting
3. Real estate brokerage
4. Land development
5. Real estate syndication
6. General management consultant
7. Property management
8. Underwriting mortgage guaranty insurance
9. Travel agency
10. Operation of a savings and loan
11. Underwriting home loan life mortgage insurance
12. Underwriting property and casualty insurance
13. Dealing in platinum and palladium
14. Publication and sale of personnel tests

financial services. Not surprisingly, as nonbanks, such as brokerage firms and insurance companies, have used the latest technology to expand their financial services and thereby impinge on banks, banks have sought to expand the range of their activities. Additional motivation in this regard was provided by the lifting of interest rate ceilings, which raised the cost of funds to banks and spurred efforts to obtain new sources of income by both product and geographic diversification. We begin our discussion with the issue of geography and bank branching, and we now focus on interstate branching.

GEOGRAPHIC RESTRICTIONS: INTERSTATE OPERATIONS

Like many historical issues involving states' rights, the question of bank branching across state lines was and is a highly emotional one. In 1923 the issue led to the first dissenting opinion of record in the history of the Board of Governors of the Federal Reserve. And in 1927, while considering legislation on the matter, for the first time ever on a domestic issue closure on debate was invoked in the Senate. Indeed, it is said that closure was invoked after a fistfight nearly erupted. Soon thereafter, the legislation in question passed. As a result of the McFadden Act of 1927, an apparently absolute prohibition on interstate branch banking was imposed.[10]

Over the years, however, the McFadden prohibition has proved to be distinctly less than absolute; interstate banking has substantially expanded, especially in the past few years. The various ways in which this has come about once again illustrate that confining financial regulations can breed ingenuity, innovation, and ultimately, circumvention of the intent of the regulations.

As we have seen, until restricted by regulation the multibank holding company offered a relatively simple way to get around the prohibition on interstate branching. The 1956 Bank Holding Company Act outlawed the continuation of this practice, but under the so-called Douglas amendment to the act, it grandfathered existing activity. As of 1982, one of these regional groups, First Interstate Bancorp, formerly Western Bancshares, had 22 banks in 11 western states, with 900 branches and several hundred automatic teller machines. The Douglas amendment obviously left a legacy of interstate banking.

By virtue of another of its features, the Douglas amendment also created the potential for future expansion of interstate banking activity. In particular, it permitted states to pass legislation allowing entry by out-of-state

[10]The McFadden Act actually liberalized a 1911 ruling by the attorney general that outlawed all branching. The act permitted nationally chartered commercial banks to operate branches in their home city but prohibited them elsewhere, even where branches were permitted by state law for state-chartered banks. The latter prohibition was relaxed by the Banking Act of 1933, which permitted national banks to branch statewide, subject to state laws. Interstate branching remained out of bounds.

holding companies. In 1975 Maine was the first state to enact legislation, but the legislation was restrictive in that it permitted entry by out-of-state holding companies only if the holding company's home state extended *reciprocal* entry rights to Maine holding companies. Until 1982, when New York adopted similar legislation, Maine was in a game in which no one else was playing. In the last few years, the number of players has jumped dramatically: by early 1985 some 14 states had enabling legislation, while 12 more were considering such legislation. These laws, however, are not identical in effect. Maine and Alaska, for example, currently allow entry without requiring reciprocity, while New York still requires reciprocity. Other states require reciprocity and further restrict entry to holding companies headquartered in specific states, usually neighboring states, to achieve some sort of regional banking zone. As should be evident, the amendment provides substantial potential for expansion of interstate branching, and an illustration of how states can influence our national banking structure.

One can, of course, expand interstate banking operations without opening a full-fledged bank or a bank branch. Indeed, one does not need any physical presence whatsoever to engage in certain kinds of banking business. Large commercial banks regularly issue certificates of deposit that are sold on a national market and can be bought by purchasers in any part of the country. A California bank can easily sell certificates of deposit to residents of New York, Kansas, Texas, and Maine, thus raising deposit funds without a physical presence. As suggested, however, in other cases banking operations do require some physical presence. Aside from a conventional branch, this can be achieved in a variety of ways.

1 *Edge Act corporations* are banking subsidiaries authorized to operate nationwide while engaging in international banking operations. These date from 1919 and were set up to facilitate international trade. As of 1985, 84 domestic banks operated a total of 127 Edge offices outside their home states.

2 *Loan production offices* are limited facilities that solicit commercial loan business but cannot accept deposits. These offices are permitted on an out-of-state basis, subject to the requirement that the home office approve each loan.

3 *Nonbank subsidiaries* that engage in allowable bank-related activities (see Table 5–7) are, by virtue of the 1970 amendment to the Bank Holding Company Act, permitted to cross state lines. This has provided a substantial national presence to many bank holding companies. At least three of these—Citicorp, BankAmerica Corp., and Security Pacific Corp.—each operate in about 40 states.

Taken as a whole, despite the prohibitions of the McFadden Act, it is clear that a substantial degree of interstate banking activity exists. The one area in which restrictions still exist is in deposit-taking across state lines. Even here, however, with the development of the so-called *nonbank bank*, matters are in a state of rapid flux.

To understand the seemingly nonsensical idea of a nonbank bank, we have to go back to the question of what is a bank. This was addressed in the McFadden Act, which defined a *branch bank* as "any place of business at which deposits are received, or checks paid, or money lent." In other words, any facility simply accepting deposits was declared a bank. In the 1970 amendment to the Bank Holding Company Act, this definition was modified. To count as a bank, an institution had to accept demand deposits *and* make commercial loans. The little word *and* was of critical importance, because now a facility could accept deposits and would not be classified as a bank as long as it did not make commercial loans. It could, of course, still make other types of loans, for example, to consumers. So was born that strange creature, the nonbank bank.

The nonbank bank obviously presented a major loophole to the geographic prohibitions of the McFadden Act, but this loophole was not exploited in a serious way until the early 1980s. Then, almost overnight, everyone seemed to want to get into the nonbank bank business. The regulatory process slowed down the entry of banks in the business, although by mid-1984 some 38 bank holding companies had filed applications to open some 283 nonbank banks. The first actual entrants into the nonbank bank business were drawn from the ranks of securities firms, diversified financial and industrial conglomerates, and other financial services organizations. By mid-1984, these nonbank institutions, such as Merrill Lynch and Shearson/American Express, owned over 50 nonbank banks as part of a more general attempt to serve as suppliers of a broad range of banking and financial services. These nationally known firms, not bound by state barriers or by most laws and regulations governing banks, were becoming a growing force in the interstate provision of banking services.

The growth of state laws permitting out-of-state entry, the interstate operation of nonbank firms, and the potential exploitation of the nonbank bank loophole by holding companies are rapidly serving to undermine the McFadden prohibitions on interstate banking. Moreover, technology in the form of automatic teller machines and their use across state lines represents yet another assault on the McFadden Act. In the face of all these developments, it is hardly surprising that many observers of the financial scene, including numerous Federal Reserve officials, fully expect that interstate banking will become an official reality in the not too-distant future.

Somewhat more controversial is the question of how this will come about and precisely what form it will take. If, for example, state laws permitting out-of-state entry continue to mushroom, we may see more interstate banking with a regional flavor, as states only permit entry by neighboring states. Many critics regard this regional approach as distinctly undesirable.[11] A

---

[11]The regional approach typically discriminates against those states such as New York and California that are headquarters for the largest banks. It may therefore exclude more efficient institutions from competing. Not surprisingly, in view of the potential for discrimination, the restrictive nature of some state laws is currently being challenged in the courts.

more critical question is the role to be played by banks and other depository institutions on the one hand and alternative providers of financial services on the other. Once again, this brings us back to the question of what is a bank, what services it should be allowed to provide, and what types of banking services nonbanks should be able to offer.

BANK PRODUCT DEREGULATION

Federal law has embodied a policy of separating banking from unrelated lines of commerce. The notion of "unrelated" in this context has come to mean two different sorts of things: unrelated *nonfinancial* activities such as those carried out by industrial, manufacturing, or retail firms; and unrelated *financial* activities such as those provided by insurance companies or investment banks. In recent years, banks have been particularly concerned with the limitations on the scope of allowable financial activities. To illustrate and appreciate this concern, it will be helpful if we review just one aspect of this issue, the separation of commercial and investment banking.

Investment bankers, sometimes also called *securities dealers*, serve as brokers and dealers in securities and equities, thereby assisting in the process of raising funds for financing new investments. At first blush, one might imagine this activity melding reasonably well with that of commercial banking. Indeed, prior to 1933, investment and commercial banking were frequently combined. In that year, however, Congress passed the Glass-Steagall Act, which separated commercial and investment banking.[12] The separation was motivated by the perception that the severe financial difficulties experienced by many investment banks during the Great Depression harmed the well-being of commercial banks as banks came to the assistance of their securities affiliates. Critics also charged that the affiliation between commercial and investment banks contributed to the growth of questionable banking practices. Congressional hearings held in connection with the Glass-Steagall Act disclosed numerous examples of serious conflicts of interest and self-dealing. For example, commercial banks were accused of dumping securities they had underwritten on their customers and on their correspondent banks. This was only one among a long list of accusations.

Overall, then, the Glass-Steagall Act was designed to eliminate these abuses, to restore confidence in the commercial banking system, and to limit the riskiness of commercial banking. To put this in context, it should be recalled that Glass-Steagall was enacted following the many thousands of bank failures of the early 1930s (see Table 5–2).

As is the case with the geographic prohibitions of the McFadden Act, the Glass-Steagall Act, and other line-of-business restrictions as well, proved to be less than ironclad. Once again, the infamous nonbank bank served as

---

[12]The Glass-Steagall Act, known also as the Banking Act of 1933, introduced federal deposit insurance as well. Senator Carter Glass, the major sponsor of the act, was also a principal architect of the Federal Reserve Act of 1913, which established the Fed.

a major vehicle for the circumvention of regulations. Indeed, as of early 1984, the majority of the nonbank banks were owned by securities firms, thus directly evading the intent of the Glass-Steagall Act, which was designed to prevent combinations of firms that underwrite securities and take deposits. Some observers, pointing to the strengthened securities laws and the existence of the Securities and Exchange Commission, which postdates the Glass-Steagall Act, regard these recent developments somewhat benignly. We shall come back to this issue below.

Nonbank banks have also provided a vehicle for other combinations of activities denied to banks. Several financial service organizations and insurance companies have acquired nonbank banks, as have a number of retail companies, such as J. C. Penney. Commercial and industrial firms such as Chrysler and the Parker Pen Company have also acquired nonbank banks. These various acquisitions clearly serve to evade the intent of the Bank Holding Company Act, which sought to prevent commerical and industrial firms from owning banks.

The developments are part of a more general transformation in which many nonbank firms are seeking to compete with banks by providing a broad range of financial services. This is true of such financial giants as Merrill Lynch and Shearson/American Express, but it is equally true of the giant retailer Sears, Roebuck. Indeed, Sears can now offer life insurance, deposits in money market funds, stock brokerage services, real estate brokerage services, consumer credit, and ATM machines, along with its more traditional lines of merchandise such as, hardware, and appliances. As one Federal Reserve official has put it: "Many small rural banks fear competition from Sears more keenly than the threat of entry by large commercial banks."[13] He could well have added that the large commercial banks may have similar trepidations.

Not surprisingly in the light of these developments, commercial banks increasingly see themselves at a competitive disadvantage with other institutions providing bank-related services. Unhappy with the asymmetrical legal and regulatory environment that permits this, they have attempted to expand the range of their permissible activities. The Federal Reserve has responded by recently adding futures commission business, discount brokerage, and the arranging of equity financing for real estate projects to the list of permissible activities under the Bank Holding Company Act. The Fed has also recommended to Congress that legislation be passed to permit banks to underwrite municipal revenue bonds and to sponsor stock and bond mutual funds.

Some would even go further. Other activities that have been proposed for commercial banks include the following: underwriting and dealing in most forms of noncorporate securities; real estate brokerage and develop-

---

[13]Emmet J. Rice, "Progress Toward Interstate Banking," speech before the National Association of Urban Bankers, June 21, 1984.

ment; insurance brokerage and underwriting; and owning a thrift institution such as a savings and loan association.[14] Some of the items on this list are motivated by the fact that some states have adopted, and others are considering, legislation to authorize state-chartered commercial banks to engage in securities, real estate, and insurance activities. Once again, the dual banking system may be showing signs of strain as individual states go their own way, putting considerable pressure on national banking policies.[15]

What are we to make of all these developments, and what does the future hold for commercial banks? While specific predictions in this area are notoriously risky, two general tendencies seem clear: There will be a continued expansion in the range of commercial bank activities, and there will probably be federal legislation to attempt to rationalize the current chaotic situation. Many perceive that legislation is necessary because we are now haphazardly deregulating by the exploitation of loopholes (e.g., the nonbank bank) and individual state actions. Moreover, legislation will be necessary if we are to achieve fairness in the treatment of nationally chartered commercial banks, state-chartered commercial banks, thrift institutions, and the growing groups of nonbanks that are providing banking services.

The specific activities that will be allowed commercial banks of the future are less clear. Moreover, the problem in choosing these activities is the age-old dilemma between safety and efficiency. While the banking legislation of the 1930s may have left us with a legacy which in the 1980s appears to overemphasize safety, safety is not something we can afford to ignore. As Chairman Paul Volcker of the Federal Reserve has noted, competition and efficiency "must be considered in the light of the crucial importance of maintaining confidence in banking institutions, continuity in the provisions of money and payments systems, and the ability of the central bank to conduct effective monetary policy."[16] What this reasonably suggests is that there is likely to be a continued separation of "banking" and "commerce." The task of public policy will be to define these terms appropriately. This, of course, is nothing other than the question of what is a bank. In leaving this issue, it is perhaps appropriate to recall the observations of Supreme Court Justice Potter Stewart in examining the notion of obscenity. Justice Stewart admitted the difficulty of providing a rigorous definition of obscen-

---

[14]Under the Garn-St. Germain Act of 1982, commercial banks are permitted to take over a failing thrift institution, even across state lines. They cannot, however, acquire a sound thrift institution.

[15]Another source of pressure on commercial banks comes from savings and loan associations, which have recently been granted greatly expanded powers. Moreover, an S&L holding company that controls a single S&L is not, in contrast to a one-bank holding company, subject to line-of-business restrictions.

[16]Paul A. Volcker, statement before the Committee on Banking, Finance and Urban Affairs, United States House of Representatives, June 12, 1984, p. 2–3.

ity, but opined: "But I know it when I see it." If only we knew a bank when we saw it, things might be a bit simpler.

SUMMARY

1 The United States has a dual banking system consisting of both national- and state-chartered commercial banks. National banks are less numerous but larger than state banks. Prior to 1980, state banks typically faced lower reserve requirements, but uniform reserve requirements are now being phased in.

2 The diversity of forms that banks may take has its counterpart in a varied regulatory structure for the supervision of commercial banks. The Federal Reserve, the FDIC, the Comptroller of the Currency, and the 50 state banking authorities all participate in this process.

3 The total number of commercial banks in the United States has remained relatively constant since 1933 at about 14,500. A significant increase in the number of banking facilities has taken place through the marked expansion of branch banking. Even with this expansion, slightly over half of commercial banks are unit banks. The prevalence of unit banks stems from the restrictions of state branching laws. This also helps explain why there are many relatively small banks in the United States.

4 Bank regulation is concerned with the safety, efficiency, and competitiveness of the banking system. The reconciliation of the potentially conflicting goals of safety and efficiency remains a thorny problem. Nevertheless, one thing is clear: Single-minded pursuit of just one of these goals can produce bad regulation.

5 Bank holding companies, of the multibank and one-bank type have provided banks with a way to circumvent a variety of regulations, including branching restrictions and interest rate ceilings.

6 At the current time there is substantial debate over the geographic markets in which banks should be allowed to participate. The McFadden Act of 1927 prohibitied interstate branching, but has not proved airtight. Indeed, despite its prohibitions, there exists a substantial degree of interstate banking activity. The nonbank bank is only the latest in the long line of evasionary mechanisms. A continued erosion of geographic restrictions is likely to take place.

7 The Glass-Steagall Act of 1933 separated commercial and investment banking, but in recent years, the separation has proved to be a bit porous. Nonbank banks owned by securities firms are one way of circumventing the act. This is part of a more general tendency for nonbank firms to compete with banks by providing a broad range of financial services. It is likely to remain a thorny and somewhat unresolved issue for the foreseeable future.

SELECTED READINGS

Benston, G. J., (editor). *Financial Services: The Changing Institutions and Government Policy,* Englewood Cliffs, NJ, Prentice-Hall, 1983.

Drum, D. S., "Nonbanking Activities of Bank Holding Companies," *Economic Perspectives.* Federal Reserve Bank of Chicago, 1977, pp. 12–21.

Economic Report of the President, Council of Economic Advisers, Washington, DC, U.S. Government Printing Office, 1984, Chapter 5.

Galbraith, J. K., *Money: Whence It Came, Where It Went.* Boston, Houghton Mifflin, 1975.

Geographical Restrictions on Commercial Banking: The Report of the President, Washington, D.C., U.S. Treasury Department, 1981.

Tussing, A. D., "The Case for Bank Failures." *Journal of Law and Economics,* October 1967, pp. 129–147.

6

COMMERCIAL BANK POLICIES

The preceding chapter examined what might be termed the *industrial organization* of commercial banking. We also discussed the wide range of activities, both actual and potential, available to commercial banks. In this chapter we continue our analysis of commercial banking from a different and somewhat narrower perspective. In particular, our emphasis will be on the bank as a financial intermediary and hence on the nature of the sources and uses of bank funds. A bank, of course, must operate in the face of uncertainty as to the future course of the economy and of financial markets, and this adds to the complexity of its portfolio decision making. As we shall see, banks seek an optimal mix of assets and liabilities, one consistent with reconciling the conflicting objectives of safety and earnings, or, as it is sometimes termed, risk and return.

The purpose, then, of this chapter is to document the menu of assets and liabilities available to commercial banks and provide an understanding of some of the problems and principles of managing a bank. This understanding will be important when, in later chapters, we discuss the workings of monetary policy.

BALANCE SHEET ACCOUNTING

In examining bank assets and liabilities, we must inevitably confront the structure of the bank as it is constructed by those wonderful creatures, accountants. To demystify this process, it may help if we briefly digress and discuss some elementary principles of double-entry bookkeeping. Lest the reader's eyes glaze over at the prospect, our discussion will mercifully be short.

In drawing up financial statements for any unit, be it a business firm, a government, or any other organization, an accountant considers the unit to be an entity, separate and distinct from its owners. The entity must therefore account to its owners as well as to other claimants against it. There are two principal types of financial statements. One is the *income statement* or *profit and loss statement*. Such statements summarize, for some stated period of time, all the gross income accruing to the entity and the claims against the gross income—claims of owners as well as others. We shall not use income statements at this point, but later we will refer back to them.

In contrast to income statements, which refer to flows over a stated period of time, the *balance sheet* refers to a stock at a point in time. One side of the balance sheet, the *assets* side, lists the types and values of everything owned by the entity. These things of value may be money itself, debt claims against others, shares of ownership in other firms, inventories, plant and equipment, and so on. The other side of the balance sheet, *liabilities and capital account*, lists the types and amounts of claims against the entity's assets. Since double-entry accounting requires that the entity account for the total value of assets, no more and no less, the total value of claims against assets must be exactly equal to the value of its assets. Any value of assets in excess of other claims against them accrues to the owners. Liabilities are claims against assets other than ownership claims. Under the law, they have priority over ownership claims. They are mostly debt claims of some sort; they may be evidenced by formal documents such as promissory notes or bills of exchange, or they may be evidenced only by book entries. *Capital account*, or *net worth*, is simply the value of ownership claims against the entity. Since owners have only a residual claim, capital account or net worth is equal to the value of assets minus liabilities.

A highly simplified balance sheet might appear as follows:

ASSETS		LIABILITIES AND CAPITAL ACCOUNT	
Cash	$ 20,000	Liabilities	$ 85,000
Investments	80,000	Capital account	15,000
Total	$100,000	Total	$100,000

This necessary equality of assets with the sum of liabilities and capital account permits us to write three simple equations which will be useful:

Assets = liabilities + capital account (1)

Capital account = assets − liabilities (2)

Liabilities = assets − capital account (3)

In analyzing the functioning of financial institutions such as commercial banks, we emphasize one aspect of this necessary equality—namely, that a bank can acquire assets only by creating an equal value of claims against itself. Of course, it may change the composition of its assets without changing the other side of its balance sheet at all. For example, it may trade some of its short-term claims against other entities for long-term claims against other entities, and so on. Such exchanges of assets may not disturb either the total value or the composition of outstanding claims against the entity. But an entity can make net additions to its assets only by creating an equal value of claims against itself. And in the process of reducing its total assets, it must draw and retire an equal value of claims against itself.

A BALANCE SHEET FOR THE COMMERCIAL BANKING SYSTEM

We now turn from balance sheet principles to an actual balance sheet for the commercial banking system. Table 6–1 reports the aggregate balance sheet for all insured commercial banks operating in the United States on September 30, 1983. In the interest of simplicity, the table lumps together various items in order to concentrate attention on major variables. For example, all types of securities are combined into a single category, as are all types of loans. The components of these categories will be discussed more fully below; for the moment we concentrate on the main features of Table 6–1.

As noted earlier, we again see the huge size of the commercial banking industry, which holds nearly $2 *trillion* of assets. We also see that banks have acquired only a very small part, about 7 percent, of their total assets by issuing net worth or capital account claims. Most of the assets of banks were acquired by creating and issuing debts of various types, primarily in the form of deposit claims. Indeed, the liability side of the balance sheet

TABLE 6–1 Aggregate Balance Sheet for the Commercial Banking System, September 30, 1983

ASSETS	Amount (in billions)	Percent of total	LIABILITIES AND CAPITAL ACCOUNT	Amount (in billions)	Percent of total
Cash	$ 204	11%	Demand deposits	$ 355	18%
Loans	1,165	60	Time deposits	648	34
Securities	415	21	Savings deposits	449	23
Other	151	8	Other liabilities	346	18
Total	$1,935	100%	Capital account	137	7
			Total	$1,935	100%

SOURCE: *Federal Reserve Bulletin*, March 1984, pp. A72–A73.

reveals that some 34 percent of the assets are supported by time deposits with an additional 23 percent backed up by savings deposits.

On the asset side, Table 6–1 lists three main categories of assets: cash, loans, and securities. Cash assets include currency and coin held in bank vaults and deposit claims against the Federal Reserve. Assets in the form of cash and deposits with the Federal Reserve yield no interest and are held largely to meet legal reserve requirements. Loans and securities do yield interest and make up the major part of total bank assets. Loans are typically debts of businesses and households, while security holdings are largely composed of debt obligations of the U.S. Treasury, federal agencies, and state and local governments.

INTERNATIONAL ASPECTS OF BANKING

Although we shall postpone a detailed discussion of the international aspects of commercial banking until Part 6, a brief comment at this juncture may help to keep things in perspective. Up to now we have not distinguished between assets and liabilities that are held in domestic offices of United States commercial banks and those that are held in foreign branches of those banks. Not too long ago this distinction would have been of minimal importance. However, the marked growth of business in foreign branches of U.S. banks has been an important development in commercial banking during the 1970s. In 1970, there were 61 U.S. banks with foreign offices. Taken as a group, those offices accounted for less than $50 billion in assets. By the end of 1982, 196 banks had foreign offices, and those offices held $390 billion of assets. Taking those banks as a group, this amounted to roughly 30 percent of total assets. Citicorp, the largest commercial bank, is most indicative of the international scope of banking. It has more than 200 branches in roughly 100 countries of the world.

Looked at from another perspective, in 1982 U.S. banks with foreign offices earned $3 billion before taxes from their international businesses, out of total pretax income of $9 billion.[1] Clearly, then, an increasingly important part of U.S. bank business is conducted abroad. Except in critical cases, however, in the remainder of the chapter we shall make no particular distinction between domestic and foreign-held assets and liabilities.

Armed with this general background, we turn now to a discussion of some of the principles of bank management. This will serve as a prelude to a more detailed discussion of bank liabilities and assets.

[1]For all insured banks, total pretax income in 1982 amounted to $19 billion. Thus, the 196 banks with foreign offices accounted for nearly half of total pretax income. Evidently then, banks with foreign offices are among the largest institutions. For details on this, see B. N. Opper, "Profitability of Insured Commercial Banks in 1982," *Federal Reserve Bulletin*, July 1983, pp. 489–507.

A BANK AS A FINANCIAL INTERMEDIARY

We previously suggested that the great bulk of deposits in banks were created through bank purchases of assets. A banker, of course, is likely to view the relationship with the roles reversed—that is, the banker will feel that bank deposits give rise to bank acquisitions of assets. The banker might put it this way: "My bank is a member of the family called 'financial intermediaries.' As such, it gathers funds from people by issuing and selling financial claims against itself. It can acquire assets to the extent, and only to the extent, that it is supplied with funds in exchange for financial claims against it."

Thus, a bank participates in financial markets in two principal roles—as a buyer of funds through issues of claims against itself and as a seller of funds or purchaser claims against others.

BANK LIABILITIES

A bank that seeks to attract funds by issuing claims against itself realizes that these claims must compete with many other types of financial claims for a place in the portfolios of asset holders—for example, these claims compete with currency, with claims against other commercial banks, with claims against other types of financial intermediaries, and with direct securities of varying maturities and varying degrees of safety and liquidity. Thus, the volume of claims against itself that a bank can persuade others to hold depends in part on both its price policy—the yields it offers—and the characteristics of these claims in terms of safety, liquidity, and conformity to the preferences of various types of asset holders.

In issuing deposit claims, a bank encounters widely differing types and degrees of competition in different segments of the market. For example, some individuals and households have only small amounts of funds, are not sophisticated in their knowledge and appraisal of financial alternatives, and would find it costly and inconvenient to explore distant opportunities. These units may be willing to hold deposit claims even at relatively low yields. At the other extreme are large corporations with millions of dollars of investable funds and expert money managers who are fully aware of all financial alternatives. These corporations are likely to hold claims against banks only if their yields are fully competitive with other alternatives. In view of such differences, it is hardly surprising that banks practice price discrimination and attach different yields to claims tailored to appeal to different classes of investors.

A banker's freedom in determining the price and characteristics of these claims is to come to some degree restricted by laws and official regulations. The prohibition of payment of interest on demand deposits and interest rate ceilings on time and savings deposits are the most obvious form of such regulations. Even prior to the interest-bearing transactions account and the recent abolition of most interest rate ceilings, bankers had some latitude in competing for deposit funds. This primarily took the form of nonprice competition, such as the free provision of costly services (free checking services), or the use of gifts to entice customers to make deposits.

Despite this ability to compete—an ability enhanced by the elimination of most interest ceilings—it would be a mistake to think of most deposit liabilities as being under the direct control of the individual bank, especially in the short run. Rather, the bank must be prepared to cope with unanticipated declines in these liabilities—for example, when holders of demand deposits or savings deposits draw down their accounts. As we shall see below, one response of the banking system to this situation has been to develop bank liabilities over which an individual bank can have some control. A second response has been to manage bank assets to provide the bank with liquidity for unanticipated deposit outflows.

THE RELATION BETWEEN ASSET AND LIABILITY POLICIES

Bank asset and liability policies are therefore interrelated. Indeed, these two sets of policies are interdependent in several different ways. First, the yields a bank can profitably pay on its deposit liabilities depend in part on the yields realized on its assets, which is influenced by the composition of its portfolio. Disaster may follow if assets and liabilities are seriously mismatched—if, for example, a bank issues liabilities that are denominated in fixed amounts of dollars and acquires assets, such as common stocks, that have values which fluctuate widely. Similarly, as we shall see, a bank may experience liquidity difficulties if the maturity of its assets and liabilities are badly mismatched.

A second connection between assets and liabilities is a more mechanical one. In particular, as we have noted, banks must keep part of their assets in the form of cash to satisfy legal reserve requirements, and they earn no interest on these reserves. Moreover, as we shall see, reserve requirements are imposed on only certain types of liabilities. So banks have an incentive to raise funds via liabilities for which there are no reserve requirements. Not surprisingly, this has proved to be an important practical consideration.

A final type of interrelationship between assets and liabilities stems from the fact that the terms on which a bank supplies one type of service affects demands for its other types of services. We have all seen bank advertisements extolling the advantages of "one-stop, full-service banking." A bank may proclaim: "This bank stands ready to meet all financial needs; it will supply all your reasonable requests for consumer, housing, and business credit; it provides the best of convenient and cheap checking services; and its savings department offers a wide choice of deposits, all safe and liquid and carrying good returns." Such a bank can offer any one of its services on favorable terms as a means of stimulating demand for other services. We stress a bank's use of its lending policies to customers as a primary means of attracting deposits.

BANK EARNINGS, SAFETY, AND LIQUIDITY

Banks, naturally, are profit-seeking institutions. If they operated in a world of perfect certainty, their motive would probably be to maximize their long-run profits. However, as we have already seen, neither a bank nor any financial intermediary operates under such conditions. It faces uncertainties, and therefore risks, of many kinds—uncertainties as to its future volume and costs of funds and uncertainties as to the future incomes and prices on the various types of earning assets that it may acquire. A bank does not, therefore, consider earnings alone; instead, it seeks some optimal combination of earnings, liquidity, and safety. And to secure more of one the bank must often sacrifice some of the others. For example, to get higher earnings it may have to incur more risk and illiquidity, and to get more safety and liquidity it may have to sacrifice some earnings.

SAFETY OF ASSETS

As noted earlier, the risk that a debt obligation will decline in value takes two forms:

1 The market risk—the risk that the price will decline because of a rise in market rates of interest. On some occasions this risk is estimated to be very small because interest rates are expected to remain stable or even to fall, which would create capital gains.
2 The default risk—the risk that the debtor will not meet promptly and fully the promise to pay interest and to repay principal.

Bankers face difficult problems in determining the types and amounts of risk to assume. If they go to the extreme, purchasing and holding only the safest assets, earnings are likely to be very low. Moreover, they may fail to meet customers' reasonable demands for loans, may acquire the reputation of being an undependable and inadeqate source of credit, and may lose customers and deposits to other banks. On the other hand, there are real dangers in assuming too much risk. For one thing, the bank may suffer such large losses on risky assets that its net return will be less than that on safer assets. Moreover, large losses, or even the prospect of such losses, can endanger the future of the bank.

Commercial banks are especially limited in their ability to assume risk because of the very high ratio of their fixed-dollar liabilities to their total assets. As noted earlier, the net worth of banks is equal to only about 7 percent of their total assets. The other 93 percent of claims are laibilities, mostly deposits, that are fixed in terms of dollars. Thus, if the assets of a bank with these ratios depreciated by more than 7 percent, the bank would be insolvent; the value of its assets would be less than its liabilities to depositors and others. The bank might have to be closed. But the bank may face serious consequences long before its assets depreciate enough to wipe out its net worth and make it insolvent. As its net worth shrinks, depositors may become distrustful, and the bank may face problems in attracting deposits and even in retaining existing deposits. This has obvious effects on the bank's lending power.

A bank can attempt to maintain an adequete degree of solvency in two different ways: (1) by increasing its net worth and (2) by maintaining the safety of its assets. One way to increase net worth is to retain profits. This method has obvious limitations. If profits are low, net worth can be built up only slowly, even if the bank pays no dividends to shareholders. And to the extent that a bank reduces dividends in order to retain earnings, it may depress the market price of its outstanding shares. The bank may also increase its net worth by selling additional stock. As it does this, it may feel justified in acquiring a larger proportion of risky assets, thereby increasing its earnings. But there is a limit to the extent that this can be done profitably. Experience indicates that banks can achieve a profit rate on net worth comparable to profit rates in other industries only if they have a large *leverage factor*—that is, only if total earning assets are a large multiple of net worth. At some stage, therefore, a bank finds it unprofitable to expand further its net worth relative to assets. It must then limit the amount of risk it assumes.

Thus, in determining portfolio composition, bankers face difficult problems in balancing safety against earnings. They must estimate the amounts of risks attached to the various types of available assets, compare risk differentials against interest differentials, consider both long-run and short-run consequences, and strike a balance. If they veer too far toward safety, they may face not only inadequate profits in the short run, but also charges that aversion to risk prevents them from adequately serving the needs of customers and the economy. But if they veer too far in the direction of assets bearing risks, they may face disaster or at least endanger their ability to attract or to retain deposits. They must also consider the need for liquidity, a problem to which we now turn.

BANK LIQUIDITY

By the *liquidity* of a bank is meant its capacity to meet promptly demands that it pay its obligations. As noted earlier, commercial banks must pay more attention to liquidity than many other types of financial institutions, such as life insurance companies. This results from the high turnover of their debt liabilities. A large part of the gross outpayments by a bank is met from current gross receipts of funds in the normal course of business. We have already noted that deposit withdrawals are expected to be offset, at least in large part, by inflows of new deposits. A bank also receives inflows of funds as income on its assets, as repayment of principal on maturing assets, and as weekly or monthly repayments on installment loans. In many cases such gross inflows are at least sufficient to meet gross payments by a bank. Nevertheless, each bank must be prepared to make net payments stemming from outflows from its deposit accounts. Some of these are seasonal or cyclical so that they can be predicted with fair accuracy and preparations can be made. Others are more erratic and less predictable. Inability to meet these drains promptly means failure or at least loss of confidence in the bank.

A bank could, of course, elect to "play it safe" and remain completely liquid by holding cash equal to all its liabilities. But the effects on its income would be disastrous. At the other extreme, the bank could select assets solely with an eye toward generating income, ignoring liquidity altogether. This, too, can lead to disaster—perhaps to sudden death rather than slow starvation. Thus, in determining its portfolio composition a bank must balance its desire for income against its desire for liquidity. It usually tries to buy any given amount of liquidity at the lowest possible cost in terms of sacrifice of net earnings. An individual bank has two principal sources of liquidity: borrowings from others and sales out of its asset holdings. By tradition, banks typically placed primary emphasis on using the asset side of the balance sheet as a source of liquidity.

Many types of assets, each with a varying degree of liquidity, are available to banks. Among the most liquid are vault cash; deposits at the Federal Reserve; call loans to other banks, brokers, dealers in government securities, and others; and Treasury bills and other short-term obligations of the federal government. Among the less liquid are loans to customers, long-term bonds, and mortgages.

It is somewhat paradoxical that vault cash and deposits at the Federal Reserve, which are the most liquid assets in the sense of being closest to cash, do not provide a bank with a great deal of liquidity. The reason is a simple one. Such assets are held largely as required reserves and are not generally available to make payments to others. Only so-called *excess reserves* are available for this purpose. Banks held substantial quantities of excess reserves in the 1930s and 1940s, but have kept their holdings quite small in recent years.

Historically, the assets that provided the bulk of the liquidity necessary to cope with a loss of deposits were U.S. government securities, particularly short-term obligations. These debt instruments enjoy an extensive secondary market, permitting them to be sold quickly at the prevailing market price and with relatively low transaction costs. Such characteristics are the hallmarks of a highly liquid asset. Sales of short-term Treasury obligations have often proved eminently well suited for dealing with a decline in deposit balances. Of course, in order to have access to this pool of liquidity, banks must hold a sizable quantity of liquid assets. These would then be drawn down as immediate needs surfaced and gradually replenished after the bank has time to make other adjustments in its portfolio.

There is a catch in all this, of course, since highly liquid assets often yield a lower rate of return than less liquid assets. This provides an incentive to consider additional sources of liquidity. And, as previously noted, the main alternative to holding liquid assets is for the bank to borrow funds from others as needed. How a bank perceives these two options depends in part on the availability and cost of borrowings. If a bank is assured that it can borrow large amounts at any time without onus and at a low interest cost relative to the yields on the assets, it may rely largely on this source for liquidity and hold few liquid assets. But if the availability of borrowings is uncertain, or if borrowing carries an onus, or if borrowing costs are high relative to yields on the bank's liquid assets, the bank will seek more liquidity via its asset portfolio. As we shall see shortly, over the past twenty years or so conditions have gradually shifted in favor of borrowing from others as a way of dealing with liquidity issues. This change has coincided with a substantial expansion in the nature and scope of bank liabilities. Indeed, the shift in liquidity strategies has been regarded as sufficiently noteworthy that it goes by the fancy name *liability management*. In order to understand what this is all about, we need to examine in detail the liabilities and assets of commercial banks.

A DETAILED COMMERCIAL BANK BALANCE SHEET

Earlier in this chapter we encountered a highly aggregated balance sheet for the commercial banking system. Such a balance sheet abstracts from many of the interesting and important features of the determination of commercial bank assets and liabilities. A considerably more detailed balance sheet is given in Table 6–2. A glance at this table reveals the extent to which such all-inclusive categories as "loans" or "securities" tend to aggregate over rather diverse components. For example, there are eight different types of loans listed in Table 6–2, and even this degree of detail involves considerable aggregation.

While the table provides us with a detailed snapshot of the commercial banking *system*, it conceals difference among the balance sheets of *individual* commercial banks. That such differences exist should hardly be surprising in view of the diversity of banks that we have previously discussed. To examine these differences, however, would take us too far afield. Rather, we shall treat Table 6–2 as though it were the balance sheet of an "average" commercial bank. Our objectives in doing so will be to elucidate the nature of the various assets and liabilities held by banks and, more important, to gain an understanding of the economic reasons that lead to a particular configuration of assets and liabilities. We begin our discussions with the liability side of the balance sheet.

TABLE 6–2 Commercial Bank Balance Sheet, September 30, 1983 (in billions of dollars)

ASSETS		LIABILITIES AND CAPITAL ACCOUNT	
Cash balances		**Demand deposits**	
Vault cash	17.4	Individuals, partnerships, and	
Deposits with Federal Reserve	20.9	corporations (IPC)	286.9
Balances with financial institutions	91.4	U.S. government	2.3
Items in process of collection	74.5	State and local government	13.6
		Other	52.3
Total cash	204.2	Total demand deposits	355.1
Loans		**Time deposits**	
Commercial and industrial	385.3	Other IPC	557.4
Agricultural	39.1	State and local governments	57.6
Real estate	318.3	Other	33.3
Consumer credit	205.1	Total time deposits	648.3
To financial institutions	72.7		
Federal funds sold and securities resale agreements	92.3	**Savings deposits**	
		Corporations	41.0
For purchasing and carrying securities	14.5	Other IPC	398.7
		State and local	9.4
Other loans	37.5	Total savings	449.1
Total loans	1,164.8		
Securities			
U.S. Treasury	158.2	Federal funds purchased and securities sold under repurchase agreements	175.2
Other U.S. government agencies	77.8		
State and local government	152.7		
Other securities	26.7	Other borrowed funds	45.0
Total securities	415.4	Miscellaneous liabilities	125.0
		Capital accounts	137.4
		Total liabilities and capital accounts	1,935.2
Other assets	150.8		
Total assets	1,935.2		

Addenda	
Time deposits of $100,000 or more	283.0
Super NOW accounts	26.5
Other NOW accounts	66.7
Money market time deposits	196.2

SOURCE: *Federal Reserve Bulletin*, March, 1984, pp. A72-A73.

A SURVEY OF BANK LIABILITIES

As we learned earlier, the bulk of claims against commercial banks is in the form of deposit liabilities. We have also previously noted that commercial banks lack close control over the quantities of most deposit liabilities. As we shall see, however, banks can control one important type of deposit liability—the so-called certificate of deposit—and this plays an important role in liability management. The other major element in liability management is the use of nondeposit liabilities. These liabilities have become an increasingly important source of bank funds and, as we shall see, are frequently subject to bank control.

DEPOSIT LIABILITIES

As Table 6–1 reveals, in 1983 deposit liabilities accounted for 75 percent of total assets. As of the same date, demand deposits amounted to 25 percent of total deposits, savings deposits accounted for 30 percent of total deposits, and the remaining 45 percent were held in the form of time deposits.

DEMAND DEPOSITS

A glance at Table 6–2 shows that there are many different types of holders of demand deposits at commercial banks. These include individuals; businesses; and various governments, federal, state, and local. The "other" category of holder includes foreign governments and foreign banks and demand balances held by one commercial bank with another commercial bank. This latter category of interbank deposits primarily reflects correspondent balances.[2]

For many years, demand deposits played a unique and pivotal role for both banks and their customers. For banks, demand deposits provided the major source of funds. For bank customers, demand deposits provided the only readily available checkable transactions account. As we have indicated earlier, in both respects demand deposits have diminished in importance.

As they have been since the 1930s, banks are still prohibited from paying interest on demand deposits. When the general level of interest rates was quite low, this restriction was not terribly bothersome. But as interest rates on alternative financial claims have risen over the years, the public has been less willing to hold demand deposits. Banks have responded by adjusting service charges on checking accounts and by other nonprice means of competition, such as free gifts. This, however, has not been enough to stem the tide. Thus, the fraction of total bank funds raised by demand deposits has declined steadily and markedly in the post-World War II period. For example, from Table 6–3, which gives the percentage of total assets

---

[2]For state-chartered banks, such interbank deposits often satisfy reserve requirements.

TABLE 6–3 Various Bank Liabilities as a Percentage of Total Bank Assets: Selected Dates

	1947	1960	1974	1983
Demand deposits	69.8	60.7	34.3	18.3
Savings deposits	17.7	21.6	14.7	23.2
Time deposits	5.2	6.9	32.3	33.5
Nondeposit funds	0.8	2.6	11.8	17.9
Capital accounts	6.5	8.2	6.9	7.1
Total	100.0	100.0	100.0	100.0

SOURCE: *Federal Reserve Bulletin* and FDIC Annual Reports, various issues.

accounted for by various liability categories, we see that demand deposits fell from about 70 percent of total assets in 1947 to about 18 percent in 1983. In recent years, if anything, the decline in the fraction of bank funds accounted for by demand deposits has accelerated. A primary reason for this is that with the advent of NOW and super-NOW accounts, demand deposits have lost their exclusivity for transactions purposes. (In Table 6–3 these accounts are included in the category of savings deposits). Lest we give the wrong impression, however, demand deposits remain the most important component of the conventional money supply, M-1.[3] Of course, in the future demand deposits could well continue to decline in relative importance as transactions balances shift to interest-bearing accounts. But this tendency would be arrested if interest payments were permitted on demand deposits, a position the Federal Reserve and many others have endorsed.

SAVINGS DEPOSITS

As Table 6–2 reveals, savings deposits comprise the second most important source of bank funds, accounting for 23 percent of these funds in 1983. While this percentage is not appreciably different from the share of savings deposits in 1960 (see Table 6–3), the apparent constancy is misleading for several reasons. First, the relative importance of savings deposits has in fact fluctuated over time. Second, and of more consequence, by 1983 the composition of savings deposits was dramatically different from what it was in 1960. Indeed the primary savings deposit of the earlier era, the passbook savings account, was on its way to extinction in the 1980s.

A *passbook savings deposit* is an interest-bearing account evidenced only by entries on the bank's books and in the depositor's passbook, and bearing

[3]As of 1984, demand deposits accounted for 46 percent of M-1 and other checkable deposits for 25 percent. The remaining part of M-1, about 28 percent, was in the form of currency. It should also be noted that due to some elements of double counting, not all of the demand deposits appearing in Table 6–2 show up in M-1. For an explanation, see the discussion of cash assets later in this chapter.

no stipulated maturity date. Banks have historically been legally empowered to require prior notice for withdrawal, but in practice they permit withdrawals at any time. While at a practical level the immediate availability of passbook savings deposits makes them similar to demand deposits, since it is necessary to withdraw the funds prior to spending, passbook savings are not well suited for making transactions. These accounts have been used primarily by individuals and households as a vehicle for financial investment. As a result, at least until the 1960s, these accounts tended to be fairly stable, not fluctuating as much as transactions accounts. From a bank's point of view, this stability meant that the greater the fraction of funds raised by savings deposits, the less it needed to worry about liquidity needs and the more it could hold high-yielding, longer-maturity, but more illiquid, assets.

In recent years, passbook savings deposits have not proved to be a reliably stable source of funds. This development stemmed from the decline in the attractiveness of the interest rate paid on passbook savings deposits as yields on alternative assets rose well above the interest rate ceiling on passbook savings deposits. Indeed, the 5½ percent ceiling on passbook savings deposits is one of the few ceilings remaining as of 1984, although it too is scheduled to disappear in 1986. In any event, passbook savings deposits in 1983 were held in roughly the same volume as a decade earlier, when the banking system was less than half its 1983 size.

The remaining three categories of savings deposits are NOW accounts, super-NOW accounts, and money market deposit accounts. These three accounts all date from the beginning of the 1980s and are the result of the deregulation of the financial system. Moreover, all three accounts can be used in varying degrees to meet transactions needs. Indeed, both NOWs and super-NOWs are counted in M-1, and it would not be surprising if in future versions of Table 6–2, the Federal Reserve chose to lump these accounts with demand rather than savings deposits.

NOW accounts became available nationwide at the beginning of 1981.[4] These accounts provide interest-bearing checking accounts to individuals but not businesses. The interest rate banks can pay on these accounts is presently constrained by a ceiling of 5¼ percent, but under current law this ceiling is scheduled for removal in 1986. Since early 1983, the banks have been permitted to offer a NOW-type account that is not constrained by interest rate ceilings. This so-called *super NOW account*, however, initially had a minimum balance of $2,500 (this minimum balance dropped to $1,000 in January 1985 and will be eliminated in the spring of 1986). Indeed, as can be seen from Table 6–4, ordinary NOW accounts remain distinctly more popular than super-NOWs at commercial banks. Banks, in fact, have

[4]NOW accounts existed prior to 1981, but were not generally available at commercial banks until this time. For an account of the deregulation of the financial system and the growth of new financial instruments, see Chapter 7.

TABLE 6–4 The Composition of Savings Deposits, 1983

	Billions of dollars	Percent of total
Passbook savings deposits	$135	30%
NOW accounts	67	15
Super-NOW accounts	27	6
Money market deposit accounts	220	49
Total	$449	100%

SOURCE: See Table 6–2.

contributed to this lack of popularity by the structure of service charges for super-NOWs and by offering interest rates below those available on another type of savings account, the money market deposit account.

Money market deposit accounts (MMDAs) were first authorized in late 1982, a few weeks prior to the advent of super-NOWs. Like a super-NOW, an MMDA initially had a minimum balance of $2,500 and is not subject to interest rate ceilings. And while it is a savings account, an MMDA can function in a limited way as a transactions account. In particular, it can be used to make up to six transactions a month by check, preauthorization, or telephone, although at most three of these can be by check. These restrictions undoubtedly limit the usefulness of MMDAs for transactions purposes.

Nevertheless, from their inception these accounts grew at an incredibly rapid rate, accumulating to some $220 billion in the first nine months of their existence (see Table 6–4). Individuals were obviously attracted by the availability of a market-related interest rate on a savings account. Moreover, as MMDAs can also be held by businesses, many small and medium-sized companies chose to hold MMDAs. One reason why banks priced MMDAs to make them more attractive than super-NOWs is that there are no reserve requirements on MMDAs, while at the margin, super-NOWs have a 12 percent reserve requirement. What this means is that a dollar of an MMDA can support a dollar of earning assets, while a dollar of a super-NOW only permits banks to hold 88 cents in earning assets. Given these circumstances, it is hardly surprising that MMDAs would be priced more attractively than super-NOWs.

TIME DEPOSITS (SMALL DENOMINATION)

As Table 6–3 reveals, *time deposits* now provide the single most important source of funds to commercial banks. Time deposits have stipulated maturity dates, are evidenced by a written instrument, and bear a rate of interest that remains fixed during the life of the contract. As Table 6–3 also indicates, time deposits come in two varieties: small-denomination deposits (under $100,000) and large-denomination deposits, typically in the form of what are called certificates of deposit. We focus first on the small-denomination variety, which in 1983 provided some $365 billion to banks (see Table 6–3).

Small-denomination time deposits are typically offered in maturities ranging from 7 days to 8 years. Holders of these claims are expected to keep them to maturity, but typically banks stand ready to redeem them before maturity, and impose a penalty in the form of some loss of interest. Moreover, since these accounts cannot be sold to others, from the point of view of the holder time deposits are less liquid than demand or savings deposits. Because potential holders of time deposits will acquire them only if they are compensated for this illiquidity, such accounts have typically paid higher interest rates than those available on savings or transactions accounts. Until quite recently, interest rates payable on small-denomination time deposits were subject to ceilings, but these have now been all but eliminated.[5]

From the point of view of the banks, despite their higher costs, time deposits have some distinct virtues. Since these funds tend to be held to maturity, the stability means that banks are better able to match the maturity of their assets and liabilities. For example, a bank that issues a substantial volume of 4-year time deposit liabilities can feel more comfortable with granting a comparable volume of 4-year-loans. By this sort of matching process, the bank can, with a high degree of confidence, assure itself a known return for its financial intermediation.

TIME DEPOSITS (LARGE DENOMINATION)

Time deposits in denominations of $100,000 or more have become a key source of bank funding in the last two decades, amounting to $283 billion in 1983 (see Table 6–2). Perhaps even more important than their sheer volume, large-denomination time deposits are critical to banks, especially larger ones, because they offer a flexible source of funds, to a large extent under bank control. As a result, these time deposits can provide a major pool of liquidity, available for coping with changes in other deposit liabilities, as well as with changes in loan demand from valued bank customers. Put another way, large time deposits are a critical element in what we have termed the strategy of liability management. To see how this all works, we first need some facts.

Large-denomination time deposits have existed for a long time. At first, these claims were simply jumbo versions of their small-denomiantion cousins, and this type of instrument is still available. Today, however, the lion's share of large-denomination time deposits, well over 80 percent, is in the form of *certificates of deposit (CDs)*. CDs date from the early 1960s. Like any time deposit, they have fixed denominations, fixed maturity dates, and fixed rates of interest, and they are not payable by the issuing bank before ma-

---

[5]As of 1984, the one exception is for accounts under $2,500 with initial maturities of 7 to 31 days.

turity. Although they are issued in many maturities, the most common are 6 months or less. What makes CDs special is that they are negotiable.[6] That is, unlike conventional time deposits, a CD can be transferred freely from holder to holder prior to maturity. Sales of CDs prior to maturity are greatly facilitated by a group of brokers and dealers who enhance the marketability of these instruments. In addition to providing a secondary market, the brokers and dealers also assist with the intitial placement of CDs.

As a result of these conditions, the negotiable CD has assumed an important role in short-term money markets. It appeals to many types of investors, including businesses, financial institutions, and state and local governments, as a prime liquid earning asset.

It is from the point of view of the banks, however, that CDs are the most interesting, since the development of CDs gave birth to the practice of liability management. A large bank might decide, for example, that it needed $2 million to offset a comparable loss of demand deposits or because it wanted to make a loan of $2 million. In normal circumstances it could raise these funds quickly by issuing $2 million of CDs, at an interest cost likely to be close to the then-prevailing market rate on CDs.

What this suggests is that CDs enable banks to engage in liability management by permitting them to achieve two objectives: (1) They provide a way of dealing with relatively short-run liquidity needs; and (2) they permit banks to have a say in the size of their total assets. This say, however, cannot be whimsical, since the optimal size of a bank will ultimately be decided by economic conditions and a balancing of risk and return considerations.

While CDs have provided the major component of liability management, nondeposit liabilities have also played an important role in this regard. Moreover, as we shall see, some nondeposit liabilities can be issued for as short a maturity as one day, making them particularly well suited for dealing with very short-run liquidity needs.

NONDEPOSIT FUNDS

Table 6–3 shows that in 1983 nondeposit funds (excluding capital accounts) amounted to about 18 percent of total bank assets. Also evident from this table is the steady and marked expansion of nondeposit funds that has taken place over the years. Clearly, nondeposit liabilities have become a major source of bank funds.

As with the case of CDs, nondeposit liabilities expanded as banks sought a convenient and economical way of dealing with liquidity problems and as they attempted to control their own asset size. Beyond this, however,

---

[6]There is some unfortunate confusion concerning the use of the term certificate of deposit. Some banks use this phrase to describe the piece of paper evidencing a small-denomination time deposit (other banks call these *savings certificates*). We reserve the term CD for a large and negotiable time deposit.

some nondeposit liabilities arose as a way for banks to circumvent interest rate ceilings. In the 1960s, for example, CDs were themselves subject to ceilings, and banks relied on the unregulated Eurodollar market for liability management. Other nondeposit liabilities arose as a way of avoiding reserve requirements and, not infrequently, as a way of avoiding both reserve requirements and interest rate ceilings.

Although not all nondeposit liabilities are easily controlled, the bulk of them do qualify as candidates for liability management. We confine our discussion to the most important items in the nondeposit category.

BORROWING FEDERAL FUNDS

The federal funds market operates through brokers and dealers, including a few very large banks that operate federal funds departments. As originally constituted, the federal funds market was a vehicle for buying and selling, or borrowing and lending, deposits at the Federal Reserve banks. In effect, banks with reserves in excess of legal requirements lend them to other banks.

Over the years the Federal Reserve has broadened the kinds of transactions that are classified as federal funds transactions, which are subject neither to basic reserve requirements nor to interest rate ceilings. Banks obviously prefer a liberal interpretation of what constitute federal funds. One step in this direction was taken in 1964, when member banks were permitted to borrow deposits, and not just reserves, of any commercial bank—either member or nonmember. Permitting member banks to borrow from nonmember banks allowed many smaller banks to lend their excess funds via the federal funds market. A second expansion of the market occurred in 1970, when the Federal Reserve broadened the eligible lenders to include the following: mutual savings banks, savings and loan associations, branches and agencies of foreign banks, securities dealers and agencies of the federal government. As a consequence of these liberalizations, the volume of borrowing in the federal funds market has risen steadily, from a daily average of $1.5 billion in 1960 to over $100 billion in recent years.

In view of these numbers, the federal funds market has obviously become a key element in fostering interbank loans, providing a convenient way for financial institutions with temporarily excess funds to lend them to banks that need funds. The borrowers in this market are usually large banks, while the lenders are frequently smaller banks. In part this happens because there is a minimum federal funds sale of $1 million that effectively rules out small banks as borrowers. They are able to lend, however, because brokers arrange for packages in which small banks can obtain a piece of a loan to a large bank.

The typical loan in this market is for one day, although renewals occur and longer-maturity loans are also made. And although the typical loan is for one day—it is called an *overnight* loan—many banks participate in the market every day. Large banks thus can borrow federal funds to acquire

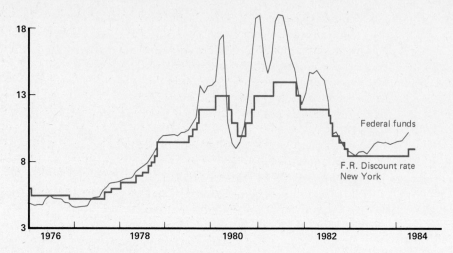

FIGURE 6–1
**Federal funds interest rate and Federal Reserve
discount rate.** (SOURCE: *Federal Reserve Chart
Book*, Washington, D.C., May 1984.)

relatively long-term assets, while small banks may lend every day in the
market instead of purchasing an alternative asset.

The interest rate on loans made in the federal funds market is determined by the continuous interplay of the forces of supply and demand.
The relative strength of supply and demand can change quickly, leading to
substantial variations in the rate from day to day or even hour to hour. This
marked variability is also evident in the monthly movements of the federal
funds rate pictured in Figure 6–1. From a low point of just over 4½ percent
in January 1977, the funds rate climbed steadily to 11 percent in August
1979. It then jumped over 17½ percent in March 1980, fell to 9 percent by
July 1980, and shot up to over 19 percent by the end of that year. At the
very least, this serves to point out that steady reliance on the federal funds
market as a source of funds can be a risky proposition.

BORROWING UNDER REPURCHASE AGREEMENTS (RPs)

A *repurchase agreement* is an arrangement under which a bank sells some
asset, typically a Treasury security, to a purchaser with an agreement to
repurchase it at some stipulated time at a stipulated price. The bank pays
interest in the form of the difference between the repurchase and sale
prices.

The RP market is closely related to the federal funds market. The interest
rate on RPs typically approximates the federal funds rate but frequently is
slightly lower, because RPs are collateralized borrowings while federal funds
are not. One important difference between the two markets is that, although

any person, firm, or government entity may deal in RPs, as we have seen, participation in the federal funds market is limited to certain institutions, such as commercial banks, mutual savings banks, savings and loan associations, and federal agencies. Institutions eligible to participate in the federal funds market can, of course, also deal in RPs. In practice, they deal in both markets and are joined in the RP market by state and local governments and business firms, among others. Like the federal funds market, the RP market grew dramatically in the 1970s. In particular, in 1970 commercial banks borrowed an average of $3 to 4 billion from the nonbank public in the RP market, while at the present time large banks have been borrowing about $75 billion in this market.

The joint impact of the federal funds and RP markets on commercial bank balance sheets is shown in Table 6–2. On the liability side, we see that banks, primarily the large ones, obtained $175 billion from these two sources in 1983. From the asset side, we see that commercial banks provided $92 billion of these funds. The difference between these two figures, $83 billion, represents the net amount of federal funds and RPs provided to the commercial banking system from outside the banking system.

Like the federal funds market, the RP market has permitted member banks to offer a nondeposit liability that bears explicit interest and is exempt from interest rate regulations and reserve requirements. In fact, by entering into a repurchase agreement with a business customer, banks are able implicitly to pay interest on demand deposits, something they are explicitly prohibited from doing. The mechanism is simple but ingenious. A business firm having excess funds in a demand deposit account buys a security from its bank under an overnight RP. The next day the security is returned to the bank, the interest on the transaction is paid, and the demand deposit is restored. This all works because the interest is technically earned on the security, not the demand deposit. As if to add insult to injury, at least as far as the Federal Reserve is concerned, the bank further benefits because there are no reserve requirements on RPs. As a consequence of the temporary relabeling of the demand deposit as an RP, a bank therefore reduces its required reserves. RPs are an outstanding example of how financial innovation provides means for evading regulatory restrictions.[7] As we proceed, we will encounter numerous other examples, not the least of which is Eurodollar borrowing.

BORROWING EURODOLLAR DEPOSITS

Eurodollar deposits are dollar-denominated deposit claims against banks domiciled outside the United States. The prefix *Euro* is misleading, since not all the banks issuing these claims are located in Europe. Eurodollar deposits are issued by foreign banks generally in exchange for deposit claims

---

[7]Needless to say, the Federal Reserve has often not sat idly by in the face of these innovations. On this see the overview on liability management later in this chapter and Chapter 12.

against banks in the United States. For example, if an American or a foreigner transfers a deposit in a U.S. bank to a foreign bank and keeps the new deposit in dollars, Eurodollars are created.

Foreign banks that have issued Eurodollar claims are naturally anxious to lend these balances, and at various times American commercial banks have proved to be willing customers. Commercial banks in the United States typically borrow Eurodollar funds through their foreign branches, receiving in return deposit claims against banks in the United States.[8] Since foreign branches are not subject to interest rate ceilings, this has been a particularly important source of funds (albeit often quite expensive) during periods of domestic credit stringency.

Banks first made extensive use of the Eurodollar market in the 1960s when there were interest rate ceilings on CDs but none on foreign branches. With the removal of ceiling on CDs, this motivation disappeared. In recent years, in fact, domestic banks have been net lenders to their branches. However, as with RPs, banks have continued to use their offshore branches to circumvent the prohibition of interest on demand deposits. The mechanism is again very simple. By electronic means, a large bank customer can shift funds overnight from the U.S. office of a bank to an offshore branch of the same bank, typically somewhere in the sunny Caribbean. Unfettered by prohibitions, the offshore branch pays a market rate of interest on the funds, which are returned electronically the next day. In some very real sense, the entire transaction is a big electronic paper shuffle, with neither the customer nor the funds ever benefitting from the Caribbean sun. The financial benefits should, however, be clear.

BORROWING VIA PROMISSORY NOTES AND COMMERCIAL PAPER

Banks began issuing promissory notes in about 1966. A similar and roughly coincident development was the use of commercial paper to raise funds. Such paper was typically issued by a one-bank holding company that passed the funds on to its bank subsidiary by purchasing some of the bank's loans. From the perspective of the individual investor, both commercial paper and promissory notes are quite similar to CDs, in that all three types of claims are slightly different forms of unsecured bank debt.

BORROWING FROM THE FEDERAL RESERVE

A final type of nondeposit liability worthy of note is borrowing from the Federal Reserve. In effect, the Federal Reserve lends reserves to a bank to meet short-term unexpected deposit withdrawals. This source of funds can be critical to a bank that is experiencing serious difficulties and finds itself unable to borrow from other sources. This lender-of-last resort function is

[8]The details of this type of transaction are spelled out in Chapter 22.

extremely important for ensuring the stability of the banking system and will be discussed below.

For more normal cicrumstances, borrowing from the Federal Reserve is of somewhat less importance as a source of funds. While a Federal Reserve bank rarely refuses to lend to a member bank having deficient reserves, it does not conceal the fact that this source should be used sparingly. It emphasizes that such borrowing is a privilege and not a right, reminds banks of the tradition against continuous borrowing, uses moral suasion to discourage "excessive" borrowing and to encourage repayment, and sometimes raises its discount rate to make borrowing more expensive. In recent years, however, there has been a movement in the direction of making such funds available with fewer strings attached, especially for explicitly seasonal needs.

The actual volume of borrowing from the Federal Reserve may vary considerably in a relatively short period of time. For example, such borrowings amounted to $3.4 billion in August 1974, $700 million in December 1974, and only $60 million in May 1975. It should be noted that when a bank borrows from the Federal Reserve it increases its reserves without decreasing the reserves of any other bank. This is not necessarily true of the other types of borrowing described; in many of these cases, the reserves that are borrowed by one bank come out of the reserves of other banks. Since borrowing from the Federal Reserve and borrowing in the federal funds market are close substitutes, we would expect the rates on these two sources of funds to exhibit similar patterns. This is generally borne out, as shown in Figure 6–1, but evidently in periods of credit restriction some banks are willing to pay a premium to avoid facing Federal Reserve lending officers.

OVERVIEW OF LIABILITY MANAGEMENT

Our survey of bank liabilities has made clear that in recent years banks have done considerably more than passively accept deposits as their sole source of funds. They have aggressively sold CDs and showed considerable ingenuity in creating marketable nondeposit liabilities. While the banks are by now quite adept at liability management, this strategy was not without its problems in the early years. Since it will shed some light on the asset side of things, it may help to review briefly this experience.

Liability management began in earnest with the development of the CD market in the early 1960s. Throughout the first half of the decade, the volume of CDs outstanding grew steadily and stood at $18.6 billion in August 1966. This growth was greatly facilitated by the Federal Reserve, which raised interest ceilings on such deposits whenever a rise in market rates threatened to impair the ability of the banks to tap this source of funds for liquidity. Such increases in ceilings were effected in 1962, 1963, 1964, and 1965. So far, so good. Then, in the credit crunch of 1966, the banks experienced a rude shock when the Federal Reserve not only refused to raise ceilings as market rates of interest rose, but actually reduced some ceilings. As a consequence, the banks were unable to "roll over" CDs as they matured, and their volume declined to $15.5 billion in November 1966.

Faced with this dilemma, banks turned to the various sources of funds examined previously. In so doing, they were exploiting the fact that the line between deposits and nondeposit liabilities was a fuzzy one. Indeed, as suggested earlier, such borrowed funds are quite similar to CDs from the point of view of the holder of the claim. From the viewpoint of the issuing bank, however, there was an important difference. In particular, borrowing sources such as promissory notes, commercial paper, and Eurodollars were not legally regarded as deposits and were not subject to reserve requirements or interest rate ceilings.

The next time a credit crunch materialized, which took place in 1969, banks again experienced a substantial decline in CDs, a decline of roughly $13 billion. However, they were able to offset these runoffs by raising large quantities of funds via repurchase agreements, Eurodollars, and the like. Needless to say, the Federal Reserve, which had created tight monetary conditions in the first place, did not look too kindly on bank efforts to blunt the restrictive effects of monetary policy. Thus began a cat-and-mouse game in which each "creative" act of bank liability management was countered by a series of regulatory changes. The most important of these was the imposition of reserve requirements on commercial paper, promissory notes, and Eurodollar borrowings. By forcing part of the funds raised from these sources to remain idle, this necessarily made such funds considerably more expensive to the banks.

With the advent of the 1970s some more order returned to liability management. In two stages (in 1970 and 1973) the Federal Reserve removed the interest ceiling on large time deposits. Banks once again were free to raise funds by the use of CDs in times of credit stringency. As a consequence, in the next period of credit stringency, which took place in 1973–1974, there was no runoff of CDs. In fact, in marked contrast to 1966 and 1969, CD volume grew throughout this period. As a result, other forms of borrowing were of less importance. For example, Eurodollar borrowings, which had exceeded $15 billion in 1969, remained under $5 billion in 1973–1974.

Since the mid-1970s, liability management has taken on a new character with the marked expansion of the markets for federal funds and repurchase agreements (RPs). This can be seen in Figure 6–2, which provides an overall picture of managed liabilities since 1973. Shown are the outstanding volume of large time deposits and total nondeposit liabilities of commercial banks. Taken together, in early 1985, these two sources accounted for over $435 billion, or about one-fifth of total assets. Liability management is evidently here to stay. This, of course, has a number of important implications for overall portfolio behavior by banks. We return to this issue after we consider the asset side of the balance sheet.

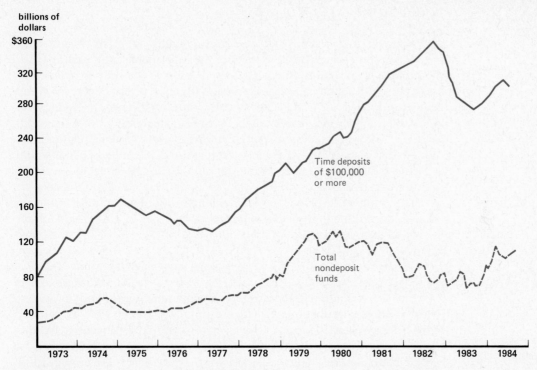

billions of
dollars

Time deposits
of $100,000
or more

Total
nondeposit
funds

FIGURE 6–2
Managed liabilities of commercial banks.

A SURVEY OF BANK ASSETS

Having examined the sources of bank funds, we now turn to the other side of the balance sheet and examine the types and proportions of assets acquired and held by banks. Reference back to Table 6–2 provides us with the composition of total commercial bank assets in 1978. The corresponding proportions or percentage distribution of bank assets are given in Table 6–5. So that we may trace the changing composition of bank assets over time, Table 6–5 provides, in addition to the data for 1983, a snapshot of asset proportions for some earlier years.

A glance at Table 6–2 reveals that several types of assets are conspicuous for their absence or scarcity. Outstanding in this respect are physical assets in the form of land, buildings, and equipment. Few banks own many more assets of this type than are needed for banking purposes. Even smaller are holdings of common stock; and most of these are in the form of stock in the Federal Reserve banks, which member banks are required to hold. The most important assets actually held are cash, loans, and securities.

CASH ASSETS

As Table 6–2 shows, four types of assets qualify as "cash"—vault cash, deposits at the Federal Reserve, balances at other banks, and cash items in the process of collection. *Vault cash* simply refers to the volume of currency and coin held in the vaults of commercial banks. It is needed for transactions purposes but also satisfies, along with deposits at the Federal Reserve, the legal reserve requirements for banks. Balances at other banks are generally held as part of the system of correspondent banking relationships described earlier. The final category, cash items in the process of collection, is a somewhat esoteric accounting device. It arises because an economic unit that receives a check may have its account credited before the account of the unit that issued the check is debited. This double counting artificially inflates the volume of demand deposits. Cash items in the process of collection measures the extent of this and is simply a way of making the books balance.

As is clear from Table 6–5, cash assets have declined from about 24 percent of bank assets in 1947 to under 11 percent in 1983. To a large extent, this reflects a reduction in required reserves that has come about for several reasons: general reductions in reserve requirements; a shift of deposits away from demand deposits, which have relatively high reserve requirements, to time deposits, which have relatively low or indeed no reserve requirements; and a greater reliance on nondeposit funds bearing no reserve requirements.

As should be apparent from this discussion, cash assets are largely determined by factors outside the direct control of banks. Moreover, since cash assets add nothing, at least explicitly, to bank earnings, and can be viewed as incurring an opportunity cost relative to other assets, banks have been quite happy with developments that permitted a reduction in the

TABLE 6–5 Various Bank Assets as a Percentage of Total Bank Assets: Selected Dates

Asset	1947	1960	1974	1983
Cash balances	24.1	20.3	13.9	10.5
Commercial and industrial loans	11.7	16.7	20.3	19.9
Real estate loans	6.0	11.1	14.2	16.4
Consumer loans	3.7	10.2	11.2	10.6
Other loans	3.1	7.5	14.0	13.3
U.S. government securities	44.5	23.7	5.9	12.2
State and local securities	3.4	6.8	10.9	7.9
Other securities	2.4	1.3	4.4	1.3
Other assets	1.0	2.3	5.2	7.9
Total	100.0	100.0	100.0	100.0

SOURCE: *Federal Reserve Bulletin*, various issues.

fraction of total assets they had to keep in cash form. As a result, banks have been able to devote more of their resources to earning assets, to which we now turn.

COMMERCIAL AND INDUSTRIAL LOANS

Let us start with the type of loan that gave commercial banking its name. The *commercial loan* theory of banking, which has been highly influential but never wholly accepted by either bankers or economists, holds that banks should confine themselves exclusively to this type of credit. They should make only short-term, self-liquidating loans based on the production, distribution, or sale of goods and services. The basic idea is that a bank should lend only on the basis of a specific transaction or process that is short-term in nature and at its termination will provide the borrower with funds that can be used to pay off the loan. For example, it is held that a merchant may properly borrow to buy an inventory of merchandise that can be sold in a few months for enough money to retire the loan. Or a manufacturer may borrow to buy raw materials and components and to meet payrolls in order to turn out a product that can soon be sold and the proceeds used to pay off the loan. Or a farmer may properly borrow to finance the planting, tending, and marketing of a crop that will be sold in a few months. On the negative side, the commercial loan theorists contend that banks should not make long-term loans and should not lend on the basis of a project or process that will bring in proceeds only over a long period. For example, a bank should not lend money to a merchant to buy a store, to a manufacturer to buy plant and durable equipment, or to a farmer to buy land. Virtually all economists now reject the commercial loan theory, and few bankers are guided by it.

Some of the loans included in "commercial and industrial" in Table 6–2 conform to the commercial loan theory, but many do not. For one thing, a sizable percentage are not short-term (their original maturity exceeded one year) but are *term loans* that may run for 3 to 5 years or even longer. Perhaps more important, many of these loans, short-term as well as term loans, are not based on a specific transaction or process. Rather, they are based on the general credit rating of the borrower as reflected by past and prospective income and expenses; the ratio of assets to total liabilities; and the ratio of short-term assets to short-term liabilities. A borrower whose rating in these respects is satisfactory may get a short-term or term loan from a bank without specifying any particular project, mix the proceeds with other funds, and use the funds as he or she sees fit, including perhaps the purchase of real estate or durable equipment.

The term *commercial banks* is appropriate in the sense that these institutions are by far the largest source of short-term, and even of term, commercial and industrial loans. In many areas and for many business firms, there is no other source of short-term loans that can compare in convenience, adequacy, and cheapness. But it remains true that these loans represent only a fraction of total commercial bank credit. This fraction, however, has grown over time. In recent years commercial and industrial loans have accounted for about 20 percent of total bank assets, or nearly twice the fraction they represented in the early post-World War II period.

OTHER LOANS

Aside from business loans, the most important types of loans made by banks are for consumer credit, real estate, and securities transactions.

CONSUMER LOANS

Commercial banks constitute one of the largest sources of installment consumer credit, providing about 45 percent of all such funds. Banks extend much of this credit directly to consumers. From Table 6–5 we see that this has amounted to about 11 percent of bank assets in recent years. However, banks also provide such credit indirectly through sales finance companies, consumer finance companies, and others who lend to consumers. Banks do this by lending directly to these institutions and by purchasing in the open market the short-term or longer-term promissory notes these institutions issue to get funds.

A smaller but rapidly growing amount of consumer credit is extended through bank credit cards and arrangements given such names as "instant credit" or "check credit." These credit systems became economically feasible as computers became available to handle the large amounts of record-keeping involved. Some banks issue their own credit cards, but the trend is toward national cards such as Visa and MasterCard which are issued by many banks and are acceptable over wide geographic areas. A bank customer who establishes creditworthiness receives, in effect, a line of credit that can be used to purchase goods and services from merchants who have joined the plan or to get cash advances from any bank that is a member of the plan. Instant credit or check credit is, in effect, an arrangement for overdrafts. After establishing a line of credit at the bank, the customer can get credit automatically by writing checks in excess of his or her deposit balance. Such methods of extending consumer credit will probably become increasingly important in the future.

REAL ESTATE LOANS

Loans for real estate have also been a growing component of bank assets, amounting to about 17 percent of total assets in recent years. Some of the loans on real estate are short-term construction loans, which are paid off when a building is finished and sold. But most of them are long-term mortgages on farms, on residential properties, and less often on commercial and industrial properties. Banks feel justified in holding these long-term mortgages primarily because of their time and savings deposits.

SECURITY LOANS

Loans on securities are for various purposes, but have the common characteristic that securities are used as collateral. Some are a type of business loan to enable security dealers to carry inventories. For example, dealers in U.S. government securities have to carry large inventories relative to their net worth and borrow heavily for this purpose, usually on a very short-term basis. Banks are an important source of such credit and also lend to dealers who hold inventories of other types of securities. Loans to brokers are primarily for the accounts of the brokers' customers who buy securities *on margin.* In effect, the broker gets a loan on the basis of the customers' securities and uses the proceeds to pay the sellers of the securities. Individuals and others sometimes borrow directly from banks on the basis of securities and use the proceeds for purchasing or carrying securities. But the proceeds from loans backed by securities are often used for other purposes, securities being used as collateral simply because the lending bank finds them acceptable. For example, you might pledge as collateral some shares of General Motors and use the proceeds to buy a car, finance a marriage, or buy business inventory. In many cases there is no relation between the nature of the collateral and the use of loan proceeds.

We need not discuss the other types of bank loans to establish the fact that commercial banks lend to many types of borrowers, for widely varying lengths of time, on many bases, and for a wide variety of stated purposes.

U.S. GOVERNMENT OBLIGATIONS

For several years after World War II, these securities made up 40 percent or more of total commercial bank assets. Thereafter they declined steadily in importance, and by 1974 these securities amounted to only 6 percent of bank assets. In the last decade or so, however, U.S. government securities have regained a bit of their former importance and now account for about 12 percent of bank assets. As previously noted, owing both to the nature of the securities themselves and to the efficiency and cheapness of the market mechanism, these securities, and especially Treasury bills and other short-term issues, have been an important instrument for adjusting cash, liquidity, and portfolio positions. Banks would typically sell such securities when economic activity was on the upswing and loan demand was strong. They would buy some of these back when opportunities for making loans deteriorated in a downswing of the business cycle. While this general pattern still prevails, banks currently hold only a relatively small quantity of such obligations. In fact, even this limited quantity is not fully available for liquidity needs. This is because many of these potentially liquid securities are *pledged assets.* Pledged assets arise from the fact that banks are required to hold U.S. government (or high-quality municipal) bonds as collateral against deposits of federal, state, and local governments. Sales of pledged assets would entail loss of a corresponding quantity of deposits, hardly the way to solve liquidity problems.

OTHER SECURITIES

Among the other types of securities held by commercial banks, obligations of the states and their subdivisions are by far the largest. Some of these are acquired directly from their issuers, others in the open market. Their special attraction to banks is the exemption of their income from the federal income tax.

In summary, banks hold a wide variety of earning assets. Far from restricting themselves to short-term business loans, banks hold debt claims of widely varying maturities against other financial institutions, governments at all levels, consumers and others. Thus, they are involved in many branches of the markets for savings and financial claims and can bring about widespread effects as they expand or contract their credit.

OPEN-MARKET AND CUSTOMER RELATIONSHIPS

As a further step in explaining the behavior of bank portfolios, it will be useful to distinguish between customer loans and earning assets acquired and sold in the open market. Like most classifications, this one presents troublesome borderline cases, but it does highlight some motivations and market differences that strongly influence a banker's decisions relative to his or her portfolio.

The very term *customer* suggests a relationship that is usually of a continuing nature and that at least one of the parties involved would be reluctant to break. *Open market* suggests a quite different sort of relationship: impersonal, not necessarily continuing, and "open to all comers."

OPEN-MARKET ASSETS

The clearest examples of open-market relationships are those in which the bank that buys or sells a debt claim does not deal directly with the ultimate debtor. A bank may buy or sell, through a broker or dealer, U.S. government securities, state and municipal obligations, acceptances, open-market commercial paper, brokers' loans, and so on. In many cases the banker knows the debtor only by reputation, and the debtor does not know who holds the claims.

Open-market relationships usually have the following characteristics:

1 The bank decides whether to buy or sell a particular debt claim solely on the basis of the asset's attractiveness relative to other available open-market assets, and is not influenced by considerations concerning other possible relations with the debtor. For example, it does not assume that by purchasing a particular debt claim, it will attract deposits from the debtor.

2 The bank is not impelled to buy or is not constrained from selling a

particular debt claim by any feeling of "loyalty" or "responsibility" to the debtor.

3 The individual bank has no significant monopoly power in the open market as a whole, or even in the market for the particular type of debt claim. From the individual banker's point of view, conditions in the open market approach the "purely competitive." Each bank controls such a small part of the total demand that its own actions in buying or selling an open-market asset are assumed to have no significant effect on the price of the asset. Bankers assume that they can buy or sell as much of the asset as they wish at the going price.

This is not to say that conditions in the open market conform completely to those required for pure competition. But they come much closer than conditions in customer-loan markets.

CUSTOMER LOANS

Relations between a bank and its borrowing customers are quite different in several respects. For one thing, the lender-borrower relationship is intertwined with other bank-customer relationships. The customer usually holds checking deposits, and sometimes time deposits, at the bank, and may also be a customer of the trust or foreign exchange departments. Customers are made fully aware that the amount of loans they can get depends in part on the bank's experience with them as depositors. The lending bank also has ways of encouraging the customer to be a depositor. For example, it may require what are termed *compensating deposit* balances from its borrowers, and let them know that the availability of loans will depend on the amount of their deposits. Indeed, this relationship is often formalized in that a business may be required to hold a compensating deposit balance in order to obtain a *line of credit* under which, at the firm's initiative, it can borrow from the bank in the future.

Looked at from the other side, bankers are equally aware that the amount of deposits they can attract and retain, and therefore their lending power, depends in part on their reputation for taking care of the legitimate credit needs of customers, even in periods of tight credit. If the bank acquires a reputation of meeting all responsible loan demands, it will be able to attract and retain more deposits, and thus to lend more. But if it becomes known as niggardly in meeting customer's needs, it will be able to attract and retain only a smaller volume of deposits, and the bank's total lending power will shrink. This is important partly because of the limited degree of price competition among banks in a local market. Where price competition is restricted, nonprice competition comes to the fore. This takes many forms: reputation for soundness, convenience of location, decor, courtesy, and so on. Not the least of these is the bank's reliability as a loan source. The advertising slogan, "You have a friend at Chase Manhattan," referred to a loan officer, but it was not meant to be ignored by potential depositors.

There are many imperfections of competition in customer-loan markets, and each bank has some degree of monopoly power relative to its customers. The amount of this power depends on many things, including the nature of the customers. No bank may have much monopoly power relative to a huge corporation with a well-known credit rating that has access to banks all over the country and can easily secure funds by selling short- or long-term claims in the open market. In fact, a huge corporation can often dominate even a very large bank by threatening, in effect, "If you do not give us the money we need at a rate of interest as low as that charged your most-favored customer, we shall find it necessary to move our multimillions of deposits to banks that are more sympathetic." At the other extreme is the small firm that is virtually unknown to any bank other than its own and that could issue securities in the open market only at prohibitive cost. For such reasons, there are wide differences among customers' price elasticities of demand for loans at an individual bank. It is not surprising, therefore, that banks practice price discrimination.

To illustrate, let us consider the intermediate case of a small or medium-sized business firm that is a good credit risk but whose credit rating is not widely known. Such a firm finds it costly and inconvenient to shift its banking business to distant banks. To hold its deposits at distant banks is possible, but usually costly in time and convenience. To borrow at distant banks is even more costly because of the time and expense incurred by those banks in investigating its creditworthiness. Thus, there are strong forces tending to confine the firm's borrowing to banks in its own area. But as it surveys the local banking structure, the firm finds a situation of banking oligopoly (few sellers) of customer credit. There are only a few local banks, all charging about the same rate of interest, and afraid to compete aggressively for loans by lowering interest rates. Each bank knows that if it lowers its rates its competitors will soon do the same, so it will gain a differential advantage for no more than a short period.

If the firm tries to "shop around" at the various banks, it is likely to meet responses of this sort: "Why don't you borrow at your own bank, where you do your other banking business? They know you, understand your credit needs, and are in a position to take care of you. It isn't sound policy to change frequently from one bank to another. Of course, if you decide to switch banks and bring all your banking business here, we can talk about the loan. Our first obligation is to meet the borrowing needs of our own customers." Such imperfections of competition give each bank some degree of monopoly power over customers. But the attachment of customers to other banks works to the disadvantage of a given bank, for that bank finds it harder to attract the business of those customers.

For large corporate customers, the situation is somewhat different. As noted earlier, an individual bank has no monopoly power over large corporations that have access to banks nationwide and to securities markets. For many years, large corporations used securities markets for longer-term financing and relied on bank borrowing for short-term needs. In the second half of the 1960s this pattern was disturbed by the inability of the banks to meet all of the loan commitments of their large corporate customers. We have already encountered the reason for this—namely, the inability of the banks to roll over their CDs when the Federal Reserve refused to raise the interest rate ceiling on CDs in the credit crunches of 1966 and 1969. By 1969 large corporate borrowers responded, out of sheer necessity, by issuing commercial paper to raise short-term funds in the open market. If anything, once having had this experience, large corporations became even less dependent on the banks. As a result, banks found it necessary to keep the interest rate on loans to large customers in line with the rate on commerical paper. As we shall see, this required some changes in bank practices and created at least a few headaches for the banks.

As the discussion should make clear, other things being equal, a bank is strongly impelled to meet customers' loan demands rather than acquire open-market assets. But "other things," such as interest rates and degrees of safety and liquidity, may not be equal. For example, open-market assets may be safer, more liquid, or higher yielding. The bank's desire to make customer loans must therefore be balanced against its demand for safety, liquidity, and, in some cases, earnings. It should be emphasized, however, that what a bank considers to be an optimal portfolio composition in one set of circumstances may not be optimal under other circumstances. The optimum can be shifted by such things as changes in the banker's estimates of the amount of safety and liquidity needed, changes in customers' demands for loans, and changes in the level and structure of interest rates. Indeed, as we shall now see, the behavior of the interest rate on loans has undergone some important changes in recent years.

INTEREST RATES: LOAN MARKET AND OPEN MARKET

As we have seen in the case of the federal funds rate, like prices in most other highly competitive markets, interest rates in the open market change frequently and quickly in response to changes in supply-demand relations. They often change every day and even several times during a day. In contrast, rates on customer loans change less frequently and more slowly. Like other "administered prices," they often go unchanged for a considerable period, even though supply-demand relationships have clearly changed. In recent years the rate on customer loans has been somewhat more flexible than in the past. This is due to some institutional changes. However, let us first consider the situation as it prevailed through the early 1970s.

The basic rate on bank loans to business customers is called the *prime rate.* This is the rate charged to "prime" customers, usually very large customers with an unquestioned credit rating and a favorable competitive position. Rates to other customers range upward from the prime, those to customers who are almost prime being only a little higher, and so on.

Historically, the prime rate was changed infrequently. The most extreme illustration of this is provided by the fact that when, in December 1947, the prime rate was moved from 1½ percent to 1¾ percent (indeed, interest rates were once that low), this was the *first* change in the prime rate since its inception in 1933. Subsequent changes in the prime rate were, by this standard, considerably more frequent, although over the next two decades there were only 19 changes in the prime rate. Such changes were typically initiated by a very large bank, usually in New York City but sometimes in another major financial center, which assumed the role of price leadership.

For the most part, changes in the prime rate occurred only after considerable pressure for change had accumulated. For example, suppose bank lending power had increased markedly relative to the demand for loans. Instead of lowering the prime rate quickly, banks sought to expand their credit in other ways. For one thing, they increased their holdings of open-market paper. In the customer-loan market they became more generous in meeting loan requests, gave some nonprime customers rates closer to the prime rate, and so on. Only after a delay, when downward pressures had already lowered rates in the open market, did they lower the prime rate. Suppose, on the other hand, that the supply of credit had decreased relative to the demand for it and that this was reflected in rate increases in the open market. Here again banks often delayed in raising the prime rate, perhaps partly because each bank feared that if it raised the rate, other banks would not follow suit. For some time they would ration loans to customers not by raising the interest rate, but by scaling down loan requests and otherwise limiting the availability of credit. Only after pressures for rate increases had accumulated and open-market rates had already risen was the prime rate raised.

A number of recent developments have led to more frequent changes in the prime rate. One of these was an innovation, introduced in October 1971, called a *floating formula prime rate*. At that time one of the largest banks announced that in the future it would adjust its prime rate weekly, floating it ½ percent above the average yield on prime open-market commercial paper during the preceding week. A number of other banks quickly followed suit and also introduced a floating prime rate, although the specific formula varied from bank to bank. Part of the banks' motivation for a floating prime rate was undoubtedly to try to insulate themselves from the political criticism that often resulted from a change in the prime rate. In this respect the innovation was not fully successful, since in 1973, under a then-prevailing program of economic controls, the banks were forced to suspend the formulas and roll back some announced increases in the prime rate. While the controls program proved short-lived, the idea of a more flexible prime rate proved its staying power, although banks have not necessarily adhered to strict formulas.

Indeed, banks have gone further by making extensive use of *floating rate loans* or, as they are also called, *variable-rate loans*. A floating rate loan does not carry a fixed interest rate over its term to maturity. Rather, the interest rate charged the customer is adjusted periodically in some well-defined way. These adjustments may take place at regular intervals, or adjustments may be tied to changes in the prime rate.

Floating-rate loans were introduced by the banks as a way of protecting themselves against unexpected changes in the cost of bank funds. Especially with increased reliance on CDs and nondeposit liabilities, banks frequently made loans with a longer maturity than the source of the funds used to make the loan. For example, a 1-year loan might be initially financed by a 6-month CD. When this CD matured midway through the life of the loan, it would have to be reissued to continue to support the loan. This need to roll over the CD subjected the bank to a certain amount of risk, since when it made the loan it would not know exactly what its own cost of funds would be. A floating-rate loan allows the bank to avoid this risk. If the cost of funds to the bank rises, the loan rate can be adjusted. According to a recent Federal Reserve survey of commercial and industrial loans, about one-third of all short-term loans and roughly three-quarters of all long-term loans are of the floating-rate variety.

As the prime rate has become more flexible, it has also changed its meaning. As noted earlier, the prime rate has historically been the rate charged "prime" corporate customers, with other smaller and less favored customers charged more than the prime rate. These days, however, the major corporations often pay a *below-prime* rate. This permits the banks to be competitive for the loan business of major corporations that have the option of going directly to the commercial-paper market to raise funds. When a bank wishes to raise its loan rate to borrowers who do not have convenient borrowing alternatives, it can at the same time vary the discount from prime that it gives to large customers. That is, it can raise rates for some but not all customers. The net effect of this is that the banks are much better able to practice price discrimination among their customers. Needless to say, this has not made all customers happy (see box, p.165).

OVERVIEW

Over the last 35 years, bank asset portfolios have changed substantially, Figure 6–3 illustrates the banks' shares of major assets, as a fraction of total assets, for the period since 1950. The growth in the importance of loans and the decline in the shares of securities and cash assets are evident. By any traditional measure, bank assets have markedly declined in liquidity. To a very substantial extent, this has come about as banks have increasingly relied on the liability side of the ledger for their liquidity needs. Through liability management, the banks have gained a tool whereby they can make rapid adjustments in their portfolios, whether these adjustments are occasioned by deposit outflows or the need to satisfy bank loan customers.

164

PART 2 COMMERCIAL BANKS AND OTHER DEPOSITORY INSTITUTIONS

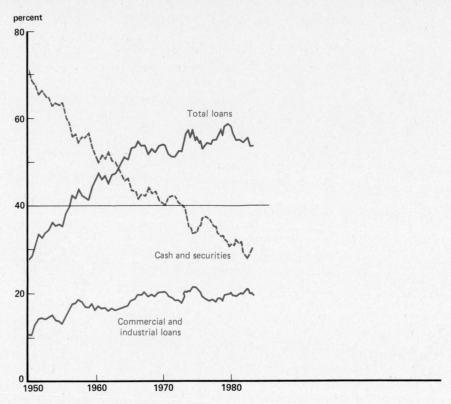

FIGURE 6–3
Holdings of various assets as a share of total
assets for commercial banks, 1950–1983.
(SOURCE: **Board of Governors of the Federal**
Reserve System, *1983 Historical Chart Book,*
Washington, D.C., p. 83.)

While changing bank portfolio practices are interesting in their own right, they also have important consequences for the conduct of monetary policy. For one, liability management has tended to cloud the precise meaning of money. (For example, should repurchase agreements, which are often demand deposits in disguise, be counted as money?) Indeed, for this and other reasons, it has been the case that bank liability management has tended to complicate the life of the Federal Reserve, especially when it wished to pursue a restrictive monetary policy. We return to this theme when we delve more deeply into issues of monetary policy.

SUMMARY

1 The basic accounting identity relevant for banks, or indeed any other finanical intermediary, is that assets equal liabilities plus net worth.

PRIME RATE SEMANTICS

When the prime rate was reserved for the best bank customers with access to alternative sources of funds, it used to be a joke that to get a loan at the prime rate, you had to prove that you didn't need it. The advent of below-prime lending has meant that the prime rate is no longer the lowest rate available to the most creditworthy corporate customers. While it is clear what it is not, it is less clear what the prime rate now actually is. Attempts by banks to define the concept have been singularly unsuccessful. For example, one bank has stated: "The prime rate is the rate of interest publicly announced from time to time by the bank as a standard for rates of interest to business loans." This sounds suspiciously like an unpoetic version of the prime is the prime is the prime. Indeed, one congressional committee has written: "Thanks to the actions of the banking industry, the prime has little meaning today, and it should be confined to the junkyard for abused banking terms."

Definitions aside, as it became more widely known that banks were offering discounts below prime, some customers who were not offered discounts were understandably miffed. Former congressman Henry Reuss compared the official prime rates to "falsies . . . that would shame the brassiere industry." Borrowers who had floating-rate loans tied to the official prime rate were particularly upset by "false" prime rates. One of the more offended borrowers, Jackie Kleiner, a professor of business, sued his bank for violating federal truth-in-lending laws. Somewhat indignantly he charged that "the banks artificially created the prime to make higher profits and then artificially discounted it. They aren't pillars of society—they're white-collar criminals in three-piece suits." Evidently there is nothing so wrathful as a borrower scorned.

The primary bank liabilities are demand deposits, savings deposits, and nondeposit funds such as federal funds, repurchase agreements, and Eurodollar borrowings. In the past twenty years, demand deposits have accounted for a declining fraction of total liabilities, while time deposits and nondeposit funds have increased in importance.

2 The three broad categories of bank assets are cash assets, loans, and securities. Loans include business loans, real estate loans, and consumer loans, while the securities held are primarily those issued by the U.S. government and by states and localities. Cash assets are largely determined by factors beyond a bank's control (e.g., reserve requirements). Cash assets have declined in relative importance in the past

twenty years, a development much to the liking of banks, since cash assets do not contribute to earnings. Holdings of U.S. government securites have also declined in importance, as banks have increased the fraction of their assets held as loans.

3 As with any financial intermediary, bank portfolio management must balance profitability or earnings with the conflicting considerations of safety and liquidity. Banks need liquidity to cope with withdrawals of deposits, but liquid assets typically yield less interest than illiquid ones.

4 Banks traditionally met their liquidity needs by keeping a pool of liquid assets such as U.S. government securities. Some twenty years ago, banks discovered liability management as a way of coping with liquidity needs, and it remains an important component of current bank portfolio strategies.

SELECTED READINGS

Bowsher, N. N. "Repurchase Agreements," *Review*, Federal Reserve Bank of St. Louis, September 1979, pp. 17–22.

Havrilesky, T. M., and J. T. Boorman. *Current Perspectives in Banking*. Arlington Heights, IL: AHM, 1976.

Mason, J. M. *Financial Management of Commercial Banks*. Boston: Warren, Gorham, and Lamont, 1979.

Mayer, M. *The Bankers*. New York: Ballantine Books, 1976.

Nadler, P. S. *Commercial Banking in the Economy*, 3rd ed. New York: Random House, 1979.

7

THRIFT INSTITUTIONS

The preceding chapter examined the largest depository financial intermediary—the commercial bank. As the modifier "commercial" implies, such institutions play an important role in financing business activity. This chapter considers saving and loan associations, mutual savings banks, and credit unions—depository institutions of particular importance to households. Indeed, these financial intermediaries, collectively known as *thrift institutions*, or just *thrifts*, were historically the first to offer households the opportunity to invest their savings and earn interest; they also pioneered in offering credit to households.

As emphasized before, these days the thrifts and the commercial banks show many similarities. Not the least of these is that both thrifts and banks offer transactions accounts which serve as the major component of the money supply. The similarities of banks and thrifts are, however, of relatively recent origin. For many years, the thrifts were quite specialized institutions. Saving and loan associations (S&Ls), for example, essentially offered only savings deposits and mortgage loans. They were hardly department stores of finance. This specialization began in a natural way, but its continuation was mandated by governmental policy, motivated by a desire to provide a reliable source of financing for home ownership.

By the late 1960s, however, enforced specialization was proving to be something of a problem, as savings and loan associations and mutual savings banks (MSBs) faced increased difficulties in coping with rising interest rates. S&Ls and MSBs were hampered by the limited diversification permitted in their assets and liabilities, and by the fact that they financed long-term assets, primarily mortgages, with short-term liabilities. This meant that the interest rate they received on assets could be below the rate they had to pay to attract funds, creating the possibilities of financial losses. One governmental response to these difficulties was to use interest rate ceilings in an attempt to "protect" the thrifts. As we shall see, these ceilings created other problems. Indeed, it was the innovations of thrift institutions, coupled with a major boost from the so-called money market mutual funds, that ultimately led in the 1980s to legislation removing interest ceilings and providing new asset and liability powers for the thrifts. It is these recent changes that make it important to study the nature of the thrift institutions if we are to understand the workings of monetary policy.

In this chapter, we first trace the origins of the historically specialized nature of the thrift institutions. We then examine the regulatory structure of the thrifts and take a look at their balance sheets. We next document the plight of the thrifts after the mid-1960s and follow their evolution in the 1970s. This evolution provides a vivid illustration of the extent to which financial innovation by the private sector can force the hand of the government to restructure the financial system. This restructuring was accomplished by two major pieces of legislation, the Depository Institutions Deregulation Act of 1980 and the Garn–St. Germain Depository Institutions Act of 1982. These acts have already had a profound impact on the shape of the financial system and will have further effects in the years to come.

A BRIEF OVERVIEW

The thrift institutions originated in the early part of the nineteenth century, and developed in response to the fact that commercial banks did not provide ordinary households with loans or deposit facilities. A first response to this gap was the establishment of mutual savings banks in 1816 in several eastern cities. MSBs were set up by wealthy individuals to encourage "thrift" by providing an attractive investment opportunity to houholds in the form of an interest-bearing deposit account. One of the first MSBs was sponsored by the Society for the Prevention of Pauperism in the City of New York. MSBs primarily invested in market securities and the earnings on these, after expenses, accrued to the depositors who mutually owned the institutions. While the MSBs did make some loans to their depositors, this was not their major function. As a consequence, the borrowing needs of most households were left unsatisfied.

To remedy this remaining gap, in the 1830s groups of households banded together to form building and loan associations—or, as they later came to be known, savings and loan associations. These were cooperative institutions in which households pooled their savings and lent to each other to finance the purchase of homes. Interest earnings on these mortgage loans permitted these institutions, like MSBs, to offer an interest-bearing deposit account. The popularity of S&Ls spread, and over time they expanded the scope of their operations by lending to households that were not depositors. A new form of S&L also developed, a stock association that was a corporation owned by equity holders. This was in contrast to the mutual S&L, which was owned by its depositors.

The establishment and growth of MSBs and S&Ls provided households a way to earn a return on their savings and a source of home finance, but throughout the nineteenth century other forms of consumer loans were not easy to come by. Credit unions, which first appeared on the scene after the turn of this century, were a direct response to these needs. Like the original building and loan associations, credit unions (CUs) were cooperative associations in which individuals pooled savings to make loans to members. These loans were typically unsecured by property and essentially relied on the promise of the borrower to repay. To minimize difficulties in this regard, membership in a credit union was generally restricted to individuals with a common affiliation, such as employment or membership in a social, fraternal, or religious organization. The requirement of common affiliation persists to this day, with most credit unions being based on common employment.

As should be apparent from this brief history of thrift institutions, the specialized nature of the thrifts and their importance to households evolved quite naturally. Later developments have changed matters in two important ways. First, other financial intermediaries have increasingly competed to attract household deposits and to make loans to consumers. For example, commercial banks are now major lenders to households, both for home finance and more generally. Second, the thrift institutions, especially with the legislative reforms of the last few years, have sought to become less specialized. While they have accomplished this to some degree, their specialized origin is still very much in evidence in their balance sheets. Before discussing these balance sheets, we need to take a brief look at the regulatory structure of the thrift institutions.

REGULATION OF THE THRIFTS

Until the 1930s, MSBs, S&Ls, and CUs were chartered and regulated exclusively by the states. The federal government got into the act after the financial crisis of the early 1930s. As we have seen, that period was marked by the failure of nearly 8,000 commercial banks and spawned much of our current regulatory framework. Compared to the commercial banks, the experience of the thrifts in the 1930s was more mixed. In particular, while S&Ls closed their doors at about the same rate as commercial banks, MSBs experienced only a modest number of failures. It was the S&L experience that prompted new legislation.

The federal regulation of S&Ls dates from 1933, when Congress passed legislation providing deposit insurance coverage, allowing for federal chartering of S&Ls, and establishing the Federal Home Loan Bank System. Loosely modeled after the Federal Reserve System, the new system has 12 regional banks coordinated by a central authority in Washington, D.C., known as the Federal Home Loan Bank Board (FHLBB). The Federal Home Loan Bank System has several functions. First, it stands ready to lend funds to S&Ls experiencing liquidity problems. Second, via the FHLBB, it charters and regulates federally chartered S&Ls. Third, through a subsidiary known as the Federal Savings and Loan Insurance Corporation (FSLIC), it provides deposit insurance. Insurance is mandatory for federal S&Ls; state associations may apply for the insurance. Overall, nearly 90 percent of all S&Ls, accounting for about 98 percent of all S&L assets, are insured by the FSLIC.

Although also affected by the reforms of the 1930s, mutual savings banks and credit unions were treated with less completeness. MSBs were permitted to obtain deposit insurance through the FDIC. They were also entitled to join the Federal Reserve System, but not many took advantage of this option. It was not, however, until 1978 that MSBs were eligible for federal charters. Not surprisingly, even today MSBs are almost completely regulated by state authorities, primarily by the states of Connecticut, Massachusetts, and New York, where three-quarters of the MSBs are located.

Credit unions received the most perfunctory treatment of all the thrifts in the reforms of the 1930s. Most significant, they were not made eligible for any federal deposit insurance. And while they did become eligible for federal chartering in 1934, the administration of the chartering was left in the unlikely hands of the Farm Credit Administration. This regulatory authority was subsequently passed around a bit, even resting for a time with the Social Security Administration. Beginning in 1970, however, credit unions began receiving more serious attention. In that year, they received a "proper" independent regulatory agency, the National Credit Union Administration, and CUs also became eligible for federal deposit insurance.

BALANCE SHEETS OF THE THRIFTS

As noted earlier, despite recent developments, the balance sheets of the thrifts still reflect their historical origins. This is particularly evident on the asset side, where mortgages figure so prominently, but it is also reflected in the nature of their liabilities.

SAVINGS AND LOAN ASSOCIATIONS

As of 1984, there were about 3,400 S&Ls, which in the aggregate had assets of nearly $1,000 billion. This made the S&Ls the second largest financial intermediary after the commerical banks. S&Ls achieved this position by growing quite rapidly throughout most of the post-World War II era. The aggregate balance sheet for all S&Ls, given in Table 7–1, reveals that mortgages are the dominant asset, accounting for over 60 percent of all assets. This reflects both the tradition of S&Ls and the reinforcement of this tradition by government policy aimed at promoting housing. Such policies include restrictions on permissible S&L assets and tax incentives designed to induce S&Ls to make mortgages available to households. As mentioned above, in recent years S&Ls have had somewhat more leeway in choosing assets, and they have used this modest freedom to reduce the fraction of their assets held in mortgages. As recently as 1979, S&Ls held over 80 percent of their assets in mortgages, although the percentages had dropped to 61 percent by 1984. The remainder of S&L assets are held in a small number of alternative ways. Cash and securities, largely issued by the U.S. government, account for 18 percent of assets, while construction loans and a limited volume of consumer and business loans make up the remaining 21 percent of total assets.

On the liability side, time and savings deposits make up the bulk, amounting to some 77 percent of total assets. As with commercial banks, the composition of time and savings accounts has changed markedly in the last few years. The traditional liability of S&Ls, the passbook savings deposit, has declined dramatically in importance, currently accounting for less than 10 percent of total assets. Other types of deposit accounts have become much more consequential, with the money market deposit account, which only came into existence at the end of 1982, making up roughly 20 percent of total assets. NOW and super-NOW accounts are also a growing source of deposit funds. Borrowed funds constitute the major nondeposit liability available to S&Ls, and this mainly consists of advances lent by the Federal Home Loan banks. As with commercial banks, only a small part of total assets is supported by net worth.

TABLE 7–1 Savings and Loan Balance Sheet, Year-End 1984 (in billions of dollars)

ASSETS		LIABILITIES AND NET WORTH	
Cash	10.6	Checkable deposits	24.7
U.S. securities	170.7	Small time and savings deposits	640.4
Mortgages	606.3	Large time deposits	131.0
Consumer credit	43.7	Federal funds and security RPs	45.5
Other assets	158.6	Other borrowed funds	90.3
Total	989.9	Miscellaneous	34.4
		Total liabilities	966.3
		Net worth	23.6
		Total	989.9

MUTUAL SAVINGS BANKS

In many respects, mutual savings banks are similar to mutual savings and loan associations. They largely obtain funds from the same type of sources and primarily invest in mortgages. As we have seen, this affinity for mortgages was not part of the early MSB tradition; it was fostered by government policy, largely via tax incentives. As of 1984, there were roughly 500 MSBs, and these institutions had over $200 billion in assets. In contrast to S&Ls, mutual savings banks have grown much more slowly during the postwar period. Indeed, in 1946 MSB assets were nearly twice those of S&Ls, whereas currently MSB assets are about one-quarter those of S&Ls. This declining importance reflects the fact that MSBs are located principally in areas of the country that have experienced below-average population and income growth in the postwar period.

The balance sheet for MSBs, given in Table 7–2, shows that 50 percent of total assets are held in mortgages, somewhat lower than the corresponding percentage for S&Ls. The remainder of the MSB asset portfolio is more diversified than that of S&Ls. In view of the historical emphasis on investing in marketable securities, this is perhaps to be expected. More particularly, in 1984 MSBs held 10 percent of their assets in corporate and foreign securities, which include commercial paper, corporate stocks, and corporate bonds. They also hold both short- and long-term government securities and make consumer and construction loans. On the liability side, we see that nearly 90 percent of assets are supported by deposits of one sort or another. This is somewhat higher than the percentage for S&Ls, reflecting the fact that MSBs do not have access to a ready source of government loans. As with S&Ls, however, the composition of deposits has moved away from conventional passbook savings toward certificates and money market deposit accounts.

CREDIT UNIONS

Although they are the most numerous of the thrifts, numbering over 20,000 institutions, aggregate assets of credit unions amounted to $115 billion in 1984, making them of far less importance than S&Ls or MSBs. While they are the smallest depository institution, they have also been the fastest growing since 1971. Table 7–3 contains a recent balance sheet. As noted earlier, credit unions played a key role in originating consumer credit in the United States, and the 59 percent of their assets devoted to member loans still reflects this emphasis. A few short years go, however, this proportion stood at about 80 percent. The marked decline in recent years in part reflects the more attractive returns available to CUs on money market investments. Recent legislation has extended the ability of CUs to make mortgage loans, but this has thus far not had a big impact on their asset portfolios.

TABLE 7–2 Mutual Savings Banks, Balance Sheet, Year-End 1984 (in billions of dollars)

ASSETS		LIABILITIES AND NET WORTH	
Cash	4.6	Checkable deposits	10.0
U.S. securities	34.3	Small time and savings	
Corporate and foreign bonds	21.0	deposits	153.9
Mortgages	103.3	Large time deposits	17.8
Consumer credit	11.3	Miscellaneous	13.4
Other assets	31.9	Total Liabilities	195.1
Total	206.4	Net worth	11.3
		Total	206.4

On the liability side, deposits account for over 90 percent of all assets. As with other depository institutions, recent developments have altered the composition of deposits. As a result, regular share accounts, the credit union equivalent of passbook savings accounts, amounted to less than half of all deposits. Money market accounts, certificates, and share drafts account for the rest. *Share drafts*, which are like interest-bearing checking accounts, were permanently authorized by Congress in 1980. Since share drafts are a form of transactions account, they are included in the official definition of the money supply.[1] These accounts, in conjunction with the NOW accounts offered by S&Ls and MSBs, remind us why it is necessary to study the nature of thrift institutions if we are to understand what lies behind the money supply. The reason is that the thrift institutions have increasingly come to play an important role in the provision of checkable transactions accounts. This is, of course, a relatively recent development.

---

[1]Unlike NOW accounts, which still have an interest ceiling, by virtue of 1982 legislation to be discussed below, share drafts are unconstrained by interest ceilings. This same legislation exempted the first $2 million of transactions deposits from reserve requirements. This was of particular benefit to credit unions, since in 1982 some 95 percent had less than $2 million in checkable deposits. These institutions thus escaped reserve requirements initially imposed by the Monetary Control Act of 1980.

TABLE 7–3 Credit Unions Balance Sheet, Year-End 1984 (in billions of dollars)

ASSETS		LIABILITIES AND NET WORTH	
Cash	1.6	Deposit accounts	108.0
U.S. securities	27.5	Net worth	7.8
Mortgages	6.6	Total	115.8
Consumer credit	67.9		
Other assets	12.2		
Total	115.8		

How the thrifts acquired the legal right to become more like commercial banks is an interesting tale that is quite instructive in the ability of the financial sector to circumvent constraining laws and regulations.

RESTRUCTURING OF THE THRIFTS: THE ORIGIN OF THE PROBLEMS

With the end of World War II, thrift institutions began an era of remarkable growth. Aided by the increasing demand for home ownership, the so-called American dream, and the associated demand for mortgages to finance home purchases, from 1946 to 1965 the total assets of thrift institutions grew at a rate of 10½ percent per year. In contrast, the growth rate of commercial banks was a distinctly more modest 5 percent per year. As a result of their more rapid growth, the thrifts went from being one-fifth the size of the commercial banks in 1946 to three-fifths in 1965. Not surprisingly, the commercial banks noticed the striking success of the upstart thrifts, and over this period there was increasing competition between thrift institutions and commercial banks.

Competition between thrifts and banks took place on both the asset and liability side of the balance sheet. While thrift institutions had led the way in lending to households, both via mortgages and other forms of consumer credit, commercial banks increasingly moved into these markets as the profitability of doing so became evident. At the same time, commercial banks began to compete actively with the thrifts in attracting household savings and time deposit accounts. The banks were somewhat hampered in this regard by interest rate ceilings that limited the rates they were permitted to pay on these deposits. At the time, the thrift institutions were not subject to interest ceilings and were frequently able to offer more attractive rates than banks. Needless to say, banks complained, and in 1957 the ceiling rates were raised for the first time since the 1930s. As interest rates gradually continued to rise, regulators found it necessary to make additional upward adjustments. However, in 1966 economic developments added a new and worrisome element to the picture.

THE ERA OF DISINTERMEDIATION

In 1966 the economy was experiencing inflationary pressures as rising defense spending for the Vietnam war was superimposed on an economy already at or near full utilization of its resources. In the face of this, the Federal Reserve was pursuing a restricture monetary policy, and market rates of interest began rising rapidly. It was these rate increases that had policymakers particularly worried about thrift institutions and their continued ability to finance housing expenditures.

To understand this concern, we need to recall that the thrifts have tended to have what might be called a "maturity mismatch" in their assets and liabilities. That is, they tended to borrow short-term funds and lend long-term ones. More particularly, in 1966 their primary sources of funds were time deposits of short maturity and savings deposits whose maturity was set by the whim of the depositor and could be withdrawn at any time. On the other hand, the bulk of the thrifts' assets were tied up in long-term mortgages on which the rate of interest was fixed. As interest rates rose, the earnings of thrifts changed only slowly. Hence, it was argued, the thrifts would not be able to "afford" to pay higher interest rates on time and savings deposits. But the thrifts themselves feared that "overly vigorous" competition would force them to pay depositors higher rates. It was at this juncture that the policymakers stepped in.

Congress, to protect the thrifts from "ruinous competition," passed legislation giving the Federal Home Loan Bank Board the power to set interest rate ceilings for S&Ls and the FDIC authority to set ceilings for MSBs.[2] The legislation also called for consultation between the various regulators to coordinate the ceilings on S&Ls, MSBs, and commercial banks. As a result, two changes were introduced. First, ceiling rates at commercial banks were *lowered* from 5½ to 5 percent in an effort to make it easier for the thrifts to attract funds. Second, the new ceiling rates for thrifts were generally set ¼ percent higher than those for commercial banks. This ¼ percent *differential* was deemed necessary for the thrifts to compete with the banks. Commercial banks, it was argued, also offered checking accounts and had a natural competitiveness advantage in attracting time and savings deposits since, other things being equal, the public would prefer the convenience of one-stop banking. It was to overcome this advantage that the differential ceiling was conceived.

Overall, it was hoped that these various actions would make it easier and cheaper for the thrifts to attract funds, thereby assuring a continued flow of funds into housing finance. So much for intentions; what actually happened is another matter. A steady flow of funds into S&Ls and MSBs was not achieved. The source of the problem is shown in Figure 7–1, which shows the pattern over time of two of the ceiling rates at S&Ls, the ceiling on passbook savings and the ceiling on time deposits with maturities of 2½ to 4 years. Also plotted in Figure 7–1 is the interest rate on 3-month Treasury bills, which can be viewed as a proxy for short-term market rates of interest in general.

As shown in Figure 7–1, in 1966, again in 1969, and still again in the mid-1970s, there were extended episodes in which market rates of interest exceeded ceiling rates. What resulted is the phenomenon that has been dubbed *disintermediation*. That is, as market rates on such instruments as Treasury bills and commercial paper rose to a point at which they substantially

[2]Given the general tendency to ignore credit unions, they were not subject to ceilings at this time. As we shall see, this is one instance in which the credit unions were delighted to be ignored.

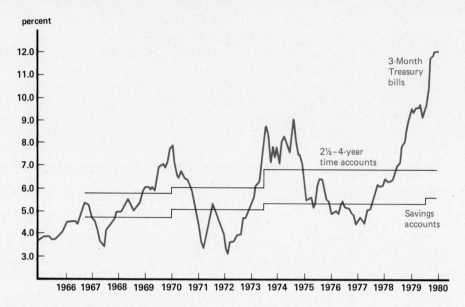

FIGURE 7.1
Ceiling rates at thrift institutions versus the
Treasury bill rate.

exceeded interest rate ceilings, depositors transferred funds out of demand, time, and savings accounts to these higher-yielding instruments. In some time periods, this produced an actual decline in deposits at commercial banks and thrift institutions; in others, deposits grew at an extremely slow rate. This process of disintermediation seriously disrupted the flow of funds to consumer and mortgage credit and put banks and thrift institutions in a rather precarious position. This undoubtedly gave the Federal Reserve pause in its pursuit of tighter monetary conditions, and in several instances may well have led to a premature easing of monetary policy. Following these experiences, the Federal Reserve itself became disillusioned with ceilings.

Overall, after several bouts of disintermediation, it became apparent that interest rate ceilings created more problems than they solved. To be sure, the ceilings limited the competition among thrift institutions and between the thrifts and the banks, but they did not insulate the thrifts from competition from money market instruments. When disintermediation took place, the volume of funds available for mortgage lending was restricted and the construction of new homes fell off sharply. Interest rate ceilings, therefore, did not accomplish the basic aim of insulating the housing market. At the same time, critics pointed out that ceilings were having other undesirable effects, bolstering their case with the following points:

1 Ceilings impair the efficiency of the financial system by inhibiting the

growth of the most efficient financial institutions and practices. That is, ceilings do not permit efficient institutions to pay a higher rate of interest to attract funds, which is precisely what would happen in a competitive environment.[3]

2 Ceilings tend to discriminate against small savers who lack information or whose limited supply of funds does not permit them to purchase higher-yielding assets.

SOME PRELIMINARY STEPS

After the imposition of interest ceilings on the thrifts, the phenomenon of disintermediation led to growing dissatisfaction with the existing financial structure and with the plight of the housing market. Two different sorts of approaches were followed to deal with these difficulties.

MORTGAGE MARKET SUPPORT

One approach used a variety of federal programs to attempt to shore up the housing and mortgage markets. Such programs, in one form or another, dated from the 1930s, but they expanded substantially after the mid-1960s. The programs were carried out by such agencies as Fannie Mae (the Federal National Mortgage Association), Ginnie Mae (the Government National Mortgage Association), and Freddie Mac (the Federal Home Loan Mortgage Corporation). One aspect of Fannie Mae and Freddie Mac activities increased the liquidity of mortgages by establishing and supporting a market for buying and selling mortgages. It was hoped this would enhance the willingness of the thrifts and banks to make mortgage loans. Ginnie Mae, which also bought and sold certain types of mortgages, was authorized to provide a direct subsidy to the mortgage market. It did this by buying mortgages at par, even though rising interest rates had lowered the market value of the mortgage. (Recall from Chapter 4 that a rise in the interest rate lowers the value of an existing security). Sellers of certain types of mortgages—more specifically those to lower-income families—thus received more for the mortgage than it was worth.

By virtue of this subsidy, it was expected that lenders would be more willing to make such mortgages in the first place. Other subsidy programs and direct loans to S&Ls by the Federal Home Loan banks also provided additional support for the mortgage market. Overall, these institutions with the funny names have become an increasingly important force in the mort-

---

[3]In response to ceilings on time and savings deposits and the prohibition of interest on demand deposits, financial institutions tend to offer free gifts (e.g., toasters, TVs, and the like) and provide services to customers below cost. This compensates depositors with *implicit interest*, but it still involves a waste of resources. Both depositors and financial institutions would be better served by a system in which competition could take the form of *explicit interest*.

gage market since the mid-1960s, undoubtedly contributing some stability to the market, although the exact quantitative nature of this contribution is open to some dispute.

REFORM PROPOSALS

A second approach to the widespread dissatisfaction with the structural defects of the financial system was to reform the system. In 1970 a presidential commission was formed to study the issue, and in its 1971 report strongly advocated establishing a financial system in which competitive forces were allowed a much freer rein. Among its findings, the commission recommended the gradual removal of interest rate ceilings and the provision for checkable transactions deposits by thrift institutions. It also recommended that thrift institutions should have a wider menu of asset choice and that restrictions on entry into banking and other financial services should be reduced.[4]

One basic aim of these proposals was to improve the lot of the thrifts by requiring banks, thrifts, and other institutions to compete on an equal basis. While this idea seems straightforward enough today, attempts in 1973 and 1975 to implement these recommendations into law were unsuccessful. The reasons for this result are speculative, but several plausible hypotheses have been offered. For one, given the comprehensive nature of the proposed reforms, each constituency in the financial community found something to be unhappy about and registered opposition. Compromise in such situations, especially in the absence of a real crisis, is difficult to achieve. The fact that we had a small and growing crisis proved insufficient to spur action.

A second reason for legislative inaction is that many individuals, including politicians, were basically distrustful of financial institutions and how they would behave in a freer competitive environment. They are much more comfortable with interest rate ceilings and the use of tax incentives to shape flows of funds. Related to this view is the populist notion that high interest rates are somehow sinful. Indeed, public figures have frequently championed usury ceilings as a way of defending the poor little consumer from big bad financial lenders. In so doing, they seem willing to ignore the fact that when usury ceilings are binding, there tends to be a shortage of funds relative to demand so that many borrowers come away empty-handed. In any event, it should be clear that many individuals are skeptical of freely determined interest rates, be they on deposits or loans.

Whatever the reasons, the fact remains that, despite reasonably widespread agreement as to need, no comprehensive reform of the financial system emerged in the 1970s. This is not to suggest that important changes

---

[4]The report of the so-called Hunt Commission (named after its chairman) was more comprehensive in scope than these recommendations imply. See *Report of the President's Commission on Financial Structure and Regulation*, Washington, D.C., U.S. Government Printing Office, 1971.

did not occur, for in many ways the character of the financial system was dramatically altered by events of the 1970s. Indeed, it was precisely these events and the crisis they created that led to the passage of the Depository Institutions Deregulation Act of 1980. Thus, rather than coming about in an orderly fashion, it was with kicking and screaming and fits and starts that we gradually groped our way toward a world not unlike that envisaged by the would-be financial reformers in 1970. The events and players in this continuing saga are spelled out in the next section.

FINANCIAL INNOVATION AND REGULATORY CHANGE

Financial reformers, as we have seen, have advocated the following actions: (1) removal of ceiling interest rates on time and savings deposits; and (2) extension of checking-like accounts to thrift institutions. Developments in the 1970s have produced progress on each of these fronts. In many respects, the events that unfolded resembled a soap opera. The major characters, at least as innovators, were the private financial institutions themselves, with an occasional assist from the regulatory authorities and some state legislatures. The courts too had a role to play, although as we shall see, they both helped and hindered progress. The final actor—Congress—had only a cameo role in the 1970s, in which, to a large extent, it grudgingly reacted to events. With the passage of the Deregulation Act of 1980, however, Congress abandoned its bit part and jumped to center stage. This section focuses on events leading up to the 1980 act; the act itself is examined in the next section.

As already noted, there was a certain theatrical quality to the evolution of the financial system in the 1970s. In any drama there are a number of "forces" that move the participants. Lust, power, greed, and progress often rank high on such a list. In the present context, greed is replaced by the more genteel-sounding profit motive, which, as interest rates rose, provided incentives to find ways to evade the shackles imposed by interest rate ceilings. Furthermore, the thrifts, in order to gain a more equal footing vis-à-vis the commercial banks, sought ways to improve their competitive position. In so doing, they were abetted by the force of progress, represented here by computer-related technological advances. Overall, as we shall see, these various forces have produced much drama,[5] but the final scene is still in the process of unfolding.

We turn now to the events themselves. A relatively complete chronological list of the major changes in the evolution of the financial structure in the 1970s is given in Table 7–4. It will, however, lead to a more instructive

---

[5]The alert reader will have noted that we provided no analogies for the forces of lust and power. In the interests of decency, these are left to the imagination.

TABLE 7–4 Selected Innovations and Regulatory Changes, 1970–1980

Date	Change
June 1970	Regulation Q ceilings on time deposits of $100,000 or more with maturities of 30–89 days are suspended.
September 1970	Federally chartered savings and loan associations are permitted to make preauthorized nonnegotiable transfers from savings accounts for household-related expenditures.
June 1972	State-chartered mutual savings banks in Massachusetts, led by the Consumer's Savings Bank of Worcester, begin offering NOW accounts.
May 1973	Regulation Q ceilings on time deposits of $100,000 or more with maturities exceeding 90 days are suspended.
January 1974	All depository institutions in Massachusetts and New Hampshire are authorized by Congress to offer NOW accounts. Accounts similar to NOWs but non-interest-bearing (NINOWs) are offered by state-chartered thrifts in additional states throughout the year.
January 1974	Under new authorization, the First Federal Savings and Loan of Lincoln, Nebraska, places electronic terminals in two Hinky Dinky supermarkets, allowing its customers to pay for groceries and make deposits to or withdrawals from their savings accounts.
Early 1974	Money market mutual funds come into existence on a large-scale basis.
August 1974	Under an experimental program selected federal credit unions are permitted to issue credit union share drafts, which are check-like instruments payable through a commercial bank.
November 1974	Commercial banks are permitted to offer savings accounts to state and local government units.
April 1975	Member banks are authorized by the Federal Reserve to make transfers from a customer's savings account to a demand deposit account upon a telephone order from the customer.
April 1975	The 1970 action is broadened to allow savings and loan associations to make preauthorized third-party nonnegotiable transfers from savings accounts for any purpose. This authority is extended to commercial banks in September 1975.
November 1975	Commercial banks are authorized to offer savings accounts to business.
February 1976	Congress extends NOW accounts to all New England states.
May 1976	New York permits checking accounts at state-chartered mutual savings banks and savings and loans.
June 1978	Six-month money market certificates (MMCs) are introduced at banks and thrifts. The ceiling rate on these fluctuates weekly and is tied to the 6-month Treasury bill rate.

TABLE 7–4 (*continued*)

Date	Change
October 1978	Congress extends NOW account authority to New York State.
November 1978	Commercial banks and mutual savings banks are authorized to offer automatic transfers (ATS) from a savings account to a checking account or other type of transaction account.
April 1979	U.S. Court of Appeals rules that share drafts, ATS, and remote-service computer terminals are illegal and must be discontinued by January 1, 1980, unless Congress acts to legalize them.
July 1979	A floating ceiling for time deposits at banks and thrifts with a maturity of four years or more is established.
December 1979	Unable to cope in time with the Court ruling, Congress temporarily extends authority for ATS and share drafts to March 31, 1980. It also extends NOW accounts to New Jersey.
January 1980	The floating ceiling is extended to time deposits with a maturity of 2½ years or more.

discussion if we group these events topically. We begin with developments related to interest rate ceilings.

CEILINGS ON TIME AND SAVINGS DEPOSITS

As noted earlier, after two bouts of disintermediation (in 1966 and 1969) the Federal Reserve became somewhat disenchanted with certain aspects of the ceilings. In both these periods the ceilings had applied to large ($100,000 or more) negotiable certificates of deposit (CDs), and as market rates exceeded the ceiling rate, outstanding CDs had declined. Banks, having embraced the strategy of liability management, had scrambled to raise lendable funds in the Eurodollar and commerical-paper markets. In June 1970 the Federal Reserve grew tired of this cat-and-mouse game and lifted the ceilings on large CDs with maturities of 30–89 days.

A glance at Figure 7–1 suggests that the next potential period of disintermediation was 1973–1974, as market interest rates again rose above ceiling rates. However, several events helped to moderate disintermediation during this period. For one, in May 1973 the Federal Reserve removed the remaining ceilings on large CDs so that commercial banks, at least, had much greater flexibility than they had had in 1966 or 1969. Furthermore, from July until November 1973 ceiling rates were suspended on time deposits of $1,000 or more with maturities of at least four years. These so-called wild-card deposits were available at both commercial banks and thrift institutions. As a result of these actions, time and savings deposits at commercial banks maintained their rapid growth during 1973–1974. The thrift institutions suffered some disintermediation, but this took the form of slower growth in time and savings deposits rather than an absolute decline in these deposits. Overall, then, disintermediation was relatively mild during this period.

With the withdrawal of the wild-card deposits, the thrifts lost a degree of flexibility that they were not to regain until 1978. In addition, individual savers lost the chance for a competitive rate of interest on time deposits. As Figure 7–1 shows, for a roughly three-year period beginning in 1975, the pattern of interest rates created little pressure for disintermediation. In the absence of a crisis, there was no major development pertaining to ceilings during this period. In the beginning of 1978, market interest rates began to diverge steadily from ceiling interest rates. Deposit growth at thrift institutions slowed in early 1978 and authorities, fearing a new and serious bout of disintermediation, felt compelled by the potential crisis to once again take action. In so doing, they were partly motivated by a relatively new player on the financial scene, the money market mutual fund. Since these funds figure prominently in the financial picture from the late 1970s until the early 1980s, it is appropriate to interrupt our chronology and say a word about them.

MONEY MARKET MUTUAL FUNDS

One of the most interesting and significant financial developments in recent years has been the emergence and phenomenal growth of money market mutual funds. Money market funds first emerged in 1971, at a time when interest ceilings on time and savings deposits were very much in evidence. Indeed, money market funds originated solely for the purpose of circumventing these ceilings. The basic idea was that if existing institutions such as thrifts and banks were constrained by ceilings, then why not invent a new institution that would be free from these constraints?

A money market mutual fund operates by issuing shares to the public and, in turn, investing these funds in so-called *money market instruments.* That is, they generally invest in short-term financial instruments that are issued in large denominations, such as Treasury bills, CDs, commercial paper, and bankers acceptances. Shareholders usually invest much smaller amounts, although there are minimum initial investments, which typically have ranged from $500 to $10,000. Most funds calculate and pay dividends on a daily basis, and shares can be redeemed at any time by wire transfer or check. The check feature is of particular significance and works roughly as follows. The fund, after making arrangements with a commercial bank, provides the shareholder with a book of checks. These can be used to make ordinary payments, although a minimum check size, such as $500, is often specified. When the check clears, the shareholder's account is reduced by the amount of the check, thus allowing the shareholder to earn interest on transactions balances.

As should be apparent from this discussion, shares in money market funds provide a highly liquid asset that, because management fees and transactions costs are kept relatively low, yield a virtual market rate of return as well. In essence, the money market funds purchased large CDs and other money market instruments that were too expensive to be purchased by a small saver and "sold" pieces of these instruments to these small savers. This was clearly a bit of clever financial intermediation.

Despite the obvious virtues of the idea, money market mutual funds remained insignificant until early 1974. Then, when interest rates began their upward march, the money market funds experienced their first period of substantial growth, expanding more than twentyfold as total assets grew from under $200 million to about $4 billion in early 1975. Growth would undoubtedly have been even faster, but the funds were restrained by regulations preventing aggressive advertising. Moreover, since money market shares, unlike deposits at thrift institutions and banks, are uninsured, households initially regarded the funds as a risky proposition. However, as the workings of the money market funds came to be understood by the public, it became more apparent that the risk was low. The reason, of course, is that these funds purchase short-term, high-quality financial instruments with little risk of default. Indeed, some funds purchase only U.S. government securities so that there is no default risk.

With the growing realization that the money market funds had relatively low risk, the public was undoubtedly more willing to hold money market shares. However, after their initial growth spurt, over the next several years interest rates moderated and the money funds did not grow any more. However, as Figure 7–1 shows, interest rates again began rising in late 1977 and continued on a sharp upward trend for about three years. This marked the beginning of a period of phenomenal growth for the money market mutual funds, with total assets of these funds expanding from $4 billion at the end of 1977 to $11 billion at the end of 1978 to $45 billion at the end of 1979. Subsequent growth was even more dramatic, but we are getting ahead of our story.

FURTHER EROSIONS IN INTEREST RATE CEILINGS

Continuing our chronology, we pick up in 1978 with rising interest rates providing policymakers with fears of another bout of disintermediation. To forestall this, in June 1978 the regulators introduced the so-called 6-month money market certificate (MMC). MMCs required a $10,000 minimum deposit and were available at both commercial banks and thrift institutions. Commercial banks were permitted to pay an interest rate on MMCs equal to the 6-month Treasury bill rate. Initially thrift institutions were able to pay ¼ percent more, but in March 1979 that differential was eliminated whenever the 6-month bill rate was 9 percent or higher.

MMCs proved to be a significant innovation for both commercial banks and thrift institutions. While from mid-1978 to year-end 1979 savings deposits and small time deposits other than MMCs declined at both banks and thrifts, the growth of MMCs was quite remarkable. By the end of 1979 commercial banks had issued more than $100 billion of MMCs, while the thrifts held about $160 billion, which amounted to roughly one-quarter of their total deposits. The thrifts also issued a substantial amount of large time deposits. Overall then, a serious bout of disintermediation was averted, at least temporarily, and with the MMCs a partial dent was made in the interest rate ceilings.

These developments, however, were not sufficient to take us out of the woods. Indeed, toward the end of 1979 signs of strain appeared at thrift institutions as deposit growth slowed noticeably. In part this was due to fierce competition from the money market funds, which grew by nearly 30 percent from September to December of 1979. To bolster the menu of deposit offerings by the thrifts, on January 1, 1980, a floating ceiling was introduced on time deposits with a maturity of 2½ years or more. On this new certificate thrifts were permitted to offer a yield ½ percent below the yield on 2½ year Treasury securities, while commercial banks were limited to a rate of ¾ percent less than the Treasury yield. This continued the gradual erosion of interest rate ceilings.

A second problem for the thrifts cropped up as the rate on MMCs rose to the point where it exceeded the usury ceilings in a number of states. This threatened to make it unprofitable to lend mortgage funds even if thrift institutions could acquire the deposits. To cope with this crisis, at the end of 1979 Congress enacted legislation temporarily suspending state ceilings for mortgage rates during the first quarter of 1980.

As should be clear from our discussion, even prior to 1980 various events had forced the monetary authorities to partially relax interest rate ceilings. However, as the decade came to and end, we were still some considerable way from a system unfettered by ceilings. Indeed, at that time there were over twenty different sorts of accounts subjected to interest ceilings of various sorts.

CHECKABLE TRANSACTIONS ACCOUNTS FOR THRIFTS

As noted earlier, a second structural problem of the financial system in 1970 was the inability of the thrift institutions to offer checkable transactions accounts. Through their power to offer demand deposits, commercial banks had a monopoly in this regard. As with the case of interest rate ceilings, financial innovations in the 1970s, notably the NOW account, ultimately undermined the banks' monopoly. Moreover, these developments also served to provide a transactions account on which the depositor could earn interest. In essence, this was an end run around the prohibition of interest on demand deposits.

PREAUTHORIZED TRANSFERS
The first step in this direction was in 1970, when some thrifts were per-

mitted to make preauthorized nonnegotiable transfers from savings accounts for household-related expenditures. In 1975 this was extended to allow such transfers for any purpose. Although this approach offers thrifts a way to make third-party payments, the necessity of preauthorization makes it rather inconvenient for the depositor except for such things as utility and telephone bills.

NOW ACCOUNTS

A more significant step toward giving the thrifts checking privileges occurred in June 1972, when the NOW account was born. A NOW account is a savings deposit that permits the depositor to withdraw funds by writing a negotiable order of withdrawal—hence the acronym NOW. NOWs were first proposed in 1970 by a state-chartered mutual savings bank in Worcester, Massachusetts, and were introduced in 1972 after the Massachusetts State Supreme Court found there was no legal basis for prohibiting NOWs. Even though the holder of such an account writes a NOW exactly as he or she would write a check, NOW accounts were deemed to be distinct from checking accounts. The legal niceties are preserved by pointing to the fact that a NOW account is technically a savings account and that financial institutions therefore have the right to 30 days' notice before they are required to make payments. Needless to say, no case of such a delay has ever been reported.

Once the NOW account had been legally blessed, other state-chartered mutual savings banks in Massachusetts jumped onto the NOW bandwagon. In September 1972 a New Hampshire savings bank joined in the fun, and others soon followed. The result of all this was that state-chartered mutual savings banks held a competitive advantage over federally chartered savings institutions and all commercial banks. As a result, commercial banks, regulators, and some members of Congress opposed NOWs and tried to have them banned. However, the reverse occurred. As of January 1974, all depository institutions in Massachusetts and New Hampshire (except credit unions) were permitted to offer NOW accounts.

While it was perhaps the hope of Congress that NOWs could be "contained" in New Hampshire and Massachusetts, other states knew a good thing when they saw it. A few states discovered that existing laws permitted checklike instruments for thrifts, while in other states the legislatures proved willing to act. For example, toward the end of 1975 legislatures in both Maine and Connecticut permitted state-chartered thrifts to offer personal checking accounts. These actions, in conjunction with the ever-present example of NOWs in New Hampshire and Massachusetts, led Congress to extend NOWs to all six New England states in February 1976. Shortly thereafter New York passed legislation permitting checking accounts, including overdraft privileges, at state-chartered mutual savings banks and savings and loans. Congress responded in October 1978 by authorizing NOWs in New York. Then, in January 1980, NOWs continued their southward trickle as Congress extended them to New Jersey.

To many observers, the only logical outcome of this process was for NOW accounts to be authorized on a nationwide basis and, as already indicated, the Deregulation Act of 1980 did precisely that. In some respects this episode provides a vindication for those who defend the curious patchwork quilt of regulation governing financial institutions. As may be recalled, one argument in favor of the chartering of financial institutions by individual states is that it encourages innovation by providing fifty "experimental laboratories." At least in the case of NOW accounts, it seems clear that we have gotten to the present state of affairs only because of innovation at the state level, which forced action at the federal level. Indeed, it was the momentum of this process that gave us NOWs on a nationwide basis.

ELECTRONIC MONEY ONCE AGAIN

While congressional action has dictated that nationwide NOWs should serve as the solution to the problem of providing checklike powers to the thrifts, as events were unfolding in the 1970s this was less than evident. Consequently, the thrifts pursued other strategies aimed at eroding the checking advantage of the commercial banks. One of these developments is worthy of note, since it may well have a role to play in conjunction with universal NOW accounts. In particular, we are referring to the use of electronic terminals to make transactions. Such terminals, which go by the name of *remote service units* (RSUs) or *point of sale* (POS) terminals, were first utilized by a savings and loan association in Nebraska that placed several RSUs in Hinky Dinky supermarkets. Account holders could withdraw cash, make deposits, make charge account and loan payments, and transfer funds from one account to another while shopping. Other savings and loans soon followed suit, locating terminals in such convenient places as airports, factories, and student centers at colleges and universities.

While it is apparent that RSUs are not a perfect substitute for checking accounts, they clearly make savings accounts at thrifts more useful for transactions purposes. Indeed, it should be apparent that even with nationwide NOWs, RSUs could well be a critical component in the financial system of the future. The status of the RSUs was temporarily clouded by an April 1979 court order declaring them illegal under existing law. However, a grace period was provided before RSUs actually had to be withdrawn, and, as we shall see, the legal issue was subsequently settled by Congress.[6]

As should be apparent from our discussion, in the 1970s savings and loans and mutual savings banks went a long way toward acquiring checklike powers. Via share drafts, which function much like NOW accounts, some credit unions had also acquired checklike powers. As far as customers are concerned, these new deposit services at nonbank intermediaries are

---

[6]Another interesting legal aspect of RSUs is that, before they had been challenged, they were not considered branch offices of the thrifts. In contrast, similar terminals introduced by commercial banks had been judged to be subject to branch banking laws.

quite similar to demand deposits at commercial banks. There is, of course, one important difference in that NOWs pay explicit interest.

AUTOMATIC TRANSFER SERVICES (ATS)

While the thrift-led NOW account revolution was in progress, commercial banks were increasingly unhappy with being left out. The Federal Reserve came to the rescue when in 1978 it authorized member banks to offer *automatic transfer services* from a savings account to a checking account or other type of transactions account.

Under ATS the customer need not keep any funds in a checking account. Transactions balances are kept in savings accounts, earning the passbook rate of interest, and funds are transferred as checks clear. In effect, ATS function much like a NOW account, and in fact it was congressional slowness in approving nationwide NOWs that led the Federal Reserve to introduce ATS. However, in April 1979, the U.S. Court of Appeals ruled that ATS were illegal and could not be maintained after January 1, 1980, unless Congress enacted appropriate legislation. At the end of 1979 Congress provided temporary authorization until March 31, 1980, and used the time to sort out the whole ATS/NOW issue. We now turn to the end result of this process.

DEPOSITORY INSTITUTIONS DEREGULATION ACT OF 1980

At the start of 1980 Congress found itself under considerable pressure to reform the financial system. The immediate source of this pressure was the court decision that had invalidated ATS, RSUs, and credit union share drafts. In addition, with the spread of NOW accounts to New York, New Jersey, and the six New England states, it became increasingly evident that containment of NOWs was no longer a viable strategy. Finally, there was the long-standing pressure to "do something" about the interest rate ceilings, and likewise to expand the scope of activities permitted thrift institutions. It was in the face of all these pressures that Congress undertook a comprehensive reexamination of the financial system and ultimately passed the Deregulation Act of 1980.[7] The act contained many important provisions, with the following among the most noteworthy:

> **NOW ACCOUNTS.** Authorized NOW accounts nationwide at all depository institutions, effective year-end 1980. NOW accounts are available to individuals and nonprofit organizations.

---

[7]Strictly speaking, the Deregulation Act pertains to interest rate ceilings, while such things as NOW accounts were authorized by the formidable-sounding Consumer Checking Account Equity Act of 1980. For simplicity we shall refer just to the deregulation act. Another part of the legislation, the Monetary Control Act of 1980, was designed to improve the ability of the Federal Reserve to conduct monetary policy. This act is discussed elsewhere.

ATS. Permitted banks to provide automatic transfer services from savings to checking accounts.

RSUs. Permitted the establishment of remote service units by savings and loan associations for such purposes as crediting and debiting savings accounts and credit payment on loans.

SHARE DRAFTS. Authorized all federally insured credit unions to offer share draft accounts, thus extending checking-like power to credit unions.

MORTGAGE USURY CEILINGS. Eliminated State mortgage usury ceilings unless a state adopted a new usury ceiling prior to April 1, 1983.

Quite evidently these actions were far-reaching and had a marked and relatively immediate impact on the nature of the financial system. Other provisions of the act, specifically those dealing with interest rate ceilings on deposits, had their effects felt more gradually.

INTEREST RATE CEILINGS

The introduction to the Deregulation Act states the following:

> The Congress hereby finds that
> (1) limitations on the interest rates which are payable on deposits and accounts discourage persons from saving money, create inequities for depositors, impede the ability of depository institutions to compete for funds, and have not achieved their purpose of providing an even flow of funds for home mortgage lending; and
> (2) all depositors, and particularly those with modest savings, are entitled to receive a market rate of return on their savings as soon as it is economically feasible for despository institutions to pay such rate.

The introduction then goes on to indicate that it is the purpose of the act to provide for an "orderly phase-out and the ultimate elimination of the limitations on the maximum rates of interest and dividends which may be paid on deposits."

To accomplish this phase-out of interest ceilings, the act established a Deregulation Committee consisting of the secretary of the Treasury and the chairmen of the Federal Reserve, the FDIC, the Federal Home Loan Bank Board, and the National Credit Union Administration Board. The Deregulation Committee was charged with bringing about the phase-out over a six-year period and with making regular reports on how the deregulation process is working. Other than providing a self-destruct mechanism for the Committee and for repealing all authority to impose interest ceilings after six years, the Act sets no specific timetable for the phase-out. It should be apparent that in the long run this provision of the Act will initiate marked changes in the nature of financial intermediation.

EXPANDING THE POWERS OF THE THRIFTS

As suggested earlier, piecemeal tinkering with the financial system is potentially dangerous in that it can sometimes upset a delicate balance. It was with this in mind that financial reformers, while proposing the elimination of interest rate ceilings, typically also proposed expanding the powers of the thrift institutions to enable them to compete effectively with the commercial banks. In shaping the Deregulation Act of 1980, Congress was also mindful of this issue and took several steps to enrich the menu of asset choices available to the thrifts. In particular, the act contained the following provisions:

1 Authorization for savings and loans to invest up to 20 percent of assets in consumer loans, commercial paper, and corporate securities.
2 Expansion of the authority of savings and loans to make real estate loans by removing the geographic restrictions on lending.
3 Permission for savings and loans to issue credit cards and extend credit in connection with such cards.
4 Authorization for savings and loans to offer trust services.
5 Permission for mutual savings banks to make commercial and business loans up to 5 percent of their assets.

These steps, in conjunction with NOW accounts and the elimination of mortgage usury ceilings, it was hoped would improve the competitive position of the thrifts. Nevertheless, it was not clear whether these steps went far enough. Doubts on this score are explicitly recognized in the act itself, which calls for the president to convene a task force to study and make recommendations regarding options available to improve the balance between assets and liabilities in thrift portfolios. Similarly, the act provides for the Deregulation Committee phasing out interest ceilings to pay due regard to the viability of the thrift institutions. What this all suggests is that Congress recognized that further legislation might prove necessary to ensure the health of the thrift institutions. As we shall now see, events proved the Congress right.

DEVELOPMENTS IN THE 1980s

A major intent of the 1980 deregulation act was to enhance the viability of the thrift institutions. Allowing thrifts to provide checkable transactions accounts and liberalizing their investment menu were certainly major steps in this direction. Nevertheless, despite these reforms, the years immediately after the provision of the new powers were among the worst ever experienced by the thrifts. They suffered record losses and many thrift institutions failed. Numerous other thrift institutions would also have failed were it not for the fact that they were absorbed by merger into healthier financial institutions. What accounted for this disturbing deterioration in the health of the thrifts? The primary culprit was the extraordinarily high, indeed, record level of interest rates that prevailed in the period 1980 to 1982.

INTEREST RATE EFFECTS ON THRIFT LIABILITIES

As Figure 7–1 reveals, the level of market interest rates from 1980 to 1982 was extraordinarily high by historical standards. The 3-month Treasury bill rate averaged over 11½ percent in 1980, over 14 percent in 1981, and nearly 11 percent in 1982. At several points, the rate hovered in the vicinity of 16 percent. The more sensitive federal funds rate reached even greater heights, averaging nearly 16½ percent in 1981 and staying at over 19 percent for months at a time. These high rates spelled trouble for the thrifts, because thrifts were still largely constrained by interest rate ceilings. The 1980 deregulation act had called for the elimination of these ceilings, but this was to be a gradual process spread out over six years. This process had barely begun when interest rates reached record levels.

As a result of the constellation of high market interest rates and interest rate ceilings, the thrift institutions found themselves unable to compete with money market mutual funds. Indeed, these funds grew at a nearly unbelievable rate from 1980 to 1982. Money market mutual funds had total assets of $45 billion at the start of 1980. By late 1982 the assets of these funds had skyrocketed to $207 billion. To attract these new shareholders, the money market mutual funds offered interest rates as high as 17 percent. The best the thrifts could do in response was to offer the 6-month money certificates (MMCs) described earlier. Even on the MMCs, where the ceiling rate was tied to the 6-month Treasury rate, the thrifts could not quite compete with the money market funds. As for their other liabilities, where the ceilings had not yet been relaxed, the thrifts found that the rates they were permitted to pay were hopelessly out of line with market interest rates. For example, on passbook savings accounts the thrifts were paying 5½ percent, while on one-year certificates they could only pay 6½ percent. It is little wonder that the money market mutual funds were able to drain away a substantial volume of funds from the thrift institutions.

As this drain was occurring, policymakers did not sit idly by. The Depository Institutions Deregulation Committee, the group charged with overseeing the gradual elimination of interest rate ceilings, helped a bit by liberalizing the ceiling on time accounts with maturities of 2½ years or more. Congress also got into the act in 1981 by authorizing depository institutions to offer something called an *all saver certificate*. The first $1,000 of interest income on these certificates was exempt from federal income tax. This tax-exempt feature enabled thrifts and banks to offer a reasonably attractive one-year certificate. While this improved the competitiveness of the thrifts and banks vis-à-vis the money market mutual funds, it made only a modest dent in the problem. The reason is that money market funds did not require tying up funds for any fixed period of time and also offered some checkwriting privileges. The all saver certificate, in comparison, was a much more rigid financial instrument. One other aspect of the all saver certificate should be noted; namely, by permitting a tax-exempt feature, Congress was reducing tax revenues and thus providing a direct subsidy to the depository institutions.

While these limited actions made the thrifts a bit more competitive, overall the money market mutual funds and, of course, direct investment in money market instruments retained the upper hand. Some called for restraints to be placed on the money market mutual funds, either in the form of reserve requirements or by use of interest rate ceilings. To many, however, the idea of imposing ceilings on money market funds when, at the same time, ceilings were in the process of being generally dismantled seemed rather inconsistent. Others called for simply speeding up the process of removing the ceilings on the thrifts. However, because of the shaky financial health of the thrifts, policymakers had serious reservations about the wisdom of this strategy.

INTEREST RATES AND THE HEALTH OF THE THRIFTS

With the era of high interest rates that accompanied the beginning of the 1980s, the thrifts found themselves in an increasingly fragile state. The basic problem was the one that had motivated the imposition of ceilings on thrifts in the first place—the maturity mismatch between their assets and liabilities. Put another way, thrifts were financing long-term mortgages with short-term liabilities. Especially important in this regard were the 6-month certificates—the MMCs—that allowed the thrifts to be competitive. By 1981, these accounted for about 35 percent of all thrift deposits.

The essence of the problem can be seen when we recognize that most of the mortgage loans made by the thrifts in the late 1970s were at interest rates of 9 or 10 percent. When these mortgages were made, the thrifts obviously thought the rates were sufficiently high to yield a profit. However, as market interest rates rose and competition from the money market funds intensified, the thrifts found themselves supporting these long-term 9 and 10 percent mortgages with 6-month certificates and other liabilities costing up to 15 percent. This was a clear recipe for financial disaster, and it struck the thrifts with a vengeance. Before giving the sad details, one response of the thrifts to the maturity mismatch is worth noting.

In the previous chapter, we noted that commercial banks have increasingly relied on floating-rate or variable-rate loans as a way of protecting themselves against unexpected changes in the cost of bank funds. In a similar fashion, thrift institutions also began to issue mortgage loans with a floating interest rate. In its simplest terms, a *variable-rate mortgage* is a loan for a fixed maturity where the interest rate is adjusted periodically in the light of some market rate of interest. In actually implementing such mortgages, a bewildering number of variations on a basic theme have emerged.

The various instruments differ in terms of how frequently the rate adjustments are made and whether or not there are limitations on the extent to which the rate can be raised. Such details aside, the basic intent of the variable-rate mortgage is to shift the risk of fluctuating interest rates away from the thrifts and onto borrowers. It does this by varying the mortgage rate in a way that is likely to compensate a thrift for its cost of funds, thus overcoming the maturity mismatch problem.

While the innovation of variable-rate mortgage may well help the thrifts in the long run, since these instruments were in their infancy, they came too late to avoid the serious problems created by the maturity mismatch and the high interest rates of 1980, 1981, and 1982. The magnitude and the consequences of these problems are illustrated by Table 7–5, which gives selected data on the performance of savings and loan associations in the years 1977 to 1982. (The MSB experience is qualitatively similar.) The first column shows the steady rise in the rate on *new* mortgages, while the second column shows the distinctly more modest advance in the *average* return on assets. This reflects the fact that S&Ls were saddled with lower-yielding mortgages issued in previous years. Thus, despite the fact that the 1982 mortgage rate was over 15 percent, the average return on assets in that year was only 10.8 percent, and the average cost of funds was 11.4 percent. With S&Ls paying more for funds than they were earning, they obviously lost money. As Table 7–5 shows, these losses were over $6 billion in 1981 and 1982. In the face of these developments, many thrift institutions failed and hundreds more merged to avoid failing. As the last column of Table 7–5 shows, from 1980 to 1982 there was a net reduction of roughly 800 in the number of S&Ls outstanding. It was these events and the prospect of further difficulties that once again led Congress to action.

TABLE 7–5 Selected Data, Savings and Loan Associations

Year	Rate on new mortgages (Percent)	Return on assets (Percent)	Cost of funds (Percent)	Net income (Billions of dollars)	Number of associations
1977	9.02%	8.44%	6.44%	$ 4,710	4,761
1978	9.61	8.73	6.67	5,832	4,725
1979	10.89	9.29	7.47	5,299	4,684
1980	12.90	9.72	8.94	1,215	4,613
1981	15.00	10.11	10.92	− 6,271	4,292
1982	15.38	10.82	11.38	− 6,010	3,833

SOURCE: A. S. Carron, *The Rescue of the Thrift Industry*, The Brookings Institution, Washington, D.C., 1983, and *'83 Savings and Loan Sourcebook*, United States League of Savings Institutions, Chicago, 1983.

THE DEPOSITORY INSTITUTIONS ACT OF 1982

In passing the Depository Institutions Act of 1982, also known as the Garn–St. Germain Act, Congress took its second major step in two years toward the deregulation of depository institutions.[8] In so doing, it helped to provide an environment that would eventually restore the thrifts to financial health. However, in recognition of the problems of getting from here to there, Congress also granted exceptional powers to regulators to cope with the many failures and potential failures of the thrifts.

To improve the long-run viability of the thrifts, the 1982 act further liberalized their investment powers. Federally chartered thrifts were authorized to engage in commercial lending and, as of 1984, were permitted to place up to 10 percent of their assets in this category. They were also provided with a related authority to offer demand deposits to customers having a business relationship with them. This moved the thrifts much closer to the "commercial" aspect of commercial banks. The act also increased the maximum amount of allowable consumer lending by thrifts from 20 to 30 percent of total assets, liberalized lending for nonresidential real estate, and enhanced the ability of the thrifts to purchase state and local securities. These various provisions, which appear in the Garn–St. Germain Act under the heading "Thrift Institutions Restructuring," should enable the thrifts gradually to diversify their assets in a substantial manner.

The same section of the act directed the Depository Institutions Deregulation Committee (DIDC) to establish a money market deposit account that is "directly equivalent to and competitive with money market mutual funds." This account was to be available at thrifts and banks, have no interest ceiling, and was to permit depositors to make up to six transactions per month, three by check. Related provisions of the act mandated that the DIDC would not impose an interest rate ceiling or a rate differential on any new type of deposit account and required the DIDC to eliminate all rate differentials between banks and S&Ls by 1984.

As mentioned, the act also provided a number of powers to deal directly with weaker financial institutions. It expanded the authority of the Federal Savings and Loan Insurance Corporation (FSLIC) in arranging mergers and acquisitions of financially troubled thrifts. Thus, for example, a commercial bank in one state could acquire a troubled S&L in another. The Garn–St. Germain Act also provided for a variety of new forms of direct financial assistance to troubled depository institutions. Many of these extraordinary powers were temporary and set to expire after three years.

---

[8]The cosponsor of the Depository Institutions Act of 1982, Senator Jake Garn, received a different sort of notoriety in 1985 when he became the first member of Congress to fly on the space shuttle.

AFTER GARN–ST. GERMAIN

The money market deposit account (MMDA) authorized by Garn–St. Germain went into effect in mid-December 1982. Unlike a share account at a money market mutual fund, the MMDA was insured by the federal government. With depository institutions emphasizing the insurance feature of the MMDA and offering an attractive rate of interest, the new account immediately proved its appeal. Indeed, banks and thrifts attracted a whopping $340 billion into these accounts in four short months. Some of these deposits were attracted from money market mutual funds whose extraordinary growth ceased at the end of 1982; their shares declined by $44 billion over the next 12 months. However, most of the MMDAs came from savings deposits and smaller-denomination time deposits at banks and thrifts.

What this meant was the thrift institutions were now paying market rates for funds they earlier had obtained at below-market rates. Other things being equal, this was a recipe for further disaster. Other things, however, were not equal. Most important, after mid-1982 market interest rates fell. For example, after averaging over 12½ percent in the first half of 1982, the 3-month Treasury bill rate dropped to 8 percent at the end of the year. And for the twelve months of 1983, the bill rate averaged 8.6 percent. This reduction in market rates translated into a lower cost of funds to the thrifts and put them on the road to recovery.

The DIDC also took other actions in the light of the Garn–St. Germain Act. For one, as discussed in the previous chapter, in early 1983 it authorized depository institutions to offer super-NOW accounts. These accounts have no limitations on the number of transactions and no interest rate ceilings. They do, however, have a number of restrictions: (1) There is a minimum balance, originally set at $2,500; (2) they cannot be held by businesses; and (3) they are subject to reserve requirements. While the attractiveness of the super-NOWs has thus far been modest, when taken in conjunction with the money market deposit account, it is clear that the earlier competitive advantage of the money market mutual funds over the thrifts and banks has been reversed.

A second set of DIDC actions dealt with interest rate ceilings. The Garn–St. Germain Act had mandated the elimination by 1984 of the interest rate differential that typically permitted thrifts to pay ¼ percent more than banks on comparable deposit accounts. The DIDC complied a bit early, removing the differential on October 1, 1983, and simultaneously lifted a number of the remaining interest rate ceilings. As of that date, there were only three remnants of what was once an extraordinarily complex set of interest rate ceilings. These covered passbook savings accounts, NOW accounts with balances below $2,500, and time deposits of less than $2,500 with maturities of 7 to 31 days. Of course, even these ceilings were set to expire in 1986.

The legislative reforms of 1980 and 1982 have clearly served to increase the long-run viability of the thrift institutions. These reforms will permit the thrifts to diversify their assets, thus reducing their specialized nature. Moreover, to the extent that mortgages remain a key asset, and this certainly seems likely, the thrifts will benefit from the growing use of variable-rate mortgages. The mere passage of the 1980 and 1982 legislation, however, did not magically restore the thrift institutions to health. Indeed, as we have seen, it was only a fairly substantial drop in market interest rates that averted a more extensive financial crisis. And even this drop was not enough to restore all the thrifts to a healthy state. Consequently, a substantial number of additional mergers of weak institutions was to be expected. These expectations were borne out by the experience of the S&Ls, whose numbers declined from 3,833 at the end of 1982 to 3,391 as of 1984. Moreover, thoughtful observers of the thrift scene suggested that the number of S&Ls could well continue to decline until the industry has between 2,000 and 2,500 firms. Whether this forecast proves accurate or not, it is clear that the thrifts of the future will be diversified institutions, with increasing similarities to the once-unique commercial banks. It is in the light of these developments that we must consider commercial banks and thrifts together when, in the next chapter, we examine the determination of the money supply.

SUMMARY

1 The thrift institutions consist of savings and loan associations, mutual savings banks, and credit unions. Thrift institutions have grown extremely rapidly since the end of World War II, outstripping the growth of commercial banks.

2 Historically the thrifts were quite specialized institutions, offering savings deposits and making mortgage or consumer loans. The specialized nature of their assets and liabilities has at times created substantial difficulties for the thrifts. Due to interest rate ceilings on their deposit liabilities, they have been subject to disintermediation during periods of high market interest rates. At the same time, since many of the thrift assets were held in the form of longer-term fixed-rate mortgages, thrifts could not reap the full benefits of higher market rates.

3 Regulatory changes and financial innovations of the last decade have done much to improve the long-run viability of the thrifts. The thrifts themselves played a major role in this via the innovation of the NOW account, which provides an interest-bearing checkable account for the thrifts. The NOW account was formally authorized by the Depository Institutions Deregulation Act of 1980, which also called for the gradual phase-out of all interest rate ceilings by 1986. The act also expanded the asset powers of the thrifts.

4 Despite the 1980 act, the extraordinarily high level of interest rates that prevailed from 1980 to 1982 proved to be a major stumbling block for the thrifts. They suffered record losses and many institutions failed.

While the thrifts could attract funds at very high interest rates, the maturity mismatch of their assets meant they were earning less on mortgages than they were paying for funds. That this crisis did not turn into a disaster largely stems from the decline in interest rates after mid-1982. The Garn–St. Germain Act of 1982 sought to improve the long-run viability of the thrifts by further liberalizing their investment powers and permitting them to offer a money market deposit account to compete with the money market mutual funds.

5 As a result of the recent regulatory changes, thrift institutions have become more similar to commercial banks. This is reflected in the fact that we now include certain liabilities of the thrifts in our definition of money. It also means that we need to take account of the thrifts in discussions of monetary policy. This will be immediately evident in the next chapter, where we discuss the determination of the money supply.

SELECTED READINGS

Carron, A. S. *The Plight of the Thrift Industry*. Washington, D.C.: The Brookings Institution, 1982.

———. *The Rescue of the Thrift Industry*. Washington, D.C.: The Brookings Institution, 1983.

Lovati, J. M. "The Growing Similarity Among Financial Institutions," *Review*, Federal Reserve Bank of St. Louis, October 1977, pp. 2–11.

Report of the President's Commission on Financial Structure and Regulation. Washington, D.C.: U.S. Government Printing Office, 1971.

8

DEPOSITORY INSTITUTIONS AND THE SUPPLY OF MONEY

In several preceding chapters we investigated various aspects of the depository intermediaries—commercial banks, mutual savings banks, savings and loan associations, and credit unions. Among other things, we saw that these institutions provide liabilities which serve as checking or transactions accounts for households and businesses. Since these transactions accounts constitute the lion's share of the quantity of money in the economy, depository institutions evidently play a critical role in the determination of the money supply. Indeed, as noted in Chapter 2, by acquiring assets depository institutions can "create" deposit accounts and hence money. Now we consider in more detail the precise nature of this process. In addition to explaining the role of the depository institutions in the mechanics of money creation, this chapter also emphasizes that the supply of money depends as well on the portfolio decisions of the public and the policies pursued by the Federal Reserve. The Federal Reserve, through its provision of reserves and the setting of reserve requirements, can play a decisive role in this process. As should be evident, then, the material in this chapter will prove to be a key ingredient in our subsequent discussion of the workings of monetary policy.

SOME PRELIMINARIES

Before considering the determination of the money supply—by which it will be recalled we mean the sum of currency and transactions deposits, denoted by the symbol M-1—we first need to introduce a convenient device known as the T-account. We next need to say a few words about reserve requirements and the mechanics of transferring funds between depository institutions. We will then be armed with enough tools to explain the determination of the quantity of money.

THE T-ACCOUNT

We have already encountered the idea of a balance sheet in previous chapters. A *T-account* is a simplified form of the balance sheet that shows the *changes* that have occurred on the balance sheet between two points in time. Quite often, the T-account is used to illustrate the effects of a single transaction on the balance sheet. Suppose, for example, that someone deposits $2,000 of currency in a bank. The bank would credit the account of this individual with $2,000 and initially, at least, put the currency in its vault, where it becomes vault cash, a form of cash reserve. The T-account corresponding to this transaction would look as follows:

Δ ASSETS		Δ LIABILITIES	
Cash reserves	+ $2,000	Deposits	+ $2,000

Several aspects of this T-account deserve note. First, it depicts only changes in the balance sheet. (Indeed, the Greek letter delta—Δ—which appears in the T-account is used by economists to denote changes.) The actual underlying balance sheet for this bank may be quite complicated—as, for example, in Table 6–2. By focusing only on changes, we can avoid listing all the items that are not altered by the deposit of currency. Second, just as a balance sheet must "balance," so must the T-account. In the present case this is obviously true, since both sides of the T-account show changes of the same magnitude.

To see another way in which a T-account can balance, let us consider a second transaction. In particular, let us suppose that the same bank decides to use $1,000 of its newly acquired vault cash to purchase a security. This transaction would be depicted as follows:

Δ ASSETS		Δ LIABILITIES
Cash reserves	− $1,000	
Securities	+ $1,000	

This T-account shows nothing on the liability side because the transaction involves only exchanging one asset—cash reserves—for another asset—

securities. This T-account balances because the net change on the asset side is zero.

Finally, should we be so inclined, we can combine the two previous T-accounts to reflect the *overall* effect of the $2,000 deposit and the $1,000 security purchase. The T-account reflecting *both* these transactions is:

Δ ASSETS		Δ LIABILITIES	
Cash reserves	+ $1,000	Deposits	+ $2,000
Securities	+ $1,000		

Again, we see that the T-account is balanced.

Armed with the useful device of the T-account, we now introduce a major ingredient in the determination of the money supply—reserves and reserve requirements.

RESERVES AND RESERVE REQUIREMENTS

As we noted in previous chapters, depository institutions must hold a percentage of certain types of their liabilities in the form of *reserves.* Under current law, only a few specific types of liabilities are "reservable"—that is, against which reserves must be held. These include checkable transactions deposits, Eurodollar borrowing, and the quaintly named nonpersonal time deposit. (A "nonperson" is a business or a government entity.) Of these, reserves against transactions accounts are by far the most significant, and to simplify our discussion, at least initially, we assume that transactions accounts are the only reservable liability.

We also assume that depository institutions must hold *at least* some fixed percentage of transactions deposits in the form of reserves.[1] The specific percentage, say 10 percent, is called the *reserve requirement,* and to calculate the dollar quantity of *required reserves*, we multiply the percentage reserve requirement by the amount of reservable liabilities. For example, a bank with transactions deposits of $10 million faced with a 10 percent reserve requirement would have required reserves of $1 million.

To be sure, as implied by the phrase "at least," banks are permitted to hold *total reserves* that exceed the level of required reserves. These additional reserves—that is, the excess of total reserves over required reserves—go by the name of *excess reserves.* Once we recall, however, that reserves must be held as vault cash or as a deposit with the Federal Reserve, neither of which contributes to the earnings of the depository institutions, we realize that the profit motive provides a strong incentive to minimize holdings of excess reserves.

---

[1]The actual structure of reserve requirements is slightly more complicated than this, since there is a sliding scale depending on the quantity of deposits. See Chapter 12 for the details.

We will see later that the Federal Reserve is empowered to set such minimum fractional-reserve requirements and to alter within limits the height of these minimum requirements. Note that to fix a minimum ratio of reserves to deposit liabilities is the same as fixing a maximum ratio of deposit liabilities to reserves. For example, to say to a bank, "You must hold reserves equal to at least 10 percent of your deposit liabilities," is the same as saying, "Your deposit liabilities may not exceed ten times the volume of your reserves."

Thus, we find that the maximum volume of deposit liabilities that may be outstanding depends on (1) the dollar volume of reserves available to the banks and (2) the size of the reserve requirement. This indicates why dollars in bank reserves are often referred to as *high-powered* money; under a fractional reserve system each dollar of legal reserves can "support" several dollars for checking deposits. And the lower the required reserve ratio, the higher-powered is each dollar of the reserves.

This also introduces us to the two principal ways in which the Federal Reserve can regulate the behavior of the money supply. Although the Federal Reserve uses a number of instruments, all are aimed at regulating either the dollar volume of reserves available to depository institutions or the level of reserve requirements.

The role of reserve requirements can be readily illustrated by use of the balance sheet and T-account. As an example, let us assume that the reserve requirement is 10 percent and that we are dealing with a bank whose balance sheet is given as follows:

ASSETS		LIABILITIES	
Reserves	$1 million	Demand deposits	$10 million
Loans and investments	$9 million		
Addenda			
Required reserves	$1 million		
Excess reserves	0		

This bank is currently holding reserves, either in the form of vault cash or as deposits with the Federal Reserve, precisely equal to its required reserves. That is, it has zero excess reserves. A bank in this position is sometimes said to be *fully loaned up*. Indeed, aside from required reserves, all the bank's remaining assets are held in the form of loans and investments.

Let us now imagine that someone deposits $1,000 of currency in this bank, and this currency is placed in the bank's vault. The T-account for this transactions looks as follows:

Δ ASSETS		Δ LIABILITIES	
Reserves	$1,000	Demand deposits	+ $1,000
Addenda			
Required reserves	+ $100		
Excess reserves	+ $900		

As a result of this deposit, total reserves have risen by $1,000—remember that vault cash counts as reserves—but, given the 10 percent reserve requirement, required reserves have increased by only $100. The remaining $900 is now held in the form of excess reserves. As suggested before, since excess reserves are idle nonearning assets, this bank is unlikely to be content with its current asset position. Rather, it is likely to put these idle assets to work earning interest. It does this by using these funds to acquire securities or to make loans. In doing so, it will contribute to the creation of deposits. Before we can spell this out, we need one last preliminary: an understanding of the mechanics of the process of transferring funds between depository institutions.

THE MECHANICS OF TRANSFERRING FUNDS

Huge amounts of payments are made by transferring deposit claims from payers to payees by check. As we have seen, coping with these pieces of paper is an expensive proposition, requiring that substantial resources be devoted to the payments mechanism. Our concern here, however, is not with this expense, but with what actually happens when a check is written by an individual and given to someone else. Typically the recipient deposits the check in an account at a depository institution. What happens next depends on some further assumptions.

The simplest case is if payer and payee are depositors at the same institution. For example, both Jones and Whyte may be depositors at bank A. If Jones gives a $1,000 check to Whyte, bank A will simply deduct that amount from its deposit liability to Jones and increase equally its deposit liability to Whyte. The bank's assets and total liabilities remain unchanged. But suppose payer and payee are not depositors in the same bank. Suppose Jones writes a $1,000 check on bank A and gives it to Whyte, who deposits it in bank B. The latter will add $1,000 to its deposit liability to Whyte and send the check to bank A, which will deduct this amount from its deposit liability to Jones. Bank A now owes bank B $1,000. To collect, bank B could send an armored car over to bank A and haul away the currency. This would be incredibly tedious and expensive if it were done for every check. Depository institutions therefore wait a bit before settling up so that things can "average out." That is, there may be some offsetting transactions that will require bank B or some other depository institutions to pay bank A.

Fortunately, only a small fraction of the check flows lead to net inter-institution payments and to net transfers of cash from one depository institution to another. In the course of every day, large amounts of checks will be drawn on a depository institution and deposited in other institutions, thus creating large liabilities for it to pay those institutions. But at the same time the depository institution will receive on deposit large amounts of checks drawn on other institutions, thus giving it claims for payment by them. Since these will usually be largely offsetting, it would be both confusing and inefficient if each had to transfer cash to meet the full value of its liability to pay other institutions and to receive cash reserves equal to all its claims for payment by other institutions. How much more efficient it would be to offset these flows to the maximum possible extent and transfer cash reserves only to cover net payments or receipts at the end of the day. This is, in fact, what is done. But what institutions do not do is settle up by sending an armored car to collect or make payments. Rather, a complex clearing and collection system has been developed for this purpose. It includes local clearinghouses, correspondent banks, and the Federal Reserve banks. At least once a day these organizations compare for each depository institution the flow of checks drawn on it and deposited with other institutions, with the flow of checks deposited with it and drawn on other institutions. Each depository institution then receives the net amount due it or pays the net amount owed by it. These net payments are usually made by transferring cash reserves. The mechanics of this can be readily illustrated with the versatile T-account.

Suppose, for example, we are dealing with a commercial bank called bank A and a savings and loan with the exciting name of S&L B. Further assume that at the end of some business day, customers of bank A have deposited checks totaling $3 million drawn on NOW accounts at S&L B, while customers of S&L B have deposited checks totaling $1 million drawn on demand deposit accounts at bank A. Finally, let us assume that these two institutions rely on the services of the Federal Reserve to clear their checks. What happens now?

In the first instance, both bank A and S&L B send the checks they have received to the Federal Reserve. Next, the Federal Reserve does something it is quite good at—arithmetic. It compares the two piles of checks and concludes that S&L B owes bank A $2 million. By the stroke of a pen or, more likely, the manipulation of a computer terminal, it then balances the books by deducting $2 million from the account that S&L B has with the Federal Reserve and credits the corresponding account of bank A with $2 million. Graphically, this looks as follows:

BANK A				S&L B			
Δ ASSETS		Δ LIABILITIES		Δ ASSETS		Δ LIABILITIES	
Deposits at Federal Reserve	+$2 million	Demand deposits	+$2 million	Deposits at Federal Reserve	−$2 million	NOW accounts	−$2 million

In other words, bank A has gained demand deposits and a corresponding deposit at the Federal Reserve, while S&L B has lost NOW accounts and had its balances at the Federal Reserve reduced. But, and this is critical, deposits at the Federal Reserve are nothing other than reserves used to satisfy reserve requirements. *Hence, we see that when a depository institution receives a check drawn on another depository institution, it increases its reserves by the amount of the check. At the same time, the depository institution on which the check is drawn loses an equal amount of reserves.* This important principle will come into frequent play as we now finally fathom the mysteries of deposit creation and the multiple expansion and contraction of deposits.

MULTIPLE EXPANSION AND CONTRACTION OF DEPOSITS

In order to examine the basic economics of deposit creation, it is useful to begin with some simplifying assumptions that permit us to focus on the details of the process. Once we have established the basic principles, we can examine the consequences of relaxing these simplifying assumptions. The key simplifying assumptions are as follows:

1 Depository institutions issue only transactions accounts.
2 All depository institutions face the same percentage reserve requirement against their transactions accounts. For illustration purposes, we assume this requirement is 10 percent.
3 Depository institutions have no desire to hold excess reserves.
4 The public does not alter its currency holdings. This is sometimes expressed by saying there is no *cash drain from the banking system.*

This set of assumptions is sufficient to tie together the quantity of transactions deposits and the quantity of reserves. That is, as we will see explicitly in a moment, the volume of deposits can change only if the volume of reserves held by depository institutions also changes.

What is it that determines the quantity of reserves? As already suggested, the policies of the Federal Reserve are the key element. There are, in fact, two basic ways in which the Fed can alter the quantity of reserves. One way, noted in Chapter 6, is for the Fed to lend reserves to depository institutions. Reserves acquired in this fashion are called *borrowed reserves* or simply *borrowings.* When the Fed increases its loans to depository institutions reserves increase, and when it decreases these loans reserves decrease.

A second way in which the Fed can alter the quantity of reserves is by purchasing or selling securities. When it purchases securities, for example, it pays for these securities by writing a check on itself. The seller of the security deposits the check with a bank, say, and the bank passes along the check to the Fed for payment. Payment is made by adding the amount of the check to the bank's reserve account at the Fed. In other words, by purchasing securities, the Fed simply creates reserves. The Fed can accomplish the destruction of reserves by selling securities. The Fed, as seller, receives a check drawn on some depository institution. When it clears this check, it reduces the reserve account of the depository institution and thus reduces total reserves.

Whatever the method utilized, then, the Federal Reserve can influence the quantity of reserves outstanding.[2] Let us now assume that the Fed purchases a security from an individual for $1,000 and that the seller of the security deposits the Fed's check in our infamous bank A. We want to trace the consequences of this change.

DEPOSIT EXPANSION: THE FIRST BANK

As a result of the Fed's security purchase, bank A finds itself with an additional $1,000 of demand deposits. Furthermore, after it has presented the check drawn on the Fed to the Fed, bank A will be credited with $1,000 of reserves. The T-account corresponding to this transaction is as follows:

BANK A			
Δ ASSETS		Δ LIABILITIES	
Cash Reserves	+ $1,000	Demand deposits	+ $1,000
Addenda			
Required reserves	+ $100		
Excess reserves	+ $900		

As shown in the T-account, bank A has $900 in excess reserves. By our assumptions, it does not want to hold excess reserves and this will convert these funds into an earning asset. It can do this by purchasing securities or by making a loan. Let us suppose bank A chooses the loan option. When a bank makes a loan, it makes the proceeds of the loan available to the customer in the form of a checking account. In other words, when it lends, bank A will *create* a transactions deposit. Since transactions deposits are money, bank A will be creating money.

How much can bank A lend? It might reason as follows. "The limit on our creation of deposits seems to be the 10 percent reserve requirement, so we could contemplate lending and creating deposits of up to ten times our excess reserves. Since we have $900 of excess reserves, let us lend $9,000 and create $9,000 of deposits." Taken by itself, the T-account for this transaction would look like this:

Δ ASSETS		Δ LIABILITIES	
Loans	+ $9,000	Demand deposits	+ $9,000

By a stroke of a pen, bank A has created $9,000 of deposits beyond the initial injection of $1,000 of deposits. To see where bank A stands, we can combine this T-account with the previous one to get the following:

[2]The process of Federal Reserve determination of reserves is described in considerable detail in Chapter 11.

Δ ASSETS		Δ LIABILITIES	
Cash reserves	+ $1,000	Demand deposits	+ $10,000
Loans	+ $9,000		
Addenda			
Required reserves	$1,000		
Excess reserves	0		

We see that as a result of the Fed's initial injection of reserves and bank A's actions, demand deposits have expanded by $10,000, or ten times the initial injection of reserves. Furthermore, in a move seemingly too good to be true, bank A has apparently converted its $900 of excess reserves into a veritable goldmine of earning assets. Unhappily for bank A, it *is* too good to be true.

What bank A has forgotten is that borrowers do not take out loans and pay interest on these loans just for the privilege of having a deposit account at bank A. These borrowers will undoubtedly want to *spend* these funds, and when they do they will write checks on their accounts. However, most of these checks will probably be deposited in *other* depository institutions by their recipients. Only if bank A were a *monopoly bank* that provided the sole depository services in the country would it be confident that checks written on it would be returned to it. But in a system with over 40,000 depository institutions, the distinctly more plausible case is that once loan funds are spent, they will disappear from bank A. And, as we have seen from the description of the clearing process, once this happens bank A will lose reserves. To take the extreme case, if all the newly created $9,000 of deposits is spent and redeposited with other institutions, bank A will lose $9,000 in reserves. Unfortunately for bank A, it has only $900 excess reserves, so it will be sadly deficient in required reserves.

What this strongly suggests is that the prudent lending limit for bank A is the amount of reserves it can afford to lose, which is the amount of its *excess reserves*. In the present case, this means bank A can lend $900, creating an equivalent amount of deposits. Until these newly created funds are spent, bank A will still have some excess reserves (draw up a T-account to convince yourself of this); but once these funds are spent and redeposited in another institution, bank A will lose its excess reserves.

The T-account showing the effects of the initial $1,000 deposit, the subsequent loan, and the ultimate withdrawal of the $900 of newly created deposits is as follows:

BANK A			
Δ ASSETS		Δ LIABILITIES	
Cash reserves	+ $100	Demand deposits	+ $1,000
Loans	+ $900		
Addenda			
Required reserves	+ $100		
Excess reserves	0		

What we now see is that bank A has adjusted to its original $1,000 deposit by adding $100 to reserves and $900 to earning assets in the form of loans. In the terminology we have used before, it is fully loaned up, and its excess reserves have been eliminated. Bank A thus satisfies all our assumptions.

Is this the end of the story? The answer is a resounding "no." There is the substantial matter of the $900 check written on bank A by the recipient of the loan. By our assumption, this sum was redeposited in another depository institution. We now need to trace the effects of this deposit.

DEPOSIT EXPANSION: THE SUBSEQUENT ROUNDS

As just noted, as a result of the loan made by bank A, other depository institutions will be the recipients of checks totaling $900. To keep things simple, let us assume that all these funds are paid to depositors who have NOW accounts at S&L B. The T-account for this transaction is:

S&L B			
Δ ASSETS		Δ LIABILITIES	
Cash reserves	+ $900	NOW accounts	+ $900
Addenda			
Required reserves	+ $90		
Excess reserves	+ $810		

We see that S&L B has $900 of reserves, but only $90 of these (10 percent of the NOW accounts of $900) are required reserves. The remaining reserves, $810, are excess reserves. Motivated by the same sort of profit considerations that faced bank A, S&L B will also seek to put these excess reserves to work earning interest. It can safely do this by making loans or purchasing securities in an amount equal to its excess reserves. Let us suppose S&L B buys $810 worth of Treasury bills. After it pays for these securities and the clearing process is completed, it will have converted the $810 of excess reserves into earning assets. The T-account reflecting the initial NOW account deposit and the subsequent security purchase is:

S&L B			
Δ ASSETS		Δ LIABILITIES	
Cash reserves	+ $90	NOW accounts	+ $900
Securities	+ $810		
Addenda			
Required reserves	+ $90		
Excess reserves	0		

S&L B is now in equilibrium and satisfies our various assumptions.

We will spare you the tedium of going through another round, but the next steps should be clear. The Treasury bills bought by S&L B were bought from someone, and that someone received $810. By our assumptions, these funds will be deposited in a transactions account. The receiving institution will have a deposit of $810, required reserves of $81 (10 percent of $810), and excess reserves of $729 ($810 − $81). These $729 can in turn be used to acquire earning assets, simply continuing the sequence.

By now there should be an obvious pattern in all this. At each step, the depository institution sets aside 10 percent of its newly acquired deposits in the form of required reserves and uses the remaining 90 percent, its excess reserves, to acquire earning assets. As the rounds mount up, the total quantity of assets and transactions accounts in the banking system increase, although at each round the increase is 10 percent smaller than the previous one. Indeed, the need to set aside 10 percent of each addition to deposits in the form of required reserves ultimately limits the size of the expansion.

This deposit expansion process is conveniently summarized in Table 8–1. As will be recalled, the first round involving bank A started with a $1,000 injection of reserves by the Federal Reserve as a result of a purchase of securities. Bank A uses $100 for required reserves and lends $900. This $900 next shows up in S&L B, which sets aside $90 in required reserves and uses its excess reserves of $810 to purchase earning assets. The first ten rounds of this process are individually identified in Table 8–1. The cumulative effects after ten rounds are also shown. As we can see, after ten rounds, transactions deposits have expanded by $6,513.22, earning assets have risen by $5,861.90, and required reserves have increased by $651.32. Since there were initially $1,000 of reserves injected into the system, after

TABLE 8–1 Deposit Expansion on New Reserves by the Depository Institution System

	Additional transactions deposits received	Additional loans made	Additional required reserves
1. Bank A	$ 1,000.00	$ 900.00	$ 100.00
2. S&L B	900.00	810.00	90.00
3. Bank C	810.00	729.00	81.00
4. S&L D	729.00	656.10	72.90
5. MSB E	656.10	590.49	65.61
6. CU F	590.49	531.44	59.05
7. S&L G	531.44	478.30	53.14
8. S&L H	478.30	430.47	47.83
9. Bank I	430.47	387.42	43.05
10. Bank J	387.42	348.68	38.74
Total, first 10 DIs	$ 6,513.22	$5,861.90	$ 651.32
Other DIs in turn	3,486.78	3,138.10	348.68
Grand total	$10,000.00	$9,000.00	$1,000.00

the tenth round there remain excess reserves of $348.68, and so the process will continue.

These rounds cease when all the excess reserves have been converted into required reserves. At that point, as Table 8–1 shows, transactions accounts have expanded by $10,000, required reserves are up $1,000, and earning assets have increased by $9,000.[3] These numbers, it should be noted, are identical to those bank A first arrived at before it realized it had overdone things. We also pointed out that when it had overdone things, bank A was acting as if it were a monopoly bank—that is, the only bank in the system. What we now see is that the *whole system* operates as if it were a monopoly bank. This actually makes good intuitive sense, because the system as a whole does have a monopoly in the provision of transactions accounts. Put another way, while individual depository institutions are subject to induced changes in reserves as the rounds proceed, under our assumptions the financial system as a whole cannot extinguish these reserves. Since we have also assumed that depository institutions ultimately hold no excess reserves, the process must ultimately convert the $1,000 reserve injection into required reserves. This can come about only if transactions deposits rise by $10,000. In this case we see that transactions accounts expand by a tenfold multiple of the initial reserve injection.[4]

Taken as a whole, the deposit expansion process illustrates a number of important points:

1 Every individual banker could properly say, "I certainly didn't engage in multiple expansion. All I did was to accept deposits, set aside the required reserve, and then lend an amount equal to the remainder." Yet for the system as a whole, there was indeed a multiple expansion of deposits and earning assets.

2 Most of the expansion occurred not at the depository institution initially receiving the increase of reserves, but in other institutions to which most of the reserves came to be transferred.

3 This illustrates the process through which initial injections of additional reserves in only one or a few depository institutions can lead to increased reserves and credit expansion throughout the system as a result of the transfer of funds between institutions.

---

[3]The total increase in transactions accounts is the sum of the increases on each of the individual rounds. That is, we need to add $1,000 + $900 + $810 + $729 + $\cdots$, where each term is 0.9 times the preceding term. That is, we need to find the sum of a geometric series of the form $a + ar + ar^2 + \cdots$ where in our present example $a = \$1,000$ and $r = 0.9$. As might be remembered, the general answer to this problem is that the sum of the series is given by the formula $a/(1 - r)$. With our given values of a and r, this works out to $\$1,000/(1 - 0.9) = \$10,000$, as shown in Table 8–1.

[4]As this logic suggests, the multiple depends on the percentage reserve requirement. For example, a 5 percent reserve requirement would allow a $1,000 injection of reserves to support an increase in transactions accounts of $20,000 (since $.05 \times \$20,000 = \$1,000$). In other words, this would be a multiple of 20. Some simple algebraic expressions for the multiple are given in the next section.

These transfers of funds are significant for several reasons. In the first place, they help to explain why depository institutions seek to attract deposits away from other depository institutions. An institution that succeeds can draw reserves from others and increase its lending power. In the second place, they make the liquidity problem of an individual institution quite different from that of the system as a whole. An individual institution must be able to meet not only its depositors' demands for coin and currency, but also its payments to other depository institutions. And in the third place, because of these depository institution transfers, an individual institution that receives an initial addition to its cash reserves usually cannot expand its loans, investments, and deposits by a multiple amount. The depository institution must recognize that at least some of the deposits it creates by making loans or buying securities will be checked out to others, necessitating transfer of all or some of the initial increase of cash reserves.

DEPOSIT CONTRACTION

To this point, we have considered only the consequences of an injection of reserves into the system. The Federal Reserve, however, is equally capable of reducing reserves. As we have seen, it can do this by reducing its lending to depository institutions or by selling securities. A reduction of reserves starts a multiround process, like that described before, with the important distinction that instead of deposits being *created* as depository institutions expand, deposits are *destroyed* as these institutions contract.

Let us assume, for example, that the Fed sells $1,000 worth of securities to an individual and is paid by check. The depository institution on which the check is drawn will find that both its deposits and its reserves decrease by $1,000. While the balance sheet of this institution is still "balanced," it now finds itself in a difficulty of a different sort; it has a *reserve deficiency*. The reduction in deposits means that required reserves decline by $100 (assuming, as before, a 10 percent reserve requirement). But total reserves have dropped by $1,000, so this institution is now short $900 worth of reserves. To remedy this deficiency, it can call loans or sell securities. If it sells securities, it will likely be paid with a check drawn on another depository institution. This second institution will then have a reserve deficiency, and the rounds will continue.

The process, results, and conclusions are symmetrical with those mentioned previously. Table 8–1 can be used to illustrate this if the column headings are changed. Change the first column heading to read, "Decrease in deposits and reserves"; the second to, "Decrease of required reserves because of loss of deposits"; and the third to, "Decrease in loans and investments" (this is equal to 90 percent of deposits lost).

Now that its reserves are deficient, the first depository institution will decrease its loans and security holdings, receive in payment checks drawn on the second depository institution, and gain reserves from the latter. The second institution will decrease its loans and security holdings, receive in payment checks on the third, and gain reserves from it. And so the contraction process spreads and continues until the system has contracted by the minimum amount required to repair the reserve position of its members. As we see from Table 8–1, suitably reinterpreted, in the present example there will ultimately be a contraction of $10,000 in deposits and $9,000 in earning assets.

SOME COMPLICATIONS

In explaining the basics of deposit expansion and contraction, we abstracted from a number of complications by the use of simplifying assumptions. While these assumptions proved expositionally convenient, you will be glad to hear that replacing these assumptions with more realistic ones will not change the essentials of deposit creation.

For example, as we proceeded, we assumed at each round that when an individual depository institution experienced an initial increase in its excess reserves and proceeded to expand its holdings of loans and securities, all the resulting so-called *derivative deposits* and an equal amount of reserves would be transferred to other institutions. Thus, it could expand its loans and securities only by an amount equal to the initial addition to its excess reserves. This is an approximation of what often happens to an individual depository institution in a system of thousands of institutions. However, in some cases a part of the derivative deposits created by an individual institution remains with it, at least for a time, so that its loss of deposits and reserves to others is less than depicted above. For example, a borrower from the depository institution may voluntarily leave some of the proceeds on deposit with the institution, or the depository institution may require the borrower to do so as a condition for granting the loan. Or the borrower may pay some of the derivative deposits to others who are depositors at the same institution. In such cases an individual depository institution may expand its loans and securities more than was indicated in the earlier example.

Nevertheless, despite this potential complication, the overall expansion of the system will be exactly as we have described it. Indeed, we have seen that the overall result would be precisely the same if there were just one monopoly bank which had cornered the market in deposits. Under our assumptions, all that matters is the size of the initial injection of reserves and the percentage reserve requirement. These two ingredients determine the ultimate expansion of the system. The precise way in which this expansion is split up among individual depository institutions has no bearing on the size of the ultimate expansion.

To be sure, we also made a number of other simplifying assumptions that could affect the size of the expansion. We assumed that depository institutions only held transactions accounts and that they held no excess reserves. We also assumed that the public held a fixed amount of currency throughout the expansion or contraction processes. Relaxation of these assumptions does not change the logic of the process, but it can alter the numerical results. The precise way in which this works can be seen if we turn to some explicit expressions for the deposit creation process.

MULTIPLE EXPANSION AND CONTRACTION IN SYMBOLS

We have just seen that an injection of reserves available to depository institutions will yield a change in transactions deposits and assets equal to some multiple of the initial change in reserves. And we have also suggested that the size of the multiple will tend to be larger as the reserve requirement is smaller. Similarly, we have seen that if depository institutions lose reserves at a time when they hold no excess reserves, they will have to reduce their deposit liabilities and assets by some multiple of the reserves lost. This multiple expansion and contraction of deposits and assets in response to a change in reserves plays a key role in the operation of monetary policy. It is therefore important that we understand what lies behind this multiple. We shall in fact explore not just one multiple, but several: those relating to (1) transactions deposits; (2) earning assets of depository institutions; and (3) the money supply. In some cases, as we shall see, the various multiples can differ significantly.

To explore these various multiples, as before, we start from some *initial* injection into the total reserves of the depository institutions. The $1,000 increase in total reserves that started the process portrayed in Table 8–1 is one example of such an initial injection. The word *initial* is emphasized here because once we permit the public to vary its holdings of currency (recall that one of our simplifying assumptions ruled this out), the quantity of reserves available to the depository institutions can change from the initial injection. Indeed, it is quite likely that as an expansion of deposits is taking place, the public will prefer to take some of the proceeds and hold them in the form of currency. In such a situation, we say there is an *induced cash drain*. Each dollar withdrawn to serve as currency in circulation removes a dollar of the initial increase of reserves and leaves the depository institutions with a smaller net increase of reserves to support deposit creation.[5]

We turn now to the analysis of the multiples of expansion permitted by an initial increase in reserves. Since we propose to do this in symbols, we need to establish a bit of notation. For convenience, although we will introduce them gradually, it will help to have all the symbols we will need in one place.

---

[5]This should hardly be surprising, since earlier in this chapter we saw that if the public voluntarily chose to deposit currency in a depository institution, this provided reserves to the institution (see p. 198). When the public adds to its currency holdings by withdrawing currency from a depository institution, the opposite happens and reserves decline.

ΔB = the initial change in the volume of total reserves.

ΔD = the change in the volume of transactions deposits.

ΔN = the change in the volume of nonpersonal time deposits. At times it will be convenient to express this as $\Delta N = n\Delta D$, thus stating ΔN as a fraction or multiple of ΔD.

r_D = the fractional reserve requirement against transactions accounts.

r_N = the fractional reserve requirement against nonpersonal time deposits.

ΔC = the net induced change in currency holdings by the public as a result of deposit expansion or contraction. This will sometimes be expressed as $\Delta C = c\Delta D$, thus stating ΔC as a fraction, c, of ΔD.

ΔM = the change in the money supply. This is equal to $\Delta D + \Delta C$.

ΔL = the change in the volume of loans and investments of the depository institutions.

ΔE = the ultimate change in excess reserves after the depository institutions have responded to the initial reserve injection. It will be convenient to express this as a fraction of the change in transactions deposits, as in $\Delta E = e\Delta D$.

THE SIMPLE CASE REVISITED

We first develop the relevant expression for the case corresponding to Table 8–1. This case was simplified in that we assumed there were no excess reserves, no cash drains, and no nonpersonal time deposits.[6] In the present instance, these assumptions correspond to $e = 0$, $c = 0$, and $n = 0$. What these assumptions mean is that no part of the initial injection of reserves is absorbed in excess reserves or in a cash drain or goes to support an expansion of nonpersonal time deposits. Stated positively, all the initial injection of reserves is available to support an expansion of transactions deposits.

EXPANSION

Suppose depository institutions receive an initial increase in reserves equal to ΔB. With this accretion to their reserves, they can proceed to create additional deposits (ΔD) by expanding their holdings of loans and securities (ΔL). They will have expanded to the maximum permitted by ΔB only when they have expanded transactions deposits so much that their required reserves ($r_D\Delta D$) have risen by an amount equal to the initial injection of reserves. In other words, maximum expansion has been reached when

$$r_D\Delta D = \Delta B$$

---

[6]In effect, we earlier assumed there were no personal time deposits as well. Since personal time deposits are exempt from reserve requirements, for our present purposes they can be safely ignored, since they do not directly affect the expansion process we are describing.

or

$$\Delta D = \frac{\Delta B}{r_D} \tag{1}$$

We thus see that the increase in the volume of transactions deposits, ΔD, is a multiple of the increase in total reserves in the system, where the *multiplier, m,* is given by

$$m = 1/r_D \tag{2}$$

In other words, we can write

$$\Delta D = m\Delta B \tag{3}$$

where the multiplier m is the reciprocal of the reserve requirement.

What happens to the quantity of money in this case? We know that in general $\Delta M = \Delta D + \Delta C$. But since we are ruling out cash drains, $\Delta C = 0$. Hence, $\Delta M = \Delta D$ in this case.

In order to see how this works, we can turn to a numerical example. To facilitate comparison with our earlier results, we assume that

$$\Delta B = \$1,000$$

$$r_D = 0.10$$

These are the numerical values that underlie Table 8–1. What we see now is that $\Delta D = \$1,000/.10 = \$10,000$. We can show the results of this by the following T-account for all depository institutions taken together:

Δ ASSETS		Δ LIABILITIES	
ΔB	+ $1,000	ΔD	+ $10,000
ΔL	+ $9,000		
Addendum			
Increase of required reserves			
= $10,000 × 0.10 = $1,000			

The addendum shows that deposits have indeed expanded to the maximum permitted, for required reserves have increased enough to absorb all the initial increase in reserves. What we immediately see is that our convenient multiplier formulas give us the same results as we obtained in Table 8–1. That is, an injection of reserves results in a tenfold expansion of transactions deposits.[7]

[7]A comparison of the T-account above with Table 8–1 suggests that we should interpret the symbol, ΔD, as the *total* increase in deposits resulting from the injection of reserves. Thus, for example, if the Federal Reserve provides the reserve injection by purchasing securities, there will be an initial deposit by the seller of the security which is the vehicle for providing the reserves. As Table 8–1 shows, this initial deposit of $1,000 is included in the $10,000 total expansion of deposits. Therefore, this initial $1,000 is also included in our symbol, ΔD. We should also note that ΔL in the above T-account is simply computed so as to make the T-account balance. However, see footnote 9 below.

CONTRACTION

As we saw before, deposit contraction can be brought about by an initial reduction in the reserves available to depository institutions. We saw also that deposit expansion and contraction are really quite symmetrical. In our present discussion, a contraction is nothing more than a process that starts with a negative number for ΔB. For example, if depository institutions should experience a loss of $1,000 of reserves, we would have $\Delta B = -\$1,000$. This would set up a reserve deficiency that would lead to a reduction of loans and investments and a reduction in transactions deposits. Our simple multiplier formula tells us precisely how much this reduction will be—namely, $\Delta D = -\$10,000$. In other words, the contraction process stops when deposits have been reduced enough so that the reduction in required reserves matches the initial reserve loss.

COMPLICATION I: THE CURRENCY DRAIN

Thus far we have assumed that as depository institutions expanded, they induced no net currency drain from the system and therefore lost none of the initial increase of reserves. And when they contracted, they induced no net currency flow and were not able to gain reserves in this way to offset some of the initial loss. In a more realistic setting, however, net cash drains or inflows frequently are induced. When these do occur, they can markedly reduce the size of the multiplier of expansion or contraction.

Why does the public tend to hold more currency as deposit expansion increases the total money suppy, and to hold less currency when the system contracts? The answers most frequently given are of two general, although not necessarily conflicting, types. One emphasizes that, given the state of institutional arrangements and public preferences, there will be some more-or-less fixed ratio of currency and checking deposits the public considers to be most advantageous. When the total money supply is increased, the public will elect to hold a major part of it in the form of deposits, but will take some part in additional currency. And when the total supply of money is decreased, the public will give up some currency as well as relinquish deposits.

The other approach emphasizes the behavior of the types of payments for which currency is widely held and used. These include consumer expenditures to retail stores, restaurants, transportation companies, nightclubs, parking meters, gasoline stations, and so on. The amounts of currency the public demands to hold will most likely vary in the same direction as, if not in strict proportion with, these expenditures. When the system expands its loans and security holdings to any considerable extent, the result is likely to be a general expansion of expenditures, including retail spending. The public is therefore likely to demand more currency. But a sizable contraction of bank credit is likely to bring the opposite results— that is, a general decrease of spending, and a net relinquishment of currency by the public.

Both approaches lead to the same qualitative conclusion—that changes in transactions deposits are likely to be accompanied by changes in the same direction of the public's demand for currency. As noted above, for simplicity we assume that there is a proportional relationship between the change in currency (ΔC) and the change in deposits (ΔD). Thus, ΔC can be expressed as a fraction, c, times ΔD. In our numerical example we shall let $c = 0.15$. Thus, $\Delta C = 0.15 \Delta D$.

Again we start with the assumption that the depository system enjoys an initial increase in reserves (ΔB) and that it proceeds on this basis to expand its loans and security holdings. The public will hold the proceeds in the desired proportions in the form of additional transactions deposits (ΔD) and additional currency ($c \Delta D$). In this case, the initial increase of reserves is absorbed, or used up, in two ways: as required reserves against the additional deposits ($r_D \Delta D$) and to meet the net induced drain of currency from the system ($c \Delta D$). The system will have expanded to the maximum only when all the initial increase of reserves has been absorbed in these forms. In short, maximum expansion is reached when $r_D \Delta D + c \Delta D = \Delta B$ or $(r_D + c)\Delta D = \Delta B$, so

$$\Delta D = \frac{\Delta B}{r_D + c} \tag{4}$$

In other words, comparing equations (4) and (1), we see that as before, the increase in transactions deposits is a multiple of the initial increase in reserves. But in this case the multiplier is given by

$$m = \frac{1}{r_D + c} \tag{5}$$

Since c is a positive number, the multiplier in equation (4) will be smaller than the multiplier in equation (1). Substituting or assumed values of $\Delta B = \$1,000$, $r_D = 0.10$, and $c = 0.15$, we get

$$m = \frac{1}{0.10 + 0.15} = 4$$

whereas previously the multiplier was $1/r_D$ or 10. From equation (4) we have $\Delta D = m \Delta B = \$4,000$, so the tenfold expansion has been reduced to a fourfold one.

The net drain of currency into circulation, ΔC, is $c \Delta D$. In this case, it is $0.15 \Delta D$, or $\$600$. Note that this represents both the amount of the initial increase of reserves that the system loses through the induced currency drain and the part of the increased money supply that the public elects to hold in the form of increased currency outside the depository system.

The final effects on the balance sheet of the depository system is shown in the following table, which is in the form of a modified T-account. The addenda indicate that the system has expanded to the maximum, because the entire initial reserve increase has been used up to meet the induced cash drain and to serve as required reserves against the increase in transactions deposits.[8]

Δ ASSETS		Δ LIABILITIES	
Initial ΔB	+$1,000	ΔD	+$4,000
Less: Cash drain	600		
Remaining increase of reserves	$ 400		
ΔL	$3,600		
Addenda			
Absorption of the initial ΔB			
Loss of reserves through cash drain			$ 600
Increase of reserves required against new transactions deposits			$ 400
			$1,000

Overall, then, the introduction of the complication of the currency drain leaves the logic of the expansion process intact, but it does reduce the size of the deposit multiplier. It therefore reduces the expansion of transactions deposits brought about by an injection of reserves. What about the money supply? The general expression is

$$\Delta M = \Delta D + \Delta C = \Delta D + c\Delta D = (1 + c)\Delta D$$

Since $\Delta D = \$4,000$ and $c = 0.15$, we have $\Delta C = \$600$, so $\Delta M = \$4,600$. What we see, then, is that while the currency drain serves to reduce the size of the deposit multiplier, this same currency drain adds directly to the change in the quantity of money. However, because the currency drain cuts down on the multiple expansion process, the money supply increase in the present case is smaller than in the preceding one. After considering the remaining two complications, we will have more to say about the size of the change in the money supply.

COMPLICATION II: EXCESS RESERVES

In deriving our results so far, we have continued to assume that depository institutions hold no excess reserves. Put another way, we have assumed these institutions to be fully loaned up. This assumption is a relatively realistic one. Indeed, we have noted before that excess reserves are a non-earning asset and that profit considerations lead depository institutions to minimize such assets. Nevertheless, despite this general tendency, a modest amount of excess reserves is usually held, typically by smaller deposi-

[8]As the table in the text makes clear, the initial reserve injection, ΔB, is ultimately split into two parts: a cash drain in the form of currency and the remaining increase in reserves. For some purposes it is useful to introduce a concept called the *monetary base*, which is defined as the sum of reserves plus currency. Given this definition, the initial change in reserves is thus identical to the change in the monetary base. This, in part, motivates the choice of the symbol, ΔB, as the initial reserve injection. It also means that the multipliers in the text are multipliers with respect to the monetary base.

tory institutions. Moreover, as we will see in Chapter 12, excess reserves have sometimes been held in substantial quantities, and marked variations in these holdings have historically posed a serious policy problem for the Federal Reserve. As a consequence, it is worthwhile to spell out how the introduction of excess reserves alters the deposit expansion story.

Introducing excess reserves into the picture is quite straightforward, and the details are similar to the case of a currency drain. To emphasize this similarity, we consider both complications at once. Permitting depository institutions voluntarily to hold excess reserves means that there are now three potential uses of an initial reserve injection: for required reserves, for a currency drain (ΔC), or for excess reserves (ΔE). Let us denote the change in required reserves by ΔRR. We can thus express the three possible uses of the initial reserve injection in symbols as follows:

$$\Delta B = \Delta RR + \Delta C + \Delta E \tag{6}$$

It will be recalled that we are expressing the currency drain by $\Delta C = c\Delta D$. As noted earlier, it will also be convenient to model the demand for excess reserves in a similar fashion—namely, $\Delta E = e\Delta D$. Finally, as in the previous cases, the change in required reserves induced by a change in transactions deposits is given by $\Delta RR = r_D \Delta D$. We can substitute these three expressions into equation (6) to yield

$$\Delta B = r_D \Delta D + c\Delta D + e\Delta D$$

$$= (r_D + c + e)\Delta D$$

This can be solved for ΔD to yield

$$\Delta D = \frac{\Delta B}{r_D + c + e} \tag{7}$$

Equation (7) summarizes the deposit creation process when both currency drains and excess reserves are taken into account. As before, it says that the expansion of transactions deposits, ΔD, will be a multiple of the initial reserve injection, ΔB, although the multiplier is now

$$m = \frac{1}{r_D + c + e} \tag{8}$$

Comparing equations (7) and (4), we see the only difference is the appearance of the symbol e in the denominator of (7). What this says, reasonably enough, is that the more depository institutions *sterilize* reserves (i.e., the higher e is), the lower the deposit multiplier will be. For lower values of e the mulitplier rises; in fact, when $e = 0$, equation (7) collapses to equation (4).

As a numerical illustration, let us assume that $e = 0.05$, and let us continue to use our earlier values: $\Delta B = \$1,000$, $r_D = 0.10$, and $c = 0.15$. Plugging these numbers into equation (8) gives us

$$m = \frac{1}{.10 + .15 + .05} = \frac{1}{.30} = 3\frac{1}{3}$$

and using (7) we have $\Delta D =$ \$3,333.33. In other words, allowing for an excess reserve drain has reduced the deposit multiplier from 4 to 3⅓.

COMPLICATION III: NONPERSONAL TIME DEPOSITS

The final complication we analyze is created by the existence of nonpersonal time deposits. These are liabilities issued to an entity other than a "natural person" and include savings and time deposits issued to businesses and governments. For the most part, nonpersonal time deposits are composed of large-denomination certificates of deposits which, as we have seen earlier, are used in liability management. As indicated above, percentage reserve requirements are applied to nonpersonal time deposits. We denote this fractional reserve requirement by the symbol r_N.

Whether or not such changes in nonpersonal time deposits will occur, and how large they will be relative to changes in transactions deposits, depend on many things, such as the nature of service charges on transactions deposits, the levels of interest rates on transactions deposits and nonpersonal time deposits, the characteristics of other available claims and their yields, changes in income levels, and so on. Without delving further into the relevant motivations, we assume that nonpersonal time deposits do expand and contract as depository institutions expand and contract and that we can express this as $\Delta N = n\Delta D$.

To analyze the effects of nonpersonal time deposits, we can use precisely the same tack we have taken before. In particular, an injection of reserves, ΔB, can be absorbed by an increase in required reserves or by a currency drain or by an excess reserves drain. This was expressed previously in equation (6), which is repeated here for convenience

$$\Delta B = \Delta RR + \Delta C + \Delta E$$

The new wrinkle in the present case is the expression for the change in required reserves, ΔRR. Up to now, only transactions deposits were permitted to change, so we had $\Delta RR = r_D\Delta D$. Now that we are accounting for an induced change in nonpersonal time deposits, we must recognize that some required reserves will be needed to support this change. Given our symbol, this additional component of required reserves is $r_N\Delta N$. The overall change in required reserves, reflecting *both* the change in transactions deposits and in nonpersonal time deposits, is given by

$$\Delta RR = r_D\Delta D + r_N\Delta N$$

Substituting this into equation (6), we have

$$\Delta B = r_D\Delta D + r_N\Delta N + \Delta C + \Delta E$$

Making use of $\Delta N = n\Delta D$, $\Delta C = c\Delta D$, and $\Delta E = e\Delta D$, we get

$$\Delta B = r_D\Delta D + nr_N\Delta D + c\Delta D + e\Delta D$$

$$= (r_D + nr_N + c + e)\Delta D$$

Solving this for ΔD gives the expansion of transactions deposits, ΔD, as

$$\Delta D = \frac{\Delta D}{r_D + nr_N + c + e} \tag{9}$$

This once again characterizes a multiplier expression of the form $\Delta D = m\Delta B$, where m is now given by

$$m = \frac{1}{r_D + nr_N + c + e} \tag{10}$$

Equation (9) is the most complex expression for the expansion of transactions deposits we consider. Indeed, with equation (9), we have now relaxed all our previous simplifying assumptions and have accounted for currency drains, excess reserves, and nonpersonal time deposits. We can evaluate the effect of this latest complication by comparing equations (10) and (8). We see that the multipliers differ in the appearance in equation (10) of the term nr_N in the denominator. Since this term is a positive number, the multiplier given by equation (10) is smaller than the one given by equation (8).

We can see how this works itself out in a numerical example with the aid of two additional assumptions: First, we assume a 5 percent reserve requirement on nonpersonal time deposits, so that $r_N = 0.05$. Second, we assume that $n = \frac{2}{3}$. That is, every \$1 of ΔD is accompanied by 67 cents of ΔN. As before, we continue to assume $\Delta B = \$1,000$, $r_D = 0.10$, $c = 0.15$, and $e = 0.05$.

Substituting our assumed values (after converting the decimals into fractions) into equation (10) we obtain:

$$m = \frac{1}{\dfrac{1}{10} + \dfrac{3}{20} + \dfrac{1}{20} + \dfrac{2}{3}\cdot\dfrac{1}{20}} = \frac{1}{\dfrac{10}{30}} = 3$$

so we see that the multiplier for transactions deposits is now 3. We can also use our various formulas and our assumed values to compute other magnitudes in which we are interested.

1 ΔD, which is $m\Delta B$, is $3 \times \$1,000$ or \$3,000.
2 ΔN, which is given by $n\Delta D$ with $n = \frac{2}{3}$, is \$2,000.
3 ΔE, stated as $e\Delta D$, with $e = 0.05$, is \$150.
4 The currency drain, ΔC, given by $c\Delta D$, with $c = 0.15$, is \$450.
5 The increase in the public's money supply (ΔM) is given by $\Delta M = \Delta D + \Delta C = \$3,000 + \$450 = \$3,450$.

The final effects on the balance sheet of the depository institutions will be as shown in the following table. The addenda indicate how the initial $1,000 injection of reserves has been used up in the expansion process to meet the induced cash drain, the induced excess reserve drain, and to serve as required reserves against the additional transactions and nonpersonal time desposits. In particular, after the cash drain of $450 a total of $550 of new reserves remain. Of these assets, $150 are held in the form of excess reserves, while the remaining $400 is used to support the expansion of transactions and nonpersonal time deposits.

Δ ASSETS		Δ LIABILITIES	
Initial ΔB	+$1,000	ΔD	+$3,000
Less: Cash drain	450	ΔN	+$2,000
Remaining increase of reserves	550		
ΔL	$4,450		
Addenda			
Absorption of the initial $1,000 increase of reserves			
Loss of reserves through cash drain			$ 450
Reserves used by excess reserves drain			150
Increase of reserves required against new transactions deposits = 0.10 × $3,000			300
Increase of reserves required against new nonpersonal time deposits = 0.05 × $2,000			100
			$1,000

OVERVIEW

We have now considered the deposit expansion and contraction process in all its glory. We began with a simple case in which there were no leakages from the initial injection of reserves. This meant that the entire initial injection of reserves was available to support a multiple expansion of transactions deposits. We then considered three alternative forms of reserve leakage: currency drains, excess reserves, and nonpersonal time deposits. Each additional source of leakage served to reduce the expansion of transactions deposits stemming from a given initial reserve injection. Stated another way, each successive leakage served to reduce the size of what we have called the transactions deposit multiplier.

Overall, the last case we considered, summarized in equation (9), is the most general one; all the preceding expressions are special cases of this more general formula. The numerical details of these various cases are summarized in Table 8–2. Evidently, the expansion of deposits declines as we move from case 1 to case 2 to case 3, reflecting the increasing leakage of reserves to uses other than supporting transactions deposits. The expansion of the money supply also declines as we move to the right in Table 8–2.

One final but important point can be brought out by comparing case 2 and case 3. We see that the expansion of transactions deposits is *lower* in

TABLE 8–2 Summary of Expansion in Three Cases
(ΔB = \$1,000, r_D = 0.10, r_N = 0.05

	Case 1 $c = 0$ $e = 0$ $n = 0$	Case 2 $c = 0.15$ $e = 0$ $n = 0$	Case 3 $c = 0.15$ $e = 0.05$ $n = 0.67$
ΔD	\$10,000	\$4,000	\$3,000
ΔN	0	0	2,000
ΔL	9,000	3,600	4,450
ΔC	0	600	450
$\Delta M = \Delta D + \Delta C$	10,000	4,600	3,450

case 3 than in case 2. Yet at the same time, the induced expansion of loans and investments, ΔL, is higher in case 3. How can this be? The answer is simple. In case 3 nonpersonal time deposits also expand (ΔN = \$2,000), so the expansion of *total* deposits in case 3 is larger than in case 2. Since depository institutions can use both transactions deposits and time deposits to acquire earning assets, it should hardly be surprising that ΔL is larger in case 3.[9]

THE SUPPLY OF MONEY

One of the major aims of this chapter is to provide an understanding of the determination of the money supply. This is important in its own right, but is critical if we are to understand the workings of monetary policy. Thus far in this chapter, however, we have made only passing reference to the money supply, concentrating instead on its major component, the quantity of transactions deposits. It is, however, quite simple to convert our general multiplier expression for transactions deposits into an expression for the total money supply.

To accomplish this, we need three ingredients. The first is equation (9), which is reproduced below

$$\Delta D = \frac{\Delta B}{r_D + nr_N + c + e}$$

and the second is the definition of the money supply as in $\Delta M = \Delta D + \Delta C$. The final ingredient is our expression for the currency drain, $\Delta C = c\Delta D$. These last two formulas can be combined to yield

$$\Delta M = (1 + c)\Delta D$$

[9]The various numbers of ΔL which appear in Table 8–2 are calculated by using the "balancing" feature of a T-account. This requires the change in assets to equal the change in liabilities. The change in assets is given as $\Delta L + \Delta RR + \Delta E$, and the change in liabilities is obviously $\Delta D + \Delta N$. Equating these two and solving for ΔL yields $\Delta L = \Delta D + \Delta N - \Delta RR - \Delta E$.

We can then substitute for ΔD from equation (9) to obtain

$$\Delta M = \left(\frac{1 + c}{r_D + nr_N + c + e}\right) \Delta B \tag{11}$$

Equation (11) expresses the change in the money stock, ΔM, as a function of the initial injection of reserves, ΔB, the reserve requirement ratios, r_D and r_N, and the three parameters relating to currency, excess reserves, and nonpersonal time deposits, c, e, and n. Equation (11) is generally called a money-multiplier formula and the quantity in parentheses in (11) is called the *money multiplier* because it is the magnitude by which a change in reserves must be multiplied to yield the corresponding change in the supply of money.[10] If we denote the money mulitiplier by m_B, we can rewrite equation (11) as

$$\Delta M = m_B \Delta B \tag{12}$$

From Table 8–2 we see how the numerical value of the multiplier changes as we alter our assumptions. Thus, for example, in case 1 the money multiplier is 10 ($\Delta M = \$10,000$ with $\Delta B = \$1,000$), while in case 2 it is 4.6 and in case 3 it is 3.45. Quite evidently the numerical value of the multiplier is sensitive to the particular values of the parameters c, e, and n, as well as to the reserve requirements, r_D and r_N.

In one sense, equation (12) tells us all there is to know about the determination of the money supply. As a consequence, it also appears to be a useful tool for a policymaker who wishes to control the supply of money. While both these notions have some truth to them, despite its deceptively comprehensive appearance, at a practical level equation (12) is not all there is to be said about the money supply. Indeed, one danger with the multiplier approach is that it gives the impression that changes in the quantity of money are brought about by a rather mechanical process. In particular, our formula suggests that, given the reserve requirement ratios, the Federal Reserve simply picks ΔB and out pops ΔM. As we shall now see, for a variety of reasons this view is terribly misleading.

THE BEHAVIOR OF THE PUBLIC

Part of the seeming simplicity of the multiplier formula stems from the way in which currency and nonpersonal time deposits appear to affect changes in the supply of money. The influence of these two quantities is captured in the parameters c and n, innocently suggesting that these are institutionally determined constants. But nothing could be further from the truth.

[10]While the money-multiplier formula has been derived and is expressed in terms of changes, the same formula holds true in terms of levels. That is, we can write $M = m_B B$. In this expression, B should be interpreted as the monetary base—that is, the sum of reserves plus currency.

Currency and nonpersonal time deposits do not move hand in hand with transactions deposits. Rather, the quantities of currency and nonpersonal time deposits the public chooses to hold vary over time in response to economic factors. In determining the quantities it will demand of currency, nonpersonal time deposits, transactions deposits, and other financial assets, the public considers their relative liquidity and safety and their relative yields. Consequently, a change in any one of these factors can alter the willingness of the public to hold currency and nonpersonal time deposits relative to transactions deposits (i.e., the parameters c and n). For example, the growth of particular kinds of transactions could alter the relative convenience of currency as compared with transactions deposits. Variations in service charges and yields paid on nonpersonal time deposits could also alter the values of c and n.

In short, the parameters c and n are economically determined variables that cannot be expected to remain constant over time. While in some circumstances they may change only slowly, if general economic conditions change rapidly, c and n may also exhibit sizable changes in a relatively brief period.

DEPOSITORY INSTITUTION BEHAVIOR

Just as economic decisions by the public influence some of the components of the money multiplier, economic decisions by depository institutions can have a similar effect. Indeed, the depository institutions can have an impact on all three parameters, c, e, and n. By altering the characteristics of their liabilities, they can directly affect the public's choice among currency, transactions deposits, and nonpersonal time deposits (the parameters c and n). Variations in service charges and in interest yields are two of the ways in which these parameters can be affected.

A vivid illustration of this is the widespread use of liability management by commercial banks. As documented in Chapter 6, this practice has grown substantially in the past two decades and now provides an important source of funds to commercial banks. One of the major ingredients on liability management is the issuance of large certificates of deposit to raise funds. As indicated earlier, such certificates are included in nonpersonal time deposits. To be sure, the commercial banks cannot simply dump these CDs on a passive public. But the banks can raise the yield they are willing to pay on CDs and induce the public to hold more of them. In this process, the banks are contributing to changing the parameter n.

Economic considerations can also affect the desirability of holding excess reserves by depository institutions (i.e., the parameter e). Excess reserves serve a useful function in keeping a depository institution liquid so that it may meet adverse clearing balances or the loan demand of its valued customers. The desirability of holding excess reserves for such purposes depends on the cost of holding such reserves—the interest income that will be forsaken—relative to the anticipated costs of meeting a deficient reserve position or new loan demand.

Clearly, this is an economic decision. We would expect that, other things being equal, depository institutions would hold more excess reserves the lower the interest rate on relatively liquid securities and hence the lower the opportunity cost on holding such reserves. In other words, e will vary with economic conditions.

FEDERAL RESERVE INFLUENCE

The remaining way in which the multiplier formula oversimplifies reality is the deceptive appearance of ΔB, the quantity we have identified as the injection of new reserves. While we have suggested that the Federal Reserve can regulate the volume of reserves, it is not endowed with a "reserve dial" that it simply sets to achieve a desired change. Rather, it must contend with a significant number of diverse factors that affect bank reserves. Among the various influences on the quantity of reserves are the following: changes in the gold stock, borrowing of reserves by the depository institutions, and the volume of foreign-owned deposits held at the Federal Reserve.[11] Each of these factors can be only imperfectly anticipated by the Federal Reserve, so that the task of regulating the volume of reserves is far from a mechanical one.

OTHER FACTORS

There are a number of other respects in which the money-multiplier formula presented in equation (11) is somewhat simplified. Here we comment on one possible complication stemming from the treatment of reserve requirements in equation (11).

As noted above, in deriving the money multiplier we have assumed that all depository institutions are subject to the same set of reserve requirements. As documented in Chapter 12, until 1980 this assumption would have been patently false. In 1980, however, Congress passed the Monetary Control Act, providing that all depository institutions should be eventually subject to *uniform reserve requirements.* For our present purposes the catch is "eventually," since the transition will not be complete until 1988. As long as reserve requirements are not uniform across depository institutions, the overall average reserve requirement can be affected by shifts of deposits between institutions with different requirements. This, of course, means that even with a given set of laws and regulations governing reserve requirements, r_D and r_N in equation (11) may move around, adding to the

---

[11]For a detailed discussion of how these affect reserves, see Chapter 11.

complications of variations in *c, e,* and *n*.[12] Fortunately, although the evidence is scanty, in practice this problem does not appear to be a particularly serious one.

OVERVIEW

We began this section by developing the money multiplier approach. We then detailed some of the hidden assumptions in this approach, suggesting that matters were somewhat more complicated than they appeared at first. The critical tone of this discussion may have gone too far in the opposite direction. It is now time to place the matter in perspective.

Briefly put, while we have stressed the fact that the multiplier formula should not be regarded as a mechanical tool, this does not mean that we should minimize the importance of the multiplier approach. The multiplier formula serves an extremely useful role in highlighting how an injection (or withdrawal) of reserves will be translated into a change in the money supply. Indeed, when properly interpreted, it serves to emphasize the importance of asset choices by the public and the depository institutions in the money supply process. Furthermore, it makes clear that the Federal Reserve, should it desire to achieve some specific change in the money supply, must be able to forecast the consequences of the behavior of the public and the depository institutions. Such anticipation is necessary, above and beyond the somewhat more technical problems of controlling the quantity of reserves.

Subsequent chapters consider in more detail the asset choices of the public. They also analyze the objectives of the Federal Reserve and spell out more precisely how the Federal Reserve goes about influencing the volume of reserves. Indeed, it is to the workings of the Federal Reserve that we now turn.

SUMMARY

1 All depository institutions are required to hold a percentage of their checkable transactions deposits in the form of reserves. Reserves amount to a nonearning asset, which can be held either as a deposit with the Federal Reserve or as vault cash. The volume of required reserves is

---

[12]There is another reason why average reserve requirements may move around. Under the 1980 law, individual depository institutions face one reserve requirement for transactions deposits below some threshold and a higher reserve requirement for deposits above the threshold. This means that smaller depository institutions will have a lower reserve requirement on transactions deposits than larger ones. Hence, a shift of transactions deposits from small to larger institutions, or vice versa, can change the overall average reserve requirement. For details on the structure of reserve requirements, see Chapter 12.

computed by applying the specific percentage, known as the reserve requirement, to the volume of reservable liabilities. Depository institutions are permitted to hold total reserves in excess of those that are required.

2 When a depository institution receives a check drawn on another depository institution, it increases its reserves by the amount of the check. At the same time, the depository institution on which the check is drawn loses an equal amount of reserves.

3 Each dollar of reserves is "high-powered" money, capable of supporting several dollars of deposits. Thus, by injecting an additional dollar of reserves into the depository institution system, the Federal Reserve can induce a multiple expansion of deposits and the money supply. Conversely, by depriving depository institutions of a dollar of reserves, the Fed can force them to reduce deposits, and hence the money supply, by some multiple.

4 The precise amount that the money supply changes for a one-dollar change in reserves is known as the money multiplier. In the simplest case, the money multiplier is just the reverse of the reserve requirement. This inverse relationship remains when complications are introduced, but the size of the money multiplier will be reduced by excess reserves, currency drains, or nonpersonal time deposits.

5 The money-multiplier approach seems to suggest that it is a relatively trivial matter for the Fed to control the money supply by picking the right quantity of reserves. However, controlling the money supply is easier said than done, since many factors impinge on bank reserves. Moreover, economic conditions can change the size of the money multiplier.

SELECTED READINGS

Burger, A. E. *The Money Supply Process.* Belmont, CA: Wadsworth, 1971.

Havrilesky, T. M., and J. T. Boorman. *Monetary Macroeconomics.* Arlington Heights, IL: AHM, 1978.

Nichols, D. M. *Modern Money Mechanics.* Chicago: Federal Reserve Bank of Chicago, 1975.

PART 3

CENTRAL BANKING

9

ORIGINS OF CENTRAL BANKING IN THE UNITED STATES

Visitors to the United States are often puzzled by the complexity of the American banking system. In most countries there is a single central bank to perform the functions of monetary management; power to charter and regulate commercial banks is usually concentrated in the central government; and the commercial banking system typically consists of no more than 20, and in many cases no more than 10, banks with numerous branches. Against such a background, the American system inevitably seems complex, if not confused and confusing. Here, there is not a single central bank, but a central banking system composed of the Board of Governors of the Federal Reserve System, located in Washington, D.C., and 12 separately incorporated Federal Reserve banks located in as many regions. Even at the federal level, jurisdiction over commercial banks is not concentrated in a single agency but divided among three—the Federal Reserve, the Comptroller of the Currency, and the Federal Deposit Insurance Corporation. Moreover, power to charter and regulate commercial banks is shared in complex and often overlapping ways among federal agencies and the various state governments. The result is the American *dual banking* system.

No one can understand this system without a knowledge of American banking history, which is closely interlinked with old and continuing political and economic controversies over such issues as the relative roles of the central and state governments in a federal system, concentration of economic and financial power, and conflicts between creditor and debtor areas. Our purpose in this chapter is not to present a complete history of American banking, but rather to concentrate on those episodes, events, and forces that contribute most to an understanding of the present system of commercial and central banking.

BANKING FROM 1781 TO 1863

In banking, as in most other aspects of American life, the period from 1781 to 1863 was one of rapid development and widespread controversy. Having gained its independence, the new nation was struggling to determine its social, political, economic, and financial patterns. On all these matters there were important differences of opinion. By far the largest part of the population lived on farms, most of which were largely self-sufficient; all except a few of the cities were small; manufacturing was still in its infancy; and trade occupied a far less important position than it does today. The nation had virtually no experience with banking of modern types, and there were wide disagreements concerning the contributions banks could make. Some people were perhaps too laudatory, overestimating the extent to which banks could stimulate capital formation and promote productivity and trade by providing credit and a more generous supply of money in the form of bank notes and deposits. Others insisted that banks merely lowered the quality of the nation's money because issues of bank notes and deposits drove out, or kept out, an equal value of good metallic coins.

Alexander Hamilton and others who shared his goal of developing an industrial and commercial type of economy were generally favorably disposed toward banking, believing that banks were an essential part of such an economy. Thomas Jefferson and his sympathizers, who believed that the country should remain largely agricultural, were generally opposed to banks, at least partly because banking was closely related to industry and commerce. The Federalists and others who favored centralization of political power believed that the power to charter and supervise banks should be exclusively federal. They questioned the constitutionality of state activities in this field. On the other hand, the anti-Federalists and their friends, who opposed centralization of political power and championed states' rights, insisted that only the states had the power to create and supervise banks and that such federal activities were unconstitutional. Much of the banking controversy of the period is understandable only as a part of the broader controversy over industrialization versus agrarianism and centralization of political power versus states' rights.

It is important to remember also that bank notes were more important than deposits as a means of payment until about the time of the Civil War. Checking deposits were used, especially in the cities, but they were not suited to a predominantly agricultural country with few towns and slow travel and communication. In fact, during the colonial period the word *bank* meant "a batch of paper money." The first bank of a modern type in this country was the Bank of North America, which was established in Philadelphia in 1782 to aid in financing the revolutionary war. The Bank of New York and the Bank of Massachusetts were established in 1784. These three were the only incorporated banks in the United States in 1790. There were, however, a few unincorporated or private banks, for under the common law everyone had a right to engage in banking as well as in other types of business. Only later, after 1800, did the states begin to limit banking by unincorporated firms.

THE FIRST BANK OF THE UNITED STATES, 1791–1811

The First Bank of the United States, the first to be authorized by the federal government, received a 20-year charter in 1791. It had a capital stock of $10 million, of which $2 million was subscribed by the federal government with funds borrowed from the bank; the remainder was subscribed by private individuals, some of them residents of foreign countries. By today's standards it was a small bank; in its day it was huge. It was not only by far the largest bank of its day, but also the largest corporation in America. It established its head office in Philadelphia and branches in the other principal cities of the country. Thus, the first federally chartered bank was a nationwide branch bank jointly owned by the federal government and private investors.

The bank made loans and purchased securities; issued both deposits and bank notes; transferred loan funds and payments from one end of the country to the other; and performed useful functions for the government in lending to it, acting as its depository, and transferring funds for it. It also performed some central banking functions, for it regulated the lending and note-issuing powers of state banks. As the largest bank in the system, its own lending policies greatly affected the reserves of other banks. When it expanded its loans, some of the proceeds flowed to other banks, augmenting their reserves in the form of deposits at the First Bank, or gold and silver specie. When the First Bank contracted its loans, it drained reserves from the other banks and limited their lending ability.

It could greatly affect their specie reserves and lending power by its disposal of the bank notes that came into its possession. By simply holding these notes or paying them out into circulation, it could permit the banks to retain their specie reserves. But by presenting their notes to the issuing banks for redemption, the First Bank could decrease their specie reserves. It was in the exercise of its central banking power, and especially in limiting the loans and note issues of state banks, that the First Bank made some of its bitterest enemies.

The First Bank seems to have functioned well, especially when compared with other banks during the first half of the nineteenth century. Nevertheless, Congress refused to renew its charter when it expired in 1811. Several arguments against recharter were advanced:

1 Much of the bank stock was owned by foreigners. Some people feared that foreigners would exercise excessive control over the economy through the bank, although foreign stockholders had no vote; it was also argued that money was drained out of the country by the payment of dividends to foreign stockholders.

2 Only "hard money" was good money. A large part of the community was still opposed to paper money of any sort, whether issued by banks or by government.

3 The bank was unconstitutional. The Constitution contained no express provision for bank charters. The anti-Federalists contended that no such power was even implied, and hence the bank had been unconstitutional from the beginning. Moreover, they feared that it would tend to centralize power in the federal government at the expense of the states, as its foremost proponent, Alexander Hamilton, hoped it would. It was frequently charged, apparently with some justice, that the bank was dominated by Federalists and that it discriminated against anti-Federalists in making loans.

4 The bank discouraged the growth of state banks. It is clear that the First Bank curbed the issue of state bank notes by presenting them regularly for redemption. Some elements of the community, including the owners and officers of state banks as well as other proponents of "easy money," wanted to eliminate the curbing effects of the bank.

Whatever the deciding motives of Congress in refusing its recharter, the First Bank of the United States expired in 1811.

STATE BANKING, 1811–1816

Freed from the restraining influence of the First Bank and favored by inflationary financing of the War of 1812, state banks went on a spree. They grew in number from 88 in 1811 to 246 in 1816, and their note issues rose from $45 million in 1812 to at least $100 million in 1817. Virtually all ceased to redeem their notes in gold or silver, and their notes depreciated by varying amounts; the notes of many banks became virtually worthless. All the banking abuses we shall study later appeared during this period. It was largely because of these gross abuses of the banking privilege by state banks and because of the extreme disorder of the monetary system that the Second Bank of the United States was established in 1816.

THE SECOND BANK OF THE UNITED STATES, 1816–1836

The Second Bank of the United States received a 20-year charter from the federal government in 1816. In many respects it resembled the First Bank, but it was much larger and some of its charter provisions were different. Its capital was fixed at $35 million, of which one-fifth was to be subscribed by the federal government and paid for with its bonds. The remaining $28 million was subscribed by individuals, corporations, companies, and states. The bank was governed by a board of directors, of whom 5 were appointed by the president of the United States and 20 were elected by the private stockholders. It established 25 branches to serve all the settled parts of the country.

Like the First Bank, the Second Bank performed both commercial and central banking functions. Moreover, it acted as a regulator of state banks, presenting their notes for redemption, insisting that they redeem their obligations promptly in specie, and limiting in general the amount of credit they created. This was one of the principal purposes for which the Second Bank was created. This regulatory function naturally proved to be a source of considerable tension between the Second Bank and the state banks. In addition, state banks did not take kindly to competition from the Second Bank in the areas of loans and deposits, and were a major source of opposition to the continued existence of the Second Bank. As with the First Bank, there were also other sources of opposition. Once again questions of constitutionality emerged, as did challenges from those who doubted the wisdom, in a political democracy, of concentrating financial and economic power in the hands of a small group.

The Second Bank might have survived this opposition, and even the charges of mismanagement leveled against it, were it not for its political activity. This became particularly troublesome with the election of Andrew Jackson to the presidency in 1828. A large majority of those in control of the Second Bank were opposed to Jackson and his party. Moreover, they were often aggressive in their political activities, with at least some of the bank's branch managers using their lending power to influence votes. The fate of the bank was sealed when its president. Nicholas Biddle, openly but vainly opposed Jackson's reelection in 1832 and made recharter of the bank one of the issues of the presidential campaign. After his reelection Jackson saw to it that federal deposits were withdrawn from the bank and placed with selected state banks, and the charter was allowed to expire in 1836. The country was to see no more federally chartered banks until 1863 and was not to have another central banking system until 1914. The clash between Biddle and Jackson thus may well have altered the course of our banking history.

Was President Jackson right in refusing to recharter the Second Bank in 1836? A full answer to this question would require far more space than we can devote to it. Two facts now seem clear, however. In the first place, it is questionable public policy to grant central banking powers to a corporation that is largely owned and controlled by private individuals and other corporations; is operated by its owners primarily for profit; and, as a profit-seeking enterprise, has interests in conflict with those of the banks it regulates. We now recognize that central banking is a governmental function that can be properly exercised only by institutions with a primary motive of not profit but financial and economic stabilization. A properly managed central bank must often follow policies that will decrease its profits. In the second place, it is quite clear that the abolition of the Second Bank without establishing another institution to assume its functions was a major blunder. It ushered in a generation of banking anarchy and monetary disorder.

STATE BANKING, 1836–1863

From the lapse of the Second Bank's charter in 1836 until the establishment of the National Banking System in 1863, our banking system was made up exclusively of private (unincorporated) banks and of banks operating under corporate charters granted by the various states. We shall not discuss the unincorporated banks except to say that, as a group, they seem to have been neither significantly better nor significantly worse than the incorporated banks. The incorporated banks, operating under widely diverse state laws, varied from those that performed their functions satisfactorily to those that engaged in practically all known banking abuses.

Prior to 1837 a bank could secure a corporate charter from a state only by a special legislative act. This method of granting bank charters gradually fell into disfavor for several reasons. It injected banks into politics and politics into banks. Loyal members of the political party in power might receive a bank charter, whereas members of the minority party had little chance of success. The controversy over bank charters threatened to corrupt state governments. Legislators were offered large sums of money to grant new charters and other large sums by existing banks to reject the applications of potential competitors. Furthermore, this method of granting charters often gave monopoly power to the favored banks.

To remedy this situation, Michigan in 1837 and New York in 1838 enacted *free banking* laws. Most of the other states later enacted laws of the same general type. These laws ended the practice of granting charters by special legislative act and provided that anyone might secure a corporate charter and engage in banking by complying with the provisions of a general bank incorporation law. Banking was made "free" to all enterprisers who met the specified general requirements. The quality of state banks came to depend on how appropriate these general requirements were and on how well they were enforced. In some states the requirements were strict; banks could issue notes only by depositing with a state official an equivalent amount of high-quality bonds and by meeting adequate capital and reserve requirements. But in the majority of states the collateral requirements for notes were hopelessly inadequate, and capital and reserve requirements were virtually meaningless.

The relationships between banks and the states varied widely. At one extreme, the banks merely received their charters from the state; they secured all their capital from private sources and made any loans that were permitted within the broad framework of the banking laws. At the other extreme, many banks were wholly owned and operated by states. There were several variations between these two extremes. Thus, some banks were owned jointly by a state and private investors. Others had to pay large sums to the state for the privilege of banking. And still others were permitted to act as banks only if they would lend stipulated amounts to canal companies, railroads, or other enterprises considered meritorious by the state legislature. In a period when "capital" was still scarce, states encouraged and even forced banks to lend large amounts for the financing of selected projects.

With the transfer of federal deposits from the Second Bank to selected state banks and the removal of the moderating hand of the Second Bank, both the number of state banks and the volume of their credit increased. This growth was far from steady, and there were often violent fluctuations in the amount of money created by the banks. The principal expansions and contractions during this period are shown in Table 9–1. Business activity and prices fluctuated widely as banks alternated between (a) inflationary periods of increased money supplies and liberal loans and (b) periods of shrinking money supplies and reduced loans. The banks' policies were not the sole causes of these fluctuations, but they were unquestionably contributory factors.

ABUSES BY THE STATE-CHARTERED BANKS BEFORE THE CIVIL WAR

The principal banking abuses during this period were so widespread that they greatly influenced both public attitudes toward banks and subsequent banking legislation. Some of the most serious were the following:

TABLE 9–1 Principal Expansions and Contractions of State Bank Notes and Deposits, 1834–1860

Period	PERCENTAGE EXPANSION (+) OR CONTRACTION (−)		
	Bank notes	Bank deposits	Total notes and deposits
1834–1837	+ 56	+ 67	+ 61
1837–1843	− 60	− 56	− 58
1843–1848	+119	+ 84	+102
1848–1849	− 11	− 12	− 11
1849–1854	+ 78	+107	+ 91
1854–1855	− 9	+ 2	− 4
1855–1857	+ 15	+ 21	+ 18
1857–1858	− 28	− 19	− 24
1858–1860	+ 36	+ 37	+ 36

SOURCE: Board of Governors of the Federal Reserve System, *Banking Studies*. Washington, D.C.: 1941, pp. 417–418.

1   **INADEQUATE BANK CAPITAL.** Many banks failed to maintain large enough capital accounts to protect their creditors. Some made no pretense of having adequate capital. Others had a large enough nominal capital, but it was paid for with the promissory notes of the stockholders, many of whom were unable to meet their obligations. Even when bank stocks were initially paid for with gold or silver, stockholders often borrowed back the coin, giving in return doubtful paper. Furthermore, bank capital was frequently dissipated by excessive dividend payments.

2   **RISKY AND ILLIQUID LOANS.** Many of the banks made highly risky, illiquid, and speculative loans without regard for the safety of their creditors, and some lent excessively to their own stockholders and officers. This combination of inadequate capital and highly risky and illiquid loans could lead to but one result: numerous bank failures and serious losses to note holders and depositors.

3   **INADEQUATE RESERVES AGAINST NOTES AND DEPOSITS.** In certain of the state banking laws the reserve requirements were either wholly absent or very inadequate, and evasions of existing requirements were widespread.

As a result of all these abuses—excessive issues of bank notes, inadequate bank capital, risky and illiquid bank assets, and highly inadequate reserves—bank notes had widely differing values. The notes of some banks were freely redeemed in gold and silver and circulated at their face value. Others circulated at small but varying discounts; still others circulated at only a small percentage of their face value; and many became completely worthless.

The period was a counterfeiter's paradise. Each of the hundreds of banks issued notes of its own design and in many denominations; the notes were made of many kinds of paper, mostly of low quality; the workmanship on the genuine notes was usually poor; and no one could be familiar with all the notes outstanding. Under these conditions it was easy to raise the denomination of genuine notes and to issue counterfeits on existent or even nonexistent banks. Bicknall's Counterfeit Detector and Bank-Note List of January 1, 1839, contains the names of "54 banks that had failed at different times; of 20 fictitious banks, the pretended notes of which are in circulation; of 43 banks besides, for the notes of which there is no sale; of 254 banks, the notes of which have been counterfeited or altered; and 1,395 descriptions of counterfeited or altered notes [then] supposed to be in circulation, from one dollar to five hundred."[1] That these conditions had not been remedied by 1858 is indicated by the fact that Nicholas's *Bank Note Reporter* gave 5,400 separate descriptions of counterfeit, altered, and spurious notes. There were 30 different counterfeit issues of the Bank of Delaware notes.[2]

[1] Raguet, quoted by Horace White, *Money and Banking*. Boston: Ginn, 1896, pp. 403–404.
[2] Ibid., p. 398.

The numerous counterfeit detectors and bank note reporters that attempted to warn against counterfeits and to indicate the current values of the various bank notes were of only limited assistance. Even with their supplements they were often out of date, they were beyond the reach of small businesses and individuals, and they could not remove the confusion in trade resulting from the fact that the price charged for an article depended on the type of bank note with which payment was to be made.

Although banking abuses during this period were widespread, we must not leave the impression that all state banks were unsound. Some states, notably New York, Massachusetts, and Louisiana, enacted highly protective banking laws and implemented them with supervision and examinations. In fact, some of these laws, especially those of New York, contributed much to the legislation establishing the national banking system.

Moreover, it should not be concluded without investigation and analysis that banks that "play it safe" are always more socially beneficial than those that assume large risks in both types and amounts of their loans. On the one hand, we want banks to be safe; we do not want them to fail; and we want them to keep their bank notes and deposits continuously at parity with other types of money. On the other hand, we want banks to stand ready to finance productive projects, some of which are inherently risky. It may well be that some of the banks which made highly risky loans contributed more to American economic development and growth than some which were overly concerned with safety. It is not always easy to find an optimal balance between these objectives.

THE NATIONAL BANKING SYSTEM, 1863–1914

In 1863, just 27 years after the expiration of the Second Bank of the United States, the federal government again entered the banking field by passing "An Act to provide a national currency, secured by a pledge of United States Stocks, and to provide for the Circulation and Redemption thereof." The 1863 law, which contained a large number of imperfections, was replaced by a new law in 1864. The latter is usually referred to as the National Banking Act.

PRINCIPAL PROVISIONS OF THE NATIONAL BANKING ACT

We have already said that the National Banking Act owed much to earlier state banking laws, especially those of New York. The new law provided for free banking. Anyone meeting the general requirements of the act was to receive a charter and permission to engage in banking. A new office, the Comptroller of the Currency, was created in the Treasury Department to grant charters and to administer all laws relating to national banks. Among its principal provisions, in order to provide for the safety and liquidity of the banking system, the act imposed several sorts of capital requirements,

238

elaborated many restrictions on the kinds of assets banks could hold, and introduced minimum reserve requirements for both circulating bank notes and deposits. Furthermore, remembering the sorry record of state bank notes, the act set forth a detailed set of regulations concerning the issuance of bank notes. Finally, in order to ensure compliance with both the letter and the spirit of the act, national banks were required to supply the Comptroller of the Currency with periodic reports on their financial condition and were made subject to examination by the Comptroller's representatives.

Thus, every effort was made to ensure the safety and parity of value of national bank notes. In these respects, the act was successful.

STATE BANKS

It was hoped that the authorization of national banks would induce state banks to take out federal charters and comply with the requirements of the National Banking Act. When it became evident that few state banks were going to do this, Congress decided to force the issue by levying a 10 percent tax on any bank or individual paying out or using state bank notes. The purpose was to end the issuance of circulating notes by state banks and to force all or most of these banks to become national banks or to cease doing a general banking business. As shown in Table 9–2, the act did succeed in reducing the number of state banks from 1,089 in 1864 to 247 in 1868. After 1868, however, the number of state banks again began to expand, and by 1914 they outnumbered national banks by more than two to one.

How were state banks able not only to survive but to expand in spite of the prohibitive tax on their notes? The first and foremost reason was that issuing notes had become much less important in banking. With the growth of cities and more rapid transportation and communication, people used checking deposits more and more. With the privilege of creating checking deposits, a bank could now operate successfully without issuing notes. But

TABLE 9–2 State and National Banks in the United States, 1864–1914

Year	State banks	National banks
1864	1,089	467
1868	247	1,640
1870	325	1,612
1880	650	2,076
1890	2,250	3,484
1900	5,007	3,731
1910	14,348	7,138
1914	17,498	7,518

SOURCE: Board of Governors of the Federal Reserve System, *Banking Studies.* Washington, D.C.: 1941, p. 418.

why did many banks prefer to operate under state rather than federal charters when national banks also had the right to create circulating notes? The answer is to be found largely in the fact that many states imposed less rigid restrictions and granted more liberal powers than those contained in the National Banking Act. In general, state banking laws provided lower capital requirements, lower reserve requirements, less supervision by the government, and more liberal powers to lend.

SHORTCOMINGS OF THE NATIONAL BANKING SYSTEM

Although the national banking system unquestionably greatly improved the general quality of banking, the system became subject to increasing criticism. Demands for further bank reform swelled during the late years of the nineteenth century and grew still more in the first years of the twentieth, finally ushering in the Federal Reserve System in 1914. Although many aspects of national banks were criticized, the greatest complaint was against their "inflexibility," or "inelasticity." The keynote of the National Banking Act was safety, especially safety of national bank notes. Less attention was paid to the safety of deposits. Critics now complained that the system was too inflexible and that it must be given a greater degree of elasticity. The meaning of these terms was often unclear, but we can discover its general import as we proceed.

Although national bank notes were safe, there was no provision for appropriate variations in their quantity over the long run, in response to seasonal variations in the need for them, and during crisis periods. One reason for this was a provision of the National Banking Act that tied the allowable quantity of national bank notes to the quantity of federal bonds owned by the banks. The effect was to restrict the volume of bank notes to at most 90 percent of the eligible bonds outstanding. Critics maintained that a note system of this type, which was subject to the vagaries of the supply of government bonds, could never provide a properly elastic currency that would respond to the needs of the economy.

National bank notes were also criticized for their lack of seasonal elasticity. The demand for currency for hand-to-hand use showed marked seasonal variations, yet the volume of outstanding national bank notes remained relatively constant throughout the year. Hence, banks could meet seasonal peak demands for currency only by draining funds from their reserves, and the inflow of currency to the banks during slack seasons increased their reserves. Critics complained that this led to seasonal credit stringencies and demanded the creation of a currency that would increase and decrease with seasonal demands for coin and currency and leave bank reserves unaffected.

Critics also complained of the inelasticity of national bank notes during crises. They pointed out that there was no existing way in which new currency could be created to satisfy general demands on the banks for cash, and that banks could not meet these demands out of the limited cash in their vaults.

The disturbing effects of an inelastic bank note system were intensified by another feature of the National Banking Act—a defective system of reserve requirements. This reserve system had three principal weaknesses. The first drawback was that a large part of the nominal reserve was fictitious in the sense that it was not available for meeting actual cash drains from the banking system. This was because a large part of the reserves was in the form of deposit claims against other banks, which in turn held only a small percentage of actual cash as a reserve against their deposit obligations. The second weakness of the system was that reserve requirements were very inflexible. Each bank was ordered to meet its reserve requirements at all times; it could not legally make any new loans while its reserves were deficient. There arose a general demand that reserve requirements be relaxed by being suspended in periods of crisis or at least by banks being allowed to meet these requirements on the average over a period of time, deficiencies at one time being balanced by overages at another. The latter method is employed for banks that are members of the Federal Reserve System.

The third shortcoming, which was widely criticized, was the "parcelation of reserves" resulting from the lack of any orderly way of pooling the reserves of individual banks to meet drains of cash from any segment of the banking system. Some compared existing reserve requirements with attempting to fight fires by placing a pail of water in each house; the greater effectiveness of pooling the water and providing a system of pipes to concentrate it at the point of need was obvious. Advocates of bank reform proposed the establishment of a similar system of pooling individual bank reserves so that they could be concentrated at the points of greatest need in times of emergency. This was another purpose of the Federal Reserve Act of 1914.

The inelasticity of national bank notes and the defects, or at least the inadequacy, of bank reserve requirements were dramatized by the recurrent banking panics that occurred under the national banking system before 1914. There were full-fledged panics in 1873, 1884, 1893, and 1907; and serious credit stringencies threatened at other times. Unable to meet their obligations to pay cash on demand, most banks suspended payments for periods of varying lengths; some of them never reopened, a mad scramble to call loans ensued, and business activity suffered. The panic of 1907 was the last straw. Popular disgust with recurrent panics made the Federal Reserve Act politically possible, although the act had objectives beyond the prevention of panics. As Carter Glass told the House of Representatives:

> Financial textbook writers in Europe have characterized our banking as "barbarous," and eminent bankers of this country ... have not hesitated to confess

that the criticism is merited. . . . The failure of the system in acute exigencies has caused widespread business demoralization and almost universal distress. Five times within the last thirty years financial catastrophe has overtaken the country under this system; and it would be difficult to compute the enormous losses sustained by all classes of society—by the banks immediately involved; by the merchants whose credits were curtailed; by the industries whose shops were closed; by the railroads whose cars were stopped; by the farmers whose crops rotted in the fields; by the laborer who was deprived of his wage. The system literally has no reserve force. The currency based upon the nation's debt is absolutely unresponsive to the nation's business needs. The lack of cooperation and coordination among the more than 7,300 national banks produces a curtailment of facilities at all periods of exceptional demand for credit. This peculiar defect renders disaster inevitable.[3]

Many other observers agreed with Glass that the primary problem was that the existing system had no "reserve force," no "elasticity" in time of strain. No existing institution was motivated to hold large excess reserves for use in time of strain, none had the power to create new bank reserves in such periods, and none was empowered to create additional currency in time of need. The remedy followed from the diagnosis; new institutions should be created that would be empowered to create new currency and new bank reserves "as needed." *Elasticity* was the central theme of the new reserve system.

Even among those who favored banking reform, and many did not, there were widely differing opinions as to the proper control and structure of any new institutions that might be established. Some thought they should be regarded as cooperative or mutual aid societies formed privately by banks, while others argued that this was properly a function of the government or its appointees. Opinions as to the proper structure of the new system also differed. Some insisted that the United States, like most other countries, should have a single central bank. Others thought such centralization both unnecessary and undesirable. It would bring a dangerous concentration of financial power, invite domination of the entire country by Wall Street or Washington, and ignore regional differences in economic and financial conditions. One congressman thought that fifty such regional institutions would be about the right number.

The Federal Reserve Act represented a compromise among such conflicting views. The country was divided into a number of districts, each with its own Federal Reserve Bank, and a central authority was established in Washington to supervise the various Reserve banks and to coordinate their policies while permitting some degree of regional autonomy.

[3]*The Congressional Record*, September 10, 1913, p. 4642.

BANKING UNDER THE FEDERAL RESERVE SYSTEM

The establishment of the Federal Reserve System in 1914 is one of the great landmarks in American banking history.[4] More than 75 years after the demise of the Second Bank of the United States, the nation again had a set of institutions capable of exercising central banking powers. We shall discuss the details of the structure of the Federal Reserve System in the next chapter. For the present, let us focus on the initial objectives of the newly established central bank, on how these objectives were modified over time, and on the important legislative developments subsequent to the passage of the Federal Reserve Act.

As we have suggested, the Federal Reserve began with the primary objectives of using its power to create currency and bank reserves, to provide "elasticity," and to prevent or deal with banking crises and panics. In addition, the Federal Reserve Act sought to replace the slow and expensive system of check clearing and collection with one that would be faster and more efficient; to provide a more satisfactory fiscal agent for the federal government; to achieve a better coordination of state and national banks, and especially to secure more effective supervision of state banks; and to provide more liberal powers for national banks, such as those of establishing trust departments and lending on real estate, to enable them to compete more effectively with state banks and trust companies, many of which enjoyed more freedom of action. These reforms were important, but they were secondary. The primary purpose of the new banking reform was to end recurrent banking panics and crises.

To accomplish this primary objective the Federal Reserve, judged by present-day standards, had only limited discretionary powers. The new, supposedly elastic, currency provided by the Federal Reserve Act was in fact tied to supplies of gold and eligible paper, with no possibility of modifying this in times of crisis. Furthermore, changes in the reserves of member banks were determined largely at the initiative of those banks rather than by the Federal Reserve. The major point to be emphasized is that the purposes of the Federal Reserve System as conceived by its originators were far different from those of today. Now, the belief is widespread that the primary purpose of the Federal Reserve is to manage money deliberately and continuously to promote the achievement of desired economic objectives. Despite the desire for an "elastic" currency, such an idea was alien and unacceptable to those who established the Federal Reserve System. They were pleased with the international gold standard then in operation,

---

[4]Despite their "landmark" status, in the early years Federal Reserve Board members were rather low on the Washington protocol list. President Wilson, to whom they complained, is reputed to have said, "They might come right after the fire department." The press, rather more sympathetically, referred to the Board as "the new Supreme Court of finance." Cited in J. K. Galbraith, *Money*. Boston: Houghton Mifflin, 1975, p. 135.

and did not want a "managed money." Indeed, there would almost certainly have been no Federal Reserve System if its advocates had heralded it as an instrument of monetary management.

With the benefit of hindsight, this view certainly seems shortsighted. As was the case with the National Banking Act, the restructuring of the banking system in 1914, despite good intentions, did not go far enough. In particular, the limited scope of the Federal Reserve, as initially constituted, was not up to handling the financial shocks created by the stock market crash of 1929 and its aftermath. As already noted, there were nearly 8,000 bank failures in the period 1930–1933. This period culminated in the major banking crisis of 1933, during which President Roosevelt was forced to declare a banking holiday and close all the banks. The result of these developments was a number of basic changes in the regulation of the banking industry. This was accomplished in large part by a significant reorganization of the Federal Reserve that led to a much greater degree of centralization. In particular, the central bank was given responsibility for implementing monetary policies that would promote economic stability and growth. Toward this end, the mechanism for borrowing from the Federal Reserve was altered to give less discretion to member banks, and the Federal Reserve was given the authority to set maximum rates of interest paid on time and savings deposits and to vary reserve requirements ratios on demand and time deposits. Although we discuss the details of these developments later, the important point to emphasize here is that as a result of the changes introduced in 1933 and soon thereafter, the Federal Reserve evolved into a full-fledged modern central bank.

SUMMARY

1 Central bank functions were initially performed in the United States by the First and Second Banks of the United States. Both performed banking functions for the federal government and regulated the lending and note-issuing powers of state banks. The state banks, in turn, did not enjoy this regulation, nor did they appreciate the fact that the First and Second Banks engaged in conventional commercial banking, thus competing with the state banks. This created political controversy that ultimately contributed to the demise of both banks.

2 From the disappearance of the Second Bank in 1836 until 1863, banking was in the hands of state-chartered institutions and private banks. There was no central bank and no national bank of any sort. This was also a period of widespread abuses, and it was in response to these that the National Banking Act was passed in 1863.

3 The 1863 act established a class of nationally chartered banks and set up the office of the Comptroller of the Currency to grant charters and to monitor the financial condition of banks. The act also regulated

bank assets and liabilities, including the issuance of bank notes. While an improvement over the previous state of affairs, the act did not provide a systematic way for varying the quantity of bank notes in circulation, nor did it provide for a lender of last resort. As a consequence, the act did not eliminate bank panics which, over the next 40 years, occurred about once a decade. The 1907 panic proved to be the last straw and ultimately led Congress to pass the Federal Reserve Act of 1913.

4 With the establishment of the Federal Reserve System in 1914, the United States finally had a full-fledged central bank, endowed with a role as a lender of last resort. However, as events of the 1930s proved, the 1913 act did not go far enough in providing for a stable banking system. Indeed, it was only after the banking crisis of 1933 that the Federal Reserve was reorganized as a modern central bank.

SELECTED READINGS

Board of Governors of the Federal Reserve System. *Banking Studies*. Washington, D.C., 1941.

Dewey, D. R. *Financial History of the United States*, 11th ed. New York: McKay, 1931.

Hammond, Bray. *Banks and Politics in America from the Revolution to the Civil War*. Princeton, NJ: Princeton University Press, 1957.

Sprague, O. M. W. *History of Crises Under the National Banking System*, Senate Document No. 538. Washington, D.C.: U.S. Government Printing Office, 1910.

Taus, E. R. *Central Banking Function of the U.S. Treasury, 1789–1941*. New York: Columbia University Press, 1943.

Trescott, P. B. *Financing American Enterprise*. New York: Harper & Row, 1963.

10

THE FEDERAL RESERVE SYSTEM

In passing the Federal Reserve Act in late 1913 and actually establishing the Federal Reserve banks in November 1914, the United States was one of the last of the great economic powers to provide itself with a central bank. The Bank of Sweden was founded in 1656, the Bank of England in 1694, the Bank of France in 1800, the Netherlands Bank in 1814, and the Bank of Belgium in 1835. In general outline, the functions of the Federal Reserve are similar to those of central banks in other countries. Like other central banks, its primary function is to regulate monetary and credit conditions. To this end it creates and destroys money and regulates the creation and destruction of money by depository institutions. It also performs many other functions, including check clearing and collection, acting as fiscal agent for the government, engaging in operations in the foreign exchange market, and so on. This chapter will focus on these subsidiary functions as well as on the structure of the Federal Reserve System. The role of the Federal Reserve in the regulation of money and credit will be taken up in the next two chapters.

THE STRUCTURE OF THE FEDERAL RESERVE SYSTEM

THE 12 FEDERAL RESERVE BANKS

The Federal Reserve Act provided that the continental United States should be divided into no fewer than 8 nor more than 12 Federal Reserve districts, each to have a Federal Reserve bank. The maximum number of districts and banks was established at the outset. The boundaries of these districts are shown on the map in Figure 10–1. Each Federal Reserve bank is named after the city in which it is located; there is the Federal Reserve Bank of Boston, the Federal Reserve Bank of New York, and so on. To facilitate their operations, some of the Federal Reserve banks have established branches in their districts. There are now 25 of these branches distributed unequally among the various districts.

To outsiders, the existence of the district banks sometimes give the appearance of the United States' having 12 central banks. In the early years of the Federal Reserve, there was an element of truth in this view. Indeed, to the designers of the Federal Reserve System it was at least plausible to argue that each broad region should have its own central bank, which could adapt its policies to the specific conditions of the region.[1] This strategy, however, inevitably gave rise to a number of complications. In particular,

[1]According to one waggish economist, the multiplicity of district banks—each of which resided in a building of "somber fiduciary classic"—had the side benefit of contributing "an impression of solid substance to such otherwise secondary financial centers as Cleveland or St. Louis." See J. K. Galbraith, *Money*. Boston: Houghton Mifflin, 1975, p. 119.

FIGURE 10–1
Federal Reserve districts, Federal Reserve banks,
and branches of Federal Reserve banks

KEY:
— Boundaries of Federal Reserve districts
— Boundaries of Federal Reserve branch territories
● Board of Governors of Federal Reserve System
● Federal Reserve bank cities
○ Federal Reserve branch cities

as originally passed, the Federal Reserve Act was rather vague as to the precise relationship among the 12 regional banks and between the 12 banks as a group and the Federal Reserve Board in Washington. As events developed, at first the district banks played a dominant role in the system, with the Federal Reserve Bank of New York assuming particular importance. The role of the New York bank reflected its size (even today it holds about 25 percent of the total assets of all the Reserve banks); the forceful leadership of its president, Benjamin Strong; and its critical location at the hub of the domestic and international financial markets. Overall, the relative importance of the district banks vis-à-vis Washington in the early years is illustrated by the fact that on several occasions the chairman of the Federal Reserve Board moved on (at a doubled salary) to head a Federal Reserve bank.[2] The struggle for power between the Federal Reserve Board in Washington and the 12 district banks continued for roughly two decades. It was not until the reorganization of the Banking Act of 1935 that Washington (and the newly renamed Board of Governors) finally achieved ascendancy. Today, despite appearances, the United States does have a single central bank.

MEMBER BANKS

Each of the 12 Federal Reserve banks has many *member banks*, those commercial banks in the district that have met at least the minimum requirements and have been accepted for membership in the Federal Reserve System. As explained in Chapter 5, by law all national banks (that is, those with a federal charter), must be members of the Federal Reserve; for state-chartered commercial banks, membership is optional. In recent years, only 10 percent of state-chartered banks have been members of the Fed. The reason is largely historical. Indeed, with the passage of the Monetary Control Act (MCA) in 1980, the very concept of a member bank became largely of historical interest. To appreciate this, we need to review the situation prior to the passage of the MCA.

Before 1980, member banks were distinguished from nonmember institutions in several ways. Nonmember banks did not have direct access to loans from the Federal Reserve and to other services provided to member banks. At the same time, nonmember banks escaped a number of costs of membership. For one, state-chartered nonmember banks, operating under more lenient state banking laws, were able to avoid the more stringent regulations applicable to member banks. Such regulations cover a broad

[2]These days the salary structure is the same, but movement is the other way. For example, Paul Volcker left the presidency of the Federal Reserve Bank of New York to assume his current position as chairman of the Board of Governors in 1979. For his pains, Volcker was rewarded with a pay cut of more than $50,000. Evidently, members of the Board of Governors are perceived as civil servants, while the heads of the district banks are viewed as bankers—and paid accordingly.

spectrum, including reporting requirements and restrictions on affiliates. Second, and most important, is the fact that member banks were subject to reserve requirements which had to be held in the form of vault cash or deposits at their Federal Reseve banks. In contrast, prior to 1980, nonmember banks were subjected to lower-percentage reserve requirements and were often able to hold their required reserves in interest-bearing form. Federal Reserve membership therefore reduced a bank's profits, and those banks with a choice largely opted for nonmember status.

As a result of this incentive structure, over the last 30 years member banks represented a declining fraction of all commercial banks. Member banks also accounted for a declining fraction of all deposits, with the fraction falling from 85 percent in 1955 to about 70 percent in 1980. The Federal Reserve saw this decline as undermining its ability to conduct an effective monetary policy and, on a number of occasions, called for legislation to make membership compulsory for all insured commercial banks. Matters came to a head in 1980 as nonbank depository institutions were about to gain authority to offer transactions accounts. What this meant was that the transactions accounts of savings and loan associations, mutual savings banks, and credit unions would join the transactions accounts of nonmember commercial banks in being largely exempt from reserve requirements. In the face of these developments, the Federal Reserve backed away from its call for compulsory membership, arguing instead that effective monetary control could be accomplished with *uniform reserve requirements* applicable to all depository institutions.

This was precisely the tack taken by Congress in the Monetary Control Act of 1980. In effect, the act subjected all depository institutions to the same set of reserve requirements. Moreover, it gave all depository institutions equal access to the services provided by the Federal Reserve. At least as far as monetary policy is concerned, the distinction between member and nonmember institutions is now largely irrelevant. There do remain some minor technical differences between member banks and other institutions, but only one of these is worth mentioning in the present context.

Member banks of the Federal Reserve System are technically its owners. Each member bank is required to subscribe to the stock of its Federal Reserve bank in an amount equal to 6 percent of its own paid-up capital and surplus, although in practice member banks have been required to pay in only half of their subscriptions.

It is important to note, however, that in this case, ownership does not carry with it control of the corporation and enjoyment of all its earnings. (The distribution of control is discussed in the next section.) Annual dividends to stockholders of the Reserve banks are limited to 6 percent of the paid-in capital stock. The remainder of Reserve bank earnings have been used to build up the surplus accounts of the Reserve banks and to provide revenue for the Treasury. Since 1947 the Board of Governors has voluntarily operated under a plan whereby it channels into the Treasury most of the earnings in excess of dividend requirements. In 1983 this amounted to over $14 billion, and in 1984 the sum transferred was a hefty $16 billion.

NONMEMBER BANKS AND OTHER DEPOSITORY INSTITUTIONS

As just spelled out, the Monetary Control Act of 1980 subjected all depository institutions to the same reserve requirements set by the Federal Reserve. All depository institutions were also given identical access to Federal Reserve services, such as borrowing from the Fed and check clearing. Despite this altered treatment of nonmember depository institutions, the MCA left intact the existing regulatory structure. What this means is that supervision and examination of nonmember depository institutions is still to be carried out by the various state and federal agencies that have historically regulated these institutions. Thus, for example, nonmember state banks are regulated by state banking authorities, and federally chartered savings and loan associations are overseen by the Federal Home Loan Bank Board.

CONTROL OF THE FEDERAL RESERVE SYSTEM

Closely related to the original controversy in 1913 over the structure of the Federal Reserve System was the issue of its control. The most widely debated questions were: (1) Who should control the Federal Reserve? (2) Should control be centralized or decentralized? Three principal groups wanted a voice in control—the federal government, member banks, and businesses that were customers of member banks. Some, arguing that central banking is essentially a governmental function and that one of its principal objectives is the regulation of member banks, demanded full government control. Many bankers, who considered the new Reserve banks to be essentially cooperative institutions for member banks, demanded that full control be placed in the hands of bankers, although small banks feared domination by larger competitors. Others argued that business customers of banks should be given a voice. No less heated were the discussions concerning the degree of centralization of control. Some wanted almost complete centralization, whereas others demanded a large degree of regional autonomy.

Here, too, the issue was settled by compromise. All the competing groups were given representation, and control was divided between a central authority in Washington, D.C., and the regional Federal Reserve banks. In the succeeding sections we shall describe the present system of control, which is summarized in Figure 10–2. Note, however, that the original division of authority proved unsatisfactory in many respects and has been changed in several ways since 1914. In general, the evolution has been toward greater centralization of authority and a greater degree of control by the federal government.

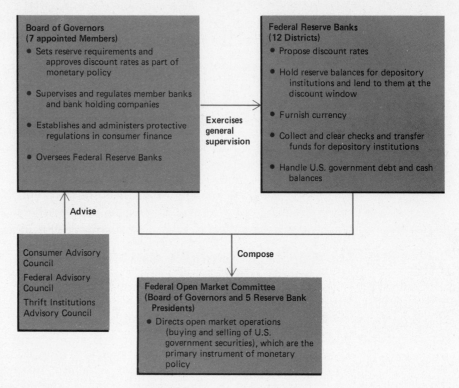

FIGURE 10–2
Organization of the Federal Reserve System.
SOURCE: **Board of Governors of the Federal Reserve System,** *The Federal Reserve System: Purposes and Functions,* **7th ed., Washington, D.C., 1984, p. 5.**

THE BOARD OF GOVERNORS OF THE FEDERAL RESERVE SYSTEM

The central controlling authority, which has its offices in Washington, D.C., is the Board of Governors of the Federal Reserve System. This Board is composed of seven members (called governors) appointed by the president of the United States with the advice and consent of the Senate. Each member devotes full time to the Board, is appointed for a term of 14 years, and is ineligible for reappointment after serving a full term. No more than one member of the Board may be selected from any one Federal Reserve district, and in making appointments the president is to "have due regard to a fair representation of the financial, agricultural, industrial, and commercial interests, and geographical divisions of the country." The president designates one of the members as chairman and another as vice-chairman.

Although the actual location of control has in the past depended greatly on economic and political conditions and on the forcefulness of the various personalities involved, the Board of Governors is now clearly the most powerful controlling force in the entire Federal Reserve System. Among its most important powers are the following:

1 To exercise general supervision over the Federal Reserve banks, to examine their accounts and affairs, and to require reports by them.
2 To approve or disapprove appointments to the positions of president and first vice-president of each Federal Reserve bank and to suspend or remove any officer or director of any Federal Reserve bank.
3 To supervise the issue and retirement of Federal Reserve notes by each Federal Reserve bank.
4 To serve as a majority of the members of the Federal Open Market Committee.
5 To permit one Reserve bank to lend to another and, by a vote of at least five members of the Board, to require it to do so.
6 To determine, within the broad limits prescribed by law, the types of loans the Reserve banks may make.
7 To approve or disapprove discount rates established by the Reserve banks.
8 To fix, within the limits established by law, reserve requirements.
9 To regulate loans on securities.

Although this list is far from complete, it indicates the general scope of the Board's authority.

THE FEDERAL OPEN MARKET COMMITTEE

As we shall see later, one of the most powerful instruments of control in the hands of the Federal Reserve System is its power to buy and sell government securities and other obligations in the open market. The Reserve banks can create additional depository institution reserves by purchasing obligations in the open market and can contract reserves by selling securities. The original Federal Reserve Act was vague as to who should control this function, with the result that the individual banks sometimes followed conflicting policies, and sharp controversies arose within the system. Attempts were made to solve the problem in the 1920s by creating an informal open-market committee made up of representatives of the Federal Reserve banks, but these efforts were only partially successful. Some Reserve banks complained that they were not adequately represented; others ignored the decisions of the informal committee; and the Board in Washington felt that it should have more control of this function.

The Federal Open Market Committee was created by amendments to the Federal Reserve Act in order to clarify the location of authority and to centralize the control of Federal Reserve open-market operations. It is composed of 12 members; 7 of these (a majority) are members of the Board of Governors of the Federal Reserve System and 5 are representatives of the

Reserve banks. The latter are elected annually and must be presidents or vice-presidents of Reserve banks. The distribution of the five Reserve bank representatives is as follows:

One from the Federal Reserve Bank of New York
One from the Federal Reserve Banks of Boston, Philadelphia, and Richmond
One from the Federal Reserve Banks of Atlanta, Dallas, and St. Louis
One from the Federal Reserve Banks of Minneapolis, Kansas City, and San Francisco
One from the Federal Reserve Banks of Cleveland and Chicago

Because of its key position, the New York Bank is always represented on the committee:

The Federal Reserve Bank of New York occupies a unique position with respect to the Federal Reserve System, the Treasury, and the banking system of the country. Its resources total approximately 40 percent of the aggregate of the twelve Federal Reserve Banks. It is located at the central money market and at the principal market for Government securities; its operations as fiscal agent of the United States and its transactions with foreign governments, foreign central banks and bankers, as well as its operations in foreign exchange, are in far greater volume than those of any other Federal Reserve Bank. It is clearly in the public interest that the Federal Open Market Committee be given at all times the benefit of counsel of the Federal Reserve Bank which is in constant touch with the domestic and international money and capital markets and has had long experience in these fields.[3]

The Federal Open Market Committee has full control of all open-market purchases and sales by the reserve banks. No reserve bank may engage in or decline to engage in open-market operations except in accordance with the regulations adopted by the committee. The committee was also given jurisdiction over Federal Reserve purchases and sales of foreign exchange soon after these began in the early 1960s.

THE FEDERAL ADVISORY COUNCIL

The Federal Advisory Council is composed of 12 members, one selected by the board of directors of each Reserve bank. The sole function of this council is to act in an advisory capacity to the Board of Governors. The only sources of its power are its eloquence and the prestige of its members, most of whom are prominent individuals.

CONTROL OF INDIVIDUAL FEDERAL RESERVE BANKS

Control of each of the 12 Federal Reserve banks is divided among the member banks in the district, businesspeople in the district, and the Board of

[3]*Federal Reserve Bulletin*, August 1942, pp. 740–741.

Governors of the Federal Reserve System. Each Reserve bank has a board of directors with nine members. Three of these are known as class A directors, three as class B directors, and three as class C directors. The class A directors represent the member banks of the district and are chosen by them. To prevent domination of the Reserve bank by any one banking group, the member banks of the district are divided into three groups based on size, and each group elects one class A director. The class B directors represent industry, commerce, and agriculture in the district and must be actively engaged in one of these pursuits at the time of their election. They may not be officers, directors, or employees of any bank. They are, however, elected by the member banks of the district in the same way as the class A directors. All three of the class C directors are appointed by the Board of Governors. One of these, who must be "a person of tested banking experience," is chairman of the board of directors and Federal Reserve agent at the bank. As such, that person acts as official representative of the Board of Governors in carrying out its legal functions. Another class C director at each Reserve bank acts as deputy chairman of the board of directors.

The chief executive officer of each Reserve bank is its president, who is appointed by its board of directors with the approval of the Board of Governors. The first vice-president of each Reserve bank is appointed in the same way. Other Reserve bank officers and employees are appointed by the bank's board of directors, although they may, of course, be removed by the Board of Governors.

Although it is now clear that the Board of Governors occupies the dominant position, some power still rests with the representatives chosen by member banks. But the Board of Governors has many sources of power:

1 Exclusive regulation of many Federal Reserve and commercial bank functions is in the hands of the Board.
2 Its members make up a majority of the members of the powerful Federal Open Market Committee.
3 The Board appoints three members of the board of directors of each Federal Reserve bank, one of its appointees at each bank being chairman of the board of directors and Federal Reserve agent.
4 The Board may disapprove appointments of presidents and first vice-presidents of the Reserve banks and may remove directors, officers, and employees.

FEDERAL RESERVE "CHORES"

Having examined the structure and control of the Federal Reserve System, we can now begin to study its functions. We shall look first at functions other than those of monetary and credit management. As one aspect of these functions, the Federal Reserve serves as a banker's bank. It also provides some banking services to the federal government. A second aspect involves the supervision and examination of banks; the Federal Reserve functions as the "maintenance man" of the financial system. We will call these various types of functions "chores". But the chores are not merely incidental or unimportant functions. Collectively, they account for the great bulk of work within the Federal Reserve. And in performing these chores, the Federal Reserve has contributed greatly to the efficiency and convenience of the banking system.

BANKING SUPERVISION

As noted earlier, the supervision and examination of banking in this country are not exclusively a Federal Reserve function, but are shared with several other authorities. The Comptroller of the Currency has jurisdiction over all national banks. State banking authorities have jurisdiction over state banks. And the Federal Deposit Insurance Corporation has jurisdiction over all banks with deposit insurance, which includes members of the Federal Reserve System and most nonmembers. Each Reserve bank has its staff of bank examiners, and member banks must periodically report their condition. In addition to requiring reports and examining member banks, the Federal Reserve exercises other important supervisory powers, among which are the powers to:

1 Remove officers and directors of member banks for continued violation of banking laws or for continued unsafe or unsound banking practices.
2 Suspend a member bank's borrowing privileges at the Federal Reserve if it is found to be making undue use of bank credit for speculation in securities, real estate, or commodities.
3 Permit national banks, where appropriate, to exercise trust powers.
4 Evaluate applications and rule on mergers between banks.
5 Establish allowable lines of business for bank holding companies.
6 Permit member banks to establish branches in foreign countries.

Overlapping jurisdictions of the chartering, supervisory, and examining authorities remain a problem despite the degree of cooperation achieved. These agencies sometimes conflict, differ in their administrative interpretations if not in basic principles, and enable banks to "play off one agency against another." To eliminate the overlapping of federal and state jurisdictions may be politically impossible. But many think it desirable, and perhaps politically possible, to eliminate at the federal level the overlapping jurisdictions of the Comptroller of the Currency, the Federal Reserve, and the Federal Deposit Insurance Corporation. Some suggest that all supervisory and examination powers should be vested in one of the existing agencies. Others think they should be concentrated in a newly created agency, which might also have jurisdiction over other types of financial institutions. We return to some proposals of this sort later in the chapter.

CLEARING AND COLLECTION OF CHECKS

The Federal Reserve System has greatly enhanced the speed, convenience, and cheapness of clearing and collecting checks and other similar items. Before 1914, a check might spend two weeks or more in the process of being cleared and collected, especially if it had to move long distances. The maximum time now required is only a few days, and banks that clear checks through the Federal Reserve receive payment in two days or less. The whole process is completed with virtually no shipment of coin or currency. Deposit accounts at the Federal Reserve banks play a central role in this process.

To illustrate the development of the clearance and collection system for checks and similar instruments, let us look at the process in a few typical situations. The processes often vary from those described below, but the principles involved are similar. Let us suppose that Smith deposits with the First Hartford Bank in Connecticut a check for $100 given him by Jones. If Jones's check is drawn on the First Hartford Bank, the clearance process is simple; the bank merely adds $100 to Smith's deposit account and deducts $100 from Jones's account.

Suppose, however, that Jones had written the check on another bank in the same city, the Second Hartford Bank. After Smith has deposited the check with the First Hartford Bank, it may be cleared in either of two general ways. The two banks may informally exchange their claims against each other at the end of the day, the net debtor then paying the other bank with a check drawn on another bank, probably the Federal Reserve bank of the district. Final payment is made by transferring a deposit credit at the Federal Reserve from the account of the Second Hartford Bank to that of the First Hartford Bank. Or the banks may clear and collect checks through a local clearinghouse. At an appointed time each day, each bank in the area takes to the clearinghouse all the checks and other matured claims it has against other members of the clearinghouse. Clearinghouse officials compare the total amounts of checks presented by each bank against all other banks with the total amount of checks presented by all other banks against it, and then pay each bank the net amount due it or collect the net amount owed by it. These net payments are usually made with checks, often with checks drawn on the Reserve bank of the district. Actual coin or currency is almost never used to pay net differences at a clearinghouse.

If the check Jones gave to Smith is drawn on a bank located in another city in the same Federal Reserve district (say, in Springfield, Massachusetts), the clearance and collection procedure is somewhat as follows: Smith deposits the check with the First Hartford Bank, which credits his account and sends the check along with others to the Federal Reserve Bank of Boston for clearance and collection. The Boston Reserve bank then sends the check to Springfield, and the Springfield bank deducts the amount of the check from Jones's deposit account. After the lapse of sufficient time for notification if the check is not good, the Boston Reserve bank deducts the amount of the check from the Springfield bank's reserve account with it and adds the same amount to the Hartford bank's reserve account. Payment of the check has been achieved quickly and with no shipment of coin or currency.

The procedure is only slightly more complicated if Jones's check is drawn on a bank in another Federal Reserve district, say, on the Los Angeles Commercial Bank. Smith deposits the check with the Hartford bank, which credits his deposit account and sends the check along with others to the Federal Reserve Bank of Boston. The latter then sends the check along with others to the Federal Reserve Bank of San Francisco, which then sends it to the Los Angeles Commercial Bank. If the San Francisco bank is not notified within the appointed time that the check is bad, it deducts the amount from the Los Angeles bank's reserve account with it. At or about the same time, the Boston Reserve bank adds the amount of the check to the Hartford bank's reserve account. At this point Smith has been paid, Jones has paid, Smith's bank has been paid, and Jones's bank has been paid. But the San Francisco bank still owes the Boston bank the amount of the check, if it has not been offset by counterclaims.

How is a net balance paid between Reserve banks? This is accomplished without any shipment of coin or currency by the simple expedient of book entries in the Interdistrict Settlement Fund, which is maintained by the Board of Governors in Washington. Each Reserve bank establishes a credit in the Interdistrict Settlement Fund. Any net balance due a Federal Reserve bank at the end of a day is added to its account in the fund, any net claim of another Reserve bank against it is deducted from its account. It is through arrangements of this type that payments can be made to all points within the country quickly and without the inconvenience and expense of shipping coin and currency.

WIRE TRANSFERS

In addition to providing a rapid and efficient system for clearing and collecting checks, the Federal Reserve transfers funds and certain types of securities by wire. Until the early 1970's the wire transfer system consisted of telegraphic linkages among the Board of Governors, the 12 Federal Reserve banks, and the 25 branches of the latter. This system was replaced in the early 1970's by one of interconnected computers. The new system has far greater capacity than the old one and can accomplish in minutes what might earlier have required hours. Partly because of the rapidly rising burden of handling checks and other paper instruments, the Board of Governors encourages the use of wire transfers.

Through the wire transfer system, the federal government, banks, and customers of banks can transfer funds from one end of the country to another almost simultaneously. Suppose, for example, that Jones in Los Angeles wishes to transfer by wire $1 million to Smith in Hartford, Connecticut. Jones gives her bank a check for that amount, and the bank wires the Federal Reserve Bank in San Francisco, asking it to transfer the funds. The San Francisco Reserve bank deducts the amount from the reserve account of the Los Angeles bank and wires the Federal Reserve Bank of Boston, telling the latter to transfer the funds to Smith at the First Hartford Bank. The Boston Reserve bank adds the amount to the First Hartford Bank's reserve account and wires the Hartford bank to credit Smith's account. The whole process is completed within minutes. The San Francisco Reserve bank settled with the Boston Reserve bank through a transfer on the books of the Interdistrict Settlement Fund at the Board of Governors.

Through its wire transfer system the Federal Reserve can also transfer federal government securities over long distances within a few minutes. Suppose, for example, that a bank in Seattle wishes to transfer $10 million of Treasury obligations to a New York dealer in government securities. The bank will take the securities to the Seattle branch of the Federal Reserve bank of San Francisco, indicating the identity of the dealer to whom they are to be delivered. The Seattle branch will retire the $10 million of certificates and wire the Federal Reserve Bank of New York to issue and deliver to the buyer new Treasury obligations of the same issue and in the same amount. After the dealer has sold these securities, the Seattle bank may be paid through the wire transfer system.

In some cases such transfers of claims against the government debt are even simpler. This is because at least some of the bank's debt claims against the Treasury may not be evidenced by certificates or any other paper document, but only by book entries at its Federal Reserve bank. This claim at the Federal Reserve indicates the particular Treasury issues against which the bank has claims, and the amounts of each. If a bank wishes to sell some of these claims, it simply sends the relevant information to the Federal Reserve, which makes the transfer on its books.

Overall, some see the growing use of wire transfers, facilitated by advances in computer technology, as leading to the development of a nationwide electronic payments system. However, even if a fully integrated electronic payments system does not emerge in the near future, its encouragement of wire transfers shows that the Federal Reserve is committed to promoting a more efficent payments system.

TRUTH IN CONSUMER LENDING

In 1968 Congress passed the Truth in Lending Act and gave the Board of Governors responsibility for formulating and issuing regulations to carry out the intent of the act—namely, to promote the informed use of credit. This responsibility has been fulfilled by the issuance of Regulation Z and the preparation of an annual report to Congress. Among other things, the report assesses the extent to which compliance is being achieved and suggests changes in the act.

DATA GATHERING AND ECONOMIC RESEARCH

Through its supervision of many aspects of banking, the Federal Reserve has also become a major source of economic data. These data are analyzed by economic researchers both in and out of government to help improve our understanding of monetary phenomena. In particular, the various Reserve banks and the Board of Governors all maintain sizable research staffs whose findings serve as inputs to the policymaking process. Both the economic data and the Federal Reserve analyses of these data are frequently communicated to the public. The Board of Governors, for example, publishes the extremely useful *Federal Reserve Bulletin* on a monthly basis and even has weekly releases of monetary data. The Reserve banks also issue publications, typically in the form of a monthly review, which present analyses of both national and regional economic developments.

PRICING OF FEDERAL RESERVE SERVICES

As noted above, prior to 1980, one of the compensations for a commercial bank that became a member bank in the Federal Reserve System was that it was provided with a variety of free services. With the passage of the Monetary Control Act of 1980, matters changed as Congress dictated that the services provided by the Federal Reserve be made available to all depository institutions and that the Fed charge for these services. Specifically, the act required the Federal Reserve to price its services so that over the long run, the fees charged would cover all costs, including the costs of taxes and capital the Federal Reserve would incur if it were a private profit-making firm.

Congress was aiming at improving the efficiency of the payments mechanism. The basic idea was that realistic pricing by the Fed would send the proper signals to those in the private sector who wished to go into competition with the Fed. With realistic pricing, competitors who could provide services at lower costs would be encouraged to enter, thus improving the efficiency of the payments mechanism. Such competition exists, for example, in the provision of check-clearing services by correspondent banks.

The Fed structured its prices to recover separately costs for each of seven service lines: (1) check collection; (2) wire transfer of funds; (3) automated clearinghouse operations; (4) safekeeping of securities; (5) safekeeping and transfer of book-entry securities; (6) cash transportation; and (7) coin wrapping.

Not surprisingly, given that it had not been required to price its services before, the Fed experienced some difficulties in implementing the new regime. But by early 1984 it reported that all services were covering costs and being made available to depository institutions regardless of size or location. Although this sounds like a happy ending to the story, we can expect further developments. First, if past experience is any guide, the Fed's actual or potential competitors are likely to criticize the accounting details and argue that the Fed is unfairly underpricing its services. Second, and more important in the long run, the payments mechanism is likely to continue evolving as new technologies are developed and improved.

FISCAL-AGENCY FUNCTIONS

As noted earlier, one purpose of the Federal Reserve Act was to provide the U.S. Treasury with a more satisfactory fiscal agent. Before that time the Treasury relied on commercial banks and on the so-called independent treasury system, which consisted of a number of regional suboffices of the Treasury. Both were unsatisfactory. Banks were unsatisfactory because some were unsafe, check clearing and collection were slow, and the limited geographic scope of each bank was not conducive to rapid regional transfers of government funds. The independent treasury system was unsatisfactory partly because its offices were so expensive to operate. Much more serious was that net movements of coin and paper money into and out of its vaults sometimes had undesirable effects on general credit conditions. Net collections of coin and currency from the public served to reduce bank reserves and restrict bank credit, whether or not this was desirable. And net outpayments of coin and currency tended to increase bank reserves and ease credit, sometimes when such results were not wanted. Treasury officials gradually learned how to avoid such undesirable results and even to use these powers in a stabilizing way. Nevertheless, it became clear that a more efficient mechanism was needed.

In acting as a fiscal agent, the Federal Reserve banks do an enormous amount of work for the federal government and its various offices and corporations. At some of the Reserve banks, the amount of work done for the government is comparable to, and even greater than, that done for the bank itself as principal. Among the functions performed by the Federal Reserve as principal banker to the government are the following:

1 Financial adviser
2 Depository and receiving and paying agent
3 Agent for issuing and retiring Treasury securities
4 Agent in other transactions involving purchases and sales of securities for a Treasury account
5 Agent for the government in purchasing and selling gold and foreign exchange

FINANCIAL ADVISER

The Treasury and other government departments do not, of course, rely solely on the Federal Reserve for financial information and advice; they have their own staffs and many other sources. Yet the Federal Reserve, which is so intimately and continuously in contact with the money, securities, and foreign exchange markets, is in a position to be especially helpful to the government in its debt management and foreign exchange transactions.

DEPOSITORY

The Federal Reserve banks, collectively, are in one sense the principal depository of federal government funds, for most government payments are made out of the Treasury's deposit accounts at the Federal Reserve. Yet the Treasury ordinarily holds only a part of its deposit balances at the Federal Reserve; the remainder are held in thousands of commercial banks. This system was evolved to minimize disturbances to bank reserves and the general credit situation that would otherwise result if the government had large net receipts or made large net payments. During some periods, especially at the peak of tax collections or when the Treasury has sold a large issue of securities, the Treasury has large net receipts, mostly in the form of checks. If all these were put into deposits at the Federal Reserve banks, the Federal Reserve would add them to its deposit liability to the Treasury and deduct them from its deposit liabilities to the banks on which the checks were drawn. The banks would lose reserves, and the supply of money and credit would tend to be restricted, whether or not this was desired. At other times, especially when tax collections are small relative to expenditures, the reverse would happen. We shall see later that the Federal Reserve can attempt to offset such disturbances by sales and purchases of government securities in the open market. But to do this smoothly and effectively when the disturbances are large presents difficulties.

It is largely to avoid such difficulties that the Treasury holds deposits in tax and loan accounts at qualified commercial banks. These banks are those that want to hold Treasury deposits, have pledged government securities to assure the safety of these deposits, and have met certain other requirements. The system works as follows: A bank or customers of a bank send checks to the Treasury to pay taxes or to pay for securities purchased from the Treasury. The Treasury records the amounts received and routes the checks back through the Federal Reserve to the bank on which they are drawn, and the latter adds the amounts of the checks to its deposit liability to the Treasury. Note that at this stage the bank has lost no reserves; it has merely increased its deposit liability to the Treasury and, if the checks were written by customers, has reduced its deposit liabilities to the public. In the meantime, the Federal Reserve maintains complete records of the amounts of Treasury deposits at every bank. Later, a few days before the Treasury wishes to use the deposits for payment, the Federal Reserve, in its capacity as fiscal agent, announces the date when a stated percentage of Treasury deposits will be called. The call states, in effect, "On the specified date, X percent of Treasury deposits will be withdrawn from your bank. On this date we shall deduct this amount from your reserve account at the Federal

Reserve and you shall deduct this amount from your deposit liability to the Treasury." This tends, of course, to reduce bank reserves. However, meanwhile the Treasury checks drawn on the Federal Reserve will have been sent to payees. As these are deposited with banks and sent by banks to the Federal Reserve, the effect is to restore bank reserves. If the timing is perfect, there will be no net change in the total volume of bank reserves, although there may be some redistribution of reserves among the banks.

In the last few years there have been some changes in these procedures. A 1974 Treasury study concluded that revenues lost by the Treasury in holding balances in non-interest-bearing tax and loan accounts were not justified by offsetting cost savings in bank services. As a result, a sizable volume of Treasury deposit balances was shifted to the Federal Reserve. This permitted the Federal Reserve to hold a larger volume of securities and thus increase its earnings. Since, as we have seen, the Federal Reserve returns the bulk of its earnings to the Treasury, the Treasury was thus better off. More recently there has been a shift back toward the old system, but with more explicit compensation of the Treasury for the value of its deposits.[4]

AGENT FOR THE TREASURY IN SECURITIES TRANSACTIONS

The Federal Reserve does a tremendous amount of work for the Treasury in issuing and retiring securities and in purchasing and selling securities for trust funds and other accounts controlled by the government. When the Treasury offers new securities for sale, the Federal Reserve publicizes the issue, receives bids and subscriptions, decides which to accept and which to reject in accordance with Treasury instructions, and collects on behalf of the Treasury. As paying agent for the Treasury, it pays interest on the federal debt and redeems maturing securities. When, as sometimes happens, the Treasury offers an issue through an investment banking syndicate, the Federal Reserve serves as agent for the Treasury in making arrangements.

AGENT FOR THE TREASURY IN GOLD AND FOREIGN EXCHANGE TRANSACTIONS

As already indicated, and as will be discussed more fully at a later point, the Treasury is sole custodian of the nation's monetary gold and buys and sells gold for monetary purposes. In almost all these transactions the Federal Reserve acts as agent for the Treasury. The Federal Reserve also buys and sells foreign exchange (claims against foreign moneys) both on its own

[4]For a description of the current system, see Joan Lovett, "Treasury Tax and Loan Accounts and Federal Reserve Open Market Operations," Federal Reserve Bank of New York, *Quarterly Review*, Summer 1978, pp. 41–46.

account and as agent for the Treasury. Some of these transactions are for the purpose of influencing the behavior of the exchange rate on the dollar. Others are merely to assist the Treasury in making or receiving international payments.

REFORM OF THE REGULATORY SYSTEM

While we have spelled out the structure and duties of the Federal Reserve as they now stand, it would be rash indeed to assume that the evolution of the system has ended. One area where there has been a recent call for substantial change in the role of the Federal Reserve is in bank supervision and regulation. In particular, as part of a proposed general overhaul of the regulatory system, in 1984 a presidential task force called for a reduced role for the Fed in regulation and supervision. At the same time, the Fed expressed the view that there were serious dangers in going too far in this direction. As this suggests, there really are two intertwined issues: (1) Should the regulatory structure be reformed, and if so, how? (2) Will the Fed be impaired in carrying out its other duties if its regulatory functions are substantially reduced? To address these questions, we need to review the current regulatory structure.

THE CURRENT STRUCTURE

As noted in Chapter 5, the Federal Reserve, along with the Comptroller of the Currency and the Federal Deposit Insurance Corporation (FDIC), comprise the major components of the federal bank regulatory structure. There are, however, other elements, and the overall structure is a quite complex one. Figure 10–3 illustrates the intricacy of the current arrangements. And even this diagram understates the complexity of the structure because it omits securities dealers, consumer protection controls administered by the Fed, and a number of other elements.

As Figure 10–3 suggests, the various regulatory agencies have different responsibilities. The Comptroller of the Currency charters national banks and examines and supervises them. Aside from its insurance function, the FDIC examines and supervises state-chartered banks that are not members of the Federal Reserve. The Fed's regulatory duties include supervision and examination of state-chartered banks that are members of the Federal Reserve. The Fed also supervises and examines all bank holding companies, regardless of charter. It is this last feature that makes for considerable overlapping jurisdiction among the regulators. For example, a one-bank holding company with a national charter would be supervised in part by the Fed and in part by the Comptroller of the Currency.

As we have seen in previous chapters, our current regulatory structure evolved in response to financial crises and the emergence of new institu-

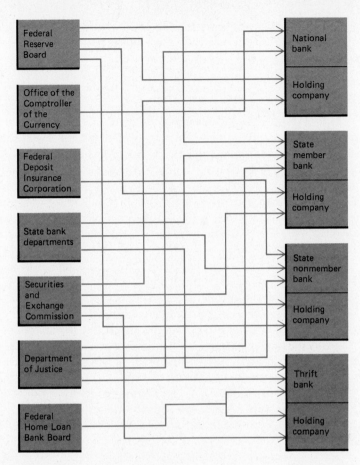

FIGURE 10–3
The regulation of banks and their holding
companies. (SOURCE: A. S. Carron, *Reforming the*
Bank Regulatory Structure, Staff paper, The
Brookings Institution, Washington, D.C., 1984,
p. 6.)

tions and forms of organization. But, critics argue, in recent years the rapid
change in financial institutions has not been matched by a corresponding
change in the regulatory structure. One harsh indictment of the current
structure has put it as follows:

> In contrast to the industry, our financial regulatory system remained static. The
> aggressive, automated, diversified multibillion dollar companies that compete in
> today's financial services industry are regulated by agencies designed for the
> Great Depression, the Panic of 1907, and the Civil War. Regulatory techniques
> are outmoded and inconsistent. The system is characterized by overlapping

authorities, duplicate controls, conflicts, and omissions. It is a disorderly structure, hard-pressed to cope with ongoing changes in the industry.[5]

Such harsh criticism must be motivated by shortcomings in the present structure, and this is indeed the case. Among the major problem areas are the following.[6]

1. If several agencies share responsibility for the safety and soundness of a depository institution, this division of duties means that no single agency is ultimately in charge. On occasion this division of duties has meant that some activities of bank holding companies have slipped through the cracks and financial difficulties were not uncovered in time to avert bank failures. It is also sometimes argued that the need for coordination among bank regulators can slow down the process of promptly and efficiently dealing with banks in financial distress, especially if regulatory agencies hold divergent views or objectives.

2. Differing regulatory views can lead to problems even when failing banks are not involved. A particularly glaring example of such a conflict occurred in the mid-1960s between the Comptroller of the Currency and other regulatory agencies. Adopting a somewhat permissive view of appropriate lines of business, the Comptroller ruled that national banks could issue corporate savings deposits, purchase corporate stock, and underwrite municipal revenue bonds. The Federal Reserve objected strongly to these changes, and a messy legal battle ensued. In the course of the dispute, the Comptroller withheld bank examination reports from the FDIC, potentially impairing its ability to deal with problems in a timely fashion. On the whole, this episode, which lasted for several years, was not the finest hour for bank regulation.

3. The increasing similarities and competition between banks and thrift institutions have prompted questions of consistency of regulation. At present, thrifts are regulated by the Federal Home Loan Bank Board, an organization that combines the functions of the Comptroller, the Fed, and the FDIC. As it now stands, there is no assurance that banks and thrifts will receive comparable treatment at the hands of the regulators. For example, as noted before, a savings and loan holding company with only a single S&L subsidiary can engage in any activity, whereas a one-bank holding company is quite constrained.

This list could be extended, but it should be sufficient to establish that shortcomings exist in the present setup. Some writers, while acknowledging these shortcomings, point to the fact that the present structure has permitted a substantial evolution of the financial system. Motivated by the view that "if it isn't broken, don't fix it," this group would leave the regulatory

---

[5]A. S. Carron, "Banking on Change: The Reorganization of Financial Regulation," *The Brookings Review*, Spring 1984, p. 12.
[6]This discussion is based on Carron, op. cit.

system pretty much as is. This was not the view, however, of the formidable-sounding Task Group on Regulation of Financial Services, chaired by Vice-President George Bush, which issued its report in early 1984.

REFORM PROPOSALS

Proposals to reform the structure of bank regulation are hardly new. Indeed, about six years after the Federal Reserve was founded in 1913, legislation was introduced in Congress to consolidate the functions of the Fed and the Comptroller. The same pattern was repeated after the FDIC was established, as legislation was introduced to make it the principal bank regulator at the federal level. Throughout the 1960s and 1970s, there were at least six major efforts to reform the regulatory structure. Viewed against this history, the Bush Task Group was just another in a long chain of attempts at reforming the regulatory system. Moreover, as with many of the previous reform efforts, the Bush proposals met with less than overwhelming enthusiasm.

In broad outline, the Bush Task Group proposed the following sorts of changes. A new institution, the *Federal Banking Agency*, would replace the Comptroller's office and, in addition to the Comptroller's current powers vis-à-vis national banks, would have authority over most bank holding companies. The Fed, which currently has this power, would retain the right to regulate only about 50 of the largest bank holding companies. The Federal Banking Agency would also inherit the Fed's authority to define those non-banking activities that are permissible for a bank holding company, although this would be subject to Federal Reserve veto. The FDIC would retain its insurance function, but forego supervision of state-chartered banks. This task would fall to the Fed. In contrast to its approach to bank regulation, the Task Group proposed to leave the regulation of savings institutions largely unchanged.

Initial reaction to the proposals was somewhat critical, even among those who favored consolidation of regulatory authority. First and foremost, critics argued that it made little sense to reform the regulatory structure without first defining what constitutes a "bank" and what general categories of activities bank holding companies might engage in. According to this view, only after legal action by Congress to address these issues would it be possible to design a rational regulatory structure. Without such action, there would be no clear statement of objectives to guide regulators. A second and related criticism was that the proposed regulatory structure does not address the need to regulate banks and thrift institutions in a consistent manner. Third, critics pointed out that instead of consolidation, in some instances the proposals would create new areas of overlapping authority. For example, under the proposals the Fed and the new Federal Banking Agency would both have some authority over bank holding companies. This would require coordination not needed at present.

As this suggests, a somewhat cleaner plan could have resulted had the proposals transferred all of the Fed's regulatory powers to the new Federal Banking Agency. Representatives of the Federal Reserve argued strongly that although such a plan might be simpler, this did not make it better. Indeed, the Fed has long held the view that it needs to maintain an effective presence in the supervisory and regulatory process in order to carry out its other responsibilities. These responsibilities include ensuring the stability and smooth functioning of the financial and payments system and the conduct of monetary policy, in which a key element is heading off or dealing with financial disturbances and crises. As the Fed sees it, to do this the Fed needs to keep a "hands on" regulatory responsibility, thus maintaining the expertise to spot unsound trends in the early stages and the ability to do something about them. While there is clearly merit in the Fed view, this remains an area of some dispute.

Overall, then, the regulatory structure remains an area of considerable controversy. Nevertheless, while there will be continual calls for reform, there is no certainty that a major overhaul of the system will soon be forthcoming. It is more likely that Congress will address the issue of defining a bank. Should this happen, questions of reforming the regulatory structure may well be put aside temporarily. The impression one gets from various Federal Reserve statements is that the Fed would not cry over this outcome.

THE INDEPENDENCE OF THE FEDERAL RESERVE

The role of the Federal Reserve in bank regulation is not the only aspect of the system that has been questioned in recent years. The relation of the Fed to Congress and to the executive branch has also come in for reexamination.

The Federal Reserve is based on the principle of independent central banking. It is, of course, responsible to Congress: It was created by Congress and must make reports to Congress. Nevertheless, a number of features tend to insulate the Federal Reserve from Congress. These include long and staggered terms for members of the Board of Governors and the fact that the Federal Reserve neither is subject to conventional government audits nor depends on congressional appropriations for operating funds. One should not, however, overemphasize the Federal Reserve's insulation, since Congress can at any time change its basic legislation, give it directives, or even abolish it.

Another aspect of "independence" is perhaps more controversial, since in the nature of things the Federal Reserve is free to follow monetary policies that may be at odds with the wishes of Congress or the administration.

This can result from different readings of the economic tea leaves as to appropriate policies or from the fact that the Federal Reserve may be pursuing somewhat different goals than Congress or the administration. Those who defend the current system of independence—especially from the executive branch—base their views on the following types of considerations:

1 The administration in power is likely to have an easy-money inflationary bias, partly because easy money and mild inflation tend to be popular and to increase the ability of the incumbent political party to remain in power, and partly because the Treasury is likely to insist on easy money and low interest rates to keep down interest charges on the national debt and to facilitate its refunding and borrowing operations.
2 Control of the central bank is likely to inject politics into the bank's operations: patronage, discrimination on the basis of party affiliation, and so on.
3 Successful monetary management requires greater continuity among top officials than would be likely to result from responsibility to the president, whose tenure will be only four to eight years.
4 The existing arrangement elicits more confidence and cooperation from the commercial banks than they would give to a politically dominated institution.

On the other hand, several arguments are advanced for terminating the independence of the Federal Reserve and making it responsible to the executive branch:

1 Monetary policy, like other governmental policies, should be controlled by people responsible to the electorate.
2 The present arrangement makes the appropriate coordination of monetary policy with the other economic policies of the government difficult. It is intolerable that the Federal Reserve should follow policies in conflict with those determined by the elected representatives of the people.

There have been, to be sure, a number of developments that have tended to reduce the level of conflict. For one, in recent years there has been considerable consultation between Federal Reserve and administration officials on economic policy. There are, for example, regular meetings involving the chairman of the Federal Reserve Board, the secretary of the Treasury, and the chairman of the Council of Economic Advisers. In addition, since 1975 the Federal Reserve has regularly consulted with Congress as to the Board's overall economic objectives and its specific targets for the growth of the various measures of the money supply. Consultation, of course, does not imply agreement, so it should not be surprising that we can still find

FEDERAL RESERVE INDEPENDENCE: A MISCELLANY

While always an issue, the question of the independence of the Federal Reserve seemed to crop up more often than usual in the early 1980s. In part this occurred because the administration seemed to go out of its way to dramatize its differences with the Federal Reserve over the conduct of monetary policy. The press may have contributed to the dispute by elevating Paul Volcker, the chairman of the Board of Governors, to the status of a cult hero in the fight against inflation. Almost daily, it seemed, the press would publish an imposing picture of Volcker in a cloud of cigar smoke, captioned "the second most powerful man in America." Needless to say, this probably irked more than a few elected political figures. But perhaps even more important in creating political heat for the Fed was the dramatically high level of interest rates that prevailed in the early 1980s. These high rates led to considerable congressional complaint and occasionally to a bit of proposed legislation.

In 1981, for example, Representative Henry Gonzalez of Texas introduced a bill to impeach the entire Board of Governors and noted:

> The Federal Reserve Board did not spring from the brow of the Greek god—it is a creature of a legislative effort by the Congress. We have turned the fate of the Government over to unelected, unresponsible, unaccountable, powerful men, the handmaidens of the most special powerful interests in the world.

Representative Byron Dorgan of North Dakota supported similar legislation, observing

> I introduced a piece of legislation that I call "the Paul Volcker Retirement Act." I did not do it so much to focus on the chairman as a person as to talk about the institution of the Federal Reserve Board that is completely and thoroughly independent.

Some months later, after this proposed legislation had dropped from sight, *Business Week* in an editorial summed up the issue as follows:

> But on balance the goal of insulating the Fed as much as possible from political pressures is proper. The image of monetary policy being decided in the White House basement or tossed around as a political football by 500 reelection-hungry congressmen is far more unsettling than the occasional lack of coordination between Fed and Administration economic objectives. Fortunately, Congress finds an independent Fed a highly convenient dog to kick when things go wrong, and it is unlikely to exchange that pleasure for a larger share of responsibility in conducting monetary policy.

The Fed not only escaped unscathed, but in 1983 Paul Volcker, who had been sniped at by various members of the administration, was reappointed as chairman. A fitting conclusion for this is the following report from the *New York Times:*

Volcker: Do Not Disturb

The Federal Reserve System is famed as a bastion of independence in a city where political influence is rarely resisted. Congress set up the Board of Governors so its chairman would never have to be subservient to the President, and that spirit seems to have permeated the institution.

The other evening, the White House called Catherine Mallardi, administrative assistant to the board chairman, Paul A. Volcker, who was traveling in Europe. The President himself got on the phone, explaining that he needed to talk with the chairman and would appreciate the name and number of his hotel abroad.

The Volcker aide was polite but firm. It was the middle of the night in Europe, she said, and she did not think the chairman should be disturbed.

The President of the United States said all right, he would try him in the morning.

evidence of acrimonious debate prominently displayed in the financial press.[7] (For some recent views, see the box.) Nevertheless, despite these periodic outbursts of anti-Fed fever, it seems unlikely that there will be a major increase in constraints put on the Fed.

SUMMARY

1 The Federal Reserve System consists of the Board of Governors, located in Washington, and 12 regional Reserve banks. Power lies largely in the hands of the Board, although in matters of monetary policy the Federal Open Market Committee has responsibility. However, as the FOMC consists of 7 Board members and 5 presidents of the district Reserve Banks, even here the Board retains the major voice.

2 Prior to 1980 there was a substantial distinction between member and nonmember commercial banks in the Federal Reserve System. As a result of the Monetary Control Act of 1980, however, all depository institutions are subject to a set of uniform reserve requirements and have equal access to the services provided by the Federal Reserve. The

[7]One proposal for reform that has often been advanced concerns the term served by the chairman of the Federal Reserve. The chairman serves for four years, but this term is not matched with the term of the president. Thus, for example, the term of the current chairman expires in August 1987, over two and one-half years after a presidential election. Those in favor of reducing Federal Reserve independence have argued for matching the chairman's tenure to that of the president.

1980 act also mandated that the Federal Reserve charge for these services so as to cover costs.

3 Aside from its basic role in the conduct of monetary policy, the Fed also provides banking services to the federal government, engages in supervision and examination of banking, is involved in the clearing and collection of checks and the provision of wire services, and has responsibilities for monitoring truth in consumer lending.

4 The Federal Reserve shares responsibilities for regulation and supervision of depository institutions with a number of other agencies. Critics of the overall regulatory system charge that it is outmoded and inconsistent and needs to be reformed. However, such charges have been levied many times in the past without producing reform, and it is not obvious that the current calls will produce many changes.

5 The Federal Reserve is a creature of Congress and therefore ultimately responsible to Congress. The Fed is, however, legally independent of the executive branch. Periodically there are calls for restricting the independence of the Fed, either by placing the Fed in the executive branch or by having Congress pass rules to circumscribe more narrowly the behavior of the Fed. Major changes in either of these directions do not appear in the offing.

SELECTED READINGS

Bach, G. L. *Making Monetary and Fiscal Policy.* Washington, D.C.: Brookings Institution, 1971.

Board of Governors of the Federal Reserve System. *The Federal Reserve System, Purposes and Functions*, 7th ed. Washington, D.C., 1984.

Carron, A. S. "Banking on Change: The Reorganization of Financial Regulation," *The Brookings Review*, Spring 1984, pp. 12–21.

Chandler, L. V. *Benjamin Strong, Central Banker.* Washington, D.C.: Brookings Institution, 1958.

Commission on Money and Credit. *Money and Credit.* Englewood Cliffs, N.J.: Prentice-Hall, 1961.

Maisel, S. J. *Managing the Dollar.* New York: Norton, 1973.

Report of the Committee on Financial Structure and Regulation. Washington, D.C.: U.S. Government Printing Office, 1971.

11

DEPOSITORY INSTITUTION RESERVES AND FEDERAL RESERVE CREDIT

Although its service functions are of substantial importance, our primary interest in the Federal Reserve is in its role as a manager of monetary and credit conditions. That is, we shall be concerned with the Fed's conduct of monetary policy—how it uses the tools at its disposal to help achieve the nation's long-term economic objectives of economic growth, price stability, and full utilization of resources. To understand this process, we will investigate the influence the Fed has on the supply of money, on the supply and price of lendable funds to businesses and consumers, and on credit conditions more generally.

As previously suggested, one of the key ways in which the effects of monetary policy are transmitted to the economy is via the depository institutions. Indeed, the liabilities of the depository institutions (DIs) in the form of transactions deposits account for the major part of the money supply. The DIs are also major lenders to both consumers and businesses. In Chapter 8 we found that the volume of liabilities depository institutions can create and have outstanding, and also the volume of earning assets they can acquire and hold, depend on the volume of reserves available to them and on the level of percentage reserve requirements. Every dollar of legal reserves is high-powered money in the sense that each dollar of reserves can support several dollars of deposits. But how high-powered each dollar of reserves is depends on the legal reserve requirements.

271

To carry out its function of general monetary and credit management, the Federal Reserve has powers to control both the height of reserve requirements and the volume and cost of reserves. As we have already seen, the Federal Reserve Act provides that only two types of assets can be counted as legal reserves for depository institutions: deposits at the Federal Reserve and cash in vault. Moreover, it empowers the Board of Governors to alter, within specified limits, the percentage reserve requirements. By raising the level of these requirements, the Board can inhibit the creation of money by the depository system and exert an antiexpansionary or even a contractionary influence. By lowering these requirements, the Board can permit and even encourage an expansion of money and credit. We shall see later that this is a powerful instrument, which the Board sometimes uses.

However, the Federal Reserve relies more usually on its power to regulate the volume and cost of reserves available to the banking system. This chapter will discuss the factors determining the volume of reserves and the process through which the Federal Reserve creates and destroys these reserves. We will emphasize the link between Federal Reserve actions and the reserve positions of depository institutions. Although the details may appear confusing at first, the principles are really quite simple. As we will see, when the Federal Reserve makes net purchases of assets it will create reserves, and when it sells assets it will destroy reserves. These purchases and sales are called *open-market operations.* The mechanics of this process are spelled out in this chapter. The next chapter considers the conduct of open-market operations in more detail in conjunction with a discussion of the entire range of monetary policy tools.

FEDERAL RESERVE BALANCE SHEETS

An analysis of the consolidated balance sheets of the 12 Federal Reserve banks will help us understand the processes through which the Federal Reserve increases or decreases the reserves of the depository institutions. We start with basic balance sheet equations of the type developed in Chapter 6:

$$\text{assets} = \text{liabilities} + \text{capital accounts} \tag{1}$$

$$\text{liabilities} = \text{assets} - \text{capital accounts} \tag{2}$$

Assets include everything of value owned by the Federal Reserve banks at the stated point in time. *Liabilities* are debt claims against the Federal Reserve banks. *Capital accounts,* or net worth, are the ownership claims against the Federal Reserve banks. At any point in time the Federal Reserve banks must have outstanding a total of debt claims and ownership claims exactly equal to the value of their assets. If they make net increases in their assets, they must pay for these assets by creating and issuing an equal net increase in debt and ownership claims against themselves. And if they decrease their total asset holdings, they must withdraw and retire an equal amount of outstanding debt and ownership claims against themselves.

An examination of the Federal Reserve balance sheet in Table 11–1 reveals that the Reserve banks have paid for only a very small fraction, about 2 percent, of their assets by issuing capital account, or net worth, claims. Thus, the Reserve banks pay for their assets largely by issuing debt claims against themselves, and they withdraw and retire debt claims when they decrease their total assets. It is precisely through this mechanism that the Federal Reserve balance sheet provides the key ingredient in understanding how DI reserves are determined. The essentials of this process can be seen in Table 11–1.

We first observe that a major component of DI reserves—namely, DI deposits with the Federal Reserve—is an entry in the Federal Reserve's balance sheet. By rearranging the balance sheet, we can therefore express these deposits as the difference between total Federal Reserve assets and the Federal Reserve liabilities *other than* DI deposits. Since elementary arithmetic and standard accounting procedures assures us that the balance sheet must balance, we inescapably come to the following conclusion: Unless it is offset elsewhere in the balance sheet, any change in an asset or liability *other than* DI deposits has to affect DI deposits. For example, if total Federal Reserve assets rise because of, say, a purchase of government

TABLE 11–1 Balance Sheet of the Federal Reserve Banks, May 1984 (end-of-month data in millions of dollars)

ASSETS		LIABILITIES AND CAPITAL ACCOUNT	
Gold certificates	$ 11,104	Federal Reserve notes	$158,727
SDR certificates	4,618	Deposits due to DIs	21,686
Coin	443	U.S. Treasury deposits	4,855
Loans to DIs	2,832	Foreign deposits	295
Acceptances	426	Other deposits	416
Federal agency obligations	8,851	Deferred availability	
U.S. government securities	154,869	Cash items	8,182
Cash items in process of		Other liabilities	2,593
collection	8,770	Total liabilities	$196,754
Foreign exchange	3,794	Capital accounts	3,346
All other	4,393	**Total liabilities and**	$200,100
Total assets	$200,100	**capital accounts**	

Addenda

Cash items in process of collection	$8,770
Minus: Deferred availability cash items	8,182
Equals: float	$ 588

SOURCE: *Federal Reserve Bulletin*, July 1984, PA10.

securities, and if no other balance sheet item changes, then DI deposits at the Federal Reserve must increase. Similarly, an increase in a Federal Reserve liability, say, in foreign deposits held with the Federal Reserve, if not counteracted elsewhere, necessarily leads to a decrease in DI reserves.

Evidently, then, it is changes in the various items in the Federal Reserve's balance sheet that contribute to the determination of DI reserves. This suggests that it will be worthwhile to take a close look at the major components of the balance sheet in Table 11–1. In the process we will be able to go beyond what may seem to some accounting gimmickry and gain a firmer understanding of the mechanics of *how* changes in Federal Reserve assets and liabilities result in movements in DI reserves.

FEDERAL RESERVE NOTES AND DEPOSITS

Federal Reserve liabilities are largely of two types: Federal Reserve notes and deposit liabilities. As indicated earlier, Federal Reserve notes make up the great bulk of paper money in the United States. Although they are impressively engraved and endowed by law with full legal tender powers, they are nothing but debt claims against the Federal Reserve banks. Deposits at the Federal Reserve banks are also merely debts owed by the Federal Reserve. They are evidenced by book entries. Table 11–1 indicates that the Federal Reserve issued deposit claims against itself to only a few types of holders. It will not accept deposits from individuals, businesses, or state and local governments. Most of its deposit liabilities are to DIs. These serve both as legal reserves for DIs and as a medium for clearing and collection, as noted earlier. Smaller deposit liabilities are owed to the federal government, and to foreign central banks. It should be evident that claims of DIs at the Federal Reserve may be decreased as these deposits are shifted to the ownership of other depositors at the Federal Reserve, and that claims of DIs at the Federal Reserve may be increased as other deposits at the Federal Reserve are transferred to the ownership of the DIs.

Changes in the volume of Federal Reserve notes outstanding reflect changes in the demand for paper money to be held in bank vaults or to be used as currency in circulation, predominantly the latter. Whenever the public wants more currency, the DIs are the first to feel the impact. Customers write checks on their deposit accounts and withdraw cash. The DIs may supply the currency out of cash in the vault, thereby losing legal reserves in this form, or they may get it by drawing down their deposits at the Federal Reserve. In the latter case, the increase in Federal Reserve notes outstanding is at the expense of DI deposits at the Federal Reserve. On the other hand, when the public wishes to hold less paper money, it deposits the excess at DIs, which may add it to their legal reserves in the form of cash in the vault or send it along to the Federal Reserve. In the latter case, the Federal

Reserve retires the net inflow of Federal Reserve notes and adds an equal amount to its liabilities to DIs.

This demonstrates several important points. First, it indicates how the volume of Federal Reserve notes is made responsive to the public's demand for paper money. Second, it shows that increases in Federal Reserve notes outstanding tend initially to be at the expense of DI deposits at the Federal Reserve, and that decreases in Federal Reserve notes outstanding tend initially to increase the volume of DI deposits at the Federal Reserve. Third, it suggests why we are justified in assuming that when the Federal Reserve makes net purchases of assets, it initially pays for them by creating deposit claims against itself; and when it makes net sales of assets, it initially collects by withdrawing an equal value of its deposit liabilities. For simplicity of exposition, we shall assume in the succeeding sections that when the Federal Reserve purchases assets, it makes payment by adding to the reserves of DIs; and that when it sells assets, it collects by deducting from the reserve balances of DIs.

FEDERAL RESERVE ASSETS

Federal Reserve banks can create or destroy their own deposit liabilities by purchasing or selling any kind of asset whatsoever. They can create deposit liabilities to pay for land, buildings, equipment, services, or any type of claim against others. Or they can withdraw their deposit liabilities by making net sales of any kind of asset. This point should be borne in mind, because even now the Federal Reserve makes several kinds of purchases and sales, and in the future it might broaden the categories of assets in which it deals.

It will be useful to distinguish between two types of Federal Reserve purchases and sales of assets:

1 **TRANSACTIONS WITH DEPOSITORY INSTITUTIONS.** When the Federal Reserve purchases assets from a DI, it pays that DI by adding to its reserve account. When it sells an asset to a DI, it collects payment by reducing the DI's reserve account.

2 **TRANSACTIONS WITH THE PUBLIC.** When the Federal Reserve buys an asset from the public—from an individual, business firm, or state or local government—it usually pays with a check drawn on a Federal Reserve bank. The seller of the asset usually deposits the check at a DI, receiving in return a deposit credit there, and the DI then sends the check to its Federal Reserve bank, which adds the amount of the check to the DI's reserve account. Thus, Federal Reserve purchases of assets from the public tend to increase directly both the public's money supply and DI reserves. Federal Reserve sales of assets to the public have the reverse effects. When a member of the public buys

an asset from the Federal Reserve, he or she usually pays with a check drawn on a DI. The Federal Reserve deducts the amount of the check from the DI's reserve account and sends the check to the DI, which deducts its amount from the cutomer's deposit account. Thus, a Federal Reserve sale of an asset to the public tends to reduce directly both the public's money supply and DI reserves. The effect on DI reserves is, of course, more important, for each dollar of change in DI reserves may induce, or even force, several dollars of change in the DI's loans, investments, and deposit liabilities.

Although the Federal Reserve can create or destroy reserves by buying or selling assets of any kind, Table 11–1 indicates that, in practice, Federal Reserve purchases and sales are largely confined to a few types of assets. We now examine these assets, and the ways in which they are acquired and sold by the Federal Reserve.

UNITED STATES GOVERNMENT OBLIGATIONS

By far the largest volume of Federal Reserve assets is in the form of debt claims against the U.S. government, including fully guaranteed obligations of federal agencies. Table 11–1 showed that in May 1984 these amounted to about $163 billion, or 80 percent of total Federal Reserve assets. This asset is of special importance not only because it is so large, but also because it has become the principal medium through which the Federal Reserve regulates the volume and cost of reserves. The Federal Reserve creates reserves by purchasing government securities, and it destroys reserves by selling government securities. It buys and sells very frequently, sometimes almost continuously, and its purchases or sales are often very large.

As already indicated, Federal Reserve purchases and sales of government securities are under the jurisdiction of the Federal Open Market Committee and are executed for the system account through the Federal Reserve Bank of New York. The manager of the account buys and sells through government security dealers, of which there are about two dozen. These, in turn, deal with every type of investor that buys and sells government securities— commercial banks, all other types of financial institutions, nonfinancial business firms, individuals, foreign central banks, and others. The manager of the open-market account usually does not know the ultimate source of the securities bought or the ultimate buyers of the securities sold. It will further our analysis, however, to distinguish two types of transactions: (1) Federal Reserve purchases from, and sales to, DIs; and (2) Federal Reserve purchases from, and sales to, investors other than DIs.

Consider first the case in which the Federal Reserve purchases $500 million of government securities from DIs. As shown in case I, the effect is to increase reserves by $500 million. The Federal Reserve pays for its additional assets by creating additional deposit liabilities to the selling DIs.

	FEDERAL RESERVE		DEPOSITORY INSTITUTIONS	
CASE	ΔASSETS	ΔLIABILITIES	ΔASSETS	ΔLIABILITIES
I	Government securities + $500 million	Deposits due DIs + $500 million	Reserves + $500 million Government securities − $500 million	
II	Government securities − $700 million	Deposits due DIs − $700 million	Reserves − $700 million Government securities + $700 million	

The total assets of DIs are not directly changed; the DIs have simply exchanged $500 million of earning assets for an equal amount of legal reserves. The public's money supply is not directly affected. However, with the addition of $500 million to the excess reserves of DIs, an expansion of credit and deposits becomes likely. Case II shows that a Federal Reserve sale of $700 million of government securities to DIs will decrease reserves by that amount. In effect, the Federal Reserve collects from the DIs by subtracting from their reserve accounts. There is no direct effect on the public's money supply, but a reduction may be induced by the decrease in reserves.

	FEDERAL RESERVE		DEPOSITORY INSTITUTIONS		PUBLIC	
CASE	ΔASSETS	ΔLIABILITIES	ΔASSETS	ΔLIABILITIES	ΔASSETS	ΔLIABILITIES
III	Government securities + $500 million	Deposits due DIs + $500 million	Reserves + $500 million	Deposits + $500 million	Deposits + $500 million Government securities − $500 million	
IV	Government securities − $700 million	Deposits due DIs − $700 million	Reserves − $700 million	Deposits − $700 million	Deposits − $700 million Government securities + $700 million	

Let us now consider the case of Federal Reserve purchases of securities from any ultimate seller other than a DI. Case III assumes that you, as an insurance company executive, a manufacturer, or an individual, sell $500 million of government securities to the Federal Reserve. As shown in the balance sheets, the direct effect is to increase by $500 million both the public's money supply and reserves. When you, as the seller of securities, receive the $500 million check, you deposit it in your DI, which adds this amount to your deposit account and then sends the check to the Federal Reserve, which adds the amount to your DI's reserve account.

A comparison of cases I and III shows that all Federal Reserve purchases of securities add to the volume of reserves, but that only purchases from non-DI sellers add directly to the public's money supply. The total effects on the public's money supply and on the supply of credit may be the same in the two cases when both the direct effects and the induced expansion of DI loans and security holdings are taken into account. In case I, where the DIs receive increased reserves without any increase in primary deposits, the entire $500 million is added to excess reserves and becomes the basis for creating new derivative deposits through an expansion of DI loans and security holdings. In case III, however, the DIs receive the $500 million of reserves in a transaction that increases their primary deposits. Some part of the increase of reserves must therefore be used to meet reserve requirements against the primary deposits, and only the remainder becomes excess reserves that can serve as a basis for creating derivative deposits.

Separation of cases I and III nevertheless serves to emphasize some important points.

1 The Federal Reserve can buy securities even when DIs do not want to sell; it can buy them from other sellers who are depositors at DIs.
2 The Federal Reserve can itself directly increase the public's money supply and need not rely solely on the willingness of DIs to expand their loans and security holdings. Quantitatively, this direct effect of Federal Reserve purchases is usually much smaller than the expansion of DI credit induced by the increase in their reserves. At times, however, it is important.
3 The Federal Reserve can directly contribute to the supply of lendable and spendable funds. Those who sell securities to the Federal Reserve are provided with funds that they can lend, spend, or use in any way they wish.

We shall emphasize the effects of Federal Reserve purchases and sales on the volume of DI reserves, and thus on the ability of the DIs to create credit and money, because these are usually so much larger. But the other effects should not be forgotten.

The effects of Federal Reserve sales of securities to purchasers other than DIs are exactly the reverse of those in case III. As shown in case IV, Federal Reserve sales of $700 million of securities would reduce by that amount both the public's money supply and DI reserves. When the Federal Reserve received the purchaser's check, it would deduct its amount from the reserve balance of the purchaser's DI and send the check to the DI, which can be relied on to deduct it from the buyer's transactions deposit account.

Later sections will discuss at length the policy problems faced by the

Federal Reserve as it must decide when, to what extent, and on what terms it will purchase or sell acceptances and government securities in the open market.

FEDERAL RESERVE LOANS

This category consists almost exclusively of loans to depository institutions. In essence, the depository institution is borrowing reserves from the Federal Reserve. Prior to 1980, such borrowings were normally available only to banks that were members of the Federal Reserve System. With the passage of the Monetary Control Act of 1980, however, all depository institutions became eligible to borrow from the Fed. Aside from depository institutions, on rare occasions the Federal Reserve has made direct loans to the Treasury, foreign central banks, and businesses.

Although the distinction has little economic significance, Federal Reserve loans to DIs are of two principal types: discounts (sometimes called rediscounts) and advances. When a DI secures Federal Reserve credit by discounting, or rediscounting, it simply endorses some of its customers' paper and sends it to a Reserve bank for *discount*. In effect, the Federal Reserve subtracts interest at its prevailing discount rate and credits the remainder to the borrowing DI's reserve account. *Advances* are simply loans to a DI on its own promissory note, although some sort of acceptable collateral is required. In recent years most Federal Reserve loans have been in the form of advances. Despite this fact, the facility for carrying out borrowing is still known as the *discount window*.

As is the case with purchases or sales of government securities, it should be clear that the Federal Reserve can create or destroy reserves by increasing or decreasing its outstanding loans. This is illustrated in the following table.

CASE	FEDERAL RESERVE			DEPOSITORY INSTITUTIONS		
	ΔASSETS		ΔLIABILITIES	ASSETS		LIABILITIES
I	Loans	+ $100	Deposits due DIs + $100	Reserves	+ $100	Borrowings from the Federal Reserve + $100
II	Loans	− $ 50	Deposits due DIs − $ 50	Reserves	− $ 50	Borrowings from the Federal Reserve − $ 50

Case I indicates that when the Federal Reserve expands its loans to DIs, it creates for them an equal increase in their reserves. Case II shows that when the Federal Reserve decreases its outstanding loans, it collects by reducing reserves.

ACCEPTANCES

A banker's acceptance arises out of a draft on a bank, typically drawn by or for the benefit of one of its customers, ordering the bank to pay to a stated party a specific sum of money on some well-defined future date. By writing "accepted" on the draft, the bank commits itself unconditionally to pay as ordered. It anticipates that the customer will provide the necessary funds to pay the acceptance when it is due. An acceptance is thus a way of substituting the credit of the bank for that of the customer. As with other securities, there is a market for bankers' acceptances. Consequently, Federal Reserve purchases and sales of acceptances have the same effects on reserves and the money supply as do similar transactions in government securities.

The importance of Federal Reserve open-market operations in acceptances has varied widely. During the period prior to the Great Depression, Federal Reserve holdings of this paper were often large, sometimes larger than its holdings of government securities. The volume of outstanding acceptances declined sharply during the Great Depression and remained very low until after the end of World War II. Federal Reserve operations in acceptances were negligible during this period. More recently, however, there has been a renewed increase in the volume of acceptances, and the Federal Reserve has resumed its purchases and sales of them. These operations are still very small, but they could grow in the future.

INTERNATIONAL RESERVE ASSETS

The next three types of Federal Reserve assets we consider—gold certificates, SDR certificates, and foreign exchange—are closely related to international monetary transactions. In particular, they are all components of, or claims against components of, the nation's international monetary reserves. As such, purchases and sales of these assets are not made for the primary purposes of affecting the reserve positions of domestic DIs and domestic monetary conditions. Instead, the primary purpose is to influence the behavior of the exchange rates between the dollar and foreign moneys. Furthermore, to an important extent the Federal Reserve does not have complete control over its holdings of these assets. This can present a problem in the conduct of monetary policy since, as we shall see, changes in these assets can affect the supply of reserves. Fortunately, the Federal Reserve can prevent such increases or decreases of reserves by making offsetting sales or purchases of other types of assets, such as securities of the U.S. Treasury.

In the aggregate, gold certificates, SDR certificates, and foreign exchange assets account for about 10 percent of Federal Reserve assets (see Table 11-1). Gold certificates are by far the most quantitatively important of these three.

GOLD CERTIFICATES

Gold certificates are Federal Reserve claims against monetary gold held by the Treasury. For all practical purposes, the value of these claims is equal to the value of the nation's monetary gold stock. This is so because the Treasury generally *monetizes* the gold stock by issuing a dollar's worth of gold certificates for each dollar of gold it holds.[1] To see how this Federal Reserve asset arises, we consider the following example.

Suppose that an American gold miner or melter of scrap offers $10 million of gold, which is purchased by the Federal Reserve for the account of the Treasury. Let us trace the direct effects in two steps.

1 The gold becomes an asset of the Treasury, which issues $10 million of gold certificates to the Federal Reserve, which adds $10 million to the Treasury's deposit account at the Federal Reserve. At this stage the gold purchase has not yet affected either the volume of reserves or the money supply.

2 The Treasury writes a check for $10 million on its deposit at the Federal Reserve and sends the check to the gold seller. The latter deposits the check in a DI, which sends it to the Federal Reserve, which deducts $10 million from the Treasury's deposit and adds it to the DI's deposit account at the Federal Reserve. All this appears on the various balance sheets as follows:

	TREASURY		FEDERAL RESERVE BANKS		DEPOSITORY INSTITUTIONS	
STEP	ΔASSETS	ΔLIABILITIES	ΔASSETS	ΔLIABILITIES	ΔASSETS	ΔLIABILITIES
1	Gold stock +$10	Gold cert. +$10	Gold cert. +$10	Treas. dep. +$10		
2				Treas. dep. −$10	Reserves +$10	Deposits due public +$10
				Deposits due DIs +$10		
Net direct effects	Gold stock +$10	Gold cert. +$10	Gold cert. +$10	Deposits due DIs +$10	Reserves +$10	Deposits due public +$10

Thus, the normal direct effects of a net purchase of gold by the Treasury are to increase by equal amounts (1) the public's money supply, (2) DI reserves, and (3) Federal Reserve holdings of gold certificates. Note that these are only the direct effects; further effects may be induced by the increase of DI reserves. Net sales of gold by the Treasury to Americans normally have exactly the opposite direct effects.

The mechanics of gold certificates are slightly different when the trans-

---

[1]For purposes of valuing the gold stock, the Treasury uses the official price of gold, currently $42.22 per ounce. The official price is in stark contrast to the market price, which as of mid-1985 was over $300 per ounce.

action is between the Treasury and an official foreign or international institution. Suppose, for example, that the Federal Reserve, acting as agent for the Treasury, purchases $100 million of gold from a foreign central bank. The Treasury adds the gold to its assets. It then creates and issues an equal amount of gold certificates to the Federal Reserve, and the latter adds $100 million to its deposit liabilities to the foreign central bank. Thus, as long as the foreign central bank continues to hold the proceeds as a deposit at the Federal Reserve, there will be no effect on either the public's money supply or the volume of DI reserves. Only when the foreign central bank withdraws these funds from the Federal Reserve will there be an effect.

Historically speaking, the size of the nation's monetary gold stock has varied over a wide range, thereby tending to have large direct effects on the volume of DI reserves and the money supply. In recent years, especially since the final demise of the gold standard in 1971, variations in the gold stock have been of considerably less importance. Those variations that have occurred have stemmed from regular monthly gold sales by the Treasury.

SDR CERTIFICATES

SDR certificates are Federal Reserve claims against Special Drawing Rights (SDRs) that are created by the International Monetary Fund and held by the Treasury. These are quite similar to gold certificates except that they are issued against "paper gold."[2] Thus, the normal effects of issuing SDR certificates are virtually identical to the effects of gold purchases. Similarly, the direct effects of a decrease of Federal Reserve holdings of SDR certificates are like those of gold sales—decreasing both DI reserves and the money supply.

FOREIGN EXCHANGE HOLDINGS

Federal Reserve assets in the form of foreign exchange are claims denominated in foreign currencies. These are in various forms—deposit claims against foreign, central, and commercial banks; short-term claims against foreign governments; and so on. When the Federal Reserve makes net purchases or sales of foreign exchange, the effects are almost exactly the same as those resulting from net purchases or sales of gold. When the Federal Reserve buys foreign exchange, it pays with checks on itself, and these are added to the money supply of the seller and to DI reserves. When it sells foreign exchange, it withdraws funds from both the money supply and DI reserves.

FEDERAL RESERVE FLOAT

Only one other Federal Reserve asset requires consideration here. This is Federal Reserve float. This is actually a net asset item arrived at by sub-

---

[2]In contrast to its normal practice with respect to gold and gold certificates, the Treasury does not issue to the Federal Reserve a volume of SDR certificates equal to all its holdings of SDRs; instead, it holds some of its SDRs inactive or unmonetized.

tracting a liability called *deferred availability cash items* from an asset called *cash items in process of collection.* Both arise out of the Federal Reserve function of clearing and collecting checks and other such claims. Checks worth billions of dollars flow into the Federal Reserve banks every day and require some time to be cleared, paid to the reserve accounts of the DIs that deposited them, and deducted from the reserve accounts of the DIs on which they are drawn. As a result, at any point in time the Federal Reserve owns a great volume of checks that it has not yet collected and has not yet paid. The asset "cash items in process of collection" indicates the value of checks in its possession on which it has not yet collected by deducting from its deposit liabilities to DIs. The liability "deferred availability cash items" indicates the value of checks it has not yet paid by adding to its deposit liabilities to the DIs that sent the checks.

If the Federal Reserve paying and collection schedule were to work out perfectly, these asset and liability items would balance out exactly, because the Federal Reserve attempts to pay DIs depositing checks at the same time that it collects from the DIs on which the checks are drawn. As checks flow into the Reserve banks, they are classified as payable "today," "tomorrow," or "the day after tomorrow," the date depending on the estimated time required for the checks to reach the DIs on which they are drawn. On the appointed day the amounts of the checks are credited to the reserve accounts of the depositing DIs. Ideally, they would on the same day be deducted from the reserve accounts of the DIs on which they are drawn. In this case "deferred availability cash items" would be exactly equal to "cash items in process of collection"; the Federal Reserve would not have paid depositing DIs before it collected from others. In the process of clearing and collection, it would have neither created nor destroyed reserves, but would have only shifted reserves from some DIs to others.

In practice, however, the Federal Reserve sometimes pays depositing DIs before it collects from the DIs on which checks are drawn. To this extent, it contributes to total reserves. This source of reserves is called *Federal Reserve float.* At any point in time it measures the net amount the Federal Reserve has contributed to reserves because it has paid some DIs before it collected from others. For example, on the date to which Table 11–1 refers, Federal Reserve float amounted to $588 million. In most of the Federal Reserve balance sheets we will use later, we will enter float as a net asset item and omit the two items from which it has been derived.

Several factors account for the existence of Federal Reserve float:

1   **UNREALISTIC COLLECTION SCHEDULES.** In at least a few cases, checks could not reach the DIs on which they are drawn within the appointed time even if their flow were unimpeded. For example, checks drawn on DIs located in remote sections of Utah and Nevada and deposited at the Federal Reserve Bank of Boston are credited two days later to the reserve accounts of the DIs that deposited them,

even though the checks cannot within that time reach the DI on which they are drawn.

2   **DELAYS IN THE TRANSIT DEPARTMENTS OF THE FEDERAL RESERVE BANKS.** The time of paying a check is determined at the time of its receipt at a Federal Reserve bank. If the process of clearing is delayed because of inadequate staff or an unusually heavy flow of work, or for any other reason, the collection of checks may be delayed.

3   **DELAYS IN TRANSPORTATION.** Anything that delays the transportation of checks after they have been received by a Reserve bank and their dates of payment have been determined can increase float. For example, a heavy fog over the eastern half of the United States could delay air mail and the collection of checks from the DIs on which they are drawn and thereby increase Federal Reserve float and reserves by several hundred million dollars.

As should be apparent, the float provides an interest-free loan from the Federal Reserve to the depository institutions. Moreover, this loan is hardly inconsequential, since from 1977 to 1980 the float averaged nearly $5 billion annually. Somewhat unhappy with what it perceived to be a subsidy to depository institutions, Congress has encouraged the Fed to reduce the float. And in the Monetary Control Act of 1980, Congress decreed that the Fed should charge for the float it provides. The Fed has only gradually introduced such charges, but by devoting additional resources to its check-clearing operations, it has succeeded in substantially reducing the size of the float.[3] In the early months of 1985, for example, the float averaged $1.2 billion.

The issue of a subsidy aside, the float can be an important factor in the conduct of monetary policy. Once the Federal Reserve has determined its schedules for clearing any check collection, and has committed a given volume of resources to collection, it has no direct control over the volume of the float. It must passively pay and collect checks in accordance with its announced schedules. Unfortunately, Federal Reserve float fluctuates widely over short periods. For example, for the week ending September 12, 1979, the float rose by nearly $2½ billion. If nothing had been done about this, it would have led to a substantial increase in DI reserves. However, as a result of offsetting sales of government securities by the Fed, reserves for the week in question actually declined. With the reduction of the size of the float in recent years, this problem still exists, but to a lesser degree. It illustrates the general point that one function of the Federal Reserve is to prevent

---

[3]The Fed has indirectly "charged" for the float by raising its fees for check clearing to reflect the added resources used to reduce the float. At least initially, however, it did not directly charge for the float, and this was the subject of a number of lawsuits by private firms that were competing with the Fed in the provision of check-clearing services. More recently, it has introduced some direct charges for the float.

fluctuations in the volume of float, and in other things that might alter the reserve positions of the DIs from exerting unwanted influences on monetary and credit conditions.

LIMITS ON FEDERAL RESERVE LIABILITIES

What, if anything, limits the extent to which the Federal Reserve can create Federal Reserve note and deposit liabilities by purchasing assets of various kinds? Historically, one type of limit has been in the form of something like reserve requirements which are imposed on the Federal Reserve. (More typically, of course, we think of the Federal Reserve doing the imposing.) The precise nature and extent of these limits have varied over time, but the requirements have typically specified that some fraction of Federal Reserve deposit liabilities and of outstanding Federal Reserve notes be backed by gold certificates. However, because it appeared that these requirements might limit Federal Reserve expansionary policies or even require restrictive action, Congress first reduced them and then eliminated them. Since March 1968, the Federal Reserve has not been subject to any requirements related to gold. It is, however, still true that each Federal Reserve bank must maintain collateral to match the volume of its outstanding Federal Reserve notes.[4] Thus far, at least, ample collateral has been readily available.[5] So that for all practical purposes the volume of Federal Reserve notes and deposit liabilities now depends on discretionary management.

DETERMINANTS OF DEPOSITORY INSTITUTION RESERVES

In the words of the Federal Reserve itself, DI reserves function as "a fulcrum for the operation of monetary policy." This, indeed, was the primary motivation for setting ourselves the objective of analyzing the factors determining the volume of DI reserves and the process through which the Federal Reserve creates and destroys these reserves. Having examined the important components of the Federal Reserve's balance sheet, we are now in good position to be able to complete this task. In particular, as suggested earlier, we can now explicitly rearrange the Federal Reserve balance sheet to focus on depository institution reserves. In so doing, we will arrive at what is commonly called the depository institution reserve equation.

[4]In case you never noticed, paper currency in the form of Federal Reserve notes does indeed bear the imprint of an individual Federal Reserve bank. Next time you have a dollar bill, look closely at the circular design on the left-hand side over the serial number.
[5]Eligible collateral includes U.S. government securities, gold certificates, SDR certificates, and collateral received in making loans.

DEPOSITORY INSTITUTION RESERVE EQUATION

The *depository institution reserve equation* is derived from a set of statistical series developed by the Federal Reserve. These statistics, which are issued in a weekly statement by the Board of Governors, are carried in the major newspapers on Thursday afternoon and Friday morning, and in the monthly *Federal Reserve Bulletin*. Table 11–2 presents such a statement for the end of May 1984.

As anticipated, Table 11–2 bears a striking similarity to the Federal Reserve balance sheet, an example of which was provided for the same date in Table 11–1, but there are a number of differences. These arise from the fact that Table 11–2 has consolidated the balance sheets of both the Federal Reserve and the monetary section of the Treasury. This accounts for the appearance of items such as "Treasury currency outstanding" and "Treasury cash holdings" in Table 11–2.[6]

The column on the left side of Table 11–2, labeled "Factors supplying reserve funds," includes all the sources of funds that are capable of being used as DI reserves. For the most part, the entries arise from the asset side of the Federal Reserve balance sheet. If there were no competing uses for these funds, the volume of DI reserves at any time would be equal to the sum of these sources. The first principal source is what is known as *Federal Reserve credit*. This is simply the volume of funds that have been created by the Federal Reserve in the process of acquiring and holding assets in the form of United States government securities, acceptances, loans, float, and other Federal Reserve assets. This source accounted for about 85 percent of all these funds. The second major source is the monetary gold stock, which represents the volume of funds supplied as the Treasury bought and held gold. The third source is the amount of SDRs monetized by the Treasury. The fourth source, Treasury currency outstanding, indicates the amount of funds supplied by the outstanding coin and paper money issued by the Treasury.

The right-hand column of Table 11–2, labeled "Factors absorbing reserve funds," shows the various uses of the total funds provided by the sources, and the amounts absorbed in each use. It is immediately apparent that large amounts of the funds supplied by the sources are not available for use as DI reserves because they are absorbed in competing uses. The volume of DI deposits at the Federal Reserve at any time is equal to the total volume of funds absorbed by the sources in the left-hand column minus the amounts of these funds absorbed in competing uses, shown in the column on the right. Thus, Table 11–2 shows reserve balances with Federal Reserve banks of $20,538 million. These are equal to the $207,528 million

---

[6]A number of other minor differences also result from consolidation. For example, gold shows up in Table 11–2 under "Gold stock" and in Table 11–1 as "Gold certificates." The difference, if any—there actually was none for the date shown—reflects unmonetized gold held by the Treasury, and this would be included in Treasury cash holdings. For a detailed discussion of the Federal Reserve's balance sheet and DI reserves, see D. M. Nichols, *Modern Money Mechanics*, Federal Reserve Bank of Chicago, 1982.

TABLE 11–2 Factors Affecting Depository Institution Reserves (end-of-month data for May 1984 in millions of dollars)

Factors supplying reserve funds		Factors absorbing reserve funds	
Federal Reserve credit		Currency in circulation	$173,803
U.S. government securities	$154,869	Treasury cash holdings	534
Federal agency securities	8,851	Deposits at Federal Reserve other	
Acceptances	426	than reserves	
Loans	2,832	Treasury	4,855
Float	588	Foreign	295
Other Federal Reserve assets	8,187	Other	7,503
Total F.R. credit	$175,753	Subtotal	$186,990
Gold stock	11,104	Reserve balances with Federal	
SDR certificates	4,618	Reserve Banks	20,538
Treasury currency outstanding	16,053	Total	$207,528
Total	$207,528		

Addenda: Total reserves

Reserve balances used to satisfy reserve requirements at the Federal Reserve	$20,538
Plus: cash in vault	16,960
Equals: Total reserves	$37,498

SOURCE: *Federal Reserve Bulletin*, July 1984, p. A4.

supplied by the various sources, minus the $186,990 million absorbed by competing uses.

Total reserves, of course, consist of both deposits of DIs at the Federal Reserve and vault cash. As indicated in Table 11–2, cash in the vaults of DIs amounted to nearly $17 billion in May 1984, so that total reserves were over $37 billion. All of this can be expressed in equation form in the so-called depository institution reserve equation:

Sources — **Competing uses**

Depository institution reserve balances at any time = {Total F.R. bank credit outstanding + Gold stock + SDR certificates + Treasury currency} − {Currency in circulation outside depository institutions + Treasury cash holdings + Treasury deposits at the Federal Reserve + Foreign deposits at the Federal Reserve + Other uses}

Since we have already examined the various sources in some detail, no further description of these is needed. However, in order to understand better the workings of the depository institution reserve equation, some of the items under "Competing uses" require comment.

COMPETING USES OF FUNDS

CURRENCY IN CIRCULATION

Of all the competing uses of funds supplied by the sources, currency in circulation DIs is by far the largest. It also shows substantial changes from one period to another. As noted earlier, when the public wishes to hold more coin and paper money, it withdraws these forms of money from DIs, which lose reserves in the form of cash in vault or deposits at the Federal Reserve. On the other hand, when the public surrenders some of its holdings of coin and paper money to DIs, the latter receive an addition to their legal reserves. As indicated in Table 11–2, the official Federal Reserve tables handle this item in a somewhat clumsy way. They first include as a factor absorbing reserve funds (or a competing use) all currency outside the Federal Reserve and the Treasury, including the cash held in DI vaults. Then, at the end, they add back as a component of DI reserves the amount of currency held by the DIs. Accordingly, in writing our reserve equation, we have adjusted the competing uses of currency to be equivalent to currency in circulation outside the DIs (and, of course, outside the Federal Reserve and Treasury as well). It is this substitution that allows us to put *total* DI reserves on the left-hand side of the reserve equation.[7]

TREASURY CASH HOLDINGS AND TREASURY DEPOSITS AT THE RESERVE BANKS

Because they are so closely related and because their fluctuations have the same effects on the general monetary and credit situation, we consider the Treasury cash holdings and Treasury deposits at the Federal Reserve banks together. Both compete with DI reserves for funds supplied by the sources. Increases in both tend to decrease reserves, and decreases in both tend to add to reserves.

The Treasury can alter both the size of its money balance and the form in which it is held. It holds its money balance in three principal forms: (1) as cash in its own vaults, (2) as deposits at the Reserves banks, and (3) as deposits with commercial banks. As noted earlier, the last are usually called "tax and loan accounts." To illustrate the process through which increases in Treasury cash holdings or in Treasury deposits at the Federal Reserve tend to reduce DI reserves, let us consider two cases.

[7]This apparent sleight of hand involves nothing more than subtracting vault cash from currency in circulation in Table 11–2 and, to keep the books balanced, adding it to DI deposits, yielding total reserves.

1 The Treasury deposits at the Federal Reserve $100 million of checks it has received from the public. These checks may represent payments of taxes or payments for securities bought by the public. On receiving the checks, the Federal Reserve will add $100 million to Treasury deposits and deduct the same amount from the reserve accounts of the DIs on which they are drawn. The checks will then go to the DIs on which they are drawn, which will deduct them from the public's deposit accounts. Thus, the effects are to decrease by $100 million both the public's money supply and DI reserves.

2 The Treasury increases its deposits at the Federal Reserve by withdrawing $100 million of deposits from commercial banks. On receiving the checks, the Federal Reserve will add them to Treasury deposits and subtract them from DI reserves.

When the Treasury draws down its cash in vault or its deposits at the Federal Reserve, it produces the reverse effects. We have already noted that fluctuations in the size of Treasury holdings of cash and deposits at the Federal Reserve often tend to have important effects on the reverse positions of DIs, especially in periods of large net receipts or net payments by the Treasury, and the Federal Reserve often takes action to prevent their having undesired effects on the general credit situation. In addition, as discussed previously, the Treasury assists in minimizing these effects by the use of tax and loan accounts.

FOREIGN DEPOSITS AT THE FEDERAL RESERVE

These are largely deposits owed by the Federal Reserve to foreign central banks. Like Treasury deposits at the Federal Reserve, foreign deposits compete with DI reserves for funds supplied by the sources. Increases in this item tend to decrease DI reserves, and decreases in it tend to add to reserves. Suppose, for example, that foreign central banks pay out to the U.S. public $100 million of checks drawn on the Reserve banks. This will tend to increase by $100 million both the public's money suply and DI reserves, because the public will deposit the checks at DIs, which will send them to the Federal Reserve to be added to their reserve accounts. If foreign central banks deposit at the Federal Reserve $100 million of checks received from the U.S. public, the effects will be just the reverse: decreases in both the public's money supply and DI reserves.

OTHER USES

This item is made up largely of the Federal Reserve net worth or capital account, with adjustments for minor liability items not accounted for elsewhere, and competes with DI reserves for funds supplied by the sources. To the extent that the Federal Reserve acquires assets by issuing ownership claims, it does not have to issue liability claims. This item usually fluctuates only narrowly over short periods.

TABLE 11–3 Factors Affecting Depository Institution Reserves, May 1983 and May 1984 (end-of-month data in millions of dollars)

Bank reserves and related items	May 1983	May 1984	CHANGES IN ITEMS DURING THE PERIOD TENDING TO:	
			Increase reserves	Decrease reserves
Sources				
Federal Reserve credit:				
U.S. Government securities	141,180	154,869	+ 13,869	
Federal agency securities	8,908	8,851		− 57
Acceptances	0	426	+ 426	
Loans	1,260	2,832	+ 1,572	
Float	850	588		− 262
Other Federal Reserves assets	8,630	8,187		− 443
Gold stock	11,132	11,104		− 28
SDR certificates	4,618	4,618	0	
Treasury currency	13,786	16,053	2,267	
Total sources	190,364	207,528		
Minus:				
Competing uses				
Currency in circulation	158,634	173,803		+ 15,169
Treasury cash holdings	532	534		+ 2
Treasury deposits at Federal Reserve	4,372	4,855		+ 413
Foreign deposits at Federal Reserve	445	295	− 150	
Other uses	6,534	7,503		+ 969
Total competing uses	170,517	186,990		
Equals:				
Reserve balances at Federal Reserve	19,847	20,538		
Plus:				
Cash in vault	16,272	16,960		
Equals:				
Total reserves	36,119	37,498		

SOURCE: *Federal Reserve Bulletin*, July 1983; July 1984.

CHANGES IN DEPOSITORY INSTITUTION RESERVES OVER TIME

The preceding discussion relates to the factors that determine the size of DI reserves as of a given date. Changes in these factors over any stated period of time determine the change in the volume of DI reserves during that period. Increases or decreases in the source items tend to increase or decrease reserves. On the other hand, increases in the amounts of funds absorbed in competing uses tend to reduce reserves, and decreases in the amounts of funds employed in competing uses tend to increase reserves. This is illustrated in Table 11–3, which compares the factors affecting member bank reserves in May 1983 and May 1984. Some factors tended to increase and some to decrease reserves during this period, but the net effect was an increase of $1,379 million. The factors tending to raise reserves were decreases in foreign deposits (a decline in a competing use) and increases in four source items: U.S. government securities; acceptances; loans; and Treasury currency. All the remaining items listed in Table 11–3, be they sources or uses, tended to change in such a way as to decrease reserves.

As Table 11–3 reveals, the single most important factor tending to change reserves during the period in question was the rise of currency in circulation, which tended to reduce reserves. The second most important factor, which largely offset the first, was the rise in holdings of U.S. government securities. For changes in reserves taken over long periods of time such as the yearly period in Table 11–3, this is typically the case. In the short run, however—say, for a week or a month or even several months—the other sources and uses are often of greater importance for potential reserve movements.

While it is informative simply to list the factors tending to increase and decrease reserves, this does not convey the true nature of the problem faced by the Federal Reserve, should it want to achieve a given volume of depository institution reserves. This stems from the fact that only a small number of items in the reserve equation are under the direct control of the Federal Reserve. These items include Federal Reserve holdings of government securities and acceptances and, to a lesser extent, loans to DIs.[8]

The remaining items fall under the control of "outsiders" or result from technical or external factors, such as the weather in the case of the float. Items controlled by outsiders include the public's holding of currency, Treasury deposits, and foreign central bank deposits with the Federal Reserve. This is not to suggest that the Federal Reserve cannot, if it wishes, offset these factors to a considerable extent. Indeed, the large net purchases of government securities shown in Table 11–3 were for the purpose of offsetting all the factors that tended to decrease reserves and to achieve a net increase. In the next chapter we consider in more detail how open-market operations are used for this purpose.

IMPLICATIONS FOR MONETARY POLICY

In carrying out its monetary policy, the Federal Reserve makes continuous use of the depository institution reserve equation to calibrate its open-

[8]Loans are determined jointly by the demand for such loans by the DIs and the willingness of the Federal Reserve to supply these loans. The precise nature of this interaction is spelled out in the following chapter.

market operations. Open-market purchases and sales are two principal types: dynamic and defensive. *Dynamic purchases* or sales are those undertaken to effect net increases or net decreases in reserves. *Defensive purchases* or sales are those undertaken to prevent other factors from bringing about unwanted changes in reserves. In effect, they are offsetting operations. These defensive operations can be in the right direction and in the right magnitude only to the extent that the Federal Reserve can forecast the behavior of the various determinants of DI reserves. The manager of the open-market account therefore seeks not only to detect changes as they occur, but also to forecast future changes.

For this purpose, the manager has several sources of information. To help in forecasting the behavior of Federal Reserve float, there are elaborate studies of its past seasonal behavior and reports from the various Reserve banks concerning any unusual conditions that might cause it to rise or fall. Nevertheless, the behavior of float has proved difficult to forecast with accuracy. The Treasury reports any significant changes that it plans in the volume of its outstanding currency and in the size and location of its money balance. Studies of past seasonal patterns are used in predicting the volume of currency in circulation. Instructions from foreign central banks assist in forecasting the behavior of foreign deposits at the Federal Reserve. The Reserve banks also report any large transactions that would significantly affect the size of other Federal Reserve accounts.

In short, an understanding of the nature and behavior of the various determinants of DI reserves is essential for both the student and the practitioner of monetary management.

SUMMARY

1 Control of depository institution reserves via Fed open-market purchases and sales of government securities is the key ingredient in the conduct of monetary policy. This chapter spelled out the mechanics of the process of controlling reserves. The primary moral of the story is that there is a substantial amount of slippage between open-market operations and the ultimate quantity of reserves. Consequently, even to sustain a given level of reserves, the Fed will have to engage in defensive open-market operations to offset the various factors impinging on reserves.

2 All the entries on the Fed's balance sheet can potentially affect DI reserves. Certain U.S. Treasury operations may likewise be of importance. All these factors are combined in the depository institution reserve equation. Over an extended period of time, the main factors at work in this equation are Fed open-market operations and currency in circulation. The other items in the equation, however, must be taken into account, especially in the short run.

SELECTED READINGS

Board of Governors of the Federal Reserve System. *The Federal Reserve System, Purposes and Functions*, 7th ed. Washington, D.C., 1984.

Nichols, D. M., *Modern Money Mechanics*. Chicago: Federal Reserve Bank of Chicago, 1982.

12

INSTRUMENTS OF MONETARY MANAGEMENT

In this chapter we analyze the various instruments of monetary management in the hands of the Federal Reserve. General monetary or credit controls—those directed toward regulating the total supply of money or credit without necessarily regulating the allocation of credit among its various possible borrowers or uses—will be discussed first. As already indicated, the Federal Reserve's powers to regulate the total volume of money and credit are of two broad types: (1) various powers to regulate the magnitude and cost of depository institution reserves, and (2) power to determine and alter depository institution reserve requirements. After discussing these, we take up the use of selective credit controls, which are intended to influence the allocation of credit. The chapter concludes with a brief discussion of the problems of conducting a sensible monetary policy.

OPEN-MARKET OPERATIONS

Open-market operations are the most important tool in regulating the cost and dollar volume of depository institution reserves. Operations are conducted primarily through purchases and sales of U.S. Treasury obligations, but the Federal Reserve also buys and sells bankers' acceptances and securities issued by federal agencies such as the Federal National Mortgage Association.

SOME MECHANICS

As noted earlier, Federal Reserve open-market operations are controlled by the Federal Open Market Committee (hereafter referred to as the FOMC), which is composed of the seven members of the Board of Governors, the president of the Federal Reserve Bank of New York, and four other presidents of Reserve banks. The FOMC meets in Washington, D.C., approximately once a month. The meetings typically begin with a review of recent and prospective economic and financial developments, in both words and pictures (via what is known as the "chart show"). Following a discussion of the objectives of monetary policy for the near-term future, the meeting culminates with the issuance of a domestic policy *directive* aimed at spelling out the broad nature of the actions to be taken. Actual purchases and sales are made by the manager of the open-market account, who is a vice-president of the Federal Reserve Bank of New York but is accountable to the FOMC.

In addition to the directive, which is rather general, the FOMC provides some operating guides for the manager by specifying acceptable ranges for certain key financial variables. We discuss later the choice of these variables and the specific nature of the directive. For the present, note that the FOMC does not set the actual quantity and nature of future open-market operations at its monthly meeting. This is left to the discretion of the manager, who, however, confers daily by telephone with FOMC members. In buying and selling, the manager deals with about two dozen government security dealers, who, as noted earlier, are at the center of a national and even international market for government securities. The manager of the open-market account is thus in a position to use open-market operations in a timely and flexible manner. The account manager can buy or sell quickly, change the rate of purchases or sales quickly, and shift quickly from buying to selling, or vice versa.

When the manager of the open-market account purchases government securities from a dealer, the dealer is paid with a check on the Federal Reserve Bank of New York. The dealer must, of course, pay these funds to the seller of the securities. If the seller is a commercial bank or other depository institution, the immediate effect is to increase the volume of reserves. If the seller is someone other than a DI, the effect is to increase directly both the public's money supply and the dollar volume of DI reserves, because the seller will deposit the check with his or her DI, which will deposit it at a Reserve bank.

Sales of government securities by the manager of the open-market account have the opposite effect. If the buyer is a depository institution, the effect is to reduce DI reserves. If the buyer is someone other than a DI, the effect is to reduce directly both reserves and the public's money supply. In effect, the dealer pays the Federal Reserve with a check received from a customer of some DI, the Federal Reserve deducts the check from the DI's reserve account and sends the check to the DI, which deducts it from the customer's account.

In actual practice, such transactions typically do not even require a check, since the process is accelerated by a computer linking the Reserve banks and the banks that act as clearing agents for the dealers. Dealer payments and debits or credits to DI reserves are thus made simultaneously, and the transaction is fully cleared during the day specified for delivery, which is often the same as the day of purchase.

Although these transactions typically occur in New York City, their effects are by no means confined to that area. Those who sell the government securities purchased by the Federal Reserve, and thereby gain Federal Reserve funds, may be located at any place within the country. So may those who buy the government securities from the Federal Reserve and thereby lose Federal Reserve funds. Moreover, the effects will be spread throughout the banking system and the financial markets regardless of the geographic location of the institution or person selling securities to, or buying securities from, the Federal Reserve. This happens because the DIs that receive the reserves created by Federal Reserve purchases will lose reserves to other DIs as they expand their own loans and security holdings. And DIs that lose reserves because of Federal Reserve sales will draw reserves from other DIs as they contract their credit. These processes may, of course, require some time.

Federal Reserve open-market operations are of two principal types: (1) outright purchases and sales, and (2) purchases under repurchase agreements and sales under matched sale-purchase arrangements. *Outright purchases and sales* are ordinary transactions in which neither the buyer nor seller makes a commitment to resell or rebuy. The transaction is final. In contrast, under a *repurchase agreement* the Federal Reserve buys securities from a dealer, with an agreement that the dealer will repurchase the securities within a stipulated period, which never exceeds 15 days and is typically less than 7 days. This is much like a short-term loan to the dealer, and the effective rate of interest is set by an auction among dealers. A *matched sale-purchase* transaction is simply the other side of the coin, in which the Federal Reserve sells securities to a dealer and agrees subsequently to buy the securities back, usually in less than 7 days.

Federal Reserve officials regard money created by repurchase agreements as "dollars with strings on them," for the very purchases that involve the issue of the dollars make provision for return of the dollars on a stipulated date. Such acquisitions are a useful instrument for at least two purposes. For one thing, they are a convenient way of supplying funds to meet a temporary need, and of withdrawing funds when the need has passed.

For example, the Federal Reserve may acquire securities under repurchase agreements during the week before Christmas, when currency is being drained from the banks, arranging for dealers to repurchase the securities just after Christmas, when large amounts of currency flow back into the banking system. This device is also useful for avoiding disorderly changes in the market price of government securities. Dealers in these securities ordinarily hold inventories far larger than they can finance with their own capital funds. They rely heavily on borrowed money. If at some time they could not borrow sufficient funds, or could do so only at very high rates of interest, they might dump large amounts of their inventory on the market, thereby seriously disturbing not only government security prices, but also money market conditions in general. Judicious Federal Reserve acquisitions under repurchase agreements can help prevent such occurrences.

Matched sale-purchase transactions work in a similar way, except, of course, that their effects are restrictive. In particular, the initial sale causes reserves to flow from DIs through the dealers to the Federal Reserve. Later, when the Federal Reserve purchase is made, the flow of reserves is reversed. Quite obviously, such arrangements are ideally suited to situations in which the Federal Reserve wishes to absorb a temporary surplus created by some external factor.

Table 12–1 contains data pertaining to open-market transactions for two years, 1974 and 1983. It shows both the extent of the various types of transactions and the securities in which these transactions were made. With regard to these data, the following points are worth emphasizing:

1 The bulk of open-market transactions are now made via repurchase agreements or matched sale-purchase arrangements and not through outright purchases and sales.[1] A comparison of the data for the two years shown reveals that this tendency has been more marked in recent years.

2 Most open-market transactions are in Treasury securities. Furthermore, although not detailed in the table, the bulk of these are in relatively short-term Treasury bills.

3 The *gross* volume of transactions is huge when compared with the *net* change in Federal Reserve holdings of Treasury securities, agency obligations, and acceptances. It is even large when compared with the stock of Federal Reserve holdings of these assets, which amounted to some $145 billion in 1984.

---

[1]The astute reader may be puzzled as to why, in Table 12–1, gross sales and purchases are not identical for repurchase agreements and matched sales-purchases. The reason is that some transactions that are initiated near the end of the year may not be completed until the following year.

TABLE 12–1 Transactions of the Open-Market Account, Selected Years (in millions of dollars)

Type of transaction	1974	1983
U.S. government securities		
Outright transactions		
Gross purchases	13,537	22,540
Gross sales	5,830	3,420
Redemptions	4,682	2,487
Matched sale-purchase transactions		
Gross sales	64,229	578,591
Gross purchases	62,801	576,908
Repurchase agreements		
Gross purchases	71,333	105,971
Gross sales	70,947	108,291
Federal agency obligations		
Outright transactions		
Gross purchases	3,087	0
Gross sales	0	0
Redemptions	322	292
Repurchase agreements		
Gross purchases	23,204	8,833
Gross sales	22,735	9,213
Bankers' acceptances		
Outright transactions, net	511	0
Repurchase agreements, net	420	−1,062
Total net change (all categories)	6,149	10,897

DEFENSIVE AND DYNAMIC OPEN-MARKET OPERATIONS

As noted earlier, *defensive open-market operations* are those undertaken by the Federal Reserve to prevent other factors, such as changes in the gold stock or in currency in circulation, from bringing about unwanted changes in the reserve positions of DIs. *Dynamic operations* are those aimed at altering the reserve positions of DIs. This distinction is useful in emphasizing that not all Federal Reserve purchases and sales are designed to bring about net increases or decreases in reserves. In fact, as one might suspect from the statistics in Table 12–1, the great majority of open-market transactions are purely defensive. Consider for a moment the data for 1983. As Table 12–1 reveals, gross purchases (outright or otherwise) of Treasury securities alone amounted to over $700 billion in 1983. The net increase in Federal Reserve holding of government securities and acceptances was a much smaller $11 billion. But even this overstates the change in DI reserves.

In particular, because of other factors in the DI reserve equation that tended to absorb reserves, DI reserves actually *decreased* by about $3 billion in 1983. It should be quite evident that the manager of the open-market account would have to earn his or her salary even if the FOMC wanted reserves to stay constant.[2]

We have stressed the prevalence of defensive open-market operations, but we should not lose sight of the importance of dynamic operations. After all, it is through dynamic changes, which purposively alter DI reserves, that monetary policy has its impact on the financial sector and thus on the economy. From this perspective, defensive operations are a technical detail from which one might well abstract. Indeed, this is precisely the tack we will take in all subsequent discussion of monetary policy. That is, whenever we talk about the impact of an open-market transaction, we will always have in mind an operation designed to change DI reserves. Let us turn now to the effects of such operations.

EFFECTS OF FEDERAL RESERVE PURCHASES OR SALES

Federal Reserve purchases or sales of government securities may have three types of direct effects: (1) effects on the dollar volume of bank reserves, (2) impact effects on the price and yield of the particular type of security bought or sold, and (3) effects on expectations concerning the future behavior of security prices and yields. In some cases one or more of these effects may fail to appear, but when they do, they may be powerful or weak, desired or undesired, anticipated or unanticipated.

Effects on the volume of DI reserves appear in every case and are usually the most powerful, for every change of one dollar in DI reserves is the basis for a change of several dollars in the money supply and DI credit. It is for this reason that throughout we shall stress the effect of open-market operations on the reserve position of the banking system. However, it would in some cases be a mistake to ignore the other effects.

When the Federal Reserve buys or sells a particular type of government security, the impact or initial tendency is to change the price and yield of that particular security. This effect may be negligible if the amount purchased or sold is very small relative to the total supply, but it may be significant if the operation is larger relative to the supply. Suppose, for example, that the Federal Reserve purchases a large amount of government securities in the 10-year maturity range. This may be described as an increase in the demand for that type of security. Or it may be described as a decrease in the supply available to meet private demands. In any case, the initial tendency is to raise the price of the security and lower its yield. This

[2]Some economists have argued that part of the explanation for the substantial volume of open-market operations displayed in Table 12–1 is that the Federal Reserve Board has tried to keep short-term interest rates from moving very much in a short period of time. This is considered briefly in the next sections and will be taken up again in a subsequent chapter..

effect is likely to be moderated and spread to other securities through private arbitrage. Private investors will tend to shun this security, and even to sell it, until its yield is as attractive as yields on other securities. However, the process may be time-consuming and imperfect, especially if the initial effects were very large. Comparable processes may be involved if the Federal Reserve sells large amounts of a particular security.

Federal Reserve attitudes toward the effects of its purchases and sales on the prices and yields of particular securities or groups of securities have varied widely. During much of its history the Federal Reserve has sought to avoid, or at least to minimize, them. It has often confined its operations to short maturities, where the impact is expected to be small, and has spread its purchases or sales over time. At other times it has consciously used this power to influence directly the prices of particular securities or groups of securities. For example, it has often bought or sold to prevent or ameliorate "disorderly movements" of security prices. From 1942 to 1951 it even went so far as to "peg" the prices and yields on long-term government securities within narrow limits. It has also engaged in "swap operations," sales of securities in one maturity range offset by purchases of securities in another maturity range. For example, in the early 1960s it sold Treasury bills and other short-term securities in order to hold down their prices and support their yields, at the same time buying long-term securities in order to support their prices and hold down their yields. We will see later that some efforts to affect the behavior of the prices and yields of securities have jeopardized the Fed's ability to control the volume of DI reserves.

Federal Reserve open-market operations may also influence the behavior of security prices and yields by influencing private expectations. These are often called "announcement" effects. Suppose, for example, that private investors see that the Federal Reserve has begun to purchase large amounts of securities with the apparent purpose of easing credit. If they come to believe that the policy will continue and will succeed, private investors will be impelled to increase their demands for securities, thereby increasing the flow of loanable funds, supporting the rise of security prices, and reinforcing the decline of yields. On the other hand, large Federal Reserve sales of securities may create expectations of higher interest rates in the future, which will tend to decrease private demands for securities and tighten credit further.

TREASURY FINANCINGS AND OPEN-MARKET OPERATIONS

We have already seen that flows of funds into and out of the coffers of the Treasury may require offsetting open-market operations to minimize the impact on DI reserves. There is, however, another way in which the operations of the Treasury impinge on the conduct of open-market operations. More specifically, large-scale Treasury debt financings—especially those involving intermediate- and longer-term debt—are regarded as having the potential to create "disorderly" financial markets. On some occasions, to avoid such problems, during a period of major Treasury financing the Federal Reserve has resorted to a policy of keeping an *even keel* in the bond markets. For example, when it was pursuing a tight money policy, the Federal Reserve has been somewhat less aggressive in carrying out open-market sales. The Federal Reserve is somewhat sensitive about this policy and is quick to point out that "in no way does [an] even keel provide a guarantee that the Federal Reserve will stabilize securities markets for Treasury financings at the expense of reserve objectives." Nevertheless, it seems clear that from time to time the Federal Reserve has given up its freedom to maneuver in the conduct of monetary policy.

PATTERNS OF OPEN-MARKET OPERATIONS

The Federal Reserve can use its powers to buy and sell in the open market in many different ways, with quite different consequences for financial markets and the economy. We will explore only a few of the possible patterns. The first is one in which the Federal Reserve retains precise control of the amount of securities held. Members of the FOMC might describe it this way: "We shall determine the amount of securities that we hold, the types and amounts that we buy and sell, and when we buy and sell. We retain the initiative and will not buy or sell simply because others wish to sell to us or buy from us." Under such a policy, the Federal Reserve can control both the volume of its holdings and the volume of DI reserves, but the prices and yields on securities can fluctuate in response to changes in demand-and-supply relationships in the market.

Another and very different pattern is the one in which the Federal Reserve passively buys and sells some security or group of securities at a fixed price and yield. For example, the FOMC might say, "At this price and yield on long-term government securities we shall buy all offered to us and sell all demanded from us." While such a policy is in effect, the price of the selected security or group of securities obviously cannot fall below the price at which the Federal Reserve will buy, nor can it rise above the price at which it will sell. However, the Federal Reserve, in adopting such a policy, loses control over both the volume of its security holdings and the volume of DI reserves. It must hold all the securities that others issue and what others do not want to hold at the fixed price and yield levels. As passive buyer and seller, it surrenders control over the volume of its holdings.

We later consider other patterns of open-market operations and some of the problems faced by the Federal Reserve in determining which pattern to follow. However, two points should be emphasized here:

1 The system must choose between accurate control of the volume of its holdings of government securities on the one hand and stabilization of interest rates on the other. If it is to control the volume of its

holdings, it must allow the prices and yields of government securities to fluctuate in response to changes in the supply of, and demand for, these obligations. If it is to stabilize their prices and yields, it must abandon accurate control of the volume of its holdings and passively buy or sell all the securities offered to it, or demanded from it, at the selected level of prices and yields. In this case, the initiative is with other investors, for it is they who determine the volume of securities offered to, or demanded from, the Federal Reserve. This means, of course, that they also determine the volume of depository institution reserves.

2 As long as investors can shift freely between government securities and other obligations, the Federal Reserve can dominate the entire structure of interest rates by regulating yields on the federal debt. This debt now makes up a sizable fraction of all the outstanding interest-bearing debt of the country, and is equal to many times the annual increase in total debt. If the Federal Reserve buys and sells these securities freely in such a way as to maintain a certain structure of yields on them, it also establishes, within narrow limits, the structure of yields on other debts. The reason is that private investors are free to arbitrage among the various branches of the debt market, to sell in one and buy in another until they see no further advantage in shifting their funds. This applies not only to DIs, but to other investors as well. In short, Federal Reserve operations in the government securities market can dominate the entire money market. However, we will see later that if this power is used to stabilize interest rates, the effect may be to destabilize the rest of the economy.

DISCOUNT POLICY AND DISCOUNT RATES

We have already noted that the Federal Reserve can create reserves by increasing its loans to depository institutions and can destroy reserves by decreasing its outstanding loans. Indeed, this lending mechanism was originally conceived of as the focal point of central banking operations in the United States. Although the Federal Reserve now relies primarily on open-market operations to regulate the volume of reserves, its discount policy, the terms and conditions on which it will lend, remains of considerable importance. And one important aspect of lending by the Federal Reserve needs to be reemphasized. Prior to 1980, only commercial banks that were members of the Federal Reserve System were normally eligible to borrow funds from the Fed. With the passage of the Monetary Control Act of 1980, this privilege was extended to all nonmember depository institutions.

TYPES OF BORROWINGS

As noted previously, depository institutions may borrow funds by means of discounts or advances. Discounting entails the sale (rediscount) of "eligible paper" to a Reserve bank. An advance is a loan to a DI on its own promissory note, secured by adequate collateral. The original notion was that most borrowing would take the form of rediscounting of short-term, self-liquidating commercial paper. This was evidently a direct result of the then-prevailing commercial loan theory of banking. With the demise of this theory, this form of borrowing has fallen into disuse. In modern times virtually all borrowing, facilitated by the marked growth in the public debt, takes the form of advances secured by government securities (although such borrowing is still loosely referred to as discounting). In addition, the Federal Reserve Act has been amended to permit advances on collateral other than government securities or eligible paper. In short, the trend has been toward greater freedom for the Federal Reserve to determine the types of loans it will make.

ADMINISTRATION OF THE DISCOUNT WINDOW

Unlike the case with open-market operations, where the impetus lies with the Federal Reserve, the initiative for discounting resides with depository institutions. As we have seen, borrowing from the Federal Reserve is but one way in which DIs can seek to augment their liquidity. Other methods include the sale of securities, the issuance of CDs, and borrowing in the federal funds or Eurodollar markets. The extent to which a DI relies on discounting depends on its opportunities with respect to these other sources, the duration of its needs, and the relative price and availability of advances from the Federal Reserve. Indeed, it is through these latter two factors that the Federal Reserve influences the volume of advances. In particular, the administration of the discount window has two major components:

1   **DISCOUNT RATE POLICY.** As noted earlier, the discount rate is simply the interest rate charged by the Reserve banks on their loans. Increases in discount rates raise the cost of acquiring reserves by borrowing, whereas decreases in discount rates make it cheaper for DIs to acquire reserves in this way.

2   **NONPRICE METHODS.** A wide array of nonprice methods is used to influence the amount of discounting. These range from moral suasion to quantitative rationing and even to outright denial of loans.

Central banks differ greatly in the extent to which they rely on discount rates and on other methods to regulate the volume of their loans and discounts. Also, the role of the discount rate and the effects of discount-rate changes are strongly influenced by the extent to which other methods are used.

Under certain conditions, a central bank's discount rate could regulate with accuracy the level of market rates of interest, or at least of short-term interest rates. Suppose, for example, that two conditions obtain: (1) The central bank stands ready to lend freely at its established discount rate; it uses no other rationing methods and relies on the discount rate alone to regulate the volume of its loans. (2) Depository institutions have no inhibitions against borrowing from the central bank. Intent on maximizing their profits, they borrow from the central bank and lend whenever market rates of interest exceed the discount rate by an amount sufficient to cover the cost of risk bearing and loan administration. They also withdraw loans from the market and repay their borrowings at the central bank whenever market rates of interest are not sufficiently higher than the discount rate. Under such conditions, the central bank discount rate could dominate market rates of interest. Increases and decreases in the discount rate would almost automatically raise or lower market rates of interest. Moreover, discount rates would be the central bank's sole method of regulating the volume of reserves that it created by lending.

These are not the conditions in American banking, and the Federal Reserve discount rate is not the only method used to regulate the volume of borrowing from the Fed. Many observers have pointed out that even before the establishment of the Federal Reserve, there was among American banks a "tradition against continuous borrowing," a feeling that it was unsound for a DI to borrow continuously or excessively. Although such a tradition did exist, it would probably be far weaker and less powerful as a deterrent to borrowing if Federal Reserve officials had not worked so hard and continuously to strengthen it. Perhaps it would be more accurate to say that the Federal Reserve developed "a tradition against continuous and excessive lending" to an individual DI and that the DIs are well aware of this.[3] Federal Reserve officials have repeatedly stated that borrowing is a privilege and not a right, that a DI should not borrow simply because it is profitable to do so, and that a DI should borrow only to meet the drains it could not foresee, and even then only for short periods, except under "unusual and exceptional circumstances."

A Reserve bank rarely refuses to lend to a depository institution that is facing an actual or prospective deficiency in reserves. But after making a short-term loan to a DI, it studies the situation carefully. If it finds that the DI has borrowed too often, too continuously, too much, or for improper

---

[3]In certain recent periods, notably 1980 and 1981, the Federal Reserve introduced an explicit cost for what it deemed excessive borrowing. This took the form of a surcharge on the discount rate of 2 or 3 percentage points. This surcharge applied to large institutions (deposits of $500 million or more) that had borrowed in successive weeks or in more than 4 weeks in a 3-month period.

reasons, it may advise the DI to contract its loans or sell securities in order to reduce or retire its borrowings. It may even go as far as to refuse to renew the loan, and in extreme cases it may suspend the DI's borrowing privilege.

Federal Reserve officials could, of course, attempt to regulate the volume of borrowing by varying their own attitudes toward lending—being very strict on some occasions and more liberal on others. Although this method is used to some extent, it is not a very flexible or effective instrument.

This combination of depository institution inhibitions against large and continuous borrowing from the Federal Reserve and the latter's unwillingness to make such loans to DIs helps to explain several aspects of monetary policy in the United States.

1 When DI borrowings from the Federal Reserve are large, credit is usually tight. Credit is, of course, less tight than it would have been if the DIs had not been able to borrow and secure reserves, but it is tighter than it could have been if the same volume of reserves had been achieved without borrowing.

2 The role of discount rates in regulating the volume of reserves is less important. The Federal Reserve does not rely solely on increased discount rates to limit borrowing. And because of the tradition against continuous borrowing, decreases in discount rates may not be very effective in inducing larger borrowings from the Fed.

It would be a mistake to dismiss changes in discount rates as ineffective and useless and to rely solely on the tradition against continuous borrowing and on Federal Reserve admonitions to regulate the amount of DI borrowing. Changes in discount rates remain important and influence the economy in several ways.[4]

1. They do have some effect on the volume of DI borrowings from the Federal Reserve. A DI faced with the question of how to deal with an actual or prospective deficiency in its reserves is tempted, despite the tradition against continuous borrowing, to repair its position in the cheapest way. If the Federal Reserve discount rate is lower than the yield it would have to sacrifice by selling some of its earning assets, a DI may elect to borrow from the Fed and may be in no hurry to repay. This is especially true of those institutions that have not been borrowing continuously and therefore fear no trouble from Federal Reserve officials. The result can be a significant increase in borrowings and reserves and a minimum of pressure toward credit restriction. However, if the discount rate is higher than the yields on assets that the DIs might sell to repair their reserve positions, many DIs will not borrow and will repay any borrowings quickly. They will attempt to repair their positions by calling loans or selling securities. The result may be to decrease borrowings and enhance restrictive pressures.

[4]For data on actual discount rate changes in recent years, refer to Figure 6–1.

2. Changes in discount rates can be an effective way of announcing to both the DIs and the public the direction of Federal Reserve policy. Open-market operations are not well suited to this purpose, partly because they are not widely understood and partly because dynamic operations are often obscured for some time by defensive operations. On the other hand, changes in discount rates are widely publicized as soon as they occur, and are generally believed to be important. In fact, many people exaggerate their importance. An increase in discount rates is generally interpreted as meaning the Federal Reserve is moving toward tighter credit and higher interest rates. This may induce some lenders to restrict their loans in anticipation of higher interest rates in the future. A reduction of discount rates, presaging an easier monetary policy and lower interest rates, may induce some lenders to increase their willingness to lend.

Of course, there is the possibility that changes in discount rates will have perverse effects. For example, if an increase in discount rates is interpreted to mean that Federal Reserve officials believe inflation is coming, such an action might encourage people to borrow and spend, thereby increasing the danger of inflation. If a decrease in discount rates is taken as a forecast of recession, it could encourage a reduction of spending and hasten a business decline. However, such announcement effects are likely to occur only if changes in discount rates create expectations about the trend of business that the public would not have had anyway, and if the public believes the Federal Reserve will not be able to achieve its objectives. The public has so many other sources of information that it would usually know about dangers of inflation or recession even if the Federal Reserve did nothing to announce its intention of combating such disturbances.

3. Changes in discount rates affect market rates of interest in various ways. We have already noted that increases or decreases in this rate may affect lenders' expectations about future rates and immediately cause them to lend less liberally or more liberally. There are other effects as well. A few (but only a few) long-term debt contracts escalate their interest rates with the Federal Reserve discount rate. The other principal effects are less direct, but nevertheless important. For example, an increase in the discount rate increases the bargaining power of lenders. Lenders may insist that "even the Federal Reserve recognizes that credit is scarcer and interest rates should go up." Reductions in discount rates generally increase the bargaining power of borrowers and tend to bring down "sticky" rates of interest. On the whole, however, these effects are rather minor, since borrowed reserves account for a relatively small part of total reserves.

SOME RECENT DEVELOPMENTS

In recent years, there has been a tendency toward liberalization of the discount mechanism for rather specific purposes. One development along these lines resulted from a decision, made in 1973, to introduce a more formal mechanism for the extension of seasonal credit to DIs that lacked access to national money markets. To be eligible for this new privilege, a DI must exhibit a seasonal pattern in loans and deposits that persists for at least eight weeks. It must also arrange for the seasonal credit prior to the need for funds. For some DIs, this new feature can provide funds for a period of several months. The primary beneficiaries of the seasonal borrowing privilege are smaller institutions, especially those that do a substantial volume of loan business in agricultural or resort areas.

The Federal Reserve discount mechanism can also be used to provide emergency credit to depository institutions facing financial stringency. Several examples of this have received widespread attention in the press in recent years. One took place in 1970 following the bankruptcy of the Penn Central Railroad. Penn Central defaulted on its outstanding commercial paper, and this had a rather chilling effect on the commercial paper market in general. Many firms found themselves unable to reissue their maturing commercial paper and turned quickly, and with substantial need, to their backup lines of credit at commercial banks. To ease the crisis atmosphere, the Federal Reserve allowed the banks involved to cover some of their added needs for funds through special borrowings at the discount window. A second use of emergency credit involved the Franklin National Bank, which ran into serious financial difficulties in 1974. It was allowed to borrow a substantial volume of funds for a relatively long period while plans for reorganizing the bank were being formulated. In short, through emergency credit the Federal Reserve is able to fulfill its traditional role as the ultimate provider of liquidity or, as it is called, "the lender of last resort." A more recent example of the same sort took place in 1984, when one of the nation's largest banks, the Continental Illinois Bank of Chicago, experienced extreme financial difficulties.

OVERVIEW

Borrowing from the Federal Reserve takes place at the initiative of depository institutions, but is subject to administrative oversight by the Federal Reserve. Such borrowing provides DIs with a simple way of meeting unexpected temporary needs for liquidity, for dealing with recurring seasonal needs, and for coping with more serious emergency situations. Nevertheless, some economists have criticized the discounting privilege, since it permits DIs temporarily to escape the effects of monetary restraint. In particular, these critics argue that discounting, by introducing "slippage" into Federal Reserve control of DI reserves, diminishes the effectiveness of monetary policy. While there is an element of truth in this, most economists do not regard it as a serious problem, certainly not one that warrants dismantling the discount mechanism. Indeed, it is generally accepted that open-market operations and administration of the discount window provide the Federal Reserve with ample flexibility to achieve its objectives, even in the face of the safety valve provided by discounting.

RESERVE REQUIREMENTS

Having discussed the two major tools for regulating the volume and cost of depository institution reserves, we turn now to the power of the Federal Reserve to determine reserve requirements. As we saw in Chapter 8, via their impact on the money multiplier, such requirements also affect the outstanding volume of money and credit in the economy. Until 1980, reserve requirements applied only to commercial banks that were members of the Federal Reserve System. With the passage of the Monetary Control Act of 1980, these requirements were extended to all depository institutions.

SOME BACKGROUND

Prior to 1935, member bank reserve requirements were rigidly set by the Federal Reserve Act and could not be altered by Federal Reserve officials. This legislation provided that nothing other than deposits at Reserve banks would count as legal reserves. Minimum reserve requirements against time and savings deposits were set at 3 percent for all member banks. In fixing reserve requirements against demand deposits at member banks, the Federal Reserve Act carried over the geographic classifications used in the National Banking Act. As a result, banks in New York and Chicago had the highest reserve requirements, banks in other large cities the next highest, and the quaintly termed country banks were subject to the lowest requirements.

The Banking Act of 1935 empowered the Board of Governors to alter reserve requirements within fairly broad ranges. For example, reserve requirements on demand deposits at banks in New York and Chicago could be set anywhere between 13 and 26 percent, while the corresponding range for their country cousins was 7 to 14 percent.

Over the years, the structure of reserve requirements was modified in a number of ways. Congress on several different occasions altered the ranges within which the Fed could vary reserve requirements. Second, in 1960 Congress empowered the Board of Governors to allow member banks to count cash in vault as legal reserves. A final change of note was brought about despite Congress. The Board of Governors had become increasingly unhappy with the historical legacy that made for differential reserve requirements based on the location of a member bank, and it strongly advocated a system in which reserve requirements would be graduated on the basis of the amount of deposits in a bank, regardless of location. After Congress had ignored several recommendations that such changes be enacted into law, the Board in 1972 took matters into its own hands. Asserting its authority to do so, the Board moved to a system of reserve requirements in which bank size, not geographic location, was the critical element. Congress was probably too shocked to complain, and the new structure was quietly accepted.

Table 12–2 gives the structure of reserve requirements as of November 1980, showing the variation in reserve requirements against net demand deposits as a function of bank size.[5] The reserve requirements on time and savings deposits that were in force on the same date are also shown. The average level of reserve requirements against time and savings deposits was distinctly lower than those against demand deposits. These differences persisted with the new set of reserve requirements enacted in 1980.

THE CURRENT STRUCTURE OF RESERVE REQUIREMENTS

The Monetary Control Act (MCA) of 1980 substantially modified the level and coverage of reserve requirements. For one, it extended reserve requirements to all depository institutions, not just member banks. Second, it applied the same reserve requirements to all checkable deposits, not just demand deposits. Third, it eliminated the reserve requirements on savings deposits and on personal time deposits.

The main features of the current structure of reserve requirements are given in Table 12–3. As the table reveals, the new structure of reserve requirements on transactions deposits retains an element of the older structure—the reserve requirement varies with bank size. The first $25 million of transactions deposits bear a 3 percent reserve requirement, while amounts

TABLE 12–2 The Old Reserve Requirements for Member Banks

Category and amount of deposit	Reserve ratio
Net demand deposits	
$0–2 million	7%
$2–10 million	9.5%
$10–100 million	11.75%
$100–400 million	12.75%
Over $400 million	16.25%
Savings deposits	3%
Time deposits	
$0–5 million, by maturity	
30–179 days	3%
180 days to 4 years	2.5%
4 years or more	1%
Over $5 million, by maturity	
30–179 days	6%
180 days to 4 years	2.5%
4 years or more	1%

[5]Demand deposits subject to reserve requirements are known as *net* demand deposits. These are defined as gross (total) demand deposits less cash items in the process of collection and demand balances due from domestic banks.

TABLE 12–3 Current Structure of Reserve Requirements

Category of deposit	Reserve ratio
Transactions accounts	
First $25 million*	3%
Amounts greater than $25 million*	12%
Nonpersonal time deposits	
Maturities less than 1½ years	3%
Maturities of 1½ years or more	0
Eurocurrency liabilities	3%

*As described in the text, the base figure of $25 million is adjusted annually and now stands at $29.8 million.

over $25 million carry a reserve requirement of 12 percent. The Fed cannot vary the 3 percent requirement, but does have authority to vary the reserve requirement in the range of 8 to 14 percent on transactions deposits over $25 million. The MCA also required that the amount of transactions accounts against which the 3 percent reserve requirement applies be modified annually in accordance with the overall growth in transactions deposits. As a consequence of this indexing, the initial $25 million cutoff stood at $29.8 million as of early 1985.[6] The Garn–St. Germain Act of 1982 added another element to the "progressive" structure of reserve requirements by exempting the first $2 million of "reservable liabilities" from reserve requirements. As noted in our discussion of thrift institutions, this feature was of particular consequence for credit unions, most of whom are quite small in size. As with the $25 million cutoff, the Garn–St. Germain Act also indexed the $2 million cutoff to grow with size of reservable liabilities at depository institutions. As of early 1985, this cutoff stood at $2.4 million.

As we can see by comparing Tables 12–2 and 12–3, the MCA drastically simplified the reserve requirements applicable to time and savings deposits. It did this by eliminating most of the previous requirements. As of the present, there remains only a 3 percent reserve requirement on nonpersonal time deposits of maturity less than 1½ years. This category of deposits accounts for only 17 percent of all time and savings deposits. As with transactions accounts, the Board of Governors has the authority to vary this requirement, and the range of variation permitted is from 0 to 9 percent. The Fed thus has the authority to eliminate this reserve requirement by setting it at zero.

Table 12–3 gives the "everyday" structure of reserve requirements, but it oversimplifies this structure in two respects.

[6]The indexing formula increases the cutoff point by 80 percent of the percentage increase in transactions accounts held by all depository institutions.

1   **THE PHASE-IN.** Since nonmember banks and the thrifts were subjected to reserve requirements for the first time, Congress provided for an eight-year phase-in of reserve requirements for these institutions. It also mandated a four-year phase-in for the new requirements for member banks. As a consequence, Table 12–3 will not be fully applicable until 1988.

2   **SPECIAL POWERS.** In addition to the basic requirements shown in Table 12–3, Congress also empowered the Board to institute a *supplemental reserve requirement* of up to 4 percent on transactions accounts at depository institutions. The Board is permitted to pay interest on these supplemental reserves at a rate no higher than the rate of return on the Fed's assets. A second form of special power, to be used only in "extraordinary circumstances," allows the Board after consultation with Congress to impose *any* reserve requirement on *any* liability at *any* class of depository institution. These extraordinary reserve requirements apply only for a period of 180 days, but they can be extended by a vote of five Board members.

As the granting of these special powers implies, Congress envisaged the possibility that the Fed would use supplemental reserve requirements in the conduct of monetary policy. In allowing for this contingency, Congress was simply acknowledging the Fed's use of such requirements in the 1970s when it imposed a variety of supplemental reserve requirements on different nondeposit liabilities. Before considering these, however, we first discuss the general use of reserve requirement changes as a policy tool.

USE AS A POLICY INSTRUMENT

Changes in reserve requirements are a powerful instrument for monetary management. A change of even a fraction of a percentage point can have a marked effect on monetary and credit conditions. To illustrate this, let us start with a situation in which DIs have neither excess reserves nor a deficiency of reserves, their deposits subject to reserve requirement total $800 billion, their average reserve requirement is 5 percent, and their actual reserve balances are $40 billion. Suppose now that the Board lowers average reserve requirements to 4¾ percent. This does not affect the total amount of reserve balances held by DIs. Rather, it changes the volume of deposits and the volume of loans and investments that DIs can support with existing reserves. In the present example the action by the Federal Reserve will reduce required reserves by $2 billion, thereby initially creating that amount of excess reserves. The latter will serve as a basis for multiple expansion by the DIs, which will tend to lower interest rates and increase the availability of credit.

Suppose, on the other hand, that the Board raises average reserve requirements from 5 to 5¼ percent. This will raise required reserves by $2 billion, thus creating a reserve deficiency of that amount. If the DIs are unable to secure additional reserves, they will have to reduce by some multiple both their earning assets and their deposits. This would decrease the availability of credit and raise market rates of interest.

Consequently, we see that although they do not directly alter the volume of reserves available, changes in reserve requirements have ultimate effects that are quite similar to those of open-market operations. This should hardly be surprising when we recall the money-multiplier formula developed in Chapter 8. Despite this equivalence, until the 1970s the Federal Reserve employed changes in reserve requirements relatively infrequently. This was consistent with the commonly held view that changes in reserve requirements were adapted only to two limited purposes:

1 Absorbing large excess reserves or offseting large losses of reserves. For example, in a liquidity crisis a reduction of required reserves offers a way of maintaining the solvency of the financial system.
2 Announcing important policy decisions to both the public and the banks. Changes in reserve requirements are overt and well-publicized actions and thus provide a way in which the Board of Governors can in effect say, "This is the direction our policy is taking, and we really mean it!"

Evidently then, the prevailing view was that variations in reserve requirements should be used to bring about relatively large changes in the reserve positions of banks, not for day-to-day or week-to-week adjustments. In part this is because it has acquired the reputation of being "more like an ax than a scalpel." This reputation, which dates largely from the late 1930s, when requirements were changed several percentage points at a time, is not wholly justified. Indeed, as already suggested, in the 1970s the Federal Reserve increasingly resorted to reserve requirement changes as a policy tool. But these changes have not been directed primarily toward the conventional liabilities of demand and time deposits. Rather, they have focused on nondeposit liabilities.

RESERVE REQUIREMENTS ON NONDEPOSIT LIABILITIES

In the 1960s, when DIs were faced with needs for funds, they turned in a significant way to certain nondeposit liabilities such as Eurodollar borrowings. Such liabilities were not originally covered by reserve requirements, but in a series of moves beginning in 1969 the Federal Reserve imposed requirements on these sources of funds as well. Reserve requirements were initially imposed by exempting certain base amounts outstanding. In effect, this introduced a *marginal reserve requirement* that penalized banks only for increases in these categories. This was done largely to minimize the shock that would have occurred had requirements been imposed on the substantial existing volume of these liabilities. Gradually, however, these exemptions were eliminated, and reserve requirements were applied to the full amounts of these categories. The percentage reserve requirement varied substantially over time. The applicable reserve percentage, which was originally 10 percent, was increased to 20 percent in 1971 and reduced to 8 percent in 1973, to 4 percent in 1975, and to zero in 1978. In October 1979 a marginal reserve requirement was reinstituted on these liabilities.

Aside from the liabilities already discussed, other nondeposit liabilities have also been subjected to reserve requirements. In 1973 and 1974 marginal reserve requirements were applied to the issuance of commercial paper by a bank's affiliates. In addition, a marginal reserve requirement was introduced—on top of the basic requirement—on time deposits of $100,000 or more.

The most recent changes in reserve requirements on nondeposit liabilities occurred in October 1979 and in March 1980 as part of major monetary policy moves involving all three tools: open-market operations, a discount rate change, and a revision of reserve requirements. More specifically, as far as reserve requirements are concerned, in October 1979 the Federal Reserve introduced a marginal requirement of 8 percent on all *managed liabilities* above a base amount. Managed liabilities were defined to include the following: large time deposits ($100,000 and over with maturities of less than a year); Eurodollar borrowings; repurchase agreements; and federal funds borrowing from nonmember institutions. As the Federal Reserve described it: "This action is directed toward sources of funds that have been actively used by banks in recent months to finance the expansion of bank credit."[7] It was clearly the hope of the Federal Reserve that the action, which increased the effective cost of nondeposit liabilities to banks, would lead to slower growth of bank credit. When the resulting growth did not prove slow enough for its liking, in March 1980 the Federal Reserve increased the reserve requirement on managed liabilities to 10 percent and expanded the base to which the reserve requirement applied.

A FURTHER REFORM?

The Federal Reserve and the depository institutions view reserve requirements from quite different perspectives. The Fed sees such requirements as a critical component in ensuring its ability to influence monetary and credit conditions. Depository institutions, on the other hand, regard required reserves as a sterile form of asset that yields them no interest. Raising reserve requirements is thus highly unpopular with DIs, since it reduces their profitability. Indeed, the sustained grumblings of DIs on this point, as well as their creativity in evading reserve requirements, has undoubtedly contributed to the marked decline of average reserve requirements in the last several decades.

[7]*Federal Reserve Bulletin*, October 1979, p. 831.

Many economists have suggested that there is a simple way to minimize the unhappiness of depository institutions with reserve requirements—namely, to pay interest on reserve balances. Indeed, the Federal Reserve has recently endorsed this view. It has suggested that by removing the incentive to find innovative ways to avoid holding reservable deposits, this could in time contribute to a more stable financial environment and to greater ease in the conduct of monetary policy.

The flip side of enhancing the profitability of the depository institutions is that the profitability of the Fed would suffer. Since about $20 billion of reserve balances are currently held at the Fed, at a 10 percent interest rate the loss of revenues would be about $2 billion per year. Since the lion's share of the Fed's revenues are returned to the Treasury, paying interest on reserves would obviously add to the federal budget deficit.[8] In view of the extraordinary high budget deficits of the 1980s, at the current time there naturally is some congressional resistance to the idea. However, Congress has already endorsed this principle in calling for interest on supplementary reserves. Many feel it is only a matter of time before Congress takes the plunge and permits interest-earning reserves more generally.

OVERVIEW

As should be apparent from this bit of recent history, changes in reserve requirements have become increasingly common. Furthermore, the introduction of marginal reserve requirement changes has added a new dimension to monetary policy. The Federal Reserve can, for example, impose an extra reserve requirement on a liability when that liability grows beyond some base period amount. This would have no immediate impact on a DI. Rather, it affects only the expansion of the DI at the margin. Despite this added flexibility, the Fed is still likely to rely largely on open-market operations and discount policy for its finer short-term adjustments, especially during the confusing phase-in period of the new structure of reserve requirements.

COORDINATION OF THE INSTRUMENTS OF GENERAL MONETARY MANAGEMENT

We have discussed the three major instruments of general monetary management: changes in reserve requirements, open-market operations, and discount policy. We now consider the interrelationships of these instruments and their coordination.

[8]Since interest paid to depository institutions would be partially recaptured through increased tax payments by those institutions and their depositors, the deficit effect would be less than the Fed's revenue loss.

METHODS

If we look only at the legal provisions of the Federal Reserve Act, we may fear that these instruments will not be used in a coordinated way, for authority over them is not fully centralized. Reserve requirements are set by the Board of Governors alone. Open-market operations are controlled by the FOMC. Discount-rate changes are usually initiated by the 12 Federal Reserve banks, subject to approval by the Board of Governors. Loan offices at the 12 Reserve banks decide whether or not to make specific loans to depository institutions, although they operate under general regulations prescribed by the Board of Governors. In practice, there is far more coordination than this dispersion of authority suggests, and it is achieved in many ways, both formal and informal. In this process the Board of Governors plays a central role. With full authority over reserve requirements, a majority of the members of the FOMC, power to approve or disapprove discount rates, and authority to prescribe regulations for lending to DIs, its legal powers are formidable. It is also in a position to persuade other Federal Reserve officials to cooperate.

In this process the meetings of the FOMC are very important. These meetings are attended not only by the members of the FOMC, but also by the seven presidents of Reserve banks who are not currently members of the FOMC, by the principal economists on the Board's staff, and by an economist from each of the Reserve banks. The presidents who are not members of the FOMC are free to participate in the meeting, but not to vote. Those assembled analyze current and prospective financial and economic conditions and discuss various alternatives. By the end of the meeting they all know what the open-market policy will be, as well as the Board's intentions with respect to reserve requirements and its attitude toward discount rates.

THE IMPORTANCE OF COORDINATION

The various instruments of monetary policy may be used singly or in combination, and they may supplement or tend to weaken one another. For example, if the Federal Reserve wishes to restrict credit, it may take one or various combinations of the following actions: raising reserve requirements, selling securities in the open market, and increasing discount rates. The net effects of using one instrument depend in part on current policies with respect to the others. Suppose the Federal Reserve increases reserve requirements enough to absorb existing excess reserves and put many DIs in a deficient reserve position. DIs may be forced to restrict credit sharply if the Federal Reserve refuses to create additional reserves by purchasing securities and if it raises discount rates to discourage borrowing. However, the restrictive effects may be largely negated if the Fed stands ready to buy at fixed prices and yields all the government securities offered to it. And the degree of restriction will be lessened if the Fed fails to raise discount rates or to take other actions to restrict borrowing.

Proper coordination does not require that all the instruments be used in every case. It requires only that the instruments not be used in such a way as to prevent the achievement of desired results. In many cases the Federal Reserve can achieve its objectives by using only one or two instruments. Open-market operations are often used alone, especially for defensive purposes or where only small dynamic effects are desired. For larger operations, they are ordinarily combined with changes in discount rates. In some cases, both are combined with changes in reserve requirements.

In a later chapter we describe the purposes for which the Federal Reserve has used its powers and the ways it has used its instruments. The succeeding examples will illustrate a few of the patterns of restrictive and expansionary policies.

RESTRICTIVE POLICIES

Suppose that to avoid an actual or threatened inflation the Federal Reserve decides to implement a *restrictive* monetary policy. Such a policy has the purpose of restricting the rate of growth of spending for output and, to this end, restricting the rates of growth of the stock of money and the stock of credit in the face of rising demand.

Suppose, for example, that the Federal Reserve decides that for some time it will permit no increase in the money supply. Sometimes it can achieve this simply by refraining from further purchases of securities. At other times it will actually sell some government securities to reduce DIs reserves and force them to borrow or to sell assets. On some occasions, it may raise reserve requirements for the same purpose. Depository institutions, facing shortages in their reserves and probably also continued increases in customers' demands for loans, try in various ways to adjust. One way a DI can improve its position is by seeking more loans from the Federal Reserve. At this stage, if not before, the Federal Reserve will raise its discount rates and may also admonish DIs that seek to "borrow too much or too frequently." DIs also try to borrow more from others—in the federal funds market, in the Eurodollar market, and so on. Moreover, they may sell earning assets, such as Treasury bills, to repair their reserve positions and meet customer demands for loans. Both the DIs' increased demands for borrowings and their sales of assets tend to raise interest rates. Eventually DIs will restrict their loans to customers by raising interest rates and perhaps through various types of nonprice rationing.

Through such processes restrictive Federal Reserve policies control the growth of credit supplies, raise interest rates, and slow down the rate of increase of spending for output.

EXPANSIONARY POLICIES

Suppose now that the country is slipping into a recession following a period of prosperity in which interest rates, including discount rates, were relatively high, and borrowings from the Fed were large. Such recession periods are usually characterized not only by declining business activity and rising unemployment, but also by declining demand for credit, which tends to lower market rates of interest. If the Federal Reserve neither lowers discount rates nor takes other positive action, it will encourage decreases in the money supply. Faced with declining demand for credit and falling interest rates, DIs that were willing to borrow and lend when interest rates were high relative to discount rates will now seek to repay their debts to the Federal Reserve. The Fed must take some positive liberalizing action if it is to prevent an actual decrease in the volume of money and credit, and still more positive action if it is to induce an expansion.

Which instruments the Fed will use, the sequence in which it will use them, and the scope of its actions will depend on its estimate of the strength and probable duration of the depressive forces. If it fears that the recession will be serious and prolonged, it may at an early stage reduce reserve requirements. If it does, the DIs will use some of the released reserves to repay borrowings at the Federal Reserve. Usually, however, the Federal Reserve "leads off" with decreases in discount rates or open-market purchases. As their reserve positions improve, DIs seek to put the money to work. At first they may buy government securities and other open-market assets, thereby depressing interest rates. At some point, usually early, the Federal Reserve will begin to lower discount rates. In a prolonged recession these are usually decreased several times as market rates decline.

SELECTIVE CREDIT CONTROLS

We have emphasized that the purpose of general monetary management is to regulate the total supply of money and credit and the general level of interest rates; it is not to determine the allocation of credit among its many possible users and uses. This allocative or rationing function is left to the private market. Those who believe in a predominantly free-market economy generally favor primary reliance on general monetary management because the allocation of credit helps to allocate real resources, which they believe should be allocated through competition in the marketplace. However, many persons, including some who favor primary reliance on general measures, believe that these measures should be supplemented by *selective controls*—that is, by measures that would influence the allocation of credit, at least to the point of decreasing the volume of credit used for selected purposes without the necessity of decreasing the total supply and raising the cost of credit for all purposes.

Selective credit controls can be negative or positive. *Negative controls* seek to decrease the supply or increase the cost of credit for certain specified purposes. *Positive controls* seek to increase the supply or lower the cost of credit for specified purposes. Although our interest is in selective controls by the Federal Reserve, it should be noted that many actions by other government agencies significantly affect the allocation of credit among potential uses and users. A few examples will suggest the range of these policies.

1 Low-cost government loans to rural electric and telephone cooperatives, to finance exports, and for certain types of housing.
2 Limitations on types of assets that may be acquired by savings and loan associations. A major purpose of this action is to increase the supply of credit for housing.
3 Government guarantees of loans for such purposes as storing farm products or housing.
4 Tax policies, such as exemption from the federal income tax, which lower the rates state and local governments must pay on their borrowings.

These examples suggest that even when selective credit controls are justified, it does not necessarily follow that they should be wielded by the Federal Reserve.

We turn now to some of the forms of selective credit controls that have been administered by the Federal Reserve.

MORAL SUASION

The Federal Reserve sometimes employs moral suasion as an instrument of general monetary management—to influence total borrowings at the Federal Reserve and the behavior of the total supply of money and credit. Moral suasion is also used for selective purposes, especially with DIs currently borrowing from the Federal Reserve. For example, in the late 1920s, and especially in early 1929, the Federal Reserve urged banks to curb their "speculative loans on securities" and to favor "loans for legitimate business purposes." In the spring of 1951, during the Korean conflict, the Federal Reserve sponsored a "voluntary credit restraint program," which encouraged banks and some other financial institutions to restrict "nonessential, nonproductive loans" while continuing to make "essential productive loans." In 1966, the Federal Reserve urged banks to curb the rate of expansion of business loans and to reduce their sales of government securities. This encouragement came in the form of a letter sent by each Federal Reserve bank president to all the member banks in the district. The letter contained a suggestion that a bank's ability to borrow at the discount window might depend on its cooperation. Also, in the mid-1960s, as part of a program to improve the nation's balance of payments, banks were first urged, and then legally required, to refrain from increasing their total loans to foreigners.

A recent example of moral suasion was contained in a 1973 letter from the chairman of the Board of Governors to all commercial banks with deposits exceeding $100 million. The letter suggested that banks should be more cautious in extending lines of credit for commercial loans and warned them that more stringent examination procedures would be employed to enforce this suggestion. A more recent attempt at moral suasion occurred in March 1980 when, with bank credit growing at 18 percent per year, the Federal Reserve introduced a voluntary program to restrain bank credit to a rate of increase of 6 to 9 percent. This voluntary program was part of a more comprehensive attempt to tighten monetary policy. To demonstrate its seriousness of purpose, the Federal Reserve summoned leading bankers to Washington and, although there is no official account of the meeting, apparently read them the riot act. After the meeting the bankers, who are notoriously not shy about getting their names in print, all refused to be quoted. Anonymously, however, they hinted at Federal Reserve threats designed to ensure compliance, and they generally expressed the view that the voluntary program was tantamount to formal credit controls. Soon after the program was announced, bank credit growth slowed substantially. However, a weakening economy and the 20 percent prime loan rate undoubtedly also had something to do with the reduced demand for loans.

From these examples it is evident that the Federal Reserve regards moral suasion as a useful supplement to its other policy tools. It should be noted, however, that many economists do not agree with this view.[9]

Let us now look at some of the more formal types of selective controls.

MARGIN REQUIREMENTS ON SECURITY LOANS

This selective control arose out of the Federal Reserve's unhappy experience with stock market speculation in the late 1920s. At that time there was nothing in the basic economic situation that called for a policy of very tight money. Employment was not overly full, commodity prices were steady, and the objective of promoting recovery and prosperity abroad called for easy money. However, the stock market was booming, and the rapid rise of prices was supported in part by large increases of loans on stock collateral. Federal Reserve officials were convinced that this was unsound and that less credit should be available for stock purposes. However, they had only two methods of dealing with the situation—moral suasion and general credit restriction. They exhorted banks not to make speculative loans on stocks while borrowing at the Federal Reserve. This did not work, partly

[9]See, for example, Edward Kane, "The Central Bank as Big Brother," *Journal of Money, Credit, and Banking,* November 1973, pp. 979–981.

because most of the banks were not in debt to the Federal Reserve and partly because of the huge and rising volume of nonbank loans on stock. They also invoked general credit restriction, which seemed to damp business activity more than stock market speculation. The outcome is now famous; stock speculation climbed until the great crash in October 1929, and the Federal Reserve's policy of general credit restriction came to be blamed in part for the ensuing Great Depression.

In 1934, largely because of this experience, Congress gave the Board of Governors power to fix, and to alter at its discretion, minimum margin requirements on security loans. These apply where two conditions are met. (1) The loan is collateraled by a security listed on a national securities exchange and not exempted—government obligations and some others are exempted. And (2) the purpose of the loan is for purchasing or carrying such securities. Minimum margin requirements are, in effect, minimum down payments stated as a percentage of the market value of the security. Setting a minimum margin requirement is an indirect way of setting a maximum loan value.

Several aspects of this selective control are worth noting.

1 It applies to borrowers as well as to lenders. It is just as illegal for a borrower to borrow in excess of the maximum loan value as it is for a lender to make such loans. Thus, this control limits the demand for such credit as well as limiting the supply for this purpose.
2 It applies not only to member banks but also to lenders of every type. Thus, for this purpose it extended the jurisdiction of the Board of Governors. This precedent was followed in later selective controls.
3 It not only enables the Federal Reserve to restrict the volume of credit used for this purpose without restricting the supply or raising the cost of credit for other purposes, but it may actually ease credit for other purposes. To the extent that less credit is demanded or supplied for this purpose, more credit tends to be made available for other uses.

Since early 1974, margin requirements have stood at 50 percent. However, the Board of Governors had changed margin requirements numerous times between their inception (in 1934) and 1974. Sometimes it has increased margin requirements to discourage borrowing and lending for these purposes (including one occasion in 1946 when the margin requirement was 100 percent). Other times it has decreased margin requirements to lessen the degree of restriction.

It is very difficult to assess precisely the effectiveness of this regulation in curbing the amount of credit used for purchasing and carrying securities. It certainly has some overall effect, and is especially effective in curbing such borrowing by those who could borrow little without pledging the securities as collateral. However, many people have found ways of evading the intent of the regulation. For example, they buy and carry these securities with funds acquired by borrowing on their general credit standing, on exempt securities, on their houses, on their businesses, and so on.

CONSUMER CREDIT CONTROLS

Selective controls on consumer credit, which were administered under Federal Reserve Regulation W, had a checkered career. They were first instituted in the autumn of 1941 under an executive order, and remained in effect until 1947, when they were withdrawn. They were reinstated in September 1948 under a temporary authorization by Congress, and expired in June 1949. After the outbreak of war in Korea, they were imposed again, but withdrawn in 1952.

This selective control employed two devices: minimum down payments and maximum periods of repayment. Both applied to consumer loans on listed articles. Raising the required down payment tended to reduce the demand for credit for this purpose, as well as to reduce the amount that could be legally supplied for it. Shortening the maximum period of repayment, which increased required monthly payments, also tended to reduce the demand for such loans. Only the latter device applied to consumer loans for unlisted purposes.

Consumer credit control proved to be almost impossible to administer and enforce. Since this control applied not only to banks, but also to other providers of consumer credit, a large number of lenders had to be kept under surveillance, and the Federal Reserve was not adequately staffed for the job. Consumers who were offered credit terms more liberal than those permitted by the regulations were not inclined to file complaints, and many suppliers of consumer credit, especially those who sold goods and services on credit, either ignored the regulations or violated them frequently.

A different sort of control was implemented in March 1980 when President Carter invoked the Credit Control Act of 1969. This act, which had received virtually no attention prior to 1980, was extraordinarily broad in scope. It provided that once the president of the United States declared that economic conditions warranted invoking the act, the Federal Reserve had the authority to regulate and control *all* forms of credit. After President Carter's authorization, the Federal Reserve introduced a 15 percent "deposit requirement" for all lenders on increases of certain types of consumer credit, including credit cards, check credit overdraft plans, and unsecured personal loans. This action amounted to a marginal reserve requirement with two novel features: (1) reserve requirements typically apply to liabilities of lenders such as bank deposits, but this applied to the asset side of the balance sheet; and (2) the requirement applied to all lenders, not just commercial banks. In addition to banks, those affected included finance companies, credit unions, savings and loans, mutual savings banks, retail establishments, gasoline companies, and firms offering travel and entertainment cards. The intent of the 15 percent requirement was to increase the cost of funds to lenders. Since these cost increases were likely to be passed on to the consumer, it would reduce the demand for consumer credit. The demand for consumer credit did moderate after this action, but almost simultaneously there was a substantial deterioration in the overall health of the economy. It quickly became apparent that the weakened economy did not warrant credit controls, and the program was ended in the summer of 1980. This episode served to remind Congress of the broad powers that had been given to the Fed by the 1969 act, and Congress had second thoughts about the matter. After considerable legislative jockeying, the Credit Control Act expired in 1982.

REAL ESTATE CREDIT CONTROLS

From 1950 until 1952, as a part of the anti-inflation program initiated after the outbreak of war in Korea, Congress authorized the Board of Governors to exercise selective control over credit extended to finance new residential construction. This it did under Regulation X. It utilized the same devices as Regulation W: minimum down payments and maximum periods of repayment. Its terms, like those of Regulation W, were not uniform for all loans of this general type. Instead, Regulation X was designed to favor lost-cost housing and housing for veterans. It therefore required larger down payments and shorter periods of repayment for higher-cost housing and on loans to nonveterans. This regulation was in effect for only a short time, and even then it did not apply to many construction projects that were already in progress or in the planning stage. For these reasons, it is difficult to predict what its effectiveness would be over a longer period. However, there are reasons to expect that it would be difficult to enforce.

INTEREST RATE CEILINGS

As we have already emphasized, the complex structure of interest rate ceilings on time and savings deposits has by now largely been dismantled. While such ceilings were in force, the monetary authorities possessed another policy instrument, since they could adjust the ceiling rates upward or downward. However, from their inception in the 1930s until the mid-1960s, interest rate ceilings were not used as a tool of monetary policy. Indeed, from 1935 to 1956, the ceiling rates were left unchanged. Over the next decade ceiling rates were adjusted upward, but in a passive way, in response to market conditions.

The first serious use of interest rate ceilings as a tool of monetary policy came in 1966, a year of inflationary pressures, highly restrictive Federal Reserve policies, and the highest interest rates in over a century. As we saw in Chapter 7, these circumstances prompted the fear that the thrift institutions would experience an outflow of funds and that the housing industry would be severely affected. To deal with this situation, the Fed used ceilings as a selective credit control device. It refused to raise rate ceilings on time and savings deposits at commercial banks, even though rates on competing assets in the open market rose to much higher levels. It was hoped that this would reduce the flow of funds to commercial banks and thereby help the thrifts. At the same time, concerned with the ability of the thrifts to "afford" to pay higher interest rates, Congress extended interest rate ceilings to the thrifts. However, in recognition of the plight of the thrifts it permitted them to offer slightly higher rates than commercial banks (the so-called differential).

These various actions only partially achieved their objectives. They did stem the flows of funds into time and savings deposits at commercial banks, especially in the form of large-denomination CDs. They did not, however, stop withdrawals from thrift institutions as customers looked to acquire higher-yielding assets in the open market. The refusal to raise ceiling rates was only partially successful in achieving another stated policy objective, slowing the expansion of bank loans to business. As we have seen in our discussion of commercial banking, banks, and large banks especially, showed great ingenuity in devising other ways of getting funds for this purpose— by selling government securities, selling participations in their portfolios, issuing commercial paper through holding companies or their subsidiaries, borrowing federal funds, borrowing Eurodollars, and so on. As the Federal Reserve itself has described it:

> The result of these developments was a great deal of churning in financial markets, a loss to some degree of the stability in financial flows and risk-taking associated with financial intermediation, and perhaps a disproportionate credit squeeze on those bank customers unable to shift to open-market sources of funds.

Understandably, these experiences somewhat diminished the enthusiasm of the Federal Reserve for the use of ceilings as a credit control device. In June 1970, following the bankruptcy of the Penn Central Railroad, ceiling interest rates on short-maturity (30 to 89 days) CDs were suspended. And in May 1973, when advances in market interest rates threatened a runoff of longer-term CDs, the ceilings on these were also suspended. After 1973, as documented in Chapter 7, ceiling rates continued to be a major element on the financial scene. But they were never again used in the same fashion to pursue a restrictive monetary policy.

OVERVIEW: ATTITUDES TOWARD SELECTIVE CONTROLS

Attitudes toward selective controls differ. Few people object to their use in time of war or rapid military mobilization, when the government will in any case intervene to regulate the allocation of resources and output. At such times selective credit controls may serve a useful purpose, both in diverting resources away from nonessential uses and in inhibiting inflation.

But their use in noncrisis peacetime periods is another matter. As might be expected, they are often opposed by those whose economic interests may be adversely affected. Some stock exchange members and officers are not friendly toward margin requirements on security loans, automobile manufacturers and dealers have criticized regulation of consumer credit, and the construction industry and realtors have opposed restrictions on credit for residential purposes.

Many economists have opposed selective controls on several grounds: (1) They may interfere unduly with the freedom of borrowers and lenders; (2) they prevent an allocation of resources and output in line with buyers' wishes; (3) they are unnecessary because general monetary management and fiscal policies are sufficient; (4) they may come to be looked upon as a substitute for more general and more widely effective measures; and (5) they are likely to become unenforceable or enforceable only with a very large staff. Other economists contend that selective controls can be a useful supplement to general monetary controls, especially when the misbehavior of credit is limited to only one or a few sectors of the economy.

FEDERAL RESERVE POLICY: THE EARLY YEARS

Previous sections of this chapter have spelled out the various tools of monetary policy as they have evolved to the present day. In its early years, however, the Federal Reserve did not have such a complete set of tools. Open-market operations in government securities were unknown, and reserve requirement changes were prohibited by law. Further hampering early monetary policy was the fact that the Federal Reserve had not yet evolved a clear set of policy objectives. This section briefly traces some of the growing pains experienced by the Federal Reserve, and the country, in the years preceding World War II.

WORLD WAR I AND ITS AFTERMATH

War had already been declared in Europe (in August) before the Federal Reserve banks first opened for business in November 1914. By the late spring of 1915, the United States was enjoying an export boom as neutrals turned to it for products formerly purchased in Europe and as the Allied Powers bought heavily to meet their needs. Foreign buyers paid for these huge net purchases in three principal ways: reselling U.S. securities, borrowing, and shipping over $1 billion of gold. Since the U.S. gold stock had been only $1.5 billion at the beginning of the war, these gold imports increased it by nearly 70 percent. No one had ever anticipated such inflows. Both the great increase in the foreign demand for U.S. exports and the flow of gold into bank reserves created strong inflationary pressures.

During the period between the opening of the Reserve banks in late 1914 and the entrance of the United States into the war in April 1917, Federal Reserve officials had no opportunity to develop meaningful objectives or to use their instruments of control effectively. It was obvious to them that they should not, in response to the gold inflow, follow expansionary policies and enhance inflationary pressures. Yet they could do nothing to offset or to sterilize the expansionary effects of gold inflows. They had almost no assets to sell, and they had no power to raise member bank reserve requirements. They had to stand by while the money supply rose from $11.6 billion in mid-1914 to $15.8 billion in mid-1917. Wholesale prices had already risen more than 50 percent when the United States entered the war.

With this country's entrance into the war, the Federal Reserve entered a new phase, "accommodating" the Treasury. The government's fiscal policy was the one common to periods of major war—large deficits representing increases in expenditures far in excess of increases in tax collections. The Federal Reserve played a central role in this process by meeting the greatly increased demand for currency in circulation, and by supplying the banking system with sufficient reserves to enable it to buy Treasury obligations, to lend to others for the purchase of Treasury securities, and to meet essential private demands for productive purposes. In sharp contrast to its policies during World War II, it did this to only a very small extent by purchasing government securities itself. It supplied the funds largely by lending to commercial banks.

The government's highly expansionary fiscal policy and the Federal Reserve's accommodating monetary policy were accompanied by inflation and monetary expansion. The nation's total money supply, which had been $15.8 billion in mid-1917, had risen to $21.2 billion by mid-1919. The wholesale price level was 25 percent higher than it was just before the entrance of the United States into the war. Inflation continued even after the end of hostilities, and by May 1920 wholesale prices were 140 percent above their prewar level. Over the six-year period from 1914 to 1920, the annual inflation rate averaged 15.7 percent.

The inflation came to an abrupt halt in May 1920. The end was signaled by a worldwide break in the prices of basic commodities. The ensuing depression, which ran into early 1922, was relatively short, but sharp and painful. The unemployment rate more than doubled, reaching 12 percent, and wholesale prices fell 45 percent. Both the solvency and the liquidity of the economy were seriously weakened. And the commercial banks, which owed the Federal Reserve about $2.5 billion, were in no position to offer easier credit. Not until April 1921, about a year after the depression started, did the Federal Reserve take a single action to ease monetary and credit conditions. The Reserve banks did refrain from putting pressure on member banks to repay their borrowings. But they did not buy either government securities or acceptances to provide the banks with reserves and enable them to reduce their borrowings, and they did not reduce discount rates. Such a policy now seems incomprehensible.

This episode was extremely painful both for the country and for the Federal Reserve. Why did the Federal Reserve follow these policies in the depression of 1920–1921? A complete answer to this question would take us far afield, but a basic point is that the Federal Reserve had not yet come to believe it had the responsibility for using its powers aggressively to promote economic stability. Also important was the fact that the Federal Reserve had not yet learned how to use open-market operations for general monetary management. Prompted by its poor performance in 1920–1921, the Fed gradually achieved both a clearer understanding of its policy objectives and an appreciation of the potential usefulness of open-market operations. Indeed, in 1924 and again in 1927 it pursued aggressively easy monetary policies to combat recessionary tendencies in the economy. While this was a first step toward becoming a force for stability, the decade of the 1930s revealed that the Federal Reserve still had much to learn.

THE GREAT DEPRESSION

At the time of the stock market crash in October 1929, and even in 1930, no one could foresee that the depression into which the world was sliding would be the most devastating in its entire history and would be a major contribution to political and economic upheavals and even to the outbreak of a second world war. This depression lasted more than a decade and ended only in World War II. At its depth in the United States, the depression reduced money national income by 50 percent and real output and income by 25 percent. One worker in four was jobless, and many others worked only part time. Business firms failed by the tens of thousands, farmers lost their farms, and families their homes. The monetary and financial system virtually collapsed. The gold standard system largely disappeared by 1932. The U.S. banking system, weakened earlier, collapsed in 1933. Many other financial institutions closed their doors, or at least ceased to function effectively in the saving-investment process. International lending came to a standstill. With hindsight, it is clear that many of the problems of the 1930s were aggravated by an ineffective performance by the Federal Reserve.

MONETARY POLICIES: 1929–1933

From October 1929 to the autumn of 1931, the Federal Reserve began gradually to relax its previously restrictive credit policy. In particular, it reduced the discount rate several times and also engaged in expansionary purchases of government securities. Despite these steps, critics have justifiably attacked Federal Reserve policies during this period as too slow and too timid. Furthermore, starting about September 1931 the Federal Reserve allowed credit conditions to tighten significantly. A major development responsible for this was an upsurge of bank failures, which damaged confidence in banks and induced large withdrawals of cash from the banking system. At the same time, banks began accumulating sizable pools of excess reserves. As might be expected from the money-multiplier formulas developed in Chapter 8, in the absence of vigorous expansionary policies by the Federal Reserve, the money supply declined dramatically. Indeed, from the peak in the fall of 1929 to the trough in March 1933 the money supply dropped by over 35 percent.

At the same time, real incomes were declining precipitously; unemployment was rising dramatically; and the solvency of individuals, businesses, and financial institutions was seriously undermined. With thousands of banks illiquid, if not insolvent, any sharp decline in confidence could topple the entire structure. The storm broke in Detroit with the failure of the Union Guardian Trust Company, which was one of the largest banks in Michigan and was also closely connected with many other banks. So great was the blow to public confidence and so panicky were withdrawals from other banks that on February 14, 1933, the governor of Michigan declared an eight-day banking holiday. The panic quickly spread to other states. By March 4, every state in the Union had declared bank holidays, and bank deposits were no longer redeemable in cash. President Roosevelt's decree of a four-day nationwide banking holiday beginning on March 6 merely recognized the existing situation.

While there has been much debate about the extent to which the Federal Reserve "caused" the Great Depression, there is little doubt that prompter and more vigorous use of monetary policy in the early 1930s might well have prevented the buildup of deflationary momentum. Similarly, policy measures to shore up the liquidity of the banking system may well have cushioned its collapse in 1933. Once again we see that, even after nearly 20 years of operation, the Federal Reserve still had much to learn.

MONETARY POLICY IN THE LATE 1930s

Following the banking debacle of 1933, although gradually improving, the economy limped along for several years. By mid-1936 about 15 percent of the labor force was still unemployed (down from a high of 25 percent) and real national output was about 5 percent below its level in 1929. During the same period commercial banks had accumulated a substantial volume of excess reserves, which stood at $2.9 billion in mid-1936 (see Table 12–4).

To a large extent, the growth in both actual and excess reserves came about as a result of the huge volume of gold inflows (review Chapter 11 for how this works). For their part, the banks were content to hold this increased volume of excess reserves. In view of the recent history of bank failures, they were quite concerned with maintaining adequate liquidity. Also, there were few opportunities to make sound loans to business.

As the economy kept up its gradual improvement, Federal Reserve and Treasury officials became increasingly concerned with the possibility that inflationary pressures would reemerge. To prevent this, they decided to

TABLE 12–4 Member Bank Reserve Positions on Selected Dates, 1933–1941 (Averages of daily figures, in millions of dollars)

Period	Actual reserve balances	Required reserves	Excess reserves
Last quarter 1933	$ 2,612	$1,839	$ 773
February 1934	2,822	1,931	891
June 1934	3,790	2,105	1,685
June 1935	4,979	2,541	2,438
June 1936	5,484	2,891	2,593
July 1936	5,861	2,954	2,907
May 1937	6,932	6,005	927
August 1937	6,701	5,951	750
May 1938	7,587	5,062	2,525
June 1939	10,085	5,839	4,246
June 1940	13,596	6,900	6,696
December 1940	14,049	7,403	6,646
June 1941	13,201	7,850	5,351
December 1941	12,812	9,422	3,390

SOURCE: Board of Governors of the Federal Reserve System, *Banking and Monetary Statistics*. Washington, D.C.: 1943, pp. 371–373.

take some slack out of the system by mopping up excess reserves. The Board of Governors for the first time used its recently acquired power to change member bank reserve requirements. In three steps—the first on August 16, 1936, and the last on May 1, 1937—it doubled all these requirements, setting them at the maximum level permitted by law. In addition, the Treasury embarked on a policy of sterilizing all gold imports, preventing them from augmenting the public's money supply, commercial bank reserves, and Federal Reserve bank reserves. It did this by selling government securities to get the funds with which to pay for the gold and then adding the gold to its own cash holdings without issuing gold certificates against it. In effect, it engaged in an offsetting open-market operation.

As a result of these actions, excess reserves were substantially reduced. Interest rates rose rather sharply. While, once again, it is debatable whether what followed was caused by the Federal Reserve, there ensued a sharp downturn in economic activity—a recession within a depression. The unemployment rate rose to about 20 percent and real output declined.

In the face of these developments, the Federal Reserve and the Treasury reversed directions, and in fact, excess reserves advanced to new heights (see Table 12–4). Nevertheless, it was not until 1940 that the economy reattained its 1937 level. The Federal Reserve, and the country, learned the hard way that excess reserves and superfluous reserves are not the same thing.

OVERVIEW

As should be apparent from this brief excursion into the history of monetary policy, there is much to criticize in early Federal Reserve actions. Indeed, to a large extent this early lackluster performance ushered in a period in which monetary policy was regarded with extreme disfavor by many economists. It was not until well after the end of World War II that monetary authorities once again played a prominent role in policymaking.

A LOOK AHEAD

To this point, our discussion of the Federal Reserve has focused largely on what might be termed the mechanics of monetary policy. That is, we have examined *how* the Federal Reserve can affect reserves and the money supply. But we have not yet addressed the broader issues of *why* the Federal Reserve might pursue one policy or another. While this will be discussed later, it may help to motivate the next several chapters if we briefly anticipate some of the relevant issues.

Rational policymaking must begin with the selection of objectives or ends. This is both difficult and controversial because there are many different objectives toward which monetary actions can be directed, and not all of these objectives are likely to be compatible. It is therefore necessary not only to identify the possible objectives, but also to have some preferences and to make choices among them. Since all individuals are unlikely to have the same view as to what the Federal Reserve should be doing, such choices inevitably leave the Federal Reserve open to potential criticism.

The second important component of rational policymaking is a theory of the relationship among economic variables. As a guide to the appropriate use of the instruments of policymaking to promote its selected objectives, the Federal Reserve must have some theory—implicit or explicit, but preferably explicit—concerning relationships among the relevant economic variables, and especially of relationships among the actions that might be taken and the effects that would flow from them. By sheer coincidence and rare good luck, a policymaker might do the thing most conducive to the promotion of the chosen objectives, even if his or her actions were not guided by an explicit valid theory. But such a happy outcome would indeed be sheer coincidence and rare good luck, unlikely to be often repeated. It is partly for this reason that we devote so much attention to monetary theory.

Much of our theory will deal with the effects of money and monetary policy on other economic variables in which we are interested. In effect, we ask: How will this specific monetary action affect such things as the aggregate demand for output, employment, real output, interest rates, and prices? How will the results differ from those that would have prevailed if this action had not been taken or if some other action had been taken? This type of analysis is important to the monetary authority, which must be concerned with, and responsible for, the effects attributable to its own action or inaction.

However, monetary theory has another related but broader function, which is to analyze all the determinants, or at least the most powerful determinants, of the behavior of the economic variables in which we are interested. It is clear that the behavior of such measures as employment, output, and prices is determined not by money and monetary policy alone, but also by many other forces. The monetary authority needs to understand these if its policy actions are to be appropriate. Much of monetary policy is of a defensive nature, designed to offset or compensate disturbances from other sources. If the roles of these other determinants of economic behavior are not understood, the monetary authority is not in a position to prescribe the appropriate action. More generally, we need to analyze all important determinants in order to view monetary policy in an overall context and to assess realistically the role that it can play.

SUMMARY

1 The Fed has three general instruments of monetary control—open-market operations, discount policy, and reserve requirements. The primary tool, open-market operations, is in the hands of the FOMC. Because of the numerous factors impinging on DI reserves, the FOMC must undertake a substantial volume of defensive open-market operations simply to keep the outstanding quantity of reserves constant. At the same time, it may engage in dynamic open-market operations designed to alter the reserve positions of DIs.

2 The quantity of reserves outstanding can also be affected by the Fed's discount policy, which influences the volume of borrowed reserves. Borrowed reserves can be influenced by the discount rate, which is the price charged the borrower, and by the Fed's willingness to accommodate the borrowing requests of DIs. Since 1980 all depository institutions, not just member commercial banks, have been eligible to line up at the discount window.

3 Reserve requirements, via their impact on the money multiplier, affect the outstanding volume of money and credit that is supportable by any given volume of DI reserves. Changes in reserve requirements are thus a substitute for open-market operations in influencing the volume of money and credit. Unlike open-market operations, however, changes in reserve requirements are not frequently used in the conduct of monetary policy. Since 1980, reserve requirements have ap-

plied to all depository institutions. The primary requirement applies to transactions accounts, but there is also a reserve requirement on nonpersonal time deposits. There seems to be some momentum developing for the idea of paying interest on reserve balances.

4 In addition to the general instruments of monetary policy, at various times the Fed has used selective credit controls. These have included moral suasion, margin requirements on security loans, consumer credit controls, real estate credit controls, and interest rate ceilings.

SELECTED READINGS

Board of Governors of the Federal Reserve System. *The Federal Reserve System: Purposes and Functions*, 7th ed. Washington, D.C., 1984.

Chandler, L. V. *American Monetary Policy, 1928–1941.* New York: Harper & Row, 1971.

Friedman, M. and A. J. Schwartz. *A Monetary History of the United States, 1867–1960.* Princeton, N.J.: Princeton University Press, 1963.

Kaminow, Ira, and J. M. O'Brien. "Selective Credit Policies: Should Their Role Be Expanded," *Business Review*, Federal Reserve Bank of Philadelphia, 1975, pp. 3–22.

Meek, Paul. *U.S. Monetary Policy and Financial Markets.* New York: Federal Reserve Bank of New York, 1982.

PART 4

MONETARY THEORY

13

THE DEMAND FOR MONEY

With this chapter we begin an extended discussion of monetary theory—that is, an analysis of the relationships between money and the behavior of other economic variables such as real output and income, employment and unemployment, interest rates, and the price level. The output and income measures that will receive attention in this and subsequent chapters are variables known as *money flows*. They measure rates of expenditure and income per unit of time, which is typically taken to be a year. Two important examples of money flow variables are gross national product (GNP) and disposable income.

While output and income are money flow measures, they should not be confused with the concept of money itself. Of course, in everyday language the terms *income* and *money* are sometimes used interchangeably. It should be stressed, however, that this is not how economists view the matter. Furthermore, measures of the money supply, however defined, are *stock* concepts. That is, as we saw earlier, data on the money supply tell us how much money is outstanding at a *point of time*. In this regard, the stock of money is analogous to other stocks encountered in economics, such as the stock of automobiles or the stock of houses. While they are different concepts, money flows and the stock of money are, of course, related. In fact, according to a simple version of what is known as the quantity theory, money flows vary proportionately with the stock of money. However, as we shall see, this simple relationship does not hold in all circumstances.

335

Our objective in the following chapters will be to develop a theory or economic model explaining the determination of key macroeconomic variables such as income, interest rates, and prices. The building blocks of our analysis will be the markets for money balances, goods, and labor. We first consider the conditions for equilibrium of supply and demand in each of the markets separately and then provide an integrated view of all three markets. Since the preceding chapters were largely concerned with the supply of money balances, we begin our excursion into monetary theory with the demand side of the market for money balances.

SOME PRELIMINARIES

What determines the community's demand for money balances? How is this demand equated with the supply of money? What effect does the process of equilibration have on the economy? These are the kinds of questions we address in this chapter. Many of the controversies in both monetary theory and monetary policy stem from the fact that different economists have given different answers to these questions.

The theory of the demand for money balances is best viewed as one part of the theory of choice in the allocation of scarce resources. All members of the community have at their command only limited resources in the form of current income and total accumulated assets. They must therefore make choices concerning their allocation. If they choose more consumption, they must hold fewer total assets. If they choose to hold more of one type of asset, they must hold less of others. They must constantly balance the advantage of holding more of one against the disadvantage of holding less of others. Putting the matter this way raises the question of why people elect to hold any money balances at all. Money has usually yielded no explicit income, or at most only a low rate of return relative to yields on other assets. But holding money costs something; the cost is the satisfaction or income forgone by holding money rather than devoting this amount of resources to other uses.

The fact that people do choose to hold some money balances at the cost of attractive alternatives suggests that holding money must yield some sort of advantage to the individual. It does, and these result from the qualities of money—its general acceptability in payments, its perfect liquidity, and its safety in the sense that it does not depreciate in terms of money. Indeed, these properties give rise to several distinct reasons for holding money.

A final point concerns the definition of money. As we have seen, money can and has been defined in various ways. This issue is of considerable importance for both empirical researchers and policymakers, and we return to it later. For our present purposes, however, beyond reminding the reader that we prefer a relatively narrow definition of money, the only explicit assumption we make is that money yields no interest return. Although this assumption serves to simplify the exposition, we emphasize that the various theories to be discussed continue to have validity if this assumption is relaxed. We will indicate why this is so as we proceed and take up the merits and consequences of the payment of interest on money in Chapter 18. We turn now to some explicit theories of the demand for money.

THE CLASSICAL QUANTITY THEORIES

Quantity theories have a long history and widespread use in economics. Such theories have appeared in many versions. As originally formulated, quantity theories were not explicitly designed as theories of the demand for money, although they can be so interpreted. They began from the assumption that the quantity (stock) of money is a significant determinant of the rate of flow of money expenditures, and focused on the problem of explaining the link between the stock of money on the one hand and the rate of money flows on the other. Some versions of the quantity theory have been concerned with expenditure flows in the most comprehensive sense, including all money expenditures or transactions. Others have been restricted to money expenditures for output. We adopt this latter approach, sometimes called the *income variant*, and represent expenditures by GNP at current prices.[1]

Two principal techniques have been used to express the link between the stock of money and the flow of money expenditures. The first employs the concept of the *velocity of money*—in this case the *income velocity of money*. This is the average number of times each dollar of the money stock is spent for output during a year. Those who employ this approach often begin with an identity:

$$MV = OP = Y \tag{1}$$

where

M = the stock of money
V = the income velocity of money, or the average number of times per year that each dollar of M is spent for output
O = real output, stated at an annual rate
P = average price per unit of output or the price level of output
Y = OP = GNP at current prices

This is often called a *Fisherine* type of equation because a similar type was used by Irving Fisher, the great Yale economist. Note that this is not a theory; it is only an identity asserting the necessary *ex post* equality be-

---

[1]The distinction arises because GNP is a measure of "final" output excluding many intermediate economic transactions. Such transactions would be included in a more comprehensive measure of money flows.

tween the flow of expenditures for output (MV) and the money value of output purchased by that flow (OP or Y).

The other technique used to express the link between the stock of money and the flow of money expenditures is the *Cambridge approach*, so called because it was used by Alfred Marshall and other economists at Cambridge University. Users of this approach also employ an identity to facilitate exposition:

$$M = KOP = KY \tag{2}$$

where

$M, O, P,$ and Y are defined as in equation (1)
K = the fraction of OP that the community holds in the form of money balances

Like the Fisherine equation, the Cambridge equation is only an identity; it expresses the necessary *ex post* equality between the left and right sides of equation (2). As a consequence, arithmetically V and K are reciprocals; that is, $V = 1/K$ and $K = 1/V$. For example, if $V = 4$, $K = \frac{1}{4}$. If we divide the Fisherine equation by V, we get the Cambridge equation, $M = (1/V)Y$, or $M = KY$. And if we divide the Cambridge equation by K, we get the Fisherine equation, $M(1/K) = Y$, or $MV = Y$.

As indicated earlier, the quantity theory can be transformed into a framework for the demand for money. Indeed, the Cambridge identity is already seemingly cast in the form of equating the supply of money to the demand for money. With the aid of few new symbols, we can make this more explicit. In particular, if we denote the quantity of money balances demanded by M^D and the quantity supplied (assumed fixed by the monetary authorities) by M^S, we can rewrite our earlier equations as follows:

$$M^D = KY = KOP \tag{3}$$
$$M^D = M^S \tag{4}$$

Equation (3) is a demand function for money, albeit an extremely simple one. It makes the demand for money balances, M^D, a proportion of GNP in current prices (or, as it is sometimes called, *nominal* GNP). Alternatively, dividing both sides of (3) by P we get:

$$\frac{M^D}{P} = \frac{KY}{P} = KO \tag{5}$$

Equation (5) indicates that the demand for *real*-money balances, M^D/P, is a proportion of real output or real GNP. Equations (3) and (5) are simply two ways of saying the same thing.

At this juncture the reader may be puzzled, since, beginning from the quantity theory *identity*, we have seemingly manufactured a theory of the demand for money. The proverbial catch lies in the apparently innocuous symbol K (or V). To see this, let us consider equation (3) a bit more carefully. On the left side of (3) we have the symbol M^D denoting the community's demand for money balances. In other words, M^D is the quantity of money balances that the community *desires* to hold, *given* the level of income, Y. Of course, in equilibrium the community's desired money balances must equal the quantity of money supplied. Equation (4), in fact, expresses this equilibrium condition. Now let us ask what happens if, at some initial level of Y, M^D is not equal to M^S. Assuming that equilibrium is ultimately established and that the authorities maintain a fixed supply of money, then clearly either Y or K (or both) must change to produce this equilibrium. Which of these occurs is naturally of considerable consequence for both the economy and the operation of monetary policy. It should be evident by now that to answer this latter question and to rescue equation (3) from the status of an identity, we must examine the determinants of K more closely.

In general, quantity theorists before the 1930s considered V and K to be relatively stable. In fact, in the short run at least, they tended to treat V and K as constants. The underlying basis for this was the view that V and K were determined by institutional considerations such as credit practices among various firms or between firms and households, and by technological factors such as the nature of communications. We will examine these factors in more detail shortly. For our present purposes, we need note only that the early quantity theorists tended to perceive these factors as changing slowly over time. Consequently, it seemed quite plausible to regard V or K as relatively constant. Before evaluating the validity of this view, it is worthwhile briefly to pursue its implications.

From equations (3) and (4) we see that a constant K implies that the stock of money is the major determinant of aggregate demand, or, expressed another way, the level of Y can be managed precisely through control of M.[2] Evidently, if the demand and supply for money are unequal at some initial level of income, since K is constant, then income must change if equilibrium is to be restored. This is clearly a strong conclusion, but unfortunately it is based on an oversimplification—namely, the assumed constancy of K. To see this, let us look at some data.

Table 13–1 shows the behavior of V and K during recent decades. Column 3 shows the behavior of income velocity, which is simply GNP/M. Column 4 shows the behavior of K, which is M/GNP, or $1/V$. This equation assumes that in each year the public had adjusted its money balances to desired levels relative to GNP. During the Great Depression and World War II, V had fallen by nearly half from its level in the late 1920s; it was still low

---

[2]It should be noted that just using equation (3) we are unable to say how a change in Y, induced by a change in M, will be split up between P and O, that is, between the price level and real output. We return to this issue in a later chapter.

by historical standards in 1947. Since that time it has shown a marked upward trend, rising from about 2.1 in 1947 to 6.6 in 1984. Consistent with this, K has shown a marked downward trend, falling from about 48 percent of GNP in 1947 to 15 percent of GNP in 1984. Clearly, V and K are not constant through time and can change substantially within a period of several years. But what about changes from one year to the next? Judged on this basis, the changes in velocity appear relatively small. Indeed, since 1947 the average arithmetic change in V is of the order of 0.12 per year, while no change exceeds 0.35 (see the third column of Table 13–1). However,

TABLE 13–1 The Income Velocity of Money and the Ratio of the Money Supply to GNP (money values in billions of dollars)

Calendar year	(1) GNP at current prices	(2) Money supply*	(3) Income velocity of money $[(1) \div (2)]$	(4) Ratio of money supply to GNP $[(2) \div (1)]$
1959	487.9	141.0	3.46	0.289
1960	506.5	141.8	3.57	0.280
1961	524.6	146.5	3.58	0.279
1962	565.0	149.2	3.79	0.264
1963	596.7	154.7	3.86	0.259
1964	637.7	161.9	3.94	0.254
1965	691.1	169.5	4.08	0.245
1966	756.0	173.7	4.35	0.230
1967	799.6	185.1	4.32	0.231
1968	873.4	199.4	4.38	0.228
1969	944.0	205.8	4.59	0.218
1970	992.7	216.6	4.58	0.218
1971	1,077.6	230.8	4.67	0.214
1972	1,185.9	252.0	4.71	0.212
1973	1,326.4	265.9	4.99	0.200
1974	1,434.2	277.6	5.17	0.194
1975	1,549.2	291.2	5.32	0.188
1976	1,718.0	310.4	5.53	0.181
1977	1,918.3	335.3	5.72	0.174
1978	2,163.9	363.0	5.96	0.168
1979	2,417.8	389.0	6.22	0.161
1980	2,631.7	414.8	6.34	0.158
1981	2,957.8	441.8	6.69	0.149
1982	3,069.3	480.8	6.38	0.157
1983	3,304.8	528.0	6.26	0.160
1984	3,662.8	558.5	6.56	0.152

*The money supply is measured by M-1 for December of each year.

while in some loose sense the numbers seem small, this is quite misleading. The reason can best be illustrated by use of an example.

Let us consider a year in which $Y = 600$, $M = 150$, and consequently, $V = 4$ and $K = \frac{1}{4}$. Now assume that the monetary authorities would like Y to grow by 6 percent, so that during the next year they would like to have $Y = 636 = 1.06 \times 600$. How much M should they supply? The answer obviously depends on their estimate of V or K. If V is expected to remain constant at $V = 4$, then clearly the appropriate quantity of money to supply is $M = 636/4 = 159$. That is, with a constant V they would let M also grow at 6 percent. But what if the actual value of V turns out to be 4.2? The value of Y that would then result would be $Y = 4.2 \times 159 = 667.8$. In other words, Y would grow at over 11 percent per year rather than the intended 6 percent. If the economy were already near full employment, this could produce a considerable amount of unwanted inflation. While the example could be done with many other assumptions, they would not change the basic message: Seemingly small fluctuations in V or K can have substantial repercussions on the level of economic activity.

Given that V and K are not constants and do fluctuate in the short run, can we say anything about the reasons for these fluctuations? In the first instance it is important to recognize that the behavior of V and K is determined by the choices of the community, not by the monetary authority. Even if the latter has firm control of the stock of money, the community is free to decide its rate of expenditures relative to M. In terms of the velocity approach, members of the community may elect to hold money balances only briefly before spending them, in which case V will be high. Or they may elect to hold money balances longer before spending, which will be reflected in a lower V. In terms of the K approach, members of the community may choose to hold only small balances relative to their rate of expenditures, which will be reflected in a high rate of expenditures relative to the stock of money. Or they may choose to hold larger balances relative to their expenditures, in which case Y will be smaller relative to M. Moreover, the choices of the community do not fluctuate in a haphazard manner, but rather are systematically related to the state of the economy.

A closer look at Table 13–1, or the corresponding velocity data that have been plotted in Figure 13–1, shows that the sharpest increases in velocity tend to occur during periods of prosperity. On the other hand, during periods of recession, indicated in Figure 13–1 by the shaded areas, velocity declines or rises less rapidly.[3] Clearly, a theory of the demand for money should capture these effects, and to do so we will rely on another variable we encountered earlier—the interest rate.

In general, classical quantity theorists tended to assume that demands for money balances were not significantly affected by the level of interest

---

[3]The 1974–1975 recession is obviously an exception. Indeed, the rapid increase in velocity after 1974 deserves particular attention. We have more to say about this in later chapters.

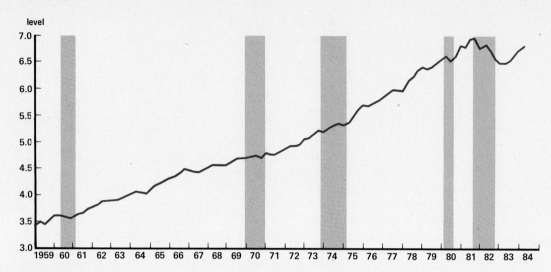

FIGURE 13–1
Velocity of M-1, 1959–1984.

rates. Since the 1930s this view has been challenged. Most monetary economists, including modern quantity theorists, now believe that demands for
money balances are sensitive to the level of interest rates, tending to fall as
interest rates rise and to rise as interest rates fall.

In explaining why demands for money balances should be negatively
related to the level of interest rates, economists stress the fact that an
interest rate is both a cost of holding money balances and a reward for
holding earning assets. (Recall we are assuming that money balances do
not earn interest.) Therefore, increased interest rates encourage the community to economize on money balances and to hold a larger fraction of
its total assets in the form of earning assets. Reduced interest rates have
the opposite effect. Since interest rates tend to rise in periods of prosperity
and to fall in recessions, this belief is certainly consistent with the data in
Figure 13–1.

To recapitulate, the quantity theory in its simplest form does not provide
a fully satisfactory theory of the demand for money. To construct such a
theory we must explicitly introduce interest rates into the determination
of the demand for money. One of the first economists to do this in a systematic and coherent way was John Maynard Keynes in his monumental
1936 work, *General Theory of Employment, Interest, and Money.*

THE KEYNESIAN APPROACH

Two of the functions of money discussed in Chapter 1 were (1) to serve as
a medium of exchange or means of payment and (2) to serve as a store of
value. Keynes, in his writings on the demand for money, distinguished

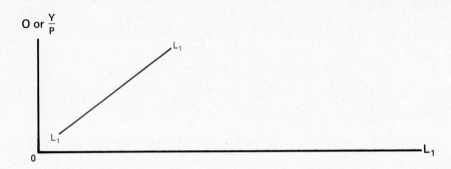

FIGURE 13–2
Transactions demand for money

between two primary motives for holding money—*the transactions motive* and the *speculative motive.*

THE TRANSACTIONS MOTIVE

Households and business firms hold money balances for transactions purposes because they think they will, or may, want to make expenditures before they enjoy a sufficient inflow of money receipts. They might hold little or no money if they were assured that money would flow to them in sufficient volume just a moment before they wanted to spend. Usually they have no such assurance. Therefore, they elect to hold some money to cover the excess of their expenditures over their receipts during some period.

It should be noted that households and business firms would hold money balances even if they could forecast perfectly and confidently both the amounts and timing of their expenditures and receipts. Realistically speaking, of course, forecasts of receipts and expenditures can rarely be made with such precision and confidence. Expected receipts may fail to materialize, or important expenditures may be earlier or larger than anticipated, or unusually attractive bargains may become available. Such contingencies provide an additional motivation for holding transactions balances.[4]

Keynes posited that the demand for money balances for transactions purposes was a function of income. This dependence is illustrated in Figure 13–2, where L_1 denotes the quantity of real money balances demanded for transactions purposes. Although the relationship between transactions balances and income is shown as a straight line—L_1L_1 in Figure 13–2—the actual relationship need not be a linear one.

[4]Keynes actually introduced a third motive, the *precautionary* one, to apply to money holdings that stemmed from the community's desire to protect itself against the possibility of unforeseen contingencies. However, this did not play a major part in his formulation of the demand for money, and we will not make use of the distinction between the precautionary motive and the other motives.

It should be evident that, at least in regard to the transactions motive, Keynes was following in the quantity theory tradition of his colleagues at Cambridge. Where he departed from this tradition was in his emphasis on the speculative motive and the role of the interest rate in determining speculative balances.

THE SPECULATIVE MOTIVE

Keynes recognized that the community may elect to hold balances in excess of its needs for transactions purposes because of its desire to hold assets that are perfectly liquid and perfectly free from risk of depreciation in terms of money. Balances that fulfill the *store of value* function constitute the speculative demand for money. In more modern terminology, this is sometimes called the *asset demand for money.*

The speculative demand for money was conceived by Keynes as primarily determined by the rate of interest. In particular, Keynes posited that higher interest rates would lead to smaller speculative balances and lower interest rates would produce larger demands for speculative balances. Keynes offered two reasons for this. First, when interest rates are high, other things being equal, this is a way of saying that the opportunity cost of holding money is high. But the second part of Keynes' argument was that other things would not be equal. In particular, he argued that capital gains on earning assets are likely when interest rates are high and capital losses are likely when interest rates are low. Since the relevant opportunity cost is the effective rate of interest taking into account capital gains or losses, this view serves to bolster the case that the speculative demand for money is inversely related to the interest rate.

But on what did Keynes base his view that capital gains (losses) are likely when interest rates are high (low)? Essentially, he reasoned as follows: First, he cited the familiar fact that increases in interest rates lower prices of outstanding debt obligations, and decreases in interest rates increase such prices. Second, he hypothesized that members of the community have some concept of "a normal level" of interest rates which is based on experience, and especially on recent experience. This level is normal in the sense that the interest rates are expected to return to this level after each significant departure from it. Thus, if actual rates are well above the normal level, the community will consider further increases of rates less likely than future declines and capital losses less likely than capital gains. It will therefore demand to hold more earning assets and thus smaller money balances. However, as actual interest rates fall well below the normal level, the community considers future rate increases to be more likely than rate decreases and capital losses more likely than capital gains. It therefore demands larger money balances and less earning assets.

The dependence of the speculative demand for money, denoted by L_2, on the interest rate is shown in Figure 13–3. The L_2L_2 curve slopes down-

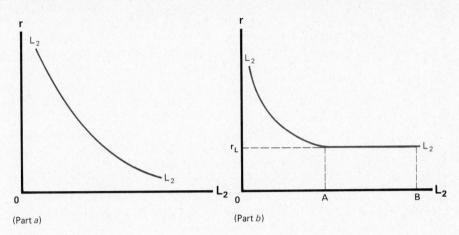

FIGURE 13–3
Speculative demand for money

ward, reflecting the *inverse* relationship between the speculative demand for money and the interest rate. Part (*a*) of the figure corresponds to what might be called the "standard" case; in (*b*) we have drawn the L_2L_2 curve to illustrate the Keynesian concept of the liquidity trap. The *liquidity trap* reflects the notion that at some positive rate of interest that is low by historical standards, the demand for money balances becomes infinitely elastic. In (*b*) the liquidity trap is represented by the flat section of the curve L_2L_2 to the right of point *A*. At the low level of the interest rate, r_L, the demand for money balances is infinitely elastic. The community will not hold any bonds at yield rates below r_L because it expects that income from holding bonds will be more than offset by capital losses resulting from future increases in interest rates.

The liquidity trap hypothesis has pessimistic implications for the adjustability of interest rates and for the efficacy of monetary policy. Interest rates could not fall below r_L, but that level of interest rates may at times be too high to be consistent with establishing a full employment level of income. Under such conditions, output and employment would be "trapped" at levels below full employment. Moreover, increases in the money supply could not lower interest rates below r_L or stimulate spending.

Few economists now accept the liquidity trap hypothesis in the extreme form just described. For one thing, it is based on a model having only two types of financial instruments—money itself and perpetual bonds—and this bears little resemblance to a modern economy with a wide array of earning assets of all maturities. In such an economy people who are unwilling to hold long-term bonds because they fear a rise in interest rates need not increase their holdings of money balances. Instead, they can buy earning assets of short maturities, which have prices that would be affected but little by a rise in interest rates. Such shifts to short maturities tend to lower at least short-term interest rates. Also, expectations concerning the future behavior of interest rates are neither so homogeneous nor so unalterable as is implied by the horizontal section of the L_2 curve. Some members of the community are likely to expect lower rates than others; this would give some negative slope to the L_2 curve. Moreover, the L_2 curve can be shifted upward or downward to some extent. For example, the monetary authority may shift the community's expectations downward by adopting an aggressive easy money policy and by announcing a determination to lower interest rates.

While economists have generally rejected the extreme version of the liquidity trap, the more basic Keynesian contribution of introducing the interest rate into the theory of the demand for money has remained to the present day.[5] Indeed, the importance of the interest rate is now even more widely accepted since the realization that the interest rate may also be an important influence in the transactions demand for money.

THE TRANSACTIONS MOTIVE RECONSIDERED

One of the primary contributions of post-Keynesian work on the transactions demand for money has been to emphasize the importance of the interest rate in determining the amount of transactions balances demanded. Keynes acknowledged the existence of this effect; yet, as we have just seen, he largely confined the role of the interest rate to the speculative motive. In order to see why it is relevant for the transactions motive as well, let us consider a simple example.

Imagine a hypothetical individual whose annual income is $9,600 and who spends all his income evenly over the year. In the first instance, let us further posit that he is paid $800 on the first day of each month. Under these assumptions his money holdings will have the sawtooth pattern shown in Figure 13–4. At the beginning of each month he has money balances of $800. These money balances are used up uniformly over the month; just when they are exhausted, he receives his paycheck for the following month; and thus the pattern is repeated. Since he begins the month with $800 and ends with zero, quite evidently his *average* money balances over the month must be half his paycheck, or $800/2 = $400. Since each month is representative of all months, his average money balance over the year is also $400. The income velocity of circulation of his money balances is the ratio

---

[5]However, it should be noted that the precise rationale on which the speculative motive is based has changed somewhat since Keynes first introduced the concept. The appendix to this chapter discusses some of the difficulties with the Keynesian approach and sketches the later developments.

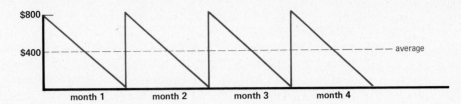

FIGURE 13–4
Transactions balances: monthly payments

of his annual income to his average money holdings, or a rate of 24 per year ($9600/$400).

Now let us ask how the situation would change if our hypothetical individual were paid $400 twice a month rather than $800 once a month. Pictorially, the situation would be as in Figure 13–5. As contrasted with Figure 13–4, the sawtooth pattern in Figure 13–5 is clearly finer. Over each half-month period, and consequently over the year as a whole, the individual's average money balances are now $200, or half as large as before. Income velocity is now 48 per year ($9600/$200).

To this point we have simply assumed that the individual responds passively to whatever frequency of payment he is presented with, but this need not be the case. In particular, an individual who is paid monthly and whom we have characterized by the pattern in Figure 13–4 could readily achieve the pattern of Figure 13–5. He can do this by putting half of his monthly paycheck ($400) into an earning asset such as a bond or savings deposit and leaving the remaining $400 in the form of money balances. Then, in the middle of the month when his cash has run down, he can convert his earning asset to cash. Thus, even though he is paid once a month, his cash holdings would have the pattern shown in Figure 13–5. That is, his average cash holdings would be $200, and his average holdings of the earning asset would also be $200.[6]

Indeed, should the individual so desire, he could make even more frequent conversions to cash and further lower his average cash holdings. For example, he could take $600 of each paycheck and place it in an earning

---

[6]He holds $400 of earning assets for the first half of the month and zero for the second half, yielding an average over the month of $200.

FIGURE 13–5
Transactions balances: semimonthly payments

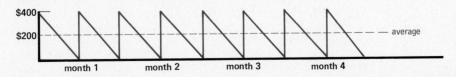

asset, leaving himself with $200 in cash. Since he makes expenditures at the rate of $800 per month, he will run out of cash after one quarter of the month has elapsed. He could then convert an additional $200 into cash, leaving $400 of his balances in earning assets. This pattern would be repeated until all balances are exhausted and he is paid again at the beginning of the new month. Clearly, this would result in average money balances of only $100, average holdings of the earning asset of $300, and an income velocity of 96 per year ($9600/100).[7]

It should be evident from these illustrations that our hypothetical individual is not necessarily constrained by the frequency with which he is paid in determining his average transactions balances.[8] But how is he to decide the optimal amount of money to hold? Or, putting the question in an equivalent way, how often should he convert from earning assets into cash during the payment period? These questions have been addressed directly in the work of W. J. Baumol and James Tobin.[9] Their formulation of the problem has two basic ingredients: (1) the rate of interest on earning assets and (2) the brokerage fee or *transactions cost* of converting an earning asset into money. When we speak of the rate of interest here, we refer to a short-term rate, such as the rate on savings deposits or on Treasury bills, which is not subject to fluctuation over the payment period. By transactions costs we mean any cost, either explicit or implicit, incurred in converting from earning assets to money. Examples of these costs might be fees and commissions paid to brokers or dealers for such a conversion. But transactions costs are also meant to cover the value of time and trouble taken by an individual in converting an asset to money. As a simple illustration, if it involves an element of inconvenience to go to a savings bank to obtain cash for one's deposits there, then qualitatively this should be treated no differently than a brokerage fee for selling stocks or bonds. Judged in this light, transactions costs are really a quite general concept.

In a frictionless world—that is, one without any transactions costs—individuals would hold no money for transactions purposes. As long as the rate of interest was positive, individuals would hold earning assets until the last instant before a transaction, converting their assets into money as

---

[7]The individual's average holding of the earning asset is computed as follows: For the first quarter of the month he holds $600 of earning assets; for the second quarter, $400; for the third quarter, $200; and for the last quarter, zero. Consequently, for the month as a whole we have ¼ × ($600 + $400 + $200 + $0) = $300 as his average balance of earning assets.

[8]In some extreme situations this need not be true. For instance, during hyperinflations, workers generally wish to get paid extremely frequently to avoid holding any liquid assets. Indeed,, during the German hyperinflation of the 1920s, workers were paid daily or twice daily. There are, in fact, many stories of workers who were met at the factory gates at noon by a family member so the family could shop immediately, thus beating the *afternoon* inflation.

[9]See W. J. Baumol, "The Transactions Demand for Cash—An Inventory Theoretic Approach," *Quarterly Journal of Economics*, November 1952, pp. 545–556, and James Tobin, "The Interest Elasticity of Transactions Demand for Cash," *Review of Economics and Statistics*, August 1956, pp. 241–247.

they were needed. In any realistic setting, however, transactions costs are not zero. As a consequence, the rational individual is faced with a tradeoff between interest earnings on the one hand and transactions costs on the other. Lower average money balances permit higher average balances of earning assets and thus greater interest income. However, as we have seen, lower money balances also mean more frequent conversions from earning assets into money and hence higher transactions costs. Conversely, higher average money balances reduce both transactions costs and interest earnings. Clearly, somewhere in the middle there must be an optimal money holding that just balances these two considerations. The precise nature of this solution need not concern us, although the interested reader is referred to the appendix to this chapter for the details. For our present purposes we only need stress the following properties of the optimal solution:

1 The optimal level of average money balances increases with the total volume of expenditures (income) during the payment period.
2 Optimal average money holdings increase with the level of transactions costs and decrease with the level of interest rates on earning assets.

The first conclusion is, of course, reminiscent of both the quantity theory and the Keynesian approaches.[10] The second conclusion is the novel one. It states, in part, than individual's demands for transactions balances—and consequently aggregate demands as well—will vary inversely with the interest rate. Higher interest rates will encourage economizing on cash balances, thereby increasing income velocity. Lower interest rates will yield higher average cash balances and will reduce velocity.

In summary, in more modern treatments the interest rate is given a prominent place in the transactions view of the demand for money. The direction of the effect is the same as in the speculative motive discussed earlier. Taken together, these two motives provide a convincing rationale for the importance of the interest rate in the demand for money.

OTHER FACTORS IN THE DEMAND FOR MONEY

To this point we have focused on the level of real output or income and the interest rate as the primary determinants of the demand for money. Restricting our attention to a few key variables is naturally of considerable analytic convenience, and we will continue to adopt this approach in subsequent discussions. Nevertheless, it is important to emphasize that other

---

[10]One important difference is that the results obtained by Baumol and Tobin suggest that the transactions demand for money will rise less than proportionately with income, indicating economies of scale in holding transactions balances (see the appendix).

factors can influence the demand for money. We can simply list some of these other factors as follows:

1 **THE WEALTH OF THE COMMUNITY.** One would expect that the richer the community, the greater will be the quantity of money that it will demand. However, with such a wide variety of highly liquid and safe earning assets available, there is no logical reason why any large part of any increase of wealth should come to be reflected in an increase of demand for money balances.

2 **THE EASE AND CERTAINTY OF SECURING CREDIT.** If credit were unavailable, or were available only uncertainly and on poor terms, both households and business firms would find it advantageous to hold larger money balances relative to their expenditures. However, as financial institutions and the use of credit become more highly developed, the community finds it advantageous to hold smaller balances relative to expenditures. Consumers need not accumulate large balances to pay for an expensive item, such as a car or a TV set; they buy it on credit and pay so much each payday. They need not hold balances to cover their expenditures between paydays; they can charge it and pay when they receive income. This also applies to business; it need not hold so much money relative to expenditures if it is assured of credit to meet excesses of expenditures over receipts. Thus, such developments as credit cards, instant credit, and confirmed lines of credit serve to reduce the demand for money balances.

3 **EXPECTATIONS OF FUTURE INCOME RECEIPTS.** The demand for money is also affected by the community's expectations as to the certainty and size of its future income receipts. Suppose, for example, that at some time the community comes to fear that its future income receipts will be less certain and may decline seriously. Community members may try to build up their money balances to tide them over the feared or expected lean period. But if they come to believe that the flow of income receipts will rise markedly in the future, they may decrease their money holdings relative to their current rate of expenditure; that is, they may increase their current rate of expenditure relative to their money balances.

4 **EXPECTATIONS FOR PRICES.** Expectations concerning the future behavior of prices are also relevant. If the members of a community believe that the prices of the things they intend to buy will remain stable, that a dollar will buy in the future just what it will buy today, they may elect to hold one quantity of money relative to their expenditures. They are likely to increase this quantity if they expect prices to fall. Both businesses and consumers may postpone purchases and hold larger balances relative to expenditures. They may elect to hold money, which they expect to increase in purchasing

power, rather than hold inventories of goods that they expect to depreciate relative to money. They try to do this by decreasing their expenditures. Expectations of higher prices have the reverse effects; the members of the community are likely to try to hold smaller balances relative to their expenditures. They try to buy before prices rise. In hyperinflations, such as that in Germany after World War I, the quantity of money demanded relative to expenditures falls to very low levels. When members of the community come to fear that each monetary unit will lose half or more of its purchasing power in a day or two, they try to avoid holding money. They refuse to accept money for their goods and services, or if they sell for money, they race to get rid of it immediately.

5 **THE NATURE AND VARIETY OF SUBSTITUTE ASSETS.** The demand for money is likely to be high if the only other assets available are highly illiquid and risky. However, the demand for money is reduced as more liquid and safer substitutes become available. We have seen that a wide variety of highly liquid and safe substitutes are available in American financial markets. These include short-term Treasury obligations, open-market commercial paper, and time and savings deposits. This also suggests that the use of a single interest rate to characterize the effects of interest rates on the demand for money is necessarily an oversimplification. Consequently, it should hardly be surprising that empirical studies of the demand for money tend to use several interest rates in explaining aggregate money holdings.

6 **THE SYSTEM OF PAYMENTS IN THE COMMUNITY.** We have already examined one aspect of this in our discussion of the frequency of income receipts. Another aspect concerns the structure of the production process. The more often that currently produced goods and services are sold for money in the process of production and distribution, the larger the demand for money is likely to be. Suppose, for example, that in producing a certain product all the processes of producing the raw material, fabricating, jobbing, wholesaling, and retailing are carried out by different firms, and that all payments among them are made with money. The demand for money relative to the final value of output is likely to be large. But the demand for money is likely to be smaller if all these processes are combined within vertically integrated firms with no money payments among the departments of each firm.

These are some of the factors, in addition to real income and the interest rate, that influence the behavior of the demand for money balances. This multiplicity of factors raises a question as to how predictable or stable is the demand for money. We address this question briefly here and more extensively in Chapter 18.

THE STABILITY OF THE DEMAND FOR MONEY

In principle, each of the factors listed above must be taken into account in predicting or explaining actual money demand. In practice, both in empirical work and in policy analysis, a number of these factors tend to be ignored. This is especially true of some of the more institutional factors—the nature and variety of substitute assets and the system of payments in the community—which are viewed as changing only slowly.

While this convenient simplification seemed to work well for many years, in the mid-1970s difficulties began appearing. Such things as NOW accounts, money market mutual funds, and convenient transfers from savings to checking accounts served simultaneously to expand the menu of assets, alter the nature of payments, and reduce the transactions costs of going from earning assets to money as then conventionally defined. As a consequence, observers found that the community was demanding a lower volume of money balances, given income, interest rates, and past behavior patterns. In addition, as noted earlier, these developments raised fundamental questions about the definition of money.

We will leave the policy implications of these developments until a later point, but these events should alert us to the fact that there may be periods during which we observe shifts in the community's money demand function.

EQUILIBRIUM IN THE MONEY MARKET

Having discussed the demand for money in some detail, we are now in position to examine the nature of the equilibrium between supply and demand in the market for money balances. This equilibrium condition will provide us with one of the important building blocks—the so-called *LM* curve—necessary for a complete theory of the determination of income, interest rates, and prices.

MONEY SUPPLY

Unless otherwise indicated, the following sections will assume that the size of the stock of money is firmly and precisely controlled by the monetary authority and that M is not allowed to respond passively to increases or decreases in demands for money balances. In short, M is a policy-determined independent variable. One consequence of this assumption is that to achieve equilibrium the demand for money must be brought into equality with the available supply by means of adjustments in the quantities demanded. Excesses of the supply of money over the demand for it must be eradicated by developments that increase the quantity demanded. And excesses of quantities demanded over the available supply must be corrected by some sort of development lowering the quantity demanded.

However, the assumption that the monetary authority has and exercises precise control over the size of M is in some cases unrealistic. For one thing, the Federal Reserve may be unable to control the size of M precisely, even if it tries to do so. There may be slippages between the instruments under its control—open-market operations, discount policy, and reserve requirements—and the size of M. Also, the intermediate policy guide that dominates Federal Reserve actions may not be that of achieving a certain size or rate of change of M, but rather a specified behavior of some other economic variable, such as interest rates.[11] For example, the objective may be to stabilize interest rates, or to achieve some other pattern of behavior of interest rates. In such cases the Federal Reserve would have to allow M to respond to the extent necessary to achieve its other intermediate objectives, and M would itself be determined, at least in part, by factors determining the behavior of demands for money balances. Some cases in which M is allowed to respond passively will be treated later.

MONEY DEMAND

In examining equilibrium in the money market, we confine our attention to a formulation of the demand for money that focuses on only two key variables—real income and the interest rates. We can write our demand function for money in a general way as

$$\frac{M^D}{P} = f\left(\frac{Y}{P}, r\right) = f(O, r) \tag{6}$$

This equation states that the demand for real money balances, M^D/P, is a function of real income or output, Y/P or O, and the interest rate, r.[12] It should be noted that in writing equation (6) we have made no distinction between money balances demanded for transactions purposes and those demanded for asset or speculative purposes. The reason we have not done so is that despite the analytical convenience of distinguishing among motives for holding money, the distinctions are really fuzzy ones. This is certainly true empirically, but it is true conceptually as well. For example, even if a dollar is to be spent for output in the near future, it serves as a store of value while it is held. Similarly, considerations of transactions costs should, strictly speaking, be introduced into the speculative or asset motive as well. Thus, for the time being at least, we will work with a single demand function for money.

---

[11]See Chapter 18.

[12]While the interest rate, r, represents the rate paid on earning assets, if interest were earned on money balances we could reinterpret r to be the *difference* between the interest rate paid on earning assets and the rate paid on money balances.

Equilibrium in the money market requires the equality of supply and demand, or

$$\overline{M}^S = M^D \tag{7}$$

where the bar over $\overline{M}^S$ is meant to indicate that the monetary authorities fix the supply of money at some given level. Combining equations (6) and (7), we can rewrite the condition for equilibrium as

$$\frac{\overline{M}^S}{P} = f\left(\frac{Y}{P}, r\right) \tag{8}$$

For the present we take the price level, P, as given. Consequently, equation (8) defines a single equation in two variables, Y and r. The equation is thus not capable of determining values for both of the variables. Rather, it defines *combinations* of pairs of values for r and Y that keep the money market in equilibrium, given the supply of money and the price level. If we were to plot the values of these equilibrium pairs, we would have the *LM* curve.

CONSTRUCTION OF THE *LM* CURVE

Although we have just indicated how we might construct an *LM* curve, actually carrying out this procedure would seem to require some specific numerical examples. We will, in fact, shortly do this by way of illustration. But in reality we can deduce the *qualitative* nature of the *LM* curve without resorting to numbers.

To do this, we must first plot the demand for real money balances as a function of the interest rate alone. Since equation (6) tells us that the demand depends on both real income and the interest rate, at first sight it may not be clear how to do this. The way around this difficulty is to plot the demand for money *given* the level of real income. Of course, this will give us a different curve for each level of income. Figure 13–6 plots two such curves for two different levels of real income, O_1 and O_2, where by assumption O_2 is larger than O_1. The first of these curves, labeled $f(O_1)$ in the figure, shows how the demand for real balances varies as a function of the interest when real income is fixed at O_1. It is downward-sloping to reflect the inverse relationship between the demand for money and the interest rate. The second curve, labeled $f(O_2)$, has the same general shape as the first but is displaced to the right. This happens because at any given interest rate, since O_2 is larger than O_1, the demand for money must be larger at O_2 than at O_1. For example, at the interest rate r_0 shown in the diagram, the demand for real balances is $(M^D/P)_1$ when income is O_1 and $(M^D/P)_2$ when income is O_2, where $(M^D/P)_2$ exceeds $(M^D/P)_1$.

We are now virtually finished. To establish the general shape of the *LM* curve we must simply examine the condition for equilibrium in the money market. This is done in Figure 13–7, where we have superimposed the fixed money supply on a slightly expanded version of Figure 13–6. The vertical

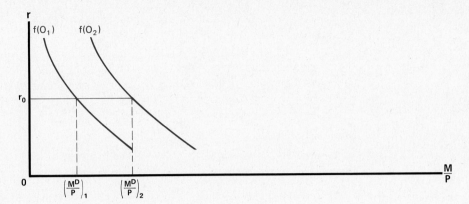

FIGURE 13–6
The demand for money and the interest rate

line in Figure 13–7 is drawn at the level of the money supply fixed by the authorities, $\overline{M}^S/P$. (It should be recalled that the price level is fixed throughout.) The points labeled A, B, and C in the figure are precisely the points where the demand for money equals the fixed supply. At point A the value of the interest rate is given by r_1 and the value of real income is O_1. Point B corresponds to both a higher level of real income, O_2, and a higher interest rate, r_2, while point C corresponds to still higher levels of both variables. If we plot these various combinations of the interest rate and real income, we have our LM curve. This is done in Figure 13–8.

While the precise shape of the LM curve will depend on the slope of the money-demand function, the important thing to note about the LM curve is that it is upward-sloping. This follows directly from the fact that as we

FIGURE 13–7
Equilibrium in the money market

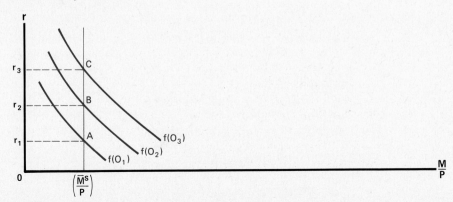

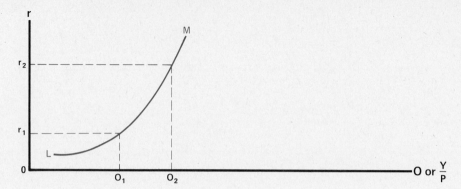

FIGURE 13–8
The *LM* curve

move from A to B to C in Figure 13–7, we are increasing *both* the interest rate and real income. A moment's thought will reveal that this upward slope could easily have been anticipated. As we raise the level of real income, the demand for money (largely for transactions purposes) must increase. However, with a fixed supply of money, equilibrium in the money market requires that the interest rate must increase to choke off this additional demand—hence the upward slope of the *LM* curve.

A SPECIFIC EXAMPLE

To clarify further the nature of the *LM* curve, consider a specific example. In constructing our example it will be helpful if we make the following simplifying assumptions:

1 The total demand function for money can be decomposed into separate parts corresponding to the transactions and asset or speculative demand for money.

2 Transactions demand will be taken to be a function of income alone, whereas asset demand will be assumed to be a function of the interest rate alone.

3 Both the transactions and the asset demand will be taken to be linear functions; that is, we assume they have constant slopes.

Thus, we can write

$$M^D = L_1 + L_2 \tag{9}$$

where

M^D = the total demand function for (nominal) money balances
L_1 = the demand function for transactions purposes
L_2 = the demand function for asset or speculative purposes

We further assume that

$$L_1 = JOP = JY \tag{10}$$

where

J = a constant giving the fraction of OP or Y demanded for transactions purposes

and that

$$L_2 = P(A - er) \tag{11}$$

where

A = a positive constant, stated in billions of dollars of constant purchasing power

$e = \dfrac{\Delta L_2}{\Delta r}$ = the "slope," stated as the number of billions of change in L_2 with each change of 1 percentage point in r

Inserting equations (10) and (11) into equation (9), we get

$$M^D = JOP + P(A - er) \tag{12}$$

Dividing both sides of equation (12) by the price level, P, yields

$$\frac{M^D}{P} = JO + (A - er) \tag{13}$$

which states that total real money balances depend linearly on real income, O, and interest rate, r. Equation (13) is thus nothing other than a linear version of our general demand for money function, equation (6).

To obtain the LM curve we must now use the equilibrium condition, equation (7), which, combined with equation (12), gives

$$\overline{M}^S = JOP + P(A - er) \tag{14}$$
$$= JY + P(A - er)$$

To use this algebraic expression to trace out an LM curve, we must, of course, put in some numbers, for example:

$\overline{M}^S$ = $250 billion

$J = \frac{1}{5}$

A = $110 billion

e = $10 billion

$P = 1$

Equation (13) then simplifies to

$$250 = \frac{1}{5}Y + (110 - 10r) \tag{15}$$

Table 13–2 shows nine of the many combinations of r and Y for which equation (15) is satisfied. This occurs at $Y = \$1{,}150$ billion and $r = 9$ percent; at $Y = \$1{,}000$ billion and $r = 6$ percent; and so on. This LM curve is depicted graphically in Figure 13–9.[13]

The fact that the LM curve is a straight line stems from the assumption of linearity in equations (10) and (11). The constant slope of the LM curve can be calculated by rewriting equation (15) with r on the left-hand side, as in

$$r = \frac{1}{50} Y - 14 \qquad (16)$$

Thus, the slope is given by

$$\frac{\Delta r}{\Delta Y} = \frac{1}{50}$$

In summary, the LM curve in Figure 13–9 represents all combinations of Y and r that satisfy the condition for equilibrium in the money market, equation (15). Any combination off the line will be one of disequilibrium, which will create pressures for adjustment. Any combination above the LM curve, such as point A, is one at which the supply of money exceeds the demand for money. We know this because there is a point on the LM curve vertically below A, at the same level of income at which equilibrium is established. At the same level of Y and a higher r, demand will be smaller and the excess supply of money will create pressure for a decrease of r, thus moving us from a point like A to the LM curve.

---

[13]Since we have assumed that $P = 1$, the horizontal axis in Figure 13–9 can be regarded as measuring nominal income, Y, or real income, O.

TABLE 13–2 A Numerical LM Example (Amounts in billions of dollars)

(1)	(2)	(3)	(4)	(5)	(6)
M	Y	$L_1 = 1/5Y$	r (in percent)	$L_2 = 110 - 10r$	Total M^D [(3) + (5)]
$250	$ 750	$150	1	$100	$250
250	800	160	2	90	250
250	850	170	3	80	250
250	900	180	4	70	250
250	950	190	5	60	250
250	1,000	200	6	50	250
250	1,050	210	7	40	250
250	1,100	220	8	30	250
250	1,150	230	9	20	250

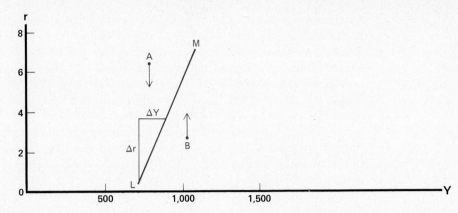

FIGURE 13–9
An *LM* curve

On the other hand, at any combination below the *LM* curve, such as point *B*, demand exceeds supply. This excess demand for money will bring pressure for an increase of *r*, again moving us to the *LM* curve.

SHIFTING THE *LM* CURVE

Before leaving the discussion of the *LM* curve, we should note that anything which shifts the demand function or the supply of money will shift the *LM* curve. For example, an increase in the supply of money shifts the *LM* curve to the right, and a decrease in the supply of money shifts the *LM* curve to the left. The reason is really quite simple. Consider first an increase in the supply of money. This creates excess supply in the money market. Reestablishing equilibrium thus requires a fall in *r*, a rise in *Y*, or both. Consequently, following an increase in the supply of money the new *LM* curve must lie down from and to the right of the original *LM* curve. This is illustrated in Figure 13–10. The original *LM* curve is labeled L_1M_1. Consider for

FIGURE 13–10
Shifting the *LM* curve

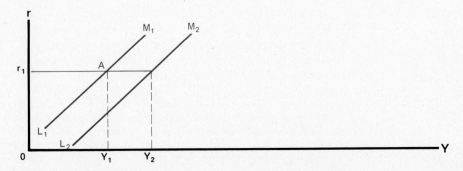

a moment point A on L_1M_1, which corresponds to the combination r_1 and Y_1. Now let us ask what value of Y will put us on the new *LM* curve *if* the interest rate stays at r_1. With the interest rate constant, the only way in which a new equilibrium can be established is if income rises to make individuals *want* to hold the new higher stock of money. Thus, we know that at the interest rate r_1 the value of income that put us on the new *LM* curve L_2M_2 must be some higher level, like Y_2, in Figure 13–10.

Conversely, a decrease in the stock of money creates excess demand in the money market, leading to an increase of r, a decrease of Y, or both. Diagramatically, in Figure 13–10 this amounts to beginning with L_2M_2 and moving left toward L_1M_1.

In examining the effects of monetary policy in subsequent chapters, we will frequently encounter such shifts in the *LM* curve. It is important, there-fore, that the logic behind these shifts be well understood.[14]

SUMMARY

1 The demand for money is a basic building block in monetary theory, which analyzes the relationship between money and the behavior of the economy. The earliest view of the demand for money stems from the classical quantity theory of money. In its simplest form, this theory posits that the demand for real money balances is a constant pro-portion of the level of real income or output. Empirical evidence sug-gesting that there is not a constant proportional relationship between money and GNP has spawned alternative versions of the demand for money.

2 Modern theories emphasize the dependence of demand on two key variables: income and the interest rate. Income enters as a measure of transactions needs, but unlike the simple quantity theory, modern theories do not assume that the relationship between money and income is strictly proportional. There are a number of explanations of why the demand for money depends negatively on the rate of in-terest. Most simply, the interest rate represents the opportunity cost of holding money. The higher the interest rate, the more individuals will try and economize in their holdings of money.

3 While we have stressed the role of income and the interest rate in money demand, other factors may also play a role. These include wealth, price expectations, the nature and variety of substitute assets, and the structure of the payments mechanism.

[14]We should note that an increase in the *real* quantity of money supplied can be brought about by either a *rise* in the nominal quality supplied, $\overline{M}^S$, or a *decline* in the price level, P. Since it is actually variations in the real quantity of money that shift the *LM* curve, we see that either a decline in the price level or a rise in $\overline{M}^S$ shifts the *LM* curve to the right. Similarly, a rise in the price level or a decrease in $\overline{M}^S$ shifts the *LM* curve to the left.

4 The *LM* curve characterizes the combinations of income and the interest rate for which the demand for money equals the supply of money. The *LM* curve is upward-sloping. Anything that shifts the demand function or the supply of money will shift the *LM* curve. For example, an increase in the supply of money shifts the *LM* curve to the right.

APPENDIX

SOME NOTES ON THE TRANSACTIONS AND SPECULATIVE DEMANDS FOR MONEY

In the preceding chapter we discussed both the transactions and the speculative demands for money. At several points we touched on some of the post-Keynesian developments in these areas, but we did not spell out any of the arguments in detail. The purpose of this appendix is to close this gap.

TRANSACTIONS DEMAND

As noted earlier, the problem faced by the individual transactor is to decide on his optimal holdings of money and an earning asset we shall call bonds. The givens of the problem are as follows:

Y = the real value of the individual's income per payment period (e.g., a month), which by assumption also equals the real value of expenditures to be made during the period

r = the rate of interest per payment period, assumed constant over the period

b = the real brokerage fee or transactions cost incurred each time the individual sells bonds[1]

The individual is assumed to sell bonds in equal-lot-size units of D, evenly spaced over the period. For example, if Y is $800 per month, D could be $800 once a month or $400 twice a month, and so on.[2] It is, of course, the optimal value of the variable D that our analysis must determine. The

---

[1] Note that this is a fixed cost per conversion of bonds into money. One can also introduce a cost that varies with the amount converted, but this would not change the results. See Baumol, op. cit.

[2] The reader will observe that we are implicitly assuming the individual is paid in bonds. This could arise, for example, if the employer deposits the employee's paycheck directly into a savings account. This assumption makes the analysis simpler, but does not change the qualitative nature of the conclusions.

problem is to choose D so as to maximize total interest earnings less total transactions costs.

Since expenditures are made at a constant rate, the individual's average balances of *both* money and bonds must be one-half his income or $Y/2$. Similarly, his average money holdings must be $D/2$. Consequently, his average bond holding over the period is the difference between these two or $(Y/2 - D/2)$. The income he receives on this will be equal to the interest rate times his average bond holdings or $r(Y/2 - D/2)$. On the cost side, if each conversion of bonds into money is in the amount $\$D$, since all balances must eventually be converted, the individual must engage in Y/D conversions during the period. Since the brokerage charge is $\$b$ per conversion, his total conversion costs are $\$b(Y/D)$.

These two elements can be combined in a total net-revenue expression:

$$N = r\left(\frac{Y}{2} - \frac{D}{2}\right) - b\left(\frac{Y}{D}\right) \tag{A1}$$

where the first term in equation (A1) corresponds to interest earnings and the second to conversion costs. To find the value of D that maximizes net revenue we must take the derivative of (A1) with respect to D, equate it with zero, and solve for D. The solution to this is[3]

$$D = \sqrt{\frac{2bY}{r}} \tag{A2}$$

Since average money holdings, here denoted by M, have been observed to equal $D/2$, from equation (A2) we derive

$$M = \sqrt{\frac{bY}{2r}} = kY^{1/2}r^{-1/2} \tag{A3}$$

where

$$k = \sqrt{\frac{b}{2}}$$

Equation (A3) is then our desired result. For obvious reasons, it is sometimes called the *square-root law* of money demand.

While we have spelled out several of the implications of this result in the preceding chapter, it is worth emphasizing the following points:

1 Both the level of interest rates and transactions costs influence optimal money holdings, with larger money holdings stemming from either lower interest rates or higher transactions costs.

---

[3]The appropriate condition is $dN/dD = (-r/2) + (bY/D^2) = 0$, which when solved yields (A2). The astute reader may observe that the optimal value of D may imply a number of transactions that is not an integer. This difficulty is more apparent than real. In this regard see Tobin, op. cit.

2 Technological or legal developments that reduce transactions costs will yield lower average money holdings. Thus, for example, if telephone or computer terminal transfers between savings and demand deposits become widespread, we would expect individuals to economize further on money balances.

3 The way in which income enters equation (A3) implies that there are economies of scale in individual money holdings. For example, if the income of an individual goes up fourfold (A3) predicts that money balances will only rise by a factor of 2.

4 While this last result cannot be directly carried over to the aggregate economy, it certainly suggests that aggregate money holdings may rise less than proportionately with aggregate income. It further suggests that aggregate money holdings may be sensitive to the distribution of income. In particular, (A3) implies that the more highly concentrated is a fixed level of aggregate income, the lower will be the demand for money.

SPECULATIVE DEMAND

As with the transactions motive, subsequent developments in monetary theory have served to clarify the concept of the speculative motive introduced by Keynes. In order to see why these developments were necessary, we first provide a brief critical review of the Keynesian approach to the speculative motive. We then outline some more recent work whose emphasis has been on providing a firm theoretical foundation for the speculative motive.[4]

As noted earlier, Keynes analyzed a world in which two assets were available—money and perpetual bonds or consols. Money yields no return, nor does it depreciate in terms of money. Bonds, of course, do yield a return made up of two components: (1) the interest payment received and (2) the change in capital value of the bond stemming from a change in the rate of interest. As we saw in Chapter 4, the formula for the price of a perpetual bond is

$$P = \frac{A}{r} \tag{A4}$$

where

P = the price of the bond
A = the dollar amount of interest paid per year to the bondholder
r = the annual rate of interest

[4]For a more complete exposition of the material in this section, see James Tobin, "Liquidity Preference as Behavior Towards Risk," *Review of Economic Studies*, February 1958, pp. 65–86.

Thus, an individual who anticipates that in the future the interest rate will be r^e must necessarily expect a bond price of P^e given by

$$P^e = \frac{A}{r^e} \qquad (A5)$$

Consequently, the expected percentage capital gain (or loss if it is negative), which we will denote by g, is given by

$$g \equiv \frac{P^e - P}{P} = \frac{A/r^e - A/r}{A/r} \qquad (A6)$$

The second part of equation (A6) is derived by substituting equations (A4) and (A5) into the definition of g. This can be simplified by canceling the A terms and multiplying the numerator and denominator of (A6) by r to give

$$g = \frac{r}{r^e} - 1 \qquad (A7)$$

This expresses g in terms of the current and expected rate of interest. For example, if $r^e = r$, then g is zero, so that no capital gain or loss is expected. Alternatively, if the current interest rate is 6 percent and is expected to fall to 5 percent, then

$$g = \frac{0.06}{0.05} - 1 = 0.2, \text{ or } 20 \text{ percent}$$

The total return from holding bonds from one year to the next is simply the sum of the interest rate and the expected capital gain. That is, we have

$$e = r + g = r + \frac{r}{r^e} - 1 \qquad (A8)$$

where

e = the one-year expected holding period yield[5]

Given equation (A8), according to Keynes the individual investor now has a simple choice. If the expected holding period yield is greater than zero—which is the expected holding period yield on money—then the individual should keep his assets in bonds. If the expected yield is less than zero, he should hold money. Since expectations were perceived by Keynes as being determined by some kind of normal rate, quite evidently the lower the current interest rate, the more likely it is that e will be negative and that money will be held. Conversely, the higher r is, the more likely it is that e will be positive and bonds will be held. Thus, the demand for speculative

[5]This concept, it will be recalled, was discussed in Chapter 4. It should also be noted that there is nothing special about our use of the time unit of one year. Any other period would work equally well.

balances will be inversely related to the current interest rate. In essence, this is a simple restatement of the Keynesian speculative motive developed earlier.

This analysis has, however, at least three troublesome aspects:

1 The analysis implies that each individual will hold all his assets in either the form of bonds or the form of money. However, it is more reasonable to suppose that individuals tend to hold *diversified* portfolios of both bonds and money, a result that does not follow from the Keynesian analysis.

2 To explain why both bonds and money are held in the *aggregate*, we must appeal to the existence of different expectations on the part of different individuals. Some of these individuals would be exclusively in bonds, others exclusively in money. However, if the market for money balances is in equilibrium for a sufficient length of time, the expectations of different individuals should tend to converge to a common expectation. When this happens, we are back to the all-or-nothing situation described previously and consequently cannot explain how both money and bonds will be held in the aggregate.

3 Despite the obvious element of uncertainty faced by the individual in making portfolio choices, the Keynesian analysis proceeds as if the individual's beliefs were held with certainty. In other words, the individual investor pays no attention to any risks associated with portfolio choice.

It was to overcome these various difficulties that the portfolio balance approach was developed.

THE PORTFOLIO BALANCE APPROACH

The *portfolio balance approach* begins from the relatively simple notion that individuals like to earn high rates of return on their assets, but that they dislike risk. Put in terms of utility, the rate of return (or the wealth that it brings) is a "good," but risk is a "bad." To gain some perspective on this, consider an individual who is presented with the following three options:

Option 1: $1,000 offered with certainty
Option 2: a 50:50 chance of getting $750 or $1,250
Option 3: a 50:50 chance of getting $250 or $1,750

All three options offer the same average or expected return of $1,000, but only the first does so with certainty. Both the second and third options have some risk attached to them; and the third option, since it has a greater dispersion of outcomes, is, in some intuitive sense, riskier than the second. To postulate that individuals like return but dislike risk, or are *risk averse*, is to argue that option 1 would be chosen by most people. Indeed, an individual might well continue to choose option 1 even if she were allowed to pick

Option 4: a 50:50 chance of getting $252 or $1,750

which has an expected return of $1,001.

However, it is clearly possible to modify option 4 further so that we raise the expected return by just enough to compensate the individual for the risk involved; that is, by sufficiently raising the expected return of a risky option, we can make the individual *indifferent* between a certain option and a risky one. This discussion is not meant to suggest that all individuals are *necessarily* risk averse, but rather that this is a reasonable assumption on which to base a theory of portfolio behavior. Let us now see how this would work in the case of the speculative motive.

As earlier, we consider an individual who wishes to divide her assets between money and perpetual bonds. Abstracting from any change in the general price level, money is a riskless asset with a zero rate of return. Bonds have an *expected* rate of return, which we previously denoted by $e = r + g$, where r was the interest component and g was the expected capital gain or loss. In contrast to e, however, the *actual* rate of return on bonds is uncertain, so that individuals holding bonds must bear some risk.

The problem faced by the individual is to choose a portfolio to maximize her utility. We first observe that negative values of e will definitely lead to an all-money portfolio, since in this case bonds offer both less return and more risk as compared with money. As a consequence, we might as well restrict our attention to positive values of e. For such values, holding more bonds increases expected interest income and hence tends to increase utility. However, this also increases the dispersion of possible outcomes, since the future value of an individual's assets can fluctuate over a greater range the higher the fraction of assets held in bonds. Viewed from this perspective, higher bond holdings tend to increase risk and thus decrease utility. The problem is clearly one of striking an optimal balance between risk and return. Even without exhibiting a specific solution to this problem, it should be intuitively clear that this will lead to an inverse relationship between speculative money holdings and the interest rate. In particular, higher current interest rates, *other things being equal*, will lead to higher expected returns from bonds. With no change in the inherent riskiness of bonds, individuals will, at the margin, find bonds more attractive than money and thus reduce their money holdings somewhat. In other words, higher current interest rates lead to lower money balances and vice versa. The plausibility of this conclusion can be buttressed by the use of some diagrams.

In Figure 13A–1 we have plotted a typical individual's *indifference curves*. Each curve corresponds to a given level of utility and thus portrays the combinations of expected return and risk between which the individual is

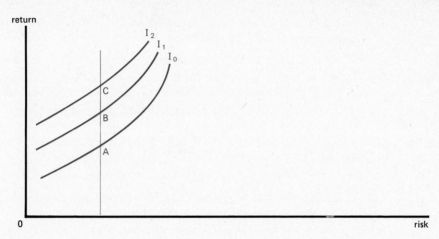

FIGURE 13A–1
Indifference curves

indifferent. The curves slope up to the right, since as we have noted earlier, increased risk must be associated with increased return to leave the individual equally well off. Similarly, indifference curve I_2 corresponds to a higher level of utility than I_1, which is in turn more desirable than I_0. This can be seen by comparing points A, B, and C in Figure 13A–1. Each point has the same riskiness, but expected return increases as we move from A to B to C. Clearly, then, the individual will prefer being on I_2 rather than on I_1 and on I_1 rather than on I_0.

To complete the givens of the problem, we must specify the set of possible combinations of expected return and risk that are available to the individual. The quantity of bonds the individual can hold ranges from zero to the total size of her assets, which we assume fixed. Denoting the quantity of bonds held by the symbol H, we have the following:

$$E = He = H(r + g) \tag{A9}$$

$$R = H\sigma \tag{A10}$$

where

E = expected return
R = total risk
σ = a measure of risk associated with $1 bonds

Equation (A9) simply says that the expected return in dollars is equal to the expected *rate* of return times the dollar value of bonds held. Equation (A10) states that total risk is given by the product of the dollar volume of bonds and the riskiness of a single bond.[6] If we divide (A9) by (A10), we can eliminate H and simplify to obtain

$$E = \left(\frac{r + g}{\sigma}\right)R \tag{A11}$$

Equation (A11) is the desired relationship between expected return and risk. It is the opportunity locus available to the individual, and it is analogous to the budget line in the conventional theory of the consumer. We have plotted several possible loci in Figure 13A–2.

The following observations on Figure 13A–2 should be noted:

1 Since (A11) expresses a linear relationship between E and R, the loci are all straight lines.
2 Again from (A11), we see that the slope of the straight lines depends on the market rate of interest, r. In particular, higher rates of interest correspond to steeper loci (that is, $r_2 > r_1 > r_0$).
3 All the loci go through the origin. The origin corresponds to the portfolio consisting entirely of money for which both the expected return and risk are zero.

We are now in a position to indicate diagrammatically the nature of the individual's portfolio choice. Given the interest rate, the expected capital gain or loss, and the riskiness of bonds (that is, r, g, and σ), the individual is constrained to choose along some particular opportunity locus. Her objective is to get onto the highest indifference curve, and this obviously is at a point where the opportunity locus is just tangent to an indifference curve.

[6]Those familiar with elementary statistics will recognize the symbol σ as a standard deviation, which is a conventional measure of dispersion. For a more detailed justification of its use as a measure of risk, see Tobin, op. cit.

FIGURE 13A–2
Opportunity curves

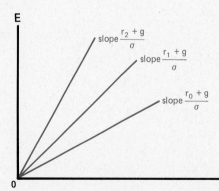

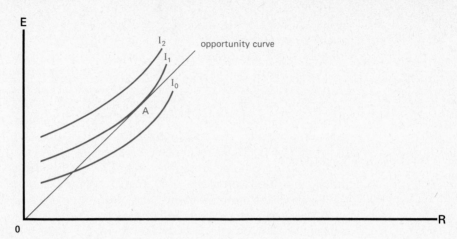

FIGURE 13A–3
Individual equilibrium: tangency between
indifference and opportunity curves

Figure 13A–3 indicates the nature of this tangency, with point A being the optimal point for the individual.

Let us now consider how an individual's portfolio will change as the interest rate changes. In Figure 13A–4 we have plotted the loci corresponding to two different interest rates. When the interest rate is r_0, the individual is in equilibrium at point A. However, if the interest rate should be at the higher level r_1, equilibrium would occur at point B. At this latter point the

FIGURE 13A–4
The effect of a change in interest rates

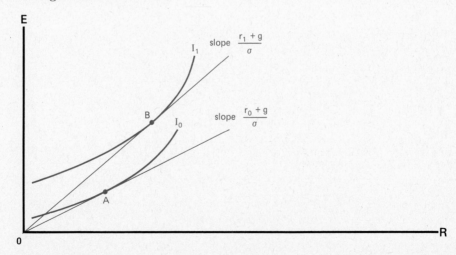

individual has a higher expected return and a higher risk as compared with point A.[7] Increased return and risk can only come about because the individual has more bonds. Consequently, the portfolio corresponding to point B contains more bonds and therefore less money than the portfolio corresponding to point A.

We now have obtained the desired result. That is, we see that higher interest rates lead to lower speculative money balances and, conversely, that lower interest rates lead to higher money balances. While this has been developed as a theory of individual behavior, it is reasonable to assume that the same general properties carry over to the aggregate demand for money. In other words, the aggregate speculative demand for money has the downward-sloping shape we have seen in Figure 13–4.

In summary, the portfolio balance approach leads to the same result as that obtained by Keynes, but it does so under somewhat more appealing assumptions. In particular, it both directly confronts the problem of uncertainty and allows for the possibility that individuals will hold diversified portfolios.

SELECTED READINGS

Branson, W. H. *Macroeconomic Theory and Policy*, 2nd ed. New York: Harper & Row, 1979.

Friedman, M. "The Quantity of Money—A Restatement." In M. Friedman (ed.), *Studies in the Quantity Theory of Money*. Chicago: University of Chicago Press, 1956.

Goldfeld, S. M. "The Demand for Money Revisited," *Brookings Papers on Economic Activity*, No. 3, 1973, pp. 577–638.

Laidler, D. E. W. *The Demand for Money: Theories and Evidence*. New York: Dun-Donnelley, 1977.

[7]In Figure 13A–4 we have ignored the possibility that the individual, feeling wealthier because of a higher interest rate, may actually assume less risk. This possible perversity of what is known as the "income effect" is discussed in D. E. W. Laidler, *The Demand for Money: Theories and Evidence*, 2nd ed. New York: Dun-Donnelley, 1977, pp. 93–95.

14

CONSUMPTION, SAVING, AND INVESTMENT

In this chapter we continue our development of the building blocks of a theory for determining the levels of income and interest rates. We saw in the previous chapter that equilibrium between the supply of money and the demand for money yields a relationship between income and interest rates—the *LM* curve—but this was not sufficient to determine the levels of these variables. Obviously, we must find another relationship between these two. To accomplish this, we turn to the market for goods or commodities. In particular, we focus on the "income and expenditure approach," which utilizes concepts such as the consumption and saving functions and the investment function. As we will see, the income approach emphasizes that a necessary condition for equilibrium of income and interest rates is that the supply of saving be equal to the investment demand for output. It is precisely this condition that will give us the additional relationship we are seeking and thus permit us to develop a complete model of the determination of income and interest rates. That is, the establishment of *joint equilibrium* in the money market and the goods market will determine both the levels of aggregate output and the interest rate.

The concept of aggregate income, measured by GNP, played a critical role in the explanation of the behavior of the aggregate demand for money. Aggregate income will receive an equally prominent role in explaining the behavior of consumption, saving, and investment. Prior to launching into the theory of saving and investment behavior, it will be extremely helpful if we understand how the concepts of income, output, saving, and investment are actually measured in practice.

NATIONAL INCOME CONCEPTS

One concept that we need to make precise is the notion of *gross national product* or *expenditure*, popularly known as GNP. There are a number of equivalent ways of measuring GNP. We begin with the most common, that of viewing GNP as the market value of the output of goods and services produced by the nation during some time period. Subsequently we exploit the wonders of double-entry balance sheet accounting to show that GNP can be equivalently viewed as a measure of the nation's income.[1]

GNP AS EXPENDITURE FOR OUTPUT

GNP is composed of three main categories of expenditures for output:[2] (1) personal consumption expenditures, (2) gross private domestic investment, and (3) government purchases of goods and services.

PERSONAL CONSUMPTION
Personal consumption expenditures include all purchases of current output by consumers. These include durable consumers' goods, nondurable consumers' goods, and consumers' services. The durables include such things as new automobiles, TV sets, refrigerators, and furniture. The nondurables include food, beverages, clothing, tobacco, and so on. Consumers' services embrace a wide variety of services such as shelter, medical care, and transportation.

GROSS PRIVATE DOMESTIC INVESTMENT
Every word in this heading is important. The term *investment*, as used here, has nothing directly to do with buying stocks, bonds, or any other type of financial instrument. We use it here and in the succeeding sections to mean simply expenditures for the current output of goods and services for the purpose of maintaining and increasing the stock of capital goods. The term *domestic* indicates that we include here only expenditures for the purpose

---

[1] Our discussion of national income accounting will be quite brief. For a more detailed treatment, see T. F. Dernburg and D. M. McDougall, *Macroeconomics*. New York: McGraw-Hill, 1976. The most recent national income data are contained in the *Survey of Current Business* published by the Department of Commerce, especially the July issue.

[2] A fourth category, net exports of goods and services, is also included in GNP. *Net exports*, which is defined as exports minus imports, is typically only a very small fraction of GNP. As a consequence, to simplify matters we postpone international considerations until Part 6.

of maintaining or increasing the stock of capital goods at home, not those for maintaining or building up capital abroad. *Private* means that only private expenditures for these purposes are included, not those by the government. The term *gross* indicates that we include expenditures for output to offset the depreciation of capital goods as well as to make net additions to the stock. If we deduct from gross private domestic investment for any period the depreciation or "using up" of capital during the period, we arrive at net private domestic investment, the net increase in the stock of these goods during the period.

Gross private domestic investment is actually made up of three broad types of investment: new construction, both residential and nonresidential; producers' durable equipment such as individual machinery, computers, and railroad cars; and *net changes in business inventories.* The last term, which perhaps requires a bit of clarification, refers to changes in the stock of business inventories from one period to another. These inventories, which may be raw materials, goods in process, or finished goods, are clearly part of the community's stock of capital goods. Hence, a net increase in business inventories is investment because it is an addition to the stock of capital goods. Historically, changes in the volume of output used to increase or decrease inventories have been an important source of fluctuations in GNP and employment.

GOVERNMENT PURCHASES OF GOODS AND SERVICES

Government purchases consist of the expenditures of the federal, state, and local governments for the current output of goods and services. These include expenditures both for the services of productive factors, primarily labor, and for the output of business firms. Government transfer payments, such as social security or welfare payments, are excluded from government purchases because they are not payments for productive services. As we shall see shortly, however, government transfer payments can indirectly affect GNP by altering household disposable income and hence personal consumption expenditures.

TRANSACTIONS EXCLUDED FROM GNP

We have just seen that government transfer payments are not directly included in the calculation of GNP. This is just one example of the fact that only transactions which represent payments for currently produced goods and services are included in GNP. Other transactions excluded by this principle are the following: purchases of existing houses or used cars, and financial transactions such as purchases of corporate stock or government bonds (regardless of whether they are "new" or "used"). A second general class of excluded transactions are those stemming from *intermediate* sales—that is, sales from one producer to another. The purchase of flour by a baker is an example. It would be double counting to include in GNP both the value of flour sold to the baker and the full value of bread sold by the baker to the consumer. As a consequence, only the *final sale* to the consumer is counted in GNP.

THE ACCOUNTING IDENTITY AND SOME DATA

We find, then, that GNP for any period is the sum of expenditures for output in the form of personal consumption, gross private domestic investment, and government purchases of goods and services.

For convenience, we denote these expenditures by the following symbols:

C = personal consumption
I = gross private domestic investment
G = government purchases of goods and services
Y = GNP, or gross national product

Thus, for any period,

$$Y = C + I + G \tag{1}$$

Table 14–1 gives some actual data on GNP and its components for several recent years. For each year, GNP is measured in terms of the average level of prices prevailing during that year. This is sometimes called *current dollar* GNP or *nominal* GNP. As an addendum, Table 14–1 also shows the value of GNP for each year at constant (1972) prices, and the corresponding price index. GNP in constant prices is called either *real* GNP or *constant dollar* GNP. The price index shown is called the *implicit GNP price deflator*. It is an index of average prices of all goods and services included in GNP, with the index constructed to have the value of unity in 1972.[3]

THE CIRCULAR FLOW OF INCOME

We noted earlier that GNP may be viewed not only as the value of output or expenditures for output, but also as the sum of gross national income shares accruing to the members of the community, including the government. We also noted that the sum of these shares accruing to the community during any period must be exactly equal to the value of output or expenditures. On reflection, this becomes almost obvious. Value created must accrue to someone; it cannot disappear in thin air. Nor can the community as a whole receive values that are not created. To state this observation in another way, expenditures made must be received by someone, but no one can receive expenditures that are not made.

A pictorial representation of this circular flow is given in Figure 14–1. It shows total aggregate demand, $C + I + G$, arriving at firms where actual

[3]In the previous chapter we denoted real GNP and the price index by O and P, respectively. Using these symbols, the relationship between real and nominal GNP is given by $Y = O \times P$ or $O = Y/P$.

TABLE 14–1 Gross National Product and its Components (in billions of dollars)

	1974	1979	1984
Consumption	888.1	1,507.2	2,341.8
Investment	228.7	423.0	637.8
Government purchases	304.1	474.4	747.4
Net exports	13.4	13.2	− 64.2
GNP	1,434.2	2,417.8	3,662.8
Addendum			
Implicit GNP price deflator (1972 = 1.00)	1.151	1.634	2.234
Real GNP in constant (1972) prices	1,246.3	1,479.4	1,639.3

SOURCE: U.S. Department of Commerce, *Survey of Current Business*, Washington, D.C., various issues.

FIGURE 14–1
The circular flow of expenditure and income

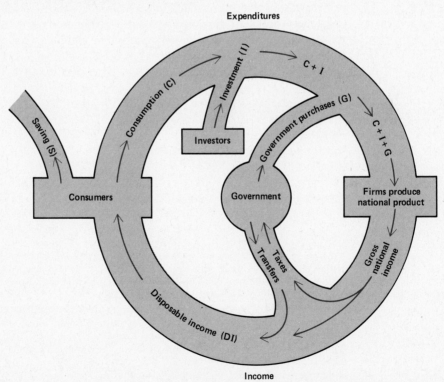

production takes place. The circular flow emerges from firms as payments to the various factors of production. We have relabled this flow "Gross national income," but as just indicated, gross national income and gross national product must be equal.[4]

Another way to see this is to consider what happens to a firm that produces and sells some dollar value of output. The bulk of these revenues must be used to pay its workers (wages), people who have lent it money (interest payments), and perhaps landlords who own the firm's building (rents). What is left over is received by the owners of the firm in the form of *profits.* But the income of these owners also counts in national income. Hence, when we add up all the factor payments, including profits, to obtain gross national income, we must also obtain the dollar value of expenditures, or GNP.

DISPOSABLE INCOME, SAVING, AND INVESTMENT

If we follow the circular flow past firms, we see that there are both some additions and some leakages in the income stream before it gets to consumers. The major leakage takes the form of taxes—on both individual and corporate incomes—collected by the government sector.[5] Partially offsetting this are government transfer payments, which may be thought of as negative taxes. Subtracting transfer payments from taxes yields *net taxes.* Net taxes thus represent the overall leakage in going from gross national income to what is known as consumer *disposable income.* In symbols, if we let DI = disposable income and T = net taxes, we have

$$DI = Y - T \tag{2}$$

As Figure 14–1 illustrates, disposable income flows to consumers, where it has two uses—it is consumed or saved.[6] We already have a symbol for consumption expenditures, C. If we denote *saving* by S, we can then express these two uses of disposable income by

$$DI = C + S \tag{3}$$

Combining equations (2) and (3), we have

$$Y - T = C + S$$

---

[4]What we have called gross national income is slightly different from the concept of national income as defined by the Department of Commerce. While for our purposes the differences are inconsequential, those who think they might be turned on by such arcane accounting matters should see Dernberg and McDougall, op. cit.

[5]As regards potential leakages, Figure 14–1 embodies a number of simplifications. For example, it assumes that all profits are paid out to owners of firms. In actual fact, some profits are retained by firms and contribute to business saving.

[6]While the saving flow appears to hit a dead end, as we saw in Chapter 3 it is recycled via financial markets or intermediaries to finance investment. This relationship between saving and investment is made more explicit in equation (6).

or

$$Y = C + S + T \tag{4}$$

Thus, we see that a third way to measure Y or GNP is by the various ways it can be disposed of—by consuming, saving, or paying taxes.

Finally, we can combine equations (1) and (4) to get

$$C + I + G = C + S + T$$

Eliminating C from both sides yields

$$I + G = S + T \tag{5}$$

Or, bringing G to the right-hand side of equation (5), we get

$$I = S + (T - G) \tag{6}$$

What equation (6) tells us is that there is an identity between investment on the one hand and saving plus the difference between net taxes and government expenditures on the other. The latter difference, $(T - G)$, is nothing other than the government surplus, if it is positive, or the government deficit, if it is negative. Another way to interpret $(T - G)$ is that it measures *government saving*— that is, government income (T) less government spending (G). Thus, the right-hand side of equation (6) can be interpreted as total saving, consisting of private saving, S, and government saving, $(T - G)$. In these terms, equation (6) simply expresses the accounting identity between saving and investment. We shall put this identity to good use as we proceed.

SOME SIMPLIFYING ASSUMPTIONS

For the remainder of this chapter, we concentrate on consumption, saving, and investment. Several characteristics of the following analysis should be borne in mind:

1 It is essentially short run in nature. That is, it does not attempt to analyze changes in the productive capacity of the economy through time; instead, it is concerned with the behavior of income and output within given capacity levels.
2 Unless otherwise indicated, it assumes that price level is constant, so that the money value of output is an index of the behavior of real output.
3 It assumes that there are no foreign transactions, so that exports and imports need not concern us for the present.
4 For the first part of the chapter, it assumes that the government engages in no economic activity, so that there are no taxes, government transfer payments, or government purchases. Thus, private disposable

income is equal to GNP. From equations (1), (4), and (6), with government spending (G) and net taxes (T) by assumption equal to zero, we have

$$Y = C + I = C + S$$

and

$$I = S$$

By temporarily ignoring the government sector we can decrease the number of variables and describe the principles involved more clearly. The government will be restored to the picture toward the end of the chapter. Our first task will be to develop consumption and savings functions.

CONSUMPTION AND SAVING

We now move from the accounting or definitional aspects of consumption and saving to the more interesting question of the determinants of consumer behavior.

THE FUNCTIONS

The most powerful determinant of private consumption and saving is the level of private disposable income, which in the absence of government is equal to total income. Both consumption and saving are positive functions of the level of income. That is, at higher levels of income, the private sectors will both consume more and save more; at lower levels of income, they will both consume less and save less. This is shown schematically in Figure 14–2. The level of income created (C + I) is measured on the horizontal axis. The amount of private disposable income (C + S) is measured on the vertical axis in part (a). As an expositional device we draw a line at a 45° angle through the origin. If a line is dropped vertically from any point on the 45° line, the vertical distance to the base is exactly equal to the horizontal distance from the origin to the point of intersection on the base. This illustrates the fact that the amount of disposable income (C + S) must be exactly equal to the amount of income created (C + I).

The CC line represents the *consumption function*. That is, it states consumption as a function of the level of income. The consumption function can also be stated algebraically:

$$C = B + \left(\frac{\Delta C}{\Delta Y}\right)Y \tag{7}$$

B = a positive constant, stated in billions of dollars. It is the height of the intercept on the vertical axis, and its size establishes the height of the consumption function

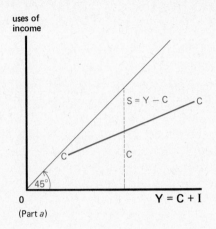

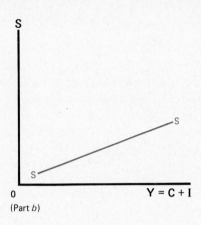

(Part *a*)   (Part *b*)

FIGURE 14–2
Private disposable income and its disposal

$$\frac{\Delta C}{\Delta Y}$$ = the slope of the consumption function

= the marginal propensity to consume

= MPC

The slope of the consumption function $(\Delta C/\Delta Y)$ indicates the marginal responsiveness of consumption to changes in the level of income. This is called the *marginal propensity to consume*, or MPC. A basic hypothesis of income theory is that the marginal propensity to consume $(\Delta C/\Delta Y)$ is greater than zero but less than one. That is, in response to a rise (or fall) of disposable income, the community will increase (or decrease) its consumption, but by an amount less than the change in income. For example, a $\Delta C/\Delta Y$ of 0.8 indicates that a given change of disposable income will change consumption by an amount equal to eight-tenths of the income change.[7]

The saving-supply function is shown in part (a) of Figure 14–2 as the vertical distance from the 45° line to the amount of consumption at that level of income. This necessarily follows from the fact that $S = Y - C$. For convenience, the saving-supply function, represented by the line *SS*, is shown separately in part (b) of Figure 14–2. It too is a positive function of income. Its slope $(\Delta S/\Delta Y)$ measures the marginal responsiveness of saving to income. This is called the *marginal propensity to save*, or MPS. The value of MPS is obviously related to the value of MPC. In fact, since $Y \equiv C + S$,

$$\Delta Y = \Delta C + \Delta S$$

[7]It is, of course, possible that the value of $\Delta C/\Delta Y$ will be different at different levels of income. We use a linear consumption function partly because of its simplicity and partly because empirical studies suggest that linear functions fit the data as well as other types of functions.

and, dividing both sides of the equation by ΔY, we get

$$1 = \frac{\Delta C}{\Delta Y} + \frac{\Delta S}{\Delta Y} \quad \text{or} \quad \frac{\Delta S}{\Delta Y} = 1 - \frac{\Delta C}{\Delta Y}$$

Thus, if $\Delta C/\Delta Y = 0.8$, then $\Delta S/\Delta Y = 0.2$. Any change in income must be equal to the changes in consumption and saving; any part that is not used to change consumption must be reflected in a change in saving.

It is important to remember that when we define either the consumption function or the saving-supply function, we are actually defining both functions because each function is simply Y minus the other function. For example, we obtain the saving-supply function by subtracting the consumption function from Y:

$$S = Y - \left(B + \frac{\Delta C}{\Delta Y} Y \right)$$

$$= Y - \frac{\Delta C}{\Delta Y} Y - B \tag{8}$$

$$= Y \left(1 - \frac{\Delta C}{\Delta Y} \right) - B$$

Since $1 - \Delta C/\Delta Y = \Delta S/\Delta Y$, we can also express the saving-supply function as

$$S = Y \frac{\Delta S}{\Delta Y} - B$$

OTHER FACTORS

Thus far we have concentrated on the effects of income on the level of consumption and saving. We did this because both a priori reasoning and empirical investigations indicate that income is the most powerful determinant of these variables.

This is not to say that the amounts of consumption and saving depend solely on the level of disposable income; many other factors help determine how any given level of disposable income will be divided between consumption and saving. Moreover, changes in these other factors can shift the consumption function up or down; that is, they can lead to more or less consumption at each level of income. Some of the more important of these factors are the following:

1 Social attitudes toward current consumption versus saving for the future.
2 Distribution of total household income by size of household income. For example, total saving out of a given level of total household income is likely to be higher if a greater part of the total income accrues to high-income classes rather than to low-income groups.

3 Age composition of the population. Both elderly and young families have higher propensities to consume than families in their middle years. A shift in age composition could shift consumption and saving functions.

4 The stock of wealth. Other things being equal, a wealthy community might be expected to consume a larger part of its income than a population with the same income but less wealth. "Windfall" capital gains or losses can increase or decrease the consumption function.

5 Expectations concerning future levels of income relative to current income levels. When future levels of income are expected to be higher than present levels, the community is likely to consume more out of its current income.

These are some of the factors that determine the height and shape of the consumption and saving functions. When we state consumption and personal saving as functions of disposable income, we implicitly assume that such other factors are constant in their effects.

DETERMINATION OF EQUILIBRIUM INCOME: A SPECIAL CASE

We can gain some insight into the workings of the consumption and saving functions by examining the determination of equilibrium income in the special case of an exogenously determined level of investment—that is, where investment is given from the outside. The major point to be made here is that income and output can be at an equilibrium level only when investment expenditure is exactly equal to the supply of saving. We have already encountered the *identity*, $I \equiv S$. This indicates that as a matter of national income accounting, saving always equals investment. Since this is always true, our equilibrium condition must be referring to a different kind of equality between saving and investment. This is indeed the case, and to see it we must distinguish between intended and unintended investment.

Intended investment is that part of investment stemming from business plans. That is, it is planned or "desired" investment. *Unintended investment* refers to the unforeseen changes in inventories arising because of unexpected changes in the level of demand or sales. Obviously, equilibrium requires that unintended investment be zero, so that we must have: intended investment = saving. This latter equality is clearly not an identity, but rather an equilibrium condition. The working of this condition is illustrated in Figure 14–3, where we have plotted a saving function, SS, and a line indicating the intended level of investment, II.

Given the II and SS functions, the only equilibrium level of Y is Y_0. Only at this level of Y is the investment demand for output exactly equal to the supply of output represented by the supply of saving—that is, to the supply of output in excess of the amount taken off the market by C. Only at this level of Y is the market just cleared of output, with neither excess demand

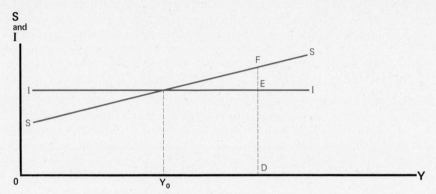

FIGURE 14–3
The equality of investment demand and the
supply of saving

nor excess supply. Any level of Y greater than Y_0 would be a level of disequilibrium, because the supply of output represented by saving would
exceed investment demand; some part of the supply would not be cleared
from the market. Consider, for example, point D in Figure 14–3, which
corresponds to some level of income greater than Y_0. At this level of income,
saving is given by DF. Actual or realized investment will, of course, equal
actual saving, DF, and this clearly exceeds intended investment which is
DE. Indeed, the difference, EF, represents the amount of unintended investment. Clearly, point D is one of disequilibrium. Producers of goods are
not selling all they would like, and some of their output is piling up in
unintended inventories. When such a situation occurs, producers will respond by reducing their rate of output, thus lowering Y. In this process
they might temporarily reduce their output below Y_0 until their excess
inventories had been sold off.

Any level of output below Y_0 would be a level of disequilibrium, because
at lower levels of Y the investment demand for output would exceed the
supply of output represented by saving. Faced by such a situation of excess
demand, producers might immediately increase their rate of output, thereby
raising the level of Y. If they did not increase the output rate fast enough,
they would experience an unwanted depletion of their inventories, which
would lead them to accelerate production in order to rebuild their stocks.
In this process they might temporarily raise their rate of output above Y_0
until their inventories had been replenished.

Thus, we see that equality of intended investment demand and saving
supply is always a necessary condition for an equilibrium level of Y. We
now turn to the question of what happens to the level of income as a result
of changes in the level of intended investment. To help answer this, we
shall introduce the notion of the multiplier.

THE MULTIPLIER

The multiplier is one of the key concepts in Keynesian models of income determination. It refers to the fact that an autonomous increase or decrease of expenditures for output can increase or decrease total expenditures for output by some multiple by inducing a change of consumption expenditures in the same direction. This effect results from the positive slope of the consumption function, which posits that the community will increase its consumption expenditures by a fraction, equal to $\Delta C/\Delta Y$, or MPC, of each increase in its disposable income. The total effect on the level of expenditures for output (ΔY) is equal to the autonomous rise of expenditure (designated by ΔE) plus the induced change of consumption (ΔC). In symbols, we have

$$\Delta Y = \Delta C + \Delta E \tag{9}$$

An autonomous change in expenditures can take any one of several forms. For example, an autonomous increase can be in the form of a rise of investment demand (ΔI) or an upward shift of the consumption function, which is the same as a downward shift of the saving-supply function.[8] To illustrate the principles involved, let us assume that the autonomous change is an increase of investment demand (ΔI), that $\Delta I = \$100$, and that investment demand remains at this higher level. Thus, in terms of our previous notation we have $\Delta E = \Delta I = 100$.

What we are interested in finding is the *investment multiplier*, which is the ratio of the change in Y to the change in I, or $\Delta Y/\Delta I$. We can do this algebraically or diagrammatically. We begin with some simple algebra.

Since $\Delta E = \Delta I$, we can write equation (9) as

$$\Delta Y = \Delta C + \Delta I \tag{10}$$

Now, from the definition of the marginal propensity to consume, we have $\Delta C/\Delta Y = $ MPC or $\Delta C = $ MPC $\times \Delta Y$. Thus, we have

$$\Delta Y = \text{MPC} \times \Delta Y + \Delta I$$

or

$$(1 - \text{MPC}) \times \Delta Y = \Delta I$$

The outcome is then

$$\frac{\Delta Y}{\Delta I} = \frac{1}{1 - \text{MPC}} \tag{11}$$

[8]Although we are temporarily excluding the government and foreign sectors from our consideration, it should be noted that an autonomous increase in expenditures can also take the form of a rise of government purchases of goods and services or a rise in foreign demand for American exports.

What equation (11) tells us that the investment multiplier is $1/(1 - \text{MPC})$. Alternatively, since $1 - \dfrac{\Delta C}{\Delta Y} = \dfrac{\Delta S}{\Delta Y}$, we have $1 - \text{MPC} = \text{MPS}$. We can then also write the multiplier as

$$\frac{\Delta Y}{\Delta I} = \frac{1}{\text{MPS}} = \frac{1}{\Delta S/\Delta Y} \tag{12}$$

To illustrate this numerically, suppose that $\Delta C/\Delta Y = 0.8$ and $\Delta S/\Delta Y = 0.2$. The multiplier is then $1/.2$ or 5. Thus, if, as assumed, $\Delta I = 100$, then $\Delta Y = 5 \times 100 = 500$.

It should be clear that as $\Delta C/\Delta Y$ increases (that is, as $\Delta S/\Delta Y$ grows smaller), the multiplier will become larger. It should also be clear that the multiplier operates downward in response to an autonomous decline of expenditures. For example, trace the effects on Y if investment falls by \$50 and remains at the lower level, and $\Delta C/\Delta Y = 0.8$.

The multiplier process can also be explained diagrammatically in terms of saving-investment relationships. For example, suppose that, starting from the equilibrium income level, Y_0 at which $I = S$, I rises by \$100 and remains at this higher level (see Figure 14–4). Y_0 is no longer an equilibrium level, because of that level of income there will now be a \$100 excess of I over S, which will drive income upward. If I remains at its new higher level, a new equilibrium will be reached only when S is also increased by \$100. But with a given saving-supply function, S can be increased only by an increase of Y. How much Y will have to rise to increase S by \$100 varies reciprocally with the marginal responsiveness of S to Y. Suppose $\Delta S/\Delta Y = 0.2$. In this case Y must rise by \$500 to increase S by \$100.

Let us consider this in steps:

1 Since I has risen \$100 and remains at the new level, S must rise by the same amount if a new equilibrium is to be established.

FIGURE 14–4
Multiplier effects of an increase in investment

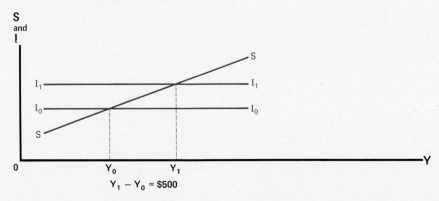

2 With a given saving-supply function, only a rise of Y can increase S, and each rise of Y will increase S by an amount equal to $\Delta S/\Delta Y$.

3 Since the required rise of $S = \$100$, we can write

$$\$100 = \Delta Y \frac{\Delta S}{\Delta Y}$$

Dividing both sides of the equation by $\Delta S/\Delta Y$ to find the required increase of Y, we get

$$\Delta Y = \$100 \times \frac{1}{\Delta S/\Delta Y}$$

If $\Delta S/\Delta Y = 0.2$,

$$\Delta Y = 100 \frac{1}{0.2} = \$500$$

Only if Y rises by this amount can it be in equilibrium with $I = S$. Any smaller rise of Y would leave S smaller than I, and the excess demand for output would continue to increase Y. On the other hand, any larger rise of Y would make S larger than I, and excess supply of output over the total demand for output would serve to depress Y.

The multiplier approach, then, provides a direct answer to the question of how equilibrium income will change following a change in autonomous investment. To clarify the multiplier principle, we have employed an elementary model and made some simplifying assumptions. One of the latter is that investment is determined autonomously and does not respond to economic forces. This, of course, is rather implausible, and we must now modify this assumption. We do so by introducing the interest rate as a determinant of investment spending. As we will see later, this will have important consequences for the interpretation of the multiplier approach.

INVESTMENT DEMAND FUNCTIONS

An investment demand function indicates the values of output demanded for investment purposes at each possible rate of interest. The latter will be denoted by r. Note that because we are interested in determining an equilibrium level of Y, we include in investment demand only intended or desired changes in business inventories. The investment demand function thus corresponds to the notion of intended investment introduced earlier.

Most of the components of investment demand (I) are demands by business for output with which to maintain or increase stocks of capital goods. These demanders are presumably motivated by a desire for profits, perhaps a desire to maximize profits. For this purpose they compare the expected returns from new investment with the costs involved. However, some of investment demand, notably expenditures by homeowners for new residential construction, may not be profit motivated. But even these demanders presumably arrive at decisions by balancing expected benefits and costs; and, other conditions being constant, they will presumably buy less when the cost to them is higher. Interest costs are an important part of the carrying charges of a house.

An investment demand function, such as that illustrated in Figure 14–5, is a typical demand curve showing the relation of quantity demanded to price. In this case the price of loan funds, or the interest rate on investable funds, is measured along the horizontal axis. The values of output demanded for investment are measured along the vertical axis. The II curve depicts the size of investment demand at the various possible levels of r. From the point of view of spenders for investment, r is the cost. If they get the money to finance investment by borrowing from othes, r is the annual interest rate they must pay to lenders. If they finance their investment spending by using their own money, r is their opportunity cost; it is the interest rate they sacrifice by using the money rather than by lending it to someone else. It is therefore plausible to assume that, other things remaining the same, a rise of interest rates will decrease the actual investment demand for output and a fall of interest rates will stimulate it.

The investment demand function can also be stated in algebraic terms:

$$I = D - \frac{\Delta I}{\Delta r}r \qquad (13)$$

where

D = a positive constant in billions of dollars. It is the intercept on the vertical axis and establishes the location of the I function

r = the interest rate

FIGURE 14–5
An investment demand function

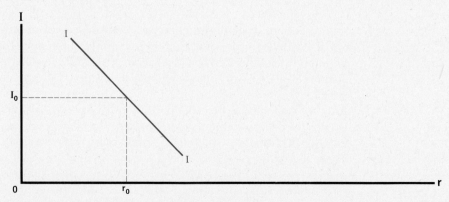

$\Delta I/\Delta r$ = the marginal responsiveness of investment to the interest rate. $\Delta I/\Delta r$ is to be interpreted as a positive number so that the negative slope to Figure 14–5 stems from the minus sign in equation (13)

We are engaging in oversimplification in assuming a single interest rate in the market. There are, of course, many rates. Moreover, other terms of lending and borrowing may change: the length of time for which lenders will make funds available, the risks that they will take at any given interest rate, and so on. Nevertheless, it will be convenient to let r represent the height of the structure of interest rates and the annual cost per dollar of borrowed funds.

In drawing any demand curve, we have to assume that all other conditions affecting demand are given and unchanged. But it is important to know what determines the position of the demand curve. We need to answer questions such as: Why is the demand curve neither higher nor lower at each level of interest rates? What forces can shift I upward at each rate of interest? What forces can shift the curve downward? To answer such questions, we need to know the motivations of those who spend for investment, and the nature of the benefits they balance against interest costs in arriving at decisions as to whether and how much to spend for investment.

MARGINAL EFFICIENCY OF INVESTMENT

The great bulk of investment expenditures are made by business firms intent on making net profits. In determining whether or not to make a capital expenditure, they ask: "Will the acquisition of this capital good add at least as much to revenues as it adds to costs?" This applies to purchases for replacement as well as to net additions to capital. Decisions as to the amount of new investment therefore depend on a comparison of interest costs and the expected annual rate of return on new investment. The latter has been given many names, including *marginal revenue product of capital* and *marginal efficiency of investment*. We use the latter term and define it as the annual amount (stated as a percentage of the cost of the capital goods) that the acquisitions of the new capital goods is expected to add to the enterprise's net revenues after deduction of all additional costs of operation except interest costs on the money used. For our purposes, we view the marginal efficiency of investment as a schedule or function showing the various amounts of new investment that are expected to yield at least various rates of return. The demand for investment is derived from the marginal efficiency of investment schedule. Enterprisers intent on maximizing their profits tend to buy those types and amounts of capital that they expect to yield a rate of return in excess of the interest cost of the money used to purchase them. Presumably, they will not buy capital whose expected rate of return is below the interest rate.

Note we have emphasized that the *expected* annual rate of return is a prime consideration in the selection of a new investment. Enterprisers select their investments on the basis of their expectations of future yields—their decisions are based on the best forecasts they can make. They cannot be certain that the returns will meet their expectations because many types of capital yield their returns only over a long period and much can change in the interim. But they must make decisions, even if they recognize the fallibility of their forecasts.

Of the many factors that affect the schedule of the marginal efficiency of investment, some of the more important are listed below.

1   **SIZE AND COMPOSITION OF STOCK.** If the existing stock of capital goods is largely obsolete and too small to produce economically the rate of output currently demanded, large amounts of new investment may be expected to yield high rates of return. But if the existing stock of capital goods is efficient and very large relative to the current demand for output, only small amounts of new investment will be profitable. If there is already excess capacity, business firms may refrain from replacing some equipment when it wears out.

2   **RATE OF INNOVATION.** If the rate of innovation is high, it may be profitable to undertake much new investment in order to produce the new types of products or to use new and more economical processes of production.

3   **EXPECTED FUTURE BEHAVIOR OF DEMANDS FOR OUTPUT.** If demands for output are expected to rise rapidly, much new investment may be expected to yield high profits. If demands for output are expected to remain at existing levels and the present stock of capital goods is adequate, the demand for new capital goods may be largely a replacement demand. And if demands for output are expected to decline, potential spenders for investment may not replace their capital equipment when it wears out.

4   **COST EXPECTATIONS.** Expectations as to future wages, other costs, taxes, and government policies also determine investment efficiency. Estimates of the profitability of new investment may be greatly affected by expectations regarding the future course of these factors.

As should be evident from this list, many factors are capable of altering the marginal efficiency of investment. This point should be borne in mind for two reasons:

1   When we draw an investment demand schedule to show the effects of interest rates on investment demand, we are assuming that the schedule of the marginal efficiency of investment is given and constant.

2   We will later want to deal with upward and downward shifts of the

investment demand schedule and their effects on Y. An upward shift of the II curve, an increase of investment demand at each interest rate, may be brought about by any force that raises the marginal efficiency of investment schedule. The II curve may be shifted downward at each level of interest rates by anything that lowers the marginal efficiency of investment schedule.

MARGINAL RESPONSIVENESS OF INVESTMENT DEMAND TO INTEREST RATES

Let us now return to the investment-demand curve drawn on the assumption that the marginal efficiency of investment is given and constant, and which therefore enables us to consider the effects of interest rates on the size of the investment demand for output. In determining the equilibrium level of Y, it is sometimes sufficient to know that I tends to be larger when r is lower, and lower when r is higher. For some purposes, however, it is useful to try to quantify this relationship, to ask how much a given change in interest rates would alter the size of the investment demand. We shall call this the *marginal responsiveness of investment to interest rates.* By this we mean the dollar change in the annual rate of investment expenditure for output in response to a change of 1 percentage point in the interest rate. As in equation (13) this will be denoted by $\Delta I/\Delta r$, the slope of the investment demand function. In Figure 14–6, $\Delta I/\Delta r$ is clearly larger on the $I_0 I_0$ investment demand curve than it is on the $I_1 I_1$ curve.[9]

[9]An investment demand curve need not, of course, be a straight line, and the value of $\Delta I/\Delta r$ may be different at different ranges of interest rates.

FIGURE 14–6
The marginal responsiveness of investment demand to the interest rate

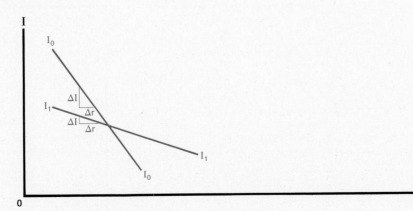

THE *IS* CURVE

In an earlier model, which assumed that investment demand is unaffected by the level of interest rates, we found not only that equality of I and S is a necessary condition for equilibrium, but also that I and S functions alone were sufficient to determine a unique equilibrium level of Y. The latter conclusion is not valid when I is responsive to the level of r. In this case, there are many combinations of Y and r that satisfy the necessary condition for equilibrium, $I = S$. This is shown graphically in Figure 14–7.

The vertical scales in parts (a) and (b) of Figure 14–7 are the same, so that the same vertical heights indicate equal amounts of S and I. Even a casual inspection of the two upper graphs reveals various combinations of interest rates and income levels that will produce the condition $I = S$. For example, $S = I$ at the low vertical level $I_0 S_0$ if r is at the high level r_0, thereby holding I to a low level, and if Y is at the low level Y_0, thereby generating only a low supply of S. $I = S$ at the somewhat higher level $I_1 S_1$ if the rate of interest is at the lower level r_1, thereby stimulating I, and if Y is at the higher level Y_1, thereby generating a larger supply of saving. $I = S$ at the very high level $I_2 S_2$ if the rate of interest is at the very low level r_2 and income is at the high level Y_2. We might thus note all the possible combinations of interest rate levels and income levels that would produce the condition $I = S$.

FIGURE 14–7
Investment demand and the supply of saving

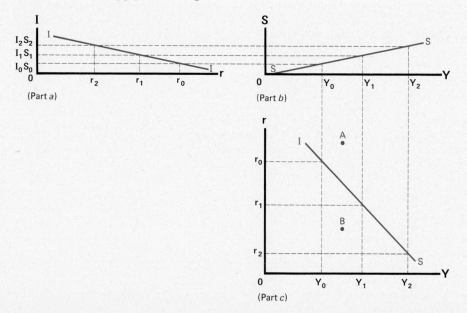

(Part a)

(Part b)

(Part c)

This is done in part (c) of Figure 14–7. The line $I = S$ plots out all those combinations of r, measured on the vertical axis, and Y, measured on the horizontal axis, at which S and I would be equal. The IS curve slopes downward to the right because the supply of S would be larger at higher levels of income, and with a given investment demand function, I can be made correspondingly larger only by a fall of r.

The same conclusions emerge from the numerical example in Table 14–2. This table is based on the types of consumption, saving, and investment functions presented earlier in equations (7), (8), and (13). The following values are assumed.

$C = 130 + 0.8Y$

$S = 0.2Y - 130$

$I = 130 - 10r$

It will be noted that $I = S$ at every combination of Y and r shown in the table. For example, $I = S = \$120$ at $Y = \$1,250$ and $r = 1$ percent; $I = S = \$70$ at $Y = \$1,000$ and $r = 6$ percent; and so on. Note also that when $I = S$, $Y = C + I$. Thus, we could also analyze total demand for output by adding together the consumption and investment demand functions.

Let us return to part (c) of Figure 14–7. No point representing a combination of r and Y that is off the IS curve can represent equilibrium conditions. For example, consider any point A that lies above the IS curve. At any such point, I would be less than S. We know this because at the same level of Y there is some lower rate of interest directly below A on the IS curve at which I is exaclty equal to S. If, by some chance, the combination of r and Y represented by point A should occur, the excess of S over I could be remedied only by a fall of interest rates to stimulate I, a decline of Y to reduce S, or some combination of changes of r and Y to a point on the IS curve. On the other hand, at any point such as B, below the IS curve, I would be greater than S. We know this because at the same level of Y there is some higher rate of interest directly above B on the IS curve at which I

TABLE 14–2 Equality of *I* and *S* with *I* Responsive to *r*

r (percent)	Y	C	S	I
1	1,250	1,130	120	120
2	1,200	1,090	110	110
3	1,150	1,050	100	100
4	1,100	1,010	90	90
5	1,050	970	80	80
6	1,000	930	70	70
7	950	890	60	60
8	900	850	50	50
9	850	810	40	40

is exactly equal to S. A disequilibrium combination such as B could be remedied only by a rise of r to reduce I, an increase of Y to increase S, or a combination of changes of r and Y to a point on the IS curve.

Any combination of Y and r that is off the IS curve is not only one of disequilibrium but also creates pressure serving to return the level of Y to some point on the IS curve. For example, a combination above the line with saving supply exceeding investment demand indicates that there is an excess of the total supply of output over the total demand for output $(C + I)$. This deficiency of demand will lead producers to reduce output and employment. On the other hand, a combination below the line with I exceeding S indicates an excess of total demand for output $(C + I)$ over the total supply of output, thus inducing producers to expand output and employment. However, the point on the IS curve to which Y returns need not to be a point of full employment.

SHIFTING THE *IS* CURVE

As we have seen, the IS curve represents the pairs of r and Y that are consistent with equality between intended investment and saving, or in other words, that are consistent with equilibrium in the market for commodities or goods. The precise location and shape of the IS curve is determined jointly by the saving and investment functions. This suggests that anything which changes either of these underlying functions will shift the IS curve. A particular example of this, the case of an upward shift in the investment demand function, is illustrated in Figure 14–8.

Assume that the initial situation from which we begin is represented by the IS curve labeled I_0S_0, which is derived from the investment demand function I_0I_0 and the saving-supply function S_0S_0. Assume further that the equilibrium level of interest rates is r_0 and the equilibrium level of income of Y_0. Suppose now that the investment demand function shifts upward at each level of interest rates by $100, rising to I_1I_1, while the saving-supply function remains unchanged. The various combinations of Y and r that formerly equated S and I will no longer do so; at each such combination I now exceeds S by $100. At any given level of interest rates, S can be raised to the level of I only by a rise of Y. As before, the amount by which Y must rise to increase S by $100 varies reciprocally with $\Delta S/\Delta Y$. If $\Delta S/\Delta Y = 0.2$,

$$\Delta Y = \$100 \, \frac{1}{0.2} = \$500$$

The new IS curve, labeled I_1S_1, lies to the right of the initial curve I_0S_0 at each level of interest rates by the amount $500. In other words, the amount by which the IS curve has shifted to the right depends directly on the size of the multiplier—that is, on the reciprocal of $\Delta S/\Delta Y$.

Unlike the case previously considered, in the present instance, where I is responsive to the level of interest rates, the multiplier analysis in its

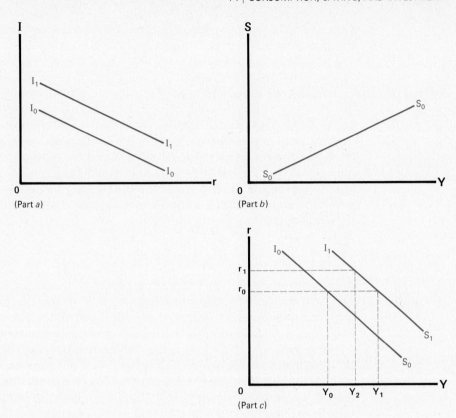

FIGURE 14–8
Shift of investment demand

simplest form is not sufficient to determine the new equilibrium level of Y. Without introducing other information, all we can say is that the new equilibrium level of Y must lie on I_1S_1, for this includes all combinations of Y and r that equate I and S. if interest rates remain unchanged at the level r_0, the full multiplier effect on income will be realized, with income rising from Y_0 to Y_1. Suppose, however, that in this process interest rates are increased, perhaps from r_0 to r_1. As we will see in the next chapter, this is quite likely to happen if monetary policy is not such as to prevent a rise of rates. In this case the full multiplier effect will not be realized. Some of the rise of investment expenditures that would have occurred if interest rates had remained constant will be "snubbed" by the rise of interest rates.

We have illustrated in detail the effects on the *IS* curve of an upward shift in the investment demand function. However, the *IS* curve can shift in other ways as well. For example, a downward shift of the *I* function at each level of r will shift the *IS* curve to the left by an amount equal to the downward shift of *I* times the multiplier. Similarly, an upward shift of the saving function (which is equivalent to a downward shift in the consumption function) will also shift the *IS* curve to the left.

INTRODUCING THE GOVERNMENT

So far we have deliberately ignored the activities of the government, assuming that both government receipts and expenditures were zero. This was done so that the number of variables could be reduced and we could concentrate on the behavior of private consumption, saving, and investment. Now we add the government to the picture. Specifically, we consider government expenditures for goods and services (designated by *G*), and net taxes (designated by *T*).

GOVERNMENT PURCHASES OF GOODS AND SERVICES (G)

As already indicated, *G* includes all expenditures by federal, state, and local governments for currently produced goods and services. Like any other form of expenditure for output, *G* is both a part of the aggregate demand for output and a contributor to the total of national income shares.

We assume that *G* is exogenously determined by the government and is not responsive to changes in the level of *Y*. The government can, of course, increase or decrease the level of *G*. Our earlier analysis suggests immediately that upward or downward shifts of *G* will serve to induce upward or downward multiplier effects, just as would similar shifts of the *I* or *C* functions.

NET TAXES (T)

As noted above, net taxes are defined as taxes minus transfers. As we will see, both taxes and transfers are responsive to the level of income, with taxes increasing as income rises and transfers decreasing as income rises. Consequently, for both reasons, net taxes tend to increase as income increases and decrease as income decreases. This is illustrated in Figure 14–9, where the net tax function, *TT*, is shown as a positively sloped function of *Y*. In keeping with our earlier assumption, government spending is shown as unresponsive to *Y* (i.e., the level of *GG* does not vary with *Y*). We now briefly explore the reasons for the upward slope of the *TT* curve, beginning with taxes.

Taxes include all receipts by federal, state, and local governments on income and product account. Thus they include not only taxes in the narrow sense of the term, but also various types of license fees and contributions by employers and employees to government-sponsored social insurance programs.

Total yields of the American tax system are highly responsive to changes

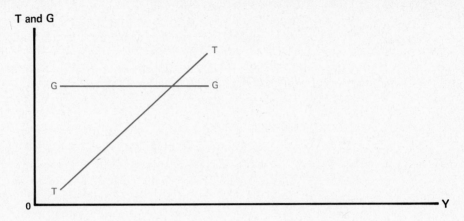

FIGURE 14–9
T and G

in the level of GNP. With a given tax program on the books, defining both the things subject to tax and applicable tax rates, total yields rise and fall sharply with increases and decreases of *Y*. This is not true of all types of taxes. For example, total yields of property taxes and certain types of fees do not respond automatically to changes in *Y* in the absence of action by the tax authorities. It is, however, true of taxes that account for the great bulk of government receipts. Corporate profits usually vary directly with *Y*, and in recent years these have been subject to marginal tax rates fluctuating around 50 percent. Yields of personal income taxes, which exempt certain amounts of household income and tax the remainder at graduated rates, are highly sensitive to changes in *Y*. So are total contributions for social insurance, which are based on payrolls. Total revenues from various taxes on production and sales, included in indirect business taxes, also vary with *Y*.

We turn now to government transfers. These, it will be recalled, are payments for which the government does not receive goods or services in return. At least some of these payments are responsive to the level of *Y* and tend to rise when *Y* falls and to decline when *Y* rises, especially to the extent that changes in *Y* are accompanied by changes of unemployment in the opposite direction. This is clearest in the case of unemployment benefits. A rise of unemployment increases total unemployment benefit payments, which serve to cushion the decline of private incomes; and a decline of unemployment reduces these payments. Some other transfer payments are also responsive to changes in income levels and employment opportunities. For example, when employment opportunities are scarce for the elderly, some retire earlier and draw old-age benefits. Direct relief payments also tend to vary directly with the amount of unemployment.

As should be apparent by now, there are ample reasons to assert that net taxes depend positively on the level of Y as portrayed in Figure 14–9. What this also suggests is that net tax receipts will fluctuate automatically as the level of Y changes. This fact is of great significance for the behavior of private disposable income and for the stability of the economy as a whole.

NET TAXES AS AN AUTOMATIC STABILIZER

As we saw earlier, total private disposable income at any level of GNP is equal to $Y - T$. Thus, the higher the level of Y, the greater the difference between Y and private disposable incomes. This is often referred to as an *automatic stabilizer effect*, although automatic *snubber* effect would be a more accurate description. These are the effects that follow automatically from an initial decline of Y even if the government makes no change in G, in its tax system or in its transfer payment program. If there is an initial decline of Y and no change at all in total T, the full impact of the decline of Y will fall on private disposable incomes. However, to the extent that the decline of Y is reflected in a decrease of T, the impact on private disposable incomes is reduced, with a corresponding decrease of pressures for further reductions of private spending. The decline of Y is snubbed.

On the other hand, an increase of expenditures for output may occur when the economy is already operating at virtually full employment levels and an undesirable rate of price inflation threatens. If total T remained constant, the full increase of Y would be reflected in private disposable incomes. To the extent that the rise of Y is absorbed by an increase of T, the rise of private disposable incomes is snubbed.

Such automatic stabilizer or snubber effects can be quite powerful. Their strength is determined by what might be called the *marginal responsiveness of net tax receipts to Y*. Pictorially, this marginal responsiveness is nothing other than the slope of the TT function in Figure 14–9, which we can denote by $\Delta T/\Delta Y$. The value of $\Delta T/\Delta Y$ depends on the nature and rates of taxes. Currently, $\Delta T/\Delta Y$ appears to be at least 30 percent. That is, each \$1 increase or decrease of GNP raises or lowers T by at least 30 cents.

While such strong snubber effects often contribute to the stability of the economy, they sometimes militate against recovery of economic activity. For example, in the early 1960s, when unemployment remained excessive, the large increases of T with each rise of Y snubbed the rise of aggregate private demands for output and slowed recovery. There was an automatic fiscal drag. This was remedied by a tax reduction in 1964—a downward shift of the TT function in Figure 14–9. On other occasions, when it becomes desirable to curb aggregate demand, the government can shift its net tax function upward. For example, by broadening tax bases or raising tax rates or both, it can increase T at each level of Y, thus serving to lower private disposable incomes at each level of Y. In subsequent chapters we explore such policy actions more fully.

THE *IS* CURVE, INCLUDING GOVERNMENT

Having investigated the basic ingredients of the government's fiscal operations, we are now in a position to modify the *IS* curve to allow for the
effect of government activity. Introduction of the government requires several important changes. For one thing, we introduce another type of expenditure for output, *G*, so that total demand for output becomes $C + I
+ G$. Also, the introduction of taxes and government transfer payments
alters the relationship between GNP and total private disposable income;
these two items would be the same in a system without taxes or government transfer programs. Finally, allowance for the government introduces
government saving into the analysis, so that total saving is now given by
the sum of government saving and private saving. Based on this observation,
in fact, we can proceed to modify the *IS* curve to take account of the
government.

This *IS* curve is, of course, defined by the condition that investment
equals saving. In the absence of the government, this was algebraically
expressed by $I = S$. As we saw previously, however, in the presence of the
government the algebraic expression for investment equals saving is slightly
more complicated. This is due to the existence of government saving,
$(T - G)$. The precise condition is given by equation (5) or, equivalently,
equation (6). For convenience, these equations are repeated here.

$$I + G = S + T \tag{5}$$

$$I = S + (T - G) \tag{6}$$

Equation (6) reminds us that equilibrium in the goods market requires that
investment equal private saving plus government saving. The equivalent
equation (5) is actually more useful for constructing the new *IS* curve.

We have graphed the two sides of equation (5) in Figure 14–10. The line
labeled $I + G$ in part (a) shows how the left-hand side of equation (5) varies
with the interest rate. This line is derived from our familiar investment
demand function, which is shown as *II* in part (a). In particular, since *G* is
exogenously determined by the government, the line $I + G$ is simply obtained by uniformly shifting up the investment demand function by the
amount *G*.

In part (b) we have graphed the right-hand side of equation (5). The *SS*
curve is the saving-supply function we have encountered earlier and corresponds to private saving. The *TT* curve, which is taken from Figure 14–9,
shows how taxes less transfers depend on *Y*. The sum of the *SS* and *TT*
curves, labeled $S + T$ in part (b), thus corresponds to the right-hand side
of equation (5).

The alert reader may have noted that in drawing *S* and $S + T$ as functions of *Y* in Figure 14–10 we have glossed over one step. As emphasized
earlier, both consumption and saving are functions of disposable income,

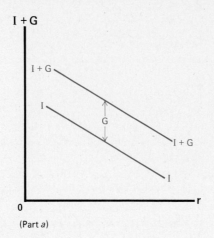
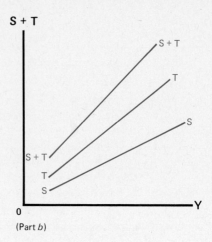

(Part *a*)   (Part *b*)

FIGURE 14–10
Investment and saving, including government

$Y - T$. How then did we get rid of the T? The trick is to recognize that net taxes, T, is itself a function of Y (see Figure 14–9). Consequently, we can use this relationship to eliminate T and express S as a function of Y rather than $Y - T$. A numerical example may help illustrate the point. Consider the following consumption and saving functions:

$$C = 100 + 0.8DI = 100 + 0.8(Y - T)$$
$$S = -100 + 0.2DI = -100 + 0.2(Y - T)$$

which clearly satisfy $C + S = DI = Y - T$. Now suppose that $T = 0.25Y$; that is, there is a flat 25 percent tax rate on Y. We then have

$$S = -100 + 0.2(Y - 0.25Y)$$
$$= -100 + 0.15Y$$

We have thus expressed S as a function of Y. This in turn can be used to express $S + T$ as a function of Y, thus fully justifying part (b) of Figure 14–10.[10] With this little detail out of the way, we are ready to proceed.

Armed with the two curves in Figure 14–10, we can now construct an *IS* curve. This is shown diagrammatically in Figure 14–11. The vertical scales in parts (a) and (b) of Figure 14–11 are the same, so that the same vertical heights indicate equal amounts of $(I + G)$ annd $(S + T)$. The resulting *IS* curve, giving the combinations of pairs of r and Y that satisfy equation (5), is shown in part (c). The reader will immediately recognize that we are following the same procedure used earlier; that is, in the absence of the

[10]Since $T = 0.25Y$, we have $S + T = -100 + 0.4Y$. Substituting for T in the consumption function also gives $C = 100 + 0.6Y$. Hence, we see that $C + S + T = 100 + 0.6Y - 100 + 0.4Y = Y$, as it should. This numerical example is taken up again in the appendix to the next chapter.

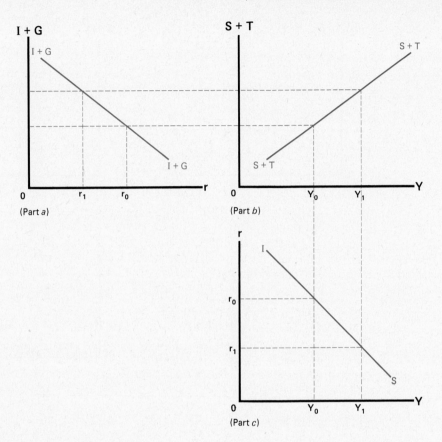

FIGURE 14–11
Construction of the *IS* Curve

government. Indeed, the only difference between our earlier derivation in Figure 14–7 and the present one in Figure 14–11 is that the curve labeled $I + G$ has replaced the *II* curve in part (a) and the curve labeled $S + T$ has replaced the *SS* schedule in part (b). Conceptually at least, this is really a minor modification.

While the *IS* curve is conceptually the same with or without the government, the actual shape and location of the *IS* curve will, of course, depend on the level of government expenditures and the nature of the *TT* function. Furthermore, shifts in the level of G or in the tax or transfer functions will induce corresponding shifts in the *IS* curve.

SHIFTING THE *IS* CURVE: A CHANGE IN G

As an example, let us first consider how the *IS* curve would shift as a result of an increase in government expenditures. The effects of this are illustrated in Figure 14–12. The direct effect of an increase in G is to shift the curve

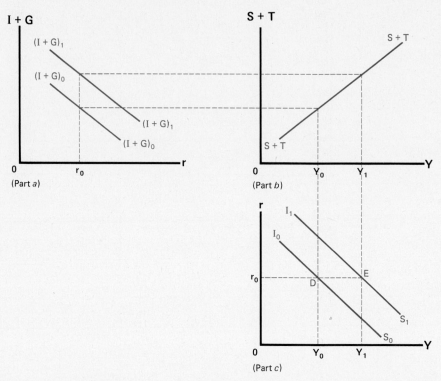

FIGURE 14–12
Shift of government expenditures

for $I + G$ upward. That is, at any given level of interest rates, $I + G$ is now higher. This is shown in part (a) as a movement from $(I + G)_0$ to $(I + G)_1$. The $(S + T)$ function in part (b) is unchanged by the increase in G. To see what happens to the IS curve let us trace our way around Figure 14–12, beginning at r_0 in part (a). Before the increase in G, r_0 was associated with the income level Y_0. This is shown as point D in part (c) on $I_0 S_0$, the original IS curve. After the increase in G, we see from part (b) that a higher income level, Y_1, now corresponds to r_0. This is shown as point E on the new IS curve, labeled $I_1 S_1$ in part (c). By choosing alternative starting values for the interest rate one can trace out the entire curve $I_1 S_1$.

Quite evidently, an increase in G serves to shift the IS curve to the right. In this respect, an increase in government expenditures is analogous to any other increase in autonomous spending which would also shift the IS curve to the right. Such increases could arise, for example, from upward shifts in the investment demand or consumption functions. It should be equally clear that a decrease in government spending will shift the IS curve to the left.

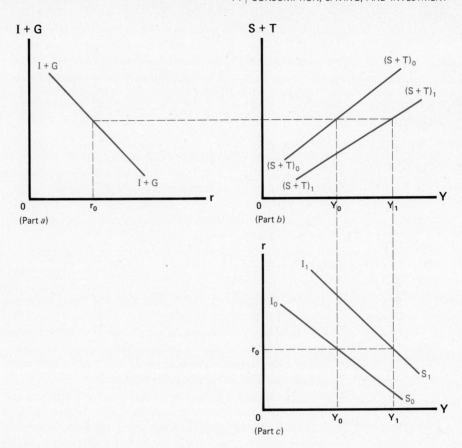

FIGURE 14–13
Shift of tax or transfer function

SHIFTING THE *IS* CURVE: A CHANGE IN *T*

As a final example, let us consider how the *IS* curve would shift as a result
of a reduction in taxes or an increase in transfer payments. Either of these
actions would serve to produce a downward shift in the *TT* function, and
this in turn would lead to a downward shift in the $(S + T)$ function.[11] This
is illustrated in part (b) of Figure 14–13, where the initial state of affairs is
given by the curve labeled $(S + T)_0$ and the relevant curve after this shift
is given by $(S + T)_1$. Again, by tracing our way around the figure we see
that the end result is to shift the *IS* curve to the right. Thus, we see that a

---

[11]The shift in the $(S + T)$ function will be less than the shift in the *TT* function. This is because
there will be a partially offsetting rise of S at each level of Y as private disposable income is
increased.

decrease in taxes tends to have the same impact on the *IS* curve as an increase in government spending, a result that makes good intuitive sense. There are, however, important economic differences between the tax cuts and expenditure increases, and these will be explored in a later chapter.

SUMMARY

1 Gross national product or GNP is composed of three main categories of expenditure for output: personal consumption, gross private domestic investment, and government purchases of goods and services. GNP can also be viewed as the gross national income generated in the economy. Another income concept, disposable income, is defined as gross income less net taxes paid.

2 Several building blocks are necessary to understand the determination of aggregate demand. The first of these is the consumption function, which states that personal consumption depends positively on the level of disposable income. The slope of the consumption function is called the marginal propensity to consume. The second key building block is the investment demand function, which posits that investment depends negatively on the interest rate. While it simplifies graphic exposition to make consumption and investment each depend on a single variable, in reality each depends on a number of other factors.

3 The *IS* curve expresses the combinations of the interest rate and output that equate savings and investment. Another way of saying this is that the *IS* curve characterizes the combinations of r and Y which assure equilibrium in the goods market. The *IS* curve is downward-sloping.

4 The fiscal activities of the government affect the *IS* curve in two ways. Government expenditures (G) are a direct component of aggregate demand, while taxes (T) influence disposable income, which in turn affects consumption spending. The equilibrium condition for defining the *IS* curve to take account of the government is $I + G = S + T$. An increase in G or a decrease in T produces an outward shift of the *IS* curve.

5 By itself, the *IS* curve is not generally sufficient to determine the level of income or output. We saw that in one simple case—when investment was exogenously determined and therefore did not depend on the interest rate—equilibrium income could be determined by the condition that investment equals saving. We also saw that a change in investment would induce a multiple change in income where the multiplier was given by the inverse of the marginal propensity to save. We will see in the next chapter that the multiplier concept remains extremely useful, even when we deal with more complicated assumptions.

SELECTED READINGS

Branson, W. H. *Macroeconomic Theory and Policy*, 2nd ed. New York: Harper & Row, 1979.

Dornbusch, R., and S. Fisher. *Macroeconomics*, 3rd ed. New York: McGraw-Hill, 1984.

Gordon, R. J. *Macroeconomics*, 3rd ed. Boston: Little, Brown, 1984.

15

THE DETERMINATION OF EQUILIBRIUM INCOME

In previous chapters we investigated the markets for money balances and for commodities, and we analyzed the conditions for equilibrium in each market separately. In the money market, this involved equating the demand and supply for money balances; in the commodity market, we saw that equilibrium occurs when investment equals saving. Out of this process emerged the *LM* and *IS* curves, which give the pairs of r and Y consistent with equilibrium in the money and commodity markets, respectively. Neither the *LM* curve nor the *IS* curve, taken by itself, is capable of determining an *overall* equilibrium combination of Y and r. Rather, as we will see, unique equilibrium levels of Y and r must be determined by the two curves simultaneously. That is, overall equilibrium can exist when we have equilibrium in both the money and the commodity markets simultaneously.

In this chapter we analyze the nature of this overall equilibrium in some detail. We first do this with given and constant supply and demand functions that underlie the *LM* and *IS* curves. This type of analysis is often referred to as *statics:* It involves those equilibrium conditions that tend to be established and maintained with given underlying supply and demand functions. The bulk of this chapter, however, will be concerned with what is called *comparative statics.* This type of analysis compares two sets of equilibrium conditions: those existing before and after a shift of a demand or supply function. It attempts to determine how equilibrium will be changed if a demand function or a supply function shifts in a specified way. This kind of analysis will be used to examine the consequences of shifts in the investment demand and saving-supply functions. It will also enable us to analyze the workings of monetary and fiscal policy.

Throughout this chapter we will continue to assume that the price level remains constant, so that money values also indicate the behavior of real values. Complications accompanying changes in price levels will be taken up in the following chapter.

REVIEW OF BASIC FUNCTIONS

Before we proceed to analyze the determination of equilibrium Y and r, it may be helpful to list briefly the basic supply and demand functions that underlie the LM and IS curves. As we have seen, the LM and IS curves are defined by the two conditions:

$$M^D = M^S \tag{1}$$

$$I + G = S + T \tag{2}$$

Corresponding to these conditions are the following underlying supply and demand functions:

1 **MONEY SUPPLY.** The supply of money (M^S) is assumed to be a policy-determined variable set by the monetary authority. The quantity of money supplied will be denoted by $\overline{M}$

2 **MONEY DEMAND.** The demand function for money balances (M^D) is a function of income and interest rates. For expositional purposes it will sometimes be convenient to think of M^D as the sum of the demand function for money for transactions purposes (L_1) and the demand function for money balances for speculative or asset purposes (L_2). It will be convenient further to assume that L_1 is a positive function of Y, such that $L_1 = JOP = JY$, and L_2 is a negative function of interest rates, such that $L_2 = P(A - er)$. Thus,

$$M^D = L_1 + L_2 = JOP + P\,(A - er)$$

or

$$M^D = P\,(JO + A - er) \tag{3}$$

Since we are assuming that the price level is constant, we can simply set $P = 1$. This, of course, makes real and nominal income equal; that is, $Y = O$. We can thus rewrite (3) as

$$M^D = JY + A - er \tag{4}$$

3 **INVESTMENT DEMAND.** Investment demand (I) is a negative function of interest rates, such that

$$I = D - \frac{\Delta I}{\Delta r} r \tag{5}$$

4 **SAVING SUPPLY.** Saving and consumption are positive functions of disposable income. Net taxes, in turn, are a positive function of total income, Y. As we have seen, this means that saving plus taxes, $S + T$, can be regarded as a function of Y. We shall write this as[1]

$$S + T = Y \frac{\Delta S}{\Delta Y} - B \tag{6}$$

As before, the basic *multiplier* for changes in autonomous spending is given by $1 \div (\Delta S/\Delta Y)$.

5 **GOVERNMENT SPENDING.** Government purchases of goods and services are assumed to be fixed by the fiscal authorities and do not vary with the level of income.

SIMPLE STATICS

We begin with the determination of equilibrium levels of income and interest rates with four given and constant functions: saving-supply, investment demand, money supply, and demand for money balances. Equilibrium does not necessarily signify a full employment level or a desirable level; it indicates only the levels that will tend to be established and maintained by the given and constant functions.

Given these functions, interest rates and income can be in equilibrium only at the point of intersection (r_e, Y_e) of the *IS* and *LM* curves. Only this combination satisfies simultaneously the two necessary conditions for equilibrium. Any other combination of r and Y would be a disequilibrium combination and would create pressures for change. We found earlier that at any combination above the *LM* curve, M^S would exceed M^D, and the excess supply of money would serve to lower interest rates. This pressure toward lower interest rates is indicated in Figure 15–1 by the downward-pointing arrows from points A and B, both of which lie above the *LM* curve. On the other hand, at any combination of Y and r below the *LM* curve, M^D would exceed M^S, and the excess demand for money balances would serve to raise interest rates. This is indicated in Figure 15–1 by the upward-pointing ar-

---

[1]For an illustrative derivation of equation (6), see p. 398 in the previous chapter. It should be noted that the symbol $\Delta S/\Delta Y$ in the present context is slightly broader than the marginal propensity to save. As equation (6) indicates, here it is the marginal responsiveness of both saving *and* taxes to a change in income. We use the same symbol because, as the text states, with the government included, the basic multiplier remains $1 \div (\Delta S/\Delta Y)$.

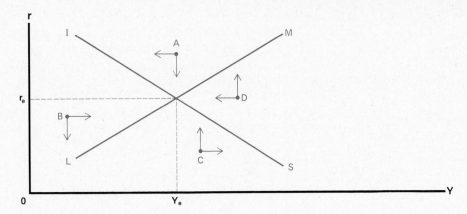

FIGURE 15–1
LM and *IS* curves

rows from points *C* and *D*. We also found that at any combination of *Y* and *r* above the *IS* curve, there would be an excess of supply of output over total demands for it, and this would induce reductions of output and employment. This is indicated in Figure 15–1 by the left-pointing arrows from points *A* and *D*, both of which lie above the *IS* curve. However, at any combination below the *IS* curve, the excess of total demand over the supply of output would lead producers to increase output and employment. This is indicated in Figure 15–1 by the right-pointing arrows from points *B* and *C*. Only at the point of intersection of the *LM* and *IS* curves (Y_e, r_e) is there no pressure for change.

COMPARATIVE STATICS

Let us now use comparative statics to analyze the effects of shifts of the investment demand and saving-supply functions. We shift the functions one at a time and compare equilibrium conditions before and after the shift.

INCREASE OF THE INVESTMENT DEMAND FUNCTION

Suppose that, starting from the equilibrium situation illustrated in Figure 15–1, there occurs an upward shift of the investment demand function, and that the function remains at the higher level. For example, investment expenditures might be increased by $10 billion at each level of interest rates. The combination r_e, Y_e is no longer an equilibrium combination because at those levels of *r* and *Y*, investment demand now exceeds saving supply by $10 billion. The rise of investment spending increases the total demand for output and also increases the community's disposable income, which will induce a rise of consumption spending. This is the multiplier process discussed earlier. A new equilibrium can be established only when $I + G$ and $S + T$ are again equated. Given the constant saving-supply function and the new investment demand function, these can be equated only by a rise of Y that will increase $S + T$, a rise of r that will decrease I, or some combination of the two. $S + T$ can be raised by $10 billion to match the rise of I at each level of interest rates only by an increase of Y, such that

$$\Delta Y \frac{\Delta S}{\Delta Y} = \$10 \text{ billion}$$

If we assume that $\Delta S/\Delta Y = 0.2$,

$$\Delta Y = \frac{\$10 \text{ billion}}{0.2} = \$50 \text{ billion}$$

This is illustrated by the horizontal shift to the right of the *IS* curve from $I_0 S_0$ to $I_1 S_1$ in Figure 15–2. The new equilibrium must be somewhere on this line.

Figure 15–2 indicates that *if interest rates remain unchanged* at the old equilibrium level, r_e, the full multiplier effect on income levels can be achieved. Actual investment expenditures will increase by an amount equal to the upward shift of the function, $10 billion, and the multiplier effect will be

$$\Delta Y = \$10 \text{ billion} \frac{1}{0.2} = \$50 \text{ billion}$$

so that income would rise from Y_e to Y_1.

However, as Figure 15–2 demonstrates, if the money supply remains constant and the M^D function is of the type assumed here, the full basic

FIGURE 15–2
Shift of investment demand

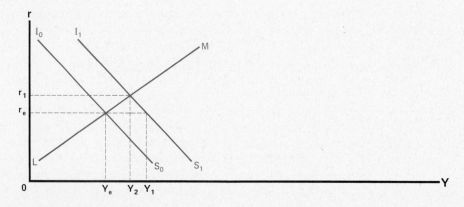

multiplier effect on income will not be realized. In particular, instead of increasing to Y_1, the new equilibrium level of income will be at Y_2, which is less than Y_1. Thus, the actual increase in income is less than the full basic multiplier effect. This is because the use of Y serves to increase the quantity of money demanded, so that the total demand for money can be equated to the constant supply only if interest rates rise, and the rise of interest rates will snub the increase of investment. How much the rise of actual investment will be snubbed depends on the extent of the rise of r and on the marginal responsiveness of investment to interest rates ($\Delta I/\Delta r$).

It is clear, therefore, that the consequences of the upward shift of the I function depends in part on the slope of the LM curve ($\Delta r/\Delta Y$). If the LM curve is nearly vertical—that is, if $\Delta r/\Delta Y$ approaches infinity—the outcome will be a large rise of r and virtually no increase of actual investment or income. However, if the LM curve approaches a horizontal position—that is, if $\Delta r/\Delta Y$ approaches zero—there will be virtually no rise of r and almost the full multiplier effect will be realized.

The value of $\Delta r/\Delta Y$ depends on both the size of J and the degree of responsiveness of L_2 to r, or $\Delta L_2/\Delta r$. This can be seen by examining equation (4). The reasoning is as follows: Each rise of Y will increase the quantity of money demanded for L_1 purposes by an amount equal to $J\Delta Y$. With total $\overline{M}$ constant, the quantity of money demanded for L_2 purposes must decline by an offsetting amount to maintain the necessary equilibrium condition, $M^D = M^S$. But with L_2 a constant negative function of r, the quantity of money demanded for L_2 purposes can be reduced only by a rise of r. If the responsiveness of L_2 to r approaches zero, very large increases of r will be required to reduce L_2 demands enough to offset each increase of L_1 demands, and the LM curve will be nearly vertical. This is illustrated by the curve labeled L_0M_0 in Figure 15–3. However, if L_2 demands for money are almost infinitely responsive to r, only a very small rise of r will be required to offset each increase of L_1 demands, and the LM curve will be almost horizontal. This is illustrated by the curve labeled L_1M_1 in Figure 15–3.

Two extreme cases will be instructive.

1 The marginal responsiveness of M^D to r is so small as to approach zero. That is, a rise of interest rates brings no decrease in the quantity of money demanded, so none is freed to satisfy the increased demand for money that would be generated by a rise of Y. In this extreme case, the upward shift of the investment demand function increases neither actual investment nor the level of income; it is reflected solely in a rise in interest rates.

2 The responsiveness of M^D to r approaches infinity; that is, even a minute rise of r will decrease by huge amounts the quantity of money demanded, and this will be available to meet the increased demand for money generated by a rise of Y; the LM curve will be virtually horizontal. In this extreme case, there will be no rise of interest rates,

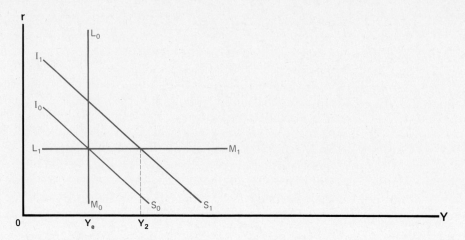

FIGURE 15–3
Some slopes of the *LM* curve

investment will rise by the full amount of the upward shift of the investment function, and the full multiplier effects on Y will be achieved.

In the usual case, the *LM* curve will be neither vertical nor horizontal; it will have a positive slope between these two extremes. From this case of an upward shift of the investment demand function we can draw several conclusions:

1 The very process of increasing the level of income generates an increase in the quantity of money demanded which, in the absence of a compensating increase of the money supply, will tend to raise interest rates and snub the increases of investment and income. Put another way, in the case of an intermediately sloped LM curve, *the relevant multiplier is smaller than what we have been calling the full basic multiplier*, $1 \div \Delta S/\Delta Y$. As we shall see, this conclusion applies to all types of shifts in autonomous spending.[2]

2 To hold the money supply constant in the face of an upward shift of the investment function will usually not suffice to prevent some rise of total expenditures for output. The ensuring rise of r will free some part of the money stock to satisfy the increased demands for money generated by the rise of the money value of output.

We need not trace in detail the effects of a downward shift in the investment demand function. In brief, at the old equilibrium levels of r and Y, the supply of saving will exceed investment demand, and a downward

---

[2]The appendix to this chapter provides a numerical illustration of the difference between the multiplier pictured in Figure 15–2 and the basic multiplier.

multiplier process will begin. This can be represented by a shift to the left by the IS curve. However, the very decline of Y will serve to reduce the quantity of money demanded, and the excess supply of money will tend to reduce r, which will snub the decline of I and Y. Here again, the extent of the actual changes of I and Y will depend in part on the shape of the LM curve in the relevant range. If L_2 demands for money are very highly responsive to each reduction of r, the LM curve will be nearly horizontal, interest rates will fall but little, and nearly the full downward multiplier effects will result. But if L_2 demands for money are less responsive to each decline of interest rates, a larger decrease of r will result, and the declines of I and Y will be snubbed.

DECREASE OF THE SAVING-SUPPLY FUNCTION

Suppose now that, starting from the initial equilibrium situation with $Y = Y_e$ and $r = r_e$, there occurs what may be viewed as either an upward shift of the consumption function or a decrease of the saving-supply function. For example, consumption demand may rise by $10 billion at each level of income, which is the same as saying that the supply of saving declines by $10 billion at each level of income. In many respects, although not all, the process and the results are the same as those following an upward shift of the investment demand function. At the old equilibrium levels of Y and r, investment demand will exceed saving supply and the total demand for output (including the rise of consumption) will exceed the total supply of output by $10 billion. Thus, an upward multiplier process is initiated. $S + T$ and $I + G$ can again be equated only by a rise of Y that will increase $S + T$, a rise of r that will reduce I, or some combination of the two. In other words, as we have seen before, a decrease of the saving-supply function serves to shift the IS curve out to the right. This means that the effects in the present case are analogous to those already portrayed in Figure 15–2. That is, a decrease in the saving-supply function leads to a new equilibrium with both a higher Y and a higher r.

Up to this point we have stressed the similarities of the case in which the investment demand function shifted upward and the present case, in which the consumption function shifted upward or the saving-supply function shifted downward. In both cases there is an upward multiplier effect on income, assuming that the LM curve is not vertical; and in both cases the actual outcome depends on the slopes of the IS and LM curves. However, there is an important difference between the two cases, and this relates to the composition of the increased output. When the investment demand function shifts upward, the resulting increase of output is composed in part of increased investment and in part of increased consumption. However, if the upward thrust on income emanates from an upward shift of the consumption function (a decline of the saving-supply function), no rise of investment will occur. Indeed, to the extent that r rises and I is responsive to interest rates, I will actually decline.[3]

The reader is invited to trace the effects of a downward shift of the consumption function or an upward shift of the saving-supply function. Note the initial autonomous decline of consumption demand, the downward multiplier effect on income illustrated by a shift to the left of the IS curve, and the relevance of the slope of the LM curve to the outcome. The outcome is, of course, some decline of output and income. This is often referred to as *the paradox of thrift;* an increase in the thriftiness of a community, in the sense of an upward shift of its saving function, can make it less prosperous. The outcome seems less paradoxical when we remember that this is a downward shift of the consumption function and note the implicit assumption that there is neither an offsetting rise of the investment demand function nor a fall of interest rates sufficient to stimulate I enough to offset the fall of C.

Having gained some familiarity with manipulating the IS–LM apparatus, we now use the tool of comparative statics to study the effects monetary and fiscal policy can have on the equilibrium levels of income and interest rates.

MONETARY POLICY: AN INTRODUCTION

In the context of the IS–LM model we have developed, the only tool of monetary policy is the supply of money. Thus far we have treated the money supply as fixed. Now we investigate the consequences of altering it. For the present, we leave aside the questions of why the monetary authorities might want to change the money supply and how they would actually accomplish this. Our only purpose here is to understand the consequences for Y and r of a change in the money supply. We focus first on an increase in the money supply.

INCREASE IN THE MONEY SUPPLY

Again starting from an initial equilibrium situation in which $Y = Y_e$ and $r = r_e$, suppose that the money supply is increased by some amount, such as $10 billion, with all the other functions remaining constant. At the old equilibrium levels of Y and r, M^S will now exceed M^D, and the excess supply of money will serve to raise demands for securities and to lower interest rates. With the demand function for money constant, M^D can again be equated to M^S only when it is increased by $10 billion by a rise of Y, a

---

[3]These conclusions depend heavily on the assumption, followed throughout this chapter, that changes in the level of income do not shift the investment demand function in the same direction.

decline of r, or some combination of the two. At a constant level of interest rates, M^D could be increased \$10 billion by some increase of Y such that

$$\Delta Y \frac{\Delta M^D}{\Delta Y} = \$10 \text{ billion}$$

where $\Delta M^D/\Delta Y$ is the marginal responsiveness of the demand for money to Y and $\Delta M^D/\Delta Y = J$ for the special case of the linear demand function of equation (4). For example, if $J = 1/5$, the rise of Y required to equate M^D and M^S would be

$$\frac{\$10 \text{ billion}}{1/5} \quad \text{or} \quad \$50 \text{ billion}$$

This is shown in Figure 15–4 as a horizontal shift to the right of the LM curve from $L_0 M_0$ to $L_1 M_1$. M^D could also be increased \$10 billion by some decrease of r such that

$$\Delta r \frac{\Delta M^D}{\Delta r} = \$10 \text{ billion}$$

where $\Delta M^D/\Delta r$ is the marginal responsiveness of money demand to r. The quantity $\Delta M^D/\Delta r$ is, of course, negative, since a decline in r increases the demand for money. In equation (4), we have $\Delta M^D/\Delta r = -e$. This is a special case. Suppose, for example, that $\Delta M^D/\Delta r = -5$; that is, each decline of r by 1 percentage point increases M^D by \$5 billion. In this case, the decline in r required to equate M^D and M^S would be

$$\frac{\$10 \text{ billion}}{\$5 \text{ billion}} = 2 \text{ percentage points}$$

In Figure 15–4 this is shown as a vertical downward shift of the LM curve from $L_0 M_0$ to $L_1 M_1'$. Thus, we see that an increase in the money supply may

FIGURE 15–4
Shift of the money supply

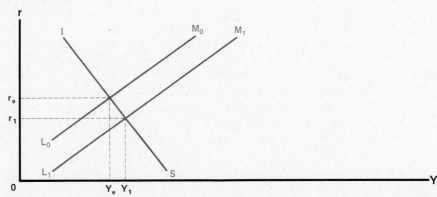

equivalently be regarded as shifting the *LM* curve either to the right or downward.

In any event, the new equilibrium for Y and r must be somewhere on $L_1 M_1$. At any combination lying below and to the right of this line, M^D would exceed M^S and the excess demand for money balances would serve to reduce demands for securities and raise interest rates. At any combination lying above and to the left of the *LM* curve, M^S would exceed M^D, and the excess supply of money would serve to increase demands for securities and to lower interest rates.

As pictured in figure 15–4, the new equilibrium occurs at $Y = Y_1$ and $r = r_1$ where the new *LM* curve, $L_1 M_1$, intersects the unchanged *IS* curve. That is, as a result of the increase in the money supply (denoted by ΔM), income increases (by ΔY) and interest rates decline (by Δr).

EFFECTIVENESS OF MONETARY POLICY

We have just seen that an increase in the supply of money is *qualitatively* an expansionary action as far as output or income is concerned. But it seems natural to ask how *quantitatively* effective it is in this regard. One common measure of the effectiveness of monetary policy is $\Delta Y/\Delta M$. This quantity, which is a monetary analogue of the multiplier concept introduced earlier, tells us the extent to which a given change in the money supply succeeds in altering Y. In this sense, larger values of $\Delta Y/\Delta M$ correspond to a more effective monetary policy. It should be emphasized that *effective* in this context has no connotation of success or desirability. It simply refers to what is also sometimes called the *bang-for-a-buck* concept of monetary policy. However, what we call $\Delta Y/\Delta M$ is of little consequence. What is important is that we understand the factors that make for larger or smaller values of $\Delta Y/\Delta M$, and it is to this issue that we now turn.

One factor that determines the effect of a given increase of the money supply is the location and shape of the *IS* curve. Beginning from an initial equilibrium of $Y = Y_e$ and $r = r_e$, we consider an increase in the money supply that shifts the *LM* curve from $L_0 M_0$ to $L_1 M_1$. As is illustrated in Figure 15–5, where Y and r end up depends directly on the slope of the *IS* curve. Two possible curves are shown in Figure 15–5—$I_0 S_0$, which is relatively flat, and $I_1 S_1$, which is relatively steep. If the relevant curve is $I_0 S_0$, then we shall move from $Y = Y_e$ and $r = r_e$ to $Y = Y_1$ and $r = r_1$. If, however, the somewhat steeper curve, $I_1 S_1$, is the appropriate one, we see that the interest rate will decline more (to r_2 as opposed to r_1) and income will increase less (to Y_2 instead of Y_1). In the extreme case, when the *IS* curve is virtually horizontal, there will be little change of r but an increase of Y approximating the shift to the right of the *LM* curve. However, if the *IS* curve is virtually vertical, the principal effect will be to lower r, with little increase of Y. It is imperative, therefore, to investigate the determinants of the shape of the *IS* curve. For this purpose, it will be convenient to deal not with the slope of the line,

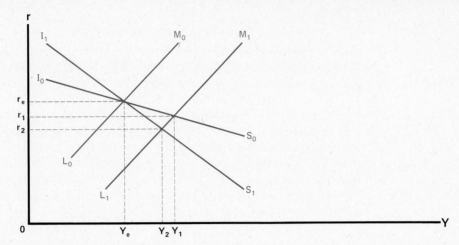

FIGURE 15–5
The effectiveness of monetary policy: the
influence of the IS curve

but rather with its reciprocal, $\Delta Y/\Delta r$. This is a measure of the flatness of the line.

If, from some point on the *IS* curve, r is lowered by some amount, Δr, this will increase I by an amount equal to $\Delta r(\Delta I/\Delta r)$. Thus, $I + G$ will exceed $S + T$. With a constant saving-supply function, $S + T$ can be increased to match the increase of $I + G$ only by some rise of Y such that

$$\Delta Y \frac{\Delta S}{\Delta Y} = \Delta r \frac{\Delta I}{\Delta r}$$

Dividing both sides of the equation by Δr and $\Delta S/\Delta Y$, we get

$$\frac{\Delta Y}{\Delta r} = \frac{\Delta I}{\Delta r} \times \frac{1}{\Delta S/\Delta Y}$$

Thus, the flatness of the *IS* curve ($\Delta Y/\Delta r$) varies directly with the marginal responsiveness of investment to interest rates ($\Delta I/\Delta r$) and with $1 \div (\Delta S/\Delta Y)$, our old friend the multiplier. For example, if investment is completely unresponsive to interest rates—if $\Delta I/\Delta r = 0$—an increase in the money supply will not increase Y. However, the more responsive investment is to interest rates, the greater will be the response of Y.

In summary, a flatter *IS* curve makes for a more effective monetary policy; and, in turn, the *IS* curve will be flatter the larger $\Delta I/\Delta r$ is and the smaller $\Delta S/\Delta Y$ is.

In addition to the slope of the *IS* curve, the effectiveness of a given change in the money supply also depends on the nature of the money demand function. It is the money-demand function that determines how far the *LM* curve will shift as a result of a given change in the money supply. To see how this works, consider the *LM* curve labeled L_0M_0 in Figure 15–6. Unlike the previous examples of this chapter, L_0M_0 is a "curved" *LM* curve. As indicated earlier, however, this is really the general case. One consequence of the curved feature of L_0M_0 is that the slope of L_0M_0, $\Delta r/\Delta Y$, is not constant. Indeed, as drawn, L_0M_0 is much flatter at lower values of Y and r and much steeper at higher values of Y and r. As a result of this, an increase in the money supply will produce a shift of the kind illustrated in Figure 15–6— that is, from L_0M_0 to L_1M_1. We will shortly explain why this kind of shift results, but first let us examine its consequences for the effectiveness of monetary policy. The main point is illustrated in Figure 15–7, where we have superimposed two different *IS* curves—with the same slope—on the *LM* curves of Figure 15–6. If the relevant *IS* curve is I_0S_0, we see that monetary policy will induce only a small change in Y, from Y_1 to Y_2. On the other hand, if the relevant *IS* curve is I_1S_1, then a much larger change in income will result, with Y going from Y_3 to Y_4. Evidently then, the effectiveness of monetary policy also depends on the nature of the *LM* curve. Before examining the consequences of this further, however, we must understand why the *LM* curve shifts in the manner portrayed in Figures 15–6 and 15–7.

As indicated earlier, the answer lies in the slope of the *LM* curve. This suggests, as was done for the *IS* curve, that it will be instructive to disentangle the underlying components of the slope of the *LM* curve. To determine this slope, we consider some point on the *LM* curve and lower r by some amount, Δr. This will increase the demand for money, M^D, by an amount equal to $\Delta r\ (\Delta M^D/\Delta r)$, and thus M^D will exceed M^S. With a given M^S, M^D can be restored to its equality with M^S only by some rise of Y such that[4]

---

[4]If we are to remain on the *LM* curve, with a given supply of money, then the change in M^D must be zero along the *LM* curve. This is the condition expressed by equation (7).

FIGURE 15–6
Shifting the *LM* curve

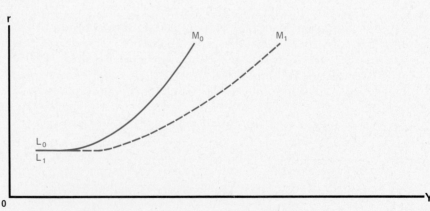

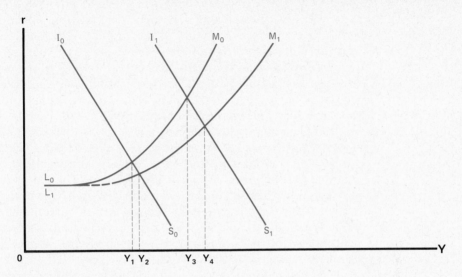

FIGURE 15–7
The effectiveness of monetary policy: the influence of the *LM* curve

$$\Delta Y \frac{\Delta M^D}{\Delta Y} + \Delta r \frac{\Delta M^D}{\Delta r} = 0 \tag{7}$$

or

$$\Delta Y \frac{\Delta M^D}{\Delta Y} = -\Delta r \frac{\Delta M^D}{\Delta r} \tag{8}$$

Dividing both sides of equation (8) by Δr and $\Delta M^D/\Delta Y$, we get

$$\frac{\Delta Y}{\Delta r} = -\frac{\Delta M^D}{\Delta r} \times \frac{1}{\Delta M^D/\Delta Y}$$

The quantity $\Delta Y/\Delta r$ is, of course, the flatness of the *LM* curve. Thus, we see that the flatness varies directly with the responsiveness of money demand to interest rates ($\Delta M^D/\Delta r$) and inversely with the responsiveness of money demand to income ($\Delta M^D/\Delta Y$). Thus, if money demand is extremely responsive to the interest rate, $\Delta M^D/\Delta r$ will be a large negative number and the *LM* curve will be quite flat. In the extreme, when $\Delta M^D/\Delta r$ approaches negative infinity—this is the case of the liquidity trap discussed earlier—the *LM* curve becomes perfectly flat. At the other extreme, when $\Delta M^D/\Delta r$ approaches zero, then so does $\Delta Y/\Delta r$ and the *LM* curve becomes vertical. Stated another way, the "curved" *LM* curve pictured in Figure 15–6 results from assuming that the demand for money behaves differently at high and low levels of interest rates..

Armed with this, we can readily see why the type of *LM* shift pictured in Figure 15–6 results. At low levels of *r* the *LM* curve is flat because $\Delta M^D/\Delta r$ is large in absolute value and people are willing to absorb substantial increases in the stock of money into speculative balances. As a consequence, equilibrium can be maintained in the money market with only small changes in *r* and *Y*, so that the *LM* curve shifts only slightly. On the other hand, for high values of *r* the *LM* curve is steep because $\Delta M^D/\Delta r$ is relatively small in absolute value. This means that most of the increase in the money stock can be used to finance transactions, so that the effect on *Y* will be substantial. That is, the *LM* curve will shift farther to the right at high levels of *r*.

Figure 15–7 has sometimes been interpreted as demonstrating that the effectiveness of monetary policy varies with the cyclical state of the economy. The reason is that periods of economical slack are likely to be ones with low *r* and *Y*, putting us on the relatively flat side of the *LM* curve. Similarly, boom periods are likely to be ones with high *r* and *Y*, corresponding to the relatively steep part of the *LM* curve. In this view, monetary policy is seen to be its most effective in a period of relatively full employment and least effective during a recession or a depression. While these results are certainly quite plausible, as we will see later, they need to be qualified.

THE ADJUSTMENT PROCESS

We are now in a position to summarize the process through which a given increase in the money supply influences interest rate and income levels and some of the factors that determine the nature and extent of the effects. We assume that the monetary authority increases the money supply by purchasing securities of various types from the public, and that spending for output is affected only through effects on prices and yields on securities. The following processes are involved.

1 In creating the additional money, the monetary institutions—the central bank and the depository institutions—increase their demands for securities and loans. This increase tends to raise the prices of debt obligations and to lower their yields. As the public sells debt obligations to the monetary institutions and acquires more money, it finds that money constitutes a larger fraction of its total assets and is impelled to buy more debt obligations, which tends to lower interest rates still more.

2 As interest rates fall, the public demands larger quantities of money balances. How much a given increase of the money supply can depress interest rates varies inversely with the marginal responsive of the demand for money to interest rates $(\Delta M^D/\Delta r)$. If $\Delta M^D/\Delta r$ is large— if each fall of interest rates greatly increases the quantity of money

demanded—the increase in the money supply can lower interest rates but little. However, if $\Delta M^D/\Delta r$ is very small, interest rates can be lowered more.

3 The size of the increase of investment demand depends not only on the size of the decrease of interest rates, but also on the marginal responsiveness of investment to interest rates $(\Delta I/\Delta r)$. The greater $\Delta I/\Delta r$, the greater will be the expansionary effects on I.

4 The size of the expansion of Y depends not only on the rise of I, but also on the value of the multiplier, which varies directly with the marginal propensity to consume.

5 The rise of Y increases the quantity of money demanded; and as the expansion of Y continues, interest rates will rise. At some point the rise of r will bring the expansion to an end. This is the point of intersection of the IS curve and the new LM curve. How large this expansion will be depends in part on $\Delta M^D/\Delta Y$.

We find, then, that the effects on Y of a given increase in the money supply depend on a number of factors: on $\Delta M^D/\Delta r$, which determines how much interest rates can be lowered; on $\Delta I/\Delta r$, which determines how much each decline of interest rates will stimulate investment; on $\Delta C/\Delta Y$, which determines the size of the multiplier; and on $\Delta M^D/\Delta Y$, which reflects the amount by which the demand for money balances will be increased by each increase of Y. The smaller $\Delta M^D/\Delta Y$ is, the larger will be the increase of income that can occur before a rise in interest rates ends the expansion.

The case of a decrease of the money supply is symmetrical with that of an increase of the money supply. With the decrease of $\overline{M}$, M^D exceeds M^S and the excess demand for money balances decreases demands for securities and raises interest rates. The effects of Y and r depend on all the factors described previously. Trace the effects, noting that the decrease in $\overline{M}$ will be evidenced by a horizontal leftward shift of the LM curve.

OVERVIEW

This section has provided an introduction to the workings of monetary policy. We have seen that an increase in the money supply will increase Y and decrease r. We have also discussed the various factors influencing the quantitative extent of these changes. Although we have focused on an increase in the money supply, the case of a decrease is really quite similar. In particular, a decrease serves to shift the LM curve leftward and upward, and in the new equilibrium we have a higher value of r and a lower value of Y. The quantitative effect on Y and r depends on all the factors just described. We will have a great deal more to say about monetary policy as we proceed, but now let us turn to fiscal policy.

FISCAL POLICY: AN INTRODUCTION

We now investigate the government's principal instruments of fiscal policy—its expenditures for goods and services (G) and its net taxes (T). To conserve space, we elaborate only on expansionary fiscal policies—that is, increases in G or reductions in T. The effects of restrictive policies will simply be the reverse of those considered below.

Before discussing the details, it may be helpful if we utilize our previous discussion to anticipate the results. The following two points should be borne in mind.

1   We saw in the previous chapter (especially Figures 14–12 and 14–13) that the effect of an increase in G *or* a reduction in T is to shift the *IS* curve upward and to the right.
2   From our discussion of increases in investment demand—which also shifts the *IS* curve upward and to the right (see Figure 15–2)—we know that such shifts generally produce an increase in both income and interest rates. Expansionary fiscal policy therefore will do likewise.

We now consider a few of the more important details, beginning with an increase in the government's demand for output, G.

INCREASE IN G

Suppose the government raises G and maintains this higher level of expenditures while leaving its tax and transfer programs unchanged. The direct impact is to increase both aggregate demand for output in the form of $C + I + G$ and also the total of gross income shares accruing to the nation. As just noted, the increase in G shifts the *IS* curve upward and to the right. This is illustrated in Figure 15–8, where the *IS* curve shifts from I_0S_0 to I_1S_1.

The original equilibrium levels of income and the interest rate, before the rise of G, are again represented by Y_e, r_e. After the rise of G this is no longer an equilibrium. A new equilibrium can be established only by a rise in the interest rate, which reduces I; a rise in income, which would raise $S + T$; or some combination of the two. As Figure 15–8 shows, with a conventionally sloped *LM* curve, r and Y will both rise, with the new equilibrium being established at Y_1, r_1. As before, the interest rate rises because increased Y increases the quantity of money demanded while the supply of money is unchanged by assumption. This rise in r tends to reduce I and thus to snub somewhat the rise of Y.

The discussion assumes that the increase in G and the ensuing rise in Y left the investment demand function unchanged. This may occur, especially if the economy is operating significantly below capacity levels. However, the rise in Y may increase the expected profitability of investment and shift the investment demand function upward at each level of interest rates.

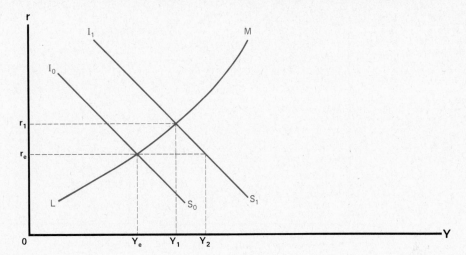

FIGURE 15–8
An increase of G

In such cases a rise in interest rates may reduce I less or not at all; in fact, the upward shift of I could be so large that I would be increased despite the rise in interest rates.

REDUCTION IN T

We now explore the case in which the government lowers its net tax collections at each level of Y, leaving its rate of expenditures for output unchanged. This result could be achieved in either or both of two ways: (1) by decreasing tax yields at each level of Y by reducing tax bases, tax rates, or both; or (2) by increasing transfer payments at each level of Y. A reduction in T does not directly affect aggregate demand for output; it does, however, increase disposable income at each level of Y. With greater disposable incomes, the private sector could be expected to consume more at each level of GNP.

As we have seen before (especially in Figure 14–13), the decrease in T shifts the $S + T$ function rightward and consequently shifts the IS curve up and to the right. Both shifts are shown in Figure 15–9. The end result, as in the case of an increase in G, is a higher level for both income and the interest rate.

INCREASE IN G VS. DECREASE IN T

We find, then, that the government can raise Y by increasing G or by lowering its T function through reducing taxes or raising its transfer payment

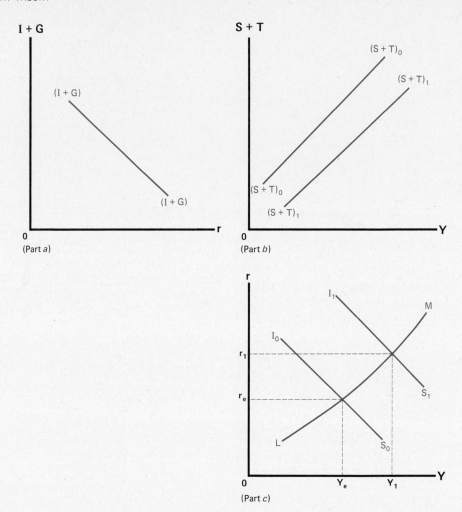

FIGURE 15–9
A tax decrease

function. A comparison of the effects of a given increase in G and an equal reduction in T brings out some interesting similarities and contrasts.

1   Both serve to increase Y. However, the rise of Y resulting from a given increase of G will be greater than that resulting from an equal decrease of T. This is because all of an increase in G is reflected in an exogenous rise of demand for output, whereas an equal decrease in T will not increase the consumption function by the full amount; some of the tax rebate will be used to increase S.

2   Both are likely to increase interest rates if the money supply is not increased. This will inhibit investment if the rise in G, the decrease in

the T function, and the ensuing rise in Y do not raise the investment demand function sufficiently to offset the rise in interest rates.

3 Effects on the composition of the increased output are different. If the expansion results from a decrease in the T function, all the increased output is in the form of consumer goods. If it results from an increase in G, the increased output is partly in the form of additional goods and services for the government and partly in the form of additional consumer goods.

THE EFFECTIVENESS OF FISCAL POLICY

We have just seen that an increase in G or a decrease in T is an expansionary action in that it tends to increase the equilibrium value of Y. As we did for monetary policy, it is possible to examine the factors that determine the quantitative extent of this—that is, the effectiveness of fiscal policy. In fact, however, our discussion can be quite brief, since we have already touched on many of the issues. In particular, as stressed earlier, both a shift in G and a shift in the investment demand function are examples of shifts in autonomous demand and have essentially the same kinds of effects. Since we have already discussed the factors that determine the size of the change in Y resulting from a shift in the investment demand function, we can simply apply those findings to the present case. In particular, we note that fiscal policy will be more effective—in the sense that a given increase in G or decrease in T will produce a larger increase in Y—under the following conditions:

1 **THE SMALLER $\Delta S/\Delta Y$ IS.** The reciprocal of $\Delta S/\Delta Y$ is, of course, the simple multiplier, and this determines how far to the right the IS curve shifts.

2 **THE SMALLER $\Delta I/\Delta r$ IS.** The smaller this quantity is, the less the increase in r will tend to decrease I and thus to snub the increase in Y.

3 **THE FLATTER THE LM CURVE IS.** With a flat LM curve, the induced rise in r will be relatively small; consequently, the decline in I will be smaller, thus lessening the extent to which the increase in Y is snubbed.

This last point is illustrated in Figure 15–10, where we are again utilizing a "curved" LM curve. If the IS curve crosses the LM curve in its relatively flat part, we see that income will increase from Y_0 to Y_1. If, on the other hand, the LM curve is steeper, the *same* increase of G will produce a much smaller increase in Y (from Y_2 to Y_3 in Figure 15–10).

As earlier, we may interpret this as saying that the effectiveness of fiscal policy depends on the cyclical state of the economy. In particular, fiscal policy is seen to work best in relatively slack economic conditions, when we are likely to be on the flat part of the LM curve. Fiscal policy will be less

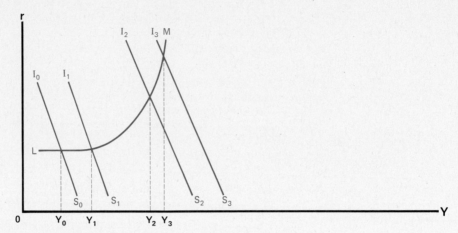

FIGURE 15–10
The effectiveness of fiscal policy

effective under conditions more closely approximating full employment, since the *LM* curve is likely to be steeper. In this respect we see that the cyclical effectiveness of fiscal policy is exactly the opposite of monetary policy, which we had earlier characterized as working best during boom periods and least well during times of economic slack. These considerations provide one element in deciding between the use of monetary and fiscal policies for stabilization purposes, but other important elements are involved in this choice.

COMPOSITION OF OUTPUT AND THE POLICY MIX

As we have seen, beginning from some initial position of equilibrium, either monetary or fiscal policy can be used to achieve some desired change in the level of *Y*. Or, for that matter, some combination or *mix* of monetary and fiscal policies could be used to produce some desired level of *Y*. Which policy mix is chosen may, of course, be affected by the cyclical state of the economy, since this influences the relative effectiveness of monetary and fiscal policy. This issue aside, however, there is another element in the choice—namely, the resulting composition of total output.

By the *composition* of output we mean the distribution of some given level of *Y* between *C, I,* and *G*. We have touched on this issue in comparing policies involving *G* and *T*, and we now expand on it. In particular, beginning from some level of *Y*, let us consider the following three policies: an increase in *G*, a decrease in *T*, and an increase in the supply of money, M^S. Let us further assume that each of these policies is quantitatively chosen to produce the *same* increase in Y. Then, drawing on the results of the previous sections, we have the following:

1   **AN INCREASE IN G.** This induces an increase in C and a decrease in I because r rises. By assumption, of course, G increases.
2   **A DECREASE IN T.** Here G is unchanged, C increases, and again I declines because r rises.
3   **AN INCREASE IN M^S.** G again remains the same, but because r decreases, both C and I rise.

Since each of these three policies is assumed to lead to the same Y, by looking at the identity $Y = C + I + G$ we see that the increase in consumption is biggest when we cut taxes and smallest when monetary policy is used to increase Y. Furthermore, monetary policy is the only policy that leads to an increase in investment.[5] This suggests that if policymakers care about the composition of output, and there is certainly evidence to this effect, this will have a direct influence on the mix of policies pursued.

As an illustration, let us consider the case in which the monetary and fiscal authorities are both quite happy with the aggregate level of output but feel that the level of investment is too low. To rectify the situation, we need a change in the mix of policy designed to produce an interest rate low enough to yield the desired level of investment while keeping the level of Y unchanged. Such a mix shift is illustrated in Figure 15–11.

By expanding the money supply, the monetary authorities shift the LM curve down and to the right, moving from $L_0 M_0$ to $L_1 M_1$. This must be balanced by a tighter fiscal policy that shifts the IS curve from $I_0 S_0$ to $I_1 S_1$. This could be accomplished by a tax increase, a decrease of transfer pay-

[5]See footnote 3.

FIGURE 15–11
A policy mix shift

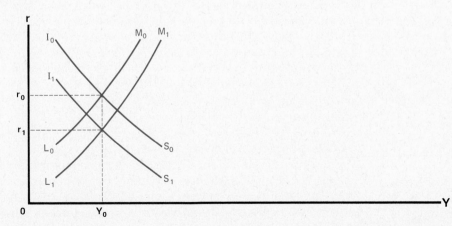

ments, or a decrease in G. As shown, the net effect of these two policy changes is to move the interest rate down from r_0 to r_1 but to leave income unchanged at Y_0.

Thus, we see how an easier monetary policy used in conjunction with a tighter fiscal policy can bring a shift in the composition of output while leaving total aggregate demand unchanged. Such a policy mix obviously requires a considerable amount of coordination between monetary and fiscal authorities. As might be suspected, this is easier said than done. We return in subsequent chapters to the problem of coordinating monetary and fiscal policies and to the question of the optimal mix of policies.

DEFICIT FINANCING

In earlier chapters we discussed the outstanding stock of government debt, while in the present chapter we have analyzed the role of taxes and government expenditures. As should be apparent, there is a direct relation between these two subjects. The connection, of course, stems from the possibility of an imbalance in the federal budget. For example, if government spending exceeds taxes, there will be a *budget deficit* that has to be *financed.* That is, if the government is going to be able to spend more than it takes in, it must somehow gain command of the necessary resources. Typically, this is accomplished by issuing Treasury securities to raise the required funds. This, in turn, adds to the outstanding stock of government debt. If tax revenues exceed government expenditures, the government has a *budget surplus*, which can be used to retire Treasury securities and reduce the outstanding stock of government debt.

ALTERNATIVE METHODS OF DEFICIT FINANCING

We have thus far assumed that budget deficits are financed by issuing government securities. There is, however, another possibility. The government may issue money (non-interest-bearing debt) to cover its deficit. This has been a popular method in some countries, especially those in which the market for government securities is not well developed. This is clearly not the case in the United States, where, furthermore, the stock of money is under the control of an independent Federal Reserve. Thus, the Treasury cannot simply "print money" to finance deficits. If the Federal Reserve is willing, however, the Treasury can accomplish the same thing by selling its securities to the Federal Reserve. In the process of paying for the securities, the Federal Reserve will create bank reserves, enabling the banking system to expand credit and the money supply by some multiple. In other words, this method of finance, which is sometimes called *monetization of the debt*, is nothing other than an expansionary open-market operation by the Federal Reserve. Hence, money finance of a deficit, since it combines expansionary fiscal policy with an expansionary monetary policy, should provide a greater stimulus to income than a bond-financed increase in government spending.

This can be readily illustrated by use of the *IS–LM* framework. We start in Figure 15–12 from the position of the equilibrium given by (r_1, Y_1), which, to keep matters simple, we assume corresponds to a balanced budget. Now suppose, because of an increase in government spending or a cut in taxes, the *IS* curve shifts upward from $I_1 S_1$ to $I_2 S_2$. If the resulting deficit is financed solely by issuing bonds, the *LM* curve remains at $L_1 M_1$ and the new equilibrium is given by (r_2, Y_2) This is the type of deficit finance that we have implicitly assumed throughout this chapter. However, if the deficit is partly or solely financed by monetizing the debt, the *LM* curve will shift to the right (to $L_2 M_2$) and yield the equilibrium (r_3, Y_3). Quite evidently, money finance is more expansionary than bond finance. Thus, whether money or bond finance is appropriate depends on the degree of stimulus that is desired.

One conclusion, which is strongly suggested by all this discussion, is that an efficient overall stabilization policy requires coordination of fiscal and monetary policy. We shall have more to say about this in later chapters.

SUMMARY

1 The *LM* curve expresses the combinations of interest rates and income that ensure equilibrium in the money market. The *IS* curve gives the pairs of the interest rates and income that are consistent with equilibrium in the goods market. The determination of the overall equilib-

FIGURE 15–12
Alternative methods of deficit finance

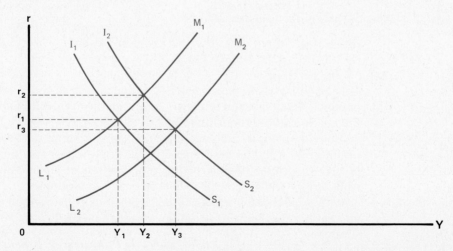

rium for r and Y requires that we simultaneously satisfy both the IS and LM curves. Graphically, this amounts to putting the IS and LM curves on the same diagram and finding the point of intersection.

2 A change in any of the ingredients that lie behind the IS and LM curves will alter the equilibrium levels of Y and r. This permits a role for both monetary and fiscal policy. For example, an expansionary monetary policy that increases the supply of money will cause an outward shift in the LM curve. This will lead to an increase in Y and a decrease in the interest rate. The size of the effect on Y will be larger the larger the responsiveness of investment to the interest rate and the larger the marginal propensity to consume. Monetary policy will also be more effective the lower the responsiveness of the demand for money to the interest rate.

3 Fiscal policy works by shifting the IS curve. Either an increase in G or a reduction in T is an expansionary fiscal action that shifts the IS curve outward. This in turn increases both Y and r. The effectiveness of fiscal policy varies directly with the size of the marginal propensity to consume.

4 In general, both fiscal and monetary policy are capable of bringing about changes in income or output. One factor in choosing which to use is the desired composition of output. This affects the choice between fiscal and monetary policy because expansionary monetary policy is likely to have more favorable effects on investment. Consequently, should the authorities wish to stimulate investment relative to consumption, expansionary monetary policy is likely to be warranted.

APPENDIX

ALGEBRAIC APPROACH TO EQUILIBRIUM LEVELS OF INCOME AND THE INTEREST RATE

This chapter relied primarily on a graphic approach to explain the determination of equilibrium levels of Y and r that would simultaneously satisfy the necessary conditions that $I + G = S + T$ and $M^D = M^S$. This can also be done by using simultaneous equations, and some readers may find it useful to have the analysis stated in algebraic terms. For the sake of simplicity, we assume that all the functions are linear. To simplify further, we work largely with some specific numerical assumptions.

With respect to the product market, personal consumption epxenditures and saving are assumed to be linear functions of disposable income, DI, such that

$$C = 130 + 0.8 \, DI \tag{A1}$$

$$S = -130 + 0.2 \, DI \tag{A2}$$

Disposable income, it will be recalled, is defined as

$$DI = Y - T \tag{A3}$$

Assuming that net taxes are given by

$$T = 0.25Y \tag{A4}$$

we can substitute equation (A4) into equation (A3) to obtain

$$DI = Y - 0.25Y = 0.75Y$$

This in turn can be substituted in the consumption and saving functions, (A1) and (A2), to yield

$$C = 130 + 0.8 \, (0.75Y) = 130 + 0.6Y \tag{A5}$$

$$S = -130 + 0.2 \, (0.75Y) = -130 + 0.15Y \tag{A6}$$

which, as before, express C and S as a function of Y or total income.

To complete the product market, we need a specific investment demand function, which we take to be

$$I = 130 - 10r \tag{A7}$$

G, of course, is exogenously determined by the government. We will shortly assume some specific numerical values for G, but for the present it will be more informative to keep it general.

We now have all the ingredients for the IS curve, which is defined by the condition

$$I + G = S + T \tag{A8}$$

Equations (A7), (A6), and (A4) give us I, S, and T. These can be substituted into equation (A8) to give

$$130 - 10r + G = -130 + 0.15Y + 0.25Y$$

which can be solved for r to yield

$$r = 26 + 0.1G - 0.04Y \tag{A9}$$

Equation (A9) is the algebraic expression for the IS curve giving all Y, r combinations that clear the product market.[1] The negative coefficient on Y indicates that the IS curve is downward-sloping. Furthermore, the positive coefficient on G indicates that an increase in G will shift the IS curve up and to the right.

---

[1]The reader may readily verify that the equation for the IS curve can also be obtained by solving $Y = C + I + G$ with C and I given by equations (A5) and (A7), respectively.

With the *IS* curve in hand, we turn to the *LM* curve. The demand for money is assumed to be given by

$$M^D = 0.2Y + (110 - 10r) \tag{A10}$$

The supply of money will be denoted by

$$M^S = \overline{M} \tag{A11}$$

As with *G*, we will shortly assume some specific numerical values for $\overline{M}$. Since the *LM* curve is defined by

$$M^S = M^D \tag{A12}$$

we can combine equations (A10), (A11), and (A12) to yield

$$\overline{M} = 0.2Y + (110 - 10r)$$

This can be solved for *r* to give

$$r = 0.02Y + 11 - 0.1\overline{M} \tag{A13}$$

Equation (A13) is the algebraic expression for the *LM* curve. The negative way in which $\overline{M}$ enters the equation shows that an increase of $\overline{M}$ will shift the *LM* curve down and to the right. This is so because at any given level of *Y* a larger value for $\overline{M}$ will yield a lower value for *r*—and this is algebraically what we mean by a downward shift.

Overall equilibrium is achieved at the intersection of the *IS* and *LM* equations, which algebraically amounts to solving equations (A9) and (A13) simultaneously. This is, we have

$$0.02Y + 11 - 0.1\overline{M} = 26 + 0.1G - 0.04Y$$

After some arithmetic, this can be rearranged to yield

$$Y = 250 + \frac{5}{3}G + \frac{5}{3}\overline{M} \tag{A14}$$

Equation (A14) is actually a most useful result because it permits us to calculate the equilibrium value of *Y* corresponding to any combination of values for *G* and $\overline{M}$. For example, if $G = 200$ and $\overline{M} = 250$, we see that

$$Y = 250 + \frac{5}{3}200 + \frac{5}{3}250 = 1{,}000$$

From either (A9) or (A13) we can then calculate that

$$r = 6$$

Thus, the equilibrium corresponding to $G = 200$, $M = 250$ is $Y = 1{,}000$, $r = 6$.

Equation (A14) can, of course, be used to produce the equilibrium values of *Y* corresponding to other values of *G* and $\overline{M}$. Table 15A–1 gives the equilibrium values for *Y*, *C*, *I*, and *r* corresponding to the values just assumed and to two other sets of assumptions for *G* and $\overline{M}$.

TABLE 15A–1 Some Numerical Examples

		EQUILIBRIUM VALUES			
		Y	C	I	r
Case I	$\overline{G} = 200$ $\overline{M} = 250$	1,000	730	70	6
Case II	$\overline{G} = 230$ $\overline{M} = 250$	1,050	760	60	7
Case III	$\overline{G} = 200$ $\overline{M} = 280$	1,050	760	90	4

Case I is the one used originally, Cases II and III both result in the same higher level of income $(Y = 1,050)$, but in case II this is achieved by an increase in G, whereas in case III this comes about from an increase in $\overline{M}$. The effects on the composition of output discussed earlier are quite evident in Table 15A–1. An expansionary monetary policy is seen to result in an increase in I and a decrease in r relative to case I, while the reverse is true for an expansionary fiscal policy.

The reader is invited to shift some of the functions and solve for the results. For example, assume that

1 G is reduced from $\overline{G} = 200$ to $\overline{G} = 180$ and $\overline{M}$ is simultaneously increased from $\overline{M} = 200$ to $\overline{M} = 220$.
2 The consumption function is shifted to $C = 160 + 0.8DI$.
3 Taxes are increased, so that $T = 0.30Y$.

Finally, we can also use our example to illustrate numerically how the full' basic multiplier or $1 \div (\Delta S/\Delta Y)$ tends to be snubbed by a rise in interest rates. From equation (6) in the text of this chapter, we recall that $\Delta S/\Delta Y$ stands for the marginal responsiveness of saving and taxes to a change in income. In the present example, combining (A6) and (A4) we get

$$S + T = -130 + 0.4Y$$

Thus, $\Delta S/\Delta Y = 0.4$ and the basic multiplier is $1/0.4 = 2.5$. This means, for example, if r were to remain unchanged, an increase in G of 30 $(\Delta G = 30)$ would raise Y by $30 \times 2.5 = 75$. Of course, as we have already seen in comparing cases I and II in Table 15A–1, when $\Delta G = 30$, r is driven up from 6 percent to 7 percent. As a consequence, the actual increase in Y is held to 50. Hence, the actual multiplier is $\Delta Y/\Delta G = 50/30 = 5/3$.[2] This is a numerical illustration of the effect pictured in Figure 15–8.

[2]As should be apparent, the relevant multiplier for a change in G is the coefficient of G in equation (A14). Similarly, the relevant multiplier for changing $\overline{M}$ is its coefficient in equation (A14). The fact that the two numbers are the same in the present case is merely a coincidence. This will not be true in general.

SELECTED READINGS

Branson, W. H. *Macroeconomic Theory and Policy*, 2nd ed. New York: Harper & Row, 1979.

Dornbusch, R., and S. Fischer. *Macroeconomics*, 3rd ed. New York: McGraw-Hill, 1984.

Gordon, R. J. *Macroeconomics*, 3rd ed. Boston: Little, Brown, 1984.

16

AGGREGATE DEMAND AND AGGREGATE SUPPLY

In previous chapters we made extensive use of the *IS–LM* framework to explore the determination of equilibrium values for income and the interest rate. Two important assumptions were made in the development of the *IS–LM* model. First, the price level was assumed to be constant, so that changes in real and nominal quantities were equivalent. Second, the notion of overall equilibrium for the economy was confined to simultaneous equilibrium in the commodity market (*IS*) and the money market (*LM*). No attention was paid to the labor market or to the production side of things. In other words, the *IS–LM* framework focuses exclusively on questions of aggregate demand, but neglects issues concerning aggregate supply.

The purpose of this chapter is to relax both these assumptions. In particular, we will be concerned with questions such as: "Suppose nominal aggregate demand increases or decreases by some specified amount. To what extent will this be reflected in price changes? In the rate of real output? In the level of employment?" Answers to these questions are important because effects on economic welfare depend heavily on the nature of the response. For example, it does matter whether a decline in aggregate demand is reflected almost entirely in decreased price levels or largely in decreased real output and employment. And it does matter whether an increase in aggregate demand is reflected solely in price inflation or in large increases in real output and employment.

DEMAND AND SUPPLY

As a first step toward understanding the responses of output, employment, and prices to demand conditions and to changes in demand conditions, it will be useful to recall some aspects of general economic theory relating to the demand and supply of a commodity that is produced and sold under conditions approximating those of pure competition. Suppose, for example, that the demand and supply conditions for this commodity are represented by the demand function, *DD*, and the supply function, *SS*, in Figure 16–1. Price (denoted by *P*) is measured along the vertical axis. The quantities demanded and supplied per period of time, such as per year, are measured along the horizontal axis (designated by *Q*). We find that as long as demand and supply conditions for this commodity continue to be those represented by the *DD* and *SS* curves, the market for this commodity can be in equilibrium only if the quantities actually supplied and demanded are at Q_0 and the price is P_0. Only this combination of *P* and *Q* will exactly clear the market, leaving no excess supply or excess demand.

This example illustrates at least two simple points that will be useful for our later analysis. First, market equilibrium is not determined by demand conditions alone, nor by supply conditions alone, but by a combination of both. Second, both price and the actual rate of output and sales are determined simultaneously.

As before, we can use comparative statics to compare two sets of equilibrium conditions: those existing before and after a shift of a demand or supply function. We can thus determine how equilibrium will be changed if the demand function or the supply function shifts in a specified way. Suppose, as in Figure 16–2, that for some reason the demand function increases from *DD* to D_1D_1. That is, the community demands more of the

FIGURE 16–1
Demand for, and supply of, a commodity

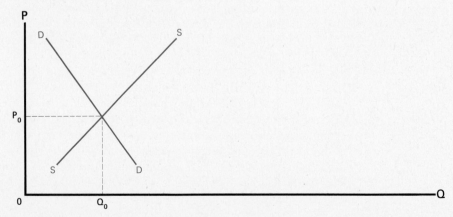

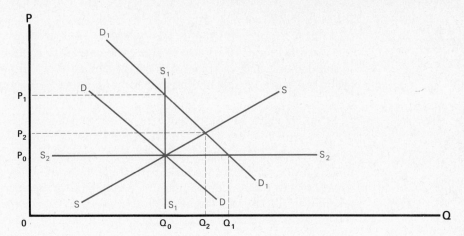

FIGURE 16–2
Shifts in demand

commodity at each price or will pay a higher price for each quantity. This will tend to raise the price, to increase the quantities actually supplied and purchased, or to raise both prices and quantities produced and sold. The actual effects of any given increase in demand will depend on supply conditions, and more specifically on the responsiveness of quantities supplied to changes in price.

Suppose supply is completely unresponsive or inelastic to price, as indicated by the supply curve S_1S_1 (Figure 16–2). In this case the entire effect of the increase in demand is to raise the price from P_0 to P_1. The quantities produced and sold and the quantities of productive factors employed in producing the commodity remain unchanged. Suppose, to go to the other extreme, that supply is completely responsive or elastic to price, as indicated by the supply function S_2S_2. That is, suppliers stand ready to supply at price P_0 any quantity that may be demanded, but will supply nothing at a lower price. In this case the increase in demand will not raise price at all; its entire effect will be to increase quantities produced and sold and to increase the quantity of productive factors employed in producing the commodity. Usually, the responsiveness of supply to price will lie somewhere between these extremes. This is illustrated by the supply function SS. In these situations an increase in demand will increase price, quantities actually produced and sold, and the quantities of productive factors employed in producing the good. The more responsive supply is to price, the less a given increase in demand will raise price, and the more it will increase quantities.

In the remainder of this chapter, we will adapt this type of analysis, which was originally developed to explain the prices and output of individual commodities, to the economy as a whole. Our supply function will relate to the economy's aggregate output of goods and services, and our demand function will relate to the quantities of that output demanded at various price levels. If we are to study the aggregate economy by analogy to the demand-supply framework, we must next focus on how one arrives at the aggregate versions of the demand and supply function.

THE AGGREGATE DEMAND FUNCTION

In Figure 16–1 we saw that the demand function for an individual commodity is a relationship between the price of the commodity and the quantity of the commodity demanded. By analogy then, the *aggregate demand function* or, as it is sometimes called, the *economy's demand curve*, is a relationship between the general price level, P, and the level of real output, which we previously have denoted by O. But how are we to arrive at such a relationship? As implied earlier, we must reconsider the *IS–LM* framework when the price level is no longer required to be a constant. This introduces an important distinction that was glossed over before. In particular, when the price level was being treated as a constant, we could afford to be casual about the differences between nominal and real magnitudes. However, this is no longer the case. It is important for our present purposes that we carefully distinguish between the following: M^D, which is the quantity of *nominal* balances demanded, and M^D/P, which is the quantity of *real* balances demanded; and between *nominal* income, Y, and *real* income, $O = Y/P$. With these distinctions in mind, we now turn first to a reconsideration of the *LM* curve.

THE *LM* CURVE

The *LM* curve is defined by the condition

$$M^D = M^S \tag{1}$$

where, as before, we assume that the money supply is exogenously fixed by the monetary authorities at $\overline{M}$. Thus, we have

$$M^S = \overline{M} \tag{2}$$

It will be recalled from Chapter 13 that the general form of our money demand function is

$$\frac{M^D}{P} = F\left(\frac{Y}{P}, r\right) = F(O, r) \tag{3}$$

which says that the demand for real balances is a function of real income (Y/P or O) and the interest rate. We have also seen a special case of equation (3) given by

$$\frac{M^D}{P} = J\frac{Y}{P} + (A - er) = JO + (A - er) \tag{4}$$

Equations (1), (2), and (3) can be combined to give

$$\frac{\overline{M}}{P} = F\left(\frac{Y}{P}, r\right) = F(O, r) \tag{5}$$

while (1), (2), and (4) yield

$$\frac{\overline{M}}{P} = J\frac{Y}{P} + (A - er) = JO + (A - er) \tag{6}$$

As earlier, equation (5) or (6) defines the *LM* curve. But there is now one important difference. With *P* taken as a constant, (5) is an equation in two variables, Y/P (or *O*) and *r*. And the pairs of *r* and Y/P that satisfy this equation give the *LM* curve. However, when *P* is free to vary, equation (5) contains three variables, Y/P, *r*, and *P*. Consequently, when *P* is variable, it is no longer true that (5) defines a *single LM* curve relating *r* and Y/P. However, it is still true that for any *given* value of *P*, (5) does define a conventional *LM* curve. Thus, we see that what equation (5) really does is to define a *family* of *LM* curves, one for each possible value for *P*. This is illustrated in Figure 16–3.

As drawn, the curve L_1M_1 corresponds to an assumed value for the price level of P_1. Now let us ask what *LM* curve will correspond to some lower price level, P_2. From equation (5) we see that lowering the price level raises the left-hand side of (5). That is, it increases the supply of real money balances. To achieve equilibrium with this new higher supply of real money balances requires that the demand for real money balances also increase. This can be brought about by an increase in *O*, or a decrease in *r*, or both. Consider, for example, point *A* on L_1M_1, which has $r = r_1$ and $O = O_1$.

FIGURE 16–3
LM **curves corresponding to alternative price levels**

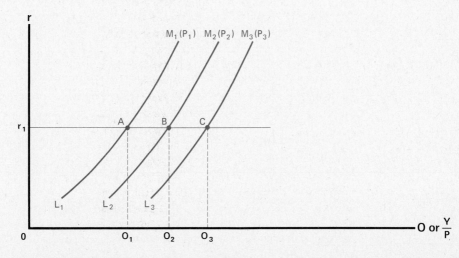

With a lower price level such as P_2, if the interest rate stays at r_1, real output must increase, say, to O_2, to reestablish equilibrium. Thus, we see that the LM curve corresponding to P_2, must lie to the right of L_1M_1, as shown by L_2M_2 in Figure 16–3. Similarly, if the price level was at an even lower value, such as P_3, we know that the corresponding LM curve, L_3M_3, must lie still farther to the right of L_1M_1.

A moment's thought should reveal that this result could have been readily anticipated. Inspecting equation (5), we see that a decrease in P has the same effect on $\overline{M}/P$ as an increase in $\overline{M}$. But we have already seen that increasing the money supply shifts the LM curve out to the right. It is thus hardly surprising that a decrease in P should do the same.

In summary then, permitting the price level to vary forces us to replace a single LM curve with a family of LM curves such as is pictured in Figure 16–3. We now turn to a reexamination of the IS curve.

THE *IS* CURVE

Here the situation is, fortunately, quite simple, since there remains a single IS curve, even when P is variable. The only difference is that the IS curve must now be regarded as a relationship between r and Y/P (or O) rather than between r and Y. The reason for a single such IS curve is as follows.

Although we were not explicit on this point earlier (it did not matter with a constant P), the expenditure functions underlying the IS curve should be regarded as expressing relationships between real or constant dollar magnitudes. Thus, for example, the proper way to think of the consumption function is that it makes real consumption expenditures depend on real income. Similarly, the investment demand function is properly specified with real investment expenditures depending on the interest rate. In each case the reason is straightforward. What lies behind a consumption function is some kind of utility-maximizing behavior by individuals. But utility can only sensibly be regarded as a function of the real quantity of goods consumed. Consequently, the process of utility maximization must lead to a consumption function expressed in real terms. As for the investment demand function, as we have seen, it results from the desire of firms to achieve an optimal quantity of capital goods for production. But clearly it is only the quantity of capital goods measured in real terms that is relevant for production. As a consequence, the investment demand function itself must be specified in real terms.

The thrust of this argument can be summarized quite briefly. With the consumption function in real terms we must have the saving function in real terms. Thus, real saving, S/P, is a positive function of real income, Y/P, and real investment, I/P, is a negative function of the interest rate. Equilibrium is now characterized by[1]

[1] We are implicitly assuming here that government expenditures are set in real terms and that the tax functions are also similarly expressed. These assumptions considerably simplify the exposition, but at best are only approximately true.

$$\frac{I}{P} + \frac{G}{P} = \frac{S}{P} + \frac{T}{P}$$

or, equivalently, by

$$\frac{Y}{P} = \frac{C}{P} + \frac{I}{P} + \frac{G}{P}$$

Consequently, the *IS* curve can be derived exactly as we did before. As already indicated, the only difference is that the *IS* curve now relates r and Y/P. A typical *IS* curve is shown in Figure 16–4, where we again have drawn a family of *LM* curves corresponding to different price levels.

As Figure 16–4 shows, when the price level is P_1, the equilibrium value of real output is O_1. At P_2, which is less than P_1, output is O_2, while at P_3 it is O_3. At each intersection, of course, there is a different equilibrium value for the interest rate. We thus see that, as far as the demand side of the economy is concerned, varying the price level produces opposite variations in the equilibrium level of output demanded. This inverse relationship between P and O is precisely the aggregate demand curve we have been seeking.

THE *DD* CURVE

In other words, to obtain the aggregate demand curve we must simply plot the equilibrium values of P in Figure 16–4 against the corresponding values for O. This is done in Figure 16–5, where the resulting curve is labeled *DD*. Thus, for example, the equilibrium pairs (P_1, O_1), (P_2, O_2), and (P_3, O_3) of Figure 16–4 all lie on the *DD* curve in Figure 16–5. We thus see that the *DD* curve, like a conventional demand curve, is downward-sloping, so that as the price level increases, the equilibrium output demanded decreases. The explanation of the downward slope is not, however, the ordinary substi-

FIGURE 16–4
IS **and** *LM* **curves for alternative price levels**

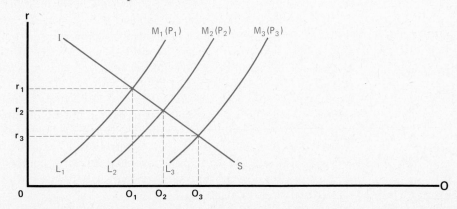

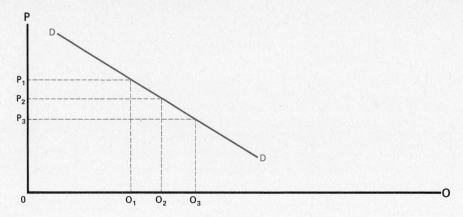

FIGURE 16–5
The aggregate demand curve

tution effect of a rising price reducing demand. Rather, an increase in P reduces output demanded, O, by tightening the money market, raising the interest rate, and consequently reducing investment. As this reemphasizes, as we move along the DD curve, the interest rate is constantly adjusting in the background to its new equilibrium level.

SHIFTING THE DD CURVE

We have earlier studied how shifts in government purchases of goods and services, in the tax and transfer functions, and in the investment and saving functions can induce shifts in the IS curve. Similarly, we have seen how changes in the money supply can shift the LM curve. As we will now see, precisely these factors will shift the DD curve. Let us first consider an exogenous change, perhaps an expansionary fiscal policy of some kind, which shifts the IS curve to the right.

This is illustrated in part (a) of Figure 16–6 as a shift from $I_0 S_0$ to $I_1 S_1$. When the relevant IS curve is $I_0 S_0$, we see that points like (P_1, O_1) and (P_2, O_2) lie on the initial DD curve, labeled $D_0 D_0$ in part (b). After the shift to $I_1 S_1$, we see from part (a) that equilibrium comes about at pairs like (P_1, O_3) and (P_2, O_4), where O_3 exceeds O_1 and O_4 exceeds O_2. Thus, we see that anything that shifts the IS curve to the right will also shift the DD curve to the right. This is shown in part (b) as a shift from $D_0 D_0$ to $D_1 D_1$. Similarly, anything that shifts the LM curve will also shift the DD curve in the same direction. Consider, for example, an increase in the money supply. We know that at any *given* price level, this must shift the LM curve to the right. This is shown in part (a) of Figure 16–7, where *both* $L_1 M_1$ and $L_2 M_2$ are drawn on the assumption that the price level is P_1. $L_1 M_1$, of course, shifts to $L_2 M_2$ as a result of the increased money supply. We thus see that (P_1, O_1) must

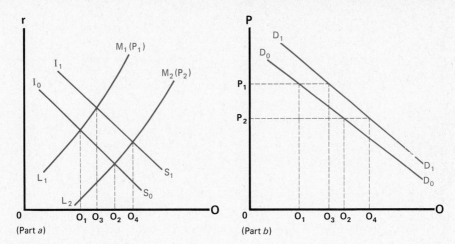

FIGURE 16–6
Shifting the *DD* curve: an *IS* shift

be on the initial *DD* curve, labeled D_0D_0 in part (b), and that (P_1, O_2) must be on the new *DD* curve. This is labeled D_1D_1 in part (b). Consequently, we see that an increase in M^S serves to shift the *DD* curve to the right.

OVERVIEW

This section has introduced the notion of the aggregate demand or *DD* curve, which gives the combinations of *P* and *O* that equilibrate the aggregate demand sector. We have also seen that anything that shifts the *IS* and

FIGURE 16–7
Shifting the *DD* curve: an *LM* shift

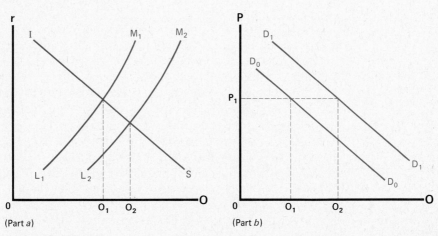

LM curves will shift the *DD* curve in the same direction. As should be readily apparent, however, the *DD* curve is not itself sufficient to determine the overall equilibrium of the price level and real income. This is because we have added a new variable, the price level, to our *IS–LM* framework, but we have added no new equations. As indicated earlier, this new equation, the aggregate supply curve, will come from the labor market, and it is to this that we now turn.

AGGREGATE SUPPLY: THE CLASSICAL CASE

We begin our discussion of the supply side of the economy with what is known as the *classical* model. John Maynard Keynes applied the term *classical* to those economists who dominated economic thought, at least in England and the United States, from the latter part of the nineteenth century until the early 1930s. Three basic assumptions are essential for the operation of the classical model:

1 All markets for output and labor are purely competitive, and all enterprises seek to maximize their profits.
2 Decisions relating to output and employment are not based on absolute levels of prices and money wage rates; instead, they are based on relative wages and prices. This is sometimes referred to as the absence of *money illusion*. This means each producer bases output decisions not on the absolute price of the product, but on its price relative to cost. Similarly, the quantities of labor demanded by firms and supplied by individuals depend not on the absolute level of the money wage rate, but on what is called the *real wage rate*, which is the ratio of the money wage rate to the price level.
3 Both prices and money wage rates are perfectly flexible, and can fluctuate both upward and downward. They change to the extent necessary in order to secure levels of relative prices and wages that lead to equilibrium in the labor market.

The consequences of these assumptions are quite straightforward. With flexible wages and prices adjusting to bring the labor market into equilibrium, there will always be *full employment* of labor. Given the prevailing state of technology and the nation's endowments of capital and natural resources, the level of labor input associated with full employment will yield what might be called the *full employment level of real output*. We denote this level of real output by the symbol O_e. A further consequence of the classical assumptions is that, barring changes in technology, the level of real output will be steadily maintained at the level O_e. As a consequence, in the classical case the aggregate supply curve is simply a vertical line at the level O_e. This is illustrated in Figure 16–8, where the aggregate supply

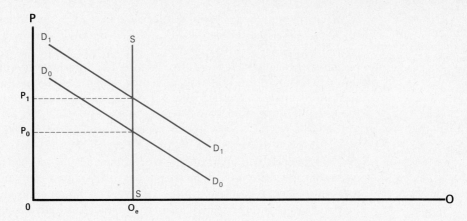

FIGURE 16–8
Aggregate demand and supply: the classical case

curve is labeled SS^2. In order to explore the consequences of this, we turn to an examination of the workings of the full classical model.

THE FULL CLASSICAL MODEL

The full classical model is summarized by the aggregate supply curve just developed and the aggregate demand curve as previously derived. These curves are illustrated in Figure 16–8, which shows the joint determination of O and P. To see how the classical model works, we again rely on the tool of comparative statics. We first consider an increase in the demand for output.

INCREASE IN THE DEMAND FOR OUTPUT

Suppose we begin from the situation illustrated in Figure 16–8, in which the aggregate demand curve is D_0D_0 and the aggregate supply curve is vertical at O_e. At the initial equilibrium the price level is P_0 and nominal income is $P_0 \times O_e$. Suppose now that, because of an autonomous increase in investment demand, the aggregate function shifts up from D_0D_0 to D_1D_1. That is, at any given level of output the community becomes willing to pay a higher price for that level of output. At the initially prevailing price level, P_0, we now have a situation of excess demand, which puts upward pressure on the price level. Since the supply of output is unresponsive to the rise of demand and prices, equilibrium will be reestablished only when the price

[2]For an explicit derivation of the aggregate supply curve, see the appendix to this chapter.

level has risen to P_1, thus eliminating the excess demand. The assumptions of the classical model also assure us that money wages will rise in proportion to prices. We know this because Figure 16–8 tells us that real output remains unchanged. This in turn means that the level of employment is unchanged after the shift in aggregate demand. Given our classical assumptions, this can happen only if the real wage is unchanged; wages must rise to match the increase in prices.

While Figure 16–8 provides an overall summary of the effects of an increase in aggregate demand, it must be recalled that behind Figure 16–8 lies the savings and investment functions and the money demand and money supply functions. In fact, we must turn to these functions if we want to see the effects on interest rates. Indeed, a moment's thought will reveal that the interest rate, r, must rise as a result of the increase in aggregate demand. Since real output is unchanged, saving, and, therefore investment, must also be unchanged in the new equilibrium. But we began from the assumption that an upward shift in the investment demand function had caused the shift in the DD function. It should be obvious, then, that with actual investment unchanged, the interest rate must rise to choke off this potential addition to investment. This point is illustrated in the IS–LM diagram of Figure 16–9. The initial equilibrium is at the intersection of I_0S_0 and L_0M_0 or at $r = r_0$ and $O = O_e$. The shift of the investment demand function in turn shifts the IS curve to I_1S_1. This creates excess demand, and the resulting upward movement in prices shifts the LM curve up and to the left—recall that an increase in the price level is like a decrease in the money supply. As we know from Figure 16–8, a new equilibrium will be established only when the LM curve has shifted to L_1M_1, which corresponds to a price level of P_1. When this happens, the level of output is maintained at O_e but the equilibrium interest rate rises from r_0 to r_1.

In summary, then, an upward shift in investment demand in the classical

FIGURE 16–9
An *IS* shift

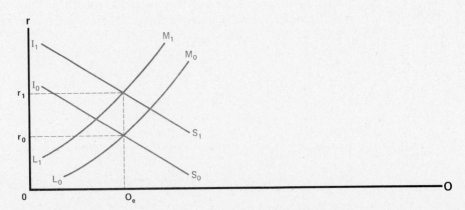

model raises the interest rate and raises wages and prices proportionately. It thus also raises nominal income. But it leaves unchanged real output, employment, and the real wage.

DECREASE IN DEMAND FOR OUTPUT

Let us turn now to the reverse case, in which the demand function for output shifts downward. We can again use Figure 16–8 for this purpose, assuming that we start from a situation in which the demand function for output is D_1D_1, the rate of real output is at the capacity level O_e, and the price level is P_1. Suppose now that the demand function shifts downward because of a decline in the investment demand function. This is shown in Figure 16–8 as a shift of the DD curve from D_1D_1 to D_0D_0. The initial equilibrium price level, P_1, is now one of disequilibrium. At this price level the amount of output demanded is below the full employment level, O_e. With flexible prices and competitive markets, this will tend to lower prices. The fall of prices will lead employers to decrease the quantity of labor demanded at the old level of money wage rates. Some unemployment will occur, at least initially. However, the unemployed will bid against each other for jobs, thereby lowering money wage rates. Such declines in money wage rates and prices will continue so long as unemployment persists.

Is it inevitable that decreases in money wage rates and prices will again make it profitable for producers to employ the entire labor supply? A decrease in money wage rates has at least two types of effects. On the one hand, as we have already seen, it serves to lower costs of production. This appears favorable to an expansion of output and employment. On the other hand, it lowers the amount of money income received by labor for each hour of work. Thus it is possible, at least in principle, that the favorable effects of reductions in money costs of production will be offset by reductions in money demands for output. The classical economists contended that this would not occur; the deflationary spiral of money wage rates and prices would be stopped and recovery of real output and employment would be induced by a phenomenon that has been called variously the *Pigou effect*, the *real balance effect*, and the *real wealth effect*. The real wealth effect is based on two propositions:

1 Real demands for output depend not only on real income, but also on real wealth. The latter is defined as (*money value of assets*/price level). In general, the greater the community's real wealth, the greater will be the level of its real consumption relative to its real income.

2 A fall in the price level raises the real wealth or purchasing power of the community's assets that are fixed in terms of monetary units. Members of the private sector, feeling richer in real terms because of the increased purchasing power of their debt claims against the government, increase their real demands for output, thereby pushing output and employment back toward full employment levels.

The net result of this process is the restoration of the equilibrium pictured in Figure 16–8 by the intersection of D_0D_0 and SS. That is, the shift in investment demand yields proportionately lower levels of prices and money wage rates, but leaves unchanged equilibrium levels of real output, employment, and real wages.

POLICY IN THE CLASSICAL MODEL

In the classical model, as we have just seen, shifts of the aggregate demand curve ultimately produce no changes in the level of real output, employment, and the real wage rate. Since both monetary and fiscal policy operate by shifting the DD curve, we know immediately that neither policy can affect any real magnitudes. While the operation of policy in the classical model is thus somewhat dull, it will nevertheless be instructive to sketch the main points.

MONETARY POLICY

Consider a decrease in the money supply. This shifts the LM curve to the left and creates excess demand in the money market. This tends to push up the interest rate, which in turn tends to reduce investment demand. As a consequence, excess supply is created in the commodity market and prices start falling. The fall in prices raises the real money supply, moving the LM curve back down toward its initial position. Equilibrium will be restored when the fall in prices exactly balances the decrease in the money supply. This is illustrated in Figure 16–10.

Thus, a decrease in the money supply leaves real output, employment, the interest rate, and real wages unchanged and merely changes prices and money wages. Both prices and money wages, in fact, decrease *exactly in proportion* to the decrease in the money supply. This can be seen by ex-

FIGURE 16–10
An *LM* shift

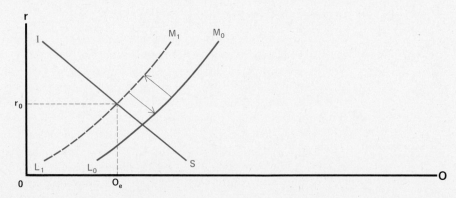

amining the condition for equilibrium in the money market—equation (5)—which is reproduced below:

$$\frac{\overline{M}}{P} = F(O, r)$$

From this equation we see that a 5 percent reduction of $\overline{M}$, for example, which leaves O and r unchanged, must produce a 5 percent reduction of the price level, P, for this is the only way in which equilibrium in the money market can be maintained.

We thus see that in the classical model there is a complete dichotomy between the real economy and nominal or money values. The only effect of a change in the money supply is to change nominal values proportionately.

FISCAL POLICY

Suppose we are dealing with a contractionary fiscal policy such as a reduction in government spending. The decline in G creates an excess supply of goods and puts downward pressure on prices. As prices fall, the real money supply increases, interest rates fall, and investment is stimulated. The details of this can, in fact, be traced with the help of Figures 16–8 and 16–9. In the new equilibrium, the price level is lower, but real output and employment remain unchanged. The interest rate, however, will decrease. This serves to stimulate investment in an amount exactly equal to the decline in government spending. Thus, fiscal policy does have an allocative effect: Resources are shifted from government spending to investment with a given level of total real output.

OVERVIEW

Having analyzed the operation of the classical model, we see that a fair characterization of the classical school is the following: "A free-enterprise economy contains within itself strong forces toward the achievement and maintenance of full employment. These forces serve to prevent departures from full employment, and any unemployment that may occur invokes automatic adjustments that restore full employment. Equilibrium at less than full employment is impossible."

It is worth emphasizing again the crucial role played in this model by the perfect downward flexibility of prices and money wage rates. It was the fall in prices that restored the community's real money balances and raised real demand for output enough to absorb the full employment supply of output. And the perfect downward flexibility of money wage rates served both to lower labor costs of production in money terms, thus rendering possible the required fall in prices, and to adjust real wage rates to the level necessary to restore full employment.

While the logic of the classical model is impeccable, its characterization of the economy has often seemed wide of the mark. This was certainly true during the 1930s, when many countries suffered extended periods of substantial unemployment. In the minds of many it is also true of the behavior of the U.S. economy in recent years. Those who are disaffected with the conclusions of the classical model have sought to reconcile economic theory and economic experience in two different ways.

One way has been to accept the premises of the classical model but to argue that the process of adjustment to a downward shift in aggregate demand—what is sometimes called the *dynamics*—is such that the economy may experience difficulties in attaining a new equilibrium. For example, the real wealth effect may be too weak and/or act too slowly to be of practical significance. Alternatively, a weak economy may set up expectations that hinder a recovery, perhaps by reducing the creditworthiness of business firms and discouraging investment. For a variety of reasons, then, it may well be that even in an economy conforming to all the assumptions of the classical model, there would be no assurance that automatic forces would restore full employment reliably, quickly, and at a minimum social cost. Under such circumstances, prompt action by policymakers could well have desirable effects.

The second way in which economists have attempted to reconcile theory and experience has been to challenge the assumptions of the model. In particular, many writers have found that actual conditions in markets for labor and output depart significantly from those assumed in the classical model. We now examine some of these criticisms, as well as the consequences of departing from the classical model.

DEPARTURES FROM THE CLASSICAL MODEL

While many economists regard the classical model as a reasonable characterization of the evolution of the economy in the long run, they view this model as inadequate for understanding the behavior of the economy in the short run. We know, for example, that recessions are not uncommon occurrences and that they are marked by extended periods of substantial unemployment of labor and productive capacity. In order to understand these phenomena, it is necessary to examine some of the crucial assumptions of the classical model. As we have seen, one of the key facets of the model is the flexibility of wages and prices. Indeed, it is this feature that gives rise to the vertical aggregate supply curve pictured in Figure 16–8. As we will now see, there are serious reasons to question the flexiblity of wages and prices in the short run. Moreover, once we relax the assumption of complete flexibility, the aggregate supply curve no longer retains its vertical shape in the short run.

LACK OF WAGE AND PRICE FLEXIBILITY

The classical model assumes that money wage rates are freely flexible both upward and downward. In effect, the classical model assumes that the labor market behaves like the market for any commodity, such as copper or wheat. However, as we look at labor markets in the United States and other industrialized countries, we are forced to conclude that these conditions are not always met. Money wages are often rigid or "sticky," especially downward, sometimes for extended periods of time. For example, when unemployment appears or increases in amount, money wage rates do not fall, or they begin to fall only after a substantial delay.

There are many reasons for this lack of flexibility. Sometimes workers and firms enter into long-term labor contracts that set money wages for up to three years ahead. Even in the absence of explicit contracts, wages tend to be adjusted relatively infrequently—say once a year. What this means is that wages are fixed for some period of time. Why this happens, of course, requires an explanation. The answer lies in the nature of the labor market. From the viewpoint of both firms and workers, a job is generally regarded as a long-term commitment. From the perspective of the firm, it is expensive to fire and hire workers. Firing requires severance pay and the loss of any special expertise the worker has accumulated on the job. Hiring involves advertising and interviewing expenses and training the new worker. In the light of these costs, a firm tends to think of much of its labor force as being reasonably attached to it. Similarly, from a worker's point of view, a job is a more than day-to-day affair. Job changes are costly, and workers are therefore also concerned with long-term arrangements.

Given that workers and firms view a job in a longer-term context, it is plausible that they would reach some explicit or implicit understanding about the terms of work. Such terms include normal working hours, overtime requirements, policies with respect to layoffs, and most important for our purposes, the level of wages. Not surprisingly, since jobs are not viewed as day-to-day arrangements, we find that wages do not adjust continuously to bring the demand and supply for labor into immediate balance. Even in the face of an increase in unemployment, firms do not rush to adjust the wages of existing workers. Simply put, in the short run the wage is not nearly as flexible as assumed by the classical model.

Similarly, prices of goods can also be less flexible than assumed by the classical model. In some instances, firms may make long-term contracts for raw materials to be delivered at prearranged prices. More generally, there may be other sorts of limitations on price flexibility. It is often argued, for example, that firms set prices with respect to longer-run or *normal standard* costs, rather than varying their prices in response to temporary shifts, either up or down. One rationale for this is that, as in commercial banking, there is often a "customer relationship" between firms and those who buy from them. Customers prefer to avoid costly searching for the best price, and

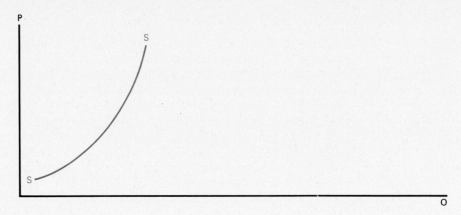

FIGURE 16–11
Aggregate supply: the nonclassical case

firms have an incentive to maintain a degree of price stability to encourage customers to return.

As a consequence of this behavior, prices may not immediately or fully respond to shifts in aggregate demand. For example, in response to a decline in nominal aggregate demand, prices may decline only slowly. This is not to say that prices will remain inflexible in such situations, especially if the decline in demand is large and prolonged. Nevertheless, the description of the economy that emerges from this view is quite different from the classical one. In particular, for some considerable period of time much of the effect of a decline in aggregate demand may be translated into a decline in real output or employment. Similar departures from the classical model may occur in response to increases in aggregate demand.

THE CONSEQUENCES OF STICKINESS

When there is some stickiness in wages and prices, the operation of the economy is distinctly nonclassical. At an analytical level, the major difference is that the aggregate supply curve is no longer vertical; rather, it has the upward sloping shape portrayed in Figure 16–11. It is easy to see why this is the case.[3]

The aggregate supply curve shows the amount of output that firms are willing to supply at various price levels. When wages are sticky, it means that business firms can purchase their major input, labor, at relatively fixed prices. This is significant because firms decide how much to produce by comparing the price they can get for their goods with the cost of producing those goods. And the major cost of producing these goods is the cost of labor. If selling prices increase while wages are relatively fixed, this com-

[3]For a more formal derivation, see the appendix to this chapter.

parison looks more promising (profitable), and firms will increase production. If selling prices decline and wages are relatively fixed, firms may well curtail production.

This is precisely the behavior that is captured in the upward-sloping aggregate supply curve in Figure 16–11: Production rises when the price level increases and declines when the price level declines. Simply put, the supply curve slopes upward because firms can purchase labor inputs at relatively fixed costs, at least for some period of time. Higher prices make input costs seem "cheaper" and spur production. To be sure, the phrase "for some period of time" warns us that the aggregate supply curve pictured in Figure 16–11 is a short-run concept. Below we take up the consequences of the fact that the short-run supply curve may not stand still. First, however, we consider the interaction of aggregate demand and aggregate supply in our alternative model.

To anticipate a bit, one major difference between our alternative model and the classical model is that our model provides a serious justification for the explicit use of monetary and fiscal policies to improve economic performance. As we have seen, if actual conditions in the economy corresponded to those assumed in the classical model, it would not be wholly unreasonable to argue that monetary and fiscal policies are of relatively little importance. Fluctuations of aggregate demand would change the price level but not employment and real output. The complete flexibility of wages and prices could be relied on to restore full employment. However, the case for deliberate management of aggregate demand becomes compelling in an economy with money wage rates that are rigid or adjust only after a long delay and then to only a limited extent, and with incompletely flexible prices. In such an economy fluctuations of aggregate demand affect not only prices and money wage rates, but also employment and output. In addition, it cannot be expected that a departure from full employment will be corrected automatically and quickly.

In such an economy, monetary, fiscal, and other policies that regulate aggregate demand can indeed be used to regulate total employment and output. For example, an increase in aggregate demand can increase total employment and output if the economy is operating below capacity levels. To see how this works, we turn to an explicit analysis of policy in our alternative model.

EQUILIBRIUM AND POLICY IN THE ALTERNATIVE MODEL

Overall equilibrium in our alternative model is portrayed in Figure 16–12. To see how this model works, we can again use the tool of comparative statics. Suppose we begin from the situation illustrated in Figure 16–12 in which the aggregate demand curve is D_1D_1. At the initial equilibrium the price level is $P = P_1$, and the level of real output is $O = O_1$. Now let us

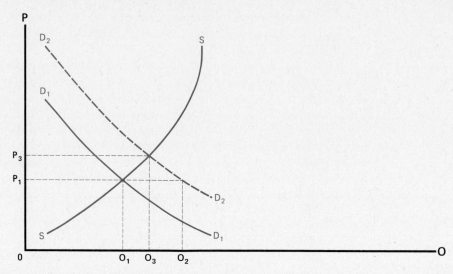

FIGURE 16–12
Aggregate demand and supply: the nonclassical
case

suppose that the authorities are unhappy with the level of employment and output at the initial position and wish to increase both. As before, we examine separately fiscal and monetary policies aimed at bringing about the desired expansion.

FISCAL POLICY

Suppose that the fiscal authorities attempt to bring about expansion by increasing real government purchases of goods and services, G/P. The immediate effect of this, shown in Figure 16–13 is to shift the IS curve from I_1S_1 to I_2S_2. This is because the increase in G/P increases GNP both directly and indirectly through the multiplier process on consumption. At the initial price level this increase in output raises the demand for money, putting upward pressure on the interest rate. Thus, with the price level at P_1, we see in Figure 16–13 that equilibrium on the demand side moves us to $r = r_2$ and $O = O_2$. But of course the price level cannot remain unchanged, since at P_1 the supply of output is O_1 but the demand is greater (O_2). Hence, prices start to rise.

The rise in P reduces the real supply of money, shifting the LM curve back to the left toward L_2M_2. This raises interest rates further, tending to reduce investment and hence total aggregate demand. The rise in prices continues until the excess demand has been eliminated—at $P = P_3$ and $O = O_3$ in Figure 16–12. At this price level, the IS and LM curves intersect at O_3 in Figure 16–13.

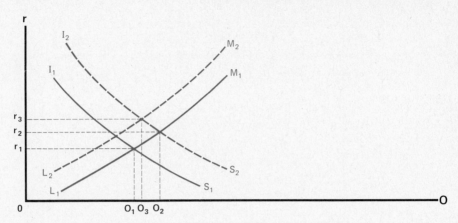

FIGURE 16–13
A fiscal policy shift

We thus see that in the present case fiscal policy is quite capable of bringing about an expansion of real output. Associated with this, of course, is a rise in employment. As for the other variables, we see that both interest rates and the price level rise as a result of the expansionary fiscal policy. However, with an upward sloping aggregate supply curve, the price level does not need to rise as much to equate supply and demand as for the classical model.

MONETARY POLICY

The same expansion of output and employment can also be brought about by an increase in the nominal supply of money. As we have seen before, however, the composition of output will differ from that obtained by fiscal policy. The detailed effects of a money supply increase on the *IS–LM* curves are shown in Figure 16–14. As far as the aggregate picture is concerned, Figure 16–12 will again suffice, with the understanding that the *DD* shift now originates with the monetary authorities.[4]

The increase in the money supply shifts the *LM* curve to the right from L_1M_1 to L_2M_2 in Figure 16–14. This puts downward pressure on the interest rate, which in turn stimulates investment. This tends to increase GNP and thus the quantity of money demanded. As a consequence, the interest rate does not fall as far as it would if output remained unchanged. With the price level fixed at P_1, equilibrium on the demand side occurs at $r = r_1$ and $O = O_2$. But once again, this is a situation of excess demand. The price level begins rising, setting up the same kinds of adjustments in commodity and money markets described for fiscal policy.

[4]In using Figure 16–12 for both monetary and fiscal policies, we are implicitly assuming that the magnitude of each policy is chosen to produce the same level of real output and hence employment.

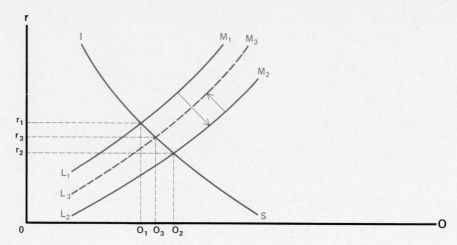

FIGURE 16–14
A monetary policy shift

New equilibrium again occurs at $P = P_3$ and $O = O_3$, where the LM curve has moved part of the way back toward the original curve, L_1M_1. We thus see that the major difference between fiscal and monetary policies in the present case is that r falls with expansionary monetary policy and rises with fiscal policy. Clearly, then, investment will be a greater fraction of GNP in the case of monetary expansion.

RECONCILING THE TWO MODELS

As we have just seen, the classical model and our alternative model with wage stickiness embody quite different views of the workings of the economy. The classical model suggests that the private economy has a self-correcting mechanism which ensures that resources will always be fully utilized. As a consequence, monetary and fiscal policy have no serious role to play. Our alternative model, on the other hand, allows for the possibility of unemployed resources and provides a role for economic policy in achieving fuller utilization of those resources. Since these models seem to yield such different conclusions, it would be nice to know which one is "right." The answer is that, properly interpreted, both are "right." To understand this seeming paradox, we need to reexamine the nature of the aggregate supply curve in the short and the long run.

AGGREGATE SUPPLY ONCE AGAIN

In presenting the short-run upward-sloping supply curve, we noted it was premised on a relatively fixed level of wages. But over an extended period of time, it is implausible to regard the level of wages as fixed. This means we need to ask what happens to the short-run aggregate supply curve as wages become more flexible in the longer run. Not surprisingly, the answer is that the short-run aggregate supply curve *shifts* its position.

We can readily illustrate this with Figure 16–15. The initial aggregate supply curve is given by S_0S_0. This curve is based on some prevailing level of wages. Let us now imagine that wages rise. Higher wages mean higher costs. Therefore, if firms are to maintain profitability, prices must rise. Put another way, firms would only be willing to supply the same output, before and after a wage increase, if the price they can sell their output for rises. What this means is that a wage increase will shift up the short-run aggregate supply curve. In Figure 16–15 this is portrayed as a shift of the aggregate supply curve from S_0S_0 to S_1S_1.

A decrease in the wage rate will, by reducing costs, make firms willing to supply output at a lower price. In Figure 16–15 this translates to a downward shift in the aggregate supply curve from S_0S_0 to S_2S_2 as a result of a decline in wages.

Armed with this insight into the nature of the short-run supply curve, we can now resolve our paradox.

EQUILIBRIUM IN THE SHORT AND LONG RUN

Complete equilibrium for the economy requires it to be in equilibrium with respect to both short-run and long-run aggregate supply curves. Such a situation is pictured in Figure 16–16. The basic ingredients in this figure are the aggregate demand curve, *DD*, the long-run aggregate supply curve, *SS*, which is vertical at O_e, and the short-run upward-sloping aggregate

FIGURE 16–15
Aggregate supply under varying wage conditions

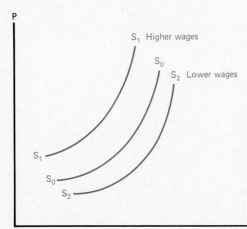

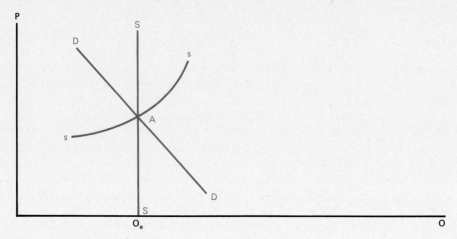

FIGURE 16–16
Equilibrium in the short and the long run

supply curve, *ss*. As shown in Figure 16–16, all three curves intersect at point *A*, making point *A* both a short-run and a long-run equilibrium.

Let us now imagine that some external event, such as a collapse in investor confidence, leads to a downward shift in aggregate demand. This is shown in part (a) of Figure 16–17, where the initial demand curve is D_0D_0 and the new demand curve is D_1D_1. Starting from point *A*, the economy first heads for point *B*, the intersection of the short-run supply curve, *ss*, and the new aggregate demand curve. At point *B* the economy is in short-

FIGURE 16–17
Response to a shift in aggregate demand

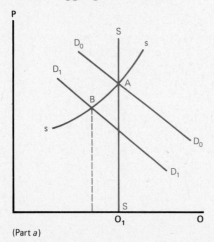

(Part *a*)

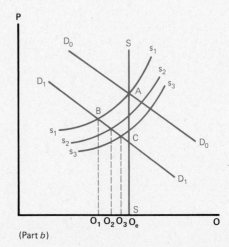

(Part *b*)

run equilibrium with real output equal to O_1. In other words, we have created a recessionary situation with real output declining from its full employment level, O_e. At point B employment will be lower and unemployment higher than at point A.

In the face of these conditions in the labor market, wages will not remain fixed indefinitely. Rather, at some time they will begin to decline, and this will cause the short-run aggregate supply curve to shift down. The stages of the process are shown in part (b) of Figure 16–17, where the supply curve shifts from s_1s_1 to s_2s_2 to s_3s_3. Ultimately, overall equilibrium will be established at point C, and output will be restored to its full employment level.

What Figure 16–17 suggests is that once we pay attention to distinctions of timing, it is possible to reconcile the classical and alternative models. To be sure, an economy that is disturbed from long-run equilibrium will eventually be restored to a new long-run equilibrium with full employment. However, during the transition period there will be a loss of real output and there will be unemployed resources. This transition period is precisely the time during which the monetary and fiscal authorities can usefully pursue policies to stabilize the economy. By expansionary monetary or fiscal policy, the authorities can produce a rightward shift of the aggregate demand curve. In part (a) of Figure 16–17, for example, sufficient stimulus could be applied to shift the aggregate demand curve from its new position at D_1D_1 to its original at D_0D_0. This would permit full employment output to be restored without putting the economy through the painful and costly adjustment process pictured in Figure 16–17.

While this discussion suggests there is room for an activist approach by policymakers to stabilize the economy, it should be noted that this position is not held by all economists. Those who have reservations on this score suggest that the adjustment process (for example, moving from point A to B to C in Figure 16–17) may take place relatively quickly, and therefore no action is needed. Critics of activist policy also point out that many practical and technical details in the conduct of policy make the job of the policymaker less simple than we have made it out to be. These very important issues will be discussed extensively in the subsequent chapters. In the remainder of this chapter, we put our aggregate demand and supply framework to work in exploring the problem of inflation.

INFLATION

At the start of the 1980s, *inflation*, the increase in the general price level over time, was solidly entrenched as public enemy number one. We examine the attempts of policymakers to "do something" about inflation in a later chapter, but for the present we can put our model of aggregate demand and supply to good use and shed some light on the nature of inflation. We begin with the oldest and simplest explanation.

MONEY AND INFLATION

The classical explanation of inflation is accurately described by the phrase "too much money chasing too few goods." This diagnosis naturally suggests the appropriate medicine to cure inflation—namely, bringing the rate of money creation under strict control.

The accuracy of this diagnosis and the curative nature of the medicine have been illustrated most vividly during periods of runaway inflation, which are known as *hyperinflation.* One case of this disease was exhibited by Germany after World War I. Prices increased about 80 percent in 1920, over 140 percent in 1921, and an astronomical 4100 percent in 1922. If this was not impressive enough, it was at this point that things got wildly out of hand—prices rose by over 100 million percent from December 1922 to November 1923. But even this was dwarfed by the greatest of all hyperinflations, which was experienced by Hungary in 1945–1946. For a period of one year, the rate of inflation averaged about 20,000 percent *per month*, while in the final month the price level advanced by an unbelievable 42 *quadrillion* percent. Overall, in the space of 13 months the price level rose more than one *octillion* times (5.2×10^{27}).

Now comes the punch line. In each of these episodes, the inflation was fueled by new injections of money in larger and larger amounts. Thus, for example, during the Hungarian hyperinflation the outstanding stock of money also rose by more than one octillion times (3.8×10^{27}), closely matching the increase in prices. Furthermore, it was only when the monetary brakes were slammed on that the hyperinflation came to end. At least in such pathological episodes, the relation between money and inflation is all too painfully clear.

Hyperinflation, of course, is relatively rare. Most of our bouts of inflation are considerably more tranquil and indeed are sometimes given the benign-sounding label *creeping inflation.* Is excessive money creation the cause of creeping inflation as well? Here the answer is considerably less clear-cut, and many economists deny that there is a mechanical one-to-one connection between money and prices, at least in the short run. Even over more extended periods of time, the connection between money and prices is sometimes quite loose. For example, from the end of 1930 to the end of 1940, the money supply grew by 70 percent. But prices, rather than rising, fell 15 percent. From 1953 to 1973, the increases in the money supply and prices were 110 percent and 80 percent, respectively. Thus, over this period the increase in the money supply was substantially more than the increase in the price level. To many, this experience suggests that inflation is not a simple "monetary phenomenon." To see what is involved, it will be helpful to turn to a demand–supply analysis of inflation.

A DEMAND–SUPPLY INTERPRETATION

Up to this point we have used the framework of aggregate demand and supply to analyze the determination of aggregate real output and the price level. Since inflation is simply an increase in the price level, we can use the same framework here. We start from the observation that in a healthy, growing economy there will normally be systematic outward shifts in the aggregate demand and supply curves. Increases in population, for example, tend to expand aggregate demand. At the same time by contributing to a larger labor force, such increases can also shift the aggregate supply curve outward. Outward shifts in aggregate supply can also come about as an economy adds to the stock of physical capital or accumulates advances in technical knowledge. Ideally, of course, shifts in demand and supply would be "balanced" to produce a growth in real output with little or no increase in the price level.

Such a situation is portrayed in Figure 16–18, where the economy's demand curve for various years shifts to the right at the same rate as the supply curve. As a result, real output increases each year, but the price level remains at P_e. Unfortunately, the idyllic pattern exhibited in Figure 16–18 has only infrequently been realized. One way in which historical experience has departed from this pattern is that the aggregate demand curve has often shifted outward too rapidly, thus putting upward pressure on prices. This case is illustrated most simply if we assume that we are dealing with a short period in which the supply curve is fixed and the demand curve shifts outward.

DEMAND INFLATION

Suppose, as in Figure 16–19, the economy starts at some initial price level, P_1, and level of real output, O_1, where (P_1, O_1) lies at the intersection of the aggregate demand and supply curves, D_1D_1 and SS, respectively. Now assume that the aggregate demand curve shifts out to D_2D_2. Such a shift could come about from a variety of factors, such as a war-induced expansion of government spending or an outward shift in the consumption or invest-

FIGURE 16–18
Demand–supply shifts over time

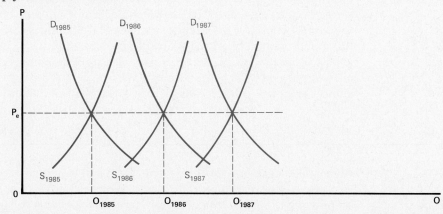

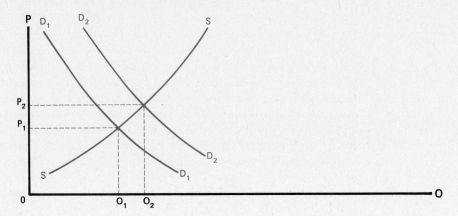

FIGURE 16–19
Demand pull inflation

ment functions of the private sector. Whatever the source, as Figure 16–19 indicates, the shift of the aggregate demand curve serves to raise both the level of real output (from O_1 to O_2) and the price level (from P_1 to P_2). This provides an example of what is called *demand pull* inflation—that is, a situation in which a shift in the demand curve "pulls up" the price level and leads to inflation. The actual amount of inflation will, of course, depend on how far the demand curve shifts and on the shape of the supply curve. If the supply curve is steep, as it is likely to be at close to full employment, there will be a larger increase in prices and a smaller response in real output than if the supply curve were less steep.

Conventional stabilization policy is well equipped to fight a demand pull inflation. In particular, through restrictive monetary or fiscal actions, policymakers can offset any outward shift in the aggregate demand curve. In Figure 16–19, for example, restrictive policy would be used to reshift the demand curve from D_2D_2 back to D_1D_1. This would curb the inflationary pressures and prevent the rise in the price level. At the same time, however, this would choke off the possible increase in real output. How one regards this policy depends on the state of the economy. If the economy were already operating at its full employment or potential level of output, then any increase in real output would likely be temporary. In such circumstances policymakers need not worry about retarding the increase in output.

Things are not so nice, however, if the economy is operating below full employment. Such a situation is portrayed in Figure 16–20. The economy is initially in short-run equilibrium at point E, which lies at the intersection of the initial aggregate demand curve, D_1D_1, and the short-run supply curve, ss. The level of real output at E is O_1, which is clearly less than the full-employment level, O_F. A shift in the aggregate demand curve from D_1D_1 to

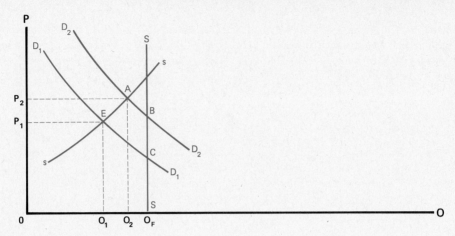

FIGURE 16–20
Policy trade-offs with demand pull inflation

D_2D_2 would tend to move the economy to point A, raising both prices and output and thereby decreasing unemployment. A policy response that shifted the economy back to point E would thus prevent the economy from moving closer to full employment. At least in this sense, there is clearly a short-run tradeoff between inflation and unemployment. Of course, in the long run, as the self-correcting mechanism emphasized by the classical economists came into play, the economy could reestablish equilibrium at a point like B or C on the long-run supply curve, SS. However, if this self-correcting mechanism were to take a substantial amount of time and involve a significantly long spell of unemployment, policymakers might welcome a rightward shift of the aggregate demand curve to D_2D_2. Indeed, one could well imagine, if such a shift did not arise in the natural course of things, that policymakers might well think about engineering one and accepting a bit more inflation as the cost of driving down the unemployment rate more quickly. We come back to the issue of such tradeoffs in a subsequent chapter.

SUPPLY INFLATION
While shifts in aggregate demand can create inflation, inflation may arise even with a fixed demand curve. For this to come about, it is necessary that the aggregate supply curve shift upward and to the left, as shown in Figure 16–21. Since we have suggested that, under normal conditions, over time the supply curve shifts down and to the right (see Figure 16–18), how can such a perverse shift come about? Unfortunately, as history has revealed, there are far too many ways. Basically, any development that restricts supply or autonomously pushes up prices will cause an upward shift in aggregate supply. Real world events that have produced such shifts

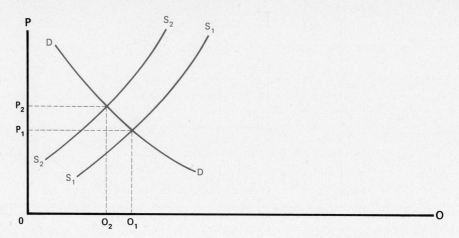

FIGURE 16–21
Cost push inflation

include crop failures, autonomous oil price increases imposed by OPEC, and declines in productivity.

The effects of a perverse supply shift are readily illustrated in Figure 16–21. As the supply curve shifts from S_1S_1 to S_2S_2, prices clearly increase—that is sometimes called *cost push* inflation, but unlike the case of demand pull pictured in Figure 16–19, real output *declines* (from O_1 to O_2). This unhappy constellation of events—rising prices and falling output—is often dubbed *stagflation* (from stagnation and inflation).

Cost push or supply inflation presents policymakers with a singularly unpleasant dilemma. As we have seen, both fiscal and monetary policy work through shifts of the aggregate demand curve. But as should be apparent from Figure 16–21, aggregate demand management cannot really solve the problem. This is perhaps illustrated more clearly in Figure 16–22, where the initial equilibrium is at point E. As in Figure 16–21, the supply curve is assumed to shift from S_1S_1 to S_2S_2. A "do-nothing" policy, which leaves the aggregate demand curve alone, will yield an equilibrium at point A, with higher prices and lower output. The decline in output and the rise in unemploymnent could be prevented by an expansionary policy that shifted out the demand curve to d_ud_u to establish point B as an equilibrium. This keeps output at its original level (O_1), but unhappily, this policy creates even more inflation than experienced at point A (P_3 vs. P_2).

Alternatively, policymakers could decide to fight inflation. For example, a restrictive policy that shifted the demand curve down to d_pd_p would yield point C. This restores the initial price level (P_1), but reduces output even further (to O_3) and creates additional unemployment. There is thus a trade-off of sorts, but not a very appealing one. In view of this discussion it should hardly be surprising that cost push inflation has proved to be a most frus-

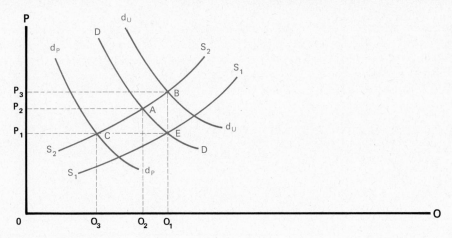

FIGURE 16–22
The dismal trade-offs with cost push inflation

trating problem for policymakers. Unhappily, as we will see when we review recent economic events, the jury is still out on the proper policy for combatting supply inflation.

THE PHILLIPS CURVE

At various points in our discussion, we have referred to the possibility of a short-run tradeoff between inflation and unemployment. That is, in certain cases it appeared that policymakers could achieve a lower rate of unemployment if they were willing to accept a higher rate of inflation. Consider, for example, the situation portrayed in Figure 16–23. Starting from an initial short-run equilibrium at point A, policymakers are presumed to contemplate two different courses of action. The first would shift the aggregate demand curve to D_2D_2, increase real output from O_1 to O_2, and raise the price level from P_1 to P_2. The second, more stimulative policy, would shift aggregate demand to D_3D_3. As compared with the alternative policy, real output would be higher (O_3 vs. O_2), and unemployment consequently lower. This lower unemployment rate would, however, be associated with a higher rate of inflation, since the price level would rise from P_1 to P_3. Hence the idea of a tradeoff.

For a period of time beginning in the 1960s, it was common to express the tradeoffs implicit in Figure 16–23 by another diagrammatic device known as the *Phillips curve*. A typical Phillips curve is shown in Figure 16–24, where the vertical axis measures the inflation rate and the horizontal axis shows the unemployment rate (the number of unemployed workers as a percentage of the labor force). The downward-sloping shape of the Phillips curve provides an explicit representation of the tradeoff. For example, in

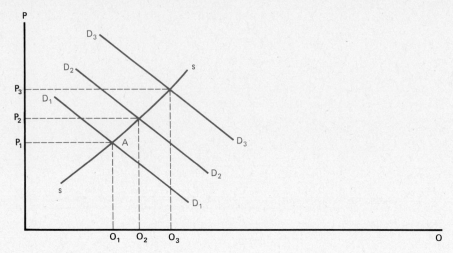

FIGURE 16–23
Equilibrium points with varying aggregate demand

moving from point *A* to point *B*, an expansionary policy would reduce the unemployment rate by 1 percentage point but simultaneously raise the inflation rate by 2 percentage points. A restrictive policy that moved the economy from *B* to *A* would reduce inflation, but increase unemployment.

The Phillips curve was first discovered empirically by the economist A. W. Phillips. Phillips worked with actual unemployment and inflation data

FIGURE 16–24
A Phillips curve

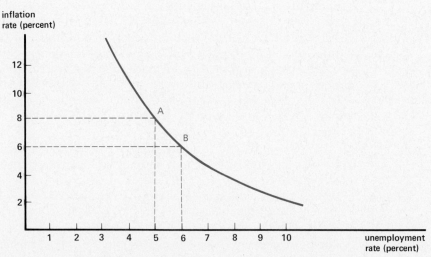

for the United Kingdom. Soon after he reported his results, economists confirmed Phillips' findings with U.S. data. As a result, in the 1960s the Phillips curve came to be viewed as a menu for policy choices. That is, it was regarded as describing the quantitative nature of the tradeoff between inflation and unemployment. For a number of years, the Phillips curve worked rather well. Then, in the 1970s, something happened. The economy behaved far worse than would have been anticipated on the basis of the historical Phillips curve. The U.S. experience is shown in Figure 16–25, where the historical Phillips curve is drawn through points up to 1970. The points since 1970 obviously lie to the right of the Phillips curve as drawn, suggesting that that original curve no longer represented the menu for policy choices in the 1970s. Indeed, subsequent examination has established that the usefulness of the Phillips curve was somewhat oversold, both for short- and long-run policy purposes.

FIGURE 16–25
An inflation–unemployment scatter for the
United States, 1954–1983. (The solid-line Phillips
curve is drawn through points for 1954 to 1969.)

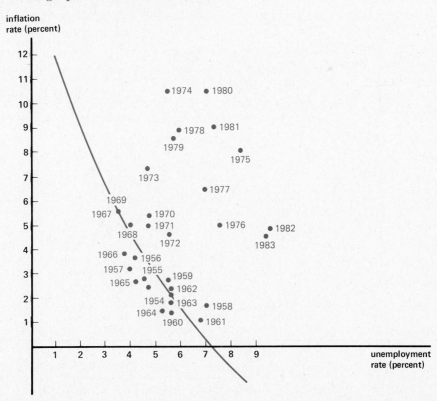

PROBLEMS IN THE SHORT-RUN

As we saw in Figure 16–23, the Phillips curve arises when we consider various possible aggregate demand curves shifting about a fixed supply curve. But what happens when there are supply shifts, such as those in Figure 16–21? What we expect to find in the face of substantial supply shifts is stagflation, a simultaneous worsening of *both* inflation and unemployment. Put another way, in the presence of stagflation, the empirical Phillips curve might actually slope *upward*. This is certainly the visual impression created by the points after 1970 in Figure 16–25. And, as we shall see below, the 1970s are generally conceded to be a period of supply shocks. What this all means is that even in the short run, the Phillips curve may not have the conventional downward-sloping shape at all times. In the long run, there are still other difficulties.

PROBLEMS IN THE LONG RUN

The difficulty with the Phillips curve in the long run can be seen most easily if we recall the primary message of the classical model. Simply put, that message is that in the long run, the economy has a self-correcting mechanism which relies on the flexibility of wages and prices. This mechanism eventually restores the economy to full employment. There is thus no way in the long run that policymakers can regard themselves as choosing from a menu of alternative unemployment rates. There is only one rate that is consistent with long-run equilibrium—namely, that rate of unemployment associated with full employment. What this means is that the long-run Phillips curve is a *vertical* line. Such a long-run Phillips curve is shown in Figure 16–26. Every point on the vertical Phillips curve corresponds to the same rate of unemployment, and it is to this rate of unemployment that the economy will tend to return. As a consequence, this rate is commonly called the *natural rate of unemployment*.[5]

THE SHORT VS. LONG RUN AGAIN

The idea of a long-run vertical Phillips curve is now accepted by most economists. Indeed, as we have just seen, it is no more than an alternative way of representing the fact that the long-run aggregate supply curve is vertical as well. This means that the conventional downward-sloping Phillips curve does not represent a long-run menu of policy choices. Does this mean that policymakers need not concern themselves with tradeoffs? Unhappily for them, the answer is "no." Indeed, whenever it takes time for long-run forces to restore the economy to full employment, there will be short run tradeoffs to be faced. Such tradeoffs are pictured in Figures 16–22

---

[5]There is no reason why the natural rate of unemployment must remain constant over time. Indeed, this rate would be expected to respond to any long-run restructuring of supply and/ or demand in the labor market. For example, an improvement in the dissemination of information about available jobs might be expected to reduce the amount of time people spend looking for jobs and hence reduce the natural rate of unemployment.

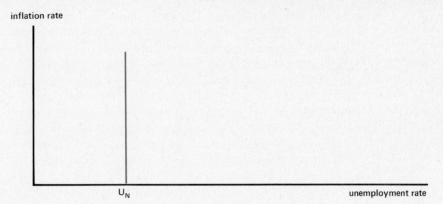

FIGURE 16–26
The long-run Phillips curve

and 16–23, and they persist whatever one chooses to think of the Phillips curve.[6] We will come back to the issue of such tradeoffs in a subsequent chapter.

MONEY AGAIN

Milton Friedman has written that "inflation is always and everywhere a monetary phenomenon." All economists agree with this statement as applied to the periods of hyperinflation, and nearly all would agree that long, extended bouts of inflation have a monetary source. Indeed, even the Federal Reserve has acknowledged the importance of money in the inflationary process. Chairman Paul Volcker, for example, has stated:

> Monetary policy is central to the process of dealing with inflation. Economic theory and experience alike indicate that inflation cannot persist without excessive growth in money and credit; or—to state the proposition in reverse—that progress toward price stability cannot be expected without appropriate restraint on the growth of money and credit. Those fundamentals underlie the strategy and execution of monetary policy—working toward growth in money consistent with a framework of greater price stability as the economy expands. Easy to state and hard to do.

There are several reasons why it is easy to state and hard to do. First, as already noted, there will be short-run conflicts between inflation and unemployment. This means that unemployment is likely to rise when anti-inflationary policies are pursued. At the same time, given the looseness of

[6]Just as one reconciles the short- and long-run aggregate supply curves by recognizing that the short-run curve can shift, one can reconcile short- and long-run Phillips curves by allowing for shifts in the short-run curve. See, for example, R. Dornbusch and S. Fischer, *Macroeconomics*, 3rd ed. New York: McGraw-Hill, 1984, chap. 13.

the short-run connection between money and inflation, it may take some time for the effects of such a policy to reduce the rate of inflation. Consequently, policymakers need a certain amount of fortitude to face up to those unwilling to bear the short-run pain of fighting inflation. A second difficulty in the design of anti-inflationary monetary policy is the changing meaning of money. Evolutionary, some might say revolutionary, changes in banking and financial markets have served to raise serious questions about the proper definition of money and the relationship between any particular definition and overall economic developments. Rather obviously, in a world in which the meaning of money is evolving, it could be a bit tricky to design a sensible anti-inflationary monetary policy. We will take up this problem, along with other practical issues in the conduct of monetary policy, in the next several chapters.

SUMMARY

1 The *IS–LM* analysis is carried out on the assumption that the price level is fixed. To explain the behavior of the price level, we need to introduce the ideas of aggregate demand and aggregate supply. The aggregate demand curve is a downward-sloping curve that gives the combinations of real output and the price level that equilibrate the aggregate demand sector. Any action that shifts the *IS* or *LM* curves will shift the *DD* curve in the same direction.

2 The aggregate supply curve is derived from considerations in the labor market and can take several forms. The classical system, based on the absence of money illusion and the perfect flexibility of prices and wages, implies a vertical aggregate supply curve. In the classical model neither monetary nor fiscal policy can affect real output. Changes in the money supply do have a proportionate effect on the price level. Overall, the classical model implies that strong forces in the economy work to bring about full employment.

3 Most economists regard the classical model as a reasonable characterization of the economy in the long run, but many feel it is inadequate to explain the short-run behavior evidenced in repeated recessions. According to this alternative view, the labor market does not behave like the market for copper or wheat. Moreover, prices and wages are not fully flexible. What this means is that in the short run the aggregate supply curve is upward-sloping but not vertical. The consequences of this are that the economy can settle down with unemployed resources, and that monetary and fiscal policy can affect real output.

4 The framework of aggregate demand and aggregate supply can be usefully applied to understanding the problem of inflation. Anything that causes the aggregate demand curve to shift outward faster than

the aggregate supply curve will lead to inflation. Inflation may also arise from an upward or leftward shift of the aggregate supply curve, typically producing the unhappy state of affairs known as stagflation.

5 The Phillips curve provides an alternative diagrammatic device for analyzing the twin problems of inflation and unemployment. While it was initially regarded as providing a menu for the tradeoff between inflation and unemployment, it is now recogized this view is rather misleading, especially in the long run. It is now generally agreed that the long-run Phillips curve is vertical at what is called the natural rate of unemployment. This is, in essence, the counterpart to the long-run vertical aggregate supply curve implied by the classical model.

APPENDIX

THE DERIVATION OF THE AGGREGATE SUPPLY CURVE

As this chapter has illustrated, economists think about the aggregate supply curve in a variety of ways. In this appendix, we sketch the derivation of several alternative aggregate supply curves. Throughout this appendix we use the following notation:

$$O = \text{real output}$$
$$P = \text{price level}$$
$$W = \text{money wage}$$
$$W/P = \text{real wage}$$
$$N = \text{employment}$$

THE CLASSICAL CASE

As noted in the text, the classical aggregate supply curve is premised on the notion that wages and prices are fully flexible and that producers and workers focus on the real wage in making labor supply and demand decisions. The consequences of these assumptions can best be illustrated with a few diagrams.

We begin in Figure 16A–1(a) with the *production function* of the economy (OO), which gives the amount of aggregate output produced as a function of N, the amount of labor employed. This function assumes a given state of technology and given endowments of capital and natural resources. The decreasing slope of the total output function as larger amounts of labor are used reflects the operation of the law of diminishing returns.

Demand and supply conditions in the labor market are shown in part (b). The marginal product of labor function (MPL) is derived from the aggregate production function; it is the amount by which total output is

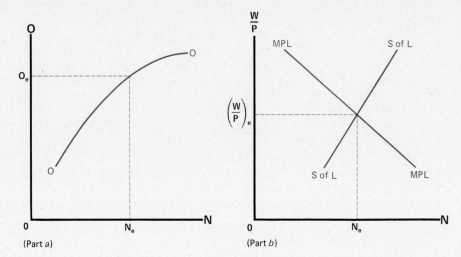

FIGURE 16A–1
**The production function and labor market
equilibrium**

changed by a change of one unit in the amount of labor used. This is the
demand function for labor, for under pure competition each enterprise will
demand all labor whose marginal product is at least as great as its real
wage.[1] The supply function of labor (S of L) is a positive function of the real
wage rate (W/P), not of the money wage rate alone. Workers do not suffer
from money illusion.

Figure 16A–1 shows the simultaneous determination of the equilibrium
levels for total output (O_e), employment (N_e), and the real wage rate ($W/P)_e$.
Only at the real wage rate ($W/P)_e$ are the supply of labor and the demand
for labor equated. At any higher real wage, the supply of labor would exceed
the demand for labor and the excess supply of labor would serve to drive
down the real wage. But at any real wage below ($W/P)_e$ the demand for
labor would exceed its supply and the excess demand would serve to drive
up the real wage. The equilibrium amount of employment (N_e) is full employment, in the sense that all labor that is offered at the real wage ($W/P)_e$
finds employment.

As Figure 16A–1 makes clear, in the classical model one and only one
level of output is possible, namely O_e. Hence it is hardly surprising that the
classical aggregate supply curve is simply a vertical line at O_e, as in Figure
16–8.

---

[1] The comparison will, of course, be made in money terms, with each enterprise hiring all
labor whose marginal value product is at least equal to its money wage. That is, equilibrium
requires that $W = P(MPL)$. But if we divide both sides by the price level (P), we get $W/P =
MPL$.

THE CASE OF STICKY WAGES

The derivation of the aggregate supply curve in the case of sticky wages is simplest if we begin with the extreme assumption that wages are rigid in a downward direction. That is, we assume that once the money wage rate rises to an equilibrium level, it will not fall from that level. We subsequently consider the less extreme case of a sticky but not rigid wage. The assumption of a rigid wage is not meant to imply any kind of permanent rigidity. Rather, it is meant to suggest that the wage rigidity lasts sufficiently long to produce a substantial observable impact on the economy.

RIGID MONEY WAGES

To see how this works, we must first examine the behavior of the labor market if we drop the classical assumption of wage flexibility and assume that money wages are rigid, at least during the period under consideration. We will continue to assume, however, that all markets for output are purely competitive and that firms attempt to maximize their profits. As a consequence, each firm hires labor up to the point where the marginal value product of labor is equal to its wage rate. The marginal value product of labor, $(MPL)P$, is the marginal product of labor (MPL) *times* the price of the unit of output produced by this labor (P). Thus, firms equate

$$W = (MPL)P \tag{A1}$$

or, dividing both sides by P,

$$\frac{W}{P} = MPL \tag{A2}$$

This gives precisely the kind of labor demand curve we used in Figure 16A–1.

In Figure 16A–2(a) we have reproduced from Figure 16A–1 the demand and supply curves characterizing equilibrium in the labor market. A similar picture is shown in Figure 16A–2(b), but the reader will note that we have relabeled the vertical axis so that it measures the nominal or money wage rate, W, rather than the real wage, W/P. This amounts, in the case of the demand for labor, to using equation (A1), instead of (A2), as the demand curve. As a consequence, the curves in (b) now have a price level attached to them and will vary as the price level varies.

Suppose we begin from the initial equilibrium position indicated in Figure 16A–2. That is, the price level is P_1, the money wage is W_1, and the real wage is W_1/P_1. The amount of labor employed is N_1, which will produce some level of total output (not shown) O_1. Suppose now that for some reason, such as a collapse in investment demand or a reduction in the nominal money supply, the aggregate demand for output declines and the price level falls to P_2. In the classical model this would shift down both the demand and supply curves in part (b)—those in part (a) are, of course,

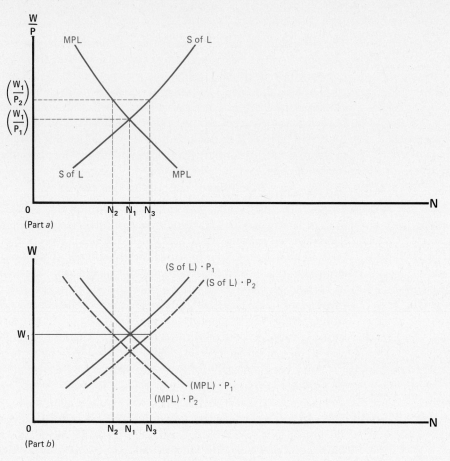

FIGURE 16A–2
Labor market equilibrium: the rigid wage case

unchanged. The resulting curves—the dashed ones in the figure—intersect at the initial level of employment, N_1, indicating that in the absence of wage rigidity the classical result would hold. The money wage, however, is assumed to remain rigid at W_1. This means that relevant supply curve is not the dashed one shown in part (b) but the horizontal line at the level W_1. The effect of this will be to lower the level of employment from N_1 to N_2 and to reduce the level of real output.

The reason for this can be stated two ways. Stating it in real terms, we can say that the fall of the price level from P_1 to P_2, while the money wage rate remained rigid, increased the real wage from W_1/P_1 to W_1/P_2, which reduced the quantity of labor demanded. Or, stating it in money terms, we can say that the fall of prices shifted downward and to the left of the $(MPL)P$ function, which is the demand function for labor. With the money wage

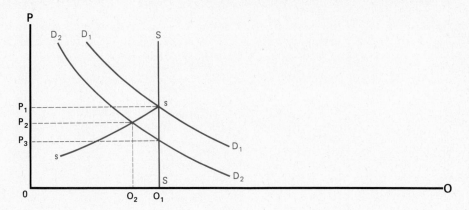

FIGURE 16A–3
**Aggregate demand and supply: the rigid wage
case**

rate rigid, less labor is demanded. Thus, the amount of labor employed can be read off either part of Figure 16A–2. We are, of course, assuming that employers cannot be forced to hire more laborers than they desire. That is, the amount of labor actually utilized is the quantity, N_2, implied by the demand for labor function. Associated with this level of employment is some reduced level of output, O_2.

This entire process is perhaps best summarized by the aggregate demand and supply diagram in Figure 16A–3. Initial equilibrium is at $P = P_1$ and $O = O_1$, where the demand curve D_1D_1 intersects the classical vertical supply curve SS. The decline in aggregate demand is shown as the downward shift of D_1D_1 to D_2D_2. In the classical model the new equilibrium would be at $P = P_3$ and $O = O_1$. That is, the level of real output would be unchanged and the price level would decline. In contrast, in the case of a rigid money wage, as we have just seen, *both* output and prices would decline. Thus, we would move along a supply curve such as ss in Figure 16A–3 to the new equilibrium $P = P_2$ and $O = O_2$. In other words, the effect of a rigid wage is to turn the vertical supply curve of the classical model into one that, below P_1, has an upward-sloping but less than vertical slope. On the other hand, if we assume that money wages are flexible in an upward direction, the classical model holds above P_1 and the relevant supply curve is again vertical above P_1.

SOME ALTERNATIVE WAGE ASSUMPTIONS
As we have just seen, the primary effect of introducing a rigid wage was to change the vertical character of the aggregate supply curve, thus making aggregate supply responsive to changes in aggregate demand and price. This can also be accomplished without resort to a rigid wage by relaxing

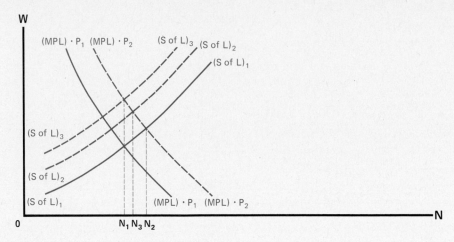

FIGURE 16A–4
Labor market equilibrium: the money wage case

the assumption that workers respond to the real wage in their labor supply decisions. In particular, if we assume that workers primarily respond to the money wage, the same kind of aggregate supply curve results. This is illustrated in Figure 16A–4.

Initial equilibrium is at the intersection of the demand for labor, $(MPL)P_1$, and the supply of labor, $(S$ of $L)_1$, giving a volume of employment equal to N_1. For variety's sake, let us suppose that an outward shift in aggregate demand *increases* the price level from P_1 to P_2. At any given money wage rate, the demand for labor increases, and this is shown as a rightward shift from $(MPL)P_1$ to $(MPL)P_2$. What happens to employment depends on the precise assumption we make concerning the behavior of workers. If we assume that workers have an extreme version of *money illusion* and respond only to the money wage, then the supply of labor function remains at $(S$ of $L)_1$. In this case employment increases from N_1 to N_2.

But we need not assume extreme money illusion to get an expansion of employment. We can allow some response to the real wage as long as the labor supply curve shifts by less than would occur in the classical case. In the classical case, the higher price level (P_2 as opposed to P_1) makes workers supply less labor at any given money wage. This corresponds to a leftward shift of the labor supply function. In fact, in the classical case the supply curve must shift to $(S$ of $L)_3$ in Figure 16A–4, which intersects the new labor demand curve at the original level of employment, N_1. Consequently, any smaller shift to the left will permit employment to expand. Thus, for example, the labor supply curve could shift from $(S$ of $L)_1$ to $(S$ of $L)_2$, as illustrated in Figure 16A–4, and increase employment from N_1 to N_3. This would correspond to somewhat less money illusion than the first case considered.[2]

What we see is that relaxing the assumption that the supply of labor is a function of the real wage means that an increase of the price level yields more employment and consequently more output than in the classical case. Similarly, a decrease in the price level will be associated with both lower employment and output. Simply put, what this means is that the aggregate supply curve is once again not vertical, but rather has the upward-sloping shape seen before in Figure 16–11.

SELECTED READINGS

Branson, W. H. *Macroeconomic Theory and Policy*, 2nd ed. New York: Harper & Row, 1979.

Dornbusch, R., and S. Fischer. *Macroeconomics*, 3rd ed. New York: McGraw-Hill, 1984.

Gordon, R. J. *Macroeconomics*, 3rd ed. Boston: Little, Brown, 1984.

[2]Note that we have omitted the multiplicative price label from the supply curves in Figure 16A–4. This is because in the presence of money illusion it is not true that S of $L = W/P$, so that one cannot simply multiply through by P. Of course, as is made clear in the text, even under money illusion the supply curve may shift with the price level. Thus, the supply curves in Figure 16A–4 may depend on P, and this should be borne in mind, despite the simple way in which we have labeled the curves.

PART 5

MONETARY POLICY
IN THEORY
AND PRACTICE

17

SOME ISSUES IN MONETARY AND FISCAL POLICY

In previous chapters we provided a framework for analyzing the effects of monetary and fiscal policy on aggregate variables such as output, employment, and prices. However, in order to keep the discussion manageable, we omitted a number of complexities of the policy process. Furthermore, except for selected instances, we have yet to examine the actual record of policy making in any detail. In this and succeeding chapters we attempt to fill this gap. In this chapter we analyze some general policy issues. In the subsequent chapter we take a closer look at the strategy and techniques of monetary policy. The final chapters of this part review the historical record of monetary policy in the United States.

A naive interpretation of the framework presented in previous chapters might suggest that policy makers could readily achieve desirable economic outcomes. But a glance at our concerns of recent years—inflation, unemployment, and difficulties with our international payments—indicates that there is a substantial gap between the promise of the textbook and actual economic performance. One could explain this gap by casting aspersions on the intentions of policy makers or even on their intelligence. And economists have not been above doing this—even, in some instances, justifiably. But, there are many other reasons why economic policy may be less than fully successful.

In the present chapter we consider these reasons, addressing the follow-

479

ing sorts of questions: What goals do policymakers pursue, and are they all attainable? What complications are presented by imperfect knowledge and the explicit allowance for lags in the policy process? What prescriptions for policymakers emerge from the monetarist view, and are these plausible? We begin our discussion by considering the goals of economic policy.

POLICY GOALS

In a general way we are all familiar with the goals of macroeconomic policy. Simply put, the primary objective of policy is to avoid the economic ills that have often beset us—inflation, unemployment, lackluster economic growth, and difficulties with our international payments. Stated more positively, these goals would be price stability, high or "full" employment, satisfactory economic growth, and equilibrium in our balance of payments. While there is now fairly widespread agreement about the desirability of these policy goals, at least in the abstract, this has not always been the case. For example, in its early years the Federal Reserve had an extremely limited scope. In particular, it was largely concerned with providing an elastic currency, with avoiding bank crises and financial panics, and with the maintenance of a smoothly functioning gold standard. It was only after the experience of the 1930s that policy, both monetary and fiscal, became increasingly sensitive to the overall quality of our economic performance. This concern, coupled with the growth of our economic understanding as to what policy could accomplish, gradually led to a more activist approach. This was partially reflected in the reoganization of the Federal Reserve in the mid-1930s, but it was not until the passage of the Employment Act of 1946 that the responsibility of government for the quality of economic performance was formalized.

SOME SPECIFIC GOALS

The Employment Act declared "that it is the continuing policy and responsibility of the Federal Government to use all practicable means ... to promote maximum employment, production, and purchasing power." This was an immense step, but the act left many questions unanswered. For example, it did not distinguish between the roles of monetary and fiscal policy in carrying out the stated objectives. As a consequence, it did not offer any mechanism to achieve coordination between monetary and fiscal authorities. Furthermore, despite the explicit statement of responsibility, the act did not provide an unambiguous set of goals. In particular, it left vague the notions of "maximum employment" and "maximum purchasing power" and certainly did not provide any specific numerical targets for unemployment or inflation. This vagueness is, perhaps, understandable.

The reasons will be more apparent if we briefly consider some of the ambiguities in making these goals more precise.

FULL EMPLOYMENT

Taken by itself, economists generally agree that a high rate of unemployment is an undesirable state of affairs. But what is a reasonable goal for the unemployment rate? While an idealist might argue that the only acceptable level is zero unemployment, this is somewhat implausible. At the very least, "full" employment is consistent with some *frictional* unemployment as potential workers (either those who have left their jobs or new entrants into the labor force) search for employment. Furthermore, some economists argue that we must accept a certain amount of *structural* unemployment, at least in the short run, since individuals without jobs may not have the skills needed by employers. But whether these considerations translate into an unemployment rate goal of 3 percent, 4 percent, 5 percent, or some other number is certainly unclear. Not surprisingly, there has been considerable dispute, among both economists and policymakers, as to what our unemployment goal should be.

PRICE STABILITY

By and large, the problem of price stability, at least in the post World War II era, has been the problem of avoiding inflation. Unlike the case of unemployment, it is perhaps less clear who is hurt by inflation. Nevertheless, there are costs of inflation, especially if it is *unanticipated*. For one thing, unanticipated inflation can redistribute income among individuals and groups in the economy. While gainers and losers may somewhat balance out in the aggregate, this redistribution can be an arbitrary and capricious thing. A second problem is created by the fact that unanticipated inflation adds a considerable degree of uncertainty to decision making and may have depressing effects on the willingness of individuals and firms to save and invest. Furthermore, unanticipated inflation erodes the usefulness of many institutional features of the economy, and individuals then devote additional resources to protecting themselves against inflation—resources that could be put to better use elsewhere.

Consider, for example, the institutional arrangements in which workers enter multiyear labor contracts that call for payment every two weeks. Such arrangements become less useful in an inflationary environment and tend to be eroded. An extreme case of this occurs during hyperinflations, when individuals may be paid several times a day at wage rates that must be renegotiated almost continuously. Indeed, under such extreme conditions individuals often resort to barter, with all its attendant inefficiences. While unanticipated inflation of a mild sort does not involve such extreme costs, even in a mildly inflationary environment individuals may become less willing to enter into long-term contracts, and the need for more frequent negotiations can waste resources.

It should be evident, then, that unanticipated inflation entails some very real costs. Many of these costs would not be present if the inflation were fully anticipated. This is so because a fully anticipated inflation, which entails no surprises, could be much more readily accounted for in individual and firm decision making.[1] While this may suggest that we could learn to live with, say, a steady 10 percent inflation rate, the historical record indicates that steady inflation is difficult to achieve at anything other than low rates. As a consequence, many would argue that, in principle at least, we should strive for zero inflation. But there are some practical problems with this. First, at least three prominent price indexes—the consumer price index, the producer price index, and the GNP deflator—do not always tell the same story. Second, it has been argued that all the price indexes suffer from an upward bias because they do not properly reflect quality improvements. These considerations might lead to a goal for inflation of 1 or 2 percent per year. However, as we shall see, the problem of price stability is not setting a goal, but achieving that goal.

OTHER GOALS

In addition to high employment and price stability, we can briefly identify a number of other goals. One is economic growth, which is typically measured by the rate of increase of real GNP. As a goal for economic growth, policymakers tend to think in terms of sustainable rate of growth—that is, one that allows demand to grow at the same rate that the capacity of the economy is expanding. Precisely what rate this is has been the subject of dispute, and this has been complicated by the fact that the rate of growth of capacity may itself be influenced by policy.

Several other goals stem from international considerations. One of these is the maintenance of equilibrium in our balance of payments. This is complicated by the difficulty of making precise the notion of equilibrium that results, in part, from the many definitions of the balance of payments. Another related goal is the one of exchange rate stability, which often requires intervention in the foreign exchange market.

A final set of goals, largely pursued by the Federal Reserve, concern financial markets. Among these are the prevention of financial panics, the facilitation of sales of government securities, the maintenance of orderly markets, and the promotion of a sound banking system. While some of these might be regarded as a *means* to achieve the previous goals, at least at some times these considerations appear to be independent goals.

---

[1] Even a fully anticipated inflation may entail some costs, especially if the economic system is not "neutral" with respect to inflation. Examples of nonneutralities include a progressive income tax rate structure, whereby inflation pushes taxpayers into a higher tax bracket even without an increase in real income. In addition, inflation leads individuals to use resources economizing on cash balances as a result of the prohibition of interest on demand deposits.

INFLATION AND INTEREST RATES: NOMINAL VS. REAL RATES

The text suggests that, unlike unanticipated inflation, inflation of the fully anticipated variety could be accounted for in individual and business decision making. One way in which this comes about is through adjustments of interest rates in response to inflation. To see how this works, let us consider a simple example.

Suppose Mr. Consumer wants to borrow $1,000 from Ms. Lender and both agree that, in the absence of inflation, a fair rate of interest would be 3 percent on a one-year loan. Thus, for the right to $1,000 currently, Mr. Consumer will pay $1,030 one year hence. In the absence of inflation, when received this sum will provide Ms. Lender with a 3 percent increase in the purchasing power of her funds.

Now assume that, instead of zero inflation, both parties expect prices to increase by 7 percent over the course of the year. While Mr. Consumer would be delighted to still borrow money at 3 percent, Ms. Lender is likely to be rather disenchanted with this prospect. As she reasons, the $1,030 she would get back on the deal actually represents a loss of purchasing power of about 4 percent (the 3 percent she receives less the 7 percent loss of purchasing power due to inflation).

The jargon used to describe this situation is that the *nominal rate of interest* is 3 percent, whereas the *real rate of interest* is negative 4 percent. The difference between the two is the 7 percent *anticipated* or *expected rate of inflation.* That is, the nominal rate equals the real rate plus the anticipated rate of inflation.

Of course, in the present example Ms. Lender is hardly going to be willing to make the loan at a nominal interest rate of 3 percent. What is likely to happen, if the market for loans is a competitive one, is that the market nominal interest rate will rise to 10 percent. This will restore the real rate of interest to 3 percent and neither party will be made better or worse off than it was originally.

What this suggests is that nominal interest rates tend to reflect fully anticipated inflation. Of course, if the actual realized inflation rate deviates from the anticipated inflation rate, then one party will be made better off and the other worse off. It is in this sense that unanticipated inflation may induce capricious redistribution of income—an effect that is absent when inflation is fully anticipated.

COMPATIBILITY OF GOALS

The existence of multiple goals immediately gives rise to the question of whether these objectives are compatible. To desire price stability, full employment, satisfactory economic growth, and a balance of international payments is one thing, but to achieve them simultaneously is another. Indeed, there are many ways in which these various goals come into conflict. For example, economic growth and full employment, which tend to be complementary, may not be compatible with either balance of payments considerations or price stability. Rapid economic growth, for instance, tends to increase our imports and worsen the balance of payments. Similarly, a monetary policy designed to bring us out of a recession is likely to be associated with lower interest rates. But as a result, foreigners may reduce their holdings of U.S. assets. The consequent outflow of capital could lead to a deterioration in our balance of payments.

However, by far the most important conflict of goals concerns the reconciliation of price stability and full employment. As we saw in the previous chapter, attempts to achieve, simultaneously, low levels of unemployment and a high degree of price stability by regulating aggregate demand for output, present serious policy problems. A higher rate of increase of aggregate demand to promote output and employment brings a higher rate of increase of money wages and prices, while a lower rate of increase of aggregate demand to promote price stability has its cost in terms of a lower rate of increase of employment and real output.

Unhappiness about such tradeoffs has led to widespread interest in measures to improve behavior patterns in labor and output markets. In particular, many economists now believe that control of aggregate demand needs to be supplemented by measures aimed at improving the supply function of output—measures that will increase the extent to which a given increase of demand will increase real output rather than prices. Various measures have been proposed. One program aims at improving the mobility of labor by means of improved employment exchanges and more widely disseminated information about employment opportunities, assistance in moving to areas where opportunities exist, job training and retraining, elimination of racial discrimination in employment, lowering of barriers to entry, and so on. Among the objectives of this program are to open "labor bottlenecks," to lessen the extent to which unemployment and excess demand for labor can coexist, and to lower the rate of wage increases while considerable amounts of unemployment persist.[2]

Although, over time, these programs may well contribute to improving

---

[2]Other measures are aimed at compelling or persuading those in labor and output markets to use their monopoly power more responsibly. These measures have been given various names, such as *wage-price guidelines* in the United States and *incomes policy* in Great Britain. To date at least, such policies have had questionable success. The reasons will be discussed in a subsequent chapter.

the tradeoffs between price stability and full employment, the fact remains that in the short run the monetary and fiscal authorities are faced with the problem of reconciling these conflicting objectives. One way of going about this would be to assign weights to the various objectives so that we could rank alternative combinations of unemployment and inflation. This would be akin to defining a *national utility function*, with price stability and full employment as the "goods." While there is some indirect evidence that policymakers may do this implicitly, they are naturally reluctant to make explicit their priorities and value judgments. As a result, outsiders have been forced to infer these priorities from the observable actions of the policymakers. And many have not liked what they have found. As a consequence, there has been much criticism of policymakers in regard to their perceived choices of relative priorities.

It is not fully clear what the answer to this dilemma is. As long as there are conflicts among objectives, some hard choices will have to be made. To do so intelligently requires that we increase our understanding of the costs and benefits of inflation and unemployment. It may also require that we make such choices openly and explicitly, and perhaps in a more democratic way. However, this is easier said than done, especially in view of the independence of the Federal Reserve.

RECENT DEVELOPMENTS

For over 30 years the Employment Act of 1946 was the major statement of goals and obligations of economic policy. However, as noted previously, the act was vague in several respects. These perceived shortcomings eventually led to the Full Employment and Balanced Growth Act of 1978 (the so-called Humphrey-Hawkins bill). This act generally amplified and extended the goals of the earlier Employment Act. Indeed, the 1978 act contained a litany of economic goals, including the following: full employment, reasonable price stability, more capital formation, a balanced budget, reduced government spending, an improved trade balance, freer international trade, and a sound and stable international monetary system. In addition to this shopping list, the act spelled out the following procedural reforms.

1 The administration must set annual numerical goals over five years for key indicators such as employment, unemployment, real income, productivity, and prices. Furthermore, the administration must present to Congress fiscal policies that are consistent with these goals.
2 The Federal Reserve is required to report to Congress twice a year on its objectives and plans for monetary policy and to comment on the plans of the administration.
3 The act stipulated that the 1983 goal for the unemployment rate shall be 4 percent for workers over the age of 16 and 3 percent for workers over 20 years of age. On the price front, the goal for 1983 was specified

as a 3 percent rate of inflation in the consumer price index. For 1988, the price goal was zero inflation, provided that achieving the goal did not interfere with the unemployment goal. Beginning in 1980 the president was permitted to change the timetable for reaching these specific numerical goals, but was supposed to indicate when they would be achieved. In the 1980 *Economic Report of the President* the unemployment and inflation goals were delayed until 1985 and 1988, respectively. By 1984, official forecasts did not see these goals being met until at least 1990. Indeed, in technical violation of the law, the administration did not specify a date when these goals would be met.

Taken as a whole, the 1978 act may well improve the level of economic discussion between Congress and other policy makers. Nevertheless, despite the list of objectives, the bill itself provided little in the way of real means to achieve or reconcile these objectives. Indeed, some have suggested that the specification of unrealistic numerical goals may turn out to be counterproductive. For the time being at least, the jury is still out on whether the 1978 act will lead to an actual improvement in the performance of the U.S. economy.

OVERVIEW

Despite general agreement on the desirability of full employment and price stability, the choice of specific goals is not a simple matter. Furthermore, goals that are incompatible need to be reconciled. As a practical matter, the process by which this happens is certainly a murky one. It is, therefore, hardly surprising that policymakers have been criticized for either (1) a poor choice of goals or (2) having a socially undesirable set of priorities. But if—and this is a big if—policymakers are consistent and intelligent in the pursuit of their chosen goals, they at least deserve our sympathy for the problems they face. Put another way, except insofar as there are policies that can be pursued to improve the tradeoffs, policymakers cannot be faulted for economic problems that result simply because there are tradeoffs. This suggests that we need to move beyond the issue of goals. In particular, we will assume that the choice of goals and the reconciliation of conflicts have been accomplished, and examine some further details of the policy process.

LAGS IN THE OPERATION OF POLICY

Our earlier discussion of monetary and fiscal policy was essentially static, or timeless, in character. We relied on comparative statics to contrast the nature of equilibrium prevailing before and after some policy change and disregarded the entire set of questions concerning timing. In other words, we have made it appear that policymakers could diagnose the state of the economy, prescribe and administer the appropriate medicine, and cure the patient all in an instant. In the real world, however, each of these steps takes time.

TYPES OF LAGS

It is convenient to decompose the total lag between the need for policy and its final effect into three parts.

The first, the *recognition lag*, refers to the elapsed time between the actual need for a policy action (such as the onset of a recession) and the realization that such a need has occurred. In terms of our medical analogy, the recognition lag thus corresponds to the time it takes to realize the patient is sick and to diagnose the specific ailment. One reason for the existence of this lag is that economic data take time to collect, so that an accurate measurement of where the economy is on some specific date will only be available some time after that date. Another reason is that, even with accurate data, reasonable individuals may take some time to arrive at a common diagnosis.

A second kind of lag, the *policy lag*, refers to the period of time it takes to produce a new policy after the need for a change has been recognized. For fiscal policy this lag may be rather long, especially if congressional approval is required (as it is in most instances). For example, the income tax reduction first called for by President Kennedy in the summer of 1962 was not enacted until early 1964. And the income tax surcharge of 1968 took nearly two years before its passage was secured. Monetary policy, on the other hand, gets distinctly better marks on this score. This, of course, stems from the fact that monetary policy is made by a relatively small group of politically independent individuals.

The final lag, termed the *outside lag*, is the period of time that elapses between the policy change and its effect on the economy. This lag arises because individual decision makers in the economy will take time to adjust to new conditions. Thus, for example, households will only gradually adjust their consumption expenditures when their disposable income changes. This may come from a certain amount of habit persistence or may reflect a desire to see whether the change in income is temporary or permanent. Similarly, if the interest rate declines, firms may not immediately increase their investment. And even if they do, it will typically take some time to produce the capital goods the firms desire.

As a consequence, the effect of a policy change will be distributed over time, and it can take a significant period before a substantial fraction of the full policy effect is felt. Comparing monetary and fiscal policy in this regard, many writers have argued that monetary policy, because it affects the economy less directly, will have a longer outside lag. Another way of looking at this is that, relative to fiscal policy, monetary policy tends to work by influencing investment. And the lags in the physical process of building plants and heavy equipment are undoubtedly longer than the lags in producing consumer goods. Overall, then, the longer outside lag of monetary policy must be balanced against the shorter policy lag in deciding on the optimal mix of policy.

LAGS AND FORECASTING

The existence of lags in the policy process, especially the outside lag, means that to prescribe the proper dosage of policy, authorities must consider both the current state of the economy as well as what the economic situation will be in the future. That is, successful policy will require accurate forecasts of the macroeconomic conditions six months, one year, or perhaps even two years into the future. To make such forecasts, economists rely on a variety of techniques.

1   **LEADING INDICATORS.** This technique attempts to make predictions by exploiting the existence of various lead-lag relationships between economic series. For example, it may have been found that, in the past, downturns in the stock market always preceded declines in economic activity, say, as measured by industrial production, by a number of months. If such a relationship could be counted on to persist into the future, this would be an extremely useful aid in forecasting. Of course, reliance on any particular leading indicator may be somewhat risky, since it can give false signals or fail to signal a change in economic conditions. To minimize these problems, those who use this technique tend to rely on an average index based on a large set of leading indicators. Although this does improve the quality of the signal, it is hardly a foolproof technique. Furthermore, the actual lead time is often considerably shorter than would be ideal.

2   **SURVEYS OF INTENTIONS.** This approach is based on the plausible assumption that if you want to know what aggregate demand will be, you should go to the "horse's mouth." That is, you should survey the spending intentions of businesses and consumers. In fact, a number of such surveys are regularly undertaken by both government and private groups. For example, the Commerce Department, in conjunction with the Securities and Exchange Commission, surveys firms as to how much they expect to invest in plant and equipment over the next one to four quarters. The McGraw-Hill Company also conducts a similar survey. As for consumers, the Bureau of the Census has collected expectations of future purchase of durable goods such as automobiles. The main difficulty with intentions or anticipations data is that they need not be realized. Should economic conditions in the future change markedly from the conditions implicit in the intentions data, actual spending can deviate substantially from in-

tentions. Nevertheless, such data are an important tool in the forecasting kit of most economists.

3 ECONOMETRIC MODELS. An econometric model is a set of empirical relationships, statistically fitted to historical data. Typical components of a model would be relationships such as the consumption function, the investment function, and the money demand function. Once estimated, an econometric model is like the numerical *IS–LM* example considered earlier, albeit with many more equations (sometimes several hundred). Like the leading indicator approach, the use of econometric model for forecasting generally requires that the structure of the economy remain fairly stable over time. This is necessary to assure that historically estimated relationships continue to be good guides to the operation of the economy in the future. However, even this condition is not sufficient to guarantee the reliability of forecasts based on an econometric model. The reason is that in using an econometric model one is required to make assumptions (forecasts) of the values of the exogenous variables that drive the model but are determined outside the model. These might include the foreign demand for products, the weather, or the incidence of strikes. Only if our model is correct *and* our forecasts of exogenous variables are accurate can we be confident that our forecasts of the endogenous variables—GNP, prices, employment, and so on—will be accurate. Clearly, this is difficult to achieve in practice.

It should be evident from this discussion that forecasting is as much an art as a science. As a consequence, no single method is likely to be unambiguously the best. Most practitioners look at the advice proffered by advocates of all three techniques discussed and then tend to make some judgmental compromise. However this is done, one can be sure that forecasts will generally be subject to error. And the magnitude of these errors is likely to increase the further ahead one attempts to forecast. The consequences of this for policy deserve to be stressed.

Given the lag in the operation of policy, we need accurate forecasts to accomplish successful stabilization policy. If our forecasts are highly inaccurate, our policy record is likely to be undistinguished, no matter how well we understand the workings of the economy. This suggests that, if the outside lag of policy is long, we must be cautious in policy because our recommendations are likely to be based on relatively inaccurate forecasts. Indeed, it is even possible that actions aimed at stabilizing economic activity may inadvertently succeed in destabilizing it. The difficulties inherent in conducting successful stabilization policy have, in fact, led some economists to conclude that we should abandon all attempts at discretionary stabilization policy. We will examine this view shortly, but we must first consider some of the other complexities of the policy process.

UNCERTAINTY AND POLICY

Another respect in which our treatment of monetary and fiscal policy in previous chapters was oversimplified was in ignoring the issue of uncertainty. In particular, our discussion proceeded as if the policy maker were sure of what would happen as a result of a policy. Under this simple view of the world, the analogy is sometimes drawn between a policy maker and a technician fine-tuning a precision instrument. This, however, is rather misleading. As one economist has expressed it:

> A better analogy might be to a novice sailor trying to steer a sailboat through a windy and shallow channel. He knows basically where he is going; but he is not sure how far away from the shoals he is. He knows in which direction the boat will respond to manipulations of the sail; but he does not know how strongly, and he does not know how fast. It all depends on such uncontrollable—and perhaps unpredictable—factors as wind, weather and currents.[3]

The appropriateness of this analogy should be readily apparent. Policy makers have a number of instruments under their control and generally have a good idea as to the direction in which each instrument will push the economy. However, they are not necessarily able to predict precisely the magnitude or timing of the effect of their policies. And even if they could, exogenous developments could always lead to an undesired outcome.

Where do these uncertainties come from? We have already touched on three sources of uncertainty in discussing the problem of lags:

1 The inability to assess perfectly the current state of the economy
2 The uncertainty associated with the timing of monetary and fiscal policy effects
3 The inevitable imprecision of the forecasts of future values of exogenous variables that impinge on the economy

There is, in addition, another source of uncertainty that deserves to be stressed. The policy maker will not have a terribly precise model of the economy with which to work. This should hardly be surprising in view of the lack of unanimity among economists as to the underlying structure of the economy. Thus, for example, economists and policy makers may have only rough estimates of critical parameters such as the marginal propensity to consume and the marginal responsiveness of both investment demand and money demand to the interest rate. Since, as we have seen, such parameters are the essential building blocks in determining the quantitative effectiveness of both monetary and fiscal policy, uncertainty means that policy makers "will not know their own strength." As a consequence, *even*

---

[3]A. S. Blinder, *Fiscal Policy in Theory and Practice*. Morristown, N.J.: General Learning Press, 1973, p. 25.

in a fully static world, they will be unable to carry out policy in a precise way.

Few economists would argue with the existence and even the importance of these various uncertainties. There has, however, been considerable debate over the proper moral to be drawn for policy making. Much of this debate has taken place in the context of a long feud between the so-called *monetarist* and *nonmonetarist* economists. It is to this that we now turn. Our discussion will follow the actual historical pattern of the debate. We first examine the monetarist view that fiscal policy is ineffective and monetary policy is all-powerful. Subsequently we consider the monetarist position that even monetary policy should not be used as part of an activist stabilization policy.

THE MONETARIST DEBATE: FISCAL VS MONETARY POLICY

Disputes among economists as to the effects of monetary and fiscal policy have focused both on the mechanisms by which each type of policy works and on their ultimate effectiveness in influencing macroeconomic activity. Views on the importance of monetary and fiscal factors, like clothing fashions, have come and gone and then come again. Prior to the 1930s, economists tended to follow the quantity theory approach, and this, of course, stressed the importance of monetary factors. With the advent of the Depression and the publication of Keynes' *General Theory*, attention focused more on fiscal factors. Indeed, for a period of over 15 years monetary policy fell into disrepute. To some extent this was due to the kinds of problems raised by the Keynesian liquidity trap. But it also reflected the view that interest rates were not a terribly important component of investment decisions. With the further passage of time, a more balanced view emerged, stressing the importance of both monetary and fiscal factors. In the past 20 or so years, however, at least part of the economics profession has come full circle with the development of monetarism.

TENETS OF MONETARISM

Monetarism is prominently associated with the name of the distinguished monetary economist Milton Friedman. However, other economists have made important contributions to the evolution of the monetarist position. And not all of these share precisely the same views; there are both "hard" and "soft" monetarists. While this makes it difficult to define precisely, the following propositions should at least serve to give the flavor of the first phase of the monetarist debate.

1 Money matters in the determination of aggregate income. Few economists of any persuasion would disagree with this statement, but what

distinguishes monetarism is the emphasis given to monetary considerations. As Friedman has put it:

> I regard the description of our position as "money is all that matters for
> changes in *nominal* income and *short-run* changes in real income" as an
> exaggeration but one that gives the right flavor of our conclusions. I regard
> the statement that "money is all that matters," period, as a basic misre-
> presentation of our conclusions.[4]

2 Fiscal policy is impotent in that it is unable to affect real income or
the price level, unless it is accompanied by an accommodating monetary policy. That is, a change in taxes or government spending with
no change in the money supply is of minuscule importance in influencing aggregate demand. However, where such changes are financed
by changes in the money supply, aggregate demand will be affected.
Of course, then it is called monetary policy.

In summary then, monetarism both denies the effectiveness of fiscal
policy and elevates money to a singular and an exalted position. A natural
question to ask is how all this might come about.

WORKINGS OF A MONETARIST MODEL

We can gain some insight into this issue by use of the model developed in
the previous chapters. In fact, under suitable assumptions that model is
perfectly capable of generating monetarist conclusions. In particular, this
will be true if the money demand function is assumed to be insensitive to
the interest rate. This can be seen as follows:

The general form of the money demand function we have used is

$$\frac{M^D}{P} = F(O, r) = F(Y/P, r) \tag{1}$$

while for illustrative purposes we have sometimes relied on a linear version
of this given by

$$\frac{M^D}{P} = JO + (A - er) \tag{2}$$

If the demand for money is insensitive to the interest rate, then the
variable r should be omitted from (1) and (2). For our present purposes we
can just as well work with (2), so that we now have[5]

$$\frac{M^D}{P} = JO \text{ or } M^D = JOP \tag{3}$$

---

[4]M. Friedman, "A Theoretical Framework of Monetary Analysis," *Journal of Political Economy*,
78 (March–April 1970), p. 217.
[5]In going from (2) to (3) we have also dropped the constant A, but this is inconsequential.

With the money supply fixed exogenously, as $M^S = \overline{M}$, we can write the condition for equilibrium in the money market as

$$\overline{M} = JOP \tag{4}$$

Equation (4) says that, given $\overline{M}$, the level of money output, OP, is determined in the money market *independently* of the interest rate. In our previous terminology this means that the *LM* curve is vertical. This is illustrated in Figure 17–1. The curve L_1M_1 is drawn on the assumption that $P = P_1$, while the curve L_2M_2 corresponds to some lower level, $P = P_2$.

As before, we can summarize the complete model by the aggregate demand and supply diagram, as in Figure 17–2. The initial *DD* curve is labeled D_1D_1. To keep matters general, we have drawn two possible aggregate supply curves—S_1S_1, corresponding to the classical case, and S_2S_2, corresponding to our alternative model with sticky wages. We can now quickly see how the monetarist propositions emerge.

Let us turn first to fiscal policy. An increase in government spending or a decrease in taxes will shift the *IS* curve up, as in the movement from I_1S_1 to I_2S_2 illustrated in Figure 17–1. However, with the money supply unchanged, the family of *LM* curves also remains fixed, and thus the *DD* curve stays at D_1D_1. This comes about because interest rates rise (from r_1 to r_2 in Figure 17–1), reducing investment just enough to offset the increase in government spending or the induced rise in consumption expenditures. Thus, equilibrium remains at (P_1, O_1) in Figure 17–2. It should be noted that this result comes about no matter which aggregate supply curve is used.

On the other hand, an increase of $\overline{M}$ will shift the *LM* curve to the right. Figure 17–1 also illustrates this if we now regard L_2M_2 as emerging from the increase of $\overline{M}$ and not from a lower price level. Unlike fiscal policy, this

FIGURE 17–1
IS–LM: **the monetarist case**

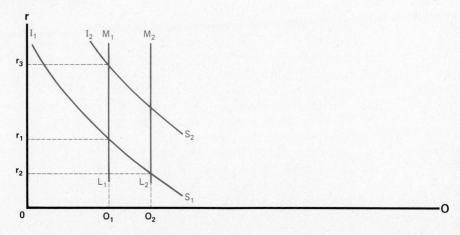

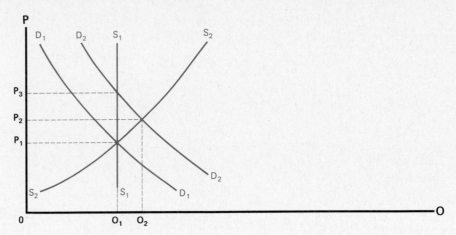

FIGURE 17–2
Aggregate demand and supply: the monetarist case

will succeed in shifting the *DD* curve—shown as the movement from D_1D_1 to D_2D_2 in Figure 17–2. If the relevant supply curve is S_1S_1, both prices and real output will increase, bringing us to (P_2, O_2). On the other hand, in the classical case of S_2S_2 real output stays at O_1 but the price level rises to P_3. Thus, we see that in either case the increase in $\overline{M}$ will raise nominal GNP, $Y = OP$. It is the labor market assumption that determines whether this will serve only to increase *P* or be split between *P* and *O*.

This discussion would seem to suggest that a relatively simple test of the validity of the monetarist view would be to settle the empirical question of whether or not the demand for money is sensitive to the interest rate. However, we have already indicated that virtually all economists (monetarists included) now accept the proposition the interest rate does influence the demand for money. Does this mean we can summarily dismiss the monetarist position? The answer, of course, is not quite. Indeed, there could hardly be an ongoing debate if the matter were so simple. There are at least two reasons why this is the case.

In the first instance, some monetarists have offered some "direct" empirical evidence to support their views. Second, as we have seen before, the effectiveness of monetary and fiscal policy depends on several factors, of which the interest sensitivity of money demand is only one. Consequently, even though the demand for money responds in a "significant" way to changes in interest rates, it is possible that these other factors offset this in such a way so as to make the economy "almost" monetarist in character. Both questions need to be examined a bit further.

SOME MONETARIST EVIDENCE

Monetarists are not impressed with existing evidence on the effectiveness of monetary and fiscal policy. To a large extent, this is because they feel we do not know enough about how the economy operates and therefore cannot sensibly specify how policy works. To try to circumvent this problem, they have adopted a rather simple approach to the question of policy effectiveness.

They begin from an assumption that income is influenced (somehow) by monetary and fiscal policy as well as by other factors. This means that the changes in nominal income (ΔY) from one time period to the next ought to be explained by the change in fiscal policy (ΔF), the change in monetary policy (ΔM), and changes in the remaining other factors. If we assume that changes in these other factors (1) either exert a constant influence on ΔY and/or (2) can be represented by a random factor, we then have

$$\Delta Y = a_1 + a_2 \Delta F + a_3 \Delta M + \text{a random factor} \tag{5}$$

We should be able to fit this equation to actual data by standard statistical procedures. And in fact, this has been done many times, most prominently by economists at the Federal Reserve Bank of St. Louis, but also by others as well. The results have varied somewhat depending on, for example, the choice of time periods, the precise definitions of the policy variables, and the statistical techniques used. Nevertheless, one finding that seemed to emerge from many of these studies is that the effectiveness of fiscal policy (measured by a_2) is very small. Indeed, not infrequently a_2 has turned out to be a small negative number, suggesting that an expansionary fiscal policy actually decreases nominal GNP. In contrast, the effectiveness of monetary policy (a_3) is always positive and typically quite large.

While seemingly offering strong support for the monetarist position, this evidence is not nearly as persuasive as might be thought at first blush. There are, in fact, three major problems with the simple approach embodied in equation (5).

1 **OMITTED VARIABLES.** It is a rather marked oversimplification to assume that the other factors influencing GNP can be adequately characterized by a constant (a_1) and/or random term. There are obviously other systematic factors influencing GNP (e.g., exports), and their omission from (5) can bias the results.

2 **IMPERFECT POLICY MEASURES.** Typically, monetary policy is represented by the stock of money or the monetary base, while fiscal policy is summarized by government spending (ignoring taxes) or by what is called the *full employment surplus*—that is, what the budget surplus or deficit would be if the economy were at full employment. Ignoring taxes is certainly inappropriate, but even use of the full employment surplus is incorrect. This measure weights government spending and taxes equally, but this is inappropriate, since, as we

have seen, they do not have identical effects on GNP. A further difficulty is that a fiscal measure calculated as if we were at full employment may not be an accurate guide to the effect of fiscal policy at less than full employment.

3 **REVERSE CAUSATION.** This difficulty can best be illustrated with an example. Suppose the following assumptions are true: We can ignore the first two difficulties; monetary policy is behaving erratically; fiscal policy is systematically trying to stabilize GNP by offsetting the random forces in (5). The fiscal authorities would thus set fiscal policy, ΔF, so that the fiscal impact, given by $a_2\Delta F$, was equal and opposite to the random forces. In this event,

$$\Delta Y = a_1 + a_3\Delta M \tag{6}$$

In other words, we would find that monetary policy explained changes in GNP perfectly but that fiscal policy did not matter. Of course, the reverse would occur if the monetary authorities were successful stabilizers and the fiscal authorities were erratic. As this example makes clear, a smart policymaker will look impotent, and this effect has generally not been allowed for in estimating equation (5).

In summary then, monetarist empirical studies suffer from a number of difficulties that render the results quite suspect. Furthermore, various writers have shown that alternative definitions of the fiscal variable or the use of more recent data tend to produce results that imply a positive and significant role for fiscal policy.[6] However, even these more recent results suffer from difficulties of omitted variables. This suggests that we ought to look at some additional empirical evidence.

OTHER EMPIRICAL EVIDENCE

As noted earlier, while investigators have found that the demand for money is sensitive to the interest rate, we still must look at a complete model to assess the effectiveness of monetary and fiscal policy. Fortunately, several econometric models are available for this purpose. Although it would take us too far afield to analyze these models in any detail, even a cursory examination suggests that the monetarist conclusions are not borne out. Rather, these models suggest that *both* monetary and fiscal policy are quite capable of altering GNP. For fiscal policy, this is illustrated in Figure 17–3, which exhibits the effectiveness of fiscal policy as calculated from seven different models. Effectiveness in this context is defined as the change in nominal GNP induced by a permanent $1 billion change in nominal government spending. Six of the models give qualitatively similar results leading to GNP changes of between $2 and $3 billion after three years.[7] Only

[6]See, for example, B. M. Friedman, "Even the St. Louis Model Now Believes in Fiscal Policy," *Journal of Money, Credit and Banking*, May 1977, pp. 365–367.

[7]Figure 17–3 also illustrated a point made earlier. In particular, it shows that effects of a policy change take time to build up. In some cases, these effects may even cycle somewhat.

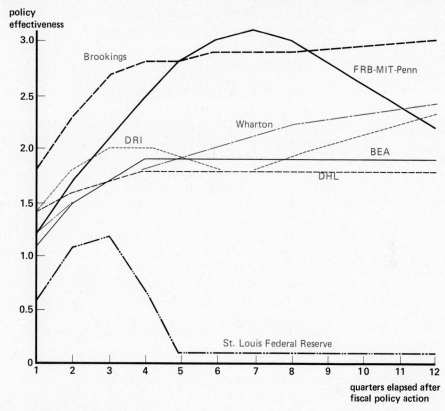

FIGURE 17–3
Effectiveness of fiscal policy: selected
econometric models of the United States
SOURCE: **Alan S. Blinder and Robert M. Solow,**
"Analytical Foundations of Fiscal Policy," in *The*
Economics of Public Finance, **Washington, D.C.:**
Brookings Institution, 1974

the monetarist St. Louis model, which is based on an equation like (5), suggests that fiscal policy is impotent.

In short, while the precise quantitative effectiveness of fiscal policy is still an open question, the monetarist contention that it is totally ineffective seems to be inconsistent with a substantial body of evidence.

OVERVIEW

One of the main tenets of monetarism is that monetary policy works, but fiscal policy does not. We have little quarrel with the first part of this statement, but it seems to us that the majority of the evidence runs counter to the second part. That is, money matters, but so does fiscal policy. As suggested earlier, in recent years this aspect of the debate between monetarists and nonmonetarists has died down somewhat, and the battle is now being fought in another arena.

THE MONETARIST DEBATE: RULES VS. DISCRETION

Earlier we touched on some of the problems created by uncertainty and lags in the policy process. A number of economists, after taking stock of these difficulties, have concluded that we would be better off if we did not use discretionary policy at all. In place of discretion, these economists would have rules to govern the behavior of monetary and fiscal policy. Aside from the alleged superiority of the rules from the viewpoint of stabilization, proponents argue that they are to be preferred on philosophical grounds as well. This view is based on the belief that economic freedom is best served when we are governed by laws, not by people who may misuse their power.

The best known of these rules is one advanced by Milton Friedman. Friedman has proposed that the Federal Reserve adopt a rule of letting the money supply steadily increase at some fixed rate of growth. That is, the same rate of growth should be followed week in, week out, month in, month out, and year in, year out. While the specific rate chosen would depend on which concept of the money supply was used, the numbers generally advanced have been in the range of 3 to 4 percent per year. Friedman, however, has been quick to point out that the specific rate is less critical than the need to keep the money supply growing *steadily* at whatever rate is selected.

The rules that have been proposed for fiscal policy have generally involved the notion that the government budget ought, in some sense, to be balanced. In the past this has often been translated into the view that the budget ought to be balanced annually. There is a basic difficulty with this view, stemming from the fact that taxes endogenously or automatically respond to changes in income. Because of this, if private demand autonomously declines, tax revenues will fall. Any attempt to balance the budget would require raising tax rates in the face of a weak economy. Judged by modern standards this would be a rather perverse policy, and in fact this rule is no longer advocated by any serious economist. Despite this, in the 1980s considerable political sentiment has developed for a constitutional amendment to require a balanced budget. Indeed, by 1984 some 32 states had passed a call for a constitutional convention to address the issue. There was speculation that Congress, fearing the potential mischief of a constitutional convention that would be free to address *any* issue once called, might be forced into passing a balanced budget amendment. As of mid-1985, however, no action had been taken.

A less rigid version of the balanced budget rule still maintains some currency. This would involve determining the level of government spending on its own merits, independent of stabilization policy, and then setting tax rates to yield a balanced budget *if* the economy were at full employment. That is, the so-called *full-employment surplus* should be zero. This rule does not suffer from the gross defects of the simple budget rule, but it would take us too far afield to discuss its specific merits and demerits in any detail.[8] We turn instead to the more general question of whether rules should replace discretionary policy.

As already suggested, economists of the monetarist persuasion have been in the forefront of those advocating rules. The essence of this debate has been well summed up in the following statement by Franco Modigliani (a prominent nonmonetarist), taken from this 1976 presidential address to the American Economic Association:

> In reality the distinguishing feature of the monetarist school and the real issues of disagreement with nonmonetarists is ... the role that should probably be assigned to stabilization policies. Nonmonetarists accept what I regard to be the fundamental practical message of *The General Theory*; that a private enterprise economy using an intangible money *needs* to be stabilized, *can* be stabilized, and therefore *should* be stabilized by appropriate monetary and fiscal policies. Monetarists by contrast take the view that there is no serious need to stabilize the economy; that even if there were a need, it could not be done, for stabilization would be more likely to increase than to decrease instability.[9]

Several key points implicit in Modigliani's statement deserve to be stressed: (1) Monetarists emphasize the basic stability of the economy; (2) as such, they view the economy as able to adapt readily to shocks and to return to a position of long-run equilibrium; and (3) monetarists, pointing to the actual historical record, infer from the evidence that policy makers have generally been a destabilizing force in the economy. Naturally, nonmonetarists have something to say about each of these points. For one thing, they regard it as self-evident that the economy is subject to numerous shocks. Moreover, they argue that while there is certainly a tendency, after a shock, for the economy to return to its long-run equilibrium, this does not happen quickly enough. As a consequence, nonmonetarists see ample opportunity for discretionary policy to improve economic performance. Reliance on rules thus removes a needed degree of flexibility.

This point can be illustrated by considering the full-employment fiscal rule given previously. That rule requires policy makers to offset any "surprises" that arise within the federal budget. Thus, if expenditures fall short of budget plans because Congress rejects some presidential spending proposals, there would be a call for a tax cut. If uncontrollable expenditures

[8]For a discussion of this specific rule, see A. S. Blinder and R. M. Solow, "Analytical Foundations of Fiscal Policy," in *The Economics of Public Finance.* Washington, D.C.: Brookings Institution, 1974.

[9]F. Modigliani, "The Monetarist Controversy or, Should We Forsake Stabilization Policies?" *American Economic Review*, March 1977, p. 1.

take a sharp jump, a tax increase would be needed. At the same time, however, advocates of this rule are determined not to respond to surprises in private demand. This seems somewhat illogical. If surprises in government demand require attention, then why not apply the same standard to unexpected shocks emanating from the private sector? Although the Friedman rule has no such problems of inconsistency, since the money supply would grow steadily no matter what economic conditions were, under this rule we would still give up the ability to respond to any shocks to the economy.[10]

Friedman has acknowledged this defect. He has even gone further, stating that his rule is "not a necessary implication of monetarist theory" and that "a believer in monetarist theory can still favor an activist monetarist policy as a way to offset other changes in the economy."[11] If one accepts the view, as Friedman does in principle, that there is scope for discretionary stabilization policy, there remains the empirical issues of whether stabilization policies have worked in the past and whether they will work in the future. We are thus reduced to this seemingly simple question: Would the actual path of the economy be more stable and would we be able to sustain higher average levels of output and employment if we abandoned discretion and followed a set of rules? Despite the apparent simplicity of the question, no readily agreed-upon answer has yet emerged. Various investigators have reached quite different conclusions from an empirical examination of the same historical evidence. A major part of the difficulty in securing a consensus on this issue is that, as we have seen, there is less full agreement as to the ways in which monetary and fiscal policy affect the economy. As a result, neither camp—neither those advocating rules nor those advocating discretion—has managed to interpret the historical evidence to the satisfaction of the other.

But even if the historical evidence is somewhat mixed, this is not sufficient cause to abandon discretionary stabilization. Policymakers are certainly permitted to (and, it is hoped, do) learn from their past mistakes. Errors committed in the formative years of both our macroeconomic understanding and practical policymaking should not be permanently held against discretionary policy.

On balance, the adoption of a set of fixed rules for monetary and fiscal

---

[10]Modigliani (ibid., p. 13) has characterized the Friedman rule as follows:

Friedman's logical argument against stabilization policies and in favor of a constant money growth rule is, I submit, much like arguing to a man from St. Paul wishing to go to New Orleans on important business that he would be a fool to drive and should instead get himself a tub and drift down the Mississippi; that way he can be pretty sure that the current will eventually get him to his destination; whereas if he drives, he might make a wrong turn and, before he notices, he will be going further and further away from his destination and pretty soon he may end up in Alaska, where he will surely catch pneumonia and he may never get to New Orleans!

[11]M. Friedman, "Has Monetarism Failed?" *Manhattan Report on Economic Policy*, 4, 3, 1984, p. 3.

policy does not appear to be a panacea for our economic ills. Discretionary policy, for better or for worse, still seems to us to have the edge. Moreover, in practice the distinction between rules and discretion is not all that precise. As Paul Samuelson has observed, a set of rules "is set up by discretion, is abandoned by discretion, and is interfered with by discretion." In other words, there is no assurance that political considerations will lead to any less tinkering in a world of rules. While this consideration is undoubtedly

RULES AND MONETARISM: SOME EARLY THOUGHTS

Today one associates the advocacy of monetary rules with the University of Chicago economist Milton Friedman. However, the intellectual foundations for this view were provided by another member of the "Chicago School," Henry Simons, who in his 1936 essay "Rules vs. Authorities in Monetary Policy," stated:

> In a free enterprise system we obviously need highly definite and stable rules of the game, especially as to money. The monetary rules must be compatible with the reasonably smooth functioning of the system. Once established, however, they should work automatically, with the chips falling where they may. . . . Political control in this sphere should be confined exclusively to regulation of the quantity of money and near money.

While Simons was thus an early monetarist, he recognized the practical problems in choosing a particular monetary aggregate to control. Indeed, he expressed annoyance with

> . . . the unfortunate character of our financial structure—with the abundance of what we may call "near-moneys"—with the difficulty of defining money in such a manner as to give practical significance to the conception of quantity.

His frustration with the world as he found it led him to suggest that regulation should seek to minimize the opportunities for the creation of substitutes for money. To accomplish this he advocated the abolition of private deposit banking and suggested drastic limitation on the borrowing powers of all private corporations.

To many this seems like a recommendation to change the world so monetarism will work better. As one waggish economist has suggested, it seems a bit like tilting Italy so as to straighten the Leaning Tower of Pisa. Whatever one thinks of Simons's recommendations, as we shall see in the next chapter, he was right to concern himself with the practical problems for monetarism that are presented by the need to choose a specific definition of money.

more relevant for fiscal policy, it carries some force for monetary policy as well.

One final point raised by the monetarist debate deserves comment. As noted above, led by Friedman, the monetarists have advocated that the money supply should be made to grow at some constant rate. While this rule has not been explicitly adopted by the monetary authorities, the monetarist argument has had a strong impact on the nature of policy. In particular, as we shall see later, in recent years the Federal Reserve has paid important attention to the growth rate of the money stock. There is more than a bit of irony in all this, because soon after the Federal Reserve tilted toward monetarism, a variety of financial innovations served to cast serious doubt on the proper definition of money. Even if one wanted to follow a Friedman-type rule, it became rather unclear as to how best to carry this out. Furthermore, the same developments that created ambiguity as to the proper definition of money also served to make it more difficult, as a practical matter, for the Federal Reserve actually to control any particular definition of the money supply. As Samuelson warned us, the Federal Reserve was thus forced to use discretion in the application of a rule.[12] We shall see how this all worked itself out in the next chapter when we discuss the role of money in monetary policy.

SUMMARY

1 As a consequence of both the Employment Act of 1946 and the Humphrey-Hawkins Act of 1978, economic policy makers are directed to pay attention to a broad range of goals. These include the following: full employment, reasonable price stability, more capital formation, a balanced budget, reduced government spending, an improved trade balance, and a sound and stable international monetary system. Unfortunately, the legislation is silent as to how these noble goals are to be achieved. It is also relatively silent about what to do should these goals come into conflict.

2 One of the major problems in the conduct of economic policy is the existence of lags in the operation of policy. There are lags in recognizing the need for action, in taking the action, and in having the action effect the economy. The existence of lags means that policies will have their effects in the future, which in turn means that policy makers must consider the likely future state of the economy. Some economists, disturbed by the difficulties of forecasting, conclude that we should minimize our attempts at discretionary stabilization policy.

[12]For a detailed discussion of all the issues raised in this section, see A. M. Okun, "Fiscal–Monetary Activism: Some Analytical Issues," *Brookings Papers on Economic Activity*, 1, 1972, pp. 23–64.

3 A second major problem confronting policy makers is the presence of uncertainty. This uncertainty can take many forms, not the least of which is the fact that policy makers will not have available a precise numerical textbook model with which to design appropriate policies.

4 Economists of a monetarist persuasion have some very particular views on economic policy. The debate between monetarists and non-monetarists has raged off and on for the past 20 years and has been fought on several different battlegrounds. One version of the debate took place in the *IS–LM* arena, with monetarists emphasizing the potency of monetary policy and the impotency of fiscal policy. Fiscalists supposedly believe the reverse. The monetarist position, at least in its extreme form, was seen to depend on a vertical *LM* curve, which in turn derives from the presumed insensitivity of money demand to interest rates. These days, this aspect of the debate has died down somewhat.

5 Although it is not a logical implication of monetarism, monetarists have also been in the forefront of arguing that the problems of uncertainty and lags and the inherent stability of the private sector favor the use of rules over discretion in the conduct of economic policy. As for monetary policy, Milton Friedman has advanced the specific rule that the money supply should be made to grow at some constant rate. The practicality of this rule is considered in more detail in the next chapter.

SELECTED READINGS

Blinder, A. S. *Fiscal Policy in Theory and Practice.* Morristown, N.J.: General Learning Press, 1973.

Okun, A. M. "Fiscal–Monetary Activism: Some Analytic Issues," *Brookings Papers on Economic Activity,* vol. 1, 1972, pp. 23–64.

Friedman, M. "A Theoretical Framework for Monetary Analysis," *Journal of Political Economy,* 78 (March–April 1970), pp. 193–238.

Modigliani, F. "The Monetarist Controversy or, Should We Forsake Stabilization of Policies?" *American Economic Review,* 67 (March 1977), pp. 1–19.

18

THE ROLE OF MONEY IN MONETARY POLICY

Some readers may think the title of this chapter a bit strange, since it probably seems self-evident that money is somehow the essence of monetary policy. Indeed, throughout our discussion of policy from Chapter 15 on, we have fostered this impression by maintaining the assumption that monetary policy involved finding the "right" quantity for the stock of money. To be sure, we have suggested that problems of conflicting goals, lags, uncertainty and financial evolution make this no simple task, but the presumption has been that money and monetary policy are virtually synonymous. While for many purposes this is a useful simplifying assumption, there is in fact more to monetary policy than just finding the "right" quantity of money.

For one thing, monetary policy does not necessarily operate by setting the money supply. From 1942 to 1951, for example, the Federal Reserve conducted policy by pegging interest rates and letting the money supply be whatever it turned out to be. In subsequent years, although it abandoned pegging, the Federal Reserve continued to pay more attention to interest rates than to monetary aggregates. It is only in recent years that policy has been seriously concerned with the money supply. Nevertheless, even here there has been more to policy than just picking a monetary target. First of all, there is the problem of defining money. When discussing general principles of monetary policy, one can afford the luxury of being somewhat imprecise as to the exact definition of money. For a more realistic policy discussion, greater precision is needed. And as we will see, in recent years such precision has been hard to achieve. Moreover, even if there were no disagreement over the definition of money, it would still be a substantial oversimplification to characterize monetary policy as merely picking a monetary target. The reason is that the Federal Reserve is not endowed with a "money supply dial" that allows it to control the stock of money. Rather, as we shall see, there are serious questions as to the best operating procedures for controlling the money supply.

The purpose of this chapter is to reexamine the nature of monetary policy. The outline of the chapter is as follows: We first reconsider some of the issues involved in defining and measuring the stock of money. We then address the question of why the Federal Reserve might pay attention to interest rates. Since the wisdom of this depends in part on the stability of the demand for money, we next examine this issue. Following this we take a detailed look at how the Federal Reserve actually conducts monetary policy, focusing particularly on its choice of operating strategies. This discussion also addresses the question of what the experience of recent monetary policies can teach us about the workability of monetarist recommendations. Finally, we consider some unresolved issues that bear on the future conduct of monetary policy.

THE DEFINITION OF MONEY RECONSIDERED

The general issues in defining money were spelled out in the first chapter. There, we expressed a preference for a narrow, transactions-based definition of money. We also indicated, however, that what constitutes a medium of payments cannot be settled once and for all. Rather, those assets which are used in transactions may change with advances in technology and the evolution of institutional practices. At an early stage of monetary development a narrow definition of money might have included only currency. Then, as commercial banking gained in importance, the commonly accepted definition of money came to include demand deposits at commercial banks. With the continuing evolution of the financial system, especially in the last decade, still other financial instruments have appeared that have been incorporated into money, even narrowly defined. A prime example of such an instrument is the NOW account authorized by the Depository Institutions Deregulation Act of 1980. A more recent example is the super-NOW account, which came into existence at the beginning of 1983.

In view of the remarkable evolution of the financial system in the last decade, it should hardly be surprising to learn that economists have been forced to rethink the proper definition of money. Indeed, in recognition of the fundamental changes that were occurring in the financial system, in

February 1980—just prior to the passage of the Deregulation Act—the Federal Reserve introduced a new set of definitions of the monetary aggregates. This set runs the gamut from the traditionial narrow definition to an extremely broad measure of liquidity. The full set of definitions, with corresponding data as of year-end 1984, is given in Table 18–1. The organizing principle underlying the redefined monetary aggregates was the functional one that at each level of aggregation one should combine similar kinds of monetary assets. To see how this principle was applied, we shall examine the narrow and broad measures in turn.

MONEY, NARROWLY DEFINED

The traditional definition of money has been the sum of currency and demand deposits at commercial banks, generally denoted by M-1. As Table 18–1 reveals, the new narrow definition of M-1 includes traveler's checks

TABLE 18–1 Various Money Stock Measures and Components, December 1984 (seasonally adjusted, except as noted; in billions of dollars)

Aggregate and component	Amount
M-1	$ 558.5
Currency	158.7
Traveler's checks	5.3
Demand deposits	248.6
Other checkable deposits	145.9
M-2	2,371.4
M-1	558.5
Overnight RPs plus overnight Eurodollars*	57.6
Money market mutual fund balances*	167.7
Money market deposit accounts*	415.2
Savings deposits	288.5
Small-denomination time deposits	885.1
M-3	2,995.2
M-2	2,371.4
Large time deposits	416.8
Term RPs*	69.7
Term Eurodollars*	83.2
Institutional money market mutual funds	62.7
L	3,544.0
M-3	2,995.2
Savings bonds	73.9
Short-term Treasury securities	271.8
Bankers' acceptances	41.3
Commercial paper	161.8

*Not seasonally adjusted. Due to the use of unadjusted data the components of M-2 and M-3 do not precisely sum to the seasonally adjusted values of M-2 and M-3.

and what are termed "other checkable deposits." The latter category, which accounted for over 25 percent of M-1 at the end of 1984, includes NOW accounts, super-NOW accounts, share draft accounts at credit unions, and automatic transfer savings accounts. While the Federal Reserve has moved to modernize the transaction-type measure of money, it has not gone as far as it might. Indeed, some of the possible candidates for inclusion are contained in the broader definitions of money. We first consider these broader definitions and then return to possible modifications to M-1.

BROADER MEASURES OF MONEY

We indicated in Chapter 1 that some economists prefer to make use of a broader definition of money that includes assets such as time and savings deposits. So this group would not feel left out, the Federal Reserve has also modernized its broad definitions of money. These are denoted by M-2 and M-3. In addition, the Federal Reserve has begun reporting a very broad measure of liquid assets, which is denoted by the symbol L. All three of these broad measures are defined in Table 18–1.

Generally speaking, M-2 includes savings and small time deposits at all depository institutions, as well as money market shares and overnight re-purchase agreements and overnight Eurodollars. A comparison of the growth of the various monetary aggregates is shown in Table 18–2. Since 1960 M-2 has grown substantially faster than M-1, reflecting primarily more rapid growth of time and savings deposits than of demand deposits. As a result, money, narrowly defined, has been a decreasing fraction of M-2, declining from about 45 percent in 1960 to under 25 percent in 1984. As Table 18–2 reveals, the M-3 measure has grown even faster than M-2.

PROBLEMS WITH THE DEFINITIONS

As we have seen, in defining M-1 the Fed has sought to provide a trans-actions-based measure. Put another way, the Fed has aimed at excluding from M-1 all those instruments not used primarily for transactions pur-poses. The problem, as one might suspect, is that the line is not that sharp. A few examples may help to convey the issues involved.

In our discussion of commercial banking, we noted that repurchase agreements (RPs) have grown dramatically in recent years. An RP, it will be recalled, is an acquisition of funds via the sale of securities, with a simul-

TABLE 18–2 Growth Rates of Various Monetary Measures (average annual rates of growth, in percentages)

Period	M-1	M-2	M-3	L
1964–1984	6.4	8.9	10.0	9.9
1964–1974	5.5	7.9	9.2	8.7
1974–1984	7.2	10.1	10.8	11.0

taneous agreement by the seller to *repurchase* them at a specified later time. RPs are frequently made for one business day (i.e., overnight).[1] The repurchase price is naturally higher than the sale price, this being the way in which interest is paid. Suppose, for example, a corporation has cash in a demand deposit account that is not needed today but is likely to be required to meet anticipated expenditures tomorrow. The corporation would naturally like to earn interest on these temporarily excess funds, and can do so by use of an RP. It can arrange to buy a government security from a commercial bank, at the same time obtaining an agreement that the bank will repurchase the security on the following day. The net effect of this is temporarily to reduce the corporation's holding of demand deposits while at the same time earning a secured market rate of return. When the RP matures, the corporation's demand deposit is restored. While the RP itself is not a medium of exchange, from the corporation's viewpoint the overnight RP and the demand deposit have much in common. Thus a case can be made for including RPs in M-1. While admitting this, the Fed had noted that "professional opinion is currently divided over whether RPs are mainly liquid investments or transaction-type balances" and has opted for including them only in a broader aggregate.

There are also other ways in which financial innovation and regulatory change have reduced the distinctiveness of money as traditionally defined and measured. Indeed, these developments have served to blur the differences between transactions deposits and savings deposits. As a consequence, how one classifies any particular instrument sometimes seems quite arbitrary. NOW accounts, which used to be excluded from M-1, have been included since 1980. Consequently, when super-NOWs were invented at the end of 1982, they too were included. However, money market deposit accounts (MMDAs) at commercial banks and thrifts, which came into existence at the same time as super-NOWs, are excluded from M-1. The reasoning is that while MMDAs can be used for transactions, the number of transactions per month is limited to six. The reader can easily see the difficulty. If six does not qualify as a transactions account, would eight? How about ten? Where one draws the line is hardly self-evident.

A more glaring problem crops up with the exclusion from M-1 of shares of money market mutual funds. As will be recalled, it was these shares that prompted the development of the MMDA. While shares of money market mutual funds were initially subject to some restrictions on the extent of permissible transactions, these retrictions have largely disappeared. The Fed's continued exclusion of these accounts from M-1 is based on surveys which show that relatively fewer transactions per month are made with these share accounts as compared with other types of accounts included in M-1. Again, there is a problem of how few is few?

---

[1]For an informative and readable analysis of repurchase agreements, on which much of our discussion is based, see N. N. Bowsher, "Repurchase Agreements," *Review*, Federal Reserve Bank of St. Louis, September 1979, pp. 17–22.

What these examples suggest is that it is difficult to construct a pure transactions-based measure of money. Moreover, even if one has a reasonably workable definition at any point in time, innovation and deregulation may make such a definition obsolete. These sorts of problems are amply illustrated by recent experience.

Although we have spared the reader the gory details, before unveiling the latest definitions of money, the Federal Reserve expended many resources on research. An Advisory Committee of Monetary Statistics, which issued its report in 1976, entailed considerable effort by economists both inside and outside the Federal Reserve. Before the recommendations of this committee were implemented, however, it became apparent that the rapid evolution of the financial system meant further study was required. Consequently, substantial additional effort was undertaken prior to releasing the currently prevailing definitions. Moreover, in the light of continued innovation and deregulation, the Fed must mount an ongoing effort to monitor the appropriateness of the various definitions of the monetary aggregates.

By now it should be clear that defining money is no simple matter. What is perhaps less clear is why this is worth worrying about.

WHY ALL THE FUSS?

To the casual observer, this scurrying about to produce the "best" definition of money might seem a bit strange. Such a person would undoubtedly agree that it was desirable, at least on esthetic grounds, to have a sensible and consistent definition of money. Yet all the effort devoted to the question suggests that more than esthetics is involved, and indeed this is the case. How one defines money can have a critical influence on the conduct and success of monetary policy. In this regard several points deserve to be stressed.

1 In carrying out monetary policy, the Federal Reserve must be guided by some model of the economy. As we have seen, a critical ingredient of such a model is likely to be the demand function for money. If such a function is to be empirically identified in a reliable way, it is clearly necessary that we define money in the behaviorally most meaningful way. Only in such circumstances is the Federal Reserve likely to be able to carry out a successful policy.

2 To put the point another way, even (or perhaps especially) if one were a monetarist who advocated the Freidman rule that the money supply should grow at a constant rate, it is clearly critical how we define the money supply.

3 As hinted at above, economists sometimes use movements in the stock of money as an indicator of the state of the economy. Again, this clearly requires a definition of money that is closely related to underlying economic variables.

4 Not all definitions of money are equally amenable to control by the Federal Reserve. If it turns out that the best definition is only controllable with significant error, then perhaps the Federal Reserve should be provided with additional tools to improve monetary control.

What this all suggests is that we need to move from definitional issues to an examination of the role of money in monetary policy.

MONETARY POLICY TARGETS: MONEY VS. THE INTEREST RATE

We have just indicated that under some circumstances the Federal Reserve, even if it could directly control the quantity of money, might choose to conduct monetary policy in some other fashion. We will consider a number of alternative possible strategies below, but here we concentrate on just one strategy that has been frequently advocated—namely, that the Federal Reserve should control the interest rate.[2] This should not be interpreted as meaning that the Federal Reserve necessarily pegs the interest rate for an extended period of time (as it did during World War II). Rather, what the advocates of this strategy have in mind is that the Federal Reserve should select a "reasonable" level for the interest rate and maintain it for some number of months. From a practical point of view, such a strategy is quite easy to carry out via open-market operations. Basically, the Federal Reserve must stand ready to buy or sell securities at the particular price that corresponds to the target interest rate. Of course, under such a strategy the Federal Reserve gives up the ability to control the money supply.

The question naturally arises as to what difference it makes whether the authorities operate by setting the money supply or setting the interest rate. As we will see, the answer depends on the nature of the uncertainty confronting the policy maker. We have noted that policy makers face various types of uncertainty. Two of the most important of these are uncertainty over the strength of aggregate demand and uncertainty over the strength of the demand for money. In terms of the familiar *IS–LM* framework, uncertainty over the state of aggregate demand means that the monetary authorities are not exactly certain where the *IS* curve is located. They know on average where it will be. But if demand is "surprisingly" strong, then the actual *IS* curve will be farther to the right than the average *IS* curve. And if demand is surprisingly weak, the actual *IS* curve will be to the left of the average *IS* curve. Similarly, because of unexpected variations in the strength of money demand, setting the quantity of money will not precisely pin down the location of the *LM* curve. Again, of course, the authorities will have some notion of where the *LM* curve will be on average.

[2]In couching this strategy in terms of "the" interest rate, we are abstracting from the real world complexity presented by the existence of many different interest rates. However, our earlier discussion of the structure of interest rates suggests that this is a reasonable simplification.

This is the setting in which we will explore the consequences of operating monetary policy by fixing either the money supply or the interest rate. Initially, we assume that the price level is fixed, but later we consider the case of a variable price level.

THE CASE OF CERTAINTY

Figure 18–1 illustrates the two types of monetary policy in the context of the *IS–LM* model. We assume that the authorities desire to bring about a full-employment level of income, O_e, and for the moment we ignore the problem of uncertainty. Thus, the position of the *IS* curve is assumed known. To bring about O_e the monetary authorities have two options. First, they could fix the money supply so that the conventional-looking *LM* curve, L_1M_1, intersects the *IS* curve at O_e. This is possible because we are temporarily ignoring uncertainty about money demand. Alternatively, the authorities could, by appropriate open-market operations, bring the interest rate to r_e and keep it there. This second option amounts to a horizontal *LM* curve, shown as L_2M_2. As is clear from Figure 18–1, in the absence of uncertainty it makes little difference which policy is pursued. In either case the equilibrium (r_e, O_e) emerges. When we introduce uncertainty, however, these two policies can diverge.

THE CASE OF UNCERTAINTY

We first consider the case in which the uncertainty is solely in the location of the *IS* curve. To keep matters simple, we assume that the *IS* curve is known to lie between the two extremes I_1S_1 and I_2S_2 in Figure 18–2. If the

FIGURE 18–1
Money stock and interest rate policies: The certainty case

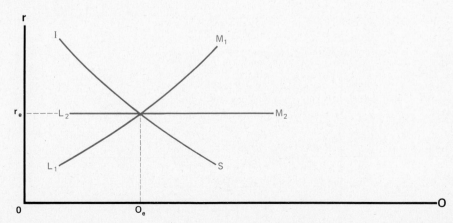

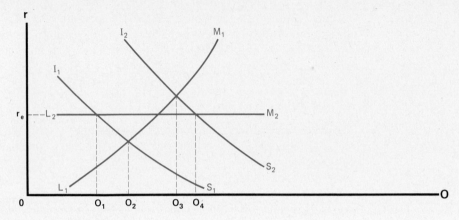

FIGURE 18–2
Alternative policies: *IS* uncertainty

money supply is set at some fixed level, then the *LM* curve will be L_1M_1. Consequently, income will fall somewhere between O_2 and O_3. Alternatively, suppose the monetary authorities fix the interest rate at r_e. The relevant *LM* curve is L_2M_2, and income will vary between O_1 and O_4, a wider range than O_2 to O_3. Since on average both policies will produce the desired level O_e, the money stock policy is superior to the interest rate policy because it produces a smaller range of variation about that average. The reason for this is that under a money stock policy a random disturbance to the *IS* curve will affect the interest rate. This in turn will induce a change in investment that partially offsets the initial disturbance.

The opposite polar case is pictured in Figure 18–3. Here we assume that there is no uncertainty about the position of the *IS* curve. However, unpredictable movements in the demand for money function will cause shifts in

FIGURE 18–3
Alternative policies: *LM* uncertainty

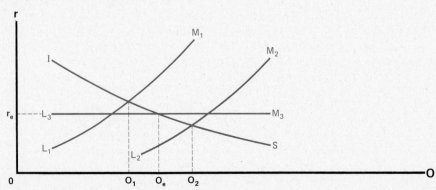

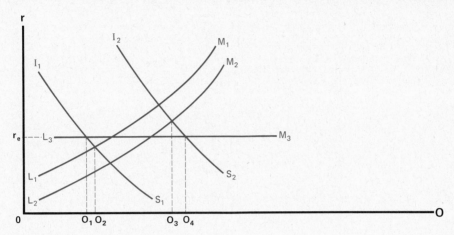

FIGURE 18–4
Alternative policies: *IS* and *LM* uncertainty

the *LM* curve if a money stock policy is followed. As illustrated in Figure 18–3, these shifts are assumed to keep the *LM* curve between L_1M_1 and L_2M_2, with the result that income ends up anywhere between O_1 and O_2. In contrast, however, an interest rate policy keeps the *LM* curve at L_3M_3, so that the desired full-employment level of income, O_e, results. This comes about because the stock of money is simply allowed to accommodate any shifts in the demand for money.

We thus see that if uncertainties arise solely from the *IS* or commodity sector, a money stock policy will be superior to an interest rate policy. On the other hand, if the uncertainties arise solely from the *LM* or money sector, an interest rate policy will be superior. In realistic situations, of course, policymakers are confronted with uncertainty in regard to *both* the *IS* and *LM* curves. Two illustrations of this are depicted in Figures 18–4 and 18–5. In Figure 18–4 the *IS* curve is more unpredictable and, as in the pure case of *IS* uncertainty, the money stock policy is superior—the range is from O_2 to O_3 instead of O_1 to O_4. In Figure 18–5 the *LM* curve is more variable and, as in Figure 18–3, the interest rate policy is superior.[3]

To a considerble extent these results serve to rationalize the policy recommendations of monetarist economists. In particular, monetarists have frequently stressed their belief that the money demand function is relatively more stable than the consumption function or the investment function. Thus, they would argue that the situation in Figure 18–4 is more realistic than the one in Figure 18–5. In view of this, it is hardly surprising that the monetarists prefer a money stock policy to an interest rate policy. Fur-

---

[3]For a detailed discussion of these points and a number of extensions, see W. Poole, "Optimal Choice of Monetary Policy Instruments in a Simple Stochastic Macro Model," *Quarterly Journal of Economics*, May 1970, pp. 197–216.

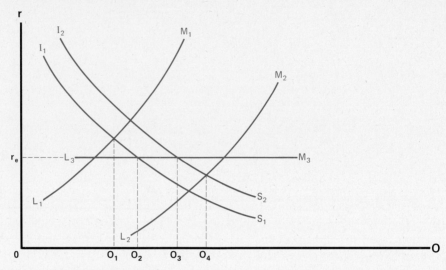

FIGURE 18–5
Alternative policies: *IS* and *LM* uncertainty

thermore, monetarists emphasize that once the price level is free to vary, there are additional grounds for avoiding an interest rate policy.

THE INTEREST RATE POLICY: A CAVEAT

As we saw earlier, in an inflationary environment there is an important distinction between nominal and real rates of interest. Furthermore, it is the real rate of interest that is more relevant for spending behavior.[4] However, since the anticipated rate of inflation is not directly observable, neither is the real rate of interest. As a practical matter interest rate policies tend to be couched in terms of nominal interest rates. There is a problem here, however, in that the nominal rate of interest incorporates an inflation premium whose size is not precisely known. It may be difficult to decide whether a given nominal interest rate represents a "tight" or an "easy" monetary policy.

This point has been stressed by monetarists, who have also pointed out the possible undesirable consequences of pursuing an interest rate policy that inadvertently attempts to keep the interest rate below its equilibrium level. They envision a scenario in which the nominal interest rate is reduced by expansionary open-market operations, which leads to an increase in the

[4]Consider, for example, a prospective homeowner faced with a 12 percent mortgage rate. Before deciding this is "high" or "low," our prospective investor obviously examines how fast house prices are likely to be appreciate. If, say, they are expected to rise at 12 percent as well, then the mortgage rate is likely to be regarded as a good deal. All we are saying here, of course, is that the investor looks at the real rate of interest (which, in our example, is actually zero).

stock of money outstanding. If this process begins at or near full employment, the initial increase in M will lead to a rise in prices—that is, inflation. The actual inflationary experience may generate a rise in the anticipated future rate of inflation. This can lead to a rise in the demand for loanable funds, which will tend to increase interest rates. Thus, still more money would have to be created to prevent interest rates from rising. This could lead to a vicious circle in which further increases in the stock of money produce more inflation, higher anticipated rates of inflation, and greater upward pressure on interest rates. Such a policy may be a perfect recipe for continuing, and probably accelerating, price inflation. In fact, once inflationary expectations become widespread, a level of interest rates that would have maintained price stability under conditions of noninflationary expectations will actually encourage inflation. In this regard it is interesting to note that during World War II, when interest rates were pegged at a low level, we also had price controls to repress the potential inflation. At the end of the war, when controls were lifted but interest rates were kept low, we experienced a serious bout of inflation.

On balance then, it would appear that caution is needed in pursuing an interest rate policy. After much badgering by monetarists, even nonmonetarists have now agreed that there are potential difficulties. Nevertheless, many nonmonetarists still maintain that if uncertainty primarily stems from the *LM* curve, interest rate policies may be desirable. This is more likely to be the case over short time horizons, when the anticipated rate of inflation does not change very much.

OVERVIEW

We have considered two alternative operating strategies for monetary policy—money targets and interest rate targets. In neither case, however, should this analysis be interpreted as implying the desirability of a fixed rate. Thus, for example, if the nature of uncertainty is such as to favor a money target, there is no presumption that this target would be chosen by a rule of the Friedman sort. Indeed, this analysis is perfectly consistent with the Federal Reserve's varying the money supply (or interest rate targets) in a discretionary way.

There remains, of course, the issue of which of the two policies we have considered is to be preferred in practice. As we have seen, this depends on whether the uncertainty stems from the *IS* or the *LM* side of things. This issue has long been debated, both theoretically and empirically, without a definitive resolution. In a way this should not be surprising, because it is quite likely that the primary source of uncertainty may switch from *IS* to *LM* and back again as circumstances change. In recent years it appears that there has been increasing uncertainty in the *LM* curve. Since the *LM* curve stems from the equilibrium condition in the money market, this uncertainty could result from the demand or supply of money. In fact, as we will see, both sides have contributed to increased uncertainty. We first take up the demand for money.

UNCERTAINTY AND THE DEMAND FOR MONEY

The recent behavior of the demand for money has been such as to impart increased uncertainty to the *LM* curve. Since uncertainty might be measured in various ways, we need to be a bit more precise on this point. What we have in mind in referring to uncertainty are the related concepts of *predictability* and *stability*. As we saw in Chapter 13, the major determinants of the demand for money are income (representing transaction needs) and interest rates. If, given these determinants, we could predict the demand for money with a high degree of accuracy, then in an intuitive sense at least, most observers would agree that money demand is not an important source of uncertainty. A precondition for successful prediction is likely to be a stable demand function for money. That is, the empirical relationship between money and its determinants should remain roughly constant from one period to the next. Until a few years ago most studies had concluded that the demand for money was both stable and quite predictable.[5] In terms of our previous analysis, other things being equal, this tended to support the use of monetary targets. Over the last decade or so, however, confidence in the stability of the demand for money has been severely shaken.[6] The first episode of instability cropped up in the mid-1970s, but uncertainty due to the demand for money has remained an important issue to this day. A brief examination of the experience of the 1970s readily illustrates the nature of the problem.

THE CASE OF THE MISSING MONEY

Since we have identified uncertainty with a lack of predictability, this suggests that we ought to take a look at the forecasting record of the demand-for-money function. This is done in Figure 18–6, where we have plotted the actual quantity of real money balances along with the quantity predicted by a conventional money demand function for the period from 1974 to 1976.[7]

The economy experienced a severe recession from the first quarter of

[5]See, for example, S. M. Goldfeld, "The Demand for Money Revisited," *Brookings Papers on Economic Activity*, 1973, no. 3, pp. 577–638.

[6]Ironically, as we see below, monetary targets were not used during the earlier period of stability but were introduced after signs of instability arose.

[7]The actual money data are based on the M-1 series. In making the predictions the money demand equation was estimated using quarterly data from 1952–1973 and then extrapolated to the period 1974–1976. For details, see S. M. Goldfeld, "The Case of the Missing Money," *Brooking Papers on Economic Activity*, 1976, no. 3, Table 2, p. 687.

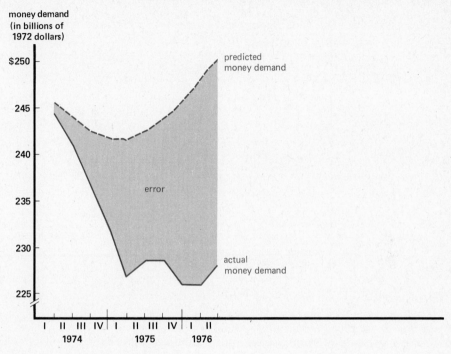

FIGURE 18–6
Actual and predicted real-money balances,
1974–1976

1974 to the first quarter of 1975 and then recovered. Consistent with this, as Figure 18–6 shows, the demand for money was predicted to decline through the first quarter of 1975 and to rise thereafter. Actual money demand did decline, but the drop was much steeper than predicted. Furthermore, as the economy recovered, the actual demand for money rose only very slightly. By mid-1976 the prediction error was a whopping 10 percent—much larger than any previous prediction error. It was thus apparent that the economy was making do with much less money, given the levels of income and interest rates, than had been predicted on the basis of past behavior. In view of this shortfall, this episode is sometimes referred to as "the case of the missing money."

The same point can be made in a slightly different way with reference to the concept of the income velocity of money. Velocity, denoted by V, it will be recalled, is defined by the condition

$$MV = Y$$

where Y is nominal GNP. In our earlier discussion we pointed out that there has been a rising trend in velocity in the period since the end of World War II. We also noted that during recessions, when both interest rates and

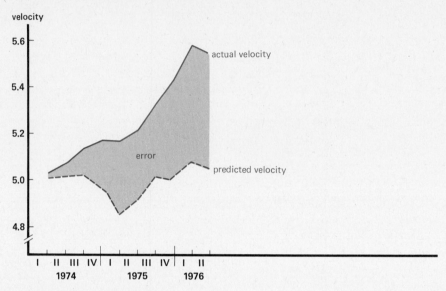

FIGURE 18–7
Actual and predicted velocity, 1974–1976
SOURCE: S. M. Goldfield, "The Case of the Missing
Money," Brookings Papers on Economic Activity,
1976, p. 3.

real income generally decline, that velocity also tends to decline. As shown
in Figure 18–7, this pattern in velocity is precisely what is predicted by a
conventional money demand equation.[8] As that figure also shows, actual
velocity continued its upward trend throughout the period, although it did
slow slightly during the recessionary quarters. In other words, actual velocity was substantially higher than predicted velocity, so that a given level
of income could be supported by a smaller amount of money than would
have been predicted.

In summary, as judged by Figure 18–6 or Figure 18–7, there is a clear
indication that the demand for money took a sharp and unexpected plunge
during the period 1974–1976. What this means is that the economy made
do with a smaller volume of currency and checkable deposits. More detailed analyses of this period suggest the further finding that virtually all
the shortfall was in checkable deposits (which, for the period in question,
simply means demand deposits) rather than currency. The question naturally arises as to how and why businesses and households modified their
behavior to make do with fewer demand deposit balances.

[8]Predicted velocity in Figure 18–7 ($\hat{V}$) is related to predicted real money demand in Figure
18–6 ($\hat{M}/P$) by the condition $(\hat{M}/P) \cdot \hat{V} = Y/P$, where P is the price level. In nominal terms this
is equivalent to $\hat{M} \cdot \hat{V} = Y$.

WHERE DID THE MISSING MONEY GO?

One basic way for both firms and individuals to economize on demand deposits is to make use of other financial instruments that serve as a substitute for demand deposits. As our discussion of financial innovation makes clear, there are an expanding number of such substitutes. For households, these include shares at money market mutual funds and money market deposit accounts; for businesses, these include the use of repurchase agreements (RPs) to manage corporate cash balances. Most of these developments, however, are of relatively recent origin and consequently explain relatively little of the shortfall pictured in Figure 18–6.[9] In other words, while a bit of the missing money went into substitutes for demand deposits, we have to look elsewhere for the rest.

The second basic way to explain the missing money starts with the observation that from the mid-1970s on, individuals and especially firms seemed to be getting by with fewer transactions balances in total (demand deposits plus substitutes). Put another way, firms were being more efficient in making transactions. If firms were making do with fewer transactions balances, we ought to be able to find evidence of innovations that permitted them to economize on such balances. There have, in fact, been numerous such innovations, and their appearance has been directly stimulated by the extremely high interest rates of recent years. While it would take us to far afield to discuss these innovations in detail, we can illustrate their nature by considering two—the lock box and the cash concentration system.

A *lock box* is a device for reducing *float*. To see how float arises, suppose that a New York customer of a California firm mails a check for payment of services. The check takes a number of days to arrive in California and is then deposited by the firm in its California bank. The bank, however, will make the firm wait until the check clears before letting it use the funds. This whole process might take something like 9 days. Enter the lock box. Instead of mailing the check to California, the New York customer mails it to a post office lock box in New York City. Most likely the check will arrive the next day and, when it does, will be collected by a New York city bank. This bank in turn will *wire* the funds to the California firm, and the firm will have immediately usable funds. The net effect is that the California firm has the use of its funds much more quickly. As a result, the company can get by with fewer demand deposit balances; put another way, it has speeded the velocity of its deposits. This is, of course, precisely what Figure 18–7 suggests has happened. The funds released by this process can be used by the firm in any way it wishes.

[9]NOW accounts were excluded from the definition of money used to derive Figure 18–6. However, in the mid-1970s these accounts were inconsequential in size and thus do not explain Figure 18–6. At one point it was thought that repurchase agreements might be a substantial factor in explaining Figure 18–6, but tests that have been performed suggest this is not the case. See R. D. Porter, T. D. Simpson, and E. Mauskopf, "Financial Innovation and the Monetary Aggregates," *Brookings Papers on Economic Activity*, 1979, no. 1, pp. 213–229.

A *cash concentration system* is a second device permitting firms to economize on demand deposits. This typically involves a wire transfer of excess demand balances from local collection banks to a central account. Such a system provides the firm with faster and more complete information on its demand balances, while centralization allows the firm to take advantage of offsetting balances at its banks throughout the country. As with the lock box, the end result is to permit a reduction in demand balances and a speedup in velocity.[10]

As should be apparent from this brief introduction to corporate cash management techniques, there are a number of ways in which firms can economize on demand deposits. Many economists feel that the use of such techniques goes a long way toward "solving" the case of the missing money. As a practical matter, however, for several reasons things are not so neat and tidy. First, no one has yet managed to produce a widely accepted way of introducing the effects of cash management techniques into an empirical demand for money function. As a consequence, changes in cash management techniques can still provide a source of unpredicatabilty or uncertainty in the demand for money. Second, these problems are compounded by continuing financial innovation and deregulation. The evolution adds to the uncertainty in the demand for money. Indeed, as we will see shortly, unexpected developments in the demand for money in 1982 and 1983 contributed to the worst recession in the post-World War II era.

OVERVIEW

The relation between the demand for money balances and its determinants is a fundamental building block in virtually all macroeconomic models. Since it is also a critical component in the formulation of monetary policy, it is not surprising that the money demand function has been subjected to extensive empirical scrutiny. This scrutiny has revealed that in recent years the demand for money has tended to shift. These shifts, while explainable in principle, have considerably complicated the task of those who conduct monetary policy. Furthermore, in the light of the uncertainty analysis of the previous section, this shifting has cast doubt on the wisdom of couching monetary policy in terms of targets for the monetary aggregates.

Our discussion in this section is obviously closely related to the issue of the definition of money. Unfortunately, as our discussion makes clear, new definitions are not sufficient to explain away all the shifts that have been observed. At the current time there remains considerable uncertainty associated with money demand, no matter how money is defined. At the very least, the Federal Reserve deserves a good deal of sympathy for having to

[10]For a more complete account of cash concentration systems and cash management techniques more generally, see the appendix to T. D. Simpson, "The Market for Federal Funds and Repurchase Agreements," Board of Governors of the Federal Reserve System Staff Study 106, Washington, D.C., July 1979.

cope with these somewhat hectic developments. Indeed, as we will see, the life of the Federal Reserve is even more complicated than we have yet let on.

THE ACTUAL CONDUCT OF MONETARY POLICY

In discussing procedures for the conduct of monetary policy, we have thus far focused on the choice of money versus the interest rate as an operating target. We have, however, yet to discuss two practical problems: (1) How does the Federal Reserve decide on numerical targets for money and/or the interest rate? (2) How does it actually conduct policy? We have implicitly caricatured these two issues as follows. The Federal Reserve first decides on its goals or objectives regarding the behavior of such measures as real output and employment. In terms of the *IS–LM* framework, for example, these objectives could be summarized by some desired level of output. The Federal Reserve then guesses where the *IS* curve is, and in conjunction with its target level of output, this tells it where the *LM* curve has to go. To accomplish this, it sets the money supply or the interest rate to pin down the *LM* curve. It then sits back and waits until some new data are available, and then it repeats the process.

As in all caricatures, there is an element of truth in this description, but needless to say, it omits many relevant aspects of policymaking. For one, the Federal Reserve is faced with incomplete information on the current state of the economy, uncertainty as to its future course, and the fact that monetary policy only works with a lag. Second, the Federal Reserve cannot simply set a dial or thermostat to control the money supply. Rather, it needs to spell out procedures for using its basic tools—open-market operations and reserve requirement changes—to accomplish this. From a practical point of view, all these issues are supposed to be settled at the meetings of the Federal Open Market Committee (FOMC).

THE FOMC AGAIN

The FOMC consists of 12 members—the 7 members of the Board of Governors of the Federal Reserve System and the presidents of 5 of the regional Reserve Banks. The committee meets approximately monthly to set monetary policy. The process consists of the following steps.[11]

1 A detailed discussion of the current state of the economy, money and financial markets, and the international situation. For this purpose

[11]For an insider's description of FOMC by an ex-governor of the Federal Reserve, see Sherman Maisel, *Managing the Dollar*. New York: W. W. Norton, 1973. The present description of FOMC procedures and the several quotes are from this source.

some several hundred statistical series are studied, their meaning debated, and their accuracy scrutinized.

2 A projection of where the economy seems to be heading. For such projections the FOMC will have to assess factors beyond its control, such as likely future fiscal policies. In actually making the predictions it relies on a mixture of judgmental and econometric forecasting techniques.

3 An analysis of goals and objectives. Here the discussion typically focuses on whether the path of the economy, if current monetary policies are maintained, is likely to lead to a desirable outcome. While in principle this would be the time for explicit discussion of objectives and proposed tradeoffs, this apparently often remains only implicit. As a former governor, Sherman Maisel, has written: "Each member remained free to vote his own value judgments and prejudices without ever having to state or defend his objectives."

4 Choice of an appropriate monetary policy. After the current path of the economy is compared, at least implicitly, with what might be desirable, a course of action is selected. Maisel describes this step as follows: "While disagreements over where the economy is and should be heading are common in FOMC meetings, they pale beside the question of what monetary policy should be adopted to achieve these goals." The basic problem, of course, is that FOMC members, like economists more generally, do not always agree on the likely effect on the economy of a given change in monetary policy. As a consequence, this step of the process is often characterized by heated debate.

5 Issuance of a *directive* to the manager of open-market operations. The function of the directive is to instruct the manager how to implement the chosen monetary policy over the next month or so. To do this, it provides various kinds of operating guides, the nature of which have changed considerably over time. Since this is a critical part of the process, we examine the directive in more detail.

THE DIRECTIVE AND OPERATING GUIDES FOR POLICY

At one end of the monetary policy spectrum we have the tools of policy, such as open-market operations and reserve requirement changes. At the other end are the ultimate policy targets, such as real output, the unemployment rate, and the rate of inflation. In between are a whole spectrum of variables that go by such names as *operating targets* or *intermediate targets.* Examples of these variables are total bank reserves, and, as we have seen, the money supply and interest rates. These variables are "in between" or intermediate in the following sense: An open-market operation first affects bank reserves and extremely short-term interest rates (e.g., the overnight federal funds rate); next it influences various monetary aggregates and longer-term interest rates; and after a still longer lag, it affects ultimate policy targets such as GNP.

In its choice of monetary policy, the FOMC naturally thinks in terms of appropriate values for one or more of these operating targets. It is these targets that are communicated, via the directive, to the manager of open-market operations. These targets serve two important purposes: (1) They provide a standard of accountability for the manager; and (2) by observing the actual behavior of the targeted variables, policymakers get some feedback. This is important, since not all variables are observed with the same frequency. For example, while interest rates may be observed daily, money supply figures are available weekly with considerable inaccuracy or monthly on a more accurate basis, and GNP data are only available quarterly. Thus, if monetary targets are used and it turns out that the actual money supply data are deviating from targeted values, the FOMC gets a chance to consider why this is happening. It may in such circumstances decide that the manager of open-market operations has fallen down on the job, or it may conclude that its targets are inappropriate and adjust them accordingly. In any event, it is clear that these intermediate variables can provide information useful to the FOMC.

Thus far we have indicated that the FOMC has a number of possible operating guides. In point of fact, it has frequently changed strategies in the last 25 years or so. A brief review of the various operating guides that have been used in the past will provide a perspective on the conduct of monetary policy past, present, and future.[12]

MONEY MARKET CONDITIONS

From 1942 to 1951 the Federal Reserve's job was to peg interest rates. Indeed, it was not until 1953 that the Federal Reserve finally made the transition to a period in which it could freely conduct monetary policy. Its first operating guides in this period were termed *money market conditions*. The particular conditions chosen consisted of changes in certain key short-term interest rates and totals for member bank borrowing and excess reserves at Federal Reserve banks.[13] Gradually the FOMC began to focus on the difference between excess reserves and member borrowing, which is termed *net free reserves* (see Table 18–3). For about a decade the directive was couched in terms of net free reserves and short-term interest rates.

---

[12]For an authoritative review of FOMC strategies prior to 1979, see H. C. Wallich, "The Role of Operating Guides in U.S. Monetary Policy: A Historical Review," *Federal Reserve Bulletin*, September 1979, pp. 679–691. For a description of the post-1979 experience, see H. C. Wallich, "Recent Techniques of Monetary Policy," *Economic Review*, Federal Reserve Bank of Kansas City, May 1984, pp. 21–30.

[13]Recall that until 1981 reserve requirements applied only to commercial banks that were members of the Federal Reserve System.

TABLE 18–3 Various Measures of the Reserve Position of Member Banks, February 1980 (Monthly average of daily figures, in millions of dollars)

Total reserves	$43,196
Less: Borrowed reserves	1,660
Equals: unborrowed reserves	41,536
Total reserves	$43,196
Less: required reserves	43,026
Equals: excess reserves	170
Less: borrowed reserves	1,660
Equals: free reserves	−1,490

SOURCE: *Federal Reserve Bulletin*, March 1980, p. A5.

Around 1960 a number of economists, both inside and outside the FOMC, began questioning the use of net free reserves as an operating target. They pointed out that the same level of free reserves could have a rather different policy impact, depending on whether credit demands at banks were strong or weak. For instance, maintenance of a given level of free reserves when a strong loan demand was tending to use up such reserves would inevitably lead to monetary and credit expansion. In effect, banks would try and lend out their excess reserves and the FOMC would replenish them. If this process were repeated for long, a dangerously expansionary situation could result. On the other hand, holding free reserves constant when loan demand was weak and banks wanted to let their free reserves rise (by accumulating excess reserves and repaying borrowing) would lead to contraction. After several episodes in which a net free reserve strategy led to undesirable effects, the FOMC began to search for other operating guides.

MONEY MARKET CONDITIONS PLUS

A gradual shift in emphasis took place in the mid-1960s as the FOMC started to concern itself more with aggregate quantities such as the volume of bank credit. In the first instance it expressed this by introducing what it termed a *proviso clause* to the directive. An example of this is contained in the directive for November 22, 1966:

> Open market operations until the next meeting of the Committee shall be conducted with a view to maintaining somewhat easier conditions in the money market, unless bank credit appears to be resuming a rapid rate of expansion.

This is basically a money market strategy with a proviso (the "unless" part). While not an official part of the directive, supporting documents for the November 1966 meeting indicated that the directive's language was consistent with a roughly zero level of net free reserves, a 3-month Treasury bill rate of about 5 percent, and bank credit expansion of from 2 to 4 percent. Interestingly enough, however, the manager was given no explicit guidance as to what to do in the event that not all these (possibly conflicting) general guides could be met.

While the proviso for bank credit represented somewhat of a change in the character of FOMC strategy, until the beginning of 1970 money market conditions remained the critical operating targets. At that time a further modification took place as the role of the proviso and the main part of the directive were interchanged. In particular, directives stressed bank credit and money as primary targets, and relegated money market conditions to the proviso. Furthermore, net free reserves were abandoned, as the proviso was typically couched in terms of a range for the federal funds rate.

Although this was a seemingly big change in the direction of a strategy based on monetary aggregates, in practice this was not the case. The FOMC specified a relatively narrow range for the federal funds rate and the manager was instructed to be bound by the proviso. As a consequence, despite the primary emphasis on money and credit, actual growth in these measures often deviated significantly from the FOMC's specified ranges.

For a brief period the FOMC experimented with various aggregate reserve measures as a substitute for the federal funds rate. These, however, proved difficult to work with. The problem was the complicated structure of reserve requirements that then applied to deposits of different types (e.g., demand vs. time) and sizes. As a result, the multiplier between a total reserve measure and the money supply proved unstable.[14] Put another way, this suggests that the simple money-multiplier approach outlined in Chapter 8 must be applied cautiously in practice. If nothing else, this experience indicated that direct control of the money supply is more difficult than might appear at first glance. In any event, after experimenting with reserve measures, the FOMC returned to a proviso based on the federal funds rate.

MONETARY AGGREGATES

The next stage in the development of an operating guide involved considerably more explicit attention to money supply. The role of bank credit was dramatically reduced and supplanted by targets for the growth of various measures of the money stock—primarily M-1 and M-2 (on the basis of the definitions then prevailing). In this regard, the Federal Reserve was spurred in part by congressional pressure to pay greater attention to monetary aggregates. From 1975 to 1978, the Federal Reserve made quarterly reports to Congress on its 12-month money growth targets. Since 1978, under the Humphrey-Hawkins bill, these reports have been semiannual, although some

---

[14]During the period the FOMC made use of both total reserves and "reserves against private deposits." Private deposits exclude Treasury balances at banks, which are quite variable and are not included in the money supply.

technical details in the nature of the reporting were improved with the passage of the Humphrey-Hawkins bill.

Despite the more prominent attention given to the money supply, the FOMC continued to rely on a proviso based on the federal funds rate, and indeed, within a monthly period a fairly narrow range was specified for the funds rate. Furthermore, in those months in which there was an incompatibility between the funds rate and the money supply, the funds rate, despite its proviso status, remained the binding constraint. There was a new wrinkle, however, in that if the actual growth of money deviated from the targeted growth rate, the range on the funds rate was adjusted at the next FOMC meeting.

This process is pictured in Figure 18–8, where we have plotted the FOMC ranges for the growth rate of M-1 and the funds rate for the year 1978. In April and May 1978, for example, the actual growth rate of M-1 exceeded the top of its tolerance range (see Figure 18–8). As a consequence, in mid-April, as shown in the figure, the FOMC both shifted up the range on the funds rate and widened the band. In terms of the analysis at the beginning of the chapter, within a month the FOMC was pursuing an interest rate policy (of course, with a range rather than a specific number). Across months, however, it was following what has been termed a *combination policy*. That is, it was adjusting both money and interest targets in the light of new information. While this combination policy in principle gave the FOMC greater control over the monetary aggregates than it would have had under a strict interest rate policy, critics still complained that control was not adequate. In 1979 these complaints grew more vociferous, especially as inflation began accelerating. For example, during 1979 the inflation rate, as measured by the change in consumer prices, was nearly 13 percent, well above the 9 percent rate in 1978 and the 6½ percent rate in 1977. Feeling the need to "do something," the Fed announced a major change in its operating strategy, to be introduced in conjunction with a tightening of monetary policy.

DEVELOPMENTS OF OCTOBER 6, 1979

On October 6, 1979, the Federal Reserve announced its intention to achieve tighter control over the money supply. To do this, it proposed to free the manager of open-market operations from the shackles of the federal funds rate and reduce the importance of the funds rate as a tool of policy. Previously this issue had been something of a vicious circle. The Federal Reserve believed that financial market participants paid close attention to the funds rate, and this inhibited the FOMC's willingness to let the funds rate fluctuate. This inhibition endowed the funds rate with significance and made the whole thing a self-fulfilling prophecy.

By word and deed, the FOMC sought to break this vicious circle. While it did not totally abandon the proviso clause, it did dramatically widen the

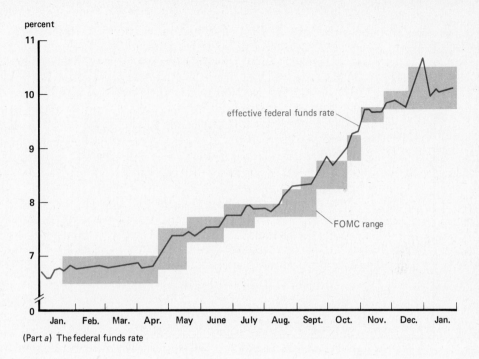

percent

(Part *a*) The federal funds rate

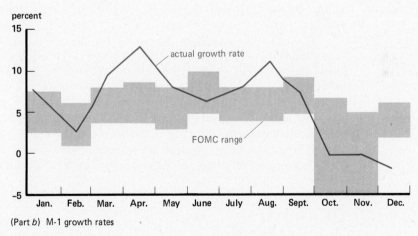

percent

(Part *b*) M-1 growth rates

**FIGURE 18–8
FOMC policy ranges, 1978**

permissible range. Thus, for example, in the directive issued on October 6, 1979, the range for the funds rate was set at 11½ to 15½ percent. In contrast, the previous directive had specified a range of 11¼ to 11¾ percent. Insofar as the federal funds rate is concerned, the dramatic impact of the new operating procedure is most vividly illustrated in Figure 18–9, which shows

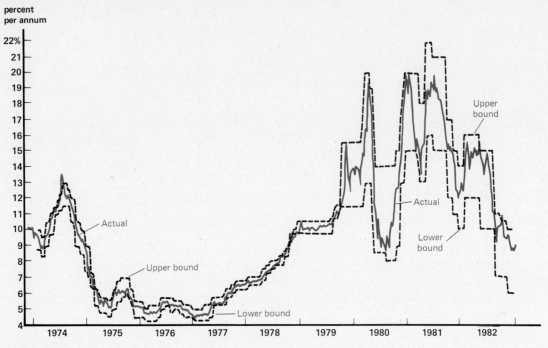

FIGURE 18–9
Federal funds rate: actual path and FOMC range

the actual funds rate and the FOMC range for 1973 to 1982. The increased width of the FOMC range after October 1979 is quite apparent. Equally striking is both the record-breaking level of interest rates and the unprecedented variability in interest rates that prevailed after October 1979. In response, the FOMC made large and frequent adjustments in the permissible range. Based on Figure 18–9, no one would deny that the new operating strategy freed the Fed from the shackles of the federal funds rate. But this freedom had its price, since the Fed was now shackled with monetarism.

THE MONETARIST EXPERIMENT

By prominently announcing adoption of its new operating procedures, the Fed aligned itself with the monetarist view that monetary targeting was the appropriate way to conduct policy. Equally, if not more, important, it set up a standard of performance—the degree of success in achieving monetary targets—by which the Fed was to be judged. Moreover, the Fed suggested that in each successive year it was likely to reduce the target rate of growth of the money supply. In taking these actions, the Fed hoped to achieve credibility as an inflation fighter.

In choosing to use monetary aggregates as an operating target, the Fed moved closer to conducting policy in simple textbook fashion. In many respects, however, the timing of this change was extremely ironic. As we have seen, due to financial innovations, there was considerable uncertainty as to how to define money. As a consequence, there was uncertainty as to what the likely impact on the economy would be of targeting some particular monetary aggregate. Put another way, past and prospective financial innovations meant that achieving some particular monetary target could turn out to be more or less restrictive than historical relationships might suggest. Similar problems could arise if there were unexpected shifts in the demand for money. It was for these reasons that a substantial number of economists raised doubts about the wisdom of the new Fed procedures; and the Fed itself was well aware of the potential frailities of its new policies. These concerns proved to be of more than academic interest. First, however, we give the good news.

After a shaky start in implementing the new procedures, the Fed managed to deliver on its promise of gradually reducing the rate of growth of money. For example the growth rate of M-1, which had been 8.2 percent in 1978, fell to 7.4 percent in 1980, and dropped again to 5.1 percent in 1981. Not only did this help establish the credibility of the Fed as an inflation fighter, it also helped to reduce dramatically the rate of inflation. So much for the good news. At the same time, however, this policy led to the most serious postwar recession on record, with the unemployment rate after the middle of 1982 heading toward 11 percent. The Fed, which had naturally expected some weakening of the economy in response to its policies, was surprised and disturbed by the seriousness of the recession. Quite evidently, the Fed's policies were proving more restrictive than intended. And the reason, once again, was another apparent shift in the money demand relationship.

The consequence of this shift can be seen most simply by the use of the notion of the income velocity of money first introduced in Chapter 13. Velocity, V, is defined from the equation of exchange $MV = Y$ as $V = Y/M$. As we have seen, the relative stability of predictability of velocity is an important pillar of the monetarist position. Table 18–4 shows what happened to velocity in the years before and after 1980. From 1970 to 1980, velocity increased at a rate of 3.4 percent per year. What this means is that a given increase in M-1 would support an increase of GNP of 3.4 percentage points more. For example, from Table 18–4 we see that from 1970 to 1980 the annual rate of increase of M-1 of 6.6 percent yielded nominal GNP growth of 10.2 percent.[15] The same table shows the marked *drop* in velocity that took place in 1982 and in 1983. This unusual behavior of velocity meant

---

[15]The fact that the 10.2 percent growth of Y almost exactly equals the growth in M (6.6 percent) plus the growth in velocity (3.4 percent) is no coincidence. It is a direct result of the relationship connecting the three variables, $MV = Y$.

TABLE 18–4 Changes in Money, Nominal GNP, and Velocity (percentage annual rates)

	M-1	Nominal GNP	Velocity
1970–1980	6.6	10.2	3.4
1981	7.1	12.4	4.9
1982	6.6	3.8	−2.6
1983	11.2	7.7	−3.1
1984	6.9	10.8	3.6

that in 1982–1983 the growth in GNP was 3 percentage points *less* than the growth in M-1.

The precise reasons for the unusual behavior of velocity in 1982–1983 are still being debated, but many economists subscribe to the view that the behavior of velocity was influenced by both financial innovations and shifts in the demand for money.[16] Whatever reason one favors, it is clear that the sharp drop in velocity was unexpected by the Fed and therefore led the Fed to pursue an unintentionally restrictive monetary policy—one that was severely depressing the economy.

As 1982 evolved and the depth of the recession became apparent, the Fed wanted to ease up. But now the shackles of monetarism got in the way. Given the decline in velocity, easing up would have meant substantial increases in the growth of M-1, increases that would have brought the growth rate of M-1 well over the target the Fed had set for itself. To the extent that the public believed that achieving these targets was essential to fighting inflation, the Fed felt its credibility was on the line and was temporarily paralyzed into inaction. Indeed, headlines in mid-1982 spoke of "The Fed's Dilemma" and "Money Supply Controls Hurt the Economy." But as of mid-1982, although the Fed was looking for a way out of the straitjacket it found itself in, it was not quite prepared to take the necessary steps.

As the Fed was pondering its actions, economic conditions continued to deteriorate. When in early October 1982 the unemployment rate jumped over 10 percent, the Fed decided it had had enough. Nearly three years to the day after embracing monetarism, the Fed announced a tactical change.

---

[16]Two sources have been cited for the increase in the demand for money in 1982 (It is a *higher* demand for money that translates into *lower* velocity). First, it is the sharp growth in the newly available NOW accounts. Second, as Chairman Volcker of the Fed has characterized it, "precautionary or liquidity motivations, during a period of economic uncertainty and turbulence, were leading to stronger than anticipated demands for money." Paul Volcker, "Statement before the Committee on Banking, Housing, and Urban Affairs," United States Senate, July 20, 1982, p. 10. For a discussion of the quantitative aspects of the shift in money demand see *The Economic and Budget Outlook: An Update*. Washington, D.C.: Congressional Budget Office, September 1982.

After pointing to the fact that the inflation rate had substantially declined, Chairman Volcker announced that the Fed's new policy objective would be to sustain economic recovery. Moreover, he announced that "distortions" were making M-1 an unreliable guide to policy and that, at least, over the foreseeable future the Fed would pay less attention to M-1.[17] The effects of this new policy were quite evident in the strong economic recovery that took place beginning in 1983.

AFTER OCTOBER 1982

As we have just seen, at the end of 1982 the Fed chose to downplay, at least temporarily, the desirability of adhering to monetary targets based on M-1. To be sure, as required by law, the Fed continued to announce ranges for the monetary aggregates. But after 1982 there were several differences. For one, the Fed began emphasizing that it was "paying attention" to a variety of monetary aggregates, including M-1, M-2, and M-3. At some times it spoke of giving "substantial weight" to the broader aggregates M-2 and M-3, while at other times the Fed talked of giving "equal weight" to all three aggregates. While this intuitively seems plausible, critics have argued that it is not really clear what the Fed meant by "paying attention" to several aggregates. What, for example, would it do if one monetary aggregate was growing faster than planned and another was growing more slowly than planned? Moreover, how does the answer depend on how much "weight" is being given to the various aggregates? Not surprisingly, some saw these ambiguities as disguising the fact that the Fed had returned to an operating strategy based on targeting interest rates. The Fed was quick to admit that it had modified its operating strategy, but sought to deny that it returned to an interest rate strategy.

For example, Governor Henry Wallich of the Federal Reserve has noted: "Changes in overall reserve positions since the fall of 1982 largely have reflected deliberate policy judgments rather than a automatic response to deviations of monetary aggregates from present target paths. Nevertheless, the Federal Reserve has not reverted entirely to the old technique."[18] Wallich went on to observe that current policy did not directly target on the federal funds rate, but rather a prechosen path for nonborrowed reserves. Others, however, have pointed out that the Fed was free to alter the chosen reserve path in the light of the behavior of interest rates, and indeed at various times seemed to do just that. In other words, under present policies the Fed could easily focus on interest rates.

[17]Volcker cited two distortions: First, that substantial amounts of all savers certificates were about to expire and some fraction of these would be temporarily placed in checking or NOW accounts, thus distorting M-1. A second distortion on the horizon was the effect of the newly authorized MMDA account to allow banks and thrifts to compete with money market mutual funds.
[18]Wallich, op. cit., p. 21.

THE TOUGH LIFE AT THE FEDERAL RESERVE

Being a member of the Fed in the early 1980s was not an easy task. As already noted, beginning in 1980 there were several episodes of high interest rates, and these prompted angry public reactions. In June 1981, for example, a headline in the *New York Times* proclaimed "Fed Officials Booed in Chicago on Rates". The article went on to note

> Consumers, business executives, local officials and home builders took the central bankers to task yesterday over economic ills ranging from the inability of home buyers to get fixed-rate mortgages to the small-businessman's cost of carrying inventory.

The demonstrators demanded a more rapid increase in the money supply and special protection for the housing industry.

In early 1982 one cement company, obviously affected by the slowdown in building caused by high interest rates, took out a full-page newspaper ad, cartooning the Fed as a vampire and stating

> Too much of our economic blood is being sucked away by the high interest rate policy of the Federal Reserve. . . . Tell your Congressman what *you* think of high interest rates. Send a copy to The Honorable Paul A. Volcker, Chairman, Board of Governors, Federal Reserve System.

This episode also caused much fretting in Congress with Senator Jake Garn of Utah noting in the *Congressional Record*

> I do not think there is anybody in this body—certainly no one on the Banking Committee—who has a lack of understanding of the problems that high interest rates have caused. Believe me, there are other years I would have preferred to become chairman of the Banking Committee than in a year when the prime rate reached 21.5 percent. Before I pray for my wife and children at night, I pray for lower interest rates, so I can have a day of peace as chairman of the committee without getting calls from automobile dealers, homebuilders, all down the line.

As we have seen, in late 1982 the Fed announced a tactical retreat from monetary targeting, and interest rates eased off. While this made some people quite happy, the Fed still came in for criticism. In testimony before the Senate Banking Committee in July 1983, Alan Blinder noted:

> I come to you today as a representative of a majority group: people who are worried about what the Federal Reserve might do. Oscar Wilde said that experience is the name we give to our mistakes. By this definition, the Fed has gained a great deal of experience in recent years. And there is reason to fear that it may be about to gain more.

> Paul Volcker once observed that "central bankers have a certain reputation: like Puritans, it is said, we have a haunting fear that someone, some place, may be happy." Quite evidently, there is an ample supply of people who don't want the Fed to be happy.

What of the future? For the moment, the Fed is clearly pursuing an eclectic sort of monetary policy. Chairman Volcker has defended this stance by observing "I doubt—during a time of profound institutional and economic change—a single rule will be so reliable that it can substitute for a degree of judgment and flexibility at times, particularly when various possible 'rules' are giving conflicting signals."[19] This is obviously a plea for discretion of a very generalized sort—one that, needless to say, makes monetarists rather unhappy. Monetarists acknowledge the somewhat stormy 1979–1982 period, but suggest that once deregulation has run its course, financial markets should settle down. At that juncture, monetarists argue, policy should once again focus on the money stock. Past experience suggests this could well happen.

OVERVIEW

As should be apparent from this excursion into the subject of operating guides, a wide variety of procedures have been employed by the Fed in the conduct of monetary policy. This variety has partially reflected the learning behavior of the Fed, once it was freed from the shackles of pegging interest rates in 1951. But the shifts in operating procedures over time have also reflected both the changing nature of economic conditions and changes in financial markets. These shifts have been particularly marked in the last few years. In 1979 the Fed turned from a policy of targeting interest rates to one of targeting monetary aggregates. As we have seen, during this episode of monetarism, the Fed's flexibility was considerably reduced. In 1982, when it became apparent that there were difficulties with its policies, the Fed took a step back from monetarism. However one chooses to characterize current policy, it clearly permits the Fed to place more weight on interest rates and generally allows policy makers to be more eclectic or judgmental in their actions. Some, of course, see this as a major defect of the current setup. Monetarists, in particular, have urged a return to monetary targeting, if not immediately, then at least in the near future. This, of course, presumes that the developments that created problems for past efforts at monetary targeting will diminish in importance. This in turn requires a bit of speculation about the future.

[19]Paul Volcker, "Statement before the Committee on Banking, Finance and Urban Affairs," House of Representatives, August 3, 1983, p. 7.

FED WATCHING AND THE M-1 JUNKIES

The pages of the financial press often feature articles that attempt to figure out what the Federal Reserve is up to. Loosely speaking, what these articles try to sort out is wheter the Fed is pursuing a "tighter" or "easier" monetary policy and what the implications of this are for the future course of the economy. As we have seen, since the Fed itself is sometimes unsure as to what its current policy really means, it should not be surprising that outside observers may sometimes be puzzled as to what is going on. This is even more understandable when we recall Maisel's observation that "the Fed has always resisted being too specific about its methods and goals, clothing its operations in a kind of mystique that left it more freedom for maneuver."

To ascertain what the Fed is up to, the interested observer can look at the following sorts of information: (1) quantitative data on the use of the basic policy instruments of the Fed, such as open-market operations, discount rate changes, and reserve requirement changes; (2) various intermediate variables, such as interest rates or money stock measures; (3) speeches and other official policy statements by the Fed members; and (4) the FOMC directive, which is released about 45 days after each FOMC meeting.

In recent years, keeping up with Fed has taken some strange forms. In early 1984, for instance, newspapers reported that Paul Volcker's Congressional testimony was subjected to a voice stress analysis. The idea, apparently, was to see how confident Volcker was in his pronouncements. But, by far the biggest efforts, seem to have gone into trying to anticipate what the money supply is likely to be when it is announced each Friday. Based on these estimates, participants in financial markets place "bets" on what is going to happen to interest rates.

Those who forecast money supply announcements sometimes go to extremes. One former Fed employee was caught trying to break into the Fed's computer (shades of *War Games!*). But the most common efforts of this sort are strictly legal, involving that mysterious type of economist known as "M-1 junkies". These analysts have spawned the Fed-watching industry. They earn their keep by accurately forecasting the money supply announcements and can be found every Friday at 4:10 pm in New York huddled around video terminals, waiting for the latest money supply data to flash across the screen.

For the Fed, this activity has been a serious source of aggravation. A few years ago one top Fed official noted "so much in the markets

has been riding on that stupid figure." He went on to state that the
market "is not even reacting to what the figure is, but to how the
figure compares to what these people thought it was going to be. It
drives me crazy. It think it's dangerous". The Fed has even toyed with
the idea of not releasing the data, but decided that this cure would
be worse than the disease. The so-called Dance of the Moneybees
thus goes on.

WHAT DOES THE FUTURE HOLD?

As this chapter has revealed, both in theory and in practice, the nature of
available financial instruments has important implications for the conduct
of monetary policy in general and the choice of an operating strategy in
particular. More specifically, we have seen that the effectiveness of monetary policy is influenced by both the interest sensitivity of the demand for
money and the degree of uncertainty about the demand for money. These
in turn are affected by innovation and deregulation in financial markets. At
least in the case of deregulation, there seems to be a reasonably predictable
built-in pattern to the process. Hence, it makes sense to ask what the world
facing the Fed might look like in the future.

INTEREST SENSITIVITY OF MONEY DEMAND

In our earlier discussion of the demand for money, the analysis was simplified by the assumption that money balances did not earn interest. The
interest sensitivity of money balances thus depended on the nature of the
substitute assets available to money holders. As the range of substitutes
expanded (e.g., by the growth of money market funds), holders of money
balances were more likely to move these balances around in response to
changes in market interest rates. In other words, these developments probably increased the interest sensitivity of money demand.

Recent and prospective developments, however, are likely to provide a
countervailing force, one that reduces the interest sensitivity of money demand. Deregulation is moving in the direction of permitting depository
institutions to pay interest on money balances. To some extent this has
already happened with NOW and Super NOW accounts, and the scheduled
additional deregulation of NOW accounts will take us further in this direction. Moreover, it is hardly farfetched to suppose that interest will one day
be paid on demand deposits, especially if the Fed has its way.[20]

[20]In 1983 the Board of Governors went on record as favoring the payment of interest on
demand deposits as well as the payment of interest on required reserves held at Federal
Reserve Banks by the depository institutions. See the Statement by J. Charles Partee in the
Federal Reserve Bulletin, November 1983, pp. 846–852.

If all money balances, except for currency, yield explicit interest, it is likely that the interest sensitivity of the demand for money will decline. The reason is that in such a world, as market interest rates change, so will interest rates paid on money balances. Consequently, any given change in market interest rates will have a smaller effect on the demand for money.[21] For example, an increase in market rates will be accompanied by an increase in rates paid on transactions balances, and there will therefore be a smaller incentive for holders of transactions accounts to purchase nonmonetary assets.

While there seems to be reasonably widespread agreement that we are likely to experience a future decline in the sensitivity of money demand to market interest rates, there is less agreement about what this means for the conduct of monetary policy. As we saw in Chapter 17, a lower sensitivity of the demand for money to interest rates is seemingly more in tune with the monetarist views of the world. On the other hand, the discussion earlier in this chapter suggests that if disturbances in the monetary sector are a source of instability in the economy, then a declining interest sensitivity of money demand will make income more sensitive to monetary shocks with a policy of targeting money. This suggests we need to address the issue of uncertainty directly.

UNCERTAINTY AND MONETARY POLICY

As noted above, it was widespread uncertainty in the demand for money that played havoc with monetary targeting in 1981 and 1982. While perhaps acknowledging these difficulties, monetarists argue that once deregulation has run its course, there will be more stability in the demand for money and hence targeting on money will be a good strategy for monetary policy. Nonmonetarists, needless to say, remain a bit skeptical. First of all, they argue, the transition period to a fully deregulated world may be fairly long. In the intervening period, there will be considerable uncertainty associated with the rapid changes that are taking place in the financial system. This uncertainty, nonmonetarists argue, dramatically diminishes the workability of monetary targeting.

Second, many nonmonetarists remain skeptical that the demand for money will be substantially less volatile, even after the transition is complete. They

[21]This can be seen algebraically as follows. A money demand function of the sort found in Chapter 13, but that allows for interest paid on transactions accounts, can be written as $M^D = d + e(r - r_m) + fY$, where r_m is rate of interest on money balances and r is the rate paid on alternative assets. When r_m is zero or fixed, then the sensitivity of M^D to r is measured by e. If we now suppose r_m varies with r as in $r_m = br$, where b is a number between zero and 1, we can rewrite money demand as $M^D = d + e(r - br) + fY = d + e(1 - b)r + fY$. In other words, the sensitivity of M^D to r has been reduced to $e(1 - b)$. This quantity will be very much smaller than e if b is close to 1, which corresponds to the case in which interest rates paid on money closely follow other market rates of interest.

point to the fact that there will be a growing array of liquid alternatives to money balances which can increase the potential movement of funds in and out of money. Moreover, this movement is likely to be facilitated by lower transactions costs such as those stemming from the greater use of electronic funds transfer systems. Finally, some point to that fact that money holdings will increasingly be decided on broader portfolio considerations, in contrast to the narrower transactions view, and that portfolio considerations can add to the volatility of money demand.[22]

What this all seems to suggest is that there is considerable uncertainty about the degrees of uncertainty we are likely to find ourselves facing in the future! Perhaps the only certain thing is that even after the pace of deregulation has slowed down, debates about the conduct of monetary policy are likely to be as extensive as those we have had in the past.

SUMMARY

1 One key issue in the conduct of monetary policy is the appropriate way to define money. The importance of this is self-evident for a policy that targets the money supply, but because any sensible monetary policy requires an empirical understanding of the demand for money, the issue is of general concern. Unfortunately, as the experience of the last decade suggests, financial innovation, deregulation, and technological change have created severe difficulties in producing a single "best" definition of money. Moreover, these potential difficulties are likely to persist for some time to come.

2 Policymakers face uncertainty over the strength of aggregate demand. In terms of the *IS–LM* framework, uncertainty can show up in surprise movements of either the *IS* or *LM* curves. When the *IS* curve is more unpredictable, a policy of controlling the money stock is superior to one of controlling the level of interest rates. The reverse is true when the *LM* curve is more unpredictable. The empirical evidence of the last decade has provided ample illustration of the unpredictability of the *LM* curve, largely stemming from shifts in the demand for money.

3 The strategy for implementing monetary policy is contained in a directive issued by the FOMC some ten times each year. The nature of the directive and the operating guides it provides for policy have varied dramatically over the last three decades. At different times, bank reserve measures, interest rates, and monetary aggregates have all served as operating guides. Monetarist recommendations favoring tar-

[22]For a discussion of these issues, see T. D. Simpson, "Changes in the Financial System: Implications for Monetary Policy," *Brookings Papers on Economic Activity*, No. 1, 1984, pp. 249–272, and John Wenninger, "Financial Innovation—A Complex Problem Even in a Simple Framework," *Quarterly Review*, Federal Reserve Bank of New York, Summer 1984, pp. 1–8.

geting the money supply were introduced in late 1979. Pursuit of these policies was clearly hampered by instabilities in money demand, which ultimately lend to their abandonment in 1982. The Fed is now pursuing a rather eclectic sort of monetary policy, but despite the experience of 1979–1982, monetarism is still a force to be reckoned with in the design of policy.

SELECTED READINGS

Board of Governors of the Federal Reserve System. "A Proposal for Redefining the Monetary Aggregates." *Federal Reserve Bulletin*, January 1979, pp. 13–42.

———. "The Redefined Monetary Aggregates." *Federal Reserve Bulletin*, February 1980, pp. 97–114.

Goldfeld, S. M. "The Case of the Missing Money." *Brookings Paper on Economic Activity*, 1976, no. 3, pp. 683–739.

Maisel, S, *Managing the Dollar*. New York: Norton, 1973.

Mayer, T. *Monetary Policy in the United States*. New York: Random House, 1968.

Porter, R. D., T. D. Simpson, and E. Mauskopf. "Financial Innovation and the Monetary Aggregates." *Brookings Papers on Economic Activity*, 1979, no. 1, pp. 213–229.

Simpson, T. D. "Changes in the Financial System: Implications for Monetary Policy." *Brookings Papers on Economic Activity*, 1984, no. 1, pp. 249–265.

Wallich, H. C. "The Role of Operating Guides in U.S. Monetary Policy: A Historical Review." *Federal Reserve Bulletin*, September 1979, pp. 679–691.

———. "Recent Techniques of Monetary Policy." *Economic Review*, Federal Reserve Bank of Kansas City, May 1984, pp. 21–30.

Wenninger, J. "Financial Innovation—A Complex Problem Even in a Simple Framework." *FRBNY Quarterly Review*, Summer 1984, pp. 1–8.

19

U.S. MONETARY POLICIES, 1941–1965

At selected points throughout this book, we have examined various historical episodes in the conduct of monetary policy. In this chapter and the subsequent one we undertake a more systematic discussion of American monetary policy. The present chapter considers the 25-year period starting with the entry of the United States into World War II; the next chapter analyzes the post-1965 conduct of monetary policy.

As noted earlier, the formulation and execution of monetary policy involve at least three elements:

1 Selection of objectives—the choice of goals or purposes to be promoted
2 Development and use of monetary institutions and instruments to promote the chosen objectives
3 The use (at least implicitly) of some theory of the economic effects of various possible monetary actions

We are interested in the evolution of all these elements in monetary policies. What have been the objectives or goals of our policies? How have these changed through time, and why? How have changing goals affected actions? How has the Federal Reserve developed its control instruments, and how has it used them? In what ways or for what reasons has it changed its use of instruments? What types of monetary theory seem to be the bases for its policies, and how have these changed through time?

Although our primary focus will be on monetary policy, in our discussion we also touch on fiscal policy and on policies related to the nature of the international payments mechanism. Like developments in the private sector, each of these influences the environment faced by monetary authorities.

The purpose of this and of the subsequent chapter is not only to tell the story of past episodes; it is also (1) to give us an opportunity to analyze policy formation and execution in specific situations, (2) to provide a basis for understanding the present status of monetary policy, and (3) to emphasize that monetary policy is always—and, at times, abruptly—in the process of change.

WORLD WAR II AND ITS AFTERMATH

We begin our analysis with the entrance of the United States into World War II in December 1941, when the Federal Reserve again became, as it has been during World War I, a servant of the government's fiscal policy. All conflicting objectives were pushed aside; its overriding objective became that of assuring that the nation's war effort would not suffer from any lack of money. Moreover, it was to assure that the huge war effort would be financed without any rise in interest rates above the low levels prevailing in early 1942.

WARTIME FISCAL POLICIES

The federal government's fiscal policy during this period followed the usual pattern for all-out war, but on a huge scale. Its expenditures rose tremendously. At the peak of the war effort federal expenditures were more than 10 times their level before the beginning of the defense program and were themselves greater than total GNP at any time during the 1930s. More than 40 percent of the nation's output was being purchased for government purposes. Between mid-1940, when the accelerated defense program began, and mid-1946, when the wartime deficits ended, the federal government spent more than twice as much as it had spent during the preceding 150 years, nearly 100 times as much as it spent during the Civil War, and 10 times as much as it spent during World War I.

Tax collections were increased greatly, but not nearly as much as expenditures. The result was, of course, huge deficits totaling $187 billion for the years 1941 to 1946 (see Table 19–1).

The Treasury therefore faced the necessity of borrowing huge amounts to cover these deficits. As it had during World War I, the Treasury tried to borrow as much as it could in ways that would not involve an increase in the money supply. It used all the devices developed during World War I as

TABLE 19–1 Federal Borrowings, Their Use, and Their Sources, 1941–1946 (In millions of dollars)

Fiscal year ending June 30	Federal cash operating deficit	Net cash borrowing	NET INCREASE IN AMOUNT OF FEDERAL INTEREST-BEARING DEBT HELD		
			By nonbank investors	By commercial banks	By Federal Reserve banks
1941	$ 4,689	$ 5,431	$ 2,143	$ 3,600	− $ 282
1942	19,294	19,652	12,869	6,300	461
1943	53,734	60,250	28,498	26,200	4,557
1944	46,095	56,757	32,913	16,200	7,699
1945	44,935	49,464	27,173	15,800	6,891
1946	17,899	7,439	5,431	200	1,991
Total increase for period	$186,646	$119,003	$109,027	$68,300	$21,317

SOURCE: L. V. Chandler, *Inflation in the United States, 1940–1948.* New York: Harper & Row, 1951, p. 72.

well as new ones to sell securities to nonbank buyers: great bond-selling campaigns, pleas by movie stars and national heroes; 100 percent clubs; payroll-deduction plans; and so on. It did succeed in getting nonbank investors to increase their holdings of Treasury obligations of $109 billion. But this was not enough; the commercial banks increased their holdings by $68.3 billion, and Federal Reserve banks by $21.3 billion.

WARTIME MONETARY POLICY

Federal Reserve assistance to Treasury financing during World War II differed in at least two important respects from that in World War I. In the earlier war, the Federal Reserve itself bought very few Treasury obligations; it gave its assistance primarily by lending to banks. In World War II, it lent very little to banks; it created additional money primarily by purchasing Treasury obligations, most of them in the open market rather than directly from the Treasury. Interest rate policies also differed markedly in the two wars. Interest rates were allowed to rise during World War I. In general, each new bond issue carried interest rates somewhat above those on earlier issues. During World War II, interest rates were not allowed to rise at all.

In March 1942 the Federal Open Market Committee agreed with the Treasury that, in general, the level of interest rates and yields on government securities should not be allowed to rise during the war, and it pledged the full cooperation of the system to this end. This promise was kept.

Interest rates in general were at that time low by historical standards, and short-term rates were abnormally low relative to longer-term rates. This was partly because of the low demand for investable funds during the Depression, partly because of the huge volume of excess reserves in the banking system. At the end of 1941 the latter were still above $3 billion. The pattern of yields stabilized by the Federal Reserve during the war period reflected these conditions. On 90-day maturities, this yield was ⅜ percent; on 9- to 12-month maturities, it was ⅞ percent, on 5-year maturities, it was 1½ percent; on 10-year maturities, it was 2 percent; and on the longest marketable Treasury issues, it was 2½ percent. The shape of this yield curve should be noted carefully, because it was to have important consequences.

The Federal Reserve's technique for preventing these various yields from rising—for preventing the prices of the securities from falling—was simple: It merely stood ready to buy without limitation all of these securities offered to it at the selected levels of prices and yields. In short, it stood ready to monetize, with high-powered reserve money, all the government securities offered to it by the banks and all other types of holders.

This passive open-market policy had several important consequences, not only during the war, but also in the postwar period.

1 The Federal Reserve thereby abandoned control over its volume of government holdings, the volume of bank reserves, and the money supply. To prevent yields from rising, it had to buy all securities offered to it, regardless of the identity of the seller and regardless of the purpose for which the newly created money would be used. Thus, banks and nonbank investors alike could get new money from the Federal Reserve at will, the only cost being the yield sacrificed on the securities sold. During the six years following 1939, the money supply rose from $36.2 billion to $102.4 billion, for an increase of 183 percent.

2 The cost of getting such funds was the low yield on short-term government securities, because banks and all other types of financial institutions held billions of these.

3 By holding down interest rates on government securities, the Federal Reserve also held down interest rates on loans to private borrowers and assured a highly liberal supply of credit for private uses. The reason was that all holders of government securities retained complete freedom to sell these holdings and to shift to other assets. Thus, not only banks but all other lenders as well could get funds from the Federal Reserve to satisfy private demands, and they would do so in great volume if yields on private obligations tended to rise.

While following a passive general monetary policy, the authorities tried to prevent or limit nonessential private borrowing by using selective credit controls. For example, in the autumn of 1941 the Federal Reserve imposed for the first time a selective control over consumer credit, fixing maximum loan values and maximum periods of repayment. Banks were admonished to refuse loans for nonessential purposes. Authorities were established to pass upon the need for new security issues. But these and other selective credit controls were far less effective in containing inflationary pressures, and even in limiting the expansion of credit for private purposes, than were the great variety of direct controls imposed on the economy early in the war.

THE ROLE OF DIRECT CONTROLS

It soon became evident that the government's fiscal policy would create strong inflationary pressure as output approached capacity levels. Indeed, with the unemployment rate dropping from its depression level of 15 percent in 1940 to 1.2 percent in 1944, and in the face of passive monetary policies, these pressures became a reality. To limit price inflation and to prevent rising private demands from diverting productive resources from the war effort, a whole series of direct controls was established.

These controls included price ceilings on virtually every type of output, ceilings on wages, and ceilings on rents. It was illegal for anyone to charge or to pay more than these prices. Also included were many types of controls over the production, distribution, and use of output. In general, both consumers and businesses were forced to spend less than they wanted and therefore forced to save far more than they would have in the absence of direct controls. The private sector used these huge savings in two principal ways: to retire debt and to acquire liquid assets.

The repression of private spending and the suppression of inflation were not, of course, complete. Consumer spending did rise, as did the wholesale and cost of living price indexes. The latter did not reflect actual price increases that occurred through quality deterioration and black markets. Yet the repression was remarkably successful in view of the strength of the inflationary pressures. By the end of 1945 consumer prices were 31 percent, and wholesale prices 39 percent, above their levels of six years earlier. Repressed inflationary pressures were very strong. The private sectors had accumulated a huge volume of liquid assets. Their money balances were now 183 percent above their level in 1939, and their total holdings of liquid assets were up 230 percent. Moreover, both business firms and households had accumulated unsatisfied wants in large volume. Many business firms that had spent little or nothing for investment purposes during the Depression, and had been prevented for spending during the war, now wanted to replace, expand, or modernize plants and equipment. Large numbers of families, feeling that they had lived like Spartans during the war, now wanted to go on a spending spree and buy the cars and other things that had not been available during the war. The inflationary potential in increased private spending was large indeed.

But there was another side to the story, a side that led many to forecast deep depression and widespread unemployment rather than inflation for the postwar period. Many feared that the decrease of government spending following the cessation of hostilities would bring disaster. The sharp drop of federal expenditures from their level of almost $100 billion a year would directly decrease the demand for output, set off a downward multiplier effect on consumption, and leave industry with so much excess capacity that virtually no investment expenditures would be justified. Such gloomy forecasts were one reason for the early dismantling of direct controls. They were also a force for a continued easy money policy. When the predicted depression did not develop immediately after the war, many people continued to insist that it was "just around the corner."

As the war drew to a close, the government quickly began to relax and to remove direct controls. Prices rose immediately. During 1946 alone, wholesale prices rose more than they had during the entire 1939 to 1945 period, and the cost of living advanced two-thirds as much as it had during the preceding six years. By August 1948, when prices reached their first postwar peak, wholesale prices had risen 120 percent, and the cost of living 76 percent, since 1939. Two-thirds of the total rise of wholesale prices and three-fifths of the increase in the cost of living had occurred since the end of the war.

POSTWAR PEGGING OF INTEREST RATES, 1946–1951

Although direct controls over the economy were removed, Federal Reserve policies remained chained to their wartime objectives and methods of implementation. The system still used its powers to peg the prices and yields on Treasury obligations, and the pegged pattern of yields for some time was the same as it had been through the war. The range was from ⅜ percent on 90-day maturities to a ceiling of 2½ percent on 25-year Treasury bonds. In short, during a period of full employment and inflation the Federal Reserve was pegging a general level and pattern of interest rates that had evolved during the nation's worst depression. Not until March 1951, more than five years after the end of the war, did the Federal Reserve abandon this pegging pattern.

This passive open-market policy of supplying additional Federal Reserve funds to anyone presenting securities at their pegged prices was potentially far more dangerous in the postwar period than it had been during the war. By limiting spending, the wartime system of direct controls had effectively limited private demands for credit. But as these limitations were removed, private buyers again became free to bid against each other for larger quantities, to pay higher prices, and to demand larger loans for the purpose. Moreover, all types of financial institutions were in a position to meet almost any foreseeable increase in private demands for credit, and to do so at low interest rates as long as the Federal Reserve pegged yields on government securities, because they held huge amounts of these obligations.

Households and nonfinancial business firms also had large holdings, which they could sell to get money to lend to others or to finance their own spending.

REASONS FOR THE PEGGING POLICY

Why did the Federal Reserve continue, despite inflation, to maintain easy money conditions through its pegging policy? In part, it was because of the widespread fear of unemployment. The long depression of the 1930s had left an indelible impression, almost a depression psychosis. Almost every year brought new forecasts of a coming decline. Moreover, the nation's new determination to promote the achievement and maintenance of "maximum employment, production, and purchasing power" was embodied in the Employment Act of 1946. Treasury and Federal Reserve officials were reluctant to take any action that might jeopardize the maintenance of prosperity.

Concern for Treasury financing and for the prices of outstanding Treasury obligations was a major reason for continuing the policy. The secretary of the Treasury was a strong and persistent advocate of pegging and a stubborn opponent of increases in interest rates. Several of the relevant arguments are worth noting.

1 Increased rates on the federal debt would add greatly to the already large interest burden.
2 Fluctuating prices and yields on governments would greatly complicate the Treasury's refunding operations, a serious matter with about 20 percent of the debt maturing within a year.
3 An increase of yields on government securities would lower the prices of securities outstanding and hence would impose capital depreciation on financial institutions and other holders. Officials worried that this might lead to panicky selling and loss of confidence in financial institutions.
4 Disturbances in the prices and yields of government securities would be transmitted to private securities and jeopardize prosperity. It was argued that not only low interest rates but also stability of interest rates and bond prices promoted prosperity.

OPEN-MARKET POLICY

For the first two years after the war, the Federal Open Market Committee continued to prevent yields on government securities from rising above the pattern selected in early 1942. The first break from the wartime pattern came in July 1947, when the Federal Reserve persuaded the Treasury to allow it to eliminate the ⅜ percent buying rate on Treasury bills. The next break came the following month, when the Treasury agreed to the elimination of the ⅞ percent rate on 9- to 12-month certificates of indebtedness.

But this did not mean that the Federal Reserve had ceased to limit increases on the yields on these shorter-term obligations. It had merely shifted its policy to one of maintaining the rates fixed by the Treasury on new issues.

Indeed, in the last analysis, it was the secretary of the Treasury who set the yields on new issues, and therefore determined the rates to be maintained by the Federal Reserve. And the secretary consented to rate increases only reluctantly, belatedly, and to a limited extent. By the end of 1948, when the first postwar inflation had reached its peak, the yield on Treasury bills had been allowed to rise only from $3/8$ percent to 1.13 percent, and that on 9- to 12-month certificates from $7/8$ percent to $1\frac{1}{4}$ percent. The results of these increases could hardly be considered high interest rates for a period of inflation. Furthermore, the continued willingness of the Federal Reserve to buy government securities in unlimited amounts robbed its other instruments of all, or almost all, of their effectiveness for restrictive purposes. In effect, this policy provided the banking system and others with a means of escape from other Federal Reserve attempts to restrict them.

After the first postwar peak of prices was reached in August 1948, there followed more than a year of mild deflation. By the end of 1949, the cost of living had fallen 5 percent and wholesale prices were down 11 percent. In fact, 1949 was a year of mild recession, with small declines in both production and employment. The Federal Reserve halted its vain attempts to restrict credit and initiated an easier monetary policy, partly by lowering reserve requirements. In addition, the Treasury lowered somewhat the yields on its new issues, and the Federal Reserve stood ready to prevent market rates from rising above these lowered levels.

Under these conditions of mild deflation, the controversy between the Federal Reserve and the Treasury died down. In such a situation there is no necessary conflict between the objective of promoting general economic stabilization, including stability of price levels, and the objectives of holding down interest costs on the national debt, facilitating Treasury financing operations, and preventing decreases in the prices of outstanding Treasury bonds.

By early 1950 the decline in business activity and prices had stopped and recovery was well under way. As to the future course of business activity and price levels, there was wide disagreement among economic forecasters. The outbreak of fighting in Korea in June 1950 ended this uncertainty and ushered in a new upsurge of inflation.

THE KOREAN WAR

The outbreak of fighting in Korea, and this country's decision to intervene, inspired a surge of buying by consumers and business firms. Remembering the scarcities and price increases of World War II, consumers rushed into the markets to get ahead of the hoarders. Business firms also hastened to replenish their inventories and to make net additions to them. Toward the end of 1950, the rise of government expenditures for military purposes also added its inflationary effects to the rise in private spending. Between May 1950 and March 1951, the cost of living rose 8 percent and wholesale prices 19 percent.

With the resurgence of inflation, the controversy between the Federal Reserve and the Treasury flared anew. The Federal Reserve wanted to restrict credit to curb the rise of prices, while the Treasury insisted that it continue to hold interest rates at an inflexibly low level. This controversy, which had seethed behind the scenes, came out into the open in August 1950, when the Federal Reserve publicly defied the Treasury. On the same day and at almost the same hour the two issued conflicting public announcements.

The Federal Open Market Committee announced the system's determination to fight the current inflation and to use all its powers to this end. At the same time, the Treasury announced a new $13 billion issue of short-term securities with yields no higher than those currently prevailing in the market. Despite this Treasury challenge, the Federal Reserve proceeded to tighten credit. To prevent the Treasury's financing from failing, the system purchased most of the new issue at the yields fixed by the Treasury. Then it sold some of its other holdings in the market on terms that raised the market yields of short-term obligations. It also raised its discount rates from 1½ to 1¾ percent. This controversy related only to short-term issues; the Federal Reserve continued to prevent the prices of long-term government bonds from falling below par.

However, the controversy spread to the prices and yields on long-term Treasury bonds. A major reason for the Federal Reserve's rebellion was its fear that its other attempts to contain inflation would be ineffective as long as it had to peg the prices of these securities. In early 1951 the conflict between the Federal Reserve and the Treasury became dramatic. In January, the secretary of the Treasury publicly announced that during the defense period all the government's issues of marketable securities (for new money as well as for refunding purposes) would bear interest rates no higher than 2½ percent. He also implied, without stating it specifically, that the Federal Reserve had agreed to this policy. Reserve officials denied that this was true. The president and the Council of Economic Advisers then entered the dispute to support the Treasury position. After a White House conference with Federal Reserve officials, the president publicly announced that the Federal Reserve had, in effect, agreed to the Treasury's announced policy. This the Federal Reserve publicly denied. Now that the controversy was common knowledge and involved the president himself, it became a hotly debated issue in Congress, in the newspapers, and in financial circles. The Board of Governors finally informed the Treasury that, as of February 19, it was no longer willing to maintain the existing situation in the government securities market. After further negotiations the Treasury and the Federal Reserve jointly announced, on March 4, 1951, their now-famous accord: "The Treasury and the Federal Reserve System have reached full accord with respect to debt-management and monetary policies to be pursued in furthering their common purpose to assure the successful financing of the Government's requirements and, at the same time, to minimize monetization of the public debt."

The Treasury–Federal Reserve accord of March 4, 1951, stands as a landmark in American monetary history because it marked the end of inflexible pegging of the prices of Treasury obligations. Nine years after it had first adopted the policy (in March 1942), the Federal Reserve had finally regained at least some freedom to refrain from purchasing all securities offered to it, to limit its creation of bank reserves, and to restrict credit when necessary to prevent inflation. To the extent that it was freed from the task of supporting Treasury operations, it could now direct them more toward promoting economic stability.

MONETARY POLICY AFTER THE ACCORD, 1951–1959

The accord thus gave the Federal Reserve the latitude to carry out the mandate set forth five years earlier in the Employment Act of 1946. That act, as we have seen, provided for government responsibility in promoting "maximum employment, production, and purchasing power." The Federal Reserve was clearly expected to participate in interpreting and implementing these objectives. In moving from the era of pegging to one of carrying out this charge, Reserve officials faced the task of developing new patterns of policy implementation. Their problem was not a lack of power; it was rather a problem of deciding how and for what purposes to use their power.

SOME EARLY PRINCIPLES

During the period of pegging before March 1951, the Federal Reserve entered the government securities market for two principal purposes: (1) to stabilize the prices of securities that were already outstanding and (2) to assist the Treasury in selling new issues. For the latter purpose the Federal Reserve frequently purchased a part of a new issue that others were not willing to buy at the yield rates fixed by the Treasury, and it sometimes bought outstanding issues of comparable maturities to "make room in the market" for the new Treasury issue.

The immediate purpose of the Federal Reserve at the time of the accord was not to withdraw completely from the government securities market and leave both the prices of outstanding Treasury obligations and current Treasury-financing operations completely on their own. To withdraw support completely and abruptly after such a long period of pegging would have been undesirable. Erratic, and perhaps even panicky, declines in the prices of outstanding securities not only would injure holders and jeopardize the future marketability of new long-term issues, but might also disturb the markets for private obligations and upset economic stability. Nor could the Federal Reserve immediately withdraw all support of Treasury financing operations. To permit a new issue to fail and perhaps force the Treasury to default on a part of the national debt was unthinkable.

The Federal Reserve's immediate purpose, therefore, was merely to secure somewhat greater flexibility—to permit the prices and yields of outstanding government securities to vary more widely and to induce the Treasury to put more realistic yields on its new issues and to rely less heavily on Federal Reserve support. However, its longer-run purpose was to work toward a situation in which its open-market policies would be shaped almost exclusively by economic stabilization objectives, and its purchases and sales would again be directed exclusively toward regulating the reserve position of the banking system rather than toward directly influencing the prices of Treasury obligations, new or old.

With respect to outstanding government securities, Federal Reserve policy for some time immediately following the abandonment of pegging was to "maintain an orderly market." Federal Reserve officials insisted that this did not mean that they would limit the extent to which the prices of these securities would be permitted to decline if the price decline was consistent with the attainment of other Federal Reserve objectives. It meant only that they would assist in keeping these adjustments orderly rather than erratic or disorderly. The system then shifted to a policy of preventing a disorderly market. This was not merely an exercise in semantics; it indicated a greater Federal Reserve tolerance of fluctuations in the prices of government securities, reduced readiness to intervene to influence these prices directly, and greater reliance on private purchasers and sellers to maintain orderly conditions.

By the spring of 1953 the Federal Reserve had arrived at a new rule that would normally or ordinarily guide its open-market operations: It would not buy or sell longer-term Treasury obligations (those with maturities of more than 1 year), but would confine its operations to short maturities, preferably Treasury bills. This has come to be known popularly as the *bills-only doctrine.* The Federal Reserve also decided that thereafter it would not ordinarily engage in *swap operations*—that is, buying some maturities to raise their prices or to limit their price declines, and selling others.

Federal Reserve officials had several closely related reasons for wanting to stay out of the market for long-term obligations and for confining their operations to bills and other short maturities where the direct effects of their purchases and sales on the prices of the securities would be much smaller.

1 They undoubtedly feared that if they continued to operate in the long-term market, they might again be shackled by an inflexible pegging policy.

2 They wished to avoid possible charges that their sales of long-term securities, or even their refusal to buy them, had unfairly imposed losses on holders.

3 The reason stressed most by Federal Reserve officials was their desire to create conditions in which private buyers and sellers would themselves develop an orderly and self-reliant market. They argued that as long as private operators in this market expected Federal Reserve intervention, they would not perform the ordinary functions of taking speculative positions, buying when they thought prices were too low, selling short when they thought prices were too high, and arbitraging among the various issues to establish reasonable yield relationships. It was hoped that after the Federal Reserve's withdrawal from the long-term market, private operators would themselves develop a broad, deep, and resilient market.

The ability of the Federal Reserve to withdraw its support from current Treasury financing operations depended to a great extent on the attitudes and policies of the Treasury. If the latter persisted in fixing low rates on its issues, the Federal Reserve would have to support them or risk being blamed for the failure of Treasury financing. In fact, however, the Treasury gradually adjusted its financing policies to the current monetary policies of the Federal Reserve and conscientiously tried to make the yields and other terms on its new issues such that they could be sold without Federal Reserve support. The Treasury's cooperation was sufficient to enable the Federal Reserve to adopt two more rules by the spring of 1953: Ordinarily it would not buy any part of a new issue at the time of sale, and it would not at that time buy any outstanding issue of comparable maturity.[1]

Thus, by the spring of 1953 the Federal Reserve had moved far from its policies during the period before March 1951 and had developed four rules that would ordinarily or normally be followed:

1 It would not deal in securities with maturities in excess of a year and would confine its open-market operations to short maturities, preferably bills.

2 It would not engage in swap operations.

3 It would not buy any new Treasury issue at the time of offering.

4 At the time of a new Treasury issue, it would not buy any outstanding securities of comparable maturity.

The Federal Reserve departed from these normal rules only twice during the first five years after their adoption. The first deviation occurred in late 1955, when the system was following a restrictive policy and the Treasury offered a large new issue with a maturity in excess of a year. The Treasury believed the issue had been made sufficiently attractive to enable all of it

---

[1]This was not interpreted as preventing the Federal Reserve from taking part of a new issue in exchange for its holdings of a maturing issue.

to be sold to private purchasers, but it soon became apparent that some of the issue would remain unsold. The Federal Reserve thereupon violated three of its rules all at once: It bought some of the new, longer-term issue and then sold some of its holdings of other maturities to mop up the reserves created by its purchases. The second departure occurred in July 1958 after the dispatch of American troops to Lebanon following the revolution in Iraq. The prices of long-term government securities, including prices on a recent issue, declined. Moreover, the Treasury had just announced a new issue, which was not attracting purchasers in sufficient volume. The Federal Reserve intervened to purchase some of the outstanding longer-term issue and some of the new issue. To mop up the reserves created by these purchases, it sold other maturities out of its portfolio.

These exceptions highlight two points. The fact that there were only two exceptions to the normal rules in over five years indicates how far the Federal Reserve had moved away from the policies it had followed before March 1951. It also indicates how far the Treasury, in its debt management policies, was willing to depart from its old objective of borrowing at continuously low interest rates and to move toward adjusting its policies to the economic stabilization policies of the Federal Reserve. But these exceptions also highlight the fact that Federal Reserve policies cannot completely ignore federal debt management.

SOME POLICY DETAILS

The rise in prices initiated by the Korean conflict ended in March 1951 with the cost of living up 8 percent and wholesale prices up 19 percent from their levels prior to the outbreak. There followed a period of more than four years of relative price stability. In mid-1955 the consumer price index was only 3 percent above its level in March 1951. The wholesale price index actually declined 6 percent. The period up to early 1953 was one of high production and employment. GNP rose substantially, and unemployment was at a minimum. Out of a total labor force of more than 66 million, unemployment averaged only 1.9 million in 1951 and 1.7 million in 1952. In the spring of 1953 it fell to the extraordinarily low level of 1.3 million.

Under these conditions the Federal Reserve allowed interest rates to rise somewhat during the remainder of 1951 and in 1952. It took no action to reduce the volume of bank reserves, but as the demand for bank credit rose it did not supply additional reserves by purchasing government securities. By early 1953 Federal Reserve officials began to fear a resumption of inflation. Prices had not begun to rise, but the economy was already operating at close to capacity levels, unemployment was at a minimum, demand was still rising, and Federal Reserve officials thought they detected a speculative buildup of inventories. They therefore intensified their restrictive policy and interest rates rose to their highest levels in 20 years. Credit stringency became severe as expectations of still tighter money and even higher interest rates led lenders to withhold funds and borrowers to rush in to anticipate their future needs. In May 1953 the Federal Reserve began to ease the situation. It now became evident that the immediate danger was not inflation, but recession.

EASY MONEY, 1953–1954

The recession of 1953–1954 was short and relatively mild. The decline in GNP was accounted for by a shift from inventory accumulation in early 1953 to inventory decumulation, and by a decrease in defense spending. Other demands for output held up very well, as consumption expenditures actually rose, due at least in part to a tax reduction at the beginning of 1954. The number of unemployed rose above its extraordinarily low level of 1.3 million in the spring of 1953, but it did not quite reach 3.5 million, or 5 percent of the labor force.

The Federal Reserve used all its major instruments to ease credit and to combat the recession. Early in May 1953, it began expansionary open-market operations, and in July it reduced bank reserve requirements. By mid-1954 credit conditions had substantially eased as the yield on Treasury bills fell below ¾ percent.

This easy money policy almost certainly helped shorten the recession, reduce its severity, and hasten recovery. Some Federal Reserve officials later wondered whether they had not eased credit too much, continued the easy money policy too long, and provided both the public and the banking system with too much liquidity. This greatly enhanced liquidity of both the public and the banks contributed to the subsequent rise in spending and prices. But it does not necessarily follow that the policies of 1953 and 1954 were too easy and too prolonged. Perhaps the error was in not moving more aggressively as business recovery approached an inflationary stage.

TIGHT MONEY, 1955–1957

The recession reached its trough in the second quarter of 1954 and was followed first by recovery and then by a boom that culminated in the third quarter of 1957. During this three-year period GNP at current prices rose 24 percent. A major contributor to this was an investment boom that, during this period, produced an increase in gross private domestic investment of more than 40 percent. Unemployment, fell to less than 4 percent of the labor force.

Prices remained stable until mid-1955 and then began to rise, slowly at first and then more rapidly. The Federal Reserve began to reduce the degree of credit ease as business activity started upward in the latter part of 1954, and then permitted tighter credit conditions to develop during the period from early 1955 to November 1957. The money supply was held approximately constant, despite a substantial increase in the transactions demand for money. Consequently, market rates of interest rose to their highest levels in 25 years, and the rise of GNP was financed almost entirely by an increase in the velocity of money.

We have already seen that these increases in interest rates did not prevent investment expenditures from rising more than 40 percent, that Federal Reserve policies did not prevent total expenditures for output from rising 24 percent. This is hardly surprising. One should not necessarily expect a rise in interest rates to prevent a rise in investment expenditures when the rise of rates is itself produced by an upward shift of the investment demand schedule. The investment function undoubtedly shifted sharply upward during this period, so that spenders for investment purposes were willing to spend much more at each level of interest rates or to spend the same amounts at much higher levels of interest rates. An actual rise in investment expenditures could have been prevented only by a sharp decrease in the supply of investable funds at each interest rate, and this did not occur.

EASY MONEY, NOVEMBER 1957–JULY 1958

The boom reached its peak in the third quarter of 1957 and gave way to recession. By the first quarter of 1958, GNP had fallen nearly 3 percent and the unemployment rate, which had been under 4 percent, rose to 7 percent. Changes in business inventory policies were a major contributor to the recession. But as so often happens, the shift in business inventory policy was induced at least in part by more basic changes in the economy. For one thing, a decline in business expenditures for plant and equipment began. For another, largely for the purpose of holding its expenditures within the total budgeted for the fiscal year and to avoid raising the debt limit, the federal government sharply reduced its new orders for military equipment. These two factors contributed to the weakness in the economy.

It was under these conditions that the Federal Reserve relaxed credit restriction and moved toward easy money. The first decisive move came in mid-November, when discount rates were reduced. The Federal Reserve also purchased government securities to increase bank reserves and then lowered member bank reserve requirements against demand deposits. These liberalizing actions were accompanied by a sharp decline of short-term interest rates. The yield on Treasury bills, which had averaged about 3.6 percent in October, had fallen well below 1 percent by May. Long-term rates proved less responsive. After dropping sharply immediately after the first reduction of discount rates in mid-November, they began to drift downward much more slowly, and by May had begun to rise. One reason for this was the extraordinarily large volume of new long-term bonds issued by both the private and government sectors. Indeed, the federal government floated several long-term issues, primarily to retire short-term debt. This became a highly controversial matter, for many believe that in periods of recession the Treasury should borrow only on short-term obligations and should refrain from issuing long-term securities that would compete with private long-term issues and tend to decrease the availability and increase the cost of long-term credit for private investment. These heavy borrowings in the long-term market while short-term loans were being repaid help to explain the disparity in the behavior of short-term and long-term interest rates. Some observers insisted that this was an occasion when the Federal Reserve should have abandoned the bills-only doctrine and bought long-term securities. A majority of Federal Reserve officials rejected this view.

TIGHT MONEY AGAIN, 1958–1959

The recession that started in the third quarter of 1957 proved to be shorter than many economists had expected, and it reached its low point in April 1958. The economy then began a recovery that continued until the first quarter of 1960. However, this proved to be the weakest recovery in the postwar period as output failed to rise as fast as the productive capacity of the economy. Consequently, this "prosperity" period was characterized by a level of unemployment comparable to the levels that prevailed during the recessions of 1949 and 1954. There were widespread complaints about the slow rate of economic growth in the United States relative to growth rates abroad. The weakness of the recovery was reflected in the stability of prices. The wholesale price index did not rise, and the consumer price index rose only 1.5 percent from early 1958 to the end of 1959. Nevertheless, fears of inflation were widespread. The almost uninterrupted rise of prices for nearly 20 years and the failure of prices to decline in the 1957–1958 recession convinced many that we were in danger of adopting inflation as a way of life.

It was largely because of fear of inflation that the Federal Reserve abandoned its easy money policy in May 1958 and initiated a restrictive policy that was to permit interest rates to rise to their highest levels in 30 years. By December 1959, when rates reached their peak, yields on 3-month Treasury bills were around 4½ percent; those on 9- to 12-month Treasury issues, about 5 percent; and those on long-term federal issues, about 4½ percent. In broad outline, Federal Reserve policy during this period was quite similar to that during the 1955–1957 boom. The Federal Reserve did not attempt to reduce the money supply; it only followed a policy of "leaning against the wind," of preventing the money supply from increasing in response to the rising demand for money balances.

After the peak of interest rates was reached around the end of 1959, the Federal Reserve began a cautious relaxation, largely because of the high level of unemployment. In the summer of 1960, as a new recession loomed, the Federal Reserve began to move more positively toward an easy money policy. Then it was faced by an unhappy fact: Even the United States could have its freedom of action limited by considerations related to balance of payments and international reserve positions.

DEVELOPMENTS IN THE INTERNATIONAL MONETARY SITUATION

We will later explore the international aspects of economic policy in considerable detail, but it is impossible to understand certain features of monetary policy in the 1960s without some brief attention to the international economic scene.

SOME GENERAL PRINCIPLES

There are three major types of economic transactions between countries: trade in goods and services, commonly referred to as exports and imports; international gifts and transfer payments; and international capital transactions whereby residents of one country purchase financial claims issued by residents of a second country. The statistical record of all transactions between a nation and the rest of the world is that nation's *balance of payments*. Speaking very loosely, a country will experience difficulties with its balance of payments whenever its expenditures exceed its receipts. Consider for a moment a situation in which a country's imports exceed its exports and it thus has a trade deficit. As with any deficit, be it of a household, a business, or a governmental unit, a trade deficit can be financed by borrowing. Borrowing, in this context, involves convincing foreigners to acquire additional financial claims (IOUs) issued by the deficit country. Obviously, other things equal, the higher the interest rate on such claims, the more willing foreigners will be to acquire them.

In the event that the deficit cannot be financed by borrowing, the deficit country will be forced to draw on its assets.[2] For this purpose, countries keep what are termed *international reserves* (historically in the form of gold or foreign currencies) that can be drawn down as needed. These reserves are generally limited, however, so that continued deficits may require more serious action. Since imports tend to be higher the larger GNP is, one possible way to eliminate a trade deficit is to use restrictive monetary or fiscal policy to damp GNP. Here we have a clear example of a conflict between domestic and international objectives.

THE EXPERIENCE OF THE UNITED STATES

Beginning in about 1950, the United States began experiencing deficits in its balance of payments. To finance these deficits, it resorted to both borrowing and drawing down its gold reserves. Through the 1950s the rest of the world looked somewhat benignly on U.S. deficits, because these deficits provided foreigners with substantial amounts of liquidity in the form of

---

[2]This is particularly true in what is termed a *fixed exchange rate system*. The United States operated under such a system until the 1970s. This is discussed further in *Chapter 21*.

both gold and claims on dollars. By about 1960, however, our short-term dollar liabilities to foreigners exceeded the remaining U.S. gold stock. In effect, the United States was a banker whose ability to deliver on demand was called into question. Foreigners began calling for the United States to do something about its payments deficits. As a result, during the period 1960–1965 there was a conflict between the objective of decreasing the deficit in the balance of payments and the desire to increase the rate of real economic growth and lower the unemployment rate. As we examine monetary policies during this period, we will see how the monetary authorities attempted to cope with this problem.

MONETARY POLICIES, 1960–1963

The economy began to slide into a recession in the first quarter of 1960. The recession was relatively mild. However, even a small decline of output, when coupled with the continuing growth of the labor force, produced a sharp rise in unemployment. By the fourth quarter of 1960, unemployment had reached 6.5 percent, and it remained at or above this level for over a year. At the same time, balance of payments deficits continued to be a problem. In October 1960, strong speculative pressures drove up the London gold price, and the U.S. gold stock declined substantially.

The first response of the Federal Reserve to the onset of the recession was to move toward a more liberal policy, just as it had done in the earlier postwar recessions. However, monetary policy during this period of excessive unemployment is best described as only moderately expansionary, and less expansionary than in earlier postwar recessions. Given this moderation, the decline in market rates of interest, and especially in short-term rates, was not as great as in earlier recessions. Partly as a consequence of all this, the recovery from the 1960 recession was a relatively weak one. While beginning in 1961 real GNP rose without interruption, its rate of growth was quite sluggish, so that extensive amounts of unemployment and excess capacity persisted. The unemployment rate, for example, averaged 6.7 percent for 1961 and fluctuated between 5½ and 6 percent throughout 1962 and 1963. It appears almost certain that in this period concern about the balance of payments did, to a considerable extent, motivate the Federal Reserve to follow less expansionary policies than it would otherwise have followed.

OPERATION NUDGE

In an attempt to reconcile its international and domestic objectives, the Federal Reserve modified its open-market policy, trying to "nudge" or "twist" short-term rates higher relative to long-term rates. The height of long-term interest rates in the United States relative to those abroad obviously influences the flow of long-term funds to other countries. However, during this period Federal Reserve and Treasury officials believed that short-term rates were more important in determining international flows of funds, whereas long-term rates were more important in determining domestic investment spending. They therefore sought to raise short-term rates relative to long-term rates. Note that they faced two separate policy problems: (1) to regulate the overall reserve positions of the banks, and thus influence the general or average level of interest rates; and (2) to influence the relative levels of short-term and long-term rates. The attempts of the Federal Reserve and the Treasury to raise short-term relative to long-term rates are usually called Operation Nudge, although some people referred to these operations as Operation Twist.

To illustrate the principles involved, we assume that the Federal Reserve has already determined the overall reserve position of the banks. The basic technique of the nudge is to increase the supply of Treasury bills and other short issues available to banks and the public relative to the supply of long-term government bonds. This can be done through both Treasury debt management operations and Federal Reserve open-market operations. For its part, the Treasury increases the supply of Treasury bills and other short maturities outstanding. It can do this in several ways: through outright "swaps" of Treasury bills for outstanding longer maturities, or by concentrating new issues in the short-term area.

In comparable ways the Federal Reserve can increase the supply of Treasury bills and other short maturities available to the banks and the public: by selling shorts and buying longs, by purchasing longs rather than shorts to supply bank reserves, and by providing banks with reserves or excess reserves by other means that do not require it to purchase shorts. To do this, however, the Federal Reserve had to abandon its controversial bills-only (or bills-usually) policy. Some steps in this direction were taken in late 1960, when the FOMC began to buy certificates, notes, and bonds with maturities up to 15 months. On February 20, 1961, it abandoned bills-only, announcing: "The System Open-Market Account is purchasing in the open market U.S. government bonds and notes of varying maturities, some of which will exceed five years." Since that time it has dealt in a wide range of maturities. However, its swaps and purchases of long maturities have been only modest in volume.

So much for principles. In actual fact, Operation Nudge was not terribly successful in raising short-term rates relative to long-term ones. The main reason was not that the principles were wrong—after all, the Federal Reserve had proved perfectly capable of pegging the interest rate structure during and after World War II—but rather that the operation was conducted on such a limited scale. For its part, the Federal Reserve swaps of short for longs were small, as were its net purchases of longer securities.

Moreover, the Treasury actually offset these operations to some extent by issuing longer-term securities. Once again, coordination on debt management issues proved to be a tricky business.

There is an interesting postscript to this failure. Recently some economists have concluded that even if Operation Nudge had succeeded in raising short rates relative to long rates, it would probably not have done much to reconcile domestic and international objectives. The reason is that both international capital flows and domestic investment now appear to respond to the entire spectrum of interest rates. As a consequence, these economists argue that the net effect of raising short rates relative to long rates would probably have been negligible.

OTHER POLICIES

While the monetary authorities were struggling to reconcile the pursuit of both domestic and international objectives, they followed what at best might be characterized as a moderately expansionary policy. In an attempt to improve the lackluster performance of the economy and to lessen the problem of conflicting objectives, the government took several steps. In particular, it adopted a more expansionary fiscal policy and introduced the so-called wage-price guideposts.

FISCAL POLICIES

The government hoped that an expansionary fiscal policy, in contrast with an expansionary monetary policy, would lead to less of a conflict between domestic and international objectives. It recognized that a fiscal policy that succeeded in raising domestic income and output would tend to worsen the balance of payments by increasing imports. But, unlike an expansionary monetary policy, it would not tend to lower interest rates or to encourage capital exports. In fact, to the extent that it succeeded in increasing the demand for domestic output and in raising the expected profitability of domestic investment, it would tend to keep funds at home.

In 1962 two steps were taken to encourage private investment. One was a liberalization of depreciation rules, which permitted firms to write off their investments more quickly for tax purposes. The other was enactment of an *investment tax credit* that permitted business firms to deduct from their income tax liabilities an amount equal to 7 percent of their purchases of new plant and equipment. This was, in effect, a subsidy for new investment.

In late 1962 President Kennedy proposed a sizable reduction of personal and corporate income tax rates, but Congress delayed the reduction until 1964. The reduction, which became effective in steps in 1964 and 1965, amounted to $15 billion at the levels of GNP prevailing in 1965. It clearly had the desired effect of increasing the rate of growth of demands for output. It would have been even more useful if it had been instituted at least two years earlier.

WAGE-PRICE GUIDEPOSTS

Although in 1962 the economy was still operating well below its potential, the desire of the government to take significant expansionary action raised the specter of a future conflict between economic growth and low unemployment on the one hand and price stability on the other. To forestall this possibility the Council of Economic Advisers set forth a set of voluntary wage-price guidelines in its *Economic Report* for 1962.

The general principle of the wage guideline was that annual increases in money wage rates should be equal to the average annual increase in output per unit of labor or productivity in the economy as a whole. For example, if productivity in the entire economy rose by 3 percent a year, it would be appropriate for money wages to rise by the same percentage. This meant that labor cost per unit of output would remain unchanged in industries where the increase in labor productivity was equal to the economywide average, would fall where the rise of productivity was above average, and would rise where the rise of productivity was below average. Exceptions to this general guideline were envisaged. For example, larger wage increases would be appropriate where the guideline wage was not high enough to attract sufficient labor or where this wage was inequitably low.

The general principle of the price guideline was that prices should be changed only by a percentage equal to the change in labor cost per unit of output. This meant that prices would remain unchanged where the rise of labor productivity was equal to the national average, would fall where the rise of productivity was above the national average, and would rise where the rise of productivity was below the national average.

In view of their voluntary nature, there has been a fair amount of controversy over whether the guideposts did actually serve to improve the tradeoff between inflation and unemployment. While the evidence seems to point to some small salutary effect, it is not fully conclusive, especially since the guideposts were abandoned when serious inflationary pressures emerged during the Vietnam war.

DEVELOPMENTS FROM 1964 TO LATE 1965

At the beginning of 1964, when the first round of the substantial tax cuts just described went into effect, the unemployment rate stood at nearly 6 percent, roughly its average of the previous three years. Then the tempo of economic activity picked up considerably. Real GNP, which over the previous three years had advanced at about a 4 percent annual rate, expanded at over a 6 percent rate during the next two years. This gradually closed the gap between actual and potential GNP, and the Kennedy–Johnson administrations' interim target of 4 percent unemployment was reached in late 1965. And all this had occurred without a change in the rate of inflation. Indeed, the rate of change in the consumer price index in 1964–1965 was comparable to the performance in 1957–1963, though some observers thought the upward movement of wholesale prices portended greater inflation in the future. About the only other stabilization problem was the nagging persistence of the deficits in the balance of payments. But even these grew somewhat smaller in 1964 and 1965. In short, who could blame the policymakers for their rosy view of the world?

But the euphoria did not last long. With the economy close to its potential, defense outlays for the Vietnam war began a significant expansion in late 1965. As these increased outlays were, initially at least, unmatched by any reduction in fiscal stimulus, monetary policy was quickly forced to bear the burden of the restraint. Thus began one of the more dismal periods in the history of economic policy.

SUMMARY

1 Monetary policy during World War II aimed at pegging the level of interest rates. This required a passive open-market policy, thereby causing the Fed to abandon control over the volume of reserves and of the money supply. The potentially inflationary effects of this policy were repressed by direct controls on prices and wages.

2 Following the end of World War II, the policy of pegging interest rates continued. With the inflationary pressures brought on by the Korean war, the Fed tried to free itself from the constraints of the pegging policy and, after a bitter political battle with the Treasury, finally got its way in 1951. Armed with its new power, the Fed was forced to develop strategies for the implementation of policy, and the recessions of 1953–1954 and 1957–1958 provided ample opportunity to practice countercyclical monetary policy.

3 Beginning with the 1960s, monetary policy was confronted with a new problem—reconciling the conflict between the objective of decreasing the deficit in the international balance of payments with the desire to increase the rate of economic growth and decrease the unemployment rate. The Fed tried to reconcile these objectives by Operation Twist, whereby short-term interest rates were to be raised relative to long-term rates, but was not terribly successful in this regard. Nevertheless, despite the problem of international payments, from 1961 to 1965 fiscal and monetary policy together brought the economy close to full employment with relative price stability. But, as the next chapter documents, there were troubles on the horizon.

SELECTED READINGS

Ahearn, D. S. *Federal Reserve Policy Reappraised, 1951–1959*. New York: Columbia University Press, 1963.

Brown, A. J. *The Great Inflation, 1939–1951*. London: Oxford University Press, 1955.

Chandler, L. V. *Inflation in the United States, 1940–1948*. New York: Harper & Row, 1951.

Fforde, J. S. *The Federal Reserve System, 1945–1949*. London: Oxford University Press, 1954.

Friedman, M. *Dollars and Deficits*. Englewood Cliffs, N.J.: Prentice-Hall, 1968.

20

MONETARY POLICY, 1965–1984

The later part of 1965 was, in many ways, a highwater mark for both the economy and economists. For the first time in nearly a decade, the actual performance of the economy was up to its potential. The unemployment rate had declined to its interim target of 4 percent, and the rate of inflation was only slightly over 2 percent per year, almost exactly in line with the behavior of prices during the preceding 10 years. Much of the credit for achieving this state of affairs belonged to monetary and especially fiscal policy. Indeed, economists who had urged a tax cut in the face of a budget deficit had been vindicated in all respects. The 1964 tax cut not only improved our economic performance, but also, precisely because of this improvement, turned around the federal budget so that it showed a surplus in 1965.

Despite this auspicious beginning, the period beginning in late 1965 proved to be an extremely turbulent and problem-filled one. The difficulties began in the last quarter of 1965 with the rapid expansion of defense spending for the Vietnam war. Federal purchases of goods and services, which had shown little increase from 1962 to 1965 (indeed, they had declined in real terms), spurted ahead. They rose steadily over the next three years, advancing by nearly 50 percent. This increase in aggregate demand, superimposed on an economy operating close to capacity, inevitably created inflationary pressures and ushered in a period of marked increases in the aggregate price level.

From 1955 to 1965 the inflation rate, as measured by the rise in the GNP implicit deflator, was about 2 percent per year. In contrast, from 1965 to 1984 the inflation rate was about 6 percent per year. Our inflationary performance was particularly dismal after 1973, with one severe bout of inflation in 1974–1975 followed by another in 1980–1981. During each of these episodes, the inflation rate averaged over 10 percent per year. Moreover, each of these episodes was accompanied by a severe recession. Indeed, the recession of 1974–1975 was the severest of the post-World War II era—until it was surpassed by the recession of 1981–1982.

In short, the years 1965 to 1984 were marked by a substantial variety of serious economic difficulties, with stagflation in evidence for much of this period. Various competing hypotheses have been advanced to explain our poor economic performance. Policy failures in the form of overly stimulative fiscal and/or monetary policies in 1965–1966, 1972–1973, and 1977–1978 have been credited with creating or worsening inflationary pressures, while overly restrictive policies have been blamed for the depth of the two most serious postwar recessions. Other observers have placed much of the blame for our stagflation on the seemingly unprecedented series of severe external shocks that buffeted the economy in the 1970s. Most prominent in this regard are the two OPEC shocks, in 1973–1974 and 1979, that taken together drove up the price of oil by a factor of 6.

As a whole, the events of 1965 to 1984 make this period an extremely instructive one for studying the workings of monetary policy. While this hardly compensates for the fact that our economic performance left much to be desired, a careful examination of the period may at least teach us how to avoid the same mistakes again.

1965 TO 1984: THE VIEW IN PICTURES

To understand economic policy in the period 1965–1984, it is perhaps best to begin by gaining an appreciation of the economic conditions that confronted (and, of course, to some extent were created by) policymakers. To keep matters relatively brief, we will resort to a few pictures showing the behavior of real GNP, unemployment, and inflation. The first of these pictures, Figure 20–1, shows the percentage change of real GNP for each quarter during the period 1965 to 1984, expressed at an annual rate. This statistic, which receives considerable attention in the press and is widely watched by economists, is the most common measure used to summarize the nation's economic growth. Overall, judged by this standard, from the end of 1965 to the end of 1984 the economy grew at the rate of 3 percent per year. However, as Figure 20–1 indicates, this growth was hardly steady. Rather, there were periods in which real GNP actually declined (i.e., the

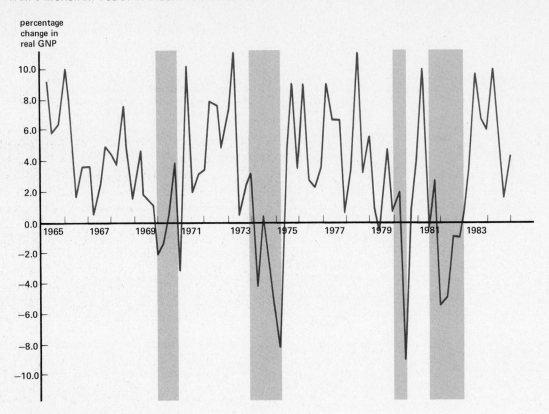

FIGURE 20–1
Percentage change in real GNP, 1965–1984.
(Quarterly data at annual rates.)

growth rate was negative). If these declines were of sufficient breadth and duration, they were labeled recessions.[1] Such recessions occurred in 1969–1970, 1974–1975, 1980, and 1982. In other periods, economic growth was substantially higher than the 3 percent average that prevailed from 1965 to 1984.

Figure 20–1, which displays these wide variations, suggests, if anything, that the magnitude of the fluctuations in the growth of real GNP tended to increase over time. This same tendency is visible in Figure 20–2, which shows the unemployment rate, and in Figure 20–3, which graphs the inflation rate. Taken as a group, these three figures tell us much of what we need to know about post-1965 economic performance. However, while each of these pictures are worth many words, a few words of summary are still in order.

[1]By custom, the job of declaring recessions falls to a private nonprofit group of economists, the National Bureau of Economic Research. The periods of recession are shaded in Figures 20–1 to 20–3.

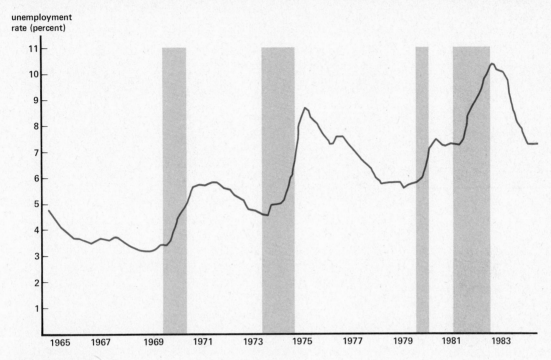

unemployment
rate (percent)

FIGURE 20–2
Overall unemployment rate. (Quarterly average
data.)

With the exception of a brief pause in 1967—not serious enough to earn
the recessionary label—real GNP expanded relatively rapidly over the period 1965 to 1969. This expansion, fueled by government spending for the
Vietnam war, brought the unemployment rate to 3¼ percent in 1969, its
lowest level since 1953. Unfortunately, however, this good news was accompanied by the gradual rise in the inflation rate evident in Figure 20–3.
Indeed, inflation continued to rise in 1969 and 1970 as the economy was
experiencing a recession. This was our first bout with stagflation, although
it was mild by later standards, with the unemployment rate peaking at 5¾
percent, and the inflation rate topping out at 6½ percent.

Economic growth was brisk during the recovery period and the subsequent expansion, which lasted until 1973. Over 1971 and 1972 the rate of
inflation declined, partly as a result of wage and price controls, but thereafter accelerated sharply as OPEC increases in oil prices were widely felt.
By mid-1974 the inflation rate had reached 10½ percent, our first experience
with double-digit inflation since 1951. Economic growth came to a halt in
1974 and a severe recession ensued. The unemployment rate reached about
8¾ percent in 1975, the highest rate since the 1930s, and the economy once
again suffered a severe dose of stagflation.

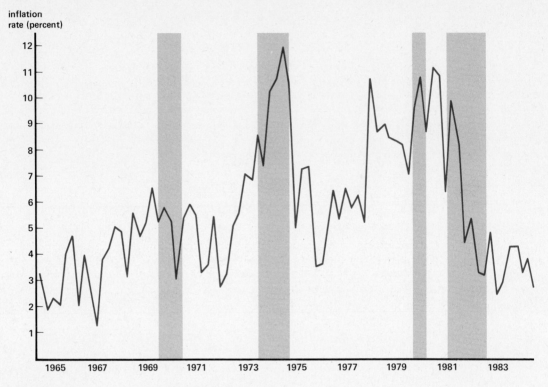

FIGURE 20–3
Overall inflation rate: percentage change in the
GNP deflator, 1965–1984. (Quarterly data at
annual rates.)

The economy began its recovery from recession in the first half of 1975. The unemployment rate fell reasonably steadily to about 6 percent in early 1978 and stayed there until early 1980. Inflation declined in 1975 and 1976, but with the expansion of the economy, surged upward starting in 1977. By 1980, after another oil price shock, we were back in double-digit inflation. Beginning in 1980, the economy experienced one of the worst and most variable periods. Real GNP fell sharply at the start of 1980, although it then recovered for several quarters. The unemployment rate, which had jumped to 7½ percent, remained at 7¼ percent until mid-1981, when the economy entered the most serious recession of the postwar period. By the end of 1982, the unemployment rate stood over 10½ percent and real GNP had not grown from its level three years earlier. As Figure 20–3 reveals, this severe recession did much to reduce the momentum of inflation and, even with the subsequent recovery in 1983 and 1984, our inflationary performance was reasonably satisfactory.

As this brief summary of our economic performance should suggest, policymakers had their hands full in the period after 1965. There were substantial economic fluctuations in which inflation and unemployment became more severe with each cycle in economic activity. It is now time to see what policymakers did in response to such gyrations and to determine to what extent economic policy may have contributed to the gyrations.

MONETARY POLICIES, LATE 1965–OCTOBER 1966

We have already described the upsurge of expenditures by the federal government after mid-1965. These were added to an economy that was already experiencing continuing increases of expenditures by state and local governments and of plant and equipment investment expenditures by private business. Taken together, these induced large increases in consumer spending. Despite these upsurges of spending, no significant federal tax increases were enacted before June 1968.

One effect of these large and rapid increases in expenditures was to reduce unemployment. Despite large additions to the labor force, the unemployment rate fell from 4.6 percent in June 1965 to 3.6 percent in November 1966. Another effect was price inflation. Price levels had been relatively stable during the seven years preceding mid-1965. For example, from 1958 to mid-1965 the consumer price index had risen at an annual rate of only 1.3 percent. However, between June 1965 and October 1966 consumer prices rose at a rate of 3 percent per year.

Thus, in the face of highly expansionary fiscal policies, it became the task of the Federal Reserve to try to contain the inflation by restricting supplies of money and credit while demands for credit were large and rising. The federal government had to borrow large amounts to finance its mounting deficits, and business firms demanded large amounts of funds in both long-term and short-term markets to finance rising expenditures for fixed equipment and inventory. The combination of a restrictive monetary policy and rising total demands for credit in 1966 raised interest rates to their highest levels in more than 40 years.

The first restrictive step was taken by the Federal Reserve in December 1965, when it increased the discount rate from 4 to 4½ percent. In retrospect, it appears that the increase should have been made earlier. However, President Johnson and many others criticized the increase, asserting that it was premature and would unduly inhibit the growth of employment and output. Perhaps partly because of such criticisms, the Federal Reserve followed a somewhat liberal open-market policy for a short time. However, in the spring of 1966 the Fed began to move toward a highly restrictive policy. By restricting its purchases of government securities, it prevented any significant rise in the supply of unborrowed reserves during the five months following April. The money supply did not increase at all between April and the end of the year, although transactions demands for money balances rose with the continued increase of GNP.

In the meantime banks—and especially large banks—were experiencing unexpected large increases in demands for business loans. Many bankers found to their consternation that while their outstanding loan commitments were far larger than they had thought, some of their most valued depositors unexpectedly demanded accommodation. To meet such demands, banks scrambled for funds. They raised their borrowings from the Federal Reserve and attempted to attract more time deposits, but the Federal Reserve refused to raise ceiling rates even though rates on other short-term assets had become higher. As a result, few banks could attract additional time deposits and some suffered net withdrawals, especially of large-denominations CDs.

This, for the first time, served notice on the banks that the strategy of liability management was not without its problems. To compensate for the runoff in CDs, the banks sold federal and state and local government securities at large losses; borrowed federal funds; and some of the most sophisticated banks raised funds expensively via the Eurodollar market. By September many banks were forced to use nonprice rationing to limit the increase of business loans, and interest rates were at their highest level in more than four decades. The entire structure of rates shifted upward, but short-term rates rose the most. For example, the rate on 3-month Treasury bills, which had averaged under 4 percent in 1965, rose to 4½ percent in June 1966 and then again to nearly 5½ percent in September 1966. While by today's standards these seem quite low, they were viewed as extremely high at the time.

DISINTERMEDIATION

As indicated in an earlier chapter, a large part of the public's saving, and especially of household saving, usually flows to financial intermediaries in exchange for such claims as shares in savings and loan associations, deposits at mutual savings banks, and claims against life insurance companies. This process was shocked severely by the sharp rise of interest rates on competing financial assets. Hardest hit were the savings and loan associations, which were accustomed to large net inflows of funds. The average monthly increase of their outstanding shares had been $881 million in 1964 and $698 million in 1965. Net inflows were far smaller in 1966, and during four months there were net outflows. Faced with the virtual cessation of net inflows, and fearing large withdrawals, savings and loan associations found it difficult to meet their outstanding commitments to lend on mortgages and were unable to make many new commitments. This was a sharp blow to the residential construction industry, which relies so heavily on these institutions for financing.

Life insurance companies faced a somewhat different problem. Flows of funds to them did not decrease. However, many of them had contracted to lend to their policyholders on demand, and at 5 percent, amounts up to the cash surrender values of their policies. As other interest rates rose, policyholders greatly increased their demand for such loans. The result was a shrinkage in the net flow of funds available to life insurance companies for purchasing other types of assets, primarily mortgages and corporate bonds.

Thus, the financial intermediaries that contribute most heavily to the financing of the residential construction industry were forced to restrict their mortgage lending. This restriction, together with high interest rates, caused a sharp fall in residential construction. Measured from their levels of a year earlier, new private-housing starts had fallen 28 percent by July 1966; in October, the decline reached 40 percent. These declines brought loud protests from the building industry, Congress, and some others.

The Federal Reserve feared that nonbank financial intermediaries would be squeezed even more and would, in at least some isolated cases, suffer large withdrawals. It was also worried about the impact of these developments on construction. Thus, it was faced with the problem of determining how to ameliorate the situation. One approach would have been to shift toward a less restrictive general monetary policy in order to curb the rise of interest rates, or even to lower them. And this consideration was a factor in the Board's refusal to approve increases in discount rates during July. (Seven of the Reserve Banks proposed that their discount rates be raised from 4½ to 5 or 5½ percent, but the Board disapproved all of these proposals.) But to relax general monetary policy would, of course, increase the danger of inflation. Therefore, the Federal Reserve sought selective measures that would enable it to slow the rate of increase of business loans by banks, reduce the flow of funds into time and savings deposits at commercial banks, and reduce the diversion of funds from nonbank financial intermediaries. It was especially concerned with large banks, whose business loans were expanding most rapidly and who were bidding most actively for funds.

SELECTIVE MEASURES

The Federal Reserve adopted several types of selective measures. One was to tighten ceilings on time-deposit rates. Board action in December 1965 had established ceiling rates of 4 percent on savings deposits and 5½ percent on all types of time deposits. As competing market rates rose sharply during the summer, there were widespread requests that the ceilings be raised to enable banks to retain deposits and perhaps attract more. This the Board refused to do. In fact, in July and again in September it actually rolled back ceilings on some types of time deposits. The maximum rate on large-denomination time deposits—those of $100,000 or more—remained at 5½ percent; ceilings on smaller denominations were reduced to 5 percent. These actions had two principal purposes. One was to reduce the diversion of funds from nonbank financial intermediaries. The other was to slow the expansion of business loans by limiting the ability of banks to attract funds.

Another action with selective effects was to increase reserve requirements on certain types of time deposits. The principal purpose of this action was to inhibit the bidding for time deposits by large banks, and thus to lessen their expansion of business loans. To accomplish this aim, the Federal Reserve also resorted to moral suasion. By early summer, Federal Reserve officials were stating that business loans were expanding too rapidly, that this was inflationary and that the investment boom might prove unsustainable in the sense that it would lead to a temporary glut of fixed capital and inventory, which would lead to a later decline. Discount officers admonished banks that sought to borrow too frequently or too much while expanding their business loans too rapidly. The moral suasion effect culminated in a letter dated September 1 that was sent to all member banks and to the press.[2] The letter made several points:

1 Some expansion of business loans is required, but the national interest would be better served by a lower rate of expansion.
2 Bank liquidation of municipal securities and other investments creates pressures on financial markets; "a greater share of bank adjustments should take the form of moderation in the rate of expansion of loans, and particularly business loans."
3 "Member banks will be expected to cooperate in the System's efforts to hold down the rate of business loan expansion—apart from normal seasonal needs—and to use the discount facilities of the Reserve Banks in a manner consistent with these efforts."
4 Banks cooperating by curtailing business loans rather than by disposing of securities will be eligible for a longer period of discount accommodation if needed.

It is difficult to assess the effects of this letter. The expansion of business loans did begin to slow down at about this time, but not necessarily as a result of the letter. One factor that may have contributed to the slowdown is that many banks had already begun to screen loan applications more closely. Also, demands for business loans were becoming less ebullient. However, it does seem likely that moral suasion by the Federal Reserve, including the September letter, played at least some small role in slowing the expansion of business loans.

The peak of the strains in the financial markets was reached in September. In October, the Federal Reserve decided to move no further toward restriction; in December, it began to move toward a more liberal policy.

---

[2]For the text of the letter, see *Annual Report of the Board of Governors for 1966*, Washington, D.C., 1967, pp. 103–104.

MONETARY POLICIES 1966–1971

LATE 1966–JUNE 1968

This shift in monetary policy was primarily in response to a weakening of private investment spending, because government expenditures continued to rise without abatement. However, expenditures for residential construction had fallen significantly by the fourth quarter of 1966, business spending for inventory accumulation fell sharply in the first two quarters of 1967, and business expenditures for plant and equipment also declined slightly. To some extent the latter drop reflected the temporary suspension of the investment tax credit in September 1966. There was considerable debate at the time as to whether the so-called credit crunch of late 1966 was about to give rise to a recession. But ultimately all that resulted is what has been termed a minipause. In particular, from the fourth quarter of 1966 to the second quarter of 1967, the annual rate of increase of real GNP slowed to 1.7 percent, a sharp drop from its 6 percent pace of the previous two years.

The Federal Reserve responded to this situation with a number of liberalizing actions. In late December, it quietly withdrew its letter of September 1. In March, it lowered reserve requirements against savings and time deposits and in April all the Reserve banks lowered their discount rates. These actions, in conjunction with open market purchases of government securities, contributed to a substantial expansion of the money supply. In the year following October 1966, the money supply rose by about 6 percent.

Market yields on short-term and long-term debts moved in disparate ways. Short-term yields fell during the first half of 1967 and then rose during the second half—although they did not reach their peaks of 1966. For example, yields on 90-day Treasury bills fell from 5.39 percent in October 1966 to 3.49 percent in July 1967 and then rose to 5.01 percent in December. The decline of market rates on competing short-term assets while ceiling rates remained unchanged permitted a large increase in time deposits at commercial banks, and also brought large inflows of funds to other financial intermediaries, especially to savings and loans associations, which helped revive residential construction. On the other hand, yields on long-term debt declined only briefly and then rose to record levels. For example, yields on corporate bonds rated AAA by Moody's declined from 5.44 percent in September 1966 to 5.03 percent in February, and then rose almost continuously to 6.19 percent in December.

This disparate behavior of short- and long-term yields resulted from a combination of factors—expectations of continuing inflation and rising rates in the future, fear of unavailability of credit in the future, and the squeeze on liquidity in 1966. Both financial institutions and other business firms had reduced their liquidity markedly by late 1966. Financial institutions preferred short-term liquid assets to rebuild their liquidity, and other business firms issued huge amounts of long-term debt to make sure that they could command funds and to reduce their reliance on bank loans.

In retrospect, it is clear that Federal Reserve policies during this period were excessively expansionary. By October 1967 these policies had become subject to criticism not only by outsiders, but also by a minority within the FOMC. Critics pointed to the continuing rise of government expenditures while Congress still refused to raise taxes, to the renewed increase of private investment spending, to the higher rate of increase of total spending, to the continuing domestic price inflation, and to the worsening of the nation's balance of payments. Such considerations led to the adoption of less expansionary monetary policies in the autumn of 1967. They probably would have been more restrictive if Federal Reserve officials had not feared that such actions would jeopardize enactment of the tax and expenditure legislation then being considered by Congress.

Both short- and long-term interest rates rose significantly. Judged on the basis of the behavior of monetary aggregates, monetary policies in this period appear less restrictive. The money supply rose at an annual rate of 7.2 percent, and time deposits at commercial breaks increased at an annual rate of 8.1 percent. In addition to these increases, nominal GNP rose at an annual rate of 9.7 percent, and the consumer price index increased at an annual rate of 4.5 percent. By this time an increasing number of people were complaining tht Federal Reserve policies were being guided too much by the behavior of interest rates and not enough by the behavior of the money supply.

JUNE–NOVEMBER 1968

In late June of 1968, a full three years after federal expenditures began their rapid rise, Congress finally passed the Revenue and Expenditure Control Act, which provided for a 10 percent surtax on personal and corporate income taxes and a reduction of $6 billion in federal expenditures. This action was widely expected to be highly effective in restricting the rise of aggregate demand, in curbing inflation, in lowering interest rates by reducing government borrowing, by lessening inflationary expectations, and by making feasible a less restrictive monetary policy. In fact, some feared overkill if the restrictive fiscal actions were not accompanied by some relaxation of monetary policies. Federal Reserve officials shared these views. At a meeting on June 18, the FOMC instructed the manager of the open-market account, "that if the proposed fiscal legislation is enacted, operations shall accommodate tendencies for short-term interest rates to decline in connection with such affirmative congressional action on the pending fiscal legislation so long as bank credit expansion does not exceed current projections."[3] Such a policy of accommodation was followed from the end of June through November 1968.

[3] *Annual Report of the Board of Governors of the Federal Reserve System*, Washington, D.C., 1968, p. 166.

By December, it had become only too clear that the fiscal actions initiated in June were less effective than had been expected. GNP was still rising rapidly, and in December 1968 the unemployment rate dipped to a 15-year low. Furthermore, inflation continued, and the balance of payments was deteriorating. It was under these conditions that the Federal Reserve shifted to a more restrictive policy in mid-December.

DECEMBER 1968–FEBRUARY 1970

The restrictive policy initiated in mid-December 1968 became more stringent during 1969 and was not terminated until February 1970. Monetary restrictions, together with rising demands for credit, raised market rates of interest, both short-term and long-term, to their highest levels in more than a century (see Table 20–1). In view of both the large rise in interest rates and the high levels reached, it is not surprising that financial markets were at times turbulent, that large amounts of funds were diverted away from financial intermediaries and into higher-yielding open-market assets, and that large amounts of funds flowed to the United States from foreign financial centers.

TABLE 20–1 Market Rates of Interest, November 1968–February 1970 (Yields in percentages per annum)

Period	3-month Treasury bills	Prime 4–6-month commercial paper	Federal funds rate	Prime rate charged by banks	U.S. Treasury bonds	Aaa corporate bonds
November 1968	5.45	5.81	5.81	6.25	5.36	6.19
December	5.94	6.17	6.02	6.50–6.75	5.65	6.45
January 1969	6.13	6.53	6.30	7.00	5.74	6.59
February	6.12	6.62	6.64	7.00	5.86	6.66
March	6.01	6.82	6.79	7.50	6.05	6.85
April	6.11	7.04	7.41	7.50	5.84	6.89
May	6.03	7.35	8.67	7.50	5.85	6.79
June	6.43	8.23	8.90	8.50	6.06	6.98
July	6.98	8.65	8.61	8.50	6.07	7.08
August	6.97	8.33	9.19	8.50	6.02	6.97
September	7.08	8.48	9.15	8.50	6.32	7.14
October	6.99	8.56	9.00	8.50	6.27	7.33
November	7.24	8.46	8.85	8.50	6.51	7.35
December	7.81	8.84	8.97	8.50	6.81	7.72
January 1970	7.87	8.78	8.98	8.50	6.86	7.91
February	7.13	8.55	8.98	8.50	6.44	7.93

SOURCE: *Federal Reserve Bulletin*, various issues.

The Federal Reserve used all its major instruments for restrictive purposes, and the banks were faced with a difficult dilemma: While the Federal Reserve refused to provide additional reserves through open-market purchases, consumer demands for bank loans were high and rising rapidly. Banks, therefore, were anxious to obtain funds from whatever source they could find. They borrowed extensively from the Federal Reserve and would have like to borrow much more at the prevailing discount rate of 6 percent. But they knew the Federal Reserve would disapprove, and some considered it prudent to conserve borrowing power for use in an emergency. Many banks would have liked to have attracted more funds by raising their rates on savings and time deposits, but the Federal Reserve refused to raise the ceilings. As yields on competing assets rose, banks in general not only were unable to attract more funds but also suffered net outflows. Withdrawals from large-denomination negotiable CDs were especially large, and the trend of total time and savings deposits at commercial banks was descending through 1969. By December, these deposits were 5 percent below their level of a year earlier.

Banks competed in many ways for the existing supply of reserves.

1 They borrowed federal funds. Increased demands for these funds, together with decreases in the supply of excess reserves, pushed the federal funds rate to very high levels. During the last half of 1969 this rate averaged about 9 percent, or 3 percentage points above the Federal Reserve discount rate.

2 They sold some of their holdings of securities, especially obligations of the federal government and of state and local governments, thereby accentuating the rise of yields on these securities.

3 They sold some of their loans and participations in their loans. Some of these sales were outright and some were under repurchase agreement.

4 Their subsidiaries and affiliates issued commercial paper and made the proceeds available to the banks.

5 They borrowed huge amounts of Eurodollars, mostly through their foreign branches. Liabilities of American banks to their foreign branches rose from $8.5 billion in January 1969 to a peak of more than $15 billion in November, and averaged above $14.5 billion during the rest of the year. On many of these borrowings, banks paid interest rates in excess of 10 percent.

Despite their competitive scramble for funds, banks were forced to curtail expansion of their loans to customers, including business firms. Moreover, as in 1966, the sharp rise in market yields was accompanied by financial disintermediation at S&Ls and MSBs, tending to reduce sharply the supply of mortgage funds, thereby depressing residential construction. Thus, no matter what criteria one may use, monetary policies in 1969 were highly restrictive. We have already mentioned the rise in interest rates to their highest levels in more than a century, the tight rein kept on the unborrowed reserves of member banks, and the shrinkage of total time and savings deposits at commercial banks. The money supply rose 3.5 percent during 1969, but the annual rate of increase during the second half of the year was only 1½ percent.

In describing this period in his *Newsweek* column in August 1969, Milton Friedman noted:

> The Federal Reserve System has done it again. Once more it is overreacting as it has so often done in the past ... Some retardation in growth and some increase in unemployment is an inevitable, if unwelcome, by-product of stopping inflation. But there is no need for—and every reason to avoid—a retardation of the severity that will be produced by a continuation of the Fed's present monetary overkill.[4]

It had been hoped that with the passage of the 1968 tax increase, monetary and fiscal policies would gradually reduce inflation with a minimum of depressing effects on employment and real economic growth. By the early months of 1970, it was becoming increasingly clear that the plan was not working. On the one hand, price inflation continued unabated. Increases for 1969 were 6 percent for the consumer price index, and 5 percent for the GNP price deflator. On the other hand, real economic growth and employment were affected adversely. Over the first three quarters of the year, real GNP grew at only a 2 percent annual rate; and in the fourth quarter real GNP declined for the first time since the end of 1960. The recession of 1969–1970 had begun. The unemployment rate, which had averaged about 3.3 percent in the first months of 1969, climbed to over 4 percent in early 1970; by year-end it had jumped to over 6 percent.

FEBRUARY 1970–AUGUST 1971

Federal Reserve officials were in a quandary as they reviewed their policies at the beginning of 1970. They knew that industrial production had been falling, that growth of real GNP had halted, and that unemployment was rising; they had good reason to believe that the situation would deteriorate further in the absence of expansionary actions. But they also knew that there were no signs of a decrease in the rate of inflation, that inflationary expectations were strong and widespread, that the balance of payments was already in bad condition, and that a more expansionary monetary policy could well lead to large outflows of funds to other countries. This mixed situation explains why there were different judgments in the Federal Reserve during the first weeks of 1970, with some officials favoring a continuation of restrictive policies and other advocating relaxation. The net effect was a cautiously expansionary monetary policy.

[4]Cited in R. Dornbusch and S. Fischer, *Macroeconomics*. New York: McGraw-Hill, 1978, p. 522.

Fiscal policy also became more stimulative in 1970 as the 10 percent surcharge on income taxes was terminated in two stages; the first of several tax reductions contained in the Tax Reform Act of 1969 became effective; and federal expenditures increased sharply, mainly through larger grants-in-aid to local governments and through transfer payments to individuals. The Fed was presented with a new challenge in the late spring and early summer of 1970 by disturbances in the commercial paper market associated with the financial distress of the Penn Central Transportation Company. The failure of this firm to meet its maturing commercial paper obligations, and rumors that other important firms might follow suit, led to a sharp reduction of supplies of funds to the commercial paper market and to fears that many businesses would be unable to roll over their commercial paper. The Federal Reserve took two actions to deal with this situation. First, it invited banks to borrow from their Reserve banks the amounts that would be needed to lend to firms that could not roll over their maturing commercial paper. Second, it suspended interest ceilings on large-denomintion CDs with maturities of 30 to 89 days, thereby enabling banks to bid freely for these funds. These actions were sufficient to prevent a financial crisis.

THE ECONOMY AS OF MID-1971

DOMESTIC ASPECTS

We have just seen that, following the highly restrictive policies of 1969 and the onset of the 1969–1970 recession, both monetary and fiscal policies became more stimulative in early 1970. The federal government increased its expenditures and lowered taxes, and the Federal Reserve adopted a quite expansionary policy. By July 1971 the money supply had risen 10 percent above its level in February 1970 and time deposits at commercial banks had grown over 30 percent. Both long- and short-term interest rates had fallen sharply.

These policies were accompanied by some increase in real output. For example, GNP in real terms rose about 2½ percent between the second quarter of 1970 and the second quarter of 1971. However, the growth rate was too small to reduce unemployment. During the summer of 1971, the unemployment rate hovered around 6 percent, about the same level that had prevailed during the preceding eight months and significantly above the levels of early 1970. At the same time, price increases continued at a rate above 5 percent with little sign of abatement and, in fact, with some evidence of acceleration. The question naturally arises as to why the relatively high level of unemployment after mid-1970 failed to slow the rate of inflation. To answer this, we must look more closely at the nature of the inflation.

We have emphasized that in the early period of the Vietnam buildup—that is, prior to the third quarter of 1968—the economy was experiencing a demand pull inflation. The same might be said, although with less certainty, of the first months of 1969. However, by the early months of 1970 the situation had clearly changed. At least partly because of more restrictive federal fiscal policies and very stringent monetary policies in 1969, the rate of increase in aggregate demand had slowed down. Moreover, underutilization of labor and plant capacity was becoming more evident. Excess capacity was appearing in industry after industry, and the unemployment rate was rising. Inflation continued unabated despite these developments.

By mid-1971 the inflationary process had become in large part a cost push and markup inflation. Hourly wage rates, including fringe benefits, rose much more rapidly than output per unit of labor, thereby increasing labor costs per unit of output. To compensate for these increased costs, most employers tried to increase their prices. Unit labor costs rose more than 4 percent in 1968 and more than 6 percent in both 1969 and 1970. They continued upward in 1971. In view of the strong inflationary expectations that had developed, it is easy to see why demanded increases in money wages were so large. Workers demanded wage increases large enough to offset not only past increases in the cost of living, but also expected future increases.

This situation of continued price inflation in the face of excessive unemployment and underutilization of other productive resources presented a dilemma for conventional monetary and fiscal policies. More restrictive policies to combat price inflation would almost certainly lead to increased unemployment, but more expansive policies to promote real economic growth and employment would probably worsen inflation and create still stronger inflationary expectations. Because of this dilemma, proposals for some sort of direct wage and price controls received increasing public support. It was thought that direct limitations on wages and prices might combat inflationary expectations, might eliminate or at least lessen cost push pressures, and might allow a larger part of any increase in aggregate demand to be reflected in increases in real output and employment.

INTERNATIONAL ASPECTS

At the same time that policymakers were faced with a dilemma in the domestic economy with regard to inflation and unemployment, there were also significant difficulties related to international payments. By 1970 these factors had produced a marked deterioration in the nation's balance of payments. In 1970 the deficit in the balance of payments, measured on an official reserve transaction basis, was $10 billion, far larger than it had been in any preceding year. This deterioration resulted in part from a shrinkage of the balance on the goods and services account, but much more from huge outflows of short-term funds on the private account. The latter was initially in response to widening differentials in interest rates as rates in the United States fell much faster than those in foreign financial centers.

Both the outflow of private funds and the balance of payments of the United States were huge during the first half of 1971. For example, as measured on an official reserve-transactions basis, the deficit for the first half of 1971 was $11 billion, and it continued to rise thereafter. In early August, a report by a congressional subcommittee asserted that the dollar had become overvalued and that the situation could be corrected through a general realignment of exchange rates. On the same day, the Treasury reported a $1 billion loss of gold and other international reserves. Outflows of funds accelerated sharply, and over the following week $3.7 billion flowed into foreign central banks. These were some of the principal developments preceding the president's announcement of August 15.

ACTIONS OF AUGUST 15, 1971

On Sunday evening, August 15, 1971, President Nixon appeared on nationwide television to announce what he described as "the most comprehensive new economic policy to be undertaken by this country in four decades." Although the accuracy of this description is debatable, there can be no doubt that the announced changes were dramatic and sweeping, that at least some of them had not only short-run but also important long-run implications, and that they represented sharp departures from the policies previously followed by Nixon's administration. Up to that time, he had staunchly defended his "game plan" for dealing with domestic inflation and unemployment, and had flatly rejected all proposals for any kind of wage-price guidelines or wage-price review board. Now he imposed a 90-day freeze on wages, prices, and rents; stated that the freeze would be followed for a temporary but indefinite period by a program providing more flexible direct controls; and proposed further tax reductions to combat unemployment. His reversal on international monetary policies was no less dramatic. Prior to this announcement he had affirmed and reaffirmed his determination to maintain the existing exchange rate on the dollar. Now he terminated convertibility of the dollar into gold and other reserve assets, declared his determination that exchange rates on other currencies should rise in terms of the dollar, and imposed a 10 percent surcharge on all dutiable imports. It was hoped that such actions would serve to equilibrate the balance of payments and give monetary and fiscal authorities greater freedom to concentrate on their domestic objectives.

The general public reaction was highly favorable, perhaps not as a result of the specific nature of the actions but as a result of a feeling of relief that "at last something is being done about the economic mess." A complex mess it certainly was: unabating inflation in the face of excessive unemployment and underutilization of plant capacities, and a deficit in the nation's balance of payments that was not only continuing but growing to mammoth proportions. Some type of comprehensive program was clearly indicated; piecemeal actions would not suffice.

COMPONENTS OF THE NEW ECONOMIC POLICY

DIRECT CONTROLS OF WAGES, PRICES, AND RENTS

As already indicated, the freeze order had several related purposes: to arrest the wage-price spiral, to weaken inflationary expectations, to enable a large part of any rise of demands for output to be reflected in increases of real output and employment, and to make more expansionary monetary and fiscal policies feasible. It was obvious that the freeze itself could be no more than a temporary stopgap, and that over a long period it would become unacceptable and ineffective. One reason was that the freeze included many inequitable and disequilibrium price and wage relationships. For example, some employers had raised wages but had not yet raised their prices; others were in the reverse position. Some recently negotiated wage increases had become effective and were therefore allowable; others had been negotiated but not yet effective and were therefore not allowable; and so on. Such maladjustments might be tolerated for 90 days, but probably not much longer. A second reason the freeze had to be only temporary was that it relied almost solely on voluntary compliance for enforcement.

When the 90-day freeze terminated in mid-November, it was followed by phase II—a flexible program to limit, but not prevent, increases in wages and prices. Administration of the program was entrusted to three bodies appointed by the president, who faced difficult problems in formulating standards for allowable wage and price increases. The standards announced were that, on the average, wages should rise no more than 5.5 percent and prices no more than 2.5 percent a year. It was believed that these wage and price standards would be mutually consistent if average productivity per unit of labor rose at an annual rate of 3 percent. However, the announcement of such average goals did not really solve the problem of standards, because it left unanswered such questions as: Which wages and prices should be allowed to rise more than the average, and how much more? Which should rise less than the average, and how much less? Under what conditions, and to what extent, should an employer experiencing an increase of wage rates be permitted to raise the prices of products? As might be expected, such questions proved to be highly controversial, and there were many well-publicized disputes in the administration of phase II.

Despite these difficulties, there is some evidence that the control system was at least partially and temporarily effective in preventing costs and prices from rising as fast as they would have otherwise. Overall, during the period of the initial freeze and phase II, which lasted until January 1973, the consumer price index rose at an annual rate of 3.3 percent.

At the same time, there were several reasons to believe that this system would become less effective with the passage of time, and especially as employment and output approached full employment levels. For example, a large number of products were exempted from price controls, and the system relied heavily on voluntary compliance due to the scarcity of enforcement facilities. These conditions virtually assured that price rises would become increasingly numerous, that those whose prices were more tightly controlled would become increasingly restive, that increases in the cost of living would militate against holding the line on wage increases, and that maladjustments of relative prices and wages would become more widespread.

In response to these kinds of considerations, the administration "decided to modify the price and wage controls program to make it more consistent with the further reduction in excess capacity seen at the time and also move toward the Administration's goal of eventually ending the controls."[5] The new program, known as phase III, generally reduced controls from those prevailing phase II and, furthermore, relied on self-administration rather than enforcement. At the time it was widely perceived that the controls were ending. While the move to phase III undoubtedly reduced the administrative burden of the controls, many economists worried that the controls were being weakened when excess capacity was declining, precisely when they might be needed most. Those fears had considerable justification.

INTERNATIONAL ASPECTS OF THE NEW ECONOMIC PLAN

Termination of convertibility of the dollar into gold and other reserve assets was a severe shock to the international monetary system. The most immediate impact was on the stability of exchange rates, because the dollar was now free to float. American authorities would no longer sell reserve assets or purchase dollars to limit declines of exchange rates on the dollar, nor would they buy reserve assets or sell dollars to depress the dollar in terms of other currencies. The behavior of exchange rates was to be determined by other participants in the market, including both private transactors and official foreign institutions. However, both the president and the secretary of the Treasury made clear their determination that exchange rates on other currencies should rise markedly in terms of the dollar. For many weeks they made no specific recommendations, but it was rumored that they would insist on an average appreciation of other currencies in the range of 12 to 15 percent.

The reaction of most foreign officials to changes of such magnitude was shock and disapproval. They contended that such large increases in ex-

[5]*Economic Report of the President.* Washington, D.C.: Government Printing Office, February 1974, p. 89.

change rates on their currencies would seriously damage both their export industries and their import-competing industries, and might precipitate an economic recession. Nevertheless, most countries allowed their currencies to float, and gradually the exchange rates on their currencies rose.

ECONOMIC DEVELOPMENTS, MID-1971–EARLY 1975

After the introduction of the new "game plan" and more stimulative monetary and fiscal policies, the pace of economic activity quickened. From the third quarter of 1971 to the end of 1972, real GNP grew at an annual rate of 6½ percent. The unemployment rate, which was about 5¾ percent at mid-1971, stayed at roughly this level for the remainder of 1971. Then, however, it gradually declined throughout 1972, reaching about 5 percent at year-end. As noted earlier, during this period, which includes the initial freeze and phase II, the consumer price index rose at an annual rate of 3.3 percent.

The economic record from the beginning of 1973 to mid-1975 is shown in Table 20–2. Starting in 1973, economic policy became more restrictive, and over the last three quarters of the year real GNP grew at 2 percent annual rate. The slowdown in the economy was brought about by fiscal and monetary policy in the hope of moderating inflationary pressures. As such, the actual behavior of prices was an extreme disappointment to policy makers. After rising at 3.3 percent rate during the freeze and phase II, the consumer price index advanced at an 8.3 percent rate from January to June 1973. Spurred by public pressure to "do something," phase III was abandoned and a second freeze was introduced in June 1973. After 60 days this was replaced by a phase IV that in several ways was stricter than phase II. Nevertheless, the rate of inflation did not abate. From June to December 1973 the consumer price index advanced at a 9.6 percent rate. Inflation, if anything, was accelerating, and the economy had yet to feel the full impact of the dramatic fourfold increase in oil prices at the end of 1973.

Quite evidently then, 1974 began with the economy in considerable difficulty. And in fact, during 1974 things got distinctly worse. The slowdown in economic growth that had taken place in the last three quarters of 1973 turned into a full-fledged recession in the first quarter of 1974. Real GNP

TABLE 20–2 Some Key Economic Indicators, Quarterly, 1973–1975 (In percentages)

	1973				1974				1975	
	I	II	III	IV	I	II	III	IV	I	II
Unemployment rate	4.9	4.8	4.7	4.7	5.0	5.1	5.5	6.4	8.1	8.7
Growth rate of real GNP	11.0	0.5	2.4	3.3	−4.0	0.4	−2.5	−5.2	−8.2	4.9
Inflation rate of GNP deflator	6.7	7.2	7.0	8.6	7.5	10.4	10.8	12.1	10.7	5.2

declined for four of the next five quarters and by the first quarter of 1975 stood 5 percent below its peak level in the fourth quarter of 1973. Particularly hard hit was housing, which over the same period declined 40 percent in real terms. The unemployment rate, which had turned up in late 1973, increased only slowly at first, hitting 5½ percent in July 1974. Thereafter it steadily and dramatically rose, reaching a peak of about 9 percent in May 1975.

Despite the dramatic slowdown in the economy that produced what was then the severest recession of the postwar period, the rate of inflation continued to be high throughout 1974. The consumer price index rose about 12 percent during 1974, the largest increase since 1947. Seemingly perversely, in the face of these developments, the controls program embodied in phase IV was abandoned in April 1974 when its authorization expired. The administration did not try to extend this authorization, nor was there substantial support in Congress for an extension. Despite the good intentions of the controls, it was perceived by many that they had failed to accomplish their objectives. Reasons for this are likely to be debated for many years to come.

MONETARY AND FISCAL POLICIES, MID-1971–EARLY 1975

As noted earlier, one of the purposes of both the system of wage and price controls and the termination of the convertibility of the dollar was to achieve greater freedom to expand aggregate demand in order to reduce the unemployment and underutilization of capacity that still prevailed in August 1971. Both fiscal and monetary policies were used for this purpose.

FISCAL POLICIES

Expansionary fiscal actions included both tax reductions and expenditure increases by the federal government. Tax reductions were granted to both business and individuals, and substantial expenditure increases in 1972 came about as a result of increases in social security benefits and a jump in federal grants-in-aid to state and local governments. At the beginning of 1973, fearing a rekindling of inflationary pressures, fiscal policy moved toward restraint and continued this restrictive stance into 1974. Parts of this restrictiveness came about from an unlegislated increase in taxation stemming from bracket creep, the phenomenon whereby inflation pushes individuals into higher tax brackets.

At the same time that fiscal policy was tightening because of the automatic responsiveness of the tax system, consideration was being given to discretionary fiscal restrictions. In early October of 1974 President Ford proposed placing a ceiling on federal spending and enacting a 5 percent temporary income tax surcharge on corporations and upper-income families. The president was advocating a more restrictive stance for fiscal policy just as the recession was assuming epidemic proportions. It was not until early January of 1975 that the president had a change of heart and conceded that it was appropriate to "shift our emphasis from inflation to recession." The result of this was the Tax Reduction Act of 1975, which was signed into law in March. The primary components of the act were a one-time rebate of 1974 taxes of about $8 billion and a temporary one-year reduction in personal income taxes of about $12 billion. Many economists were disappointed by both the size and the temporary nature of these actions. They regarded them as too little, too late.

Taken as a whole, the fiscal policy record from 1971 to 1975 left much to be desired. As summed up by one perceptive analyst of fiscal matters, Alan Blinder:[6]

> It would be hard to imagine a period of time that provided more ammunition for the opponents of discretionary fiscal policy than did the years 1972 to 1975, when, it seems, fiscal policy did almost everything wrong. With the advantages of hindsight, at least, it is clear that the government pumped up aggregate demand to an unhealthy degree before the 1972 election. Not only did this undermine the controls program, ... but also added to the stockpile of suppressed inflation that was awaiting us when controls were lifted. While a shift in policy was clearly imperative in 1973, the turn toward restriction was much too abrupt ... Only as the recession hit bottom were antirecessionary tax cuts enacted. And then the authorities weakened the effects by making them temporary.

> This is clearly not a record to be proud of.

MONETARY POLICIES

Monetary policy during this period has been indicted along similar lines as fiscal policy. As suggested by Table 20–3, the expansionary monetary policies that had been in effect since early 1970 were maintained after August 1971. During 1972 and early 1973 the growth rate of money was particularly rapid, and by now there is relatively wide agreement that the Fed pumped up the economy to an unhealthy degree during this period. Some have suggested that the Fed was misled by the rising Treasury bill rate during 1972 (see Table 20–3), and therefore interpreted its policy as a

[6]A. Blinder, *Economic Policy and the Great Stagflation.* New York: Academic Press, 1979, p. 141.

TABLE 20–3 Key Financial Variables, 1971–1973 (In percentages)

	1971		1972				1973			
	III	**IV**	**I**	**II**	**III**	**IV**	**I**	**II**	**III**	**IV**
Treasury bill rate	5.0	4.2	3.4	3.8	4.2	4.9	5.7	6.6	8.3	7.5
Corporate bond rate	7.6	7.3	7.2	7.3	7.2	7.1	7.2	7.3	7.6	7.7
Growth rate of M-1	4.9	4.3	10.2	4.9	11.2	10.7	3.0	8.1	2.3	7.7

restrictive one. If so, we have yet another example of the danger of using interest rates alone as an indicator of the thrust of monetary policy.

Like fiscal policy, monetary policy became somewhat more restrictive in 1973. The money supply increased at about a 4½ percent rate in the first three quarters of the year, a sharp drop from the 9¼ percent rate experienced during 1972. Short-term interest rates soared during the first three quarters of 1973 and reached record-breaking levels. For example, the Treasury bill rate, which had stood at about 5 percent in December 1972, jumped to over 8½ percent in August 1973. The federal funds rate rose to about 11 percent in September, up from about 5½ percent at the beginning of the year.

As market interest rates rose, as in 1966 and 1969, deposits at commercial banks became less attractive than alternative open-market assets. Contrary to the earlier experience, when there were large outflows of funds from commercial banks, measures were taken to ensure that commercial banks could compete for funds. In particular, interest rate ceilings on large certificates of deposits maturing in 90 days or more were lifted in May 1973. The ceilings on large short-term CDs had been lifted in 1970. As a consequence of these two developments, the volume of large CDs increased from $44 billion in January 1973 to $67 billion in August, a sharp contrast to the sizable decline in 1969. At the same time, however, restraint was maintained by more than doubling the marginal reserve requirement on large CDs.

In late 1973 monetary policy had adopted a slightly easier posture, largely in response to the economic dislocations stemming from the Middle East oil embargo, and short-term interest rates eased off a bit. After February 1974, however, the Federal Reserve, once again concerned with inflationary developments, returned to its earlier restrictive stance. In the months that followed, monetary restraint in conjunction with continued rapid inflation and strong business demands for credit combined to produce new historical highs in interest rates. The Treasury bill rate rose to 8¾ percent, and the federal funds rate to 13½ percent, shortly after midyear.

The tightening of credit was accompanied by fears of a general liquidity squeeze. These fears were fueled by the well-publicized difficulties (and eventual failure) of the Franklin National Bank in New York. There was also concern that a number of nonfinancial business failures were imminent. To damp these apprehensions, the Federal Reserve announced its willingness to serve as a lender of last resort to nonbanking firms as well as to banks. This helped calm financial markets regarding the possibility of serious financial instability.

Monetary policy during the 1974–1975 recession has been subject to some debate. As the extent of the recession became more apparent, the Fed did take some steps to ease monetary policy. At the time, however, observers with such diverse views as Paul Samuelson and Milton Friedman joined in condemning the Fed for pursuing an overly restrictive policy. Testifying before Congress in February 1975, Friedman cited the small money growth rates between June 1974 and January 1975 and argued that they "surely contributed to the recent deepening of the recession." Soon thereafter Samuelson echoed this view and charged that "if we go into a depression, the Fed will justly bear much of the blame."[7]

In retrospect, while the Fed certainly did not carry out a vigorous anti-recessionary program, these assessments probably overstate the restrictive position of monetary policy. The reason for this is, as we have seen earlier, that it was during this period that the demand for money was undergoing a substantial shift. This produced an increase in velocity, which meant that a given volume of money could support a larger volume of transactions. Consequently, the apparently anemic money growth rates during the last two quarters of 1974 and the first quarter of 1975 were not as restrictive as might be thought at first blush. Indeed, by March 1975 the federal funds rate had dipped to 5½ percent, a far cry from its peak of 13½ percent eight months earlier. In this instance we may have a situation in which money proved to be the deficient indicator and interest rates were perhaps somewhat more reliable. Nevertheless, it should be emphasized that had the shift in money demand not taken place, Samuelson's assessment might have unhappily proved true. Whether one should credit the Fed with blind luck or consummate skill in this matter we leave to the intrepid reader to decide.

THE RECOVERY AND EXPANSION, 1975–EARLY 1980

The economy bottomed out in the first quarter of 1975. At that point real GNP stood about 6 percent below its previous peak in the fourth quarter of 1973. Beginning with the spring of 1975, production, employment, and income all started to rise. Over the next year real GNP advanced at a healthy clip, which, however, only served to restore real GNP to slightly above its level at the end of 1973.

The unemployment rate, which had reached a peak of about 9 percent in May 1975, declined to just under 8 percent in January 1976. However, after the first quarter of 1976 real GNP advanced at a much-reduced rate and progress on the unemployment front slowed. At year-end 1976 the unemployment rate stood at about 7½ percent. The improvement in inflation was somewhat more dramatic, as the earlier extended decline in real output finally served to bring down the rate of inflation. From April 1975 to the end of the year, the various price indexes increased in the range of 6–7 percent. And for 1976 as a whole, the consumer price index rose at a 5 percent rate. While these rates might have seemed high by historical standards, they marked a substantial slowdown from the double-digit rates that had prevailed during 1974.

[7]Cited in Blinder, op. cit., p. 189.

POLICY DURING THE RECOVERY

In retrospect, the recession appears to have ended at just about the time that Congress was enacting the 1975 tax cuts. Because of their temporary nature the effectiveness of these tax cuts has been subject to heated debate, but they undoubtedly provided support for the recovery. A further stimulus was provided by the extension of these tax cuts into the first half of 1976.

As for monetary policy, there was much debate over the proper course of action during the initial stages of the recovery. In May 1975, for the first time, the Fed publicly announced its target ranges for money growth rates: 5–7½ percent for M-1 and 8½–10½ percent for M-2. Many observers, including some in the Fed, thought these rates would not be adequate to finance the recovery. The chairman of the Board of Governors, Arthur Burns, insisted that they would be adequate because of the rise in velocity that typically accompanied a cyclical upswing. With hindsight he proved correct, although as we have seen, his case was aided by the greater-than-normal increase in velocity stemming from the shift in money demand. Monetary policy in 1976 continued on roughly a 6 percent track for M-1 growth. One observer has described policy during this period as follows:

> The proceedings of the FOMC in 1976 were characterized by nothing if not blandness. During the entire year, the Committee's basic policy directive never changed, its short-run operating instructions had only minor changes, and there were hardly any dissents from the majority views.[8]

ECONOMIC DEVELOPMENTS, 1977–1980

The recovery of the economy continued in 1977. The growth rate of real GNP picked up from its pace in the last part of 1976 and advanced at a strong clip in 1977. The unemployment rate registered a further improvement and stood at 6.6 percent in the fourth quarter of the year. While the inflation rate did accelerate a bit, it had not yet advanced to a worrisome stage.

The economic expansion continued throughout 1978, and unemployment registered a further improvement. Inflation, however, accelerated to 9 percent. This generated sufficient concern among policymakers that they began implementing aggregate demand policies to restrict economic growth.

Economic growth did slow in the first quarter of 1979, and in the second quarter, GNP actually declined —the first drop in real GNP since 1975. At the time, many economists were forecasting the onset of a full-fledged recession. From the point of view of numerous observers, the recession appeared to be just what the doctor ordered to restrain what by now had turned into a serious inflation. Indeed, at the start of 1979 inflation was racing along at a 13 percent rate. The economy, however, like a recalcitrant

---

[8]Blinder, op. cit., p. 195.

patient refused to take its medicine, as real GNP growth picked up after midyear. This did nothing to help the inflation situation, which was further aggravated by a huge rise in energy prices (37 percent for 1979 as a whole).

To many economists, the resilience of the economy proved surprising. There was some speculation that consumers, rather than being turned off by inflation, actually accelerated their purchases because they expected prices to be still higher in the future. Such considerations are probably particularly important for durable goods, including housing. Thus, for example, high *nominal* mortgage interest rates may have been perceived as quite low (or even negative) *real* rates. Relative to previous periods of high nominal interest rates, in 1979 housing was also spared the effects of financial disintermediation. As we have seen, the major reason for this was the growth of money market certificates, which helped to bolster deposits at thrift institutions.

The consequences of the resilience of the economy were all too evident as 1980 began. From November 1979 to March 1980, the CPI advanced at a 16 percent rate, while lurking in the background were further rises in energy costs. The somewhat hectic economic developments from 1977 to the present considerably complicated the task of monetary and fiscal policy.

FISCAL AND MONETARY POLICY, 1977–1980

We begin our discussion at the start of 1977, when the task of policymakers seemed simple enough—to continue support for the recovery while keeping an eye out for inflationary pressures. As we have seen, of course, our tale does not have a happy ending.

FISCAL POLICY

Soon after the Carter administration came to office in 1977, it proposed a fiscal stimulus package to raise growth in real output and to make further inroads on unemployment. However, during the first quarter of 1977 real GNP growth accelerated. As a consequence, Congress considerably trimmed this proposal. When ultimately enacted, the Tax Reduction and Simplification Act of 1977 provided a relatively minor stimulus package.

Another tax development in 1977, and of considerably more consequence, was the passage of the social security amendments. These provided for major increases in social security taxes, both by raising the maximum amount of wages subject to social security tax and by increasing the tax rate. The first of these changes went into effect on January 1, 1978. One consequence of these amendments was that a considerable degree of fiscal drag was built into the system. A second source of fiscal drag came from the interplay of inflation and the progressive structure of individual income tax rates. In particular, as inflation accelerated, more individuals moved into higher tax brackets, and inflation once again was the source of an unlegislated tax increase. It was largely to counter this drag that the Revenue Act of 1978 was enacted. It provided for a small cut in business and personal taxes—less than the tax increase stemming from social security and inflation.

Despite the several tax cuts, over the three years 1977–1979 fiscal policy assumed a progressively tighter stance. Perhaps the simplest measure of this is what we have called the full employment budget—that is, the surplus or deficit that would prevail if the economy were operating at full employment. In 1977 this budget showed a deficit of $19 billion, in 1978 a smaller deficit of $12 billion, and in 1979 a surplus of about $10 billion. By any standard this represented a steady swing toward fiscal restraint. Nevertheless, while the qualitative direction of fiscal policy was appropriate, in view of the deteriorating inflation performance in 1978, 1979, and early 1980, one can obviously take issue with whether there was a sufficient quantitative degree of restraint.

MONETARY POLICY

Throughout this period, the task of monetary policy was complicated by many new developments in the financial system. These developments served to shift the demand for money about in somewhat unpredictable ways. As a consequence, it was a somewhat tricky business to know the precise degree of restraint represented by any of the monetary aggregates. Furthermore, with high and varying rates of inflation, nominal interest rates were also of questionable use as a target of policy. Thus, if it appears that the Fed muddled about in this period, we at least have some idea of why this happened.

Figures 20–4 and 20–5 show some of the key financial variables. During both 1977 and 1978, the money supply, as measured by M-1, grew at a quite rapid rate, exceeding 8 percent in each year. The Fed at the time, however, was paying somewhat more attention to interest rates and, judged by this measure, seemed to be gradually tightening monetary policy. For example, the FOMC target for the federal funds rate increased from a range of 4¼–5 percent in January 1977 to a range of 6½–7 percent in January 1978. The increase in the tolerance range continued through 1978, and in December it stood at 9¾–10½ percent. Other short-term interest rates generally followed this same upward trend, with the Treasury bill rate rising from about 4½ percent in early 1977 to over 8½ percent at the end of 1978. These moves, intending to tighten monetary policy, were clearly prompted by a deteriorating inflation picture. Somewhat ironically, this same increase in inflation clouded the interpretation of nominal interest rates as measures of monetary tightness and probably meant that the Fed was not as stringent as it intended.

FIGURE 20–4
Percentage change in M-1, 1977–1980. (Quarterly data; changes expressed at annual rates.)

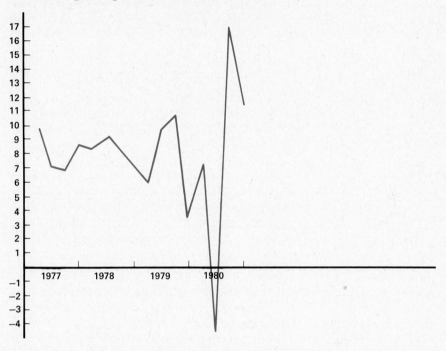

FIGURE 20–5
Short-term interest rates (in percent)

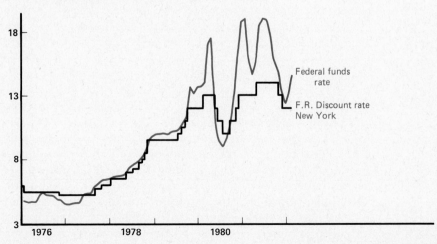

The economy received another inflationary jolt in December 1978 when the larger than expected increase in OPEC oil prices set the stage for poor performance on the inflation front in 1979. To be sure, this meant that the principal objective of monetary policy in 1979 was to help check accelerating inflation. The extent to which the Fed accomplished this, especially during the first three quarters of the year, is open to question. It is true that as the year progressed, the Fed became increasingly uneasy with the rapid growth in the monetary aggregates, and as the fourth quarter began, the Fed decided to get serious.

As noted in a previous chapter, on October 6, 1979, the Federal Reserve announced a major shift in its technique for implementing monetary policy. In particular, it abandoned adherence to a narrow range for the federal funds rate and proposed to address directly the control of the monetary aggregates via the provision of bank reserves. This, of course, did nothing to clarify the meaning of any particular aggregate. It simply promised better control over the aggregates, whatever they might mean. At the same time, the Federal Reserve raised the discount rate to 12 percent and established an 8 percent marginal reserve requirement on managed liabilities of member banks (see Chapters 6 and 12). As we will see, the new techniques did not prove to be an immediate success. First, however, we consider the next major policy move.

CREDIT CONTROLS

Inflationary pressures continued to mount during the last quarter of 1979 and inflation surged upwards in early 1980. In response, in February 1980 the Fed jacked up the discount rate and, through open-market operations, forced the federal funds rate to near 15 percent. Market interest rates established record highs, and the bond markets, to quote the financial press, "were in a state of shock." These records, however, did not last for very long. In the face of continued bad news on the inflation front, in mid-March the Fed announced yet another tightening of the monetary screws. Some of the actions taken at this time (see the box "Monetary and Credit Actions: March 14, 1980"), stemmed from the fact that President Carter declared an emergency under the Credit Control act of 1969, thus permitting the Fed to impose credit controls on the economy. Indeed, once the president had declared an emergency, under the 1969 act the Fed had virtually unlimited powers to control credit.

The Fed used these powers to introduce a series of special reserve requirements and voluntary programs to restrict the growth of both consumer and business loans. While the specific actions taken were not terribly extreme, the imposition of controls created an extraordinary amount of public confusion. There were reports that individuals thought the use of credit cards had been banned or retail stores were unsure that credit transactions were permissible. This confusion probably meant that the credit controls had some added bite.

MONETARY AND CREDIT ACTIONS: MARCH 14, 1980

In mid-March the Federal Reserve announced a series of monetary and credit actions as part of a general government program to help curb inflationary pressures. A number of the actions were specifically authorized by the president under the provisions of the Credit Control Act of 1969. Overall, the program included the following steps.*

1 A voluntary restraint program on the growth of bank credit aimed at keeping credit growth in the range of 6–9 percent per year.

2 A program of restraint on certain types of consumer credit. The cutting edge of this program was a 15 percent marginal "reserve requirement" on increases in specified kinds of consumer lending.

3 An increase from 8 percent to 10 percent in the marginal reserve requirement on the managed liabilities of large banks and an expansion of the applicability of the requirement. Large non-member banks were also subject to the 10 percent requirement on managed liabilities.

4 A 15 percent marginal reserve requirement was imposed on increases of total assets of money market mutual funds above the level of March 14.

5 A three percentage point surcharge on discount borrowings by large banks to discourage frequent use of the discount window. Including the surcharge, the discount rate was 16 percent.

*For a detailed description of the program, see the *Federal Reserve Bulletin*, April 1980, pp. 314–318.

The growth of business loans and consumer credit fell after the imposition of credit controls. At the same time, the growth of all the monetary aggregates slowed, with M-1 actually declining at annual rate of over 4 percent during the second quarter of 1980. With hindsight, it is apparent that this stringency in money and credit came at a time when the level of economic activity was already weakening. The net effect was that in the second quarter of 1980, real GNP declined at a record annual rate of 9 percent. Interest rates also fell dramatically, with the federal funds rate dropping from nearly 18 percent in March to about 9 percent in July (see Figure 20–5). The immediate objective of economic policy now turned to addressing the severe collapse in economic activity. The credit control program was abandoned in July of 1980. While the precise effects of this program are still being debated, the consensus seems to be that in a mere four months it had a substantial and rather unexpected impact on the economy.

Knowing what we know now, if we had it to do over again, it seems unlikely that such a program would have been put in place in 1980. Indeed, Congress was sufficiently disturbed by the use of the Credit Control Act in 1980 that it subsequently enacted legislation to remove it from the books.

DEVELOPMENTS SINCE 1980

As we have just seen, at least as far as the economy was concerned, 1980 did not begin in a particularly auspicious way. Indeed, as previously portrayed in Figures 20–1 and 20–2, after the first quarter of 1980 the economy entered a prolonged 2½ year period in which it was seemingly in a perpetual state of recession. The economy did bounce back a bit after its record decline in the spring of 1980, but real GNP again began declining in the spring of 1981 and by the end of 1982 real GNP was 1 percent below where it had stood three years earlier. Reflecting this weakness in the economy, the unemployment rate rose from 7½ percent at the end of 1980 to about 10¾ percent some two years later.

All this weakness was not without its payoff: Inflationary pressures gradually receded (see Figure 20–3). As measured by the GNP deflator, the inflation rate dropped from the 9 to 10 percent range during 1980 and 1981 to the 4 percent range during the following three years. The stability in the inflation rate in 1983 and 1984 was particularly noteworthy, given that this was a period in which the economy expanded briskly. When 1985 rolled around, there were, however, some worrisome signs on the horizon. To understand their origin, we need to look at fiscal and monetary policy.

FISCAL POLICY

One of the cornerstones of Ronald Reagan's 1980 presidential campaign was a promise to reduce taxes substantially for both individuals and businesses. At least qualitatively, this was in keeping with the general view prevailing at the time that the interaction of inflation and the tax system—via the infamous disease of bracket creep—was likely to raise individual tax burdens over the 1980s to unreasonable or at least politically unacceptable levels. Once elected, President Reagan delivered on his promise, and Congress passed the Economic Recovery Tax Act of 1981. The act contained large cuts in personal income taxes (roughly 23 percent spaced over three years), and substantial reductions in business taxes as well.

In selling the program, the administration emphasized the likely "supply-side" effects due to the stimulus the tax cuts would provide for both saving and investment. This was greeted with some skepticism, as were two other administration projections. The first was that the budget would be balanced in 1984, a forecast that was soon revised to be replaced by a projection of a $200 billion deficit. Indeed, the deficit problem remains to this day. The second projection was that the economy would grow strongly in 1982, even though monetary policy was restrictive. This came to be termed the "velocity problem" with the forecast. To understand this, we need to review what monetary policy was up to.

MONETARY POLICY

As noted earlier, in October 1979 the Fed embarked on an anti-inflationary policy involving the adherence to preset monetary targets. Moreover, officials announced an intention systematically to lower the target ranges as time passed. The actual outcome of the Fed's policy insofar as M-1 and interest rates are concerned is portrayed in Figures 20–4 and 20–5. What is perhaps most evident is the dramatic increase in variability in both M-1 and interest rates after the adoption of the new operating procedures in October 1979. The year 1980 stands out as one extreme example when the money supply grew at a 7 percent rate in the first quarter, declined at a 4 percent rate the second quarter, and then grew at a 14 percent rate over the last half of the year. The federal funds rate fell from 17 percent at the beginning of the year to 9 percent in midyear and then shot up to 19 percent by year end.

What is perhaps less evident from Figure 20–4 is that, despite these gyrations, the Fed did manage to reduce the growth rate of M-1 from 7.2 percent in 1979 to 6.6 percent in 1980 and 6.5 percent in 1981. It was a projected continuation of this pattern that raised serious doubts about the Reagan administration's forecast of healthy growth in 1982. As we have seen earlier, on average over the postwar period, a given growth in the money supply has supported a growth in nominal GNP of some three percentage points more. Thus, for example, if the money stock expanded by 4 percent from one year to the next, nominal GNP might expand by 7 percent. How this 7 percent was split into inflation and growth in *real* GNP depended on many factors. These aside, as a matter of arithmetic, if the rate of inflation was 4 percent, say, then real GNP could grow by 3 percent.

This average three percentage point difference between the growth of nominal GNP and the growth of the money stock is another way of saying that money turned over 3 percent faster each year or that velocity increased by 3 percent per year. However, the three percentage point growth in velocity is not an immutable constant. Rather, it reflects the fact that interest rates have generally risen over the postwar period. Put another way, in an environment of stable or declining interest rates, velocity would probably increase at a somewhat slower pace than history might suggest.

We are now able to see why adherence to restrictive monetary targets could give rise to a "velocity problem." If the Fed adhered to monetary growth of 5 percent, this would support growth in nominal GNP of at most 8 percent. As a matter of arithmetic, if nominal GNP were to advance by 8 percent, and if real GNP were to advance by 5 percent, then the rate of inflation would have to be 3 percent. If, on the other hand, inflation were to decline more slowly, then a 5 percent monetary target could lead to lackluster economic growth. Those who were pessimistic about the speed with which inflation could be reduced thus foresaw tight money leading to an extremely weak recovery in 1982.

As we saw in Chapter 18, if anything, the economy was weaker than expected as velocity, rather than increasing by 3 percent, declined by 3 percent in 1982. Indeed, as noted earlier, it was in the face of this extreme weakness in the economy that the Fed abandoned rigid monetary targeting in October 1982. Since that time, a rather more eclectic monetary policy has been pursued, and economic performance has improved. Flexibility in the conduct of monetary policy was also evidenced in a different way in 1984 with the financial difficulties experienced by the Continental Illinois Bank of Chicago. The Fed and other regulatory authorities took prompt action to assure that this one bank's difficulties did not spread to the banking system as a whole.

THE LEGACIES OF PAST POLICIES

While the behavior of the economy in 1983 and 1984 was most welcome after the three previous years of lackluster performance, a number of interrelated problems remained. In one way or another, all stemmed from an inappropriate *mix* of fiscal and monetary policies. Simply put, the tax cuts of the early 1980s, coupled with the substantial stepup in the growth of defense spending, have led to past, current, and prospective deficits in the federal budget of an extraordinary size. Not surprisingly, at the same time interest rates in the United States have remained high relative to other countries. At least judged by current inflation rates, long-term real interest rates have been especially high.

The level of interest rates in the United States has had consequences for our international payments as capital has flowed in from abroad. This in turn has raised the value of the dollar in terms of other currencies, making it extremely difficult for our export industries and encouraging imports. Indeed, for 1984 as a whole, we experienced a record trade deficit of $123 billion. While the mechanics of these international transactions are taken up in the next two chapters, common sense tells us that the United States is unlikely to be a capital importer on such a scale for an indefinite period of time. We need to address the problems of budget deficits to be able to refigure the mix of fiscal and monetary policy. Economists generally agreed that this was the number one item on the policy agenda in 1985.

OVERVIEW

With this chapter we conclude our examination of monetary and fiscal policy. It may be helpful to review quickly the progress and problems of policymaking, if only to emphasize that we have a lot to learn.

The Employment Act of 1946 was a major landmark in the history of American economic policy. Even as late as the early 1930s, few people would have believed that in less than two decades the federal government would accept responsibility for promoting "maximum employment, production, and purchasing power." As of 1985, we have achieved one major objective of the Employment Act; we have not had a major depression in the 40 years that have elapsed since World War II. Yet the performance of the economy has failed to meet fully the rising aspirations of the American people. Very large amounts of potential output and employment have been lost during eight economic recessions and some other periods of sluggish economic growth. Also, the economy has proved to be prone to price inflation. Much of the early inflation was associated with the aftermath of World War II, the Korean conflict, and the Vietnam war. While inflation in these periods seems readily explainable as a consequence of excess demand pressures, our recent inflationary experience appears to be a more complex beast. To be sure, excesss demand still very much matters, but we have had increasingly to contend with a variety of supply shocks such as OPEC oil price hikes, bad harvests, and our poor productivity performance. As events made clear, we knew a lot more about getting to full employment than we did about staying there in a noninflationary way. Evidently, then, the nation still faces the problem of reconciling its objectives of price stability, continuously high levels of employment, and economic growth.

Problems of implementation still remain. It was expected that the objectives of the Employment Act would be promoted primarily through the use of monetary and fiscal policies to regulate the behavior of aggregate demand, but the relative roles of monetary and fiscal policies were not specified. The record of fiscal policies for stabilization purposes has been spotty. The automatic fiscal stabilizers have been helpful on many occasions— although they have sometimes inhibited economic recovery, as in the early 1960s—and discretionary tax and expenditure policies have at times contributed to stability. In general, however, fiscal policies have disappointed those who expected them to be adjusted flexibly and quickly. There are many reasons for this: sluggish congressional procedures and an unwillingness to delegate authority to the president; continued lack of conviction on the part of some congressional leaders that economic stabilization should be a dominant consideration in fiscal policies; partisan politics; and so on.

The spotty performance of fiscal policy has shifted a major part of the stabilization burden to monetary policy, and fortuntely, monetary policies since World War II have been superior to those in earlier periods. The Federal Reserve has shown more wisdom in selecting its objectives and more sophistication in the use of the instruments at its command. However, even in the postwar period it was far from able to carry out policy in a precise way. This is partly because of the associated problems of inadequate economic forecasting and lags in the effect of monetary policy. However, in many instances the Federal Reserve was itself to blame for a poor choice of operating strategies. In more recent years the Federal Reserve has had the added burden of coping with a rapidly changing financial system. It remains to be seen what form the system will ultimately take and whether the Federal Reserve will be able to innovate as quickly as the participants in financial markets seem able to.

SUMMARY

1 The two decades after 1965 have been extremely turbulent ones, both for the economy and for policymakers. Troubles began at the end of 1965 when a rapid Vietnam defense buildup was added to an economy already close to full employment. In the absence of any offsetting fiscal action, the task of restraining the resultant inflationary pressures fell to monetary policy alone. As a consequence the country was beset by the highest interest rates in more than 40 years, which had heavy impacts on the construction industry and the thrift institutions.

2 After the mini-pause in the economy in 1967, the inflation rate continued its upward march, rising to a peak of over 6½ percent in the autumn of 1969. In response, both fiscal and especially monetary policy turned restrictive in 1969, and this ultimately produced the 1969–1970 recession. When the inflation rate proved stubborn—a hint of things to come—the Fed at first resisted responding to the recession, but after several months the Fed did turn more stimulative.

3 By 1971 fears of inflation were again widespread, and in August the administration launched the first phase of a program of direct controls, aimed at moderating price and wage increases. While it is generally agreed that the program temporarily slowed inflation, by 1973 inflation was steadily worsening. To make matters worse, in late 1973 the economy was hit with an inflationary supply shock brought about by the price hike in OPEC oil. Somewhat ironically, soon thereafter the controls program was abandoned.

4 In the face of worsening inflation, economic policy became more restrictive in 1973. The economy slowed down in the spring of 1973 and entered a full-fledged recession in early 1974. The recession was extremely deep, but despite the dramatic drop in GNP, as the effects of the OPEC shock spread through the economy, inflation accelerated to double-digit levels. Stagflation had arrived in full force. While the recession was severe, fearing the inflationary consequences policymakers were slow to ease up.

5 The economy was hit with another oil shock at the end of 1978 and, over the next year, inflationary performance deteriorated. Monetary policy responded by tightening and by shifting techinques for implementing policy to place greater emphasis on control of the money supply. In early 1980, authorized by the president, the Fed also im-

posed credit controls. Interest rates soared to new records. The economy then entered a recession and interest rates fell sharply. But by year-end short-term interest rates were setting new records of over 20 percent.

6 Monetary policy continued to be tight in 1981 and by mid-year we began a prolonged recession which lasted until the end of 1982. With financial innovation and deregulation changing the normal behavior of the monetary aggregates, the Fed was probably restrictive to an unintentional degree. Realizing both the severity of the recession and its cause, in late 1982 the Fed modified its policy of strictly controlling the money supply, becoming more expansive. Thereafter the economy entered a period of strong economic growth.

SELECTED READINGS

Blinder, A. S. *Economic Policy and the Great Stagflation.* New York: Academic Press, 1979.

Economic Report of the President. Washington, D.C.: U.S. Government Printing Office, 1980–1985.

Heller, W. W., and M. Friedman. *Monetary vs. Fiscal Policy.* New York: Norton, 1969.

Okun, A. M. *The Political Economy of Prosperity.* Washington, D.C.: The Brookings Institution, 1970.

PART 6

INTERNATIONAL MONETARY RELATIONS

21

INTERNATIONAL PAYMENTS AND THE EXCHANGE RATE

Most of the discussion up to this point has concentrated on domestic aspects of money and finance. However, our financial institutions play an important role in transactions across national boundaries. In addition, our monetary policy has profound effects on other countries, and the financial policies of other countries affect monetary and financial conditions in this country.

The following two chapters explore some of the most important aspects of international financial relationships. In this chapter we examine the functions of money and finance in international transactions, the types of transactions that give rise to international payments flows, and the foreign exchange market. In the following chapter, we explore the principal institutional arrangements that facilitate international payments, international economic interdependence, and the recent history of the international financial system.

FUNCTIONS OF MONEY IN INTERNATIONAL TRANSACTIONS

The basic functions of money and finance in international trade are the same as those in domestic exchanges—that is, to facilitate exchange by decreasing the real cost of transacting, and thereby enable traders to exploit potential gains from trade.

International trade is, in the final analysis, the exchange of goods and services produced in one country for those produced in another. Because of international differences in preferences, endowment of productive factors, and relative efficiencies of producing specific types of commodities and services, the residents of two countries may be able to increase their welfare by trading with each other. Similarly, financial transfers that take advantage of international differences in real rates of return to capital may increase total real income in each of the countries taking part in the transactions.

The extent to which potential gains from trade can be realized depends on the efficiency and smooth functioning of international exchange processes. All the above types of exchanges might be possible under a barter system, but such a system would be clumsy and inconvenient. It would also be possible to make international payments by shipping precious metals in the form of coin or bullion, or by shipping paper money. However, the shipments of gold or paper money across national boundaries would be expensive and risky. Freight costs would be high, the risk of loss would be omnipresent, and the speed of transferring payments would depend on the speed of the transportation facilities. To avoid these costs and inconveniences, nowadays international payments, like many domestic payments, are generally made by quick electronic transfers of financial claims from payers to payees. The financial claims that serve as *quid pro quo* in international payments are usually deposit liabilities of commercial banks. In the next chapter we discuss the role commercial banks play in international financial systems.

TYPES OF INTERNATIONAL TRANSACTIONS AND THE BALANCE OF PAYMENTS

Three broad categories of international transactions give rise to payments between nations: purchases and sales of goods and services, gifts and grants, and purchases and sales of financial claims. The statistical record of all transactions taking place between one country's residents and the rest of the world is the nation's *balance of payments account*.

TRADE IN GOODS AND SERVICES

American exports of goods and services include not only exports of many types of commodities, but also many types of services, such as transportation services, financial services, services to foreign tourists in the United States, and services rendered by American property located abroad. On the other hand, Americans purchase from the rest of the world large amounts of imports of goods and services, including services supplied to American travelers abroad and services rendered by foreign property in the United States.

Our exports of goods and services (X) may be viewed not only as a receipt item in our balance of payments, but also as the value of foreign demands for output and as the value of our output made available for use by the rest of the world. Our imports (M) may be viewed not only as a payment item in our balance of payments, but also as the amount of our national income that is used to demand output from the rest of the world. The quantity $(X - M)$ is usually referred to as the *balance on goods and services*. This has been a net receipt item for the United States during most years since World War II, although it was a net payment item in 1977, 1978, and 1982 to 1984.

INTERNATIONAL GIFTS AND GRANTS

International gifts and grants are similar to domestic transfer payments in that the donor surrenders goods, services, or purchasing power without directly receiving anything of value in return. In the balance of payments accounts, gifts and grants are called *unilateral transfers*. They are a source of receipts when the United States receives gifts and grants from abroad and a payment item when Americans or the U.S. government export goods, services, or purchasing power without receiving compensation. In most years unilateral transfers are a net payment item for the United States.

TRADE IN FINANCIAL CLAIMS

All other transactions in the balance of payments involve purchases and sales of various types of financial claims. There are three broad categories of international transactions between the residents of different countries:

1 **DIRECT INVESTMENT.** Residents of one country purchase stocks in order to acquire entrepreneurial control over a business or enterprise in another country. In addition, direct investment occurs when an enterprise of one country starts a new subsidiary in another country.
2 **LONG-TERM PORTFOLIO INVESTMENT.** International transactions in securities with original terms to maturity of greater than one year.
3 **SHORT-TERM CAPITAL FLOWS.** Securities with original terms to maturity of less than one year.

Differences in the marginal productivity of capital among countries constitute a basic, long-term force inducing international flows of capital funds. These differences in the marginal productivity of capital from country to country result from differences in stocks of savings and capital goods relative to supplies of natural resources and labor, differences in technology, differences in managerial capacity, and so on. In a world characterized by perfect competition, absence of risk, and unfettered movements of funds, differences in the marginal productivity of capital would be reflected in differences in interest rates; residents in areas with high interest rates would sell financial claims in areas with low interest rates in order to command more capital; and the process would continue until the marginal productivity of capital and interest rates were equal in all areas. There are, of course, many obstacles to international purchases and sales of financial claims, including government restrictions, imcomplete knowledge of opportunities, and fear that property rights will not be protected. However, very large international capital flows do occur. Some of these are in response to basic long-term forces of the type described above, while others are in response to short-run factors such as cyclical fluctuations in national economies. In addition, basic portfolio considerations affect the international flow of financial claims.

For example, when comparing financial investment alternatives at home to those abroad, sophisticated investors seek to achieve the most favorable combination of yield, safety of principal, and liquidity. Other things being equal, the proportion of assets held in the form of claims against other countries will vary directly with the level of interest rates abroad relative to those at home. When interest rates rise in some countries and not in others, funds tend to flow from areas with lower rates to areas with higher rates. Residents of countries with the higher interest rates tend to lend more at home and less abroad, while residents of countries with the lower interest rates tend to lend less at home and more abroad.

A second factor affecting investors' choices among claims on domestic and foreign entities is relative safety of principal. Both domestic and foreign claims are subject to default risks and to the market risk that interest rates may increase in the future. Two other related types of risk should be mentioned. The first type, called political risk, results from possibilities of confiscation, refusal to allow payments to foreigners, emergence of a government that will not enforce private property rights, and so on. When such events are expected in a country, large capital outflows are often induced. The other type of risk is exchange risk. Exchange risk arises from the possibility of fluctuations in the *exchange rate*—that is, in the rate at which one currency trades for another.

Relative liquidity is a third factor affecting investors' choices among domestic and foreign financial claims. The very high liquidity of short-term claims against dollars makes them a popular investment for foreigners. However, expected changes in relative liquidity can induce large-scale movements of funds. For example, threats of war or other developments abroad that reduce expected liquidity of foreign claims can lead to large shifts of funds to the United States.

It is sometimes useful to lump together private sector transactions in short- and long-term financial claims. Americans pay for their purchases of both short- and long-term financial claims by sending liquid purchasing power abroad. Such purchases can be thought of as generating capital outflows or capital exports. On the other hand, the payments generated by sales of both short- and long-term financial claims by Americans to foreigners can be thought of as capital inflows or capital imports to the United

States. The quantity (capital exports − capital imports) measures the increase in a country's net financial claims on foreigners and is sometimes called the *balance on capital account.*

The final type of trade in financial claims is trade between central banks. Central banks hold stocks of "official reserve assets" in the form of claims against foreign moneys or other things that can be readily exchanged for foreign money, such as gold. When a central bank adds to its stock of official reserve assets by purchasing foreign exchange, it sends its home currency abroad. Sales of official reserve assets, on the other hand, are a source of receipts because buyers must pay for them.

THE BALANCE OF PAYMENTS IDENTITY

As already noted, a nation's balance of payments account shows for some stated period the flows of that nation's receipts from the rest of the world and its payments to the rest of the world. A schematic version of the balance of payments is given in Table 21–1.

Table 21–1 shows that for any stated period a nation's total receipts from international transactions must equal its total payments on international account. To look at this accounting requirement another way, we can rearrange Table 21–1 as follows:

(exports of goods and services − imports of goods and services)
    + (unilateral receipts − unilateral payments)
= (capital exports − capital imports) + net change in official reserves

The left-hand side of this equation, which is the sum of the balance on goods and services and net unilateral transfers, is called the *balance on current account.* Also, as defined above, the term (capital exports − capital imports) is known as the *balance on capital account.* Hence, an equivalent way to express Table 21–1 is as follows:

balance on current account
= balance on capital account + net change in official reserves

This equation, in either of its two equivalent forms, is sometimes called the *balance of payments identity.* It indicates that if the United States has a

TABLE 21–1 Components of the U.S. Balance of Payments

Receipts	Payments
1. Exports of goods and services	1. Imports of goods and services
2. Unilateral receipts	2. Unilateral payments
3. Sales of long-term claims	3. Purchases of long-term claims
4. Sales of short-term claims	4. Purchases of short-term claims
5. Sales of reserve assets	5. Purchases of reserve assets

deficit on current account, it must somehow decrease its claims against the rest of the world. This may be done by having the private sector import more capital than it exports. For example, capital imports will increase whenever U.S. citizens sell previously held foreign securities or foreign citizens decide to increase their holdings of dollar-denominated assets. However, with a current account deficit, if the balance on capital account is not sufficiently negative, then, from the identity above, we see that the government must fill the gap by selling foreign exchange (i.e., decreasing its stock of reserve assets).

SUMMARIZING THE BALANCE OF PAYMENTS ACCOUNTS

Either from Table 21–1 or, equivalently, from the balance of payments identity, we see that total receipts and payments must be equal. Yet a nation is sometimes said to have a surplus or a deficit in its balance of payments. These apparently conflicting views are easily reconciled. It would indeed be rare for a nation to have an exact balance of receipts and payments on every major class of transactions entering into its balance of payments. Instead, it usually experiences net receipts on some types of transactions, which must be balanced by net payments on others.

The general notion of a surplus or deficit is fairly straightforward: A nation is considered to have a surplus during a stated period if its net receipts on account of some types of transactions are balanced by net payments on other accounts in such a way as to improve its net international reserve position or its net international liquidity position. This can be reflected in a net increase in its stock of official international reserve assets, a decrease of selected types of debt liabilities to foreigners, or some combination of the two. A nation is said to have a deficit when its net payments on account of some types of transactions are balanced by net receipts on other accounts in such a way as to deteriorate its net international reserve or net international liquidity position. This can be reflected in a net decrease in its stock of official reserve assets, an increase of selected types of debt liabilities to foreigners, or a combination of the two. Unfortunately, however, there is no general agreement on specific definitions of these key terms. Nations use differing definitions, and the United States has employed several.

Since a nation's balance of payments must balance, the key to determining when a country faces an international payments imbalance is the distinction between autonomous and accommodating transactions. *Autonomous transactions* are transactions undertaken for normal commercial motives. Frequently autonomous transactions are influenced by the exchange rate—that is, by the rate at which one currency trades for another. International traders use exchange rates to transfer prices denominated in foreign currencies into their domestic currency equivalent so that they can "comparison shop" in the international market. We discuss exchange rate determination in the following section. *Accommodating transactions* differ from autonomous transactions in that they are not undertaken in pursuit of commercial profit. One common type of accommodating transaction is undertaken by a government or central bank in order to preserve or enforce a price (the exchange rate) in the foreign exchange market. It should be noted that the balance of payments identity implies that the sum of all accommodating transactions must be equal to but opposite in sign from the sum of all autonomous transactions.

Once all international transactions have been classified as autonomous or accommodating, a payments imbalance is defined as a situation in which the sum of all accommodating transactions is nonzero. Furthermore, it is the dollar size of the sum of the accommodating transactions that is taken as the numerical measure of the surplus or deficit in the balance of payments. From this discussion, it might seem to be a simple matter to measure the state of the balance of payments. Unfortunately, this is not the case. The reason is that the distinction between autonomous and accommodating transactions is not that clear-cut. It is possible to construct a wide variety of measures of imbalance. The conceptual basis for the various measures can be seen with the aid of Table 21–1.

One possibility is to define autonomous transactions as exports and imports of goods and services—that is, the first row in Table 21–1. If there is an excess of exports over imports, we would then say we have a surplus as measured by the *balance on goods and services account*. Alternatively, if imports exceed exports, we have a deficit on this account. A slightly expanded definition of autonomous transactions would include the second row of Table 21–1, unilateral receipts and payments. As we have seen, this gives rise to what we have termed the balance on current account.

A third possible measure of the balance of payments position would include the third row of Table 21–1, long-term capital flows, as autonomous transactions. Finally, if we also include the fourth row of Table 21–1, we arrive at the *official reserve transactions balance*. In other words, according to this definition, all transactions on the current and private capital account are autonomous. Put another way, the accommodating transactions are the net change during a period in U.S. official reserve assets plus the net change in U.S. liabilities to foreign official agencies.

Table 21–2 reports some of the various measures of the balance of payments for selected years. As Table 21–2 illustrates, the various measures do not always tell the same story, so these numbers need to be used with caution. Indeed, in recognition of this, in the mid-1970s the government agency responsible for these statistics stopped publishing any official measures of the balance of payments. Rather, it publishes the raw data and lets everybody roll their own favorite definition.

Aside from this embarrassment of riches in available definitions, there is another important problem of interpretation. To illustrate this point, let us keep things simple and suppose that we have somehow selected one of

TABLE 21–2 U.S. Balance of Payments: Various Measures (In millions of dollars)

	Balance on goods and services	Balance on current account	Official reserve transactions balance
1960	$ 5,132	$ 2,824	$ − 3,618
1970	5,625	2,331	− 9,389
1980	8,950	1,873	− 7,342
1981	13,186	6,339	215
1982	84	− 8,051	1,293
1983	− 31,937	− 40,790	− 4,599
1984	− 90,119	− 101,532	− 293

these measures as the basic measure of interest. The question we now need to answer is this: What does it mean for there to be a surplus or deficit in the chosen measure?

ECONOMIC INTERPRETATION

Perhaps the simplest way to see what is involved is to refer back to the balance of payments identity. As the use of the term *identity* implies, as a matter of accounting this expression must always hold. It is thus analogous to the identity of saving and investment encountered earlier. In that case, we saw that simply satisfying the saving-investment identity did not ensure equilibrium. Equilibrium required that *desired* saving and *desired* investment should be equal. If these two were not equal, income or interest rates had to change to bring about equality. Similar considerations apply in the case of the balance of payments.

In particular, equilibrium requires that the quantity of dollars foreigners desire to hold must be equal to the quantity of dollars Americans are willing to supply. If these two quantities are not equal, we have disequilibrium. And it is the extent of this disequilibrium that some particular surplus or deficit measure is trying to capture.

As with saving and investment, if there is a disequilibrium, certain adjustments must take place. In the short run this may simply take the form of the government stepping in and using its international reserve assets to bring about equality between supply and demand. But this can only temporarily remove a disequilibrium. In the longer run there must be an adjustment in some or all of the following—income, interest rates, prices, or exchange rates—for it is these variables that influence the various entries in the balance of payments identity. For example, U.S. income levels and the relative prices of foreign and domestic goods influence the extent to which we will import foreign goods. Similarly, interest rates, both here and abroad, influence the magnitude of capital flows. In the next chapter we examine in greater detail the ways in which nations adjust to balance of payments disequilibriums.

FOREIGN EXCHANGE MARKETS

The types of international transactions we described in the preceding sections give rise to a huge volume of exchanges of national moneys. For example, an American who receives a claim against French francs and does not want to spend in France or to hold French francs will offer them in exchange for dollars or for some other nation's money he or she wants to spend or hold. Other Americans who want to spend or hold moneys of other nations offer dollars in exchange for them. Similar transactions occur all over the world. The term *foreign exchange market* refers to all the facilities and processes involved in the exchange of claims against the various national moneys. The things bought and sold include small amounts of coin and larger amounts of paper money, but the great bulk of trading is in claims against banks denominated in the various national moneys. Some of these are payable on demand; others, only after a lapse of time. Short-term claims against nonbank debtors are also exchanged in these markets.

Whenever things are exchanged against each other, there must, of course, be some rate or ratio of exchange between them; there must be some type of "price." By the *exchange rate* between two monetary units we mean simply the number of units of one money required to buy one unit of the other. Either monetary unit may be employed as the unit for stating the price of the other. For example, a situation in which 2 German marks exchange for 1 U.S. dollar could be stated either as $1 = 2 marks or as 1 mark = ½ dollar. Also, a change in the exchange rate to $1 = 3 marks can be expressed either as a rise in the exchange rate on the dollar relative to the mark or as a decrease in the exchange rate on the mark relative to the dollar. An exchange rate may be determined like any other price—that is, by the supply and demand functions for foreign exchange. The exchange rate may also be pegged by an official agency that intervenes in the foreign exchange market by buying or selling official reserve assets to maintain the rate at a certain level.

Virtually all countries have some type of foreign exchange market, but some markets are more highly developed than others. Among the largest and most active are those in New York, London, Paris, Amsterdam, Brussels, Zurich, Frankfurt, and Rome. Exchange rates in different financial centers are kept nearly identical by arbitrage.

ARBITRAGE

Arbitrage is a general term in economics for buying something where it is cheap and selling it where it is dear. If the price of Japanese yen in New York falls below that in London by more than a small cost of transacting, profits can be made by buying yen in New York and selling them in London; such a transaction is called *foreign exchange arbitrage*.

Arbitrage also keeps exchange rates consistent across markets. Disregarding transactions costs, suppose you buy $10,000 worth of yen in New

York, sell it in London for German deutsche marks (DM), and then sell the DM for dollars in Paris. If you wind up with either more or less than $10,000, the exchange rates were inconsistent across the New York, London, and Paris foreign exchange markets. If you made a profit, and you and other arbitragers would continue to transfer funds across the three markets until the exchange rates were driven into consistency. If the proposed transaction involves a loss, of course it will not be undertaken. However, it would be possible to "reverse" the transaction and make a profit. (Make sure you see why this is so.)

This brings up the question: How are market exchange rates established?

THE EXCHANGE RATE

Exchange rates may be determined by free market forces—that is, by demand-supply conditions in exchange markets. The free market of freely floating exchange rate is said to be in equilibrium when it reaches a level at which the nations autonomous receipts from international trade in goods, services, and financial claims equal its autonomous payments. Equivalently, the equilibrium exchange rate is that rate which clears the market for foreign exchange.

Official agencies may intervene in foreign exchange markets to peg exchange rates at particular levels or to influence the behavior of exchange rates. When a government intervenes in the foreign exchange market by buying foreign exchange, the transaction is recorded in the balance of payments accounts as an increase in official reserve assets. In addition, the transaction may be interpreted as an accommodating transaction and an indication of balance of payments disequilibrium. Similarly, when a government intervenes by selling foreign exchange, the balance of payments accounts record a decrease in official reserve assets.

We will now describe exchange rate determination in detail for each of these two cases. We begin with the case in which there is no official intervention in foreign exchange markets.

FLEXIBLE EXCHANGE RATES

When official agencies do not peg exchange rates or otherwise intervene in the foreign exchange market, the exchange rate is determined by freemarket forces. To illustrate the principles involved in a system of freely floating exchange rates, we analyze the dollar price of the British pound sterling. We state our analysis in terms of the supply of and demand for sterling.

By the supply of sterling we mean a function or schedule showing the quantities of sterling that would be supplied in exchange markets per period of time at each of the various possible dollar prices of sterling. Its components are the payment items in the British balance of payments—amounts of sterling supplied to purchase imports of goods and services and to buy various types of financial claims from foreigners. By the demand for sterling we mean a function or schedule showing the quantities of sterling that would be demanded in exchange markets at the various possible dollar prices of sterling. The components of these demands for sterling are the receipt items in the British balance of payments—that is, quantities of sterling demanded to pay for British exports of goods and services and to purchase various types of financial claims from the British. Let us now use simple statics to show how supply and demand functions determine exchange rates.

THE SUPPLY FUNCTION FOR STERLING

The purpose of a supply schedule stating supply as a function of price is the usual purpose of isolating the effect of price (in this case, the exchange rate) on quantities supplied. Such a curve can be drawn only if we assume that all other conditions affecting supply are given and constant. Listed next are the principal factors that, for the moment, we assume to be given and constant.

1 The level of real income in Britain
2 The level of prices and costs in Britain relative to those of other countries
3 Levels of interest rates in Britain relative to those of other countries
4 Expectations as to future exchange rates on sterling
5 Tastes for British products relative to those of other countries
6 Other factors relevant to the productivity and comparative costs of British and foreign products

Later we will see how changes in these conditions tend to shift the supply function for sterling.

The supply function of sterling is represented by the *SS* line in Figure 21–1. It is shown as a positive function of the exchange rate on sterling; that is, the higher the exchange rate on sterling, the greater will be the quantity of sterling offered in the exchange market. The reason for this is that the higher the dollar price of sterling, the cheaper will be the sterling price of imports, the greater will be the quantity of imports demanded by Britain, and the greater will be the sterling value of imports if the price elasticity of British demands for imports, stated in terms of sterling prices, is greater than unity. This becomes clearer as we remember that increases in the dollar price of sterling are accompanied by decreases in the sterling price of the dollar. For example, a rate of £ = $1 is obviously the same as $1 = £1; £1 = $1.50 is equivalent to $1 = £⅔; and £1 = $2 is equivalent to $1 = £½. Suppose the American price of some export to Britain is $1 per unit. In terms of sterling, the cost of the import to the British will be £1 if the exchange rate is £1 = $1 and only £½ if the exchange rate is £1 = $2.

THE DEMAND FUNCTION FOR STERLING

The demand function for sterling, represented by the *DD* line in Figure 21–1, asssumes that all other conditions except the exchange rate are given and constant. The most important of these conditions are those just listed as influencing the supply function of sterling, with the exception that we would now substitute the level of real income in the rest of the world for the level of real income in Britain. Later we see how changes in these conditions can increase or decrease the demand function for sterling. The demand function for sterling is shown as a negative function of the exchange rate on sterling; that is, the higher the exchange rate on sterling, the smaller will be the quantity of sterling demanded in exchange markets. This is because higher exchange rates on sterling make British exports of goods and services more expensive in terms of other currencies. For example, suppose that the sterling price of some British good is £1. The dollar cost of the good will be $1 at an exchange rate of £1 = $1, and $2 at an exchange rate of £1 = $2.

Thus, we find that, other things being equal, a nation's exports are discouraged by a rise in the exchange rate on its currency and encouraged by a decrease in the exchange rate on its currency.

We are dealing with the case in which the authorities do not attempt to peg exchange rates or intervene directly to affect their behavior, but allow exchange rates to be determined by market forces. In this case the exchange rate can be in equilibrium only when the quantity of sterling demanded is exactly equal to the quantity supplied, leaving neither an excess demand nor an excess supply. Figure 21–1 shows that, with the given *DD* and *SS*

FIGURE 21–1
Demand for and supply of sterling

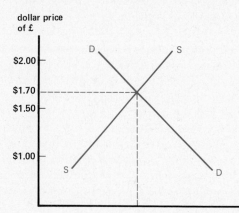

Quantity of
£ per period

curves, this can occur only at the exchange rate of £1 = $1.70. At any higher rate there would be an excess supply of sterling because British imports would be cheaper in terms of sterling, and the demand for sterling would be smaller because British exports would be more expensive to foreigners. On the other hand, there would be an excess demand for sterling at any lower exchange rate on sterling. Demands for sterling would be larger because the cost of British exports in terms of foreign currencies would be lower, and supplies of sterling would be smaller because the sterling price of imports would be higher.

SHIFTS OF SUPPLY AND DEMAND FUNCTIONS IN EXCHANGE MARKETS

We will now use comparative statics to show how changes in selected economic and financial conditions can shift demand and supply functions in exchange markets, thereby tending to change exchange rates. We pay special attention to changes in price levels, income levels, and interest rates.

CHANGES IN LEVEL OF BRITISH PRICES AND COSTS RELATIVE TO LEVELS ABROAD

Suppose, for example, that Britain experiences a domestic inflation of its price and cost levels. As the sterling prices of British products rise, the demand curve for sterling will shift to the left and downward. British goods will now be more expensive at each level of exchange rates, and British exports will be discouraged. This rise in price levels will also shift the supply curve of sterling downward and to the right. As the prices of competing domestic products rise, the British will demand more imports at each exchange rate on the dollar.

Thus, we find that if British prices rise more than prices elsewhere, the exchange rate on sterling will tend to be lowered, both by a shift in the demand function for sterling downward and to the left and by a shift in the supply function of sterling downward and to the right. When a country inflates its domestic price levels significantly while prices elsewhere remain relatively constant, it usually cannot balance its receipts and payments without reducing its exchange rate to maintain its exports and discourage imports.

CHANGES IN LEVEL OF REAL INCOME IN BRITAIN

A rise of real income in Britain would tend to increase British imports at each level of exchange rates and thereby to increase the supply of sterling in exchange markets. It would therefore tend to lower the sterling exchange rate if the demand schedule for sterling remained constant. On the other hand, a fall of real income in Britain would tend to decrease the British demand for imports at each exchange rate, to decrease the supply of sterling at each exchange rate, and to raise the sterling rate in exchange markets.

CHANGES IN LEVEL OF REAL INCOME IN THE REST OF THE WORLD

An increase of real incomes in the rest of the world tends to raise the demand for British exports at each exchange rate, to increase the demand for sterling at each exchange rate, and to raise the rate on sterling. Note that, to the extent that the rise of foreign demands for British exports is allowed to raise the exchange rate on sterling. Britain may be enabled to escape inflationary effects on its domestic price level. On the other hand, a decline of real incomes abroad tends to decrease the demand for British exports at each exchange rate, to lower the demand for sterling at each rate, and to reduce the exchange rate on sterling. By allowing the sterling exchange rate to fall, thereby making British exports cheaper in foreign moneys, Britain may be able to reduce the extent to which the decrease of foreign demand will reduce British exports, and may do this without reducing the sterling prices of its exports.

CHANGES IN LEVEL OF INTEREST RATES IN BRITAIN RELATIVE TO LEVELS ELSEWHERE

Suppose British interest rates rise relative to those elsewhere. This will at least reduce capital outflows from Britain, and may induce inflows. Thus, by decreasing the supply of sterling or increasing the demand for sterling, it will tend to raise the sterling exchange rate. A fall of interest rates in Britain relative to levels elsewhere tends to have the opposite effect—that is, to reduce the demand for sterling and increase the supply of sterling for international capital flow purposes.

CHANGES IN EXPECTATIONS CONCERNING FUTURE STERLING EXCHANGE RATES

Changes in expectations may be very important in evoking speculative capital flows. Suppose, for example, that expectations arise that the rate on sterling will fall sharply in the future. The demand curve for sterling may be shifted to the left and downward immediately as people postpone purchases of sterling. The supply curve of sterling may be shifted to the right and downward as people sell sterling and buy foreign moneys. Both the decrease in the demand for sterling and the increase in its supply will cause a decrease in the exchange rate on sterling. This decline in the sterling rate will, of course, stimulate British exports and discourage British imports.

Quite evidently, in a system of flexible exchange rates many factors can cause movements in exchange rates. We will now discuss exchange rate determination in the presence of government intervention.

PEGGED EXCHANGE RATES

Until quite recently, the most common exchange rate policy has been that of *pegging* exchange rates within narrow limits over considerable periods of time. Almost all the major national currencies were linked through fixed rates under the international gold standard that prevailed during the years preceding World War I. Most nations returned to pegged rates during the 1920s following the breakdown of the old system during World War I. After World War II, an international organization known as the International Monetary Fund (IMF) was established to oversee the functioning of the pegged exchange rate system.

Under the initial IMF agreements, the exchange rate was permitted to fluctuate within a band from 1 percent above to 1 percent below some fixed rate. Thus, for example, if the dollar price of the British pound was pegged at $2.00, the actual exchange rate could fluctuate between $1.98 and $2.02. We discuss the functions of the IMF in greater detail in the next chapter.

The technique of pegging exchange rates, like that of pegging the price of wheat, the price of gold, or the price of a government security, is basically simple. A monetary authority or someone else stands ready to supply at some fixed price all the nation's money that is demanded from it at that price, and to demand at some fixed price all the nation's money that is offered to it at that price. As we saw earlier, actual transactions take place in the foreign exchange market when national moneys are bought and sold. For example, suppose the British monetary authority undertakes to prevent the exchange rate on sterling from rising above $2.02 and from falling below $1.98. Whenever the exchange rate on the pound rises to $2.02 (that is, when the rate on the dollar falls to £1/$2.02), the monetary authority uses sterling to demand dollars. On the other hand, when the exchange rate on the pound falls to $1.98 (i.e., the exchange rate on the dollar rises to £1/$1.98), the monetary authority sells dollars in exchange for sterling. For this purpose it needs a sufficient supply of dollars, gold, or other official reserve assets that can be sold for dollars, or the ability to borrow dollars.

If nonofficial demands for and supplies of sterling are such as to equalize the demand for and the supply of sterling at some rate between $2.02 and $1.98, the government authority need not intervene at all. But the supply of sterling may exceed other demands for it at the support price. For example, at the rate £1 = $1.98 the supply of sterling may greatly exceed other demands for sterling, so that the authority must sell large amounts of its gold and foreign exchange holdings to buy an amount of sterling equal to the difference between its supply and the demand. Such a situation is depicted in Figure 21–2, where the amount of disequilibrium is indicated by *AB*. If this disequilibrium continues for very long, Britain may be drained of all its holdings of gold and foreign exchange.

It should be noted that a government can intervene in the foreign exchange market to influence exchange rate behavior without committing itself to pegging the exchange rate at a particular level for any length of time. When central banks intervene intermittently, we have a system that combines features of freely floating and pegged exchange rate systems. Such a combined system of exchange rate determination is known as a *managed float* or sometimes, more pejoratively, as a *dirty float*. We describe

FIGURE 21–2
Disequilibrium with pegged exchange rates

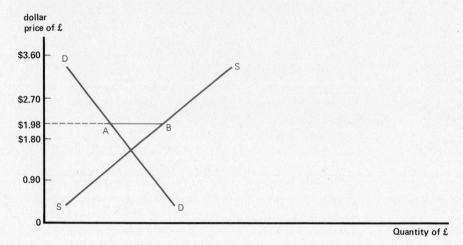

the considerations that influence a nation's choice of an exchange rate system in the following chapter.

FORWARD EXCHANGE MARKETS

Trading in foreign exchange markets includes not only currencies for immediate delivery, or *spot exchange*, but also *forward exchanges*, or currencies to be delivered on a specified date in the future. Forward contracts generally mature in 30, 60, 90, or more days from the date of execution. Transactions in forward exchange markets are similar to futures transactions in commodity markets.

Participants in forward exchange markets have several different purposes. One is to speculate. For example, suppose today's exchange rate on sterling for delivery in 90 days is £1 = $1.30. A speculator will contract to buy sterling at this rate if she believes that the spot exchange rate in 90 days will be higher than £1 = $1.30. On the other hand, she will sell sterling forward (i.e., promise to deliver sterling in 90 days) if she believes that she will be able to cover the contract by purchasing spot sterling at a rate less than £1 = $1.30 three months hence.

A second major function of forward exchange markets is to reduce exchange risks in international transactions. The following example illustrates the presence of exchange risk in international trade and shows how traders protect themselves from it.

Suppose that an American importer of British goods is obliged to pay the shipper in sterling 90 days hence. The importer can simply wait until the payment is due and then go to the spot market and purchase enough sterling to cover the obligation. However, if he postpones the purchase of sterling for 90 days, he runs the risk that the dollar price of sterling will rise in the interim, thus increasing the dollar equivalent of his original sterling liability. To avoid this risk, the importer can go to the forward exchange market to purchase a contract that promises delivery in 90 days of enough sterling to cover his sterling obligation. This type of transaction in the foreign exchange market is called *hedging*. Hedging reduces or eliminates exchange risk for international traders. International borrowers and lenders also use the forward exchange market to eliminate or reduce their exposure to exchange risk.

Because the currency in which an international loan is denominated may decline in value before the loan is repaid, international lenders face exchange risk. On the other hand, international borrowers face the risk that the currency in which their borrowings are denominated may increase in value before the debts are repaid, thus increasing their liabilities. The forward exchange market allows borrowers and lenders who do not want to risk an exchange rate change to "cover" the exchange risk and insure the domestic currency value of their debts or assets. Such transactions are called *covered interest arbitrage.*

Covered interest arbitrage is not complex in principle, but its mechanics are difficult to remember. An *interest arbitrageur* is an international lender (borrower) who compares interest rates across countries looking for the highest yield (the lowest-cost funds). However, the decisions of interest arbitrageurs are also influenced by spot and forward exchange rates. The following example shows how interest rates and exchange rates interact to determine the most profitable course of action.

We concentrate on two countries, the United States and Britain, and assume that an American lender wishes to invest funds for 3 months in a government security of one of the two countries. A simplistic approach, which ignores the possibility of changes in the exchange rate, is to compare the U.S. interest rate, r, to the British interest rate, r^*, and invest in Britain if $r^* > r$. However, to avoid the risk associated with potential changes in the exchange rate, the lender must calculate the rate of return of a series of transactions. More specifically, if our investor starts with $1,000 and wishes to make a covered investment in a British government security, she must take the following steps:

1 Convert her initial pool of dollars into sterling at the spot exchange rate. If the dollar price of sterling in the spot market is denoted by s, this conversion will produce $1,000/s$ pounds.

2 Take the proceeds of this conversion and purchase a three-month British government security. Since for every pound invested this will yield $(1 + r^*)$ pounds, she will receive sterling proceeds after three months of $1,000 (1 + r^*)/s$.

3 Simultaneous to purchasing the security, she makes a forward sale of the sterling proceeds she will receive when the bill matures. If we denote by f the dollar price of sterling for delivery 90 days hence, the value of her proceeds in dollars can be expressed as

$$1,000 \ (1 \ + \ r^*)\left(\frac{f}{s}\right)$$

Of course, to see whether this is the better of the two investment decisions, our lender must compare this amount with the amount forthcoming from investing $1,000 in a 3-month U.S. Treasury bill. This amount is clearly $1,000 \ (1 \ + \ r)$ dollars. Thus, for covered interest arbitrage to be more profitable than an investment in a U.S. Treasury bill, it is necessary that

$$1,000(1 \ + \ r) < 1,000(1 \ + \ r^*)\left(\frac{f}{s}\right)$$

Another way to write this condition is

$$\frac{1 + r}{1 + r^*} < f/s$$

In this form the condition can be interpreted as follows: Covered interest arbitrage investment in British securities is profitable when the proportion by which the U.S. interest rate exceeds the British interest rate is less than the proportional forward premium on the pound (i.e., f/s). This condition indicates that for foreign investment to be profitable it is not necessary that the foreign interest rate exceed the domestic interest rate. If sterling is trading at a forward premium $(f > s)$, interest arbitrageurs might profit by investment in Britain even if Britain has a lower interest rate. Whenever market conditions fail to yield equality between the two sides of the above condition, capital movements are profitable in one direction or the other.

SUMMARY

1 There are three broad types of international transactions: purchases and sales of goods and services; gifts and grants; and purchases and sales of financial claims. These transactions give rise to transactions between nations, and the statistical record of these transactions between a country and the rest of the world is the nation's balance of payments account.

2 As a matter of arithmetic, the overall balance of payments must balance. Nevertheless, not all parts of the balance of payments need balance. For example, exports of goods and services need not match imports of goods and services, thus implying an imbalance on the goods and services account. The balance on goods and services ac-

count is only one of several possible measures of the state of a nation's balance of payments.

3 Economists focus on some measure of the surplus or deficit in the balance of payments in order to identify the existence of a disequilibrium in international payments. Such a disequilibrium would imply the need for some sort of adjustment. In the short run, this may involve the government using its stock of international reserve assets to equalize imbalances, but in the longer run restoring equilibrium requires changes in one or more of the following: income, interest rates, the price level, and the exchange rate.

4 The exchange rate between two types of monetary units is the number of units of one money required to buy one unit of the other. In a world of floating or flexible exchange rates, these rates are free to move in response to the forces of demand and supply. Until the 1970s, exchange rates were pegged or fixed by agreement. In such an environment, government action was frequently necessary to prevent changes in the value of a currency. Even today, when rates are flexible, countries sometimes intervene in foreign exchange markets, achieving what is called a managed float.

SELECTED READINGS

Chacholiades, M. *International Monetary Theory and Policy.* New York: McGraw-Hill, 1978.

Kenen, P. B. *The International Economy.* Englewood Cliffs, N.J.: Prentice-Hall, 1985.

Kubarych, R. M. *Foreign Exchange Markets in the United States.* New York: Federal Reserve Bank of New York, 1983.

Stern, R. *The Balance of Payments.* Chicago: Aldine, 1973.

Yaeger, L. B. *International Monetary Relationships*, 2nd ed. New York: Harper & Row, 1976.

22

INTERNATIONAL FINANCIAL RELATIONS

The preceding chapter discussed international transactions and foreign exchange markets. This chapter will survey the principal institutional arrangements that facilitate international payments.

The international financial system is composed of more than 150 national monetary systems, each of which has its own central bank and determines its own monetary policy. The principal components of each national monetary system are its central bank and financial intermediaries. In addition, there exists one truly international monetary institution, the International Monetary Fund (IMF), which operates through the various national monetary authorities, serving as a source of international liquidity for them and as a channel for consultation and cooperation.

BANKS AND INTERNATIONAL PAYMENTS

The process of making international payments is greatly facilitated by a network of banking offices within each country and by interrelationships among the banks of the different countries. We have already seen how the thousands of banks in the United States are intertwined in a nationwide system for clearing and collection and in a correspondent banking system. Practically every bank in the country has a correspondent relationship with a bank in New York or with some larger bank that, in turn, has a correspondent in New York. Thus, virtually every bank, large or small, can provide customers who wish to make payments abroad with checks drawn on a well-known New York or other metropolitan bank and even with checks drawn on foreign banks with which its city correspondent maintains close relations. In most other countries, similar results are achieved through nationwide branch banking systems.

The financial centers and commercial banking networks of various countries are interconnected in two principal ways. First of all, many of the world's largest banks, including such U.S. banks as Chase Manhattan, First National City Bank, Bank of America, and Morgan Guaranty Trust, operate foreign branches. Foreign branches usually become members of the clearing and collection system of the country in which they are located, establish relations with banks in that country, and engage in banking activity insofar as the laws of the country permit it. For the head office and its correspondents and customers, foreign branches perform many types of services. They supply credit and market information, draw and sell drafts, collect drafts, pay drafts, accept drafts, and so on. In addition to their foreign branches, some American banks have established subsidiaries for the primary purpose of financing international trade. These finance not only trade between the United States and other countries, but also trade among foreign countries. Also, some American banks have joined with banks of other countries in establishing and operating banks abroad.

The second type of international connection between commercial banks takes the form of international correspondent relationships. The nature of these relationships can be illustrated by a hypothetical example in which the Chase Manhattan Bank of New York and the Midland Bank, Ltd., of London become correspondents. Under such arrangements each performs many services for the other, compensation being fixed by prior agreement or by later negotiation. Each acts for the other and for the customers and correspondents of the other in paying and collecting checks and other items, presenting bills of exchange for acceptance, and buying and selling securities, and at least one of the banks maintains a deposit account with the other.

It is easy to see how this vast network of correspondent relationships facilitates international payments. Americans are enabled to make payments abroad with written, telegraphic, or cable orders drawn by their banks on American banks or on foreign correspondent banks. And foreigners can make payments in the United States with written, telegraphic, or cable orders drawn by foreign banks on foreign—or U.S.—correspondent banks.

We have emphasized the importance of commercial banks in international transactions. These transactions have also come to play a critical role in the economic well-being of commercial banks. Between 1970 and 1976, the top ten commercial banks in the United States achieved a 30 percent annual rate of growth in overseas earnings. From just 17½ percent of total profits in 1970, their overseas contribution jumped to over half of total profits, in 1976. As of 1983, the overseas earnings of the large commercial banks still accounted for about half of their total aftertax profits. Internationalization of U.S. commercial banks had obviously become a permanent feature of the banking scene.

THE EURODOLLAR MARKET

Much of the recent rapid growth in the overseas profits of U.S. banks was a result of their participation in the Eurodollar market. *Eurodollars* are dollar-denominated deposits in foreign commercial banks and in the foreign branches of U.S. banks. The phrase "dollar-denominated" signifies that the deposit, which, for example, might be held at a German commercial bank, is stated in terms of dollars rather than in the local currency, which in this case is marks.

The Eurodollar market is one of the leasing institutions associated with international short-term capital mobility. The Eurodollar market deals in loans and interest-bearing time deposits. It is like any other market for bank loans and bank deposits, except that Eurocurrency transactions are not denominated in the currency of the country in which they take place. Originally, nearly all the banks issuing Eurodollar deposits were located in Britain and continental Europe. Increasingly, however, banks in the Bahamas, Canada, and Southeast Asia also participate in the Eurodollar market. The term *Eurodollar* is becoming obsolete not only because banks outside continental Europe participate in the "Eurodollar" market, but also because banks located in some countries are now issuing deposits denominated in other foreign currencies, such as British sterling, Dutch guilders, German marks, and Swiss francs.[1]

A SAMPLE TRANSACTION

The following example illustrates a typical Eurodollar transaction. Suppose a large corporation, say IBM, moves $5 million from its account at Chase in New York to a time deposit account at the London branch of Citibank.[2] It is simplest to think of IBM as writing a check against Chase and depos-

---

[1]The growth of the Eurodollar market tended to give a competitive advantage in dealing with non-U.S. residents to depository institutions located outside the United States. To bring this banking business back into the United States, in December 1981 the Federal Reserve Board authorized the establishment of international banking facilities (IBFs). IBFs are free of reserve requirements and interest rate limitations, but you should not run out and try to deal with one, since they are prohibited from doing business with local residents.

[2]With the exception of call money, Eurodeposits have a fixed term. These terms vary from overnight to 5 years, although the bulk of the transactions are for 6 months or less.

iting it in Citibank, London, but the actual transaction is effected by wire or telex. Of course, the deposit at Citi London is denominated in dollars.

Table 22–1 spells out what happens to the various balance sheets. It shows that IBM exchanges one asset, $5 million of demand deposits at Chase in New York, for another, $5 million of Euro time deposits at Citi London. As a result of this transaction, Chase loses $5 million in reserves and demand deposits. These reserves and deposits are gained by Citibank, but as Table 22–1 shows, the accounting is a bit complicated. In effect, Citi London has received the deposit but Citi New York has received the reserves. Consequently, Citi New York owes Citi London money, which is reflected in the item "New York office dollar account." This can be thought of as a checking account Citi London holds with Citi New York. It shows up on the asset side of the balance sheet of Citi London and on the liability side of Citi New York (as "London office dollar account").

Two things are noteworthy about Table 22–1. First, while IBM thinks of itself as now holding dollars in London, the dollars never actually left the United States. All that happened was a shift of reserves from Chase to Citi New York. The second point is that Table 22–1 is not the end of the story. Citibank in London, which has a new time deposit on which it has to pay interest, is naturally going to lend those dollars out. As we saw in our discussion of domestic bank expansion, this will set up a process of multiple expansion of Eurodollars. The precise size of the multiplier will depend on the size of various leakages (e.g., deposits out of the Eurobank system and back to the United States) and on reserve requirements. While the details of this process need not concern us, it should be noted that as a result of both initial injections of Eurodollars and the subsequent multiplier process, the Eurodollar market has grown from $65 billion at the end of 1970 to over $1 trillion in recent years.

TABLE 22–1 A Sample Eurodollar Transaction

IBM		CHASE, NEW YORK	
ASSETS	**LIABILITIES**	**ASSETS**	**LIABILITIES**
Demand deposits, Chase, N.Y. − $5 million		Reserves − $5 million	Demand deposits − $5 million
Euro time deposits Citi London + $5 million			

CITI N.Y.		CITI LONDON	
ASSETS	**LIABILITIES**	**ASSETS**	**LIABILITIES**
Reserves + $5 million	London office dollar account + $5 million	New York office dollar account + $5 million	Euro time deposits + $5 million

EURODOLLARS AS A SOURCE OF COMMERCIAL BANK FUNDS

As noted previously, commercial banks in the United States have increasingly tended to rely on nondeposit liabilities as a source of funds. They have, for example, made extensive use of the federal funds market to acquire reserves and lendable funds. In this same spirit, they have at various times utilized the Eurodollar market for similar purposes.

The most critical use of Eurodollars as a source of funds for commercial banks in the United States took place in the late 1960s. In particular, in 1968 and 1969 the ceiling kept interest rates on certificates of deposit below those available on other money market instruments. As a consequence, lenders who would normally have purchased CDs turned to other outlets, including Eurodeposits. Commercial banks in the United States, in turn, borrowed these funds back from their overseas branches (the mechanics are, in effect, spelled out in Table 22–1). After 1970, with the lifting of the ceiling on large CDs, commercial banks in the United States reduced their use of Eurodollar borrowings. Moreover, as noted in Chapter 6, in recent years banks have been net lenders to their overseas branches. Overall, the growth of the Eurodollar market has permitted overseas branches of American banks to vastly expand their operations, and has contributed to American bank profits.

OVERVIEW

The Eurodollar market is extensive and complex. It is not the only means of transferring short- and medium-term funds across national boundaries, but it has greatly increased international capital mobility, and in so doing, it has served several important functions. First, the Eurodollar market intermediates the preferences of suppliers and users of funds. Second, international flows of Eurodollars have improved economic efficiency: Eurodollar deposits flow from low-interest-rate countries to high-interest-rate countries and thereby reduce interest differentials among nations. However, the Eurodollar market has also compounded the problems of countries whose policy objectives require control of international capital movements.

The Eurodollar market and related international capital markets underwent a severe test after the oil price increase of 1973. In 1974 the oil-exporting countries' export revenues exceeded their import payments by nearly $60 billion. That sum constituted an enormous transfer of purchasing power from importers to exporters. For the most part, importers sold securities to pay their bills. If the exporters had been willing to hold the securities the importers sold, the purchasing power transfer would not have disturbed international capital markets. However, oil exporters sought highly liquid, low-risk, short-term investments while oil importers were selling longer-term, riskier assets. Eurocurrency banks were hard pressed to find borrowers who would absorb all the funds that oil exporters had placed in short-term deposits. They found themselves exposed to great risk because their deposits had grown rapidly while their equity capital had remained unchanged. A few banks failed as a result of unsuccessful forward exchange dealings. However, for the most part the system hung together in the face of this massive disturbance.

CENTRAL BANKS AND INTERNATIONAL LIQUIDITY

Each nation makes most of its payments to other countries by transferring to them deposit claims against banks. The major source of a nation's capacity to make payments to others is its flow of current receipts from these other countries. However, not infrequently a nation's residents collectively need to be able to spend abroad more than they receive in payments from abroad. In such cases a nation requires a stock of reserve assets that will be acceptable as payment in other countries. This is comparable to an individual's need for a stock of money balances to bridge the gap between excess expenditure and receipts. One of the earliest functions of central banks was to serve as a custodian of the nation's international reserves.

A nation can prepare for a future excess of international payments over receipts by holding a stock of assets in the form of claims on foreign money or claims on other assets that are readily exchanged for foreign money. For reasons described earlier, gold has long been a popular form of international reserves. However, gold has some disadvantages for its holders. Perhaps most important, it yields no interest or other explicit income. Also, its shipment to make payments is expensive and requires time. It should not be surprising, therefore, that nations have sought some form of asset that would be as good as gold, or almost as good, in terms of acceptability, and would be better than gold in the sense that it would not be inconvenient or costly to ship and would yield an income. Indeed, the importance of gold as a reserve asset has declined markedly over the years.

Most countries now hold the largest part of their international reserves in the form of claims against foreign moneys. The U.S. dollar is by far the most important international reserve currency; however, nations also hold some other currencies for this purpose, including British sterling, German deutsche marks, and Swiss francs. These claims against dollars and other reserve currencies take several forms, such as deposit claims against the central bank, demand deposits against commercial banks, time deposits, Treasury bills, and other short-term government securities. Generally, nations hold working balances of reserves in the form of demand deposits and other nonearning claims and place the remainder of their international reserves in earning assets.

Income-yielding claims against a foreign money may be considered superior to gold as an international reserve as long as that money is freely convertible or exchangeable into the moneys of other nations and there is confidence that it will not depreciate in terms of gold or other moneys. But if fears arise that the money will depreciate, an international reserve system depending heavily on claims against national moneys can create problems not only for the country whose money is used as a reserve, but also for the world's monetary system.

The responsibilities of a central bank in the international financial system do not end with serving as a custodian of a nation's international reserves. As we saw in the preceding chapter, a central bank may intervene in the foreign exchange market to influence exchange rate behavior. Where a central bank intervenes to keep the exchange rate from reaching its equilibrium level—that is, to keep the exchange rate from reaching the level at which the nation's international receipts equal its international payments—the central bank must make sure that its international reserve position is adequate to meet the demands for foreign payments that may arise.

The need for international reserves raises some of the most difficult and controversial questions in the field of international financial policy. These include the following:

1 How much international liquidity do nations need, both individually and collectively? This obviously depends in part on the behavior of flows of receipts and payments, because these determine the size of the payments gap that needs to be bridged. In addition, the need for international liquidity depends on the central bank's exchange rate policy. We discuss exchange rate policies in subsequent sections of this chapter.

2 On what sources of liquidity should nations rely? To what extent should they rely on holdings of assets in the form of foreign money or things that can be readily exchanged for foreign money, and to what extent on arrangements for borrowing foreign money when needed? What forms of assets should they hold and in what proportions? What types of borrowing arrangements should be made?

3 Who should manage the international liquidity positions of nations, both individually and collectively? To what extent should this be done by private sectors, by individual central banks and governments, by central banks in cooperation, and by international institutions?

Central banks also serve as agencies for international monetary cooperation. One of the most important forms of cooperation is the extension of credit among central banks. Some central banks borrow from others to meet unusual short-term needs for international reserves. These loans can take many forms. In some cases, these are bilateral transactions; in other cases, large numbers of central banks are involved. For example, ten or more central banks sometimes participate in a loan to a country that is experiencing or is threatened with a crisis in its balance of payments. Central banks also enter into *reciprocal currency* or *swap* agreements in which one agrees to give the other a certain amount of its own money in exchange for an equivalent amount of the money of the other and each allows the other free use of the swapped money as it is needed.

Often central bank cooperation is orchestrated by the IMF. In the following section we explore the role of the IMF in the international financial system.

THE INTERNATIONAL MONETARY FUND

The International Monetary Fund is an international financial institution established in 1946 as a result of a conference held in Bretton Woods, New Hampshire, in July 1944. The Fund has many purposes, of which the following are more important:

1 Reestablishment of a system of free multilateral payments, and reduction of other barriers to trade. During the Great Depression and World War II, many countries had adopted various types of exchange restrictions—limitations on freedom to make payments to other countries. One purpose of the Fund was to eliminate these as quickly as possible and to work toward lowering other trade barriers as well.

2 Provision of an orderly system for setting and altering exchange rates. During the period following World War II and into the 1970s, the Fund agreement provided that each member country—of which there are now about 150—establish with the Fund an initial exchange rate, and that the exchange rate should thereafter be kept within narrow limits except when the Fund gave permission for a change "to correct a fundamental disequilibrium." In 1978 the IMF officially altered its articles to permit its member countries to choose the option of a floating exchange rate. Floating, however, had been widespread since the early 1970s.

3 Provision of financial aid to member countries needing assistance to meet actual or threatened deficits in their balance of payments. It is in this function of the Fund as a source of international liquidity that we are especially interested.

FINANCIAL AID BY THE FUND

The transactions through which the Fund makes foreign moneys available to a member are called *sales of currencies* or *drawings on the Fund*. The drawing country obtains foreign money in return for an equal amount of claims on its own money. The amount a country can obtain in this way is related to its quota—the amount of gold and its own currency that it has contributed to the Fund—although by presenting justification acceptable to the Fund it can exceed its quota. When a country draws funds that exceed the amount of gold it has subscribed to the Fund, new international reserves are created. In effect, other members, through the intermediary of the Fund, have extended credit to help finance the drawing members' needs. It should be evident, then, that through this mechanism the Fund contributes to the provision of international liquidity. In recent years it has developed another important way to supply international reserve assets: through the use of *special drawing rights.*

SPECIAL DRAWING RIGHTS

At the beginning of 1970, as mentioned earlier, the IMF initiated a scheme for the creation and issue of special drawing rights (SDRs), sometimes referred to as *paper gold.* These are unconditional rights to draw currencies of other countries and are described by the IMF as "unconditional reserve assets created by the Fund to influence the level of world reserves; they are allocated to participating members in proportion to their Fund quotas."

Since the middle of 1974 SDRs have been valued by using an index constructed from a "market basket" of currencies. In early 1985 there were 17 billion SDRs outstanding, and each SDR was valued about $1.00.

SDRs, then, are intended to be used in a fashion similar to foreign exchange reserves in financing balance of payments deficits. Within certain limits, members can transfer their SDRs to other members, who are required to accept them in international payments. The receiving country thus extends credit to the paying country. With the development of SDRs, the IMF took a step toward becoming an international central bank in that it now issues liabilities that are acceptable as international money. However, the creation of new SDRs requires approval by members, so that considerations of international politics can well influence the outcome.

Some argue that SDRs or some similar type of asset should play an increasing role in the international liquidity system in the future. Such a scheme provides a mechanism through which the world can deliberately regulate the size of total international reserves and their rate of growth, rather than allow them to be determined by the vagaries of gold production, nonmonetary demands for gold, and the balance of payments position of a major nation such as the United States. It remains to be seen if SDRs will come to play such a role.

TOTAL INTERNATIONAL RESERVES

We have touched on several types of international reserves but not yet given a complete picture. This is provided in Table 22–2, which shows the international reserve position as of year-end 1983 for the United States, and the total international reserves of all countries that are members of the IMF. As officially defined by the IMF, the *international reserve position* of a country is the sum of the holdings of gold, SDRs, and foreign exchange by the country's government and central bank plus its reserve position in the IMF.

TABLE 22–2 Official International Reserves, United States and World (End of 1984, in billions of dollars)

	United States	All countries
IMF reserve position	11.5	41.6
Special drawing rights (SDRs)	5.6	16.7
Foreign exchange	6.7	346.5
Gold	11.1	39.9
Total	34.9	444.7

The last-named item is any unused part of its gold quota at the Fund against which it can draw automatically.

As is evident from Table 22–2, for IMF members countries as a whole, the bulk of international reserves consists of official holdings of foreign exchange. To a large extent these consist of claims against American dollars. While total reserves appear sizable, what is masked by Table 22–2 is the fact (which is not surprising) that reserves are unevenly distributed across countries. As a consequence, some countries are much better able to withstand balance of payments shocks (e.g., oil price increases). We will examine the effects of this difference as we proceed.

INTERNATIONAL ADJUSTMENT MECHANISMS

We noted in the preceding chapter that, in principle, a nation which allows its exchange rate to float freely never experiences a disequilibrium in its balance of payments. Its exchange rate is free to increase or decrease to a level that equates demand and supply in the foreign exchange market and, equivalently, equates the nation's international receipts and payments. However, historically many nations have been unwilling to let their exchange rate adjust to clear the foreign exchange market. These nations have pegged their exchange rates through intervention in the foreign exchange market—that is, by adding to or subtracting from their stocks of international reserve assets or by borrowing reserves to meet their needs for international liquidity. Indeed, as we have just seen, the concept of pegged exchange rates was a cornerstone of IMF policy for 30 years.

The existence of international reserve assets and international borrowing facilities do not free a nation from the need to balance its international receipts and payments over a longer period. A country with large and persistent deficits would exhaust its holdings of international reserves and also its borrowing facilities. On the other hand, a country with large and persistent surpluses would be forced to purchase large amounts of foreign exchange and other international reserve assets, thereby creating reserves for its commercial banks and a potential for domestic price inflation. We now discuss some of the methods by which a country can equilibrate its balance of international payments in a regime of pegged exchange rates.

What policy should a nation follow when it faces a disequilibrium in its balance of international payments and is balancing its receipts and payments only by drawing down its holdings of international reserve assets or building up large short-term debts to foreigners? Historically, this has been one of the most important policy problems in the entire field of international finance. The nation may, of course, adjust its exchange rate to equalize the demand for and supply of its currency and, equivalently, to equalize its international payments and receipts. Or it may resort to direct controls over its trade and payments in order to eliminate the payments imbalance. However, we will examine a hypothetical example in which Britain runs a balance of payments deficit at its pegged exchange rate of £1 = $1.30 and refuses to resort to exchange rate adjustment or exchange controls to eliminate the imbalance.

Figure 22–1 indicates that the drain on Britain's international reserves at the pegged exchange rate of £1 = $1.30 can be ended only by developments that will shift the demand curve for sterling upward and to the right (e.g., from *DD* to *D¹D¹*) or shift the supply curve for sterling upward and to the left (e.g., from *SS* to *S¹S¹*, or shift both to a sufficient extent to equalize the demand for sterling and the supply of sterling at a rate equal to or more

FIGURE 22–1
Adjustment to disequilibrium under pegged exchange rates

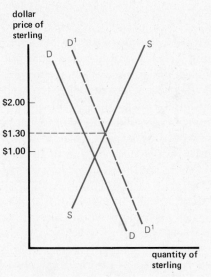

(Part *a*) Demand adjustment

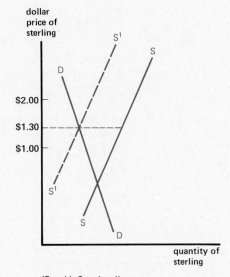

(Part *b*) Supply adjustment

than £1 = $1.30. Several types of developments in other countries can assist in this process:

1 A rise in price levels abroad would increase the demand for sterling at each exchange rate by increasing the demand for British exports. It would also tend to reduce the supply of sterling by discouraging British imports.
2 A rise in real incomes abroad would shift the demand curve for sterling to the right.
3 A decrease in interest rates abroad, to the extent that it lessened capital flows out of Britain and induced or increased a flow of capital to Britain, would reduce the supply of, and raise the demand for, sterling.

All these developments could help to raise the demand for sterling relative to the supply of it and to ease the drain on Britain's international reserves. However, if these developments do not occur abroad, or are not sufficiently strong to close the payments gap, one or more of the following things will have to happen in Britain:

1 A fall in British price levels, which would tend to increase the demand for sterling by cheapening British exports and to decrease the supply of sterling by reducing British imports.
2 A fall in real income in Britain, which would decrease British imports and the supply of sterling.
3 A rise in interest rates which, to the extent that it reduced the outflow of capital from Britain or increased capital inflows, would tend to reduce the supply of sterling or raise the demand for sterling.

Adjustments of precisely these types will tend to be made "automatically" if the deficit and surplus countries subject their monetary policies to the "discipline of their balance of payments" and "follow the rules of the international gold standard game." These rules originally applied to international gold movements, but they are also applicable to a system of pegged exchange rates in which the central bank buys and sells foreign moneys, thereby tending to create and to decrease bank reserves within the country. The essence of these rules is that the deficit country should allow its loss of gold or other international reserves to restrict its money supply, and that the surplus countries should allow their increases of gold and other international reserves to expand their money supplies.

Suppose that the deficit in the British balance of payments resulted from a decrease of its exports as other countries shifted their demand from British products to their home products. First there are the income effects. Both the decline of demand for its exports and the induced decrease of consumption expenditures at home serve to lower total demands for British output. In the surplus countries the opposite occurs; demands for their output are increased both by the shift from British products to home products and by the induced rise of consumption expenditures.

Then there are the monetary effects. As the Bank of England makes net sales of international reserve assets, it reduces the reserves of British banks, thereby tending to restrict credit and to raise interest rates. It can accentuate monetary restriction by selling securities or calling loans. The monetary restriction and rise of interest rates in Britain serve both to attract funds from abroad (or at least to reduce outflows) and to lower domestic demands for output.

As central banks in the surplus countries make net purchases of international reserve assets, they create reserves for their banks, thereby encouraging expansion of their money supplies and a decrease in interest rates. They can accentuate this if, as their international reserves increase, the central banks buy securities or expand their loans. The fall of interest rates in these surplus countries serve both to encourage outflows of funds to the deficit country and to increase demands for output in the surplus countries.

Such are the automatic processes of equilibrating international receipts and payments if both deficit and surplus countries follow the rules of the game. Capital flows to the deficit country tend to be induced by both the rise of interest rates there and the fall of rates in the surplus countries. More fundamental is the fall of demands for output in the deficit country and the rise of demands for output in the surplus countries. Suppose first that money wage rates and prices are quickly and completely flexible and that changes in demands for output are reflected only in changes in prices. The fall of prices in the deficit country and the rise of prices in the surplus countries will serve to equate international receipts and payments by increasing exports and decreasing imports in the deficit country, and causing the reverse effects in the surplus countries. Thus, if money wage rates and prices are quickly and completely flexible, international payments and receipts may be equated through adjustments of the price levels in the various countries.

What if money wage rates and prices are inflexible, at least in the downward direction? Changes in demands for output can still equate international receipts and payments, but by changing levels of real income. Increases of demands for output in the surplus countries can, by raising their real incomes, increase their demand for the exports of deficit countries. And the fall of demands for output in the deficit country can, by lowering its level of real output and income, decrease its expenditures for imports. The deficit country can become too poor to demand imports in excess of its current international receipts. In other words, it can eliminate the deficit in its balance of payments by creating a deficit in its real income or output.

It is easy to see why countries intent on promoting such domestic objectives as maximum employment and output, rapid economic growth, and price level stability are often highly reluctant to follow rules of the game, which require that their monetary and fiscal policies be dominated by their balance of payments and international reserve positions. Countries with surpluses in their balance of payments are sometimes reluctant to expand their money supply for fear of inflationary consequences. Countries with deficits are even more reluctant to follow restrictive monetary and fiscal policies if this threatens their employment and growth objectives. They often take offsetting actions, such as central bank purchases of securities, to prevent their loss of gold or other international reserves from restricting credit and raising interest rates.

However, if a country insists on pegging its exchange rates at a fixed level and will not adopt restrictive fiscal or monetary policies despite a persistent deficit in its balance of payments, it is likely to be drained of its international reserves, to be forced to impose direct controls over its international trade and payments, or both.

EXCHANGE RATE SYSTEMS

The preceding discussion indicates that a country's choice of balance of payments adjustment policies is closely related to its choices concerning exchange rate systems. For example, to the extent that a nation allows its exchange rate to float freely to eliminate surpluses and deficits, it need not rely on other methods of adjustment. On the other hand, if a country adamantly pegs its exchange rate and if its command over international reserves is limited, it can absorb deficits only for a limited period. In addition, if that country is unwilling to restrict trade and payments, it must fall back on adjustments of levels of income, prices, and interest rates, brought about by monetary and fiscal policies, to equilibrate its payments imbalances.

Evidently then, the choice of an exchange rate system is a major policy decision that critically influences the options available to a nation in dealing with imbalances in international payments. As we have already noted, there are two broad alternatives: fixed (pegged) exchange rates and floating (flexible) exchange rates. We now examine some of the features and controversies associated with each system. We first consider the general principles involved and then examine the recent history of the world's exchange rate systems.

FLEXIBLE EXCHANGE RATES

The great advantage claimed for a policy of freely floating exchange rates is that it gives a nation the freedom to pursue domestic economic objectives. If its exchange rate is allowed to adjust in such a way as to equilibrate its balance of payments, a nation need not for this purpose resort to direct controls over international trade and capital movements. And it need not allow concern over the state of its balance of payments and international reserves to influence its monetary and fiscal policies. Such policies can be directed solely to promoting such domestic objectives as full employment, rapid economic growth, and relatively stable price levels.

While the advantages of flexible exchange rates would seem to be considerable, most central bankers and many economists have long resisted the idea. Among the arguments advanced against such exchange rates are the following:

1 Uncertainty as to future exchange rates creates exchange risks and may impede international trade and capital movements. For example, an American who buys exports from Britain and promises to pay in sterling runs the risk that the dollar price of sterling will rise above expected levels. And a British exporter who sells for dollars runs the risk that the sterling price of dollars will fall below expected levels. Exchange risks can be even more serious for capital movements, and especially for long-term capital. As we saw in the preceding chapter, forward exchange markets can lessen the burden of these risks, but these facilities are sometimes expensive and inadequate. They usually are not available to bear exchange risks on long-term lending and borrowing. It is, however, important to note that exchange risk is not necessarily absent under a system of pegged exchange rates, because pegged rates may be changed, sometimes by significant amounts.

2 Changes in a nation's exchange rates that are not necessary for longer-run equilibration of its receipts and payments may cause unnecessary disturbances in that nation's economy, and especially in its import-competing and export industries. Suppose, for example, that there is an abnormal flow of short-term capital to nation A, which raises the exchange rate on its currency significantly above its longer-term equilibrium level. This increase of its exchange rate will tend to increase the cost of A's exports in terms of foreign currencies, and thus will lower output and employment in its export industries. The rise in the exchange rate will also lower the cost of imports, thus discouraging output and employment in A's import-competing industries. Such domestic disturbances resulting from erratic changes in exchange rates would not be welcome in any nation, least of all in nations heavily dependent on exports and imports.

Attitudes toward a policy of freely floating exchange rates differ widely, largely because of differences of judgment concerning the behavior patterns of rates under such a system. The optimists believe that actual rates would deviate only slightly from their longer-term equilibrium, and that through time adjustments would be relatively smooth and orderly. The pessimists disagree. A basic issue is this: Would private speculation in exchange markets be predominantly and reliably stabilizing, or would it, at least on some occasions, be destabilizing? The optimists argue essentially as follows: Private speculators, or at least those persons who speculate successfully, base their decisions on a careful analysis of the basic factors that determine the longer-run equilibrium level of an exchange rate. When the market rate rises significantly above this level, the speculator will sell the currency, thereby pushing its rate back toward equilibrium. On the other hand, if the speculator buys the currency when its price falls significantly below the long-term equilibrium level, this will tend to raise the currency's price. Thus, the speculators who make money and survive are those who correctly estimate the longer-term equilibrium level of the exchange rate and operate in a stabilizing way. Financial failure will eliminate those who are wrong in their estimate of the level of the longer-term equilibrium rate or who speculate in a destabilizing way.

Pessimists challenge both the conclusion that stabilizing speculation will always predominate and the conclusion that destabilizing speculators will lose money and be eliminated. To make their point, they sometimes use stock market speculation as an analogy. They admit that much speculation in shares of stock tends to be stabilizing. However, they contend that for considerable periods of time destabilizing types of speculation may predominate and even be highly profitable. For example, suppose that at some time the price of a particular stock is already above what you consider to be its longer-run equilibrium level, but that you expect its price to rise further because of a developing *bullish* sentiment among other participants in the market. Your purchases will be destabilizing in the sense that they will tend to push the price still further above its longer-term equilibrium level, but they will be profitable if you succeed in selling before the price again falls to the level of your purchase price. Similarly, you can reap a profit by selling a stock that is already priced below its longer-run equilibrium level, thereby tending to depress the price, if you are correct in your expectations that other *bearish* sellers will depress the price still further before it rises again. Pessimists may exaggerate the dangers of destabilizing private speculation, but they properly cast doubts on the optimistic contention that such speculation will be predominantly reliably stabilizing.

Largely because of such doubts, many advocates of flexible exchange rates favor official intervention on at least some occasions. Under such a system the authorities do not peg exchange rates within narrow limits, but they do intervene at times to buy and sell moneys in exchange markets to influence exchange rate behavior. The nature and degree of intervention vary widely. At one extreme, the authorities intervene only infrequently and only for the purpose of preventing "disorderly movements"; they do not attempt to influence the longer-term trends of exchange rates. In other cases, they intervene more frequently and do attempt to affect the level of exchange rates over longer periods. As the authorities try to hold fluctuations within narrower and narrower limits, the system assumes the characteristics of pegged exchange rates.

Official intervention under a policy of flexible exchange rates raises important problems. One is the estimation of the longer-term equilibrium level of an exchange rate. There is no assurance that official judgments will be any better than those of private speculators. Moreover, official decisions may be unduly influenced by pressures from economic groups such as exporters and industries competing with imports. When official intervention influences the longer-term level of an exchange rate, there is the problem of determining what that level should be. There is a real danger that some nations will try to manipulate the rate to achieve an undue national advantage. For example, nation A may try to drive down the exchange rate on its money to give greater advantage to its export industries and greater protection to its import-competing industries; nation A may do this despite the fact that it already has a surplus in its balance of payments. Nations B, C, and D may retaliate.

The result may be a "war of exchange rates," with disruptive effects on trade and capital movements. Such behavior is most likely to occur in depression periods, when nations try to export their unemployment, but it is by no means unknown in periods of prosperity. These disadvantages of the manipulation of exchange rates highlight the need for an international understanding or agreement concerning the appropriate behavior of exchange rates, as well as the need for some means of promoting cooperation among national exchange authorities.

PEGGED EXCHANGE RATES

One of the most controversial issues that arises under a system of pegged exchange rates is the following: What should be the relative responsibilities of surplus and deficit countries for eliminating surpluses and deficits under an international system of fixed exchange rates? Deficit countries usually reply that the surplus countries should solve the problem by increasing their imports, by lending more, or by giving more aid. Surplus countries, on the other hand, often report that the deficit countries should tighten their belts, show some self-discipline, and cease trying to live beyond their means.

Few would contend that surplus countries should make the adjustment when they are already maintaining approximately full employment and stable or rising price levels, and when the deficits of the deficit countries are clearly attributable to their own highly inflationary monetary and fiscal policies. It would be too much to ask surplus countries to eliminate their surpluses by inflating prices at a rapid rate. A more appropriate remedy in this case is for the deficit countries to reform the domestic policies that created their deficits. This may include a realistic adjustment of their exchange rates, accompanied by domestic reforms.

Consider, however, a quite different case, in which the deficit countries have relatively stable price levels and their deficits were created by a sharp fall of real incomes and output in the surplus countries. The surplus of the latter countries was created by the decline of their demands for imports. The deficit countries could, of course, eliminate their deficits by adopting deflationary policies to lower their levels of real incomes and prices. However, a more attractive alternative is for the surplus countries to adopt expansionary monetary and fiscal policies to raise their levels of real income and increase their expenditures for imports.

The following rules of conduct seem appropriate under a system of fixed exchange rates.

1 A deficit country undergoing domestic inflation should solve both problems by adopting restrictive monetary or fiscal policies.
2 A surplus country with domestic output and income well below full employment levels should solve both problems by adopting expansionary monetary or fiscal policies.

Unhappily, there are many situations that are not covered by these rules. For example, suppose some countries have large surpluses in their balance of payments along with actual or threatened inflation, while others have deficits in their balance of payments despite the presence of unemployment and excess capacity at home? Should the surplus countries inflate still more to equate the balance of payments? Should the deficit countries create still more unemployment to eliminate their deficits? A sensible alternative, if the imbalance of international payments is large and persistent, would be to adjust exchange rates.

ADJUSTMENTS OF PEGGED RATES

Although the IMF agreements envisaged virtually a worldwide system of pegged exchange rates, they also provided for adjustments of exchange rate parities "to correct a fundamental disequilibrium." The latter term was not defined, but its general meaning was clear: Exchange rate adjustments were not only permissible but encouraged as a means of dealing with imbalances in international payments that could be remedied otherwise only at excessive cost. Faced with such a basic disequilibrium, a deficit nation should lower its exchange rate to an equilibrium level and peg it there. On the other hand, a nation with a large and persistent surplus should raise the exchange parity on its currency.

The IMF agreements provided no guidelines to regulate the size or frequency of the adjustments of exchange parities. Such decisions were postponed until they could be based on experience. As the years have gone by, more and more economists and some public officials have come to believe that, in practice, adjustments of parities have been too infrequent and individually too large. Too often adjustments have been made only after a large maldistribution of international reserves has occurred, trade and capital movements have been restricted, and some nations have paid too high a price in terms of output and employment. Such critics believe that if a system of pegged rates is to be retained, parities should be adjusted more promptly and in steps small enough to avoid the large speculative flows of funds often induced by prospective large changes in exchange rates.

One proposal for accomplishing this is a scheme of "sliding" or "crawling" parities. These would provide for slow and gradual adjustments of parities in response to the behavior of actual exchange rates during a preceding period. For example, parities might be altered once a month; the parity for a currency during any month would be determined by taking the average of the actual rates for the 12 months immediately preceding the month in question. Thus, as the trend of actual market rates descended from the old parity, both the parity and the band limits would be adjusted downward, but at a pace slow enough to avoid large disturbances to capital flows. The same principles would apply as the trend of actual market rates on a currency increased from its old parity. If such automatic adjustments proved to be inadequate or inappropriate, they could be supplemented or modified through discretionary changes.

THE EVOLUTION OF THE INTERNATIONAL MONETARY SYSTEM

In the preceding sections we have examined the principal features of fixed and flexible exchange rate systems. We have also indicated that since the early 1970s fixed exchange rates have to a large extent been supplanted by floating rates. The purpose of this section is to explore why this development came about and, in the process, shed a bit more light on exchange rate issues.

FROM WORLD WAR II TO 1960

The restructuring of the international monetary system after World War II had as its foundation a system of pegged exchange rates based on the "golden dollar." Specifically, the price of gold was fixed at $35 an ounce and all other currencies were pegged in relation to this. Gold and the dollar were the two major international reserve assets, and the United States guaranteed the convertibility of dollars in the hands of foreign governments. The U.S. gold stock, which in 1946 accounted for about three-quarters of all Western monetary gold, in effect became the central gold reserve for the entire world. These were the essential elements of the international monetary system as reconstituted at the end of World War II.

In the years immediately following World War II, while war-torn and war-deprived countries were still in the process of restocking and reconstruction, demands for American exports were almost insatiable. Our net exports of goods and services were large enough to enable us to make large loans and grants of foreign aid to the rest of the world and still increase our gold reserves.

By the end of 1949 our gold stock had reached the huge value of $24.6 billion, which was about two-thirds of the world total. However, the situation began to change at about the time of the outbreak of war in Korea,

FIGURE 22–2
International reserves and foreign liabilities of
the United States

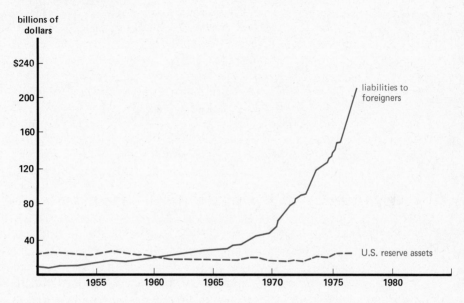

and the large surplus in the U.S. balance of payments was gradually replaced by chronic deficits. Major contributors to this turnabout were the recovery of productive capacity in other major industrial countries, the devaluation of the British pound and several other currencies in 1949, and inflation in the United States during the Korean conflict.

As a result of the large and prolonged deficits in the United States, foreign central bankers added to their foreign exchange reserves by accumulating substantial volumes of dollar claims. Of course, some of these dollars were turned back to the United States for gold, and as shown in Figure 22–2, the net international reserve position of the United States declined markedly. As Figure 22–2 also shows, by 1960 short-term dollar liabilities to foreigners exceeded U.S. international reserves. In essence, the United States was a banker whose ability to deliver on demand was called into question.

SIGNS OF STRAIN, 1960–1967

From their first appearance, in 1950 until about 1960, deficits in the American balance of payments were welcomed as almost wholly beneficial to the rest of the world. Our deficits provided the rest of the world with tremendous amounts of liquidity in the form of both gold and claims on dollars. Attitudes toward deficits in the U.S. balance of payments had begun to change by 1960, and they changed even more as the deficits continued, as American international reserves shrank and its liquid liabilities to foreigners rose, and as it became increasingly clear that the United States would not follow monetary and fiscal policies restrictive enough to terminate the deficits. Deficits that were earlier considered to be beneficial now came to be regarded as at best dangerous and at worst catastrophic for the international monetary system.

Major criticisms of the balance of payments situation were of two related types. The first was that if American deficits were not eradicated, or at least reduced markedly, confidence in the exchange rate on the dollar would deteriorate and the dollar would depreciate in terms of gold. A second criticism was that it was basically unsound to allow the world's supplies of international reserves and liquidity to be so heavily influenced, and even dominated, by the state of the American balance of payments.

As U.S. deficits persisted into the 1960s, the nation's international reserves continued to decline and its liabilities to foreigners grew markedly. This situation gave rise to speculation that the United States might devalue the dollar, thus increasing the value of its gold stock. The price of gold on the London market rose to $40 an ounce. This raised the possibility that foreign central banks would turn in dollars for gold at $35 and resell the gold at a higher price. A crisis was avoided when a group of leading central banks banded together to form a *gold pool* aimed at keeping the price of gold at $35. Although the gold market continued to be subjected to speculative waves, the international monetary system managed to limp along. But then, in late 1967, another crisis struck.

INCREASING TENSION, LATE 1967–LATE 1971

In late 1967, with the Vietnam war accelerating the outflow of dollars, it became apparent that attempts to maintain the gold price at $35 would substantially drain the resources of the gold pool. As a consequence, in March 1968 the central banks in the gold pool threw in the towel and a new so-called *two-tier* gold policy was introduced. Under this policy, which sharply distinguished between monetary gold and private gold, the price of gold in the free market was no longer pegged at $35. Existing gold stocks of central banks were still a reserve asset suitable for official international settlements, but only at $35 an ounce. At the same time, the United States stood ready to buy and sell gold for "legitimate monetary purposes" at this price. These actions temporarily served to avert the crisis, but the introduction of the two-tier system did little to solve the longer-run question of international liquidity.

The U.S. gold stock continued to decline, and the U.S. balance of payments continued to deteriorate in a dramatic fashion. In 1970 the deficit on the official reserve transactions basis was a huge $10 billion, and this soared to over $20 billion for the first three quarters of 1971. Other countries were forced to buy up huge quantities of dollars to maintain fixed exchange rates. As a consequence, in the first four months of 1971 alone, dollar holdings of foreign central banks mushroomed from $20 to $32 billion. The new effect was that these countries found themselves losing control over their domestic money supplies. West Germany and the Netherlands were the first to give up the game. Both abandoned fixed exchange rates and let their currencies float. While this eased the situation for a short period of time, in the first half of August 1971 the dollar came under strong attack once again. Faced with $35 billion of outstanding liabilities and with only $10 billion of gold, the United States finally gave up trying to play by the Bretton Woods rules.

DEVELOPMENTS FROM 1971 TO 1976

On August 15, 1971, President Nixon announced that the United States would no longer redeem dollars for gold and that it would not intervene in foreign exchange markets to maintain exchange rates relative to other currencies. The dollar was thus allowed to float, with the expectation that the dollar would be devalued. This indeed happened, although other countries intervened in foreign exchange markets to limit the appreciation in their currencies and thus preserve their relative attractiveness as exporters.

In a last-gasp effort to preserve fixed exchange rates, the major industrial nations met at the Smithsonian Institution in Washington, D.C., in December 1971. The United States agreed to devalue the dollar in terms of gold, raising the price of gold by 8½ percent to $38 an ounce. A number of other countries revalued their currencies in terms of the dollar so that, on average, the dollar was devalued by 12 percent. Pegged exchange rates were reestablished, although fluctuations were allowed within somewhat wider bands. The dollar, however, remained inconvertible into gold.

Viewed with hindsight, the Smithsonian agreement was at best a patchwork effort. It did not deal with the more fundamental problems of international liquidity and adjustment of exchange rates under a system of pegged rates. The system did limp along for about a year, but the international monetary situation again reached critical proportions in early 1973. In February 1973 the United States again devalued the dollar, this time by 11 percent, raising the price of gold from $38 to over $42 an ounce. But even this was not enough to stem the tide, and one month later floating exchange rates were back to stay.

After March 1973 exchange rates floated, albeit in somewhat "managed" fashion. There were, however, substantial movements in exchange rates, and despite the pessimism of some as to the workability of flexible rates, the international monetary system functioned reasonably well during this period. Indeed, flexible exchange rates were given a rather severe test by quadrupling of the export price of OPEC oil at the end of 1973, which brought about a fundamental change in the international payments structure. In the assessment of the Council of Economic Advisers:

The financing of the large external deficits of oil importers over the past 2 years has been accomplished considerably more smoothly than had been anticipated earlier. Financial markets turned out to be very adaptable, and the more flexible exchange rate system helped to avoid the market disruptions so often experienced during past periods of strain.[3]

REFORM OF THE IMF

It should be emphasized that virtually all the developments from 1971 to 1976 in regard to exchange rates were in technical violation of the rules of the game applicable to members of the IMF. Indeed, it was not until a broad package of amendments to the IMF's Articles of Agreement was formally approved in 1978 that the status quo was legitimized. These amendments accomplished the following: They "legalized" flexible exchange rates; raised quotas to increase the Fund's resources by over one-third; phased out gold in Fund transactions; and established a trust fund for the benefit of the poorer members of the IMF.

As far as exchange rates are concerned, the new agreement allowed for a number of other possibilities in addition to floating rates. A country could, for example, choose to peg its currency in terms of SDRs (but not gold). Or a group of countries could cooperate in maintaining their currencies in some fixed relationship to the value of the currency or currencies of other members. The revised articles even permit, with approval of an 85 percent majority vote, the reestablishment of a set of pegged exchange rates. However, as the United States has approximately 20 percent of the voting strength, this could not be done without U.S. approval.

EVENTS SINCE 1976

In mid-1976 the dollar began a gradual decline against other currencies that persisted for about a year. Soon thereafter, the United States began to run a current account balance of payments deficit, its first since 1972. As a result, the decline in the dollar picked up steam in mid-1977 and the dollar continued to weaken until late 1978. This decline is evident in Figure 22–3, which plots movements in the value of the dollar versus 17 other major currencies via what is called the *effective exchange rate index.*

In the face of a continuing depreciation of the dollar, on November 1, 1978, the Federal Reserve announced a major policy move designed to "restore exchange market stability." This new policy included the following measures:

1 A tightening of monetary policy designed both to curb inflation and raise interest rates, thereby increasing the attractiveness of U.S. financial claims

[3]*Economic Report of the President.* Washington, D.C.: Government Printing Office, January 1976, p. 140.

  2 An increase in the magnitude of Treasury gold sales
  3 An $8 billion increase in swap arrangements with Germany, Switzer-
     land, and Japan
  4 The drawing of $3 billion of foreign currencies from the IMF
  5 The sale by the Treasury of up to $10 billion of securities denominated
     in foreign currencies

As Figure 22–3 indicates, after November 1 the dollar did improve against
other currencies, but then, in mid-1979, it again took a turn for the worse.
As a consequence, in October 1979, with one eye in international markets,
the Federal Reserve was forced to take additional steps in tightening monetary policy. As we saw in Chapter 20, this launched a 3-year period of high
interest rates and weakness in the U.S. economy. As Figure 22–3 illustrates,
shortly after the October 1979 change in monetary policy, the dollar began
an extraordinary five-year climb which, by early 1985, had brought the effective exchange rate to over 50 percent above its level in mid-1980. Not
surprisingly, this period of high interest rates and a rising dollar had some
striking consequences for the international economy. The second oil shock,
which raised the OPEC price from under $13 per barrel in mid-1978 to

FIGURE 22–3
The value of the U.S. dollar versus other major
currencies: the effective exchange rate index
(1980 = 100). (SOURCE: International Economic
Conditions, Federal Reserve Bank of St. Louis,
April 1985, p. 2.

nearly $32 per barrel in mid-1980, also played a major role in these developments.

One critical problem that emerged in the period after 1978 was the growing level of the debts of less-developed countries.[4] By the end of 1982, these debts, excluding those of OPEC countries, amounted to more than $630 billion. In the face of the high level of interest rates prevailing in international capital markets, there were serious doubts about the ability of the less-developed countries to service their debts. Some countries found themselves in the unsustainable situation of having to pay more in interest on their old loans than they could raise by floating new loans.

Poland was the first country to experience a major debt crisis when, in 1981, it could not meet its obligations. It asked its creditors to "reschedule" its maturing debts—a quaint phrase whereby the creditors would turn maturing debts into long-term obligations, thus technically avoiding default. A second set of crises took place in 1982, when Mexico, Brazil, and Argentina, among others, had to make similar requests. The problems of Mexico and Brazil led to considerable concern in the United States because these countries were heavily in debt to American commercial banks. Indeed, the claims of a number of large American banks on Mexico and Brazil exceeded the banks' capital. In other words, these banks would have been insolvent if they had had to write off their claims on Brazil and Mexico.

This unhappy state of affairs caused massive efforts to avert a calamity. The efforts involved the U.S. government, the IMF, and the commercial banks. The negotiations were drawn out and complicated, but eventually did succeed. It should be noted, however, that negotiations by themselves probably would not have been sufficient to save the day. A major factor in improving the position of the less-developed countries was the decline in interest rates and the restoration of a more substantial rate of economic growth worldwide. What this all suggests is that we are not yet fully out of the woods and that the working out of the debt problem could easily take until the end of the 1980s.

While high interest rates and a strong dollar had effects on less-developed countries, these factors also had direct consequences for our own economy. The strong dollar made imports cheaper and hence more competitive. Our export industries faced the opposite problem, in that they found it more difficult to sell abroad. The net effect was the substantial trade deficit—over $120 billion in 1984 alone—and an intensified call for protectionist measures in the United States. As of early 1985, the strength in the dollar was still in evidence. Many, however, were keeping an uneasy eye on the growing indebtedness of the United States to the rest of the world. The concern was that foreigners might not be willing to go on absorbing our debt indefinitely, at least on the same terms. It was this con-

---

[4]For a more detailed discussion of the issue, see P. B. Kenen, *The International Economy*, Englewood Cliffs, N.J.: Prentice-Hall, 1985, on which much of the following discussion is based.

cern, in fact, which led many economists to urge the government to do something about the substantial deficits in the federal budget—deficits that were contributing to the need for foreign capital.

FLOATING RATES—A REPORT CARD

As of this writing, floating rates have been with us for over a decade, and a brief report card seems in order. This is easier said than done, because the record is clouded by two oil shocks, high inflation and interest rates, and deep recessions, events that should not be blamed on floating rates.

As indicated earlier, it is generally agreed that floating rates have helped cushion the world economy from a number of major shocks such as the dramatic runup in oil prices. However, while floating rates have clearly performed substantially better than the pessimists had anticipated, the floating system had not lived up to the hopes of its most fervent supporters. As noted above, optimistic supporters of floating thought that the system would allow each country to pursue domestic policies of its choice unimpeded by balance of payments constraints. It was also hoped that floating rates would insulate national economies against international disturbances. Actual events, however, turned out somewhat differently, as we see in the following statement by a governor of the Federal Reserve system:

> The promise of speedy adjustment of payments imbalances through exchange rate movements has remained unfulfilled, perhaps because the very ease with which exchange rates could move has diminished political pressure to adopt appropriate fiscal and monetary policies.[5]

While all economists would accept the fact that floating rates have not been a panacea, some would go to the other extreme and blame floating rates for many of the problems of the 1970s and 1980s. This group argues that a return to pegged exchange rates, or even the gold standard, is necessary to "discipline" governments. For most economists, however, the history of pegged exchange rates suggests that this policy would be unwise and impractical in the current environment. It seems likely, therefore, that for better or worse, floating rates are not likely to be supplanted in the foreseeable future.

SOME UNSOLVED ISSUES

We have now completed our survey of the international monetary system and of international monetary interrelationships and policies. We have devoted special attention to international reserve or liquidity systems, ex-

---

[5]H. C. Wallich, "The International Monetary and Cyclical Situation," speech delivered at Lendeszentralbank, Berlin, Germany, June 18, 1979.

change rate systems, and methods of equilibrating international receipts and payments. Each of these fields presents many policy issues with important implications not only for international trade and capital movements, but also for the behavior of output, employment, and price levels in the various countries. Moreover, policy choices in any one of these fields have significant consequences for the others.

The following list of some of the basic policy questions in the various fields will suggest both the large number of issues and their interrelatedness.

ISSUES RELATING TO THE INTERNATIONAL LIQUIDITY SYSTEM

1 How much international liquidity does the world need, and at what rate should it grow to avoid restriction of trade and capital movements and both deflationary and inflationary pressures? The answer depends in part on the nature of the exchange rate system and on the readiness of nations to eliminate deficits and surpluses in their balance of payments. A huge amount of reserves may be required if exchange rates are rigidly pegged over long periods and if nations fail to take quick and effective action to equilibrate their receipts and payments. The reserve requirement will be smaller if exchange rates are flexible or if other actions are taken quickly to equilibrate receipts and payments.

2 What should be the forms and proportions of the various components of international liquidity? What should be the roles of gold, of SDRs, of holdings of claims against foreign moneys, and of borrowing facilities?

3 Should the existing system be supplemented or replaced by an international central bank with discretionary power to create and regulate international reserves?

ISSUES RELATING TO THE EXCHANGE RATE SYSTEM

1 Should exchange rates be rigidly and narrowly pegged over long periods regardless of the cost in terms of other objectives?

2 Should exchange rates be pegged, but adjusted if defense of an existing rate becomes costly? If so, what principles should guide adjustments and what techniques of adjustment should be used?

3 Should rates be allowed to float freely without official intervention?

4 Should rates be flexible, but with official intervention? If so, what should be the criteria for intervention?

ISSUES RELATING TO METHODS OF ELIMINATING DEFICITS AND SURPLUSES

1 As a means of equilibrating international receipts and payments, what should be the relative roles of direct controls over trade and payments, adjustments of exchange rates, and adjustments of income, price lev-

els, and interest rates? These policy questions are obviously related to those concerning the international liquidity and exchange rate systems.

2 What should be the relative responsibilities of surplus and deficit countries in eliminating imbalances in international payments?

ISSUES RELATING TO NATIONAL SOVEREIGNTY AND INTERNATIONAL ECONOMIC INTERDEPENDENCE

Among the sovereign rights claimed by each nation is the right to determine its own monetary and fiscal policies. Yet it is an incontrovertible fact that the economic policies of each country affect significantly, and in some cases powerfully, economic developments and welfare in other countries. This situation poses serious economic and political questions.

1 What basic principles should serve as a guideline to resolve these issues?

2 What types of international understandings, agreements, and institutions would best promote workable solutions?

While the recent reform of the IMF answers many of these questions, it by no means settles them all. Furthermore, if the history of international monetary relations has taught us anything, it is that answers to policy questions in this area tend to be less than permanent.

SUMMARY

1 Large American banks have increasingly extended the scope of their international operations and frequently earn more of their income from these operations than from their domestic activities. A major focus of these operations is the Eurodollar market, which provides a direct source of bank profits and a vehicle for bank liability management.

2 The International Monetary Fund is an international financial institution set up in 1946 to promote freer trade, to provide an orderly system for setting and altering exchange rates, and to provide financial aid to member countries needing assistance. The IMF's role as a source of international liquidity has been particularly evident in the face of the two oil shocks of the 1970s and the serious debt problem of the less-developed countries in the 1980s.

3 Under fixed or pegged exchange rates, which prevailed in the postwar period until 1973, deficit countries have to use their international reserves to support the fixed exchange rate. Alternatively, they have to use restrictive monetary and fiscal policies to restore a balance of payments equilibrium. This, of course, has rather undesirable consequences for domestic output and income. Only in the case of a

fundamental disequilibrium were changes in the fixed exchange rate to be contemplated.

4 Floating exchange rates emerged in 1973 and have generally provided individual countries more flexibility in the conduct of monetary and fiscal policy. But they have not fully lived up to expectations in this regard. Despite this, most economists agree that they have been a distinct improvement over the workings of fixed exchange rates.

SELECTED READINGS

International Monetary Fund. *Annual Reports* and *International Financial Statistics* (monthly), Washington, D.C.

Kenen, P. B. *The International Economy.* Englewood Cliffs, N.J.: Prentice-Hall, 1985.

Solomon, R. *The International Monetary System, 1945–1976.* New York: Harper & Row, 1977.

Stigum, M. *The Money Market.* Homewood, Ill.: Dow-Jones-Irwin, 1978.

Tresize, P. H., ed. *The European Monetary Systems: Its Promise and Prospects.* Washington, D.C.: The Brookings Institution, 1979.

INDEX